CW01261042

Palgrave Studies in the History of Finance

Series Editors
D'Maris Coffman
Bartlett Faculty of Built Environment
University College London
London, UK

Tony K. Moore
ICMA Centre, Henley Business School
University of Reading
Reading, UK

Martin Allen
Department of Coins and Medals, Fitzwilliam Museum
University of Cambridge
Cambridge, UK

Sophus Reinert
Harvard Business School
Cambridge, MA, USA

The study of the history of financial institutions, markets, instruments and concepts is vital if we are to understand the role played by finance today. At the same time, the methodologies developed by finance academics can provide a new perspective for historical studies. Palgrave Studies in the History of Finance is a multi-disciplinary effort to emphasise the role played by finance in the past, and what lessons historical experiences have for us. It presents original research, in both authored monographs and edited collections, from historians, finance academics and economists, as well as financial practitioners.

More information about this series at
http://www.palgrave.com/gp/series/14583

Nicolas Barreyre • Nicolas Delalande
Editors

A World of Public Debts

A Political History

palgrave
macmillan

Editors
Nicolas Barreyre
Mondes Américains/CENA
EHESS
Paris, France

Nicolas Delalande
Centre d'Histoire
Sciences Po
Paris, France

ISSN 2662-5164　　　　ISSN 2662-5172　(electronic)
Palgrave Studies in the History of Finance
ISBN 978-3-030-48793-5　　　ISBN 978-3-030-48794-2　(eBook)
https://doi.org/10.1007/978-3-030-48794-2

© The Editor(s) (if applicable) and The Author(s), under exclusive licence to Springer Nature Switzerland AG 2020, corrected publication 2020
Chapters 13 and 19 are licensed under the terms of the Creative Commons Attribution 4.0 International License (http://creativecommons.org/licenses/by/4.0/). For further details see license information in the chapter.
This work is subject to copyright. All rights are solely and exclusively licenced by the Publisher, whether the whole or part of the material is concerned, specifically the rights of translation, reprinting, reuse of illustrations, recitation, broadcasting, reproduction on microfilms or in any other physical way, and transmission or information storage and retrieval, electronic adaptation, computer software, or by similar or dissimilar methodology now known or hereafter developed.
The use of general descriptive names, registered names, trademarks, service marks, etc. in this publication does not imply, even in the absence of a specific statement, that such names are exempt from the relevant protective laws and regulations and therefore free for general use.
The publisher, the authors and the editors are safe to assume that the advice and information in this book are believed to be true and accurate at the date of publication. Neither the publisher nor the authors or the editors give a warranty, expressed or implied, with respect to the material contained herein or for any errors or omissions that may have been made. The publisher remains neutral with regard to jurisdictional claims in published maps and institutional affiliations.

Cover illustration: © Vincenzo Dragani / Alamy Stock Photo

This Palgrave Macmillan imprint is published by the registered company Springer Nature Switzerland AG.
The registered company address is: Gewerbestrasse 11, 6330 Cham, Switzerland

Introduction

"I try and talk economics in the Eurogroup, which nobody does," Yanis Varoufakis recounted after his brief tenure as finance minister of Greece in 2014–2015. "It's not that it didn't go down well—it's that there was point blank refusal to engage in economic arguments. Point blank."[1] This confessed culture shock by an academic suddenly thrown into the midst of professional politicians at the height of an unprecedented crisis within the European Union unveils, perhaps, a certain political naiveté as much as it reveals the diplomatic disadvantage at which Greece, which he represented, then stood. Yet it also highlights that the sovereign debt crisis within the Eurozone was not only, or even mainly, about the economy: it was about politics, institutions, and solidarity. If anything, it put the lie to the usual mantra that managing a public debt, and public finances more generally, is a matter of technical expertise best left to those who know the laws of economics. Experts, it appeared, made decisions which were no less political than that of others.

This is not to say that the problem was to let politics enter the management of an economic problem, somehow distorting the "pure" economics of a solution. This is not to say, either, that public debt is *only* politics, and that its economic parameters could only yield to political will. It is to say, however, that public debts are inherently political objects as much as they are economic. The Greek crisis did not inject politics into an economic domain that gently hums in the background in fair weather. It unveiled how political public debt *always* is, even when it is not the focus of political debate. For public debt raises issues about the distribution of power and resources within and across societies, revealing as well as enhancing transfers of liabilities between social groups and generations.

This book sets out to explore exactly this political nature of public debt, both domestically and internationally. While public debt is a financial transaction—creating a relation between (mostly) private investors and a sovereign body (the former lending money to the latter, who pledges to repay the principal plus interests in a more or less distant future)—it is also, and inseparably, an *instrument of power*, a *social relationship*, and a *political arena* in which interests and values collide.[2] Public debt binds together major political issues, such as the power of the state to tax and spend, its legitimate role to regulate markets, and the social distribution of collective resources between bondholders and taxpayers. Drawing inspiration from the "new fiscal sociology" and the renewed interest of political historians in economic matters, this book aims to grasp public debt issues in all their dimensions, be they economic or political, legal, intellectual, social, or moral.[3] For we need this kind of "total history" to understand why our present is so deeply framed and impacted by public indebtedness.

THE POLITICS OF PUBLIC DEBTS IN THE LONG RUN

Public debt is hardly a new subject, and considering its importance both in the economic life of nations and in the political turmoil of our time, it is not surprising. Why, thus, a new volume? We contend that a historical perspective in the long run, from the eighteenth century to today, with a detailed attention to diverse cases as well as the circulation of ideas, systems and capital, can significantly revise our understanding of modern public debt.

There has been abundant historically oriented scholarship on public debt, contributed by economic historians, political scientists, legal scholars, and international relations specialists. Although it is a rich and variegated scholarship, we think it fair, for the sake of clarity, to distinguish three main lines of questioning that have dominated the research and debates of the last thirty years.

A first powerful line of enquiry has explored the historical and theoretical relationships between political institutions and the development of financial markets. In a 1989 seminal article, neo-institutionalist economists Douglass North and Barry Weingast argued that, in England, the political and institutional reforms brought by the Glorious Revolution of 1688 created a "financial revolution." The rise of Parliament and the limitations imposed on the king's power played a crucial role in securing property rights, thus reassuring lenders that the Crown would honor its obligations and abstain from defaulting on its outstanding debts (a common practice in early-modern Europe). Simultaneously, the creation of the Bank of England in 1694 helped channel private capital towards public bonds, and made the British *consols* one of the most attractive long-term assets for two centuries. North and Weingast thus concluded that, by creating "good institutions"—limited executive power, parliamentary oversight, and secured property rights—England showed "credible commitment" to investors who flocked to its bonds, making its state into a financial powerhouse.[4]

This article was influential in erecting the British historical experience into a sort of universal model, with which all the other national trajectories had to be compared and assessed. However, this "credible commitment" hypothesis has been qualified on many grounds since then. British historians have shown that public borrowing had started to improve well before the late seventeenth century, that "limited government" was only part of the story of the rise of the fiscal-military state, and was also based on centralized fiscal power and aggressive imperial expansion.[5] Political scientists and economic sociologists have insisted on the social interpenetration between bondholders and elite politicians to make sense of the British parliament's continuous commitment to repay debts.[6] Scholars of other countries have contested the idea that there was one single path to political and financial modernity, showing that other experiences could be equally sustainable.[7] Finally, a blindspot in this model is how historically specific it was: though it might be useful to analyze the eighteenth and nineteenth centuries,[8] it is far less efficient to account for twentieth century history, marked by a massive increase in executive power, state intervention, and market regulation.

The long-term approach we adopt in this book is meant to avoid such pitfalls. Widely extending the chronological and spatial scope of our enquiry, and considering other historical experiences, allow us to show how historically grounded the institutions in charge of public debt were, how context made them evolve, and also how their workings depended on specific political situations and debates. Against the view that there is one set of good "liberal democratic institutions,"[9] our research shows how public debt and the efficacy of institutions underpinning it vary historically, as their political legitimacy was never assured.

This issue of legitimacy is at the core of a second line of scholarly enquiry that has powerfully shaped the historiography on public debt, especially among legal scholars, political scientists, and international relations specialists. This body of literature focuses on "sovereign debt," that is, the problem of the uneven power relationship between a sovereign borrower and individual lenders. This raises complex political and legal issues about a state's commitment to repay its debts, given that there is no international legal order that may force a sovereign state to comply with its obligations towards foreign bondholders. Why does global public indebtedness keep growing while there is so little guarantee given to lenders that they will get their investment back in the event of default or systemic crisis?[10]

To answer this conundrum, the literature has taken three main directions. The first underlines the role of extra-contractual *sanctions* (what some call "supersanctions"), mainly the use of military force, trade retaliation or the imposition of international financial controls.[11] A second type of explanation focuses on *reputation* as a key factor, given that defaulting states run the risk of losing access to financial markets or of suffering from high premiums in future borrowing attempts.[12] Empirical research has demonstrated, however, that it was not always the case, since many states which had suspended their payments could later go back to the markets without being subjected to harsher conditions than "virtuous" ones.[13] That's why a third stream of studies has started to historicize and politicize debt *repudiation*, investigating the intellectual, political, and economic conditions on which a state could default without many adverse consequences. While today's "common sense" is that states should always repay their debts, historically there were times when states could suspend or cancel their obligations without much retaliation on the international scene. Different notions of sovereignty could serve to justify debt write-offs, and political legitimacy (and not only market discipline or legal contracts) was held to be crucial to decide whether a debt had to be honored or not. This was especially the case when a successor state inherited financial obligations from a previous overthrown regime, for example, in instances of decolonization.

Although it is in dialogue with the first two lines of scholarship, our approach is more aligned with the third one, which insists that "the debt continuity norm is intrinsically political and historically variable."[14] Sanctions, reputation and (il)legitimate repudiation were all key dimensions of public borrowing and debt repayment through the last three centuries. But our long-term perspective and attention to local, as well as international political conditions allows us to revise the collective conclusions of this body of literature. If, indeed, sovereign debt involves obligations both towards a state's own citizens as well as its domestic and foreign lenders, it follows that its repayment is as much an issue of political legitimacy sustained over time as of financial creditworthiness. The empirical studies assembled here show that, in the longer term, what supports legitimacy changes over time, depending on the mutations of the global political economy as well as local situations. But they also complicate our understanding of sovereign debt, for there were periods when most public debt was contracted by public entities that were not nation-states.

The third debate that has recently structured the literature on public debt, especially in sociology and political science, has revolved around the issue of the compatibility between public debt, capitalism, and democracy. Although this is not a new question—liberal thinkers in the eighteenth century already warned against the antidemocratic nature of public debts[15]—it has been revived with new urgency since the crisis of 2008, as Wolfgang Streeck's hotly debated book *Buying Time* exemplifies.[16] In the wake of the "credible commitment" hypothesis, some scholars tried to defend the opposite argument, to show that *only* liberal democracies were able to sustain large and stable public debts, while authoritarian regimes, because of their excessive power, would fail to attract investors because of a loss of confidence.[17] However, this so-called democratic advantage thesis has not been supported by empirical research.[18] On the contrary, public choice economists and international lending actors over the last thirty years have insisted on the necessity to *constrain* democratic practices rather than *expand* them for a country to build "credible commitment" mechanisms. Hence the move towards independent central banks, the adoption of constitutional rules on budgetary issues, or the refusal to align economic policies with the wishes expressed by the people at the polls (as was the case after the Greek referendum of June 2015).[19] For some of its most vehement critics, public debt is nothing but than an infernal tool used by capitalism to stifle democratic debate and accelerate a massive transfer of wealth from the public to the private sector, thereby increasing economic and social inequality to an unprecedented scale.[20]

There is, of course, much insight in this debate, but it is singularly focused on the very recent period. Our volume, on the contrary, takes a longer-term and wider comparative perspective. This allows us to depart in three significant ways from the existing literature. First, a *historical and non-teleological perspective*, open to a variety of political historical experiences across the globe (empires, nation-states, regional federations, municipalities), helps relativize the expansion of the peculiar British historical case as a primary yardstick for studying public debt. Second, we disconnect the issue of *political legitimacy* from *the nature of political regimes*: as we show, public debts can be sustained by democracies, but also by imperial bodies, authoritarian or oligarchic regimes, which may rely on different debt management techniques or have them in common. Third, we study the *historical transformation of the state/market relation in the long run*, which helps avoid the pitfalls of a short-sighted narrative that opposes the current "tyranny" of markets with the supposed "golden age" of state power and market embeddedness in the twentieth century.

This is why this book starts in the eighteenth century, when an understanding of public debt emerged in Europe that still informs ours today. Publicists and philosophers started crafting arguments to make sense of the "public" side of a debt contracted not by an identifiable sovereign but by more abstract "states." What that "public" meant, and whether it made for a different kind of debt from those contracted between individuals, were questions at the core of debates that arose then, and whose answers still resonate surprisingly cogently today, even though the economic and accounting realities of public debts have shifted far from what they were then. It was also in the late eighteenth century that public debt started feeding the intertwined emergence of a more globalized capitalism and the violent formation of imperial nation-states.[21]

It led us to bring together cases that, historically, have been studied separately because of strong differences in institutions or cultures, as if trust and credibility had always been the monopoly of liberal parliamentary regimes. Comparing vast empires (the Spanish Empire, Qing China, British colonial Africa) with smaller nation-states allows the reconsideration of historical experiences that have often been overlooked by the literature on the eighteenth and nineteenth centuries. In the twentieth century, bringing together the cases of liberal democracies (France, United Kingdom, United States) with authoritarian or totalitarian regimes (Nazi Germany, Soviet Russia) sheds light on common patterns underlying jarringly different political experiences, especially during the age of the "Great Compression," from the 1930s to the 1960s, when new instruments of market regulation were invented on a national and international scale. To understand the reordering of global capitalism in this period and the advent of the Bretton Woods system (1944), one cannot simply look at Western democracies and how they coped with economic collapse, unemployment, mounting debts, and monetary instability. What we need is a global analysis of the structural changes in the relations between states, markets, and societies, which occurred at the same time (though in different forms and degrees) in the American New Deal, in Nazi Germany's authoritarian economy, or in the Soviet planned economy.[22] Later in the century, observing the turn to financial markets for public debt in Italy, in France and in India from the 1970s to the 1990s changes the familiar story about the rise of neoliberalism, which rarely goes back farther than World War II.[23] Differences in political institutions and cultures should not obscure the common features and transformations affecting various countries in a given context, when economic ideas, capital flows, and political power are widely reconfigured.

This book thus defends an approach to global history that does not make a claim for exhaustivity, but that carefully selects and studies contextualized cases in connection to one another to reveal broader patterns and, simultaneously, local variations. It has two benefits: it makes possible an attention to multiple scales (including national debts, of course, but also imperial and local debts, which were often neglected or thought of separately)[24] and to the way sovereign bodies were transformed and hybridized across time (the "sovereign" in "sovereign debt" is not a *given*, and cannot be solely equated with the nation-state); and it allows for an integration of multiple historiographies, rather than the mostly English-language (more homogenized) historiography that single-authored global histories tend to rely on. Instead of the all-encompassing master narrative or the macro-economic perspective, this book offers a contextualized, fine-grained approach that draws strong linkages between illuminating historical cases. The international collaborative network we built for writing this book aims to avoid the pitfalls of a purely Western-centered perspective, by comparing cases taken across four continents, from China to North America, from British colonial Africa to Latin America and Europe.[25]

The Construction and Demise of Successive Public Debt Regimes

The longer view we take in this book allows us to show that, even as history does not repeat itself, relevant historical parallels illuminate our present moment in much more interesting ways. This approach makes it possible to break both with the teleology of models and with the more traditional chronology. As we show, the world has gone through successive *public debt regimes* since the eighteenth century. By public debt regime, we mean a stable, dominant configuration defined by a specific articulation between the distribution of capital and markets (or the "structural power of finance" in political science terms), the nature of state power (what tools and expertise it can use), and the shape of the political arena (where political legitimacy comes from; how different social groups mobilize to defend their views and interests).[26] Our hypothesis is that there is much interdependence between the domestic side of public debt and the structure of the international political economy (shaped by its monetary regime, the geography of capital flows, or global inequalities of power).

These regimes can be hegemonic but never without contemporary alternatives; and they are not eternal. It is precisely when debt crises occur that these regimes are challenged and redefined, through multiple negotiations, conflicts, and reordering. With this definition in mind, we can understand why global public debt crises (in the 1820s, 1880s, 1930s, 1980s, and 2010s)[27] were critical junctures during which the organization of, and boundaries between, markets, states, and citizenries were displaced and rearranged, both from a material and an intellectual point of view.[28] This notion can help us think about moments of stability and crisis together, as well as the interaction between political orders and economic systems. Our redrawing of the usual chronology and its meaning allows us to identify periods when a particular political-economic configuration of public debt became dominant, or even hegemonic, such as the era from the mid-nineteenth century to the 1910s (known to economic historians as the "First Globalization"[29]), and periods when the plurality of practices and trajectories was more pronounced (the "long revolutionary" period from the 1770s to the 1820s; or the interwar years in the twentieth century). Studying how particular regimes became dominant and shaped other configurations, we show how public debts in the modern era did not follow invariant "models." We propose an understanding of political economy that avoids teleology and can explain variations as something that goes far beyond the reconstruction of long-term statistics and the isolation of repeated patterns, or the identification of an anthropological moral invariant of debt.[30]

So, what debt regimes can we collectively identify from our historical cases? We start our investigation in the revolutionary age of the late eighteenth century, when early modern debt regimes were challenged and redefined by new political principles and aspirations. "Part I: Political Crises and the Legitimacy of Public Debts" shows that sustainable public debt had little to do with market mechanisms, or even "credible commitment," but was rather anchored in the capacity of a political regime to support its legitimacy. In a bold reinterpretation, Regina Grafe uncovers in the Spanish American Empire a strong decentralized network of public credit and merchant capital that moved money across space when needed, while unburdening the Crown with accumulated debt. Based on the political and religious legitimacies of the Monarchy and the Church, it sustained the largest empire of the time. Only the political shock of European wars and American independences upended it. The English-liberal model with which the new fledgling nations replaced it, however, proved unsuitable and failed to bolster their legitimacy. This liberal vision of public debt was also, as Rebecca Spang tells us in Chap. 2, part of what went wrong with the French Revolution. The French Monarchy's debt was not economically unsustainable, but it became politically so in the 1780s. This is why the first revolutionaries, far from proclaiming a clear break with the past, immediately declared their commitment to the public debt. In doing so, they created growing political instability. The Revolution's radicalization was the product less of extreme ideology than of the contradictions between existing property relations and new models of citizenship and participation. Maybe the French should have looked at Sweden, a peripheral country whose case is particularly illuminating. Since the mid-eighteenth century, as Patrik Winton writes in Chap. 3, public debt had been at the center of several shifts of political power within the realm, sometimes bolstering the parliamentary system, at other times helping the king confiscate more power. That story ended when the new king, Bernadotte, built his own political legitimacy by defaulting on two-thirds of the existing public debt and tying the new credit to his own person. The period from the mid-eighteenth to the mid-nineteenth century was thus a moment of political transformation when public debt became closely tied to political regimes' legitimacy. After the Revolution, the French indeed managed to create a public debt system that would sustain its new political regimes through public participation. In Chap. 4, David Todd and Alexia Yates weave together this story of intellectual reconceptualization and material popular involvement in public subscriptions. This provided the French state with renewed political legitimacy, and made Paris into one of the main capital export markets in the world, barely a few years after the infamous "*banqueroute des deux tiers*" (1797).

Thus, by the mid-nineteenth century, a *liberal debt regime*, especially as promoted by the British, had become dominant in Europe, marginalizing the different varieties of public debts that had characterized the eighteenth century. It is that regime, although there were important variations within it, that the Europeans globalized in the second half of the nineteenth century through capital flows, imperial conquests, and other forms of coercion. Yet even if pressures for increased standardization were powerful at that time, as with the global expansion of the gold standard for instance, the political conditions were diverse, leading to differing historical experiences. "Part II: Global Capital, Imperial Expansions, and Changing Sovereignties" addresses the contested diffusion of public debts across the world and how they reconfigured the distribution of wealth, fed growing inequalities, and transformed global politics. Newly independent Latin American countries were the first to import liberal understandings of public debt from Europe, but throughout the century, they mostly evaded "supersanctions" in spite of defaults. As Juan Flores argues in Chap. 5, this had mostly to do with strong citizenries with competing interests that made European military intervention or trade sanctions difficult to work out unilaterally. Similarly, the Ottoman case examined by Coşkun Tunçer in Chap. 6 complicates the usual view that public debt imperialism was a simple game of nation versus nation. The Porte was able to leverage its public debt and financial control negotiated with Western powers to push internal institutional reforms while evading much of its political cost. Not all countries could pull off that game, though. Egypt might be the prototypical case of imperialism through public debt. But to understand those evolutions, as Malak Labib shows in Chap. 7, we need to follow competing groups of experts, local and international, in defining concepts and assembling financial knowledge. While their circulation would help build international norms, their work had more to do with their entanglement in power relations than expertise. Thus, access to European capital was never a pure market transaction, as Leigh Gardner also demonstrates in Chap. 8 with the comparative West African cases of independent Liberia and the colonial Gold Coast, Nigeria and Sierra Leone. In Britain, it involved public and private interests enmeshed in the hybrid institutions of Empire, which mediated lending through actors who were both private financiers and agents of the British state. Such blurring between European lenders and their governments was, indeed, a feature of the "liberal debt regime" that became prominent in those years. In Late Qing China, on the contrary, foreign capital enabled the more commercial regions to increase commerce and develop infrastructure, at the expense of a moral political economy that emphasized the Emperor's benevolence through regional redistribution. As Dong Yan recounts in Chap. 9, European-style public debt sapped the political legitimacy of the regime, fostering nationalist unrest and wars. Across Europe and North America too, public debt allowed for massive investment in infrastructure but also contested redistribution of wealth and political power. As Noam Maggor and Stephen Sawyer show for France and the United States in Chap. 10, most of this happened at the municipal level—thus redrawing their political geography as surely as it did in China. As Part II concludes, the height of the financial globalization of the gold standard era was never the liberal world that some look back to with nostalgia. Public debts were always embedded in power relations that had little to do with market relations, but in that period they fed growing inequalities and imperial designs that made the world increasingly unstable.

This first global age of public debts exploded in World War I, and "Part III: The Great Transformation of Public Debts" explores the challenge for states to rebuild their political legitimacy, with their capacity to borrow and tax at stake, and shows the progressive and chaotic advent of a new *"dirigiste debt regime,"* with variations across political systems. World War I put tremendous stress on even the most solid states that had spent more than a century building confidence in their public debts. As Nicolas Delalande analyzes for France and Britain in Chap. 11, the need to borrow massively to wage total war was foremost a democratic challenge involving nationalism, regime legitimacy, and international standing. It led to unprecedented state reach deep into civil society, and postwar disillusionment (fueled by hyperinflation and monetary volatility) that bred political instability and social upheaval. Victors and vanquished countries all scrambled in search of a new debt regime, prodded by the urgent need of both political legitimacy and financial stability. Stefanie Middendorf recounts in Chap. 12 how, in Germany, political turmoil and the fragility of the Weimar Republic helped the emergence of a new, technical, "depoliticized" financial regime that tapped savings into a closed circuit that would serve radically different regimes, from the troubled republic of the 1920s to the Nazi state of the 1930s and the reformed postwar Federal republic. Yet it never meant that public debt could actually escape politics. In Germany, "financial repression" was intimately, and necessarily, linked to mass propaganda. So was it in the USSR. In Chap. 13, Kristy Ironside and Étienne Forestier-Peyrat take us on a fascinating tour of Soviet public borrowing. The denunciation of the prewar "liberal" regime had included repudiating the Czars' debts. Mobilization of resources meant finding ways to tap private funds where only public ownership of means of production was tolerated, leading to a mix of old-fashioned devices and institutional inventions. The heightened importance of state control of borrowing and public debt was acute throughout those decades in old European countries, new communist countries, and maybe even more in newly decolonized countries after World War II. In the Middle East, as Matthieu Rey explores in Chap. 14, public debt had been a tool of colonial domination, but after independence it became a political touchstone to build the new regimes, in a bargain where public debt both signified sovereignty and allowed to avoid taxing the population. This new "dirigiste debt regime" was less globalized than the previous one, but everywhere it helped build states, and bolster political regimes, with market operations under severe controls—in this dominant regime, only a few public debts were at the mercy of markets.

The rupture introduced in the 1970s is the subject of "Part IV: The Political Roads to Financial Markets and Global Debt Crisis." The turn to a *"financialized debt regime"* was not so much the result of a retreat of the state as a choice made by many political and economic actors to reorganize the relations between states and markets, at a time when inflation ceased to be a legitimate tool of regulation, and social spending put increasing pressure on public finances. As Anush Kapadia and Benjamin Lemoine show in their comparative take on France and India (Chap. 15), financial deregulation was conceived as a way to bypass the political and social conflicts that "embedded liberalism" could no longer cope with. The complete change in public debt management led to a shift of power, from state treasuries to central banks and international financial markets—as the Italian example studied by Alexander Nützenadel in Chap. 16 illuminates—through a mix of half-improvised solutions to short-term crises and willful restraints put on state intervention in the economy. States remained crucial actors, as their reaction after the 2008 crisis demonstrated (through bailout plans). They still have the capacity to sustain high debts, but at a political cost that weakens democratic institutions. The international relations of public debts highlight this marginalization of polities, Jérôme Sgard shows us in Chap. 17, as the diplomatic setting of debt settlement experimented by the IMF in the 1980s, however decried at the time, gave way to adjudication before national courts in a handful of jurisdictions (with large financial markets), emphasizing the loss of sovereignty of many nations and a form of legal imperialism. In the triangular relation between states, markets, and polities, the latter feel more and more excluded. The discrepancy between the financial networks of globalization and its political regime has never been so wide, and that explains many of the political developments and crises that have occurred in the 2010s. In Chap. 18, Adam Tooze chronicles those shifts through a focus on the men who styled themselves "bond vigilantes," and their role in working this new financialized debt regime to its limits. In doing so, he highlights the close connection between the new forms of high public indebtedness, the growing economic inequalities, and the widespread dissatisfaction with democratic institutions that feed the dangerous political reactions that have swept across a large part of the world in recent years.

In a concluding section, entitled "On the Historical Uses of Numbers and Words," two chapters decisively show that the meaning and understanding of "public debt" has never been stable, even among professional economists and financiers. Éric Monnet and Blaise Truong-Loï uncover how public debt accounting has actually evaded experts, civil servants, and financiers alike, for two centuries, even after massive international normative projects in the wake of World War II. Building on the detailed cases of Germany, France, and China, they show that every accounting decision (especially for comparative purposes) has been rife with political implications in the balance of power between states, creditors, and polities. Their work is a clear warning that we should be cautious about any economic study that uses long-term statistics of public debt without anchoring them in their specific intellectual and political contexts. Also taking the long view, Nicolas Barreyre and Nicolas Delalande retrace how seemingly unchanging arguments over public debt varied widely over more than two centuries. They study how political actors fighting over public debts used a shared repertoire of arguments that started building in the eighteenth century but was repeatedly transformed. Contexts changed and re-sorted those ready-made ideas. This is a call for a political history that highlights the circulation of ideas while understanding that their meaning is always *locally* contested. It makes all the more urgent the kind of political history proposed in the chapters of this book.

This narrative of successive dominant debt regimes should not be confused with a typology: we did not uncover different competing models of "doing" public debt, but rather teased from our historical cases different dominant organizations of public borrowing and management that were particular to historical moments. What we take from this first exploration, which we hope will inspire others, are three main points. The first one is that public debt has never obeyed timeless laws, as there is no impersonal mechanics attached to it. It is an inherently political object whose workings are deeply tied to modes of political legitimacy. Second, there is thus no universal "good institution" to build public debt on, and thus no inevitability to the legal rules and institutional makeup that would be "necessary" for borrowing states to establish. Finally, political legitimacy is a key feature of public debt, as well as of creditors' claims. We believe that such conclusions are important when we observe the shape of contemporary debates over national indebtedness in the new global capitalist order now in crisis, reaching unprecedented proportions with the deep impact of the COVID-19 pandemic.

Public Debt and Capitalism

By looking at past historical configurations, the book shows that global public debt crises are related to deep transformations in the relation (and boundaries) between states, markets, and polities, as well as shifting power relations across the globe. Today's tendency to consider public debt as a source of fragility or economic inefficiency misses the fact that, since the eighteenth century, public debts and capital markets have on many occasions been used by states to enforce their sovereignty and build their institutions, especially (but far from only) in times of war. Considering that access to capital is crucial to state-building, it should be no surprise that states decided to bail out banks and insurance companies after 2008, or that central banks intervened so massively to buy sovereign bonds and keep interest rates at low levels. But it is striking to observe that certain solutions that were used in the past to smooth out public debt crises (inflation in the 1920s, default in the 1870–1880s or 1930s, or capital controls after 1945) were left out of the political framing of the current crisis, thus revealing how the balance of power between bondholders, taxpayers, pensioners, and wage-earners has evolved over the past forty years.

Given the acuteness of the current debt crisis, we would like to spell out how this volume could add to the historical understanding of capitalism that has been, of late, a growing concern of scholarship.[31] It aims at recapturing the relations between private capital and public authorities, looking at the role of finance and credit in the shaping of state sovereignty, economic inequalities, democratic institutions, or imperialist endeavors.[32] By reviving "political economy" as a key concept in the study of capitalism, historians, sociologists, and political scientists insist on the deep interplay between markets and politics, as soon as we accept that the "economy" is a historical construct, embedded in social relations, moral values, and political conflicts, rather than a natural order whose laws apply at every period and in every context.[33] For all its exciting and fruitful developments, however, this "new history of capitalism" has mostly focused on the American experience. Our global history of public debts sheds light on the role played by capital flows and debt relations in the global expansion of capitalism since the late eighteenth century, and in the process "de-americanizes" (and also "de-anglicizes") the history of capitalism. Here, we show that putting the political analysis at the center of our enquiry can make sense of the history of capitalism in all its avatars through time, as capitalism is constantly reshaped in localized, interconnected political dynamics. Our contribution to this larger reflection takes four directions.

First, we argue that public debt has always been a powerful driver for the expansion of capitalism. State borrowing went far beyond the mere circulation of money and bonds. It spurred the construction of knowledge (e.g. statistics and economic categories) and the diffusion of economic ideas (classical liberalism, Keynesian macroeconomics, public choice economics, ordoliberalism, and so on), shaped financial, political, and administrative institutions, and fed the competition between moral categories and political visions.[34] Beyond financial transfers, public debts imply many circulations, of experts and scientists, of books and newspapers, of intermediaries and merchants, of institutions and specific economic policies, as shown in most chapters of this volume. When borrowing money, states need to find lenders—and it often led them to adopt the words and categories of financiers when the latter had the upper hand, because they had established themselves as the experts or when they had the power to decide the success or failure of a loan. In the nineteenth century, as many national and local governments strove to issue bonds in London, Paris, Amsterdam, Vienna (or later New York) to modernize their institutions and promote economic development (through railway construction, mining industries, administrative reforms), they increasingly bought into a financial system that sought to impose its own values and measurements on their institutions. To understand how global capitalism was shaped, we need to pay close attention to the many efforts (and disputes) to produce standardized measures and concepts about public finances and financial markets, assets and liabilities, debt ratio and so on. However this story has always been a highly contested one, marked by the contradiction between two diverging principles, the need for states to offer transparency about their public accounts (to reassure foreign or national bondholders) and the kind of opacity and secrecy that dominates many discussions between central bankers, political elites, and financial companies in times of crisis, especially today.[35]

Second, this global history of public debts compels us to think about the relationship between capitalism, imperialism, and violence. The use of sovereign debt as a tool used by Western countries to exert their domination over the rest of the world, both in colonial and postcolonial settings, is looked at afresh in the second part of the volume. Over the nineteenth century, the expansion of financial capitalism was directly connected to slaveholding, the rise of empires, the formation of nation-states, and the multiplication of wars and social conflicts.[36] If globalization rode the wings of European imperialisms, then it remains to account for an expansion of capitalism wedded to the new, triumphant nation-states. A "postcolonial" reading of sovereign debt issues insists on the oppressive nature of financial claims and duties, and its connection with violence. But looking at different scales and comparing various cases help deconstruct such a global vision, without overlooking the relation between debt and domination. Some countries searched for foreign capital precisely to reinforce themselves and wage war (see Sweden in the late eighteenth century, Greece in the 1890s); in other cases local elites wanted to leverage the external supervision of national finances to promote unpopular domestic reforms and increase their economic position and political power (as in many Latin American countries during the nineteenth century, or in newly independent states such as Iraq and Syria in the 1950s and 1960s). Exporting capital could also lead to reverse effects on creditor powers, especially when debts were canceled or repudiated, weakening the core of financial capitalism.[37] This story also points to a reinterpretation of the many experiences in international financial control and regulations, from the 1860s-1870s in Tunisia, the Ottoman Empire and Egypt, to the recent implementations of structural adjustment programs by the IMF in postcolonial African countries (in the 1980s) or the role played by the now famous *"troika"* (composed of members of the European Commission, the European Central Bank and the IMF) in Greece after 2010.

Third, this history contributes to the vivid debate, launched by political scientists in the 1990s, on the "varieties of capitalism."[38] Capitalism has indeed always taken different historical forms (not only in space, but also in time); so, we should not be surprised if the crisis we are living through has reopened urgent debates about the sustainability and future of liberal and capitalist democracies. The successive debt regimes ("liberal", "dirigiste", and "financialized") that we uncover are a start in this direction.

They are based on an analysis of how capital globalization went hand in hand with local, national, and regional differentiations across time, and how political configurations and events were a key factor—thus shedding light on power relations, economic inequalities, and social redistribution in the modern era. They also make room for alternatives to the English-liberal model which has been improperly erected as the "correct," because historically "successful," model. Not only did England *not* look like that model of "credible commitment" in the past, there existed other political economic paths that proved entirely sustainable until upended by the political upheavals that shook the world across the "age of revolutions."

Finally, this global history tries to look at how public debt has entered the everyday life of individuals and societies, how it has been appropriated by them and at times contested.[39] Combining the macro and the micro is essential if we want to understand how this abstract phenomenon of public indebtedness, saturated with figures, long-term commitments, and byzantine mechanisms, has affected the social, economic, and political life of millions of people over time.[40] The divide between theoretical and statistical macro-approaches, on the one hand, and the type of microhistory that social and cultural historians are crafting, on the other, needs to be filled if we want to get a sense of what "public debt" really meant for societies in history. The various chapters gathered in this volume mark a first step in this direction; they look at the "global chains" of capital and public debt, which connect people and institutions from different social backgrounds, countries, and continents, not only today but already in the late eighteenth century. That's why this history cannot rely solely on bankers, diplomats, and international lawyers, those "big players" whose role is often already well-known, but must also rely on the millions of small investors, taxpayers, pensioners, consumers, wage-earners, whose economic and political power has been shaped and constrained by long-distance financial transfers. Public debt entered their daily lives when they bought bonds, subscribed to life insurance policies or private pension schemes, or when inflation and debt cancelation eroded their real incomes. It also triggered political movements and upheavals, in times of war and crisis, or when financial demands and austerity measures increased inequalities while foreclosing democratic choice.[41]

* * *

In our contemporary crisis, reconnecting the history of capitalism and that of democracy seems one of the most urgent intellectual and political tasks of our time. This global political history of public debt is a contribution to this debate. The urgent task of our day is to elaborate a new understanding to articulate state power, market mechanics, and democratic agency. The issues at stake are crucial for the future of our societies. Where to draw the line between transparency and opacity in the management of public debts? What kind of responsibility do experts, central bankers, and international leaders have towards societies and people whose wellbeing is dependent upon public debts and their repayment? Can public debt be used to other ends than increased inequality and diminished political choice? These questions are not new, but they are still ours. We hope this book will bring history back into this debate, and help consider that there are always several alternatives open for political discussion, even when we speak of public debts.

Nicolas Barreyre
Nicolas Delalande

Notes

1. "Yanis Varoufakis Full Transcript: Our Battle to Save Greece," *The New Statesman* (July 13, 2015); Yanis Varoufakis, *Adults in the Room: My Battle With Europe's Deep Establishment* (London: Bodley Head, 2017).
2. Kenneth Dyson, *States, Debt, and Power: "Saints" and "Sinners" in European History and Integration* (Oxford: Oxford University Press, 2014).
3. Isaac Martin, Ajay K. Mehrotra and Monica Prasad, eds., *The New Fiscal Sociology: Taxation in Comparative and Historical Perspective* (Cambridge: Cambridge University Press, 2009); Jeremy Adelman and Jonathan Levy, "The Fall and Rise of Economic History," *Chronicle of Higher Education* (December 2014).
4. Douglass North and Barry Weingast, "Constitutions and Commitment: The Evolution of Institutions Governing Public Choice in Seventeenth-Century England," *Journal of Economic History* XLIX, no. 4 (1989): 803–32; P.G.M. Dickson, *The Financial Revolution in England. A Study in the Development of Public Credit, 1688–1756* (London: Macmillan, 1967).
5. For a synthesis, see D'Maris Coffman, Adrian Leonard and Larry Neal, eds., *Questioning Credible Commitment: Perspectives on the Rise of Financial Capitalism* (Cambridge: Cambridge University Press, 2013). On the eco-

nomic history side, see for instance Larry Neal, *The Rise of Financial Capitalism* (Cambridge: Cambridge University Press, 1990); Anne L. Murphy, *The Origins of English Financial Markets: Investment and Speculation before the South Sea Bubble* (Cambridge: Cambridge University Press, 2019); Carl Wennerlind, *Casualties of Credit: The English Financial Revolution, 1620–1720* (Cambridge, Mass.: Harvard University Press, 2011). On the history of the fiscal-military state, see John Brewer, *The Sinews of Power. War, Money and the English State, 1688–1783* (London: Unwin Hyman, 1989); Marjolein t'Hart, *The Making of a Bourgeois State: War, Politics and Finance during the Dutch Revolt* (Manchester: Manchester University Press, 1993); Philip T. Hoffman and Kathryn Norberg, eds., *Fiscal Crises, Liberty, and Representative Government, 1450–1789* (Stanford: Stanford University Press, 1994); Katia Béguin, *Financer la guerre au XVIIe siècle. La dette publique et les rentiers de l'absolutisme* (Seyssel: Champ Vallon, 2012); D'Maris Coffman, *Excise Taxation and the Origins of Public Debt* (Basingstoke: Palgrave Macmillan, 2013); Mauricio Drelichman and Hans-Joachim Voth, *Lending to the Borrower from Hell. Debt, Taxes, and Default in the Age of Philip II* (Princeton: Princeton University Press, 2014); Steven Pincus, *1688: The First Modern Revolution* (New Haven: Yale University Press, 2011); Rafael Torres Sanchez, *Constructing a Fiscal Military State in Eighteenth Century Spain* (Basingstoke: Palgrave Macmillan, 2015).

6. Bruce Carruthers, *City of Capital: Politics and Markets in the English Financial Revolution* (Princeton: Princeton University Press, 1996); David Stasavage, *Public Debt and the Birth of the Democratic State: France and Great Britain, 1688–1789* (Cambridge: Cambridge University Press, 2003).

7. Regina Grafe, *Distant Tyranny: Markets, Power, and Backwardness in Spain, 1650–1800* (Princeton: Princeton University Press, 2012); Wenkai He, *Paths Toward the Modern Fiscal State: England, Japan, and China* (Cambridge, Mass.: Harvard University Press, 2013); Katia Béguin and Anne L. Murphy, eds., *State Cash Resources and State Building in Europe, 13th-18th Century* (Paris: IGPDE, 2017), https://books.openedition.org/igpde/3806.

8. David Stasavage, *States of Credit: Size, Power, and the Development of European Polities* (Princeton: Princeton University Press, 2011); Bartolomé Yun-Casalilla and Patrick K. O'Brien, eds., *The Rise of Fiscal States: A Global History, 1500–1914* (Cambridge: Cambridge University Press, 2012); José Luis Cardoso and Pedro Laines, eds., *Paying for the Liberal State: The Rise of Public Finance in Nineteenth-Century Europe* (Cambridge: Cambridge University Press, 2010); Mark Dincecco, *Political Transformations and Public Finance: Europe, 1650–1913*, (Cambridge: Cambridge University Press, 2011).

9. See for instance Daron Acemoglu and James A. Robinson, *Why Nations Fail: The Origins of Power, Prosperity, and Poverty* (New York: Crown Business, 2012).
10. For synthetic overviews of the field, see Kim Oosterlinck, "Sovereign Debt Defaults: Insights from History," *Oxford Review of Economic Policy* 29, no. 4 (2014): 697–714; Jerome Roos, *Why Not Default?* (Princeton: Princeton University Press, 2019), 21–39.
11. Edwin Borchard, *State Insolvency and Foreign Bondholders* (New Haven: Yale University Press, 1951); David Landes, *Bankers and Pashas: International Finance and Economic Imperialism in Egypt* (Cambridge, Mass.: Harvard University Press, 1958); Kris James Mitchener and Marc D. Weidenmier, "Supersanctions and Sovereign Debt Repayment," in *Sovereign Debt: From Safety to Default*, ed. Robert W. Kolb (New York: Wiley, 2011), 155–67; P. J. Cain and A. G. Hopkins, *British Imperialism, 1688–2000*, 2nd ed. (New York: Longman, 2001); Ali Coşkun Tunçer, *Sovereign Debt and International Financial Control: The Middle East and the Balkans* (London: Palgrave Macmillan, 2015); Marc Flandreau, *Anthropologists in the Stock Exchange: A Financial History of Victorian Science* (Chicago: University of Chicago Press, 2016).
12. Michael Tomz, *Reputation and International Cooperation: Sovereign Debt Across Three Centuries* (Princeton: Princeton University Press, 2007).
13. Barry J. Eichengreen and Peter L. Lindert, eds., *The International Debt Crisis in Historical Perspective* (Cambridge, Mass.: MIT Press, 1989); Eichengreen, "The Interwar Debt Crisis and its Aftermath," *The World Bank Research Observer* 5, no. 1 (1990): 69–94.
14. Odette Lienau, *Rethinking Sovereign Debt: Politics, Reputation, and Legitimacy in Modern Finance* (Cambridge, Mass.: Harvard University Press, 2014), 3; Kim Oosterlinck, *Hope Springs Eternal: French Bondholders and the Repudiation of Russian Public Debt* (New Haven: Yale University Press, 2016); Hassan Malik, *Bankers and Bolsheviks: International Finance and the Russian Revolution* (Princeton: Princeton University Press, 2018).
15. For eighteenth-century intellectual and political debates on the nature of public debts, see Istvan Hont, "The Rhapsody of Public Debt: David Hume and Voluntary State Bankruptcy," in Phillipson Nicholas and Skinner Quentin, eds., *Political Discourse in Early Modern Britain* (Cambridge: Cambridge University Press, 1993), 321–348; Michael Sonenscher, *Before the Deluge: Public Debt, Inequality, and the Intellectual Origins of the French Revolution* (Princeton: Princeton University Press, 2007); Max M. Edling, *A Hercules in the Cradle: War, Money, and the American State, 1783–1867* (Chicago: University of Chicago Press, 2014).

16. Wolfgang Streeck, *Buying Time: The Delayed Crisis of Democratic Capitalism* (London: Verso, 2014); Greta R. Krippner, *Capitalizing on Crisis: The Rise of Financial Capitalism* (Cambridge, Mass.: Harvard University Press, 2012); Mark Blyth, *Austerity: The History of a Dangerous Idea* (Oxford: Oxford University Press, 2013); Florian Schui, *Austerity: The Great Failure* (New Haven: Yale University Press, 2014); Adam Tooze, *Crashed: How a Decade of Financial Crises Changed the World* (New York: Viking, 2018).
17. Kenneth A. Schultz and Barry R. Weingast, "The Democratic Advantage: Institutional Foundations of Financial Power in International Competition," *International Organization* 57, no. 1 (2003), 3–42; James McDonald, *A Free Nation Deep in Debt: The Financial Roots of Democracy* (Princeton: Princeton University Press, 2006).
18. Roos, *Why Not Default*, 32–37.
19. Johanna Hanink, *The Greek Classical Debt: Greek Antiquity in the Era of Austerity* (Cambridge, Mass.: Harvard University Press, 2017).
20. Coming from different academic backgrounds and political cultures, but with potentially overlapping conclusions, see for instance David Graeber, *Debt: The First 5000 Years* (New York: Melville House, 2011); Thomas Piketty, *Capital in the Twenty-First Century*, trans. Arthur Goldhammer (Cambridge, Mass.: Harvard University Press, 2014).
21. Jeremy Adelman, *Republic of Capital: Buenos Aires and the Legal Transformation of the Atlantic World* (Stanford: Stanford University Press, 1999); Jane Burbank, Frederick Cooper, *Empires in World History: Power and the Politics of Difference* (Princeton: Princeton University Press, 2010); Ali Yycioglu, *Partners of Empire: The Crisis of Ottoman Order in the Ages of Revolutions* (Stanford: Stanford University Press, 2016); Josep M. Fradera, *The Imperial Nation: Citizens and Subjects in the British, French, Spanish, and American Empires* (Princeton: Princeton University Press, 2018).
22. Adam Tooze, *Wages of Destruction: The Making and Breaking of the Nazi Economy* (London: Allen Lane, 2006); Kiran K. Patel, *The New Deal: A Global History* (Princeton: Princeton University Press, 2017); Jamie Martin, *Governing Global Capitalism in the Era of Total War* (forthcoming).
23. Niall Ferguson, Charles S. Maier, Erez Manela, and Daniel D. Sargent, eds., *The Shock of the Global: The 1970s in Perspective* (Cambridge, Mass.: Harvard University Press, 2011); Marc Buggeln, Martin Daunton, and Alexander Nützenadel, eds., *The Political Economy of Public Finance: Taxation, Public Spending, and Debt since the 1970s* (Cambridge: Cambridge University Press, 2017). Most intellectual histories of neoliberalism start with the creation of the Mont Pèlerin Society in 1947, while the term itself goes back to the late 1930s in Europe: Philip Mirowski and Dieter Plehwe, eds., *The Road from Mont Pèlerin: The Making of the*

Neoliberal Thought Collective (Cambridge, Mass.: Harvard University Press, 2012); Angus Burgin, *The Great Persuasion: Reinventing Free Markets since the Great Depression* (Cambridge, Mass.: Harvard University Press, 2012); Daniel Stedman Jones, *Masters of the Universe: Hayek, Friedman, and the Birth of Neoliberal Politics* (Princeton: Princeton University Press, 2012). One recent exception, going back to World War I, is Quinn Slobodian, *Globalists: The End of Empire and the Birth of Neoliberalism* (Cambridge, Mass.: Harvard University Press, 2018).

24. On imperial debts, see for instance Niall Ferguson and Moritz Schularick, "The Empire Effect: The Determinants of Country Risk in the First Age of Globalization," *Journal of Economic History* 66, no. 2 (2006): 283–312; Olivier Accominotti, Marc Flandreau and Riad Rezzik, "The Spread of Empire: Clio and the Measurement of Colonial Borrowing Cost," *Economic History Review* 64, no. 2 (2010) 385–407.

25. Maxine Berg, ed., *Writing the History of the Global: Challenges for the Twenty-First Century* (Oxford: Oxford University Press, 2013); Sebastian Conrad, *What Is Global History?* (Princeton: Princeton University Press, 2016). For concrete applications in the history of taxation, see for instance Yun-Casalilla and O'Brien, eds., *The Rise of Fiscal States*.

26. For a source of inspiration, see for instance how Thomas Piketty thinks in terms of "inequality regimes" in *Capital and Ideology* (Cambridge, Mass.: Harvard University Press, 2020).

27. To follow Carmen Reinhart and Kenneth Rogoff's chronology of financial crises in *This Time is Different: Eight Centuries of Financial Folly* (Princeton: Princeton University Press, 2009).

28. For a similar argument on "boundary struggles," see Nancy Fraser, "Legitimation Crisis? On the Political Contradictions of Financialized Capitalism," *Critical Historical Studies* 2, no. 2 (Fall 2015), 157–89.

29. Kevin H. O'Rourke, Jeffrey G. Williamson, *Globalization and History: The Evolution of a Nineteenth-Century Atlantic Economy* (Cambridge, Mass.: MIT Press, 1999); Marc Flandreau and Frédéric Zumer, *The Making of Global Finance, 1880–1913* (Paris: OECD, 2004); Emily Rosenberg, ed., *A World Connecting, 1870–1945* (Cambridge, Mass.: The Belknap Press of Harvard University Press, 2012).

30. Adam Tooze, "History and America's Great Recession," *Books and Ideas*, November 25, 2013, https://booksandideas.net/History-and-America-s-Great-2477.html

31. Among a profusion of articles and books, see for instance Sven Beckert and al., "Interchange: the History of Capitalism," *Journal of American History* 101, no. 2 (2014): 503–36; Mary O'Sullivan, "The Intelligent Woman's Guide to Capitalism," *Enterprise and Society* 19, no. 4 (2018): 751–802; Jürgen Kocka, *Capitalism: A Short History* (Princeton: Princeton University

Press, 2016); Jürgen Kocka and Marcel van der Linden, eds., *Capitalism: The Reemergence of a Historical Concept* (London: Bloomsbury, 2016); Nicolas Barreyre and Alexia Blin, "À la redécouverte du capitalisme américain," *Revue d'histoire du XIXe siècle*, no. 54 (2017): 135–48; Sven Beckert and Christine Desan, "Introduction," in *American Capitalism: New Histories* (New York: Columbia University Press, 2018).

32. Piketty, *Capital in the Twenty-First Century*.
33. Timothy Mitchell, "Fixing the Economy," *Cultural Studies* 12, no. 1 (1998): 82–101.
34. In a similar vein, see "Follow the Money: Banking and Finances in the Modern World," *American Historical Review* 122, no. 5 (2017), special issue.
35. Pepper D. Culpepper, *Quiet Politics and Business Power. Corporate Control in Europe and Japan* (Cambridge: Cambridge University Press, 2012); Cornelia Woll, *The Power of Inaction. Bank Bailouts in Comparison* (Cornell: Cornell University Press, 2014).
36. Carlos Marichal, *A Century of Debt Crises in Latin America: From Independence to the Great Depression, 1820–1930* (Princeton; Princeton University Press, 1989); Sven Beckert and Seth Rockman, eds., *Slavery's Capitalism: A New History of American Economic Development* (Philadelphia: University of Pennsylvania Press, 2016).
37. Lienau, *Sovereign Debt*; Kim Oosterlinck, *Hope Springs Eternal*.
38. Peter A. Hall and David Soskice, eds., *Varieties of Capitalism: The Institutional Foundations of Comparative Advantage* (Oxford: Oxford University Press, 2001).
39. William H. Sewell, "A Strange Career: The Historical Study of Economic Life," *History and Theory* 49, no. 4 (2010): 146–66.
40. Francesca Trivellato, *The Familiarity of Strangers: The Sephardic Diaspora, Livorno, and Cross-Cultural Trade in the Early Modern Period* (New Haven: Yale University Press, 2009); "Is There a Future for Italian Microhistory in the Age of Global History?" *California Italian Studies* 2, no. 1 (2011); Fahad Ahmad Bishara, *A Sea of Debt: Law and Economic Life in the Western Indian Ocean, 1780–1950* (Cambridge: Cambridge University Press, 2017); "Global History and Microhistory," *Past and Present* 242, no. 14, special issue (2019).
41. Gerald D. Feldman, *The Great Disorder: Politics, Economics, and Society in the German Inflation, 1914–1924* (Oxford: Oxford University Press, 1993); Guya Accornero and Pedro Ramos Pinto, "'Mild mannered': Protest and Mobilisation in Portugal under Austerity, 2010–2013," *West European Politics* 38, no. 3 (2015): 491–515; Wolfgang Streeck and Armin Schäfer, eds., *Politics in the Age of Austerity* (London: Polity, 2013).

Acknowledgements

There was little sense, at the beginning, that our informal conversations over coffee about public debt in France and the United States in the nineteenth century would develop into such an ambitious collaborative project. We owe it first to the enthusiasm conveyed by the few historians to whom we confided—Adam Tooze deserves special mention here. And a generous grant from the City of Paris ("Emergences" program, 2015–2019) made it possible for us to gather the outstanding team of scholars who have been part of this project since, and whose work we happily share in these pages.

Many institutions helped along the way. The Center for History at Sciences Po (Paris) hosted and managed the grant through its five years, and we owe our deep gratitude to Marie-Laure Dagieu for handling all the administrative work with unfailing attention and efficiency. The Center for North American Studies (CENA) at EHESS shouldered some of the organizational brunt. Special thanks to Camille Amat for her gracious support and suggestions. Additional funding was provided by the Mondes Américains research center and the *laboratoire d'excellence* TEPSIS.

This allowed us to put together a truly collaborative research network of 25 scholars from 10 different countries. We could meet three times to really develop this global political history together, organically. Our first meeting was hosted at the Center for History and Economics at the University of Cambridge, with financial support from the Cambridge History Department and the Economic History Society. Our thanks go to Alexia Yates for organizing it with us, as well as to Blaise Truong-Loï for his research assistance. Our second meeting was hosted at Sciences Po, in

Paris, with the organizational help of Étienne Forestier-Peyrat, the then postdoctoral researcher attached to the project. Our third and final conference met in Athens, and was generously hosted by the French School of Athens at the initiative of Anastassios Anastassiadis. Staying in Athens allowed us to finalize our project while confronting our thinking to the urgent situation facing Greece.

Over the years, we benefited from insights and generous feedback from numerous scholars during those meetings. Thanks to Martin Daunton, Pedro Ramos Pinto, and Duncan Needham at Cambridge; Katia Béguin, Mario Del Pero, Mathieu Fulla, Romain Huret, Annick Lempérière, David Priestland, Jakob Vogel, and Charles Walton in Paris; and Maria-Christina Chatziioannou, Andreas Kakridis, and Socrates Petmezas in Athens.

In its final stages, we presented the project in several seminars and conferences. We would like to thank Emmanuel Bouju and Mary Lewis for the "Europe on Credit" conference at Harvard in April 2017, Pierre de Saint-Phalle who invited us to the University of Lausanne for a conference on "Disciplining through Debt: A Long History," and Juan Pan-Montojo and his colleagues for a joint panel at the World Economic History Conference at MIT, where Marc Flandreau's comments were particularly helpful. We would also like to thank Stephen W. Sawyer and Noam Maggor, whose opinions we solicited often and who generously shared their thoughts and encouragement on the whole project.

At Palgrave, D'Maris Coffman and the editors of Palgrave Studies on the History of Finance enthusiastically welcomed this volume in their series. We thank Tula Weis and Lucy Kidwell for steering it so efficiently through the editorial process, as well as the anonymous reviewers who helped us improve our general argument. As an international team only partly made up of native speakers of English, we owe much to Elizabeth Rowley-Jolivet's skills in editing the chapters.

Finally, we want to warmly thank all the colleagues who accepted to join this international project, beyond their disciplinary- or time-specializations, and devote time to build this truly cooperative endeavor. We greatly appreciate their scholarly commitment and continuous support.

Contents

Part I Political Crises and the Legitimacy of Public Debts
        (1770s–1860s)   1

1 An Empire of Debts? Spain and Its Colonial Realm   5
   Regina Grafe

2 Publicity, Debt, and Politics: The Old Regime and the
   French Revolution   37
   Rebecca L. Spang

3 Politics of Credit: Government Borrowing and Political
   Regimes in Sweden   57
   Patrik Winton

4 Public Debt and Democratic Statecraft in Nineteenth-
   Century France   79
   David Todd and Alexia Yates

Part II Global Capital, Imperial Expansions, and Changing
          Sovereignties (1860s–1914)   107

5 The Entanglements of Domestic Polities: Public Debt
   and European Interventions in Latin America   111
   Juan H. Flores Zendejas

6 Leveraging Foreign Control: Reform in the Ottoman
   Empire   135
   Ali Coşkun Tunçer

7 The Unforeseen Path of Debt Imperialism: Local
   Struggles, Transnational Knowledge, and Colonialism
   in Egypt   155
   Malak Labib

8 Trading Sovereignty for Capital? Public Debt in West
   Africa, 1871–1914   175
   Leigh Gardner

9 The Domestic Effects of Foreign Capital: Public Debt
   and Regional Inequalities in Late Qing China   201
   Dong Yan

10 Fiscal Federalism: Local Debt and the Construction
   of the Modern State in the United States and France   231
   Noam Maggor and Stephen W. Sawyer

Part III The Great Transformation of Public Debts
           (1914–1970s)   259

11 The Financial Challenges of Total War: Britain, France,
   and Their Empires in the First World War   261
   Nicolas Delalande

12	Beyond Democracy or Dictatorship: Structuring Sovereign Debt in Germany from Weimar to the Postwar Period Stefanie Middendorf	287
13	The Communist World of Public Debt (1917–1991): The Failure of a Countermodel? Étienne Forestier-Peyrat and Kristy Ironside	317
14	Debt Without Taxation: Iraq, Syria, and the Crisis of Empires from the Mandates to the Cold War Era Matthieu Rey	347
Part IV	The Political Roads to Financial Markets and Global Debt Crisis (1970s–)	371
15	From Debt *Dirigisme* to Debt Markets in France and India Anush Kapadia and Benjamin Lemoine	373
16	The Political Economy of Debt Crisis: State, Banks and the Financialization of Public Debt in Italy since the 1970s Alexander Nützenadel	405
17	From a Multilateral Broker to the National Judge: The Law and Governance of Sovereign Debt Restructuring, 1980–2015 Jérôme Sgard	427
18	Of Bond Vigilantes, Central Bankers and the Crisis of 2008 Adam Tooze	453

Part V	Conclusion: On the Historical Uses of Numbers and Words	479
19	The History and Politics of Public Debt Accounting Éric Monnet and Blaise Truong-Loï	481
20	The Words of Public Debts: A Political Repertoire Nicolas Barreyre and Nicolas Delalande	513

Correction to: A World of Public Debts   C1

Index   541

List of Figures

Fig. 1.1	Military, civilian, and debt service expenditure in European Britain, France, and Spain in the late eighteenth century. In percent of total. (Source: Grafe and Irigoin, "A Stakeholder Empire")	9
Fig. 1.2	Military, civilian, unspecified, and debt service expenditure in peninsular Spain and Spanish America in the eighteenth century. In the case of Spanish American districts, the share is of expenditure without transfers to Spain or intra-colonial transfers. (Source: Grafe and Irigoin, "A Stakeholder Empire")	11
Fig. 1.3	Mapping governance structures: Treasury districts (*cajas*) in late eighteenth-century New Spain. (All the maps in this chapter were created with financial support from a British Academy Small Grant SG-113363. We thank Alejandra Castrodad for her assistance)	14
Fig. 1.4	Mapping governance structures: Treasury districts (*cajas*) in Ecuador, Peru, Upper Peru, Rio de la Plata, and Chile (late eighteenth century)	15
Fig. 1.5	The evolution of fiscal districts (sixteenth to eighteenth century): New Spain	17
Fig. 1.6	The evolution of fiscal districts (sixteenth to eighteenth century): Spanish South America	18
Fig. 1.7	Revenues per capita, 1785–89: France and the Spains. In pesos. Revenues are net of intra-colonial transfers and carry-overs in the case of Spanish America. (Source: Grafe and Irigoin, "A Stakeholder Empire")	20

Fig. 1.8   Yields of old bonds in eighteenth-century peninsular Spain (*juros*), newly issued bonds (*vales*), English and French bonds. (Sources: Grafe, *Distant Tyranny*; Mark Dincecco, *Political Transformations and Public Finances: Europe, 1650–1913* (Cambridge: Cambridge University Press, 2011))   23

Fig. 1.9   Intra-colonial revenue transfers (ICTs), 1729–1800. In percent of net expenditure. (Source: Grafe and Irigoin, "A Stakeholder Empire")   27

Fig. 1.10   Self-reinforcing polycentrism: ICTs as a share of total revenue for each district (1720s–1800)   29

Fig. 6.1   Revenues controlled by the Council, 1882–1913 (Source and notes: Tuncer, *Sovereign Debt*, 73. Six indirect revenues were from silk, salt, spirits, tobacco, stamps, and fisheries. Political revenues refer to the annual taxes from the tributary states (Egypt and Cyprus) of the Ottoman Empire)   143

Fig. 6.2   Bond spreads, 1880–1913 (Source and notes: Latin America represents the average of Brazil, Chile, Colombia, Uruguay and Mexico. European periphery is the average of Greece, Hungary, Portugal and Spain. Calculated from Tuncer, *Sovereign Debt*, 187; P. Mauro, N. Sussman and Y. Yishay *Emerging Markets and Financial Globalisation Sovereign Bond Spreads in 1870–1913 and Today*. (Oxford: Oxford University Press, 2006); N. Ferguson and M. Schularik, "The empire effect: the determinants of country risk in the first age of globalization," *Journal of Economic History*, Vol. 66, No. 2, (2006), 283–312)   147

Fig. 8.1   West African bond spreads. (Source: Gardner, "Colonialism or supersanctions")   182

Fig. 8.2   West African bond spreads in comparative perspective, 1900–1914. (Source: Gardner, "Colonialism or supersanctions.")   183

Fig. 16.1   Savings and interest rates (1970–85). (Source: Ministero del Tesoro, *Ricchezza finanziaria, debito public e politica monetaria nella prospettiva international*, Rapporto della Commissione di studio nominate dal Ministero del Tesoro (Roma: 1987), 157)   417

Fig. 16.2 Balance of financial assets/liabilities (1971–89). (Source: Mario Baldassari and Maria Gabriella Briotti, "Bilancio pubblico ed economia italiana negli anni '70 e '80: dalle radici del debito alla manovra di risanamento, una 'ristrutturazione' da fare," *Rivista di Politica Economica* LXXX (1990), 371–438, 405) 418

Fig. 16.3 Rate of return: state bonds, private bonds, stocks and deposits (1960–80). (Source: Ministero del Tesoro, "La difesa del risparmio finanziario dall'inflazione," in *Rapporto della Commissione di studio nominate dal Ministero del Tesoro* (Roma: 1991), 42) 419

LIST OF TABLES

Table 1.1	Sources of income of Mexico City's Poor House, 1811	26
Table 8.1	Loan issues to sub-Saharan Africa, 1871–1913	179
Table 9.1	Public investment in Chinese state-owned industries, 1863–1894	208
Table 9.2	Provincial revenue and foreign debt service, 1910	211
Table 9.3	Railway revenue, 1907–1909	214
Table 9.4	Official and undeclared sources of revenue for Guangdong, 1908–1910	216
Table 9.5	Revenue forecast for the 1911 budget	217
Table 10.1	Government debt by level of government in levels and shares in the United States (1838–1992)	236
Table 10.2	France's Public Debts from 1852 to 1897	237
Table 16.1	Distribution of public debt in Italy (1970–92)	416

Notes on Contributors

Nicolas Barreyre is Associate Professor in American History at EHESS (Paris). He is the author of *Gold and Freedom: The Political Economy of Reconstruction* (University of Virginia Press, 2015), and coeditor of *Historians Across Borders: Writing American History in a Global Age* (University of California Press, 2014).

Nicolas Delalande is Associate Professor in European History at the Centre d'Histoire at Sciences Po (Paris). He is the author of *Les Batailles de l'impôt. Consentement et résistances de 1789 à nos jours* (Seuil, 2011), and coeditor of *France in the World: A New Global History* (Other Press, 2019).

Juan H. Flores Zendejas is Professor of Economic History at the Paul Bairoch Institute of Economic History of the University of Geneva. He is the author, with Yann Decorzant, of "Going multilateral? Financial markets' access and the League of Nations loans, 1923–1928," *Economic History Review* 69, no. 2 (2016): 653–78.

Étienne Forestier-Peyrat is Associate Professor of History at Sciences Po (Lille). He is the author of *Histoire du Caucase au XXe siècle* (Fayard, 2020).

Leigh Gardner is Associate Professor in Economic History at the London School of Economics and a Research Associate in African Economic History at Stellenbosch University. She is the author of *Taxing Colonial Africa: The Political Economy of British Imperialism* (Oxford University Press, 2012).

Regina Grafe is Professor of Early Modern European History at the European University Institute (Florence). She is the author of *Distant Tyranny: Markets, Power and Backwardness in Spain, 1650–1800* (Princeton University Press, 2012).

Kristy Ironside is Assistant Professor of Russian History at McGill University (Montreal). She has written numerous articles on the wartime and postwar Soviet economy, including "Rubles for Victory: The Social Dynamics of State Fundraising on the Soviet Home Front," *Kritika: Explorations in Russian and Eurasian History* 15, no. 4 (2014): 799–828.

Anush Kapadia is an Assistant Professor in Humanities and Social Sciences at the Indian Institute of Technology (Bombay).

Malak Labib is a postdoctoral fellow at the Free University of Berlin and at the EUME program (Forum Transregionale Studien).

Benjamin Lemoine is a research fellow at CNRS (Paris Dauphine). He is the author of *L'Ordre de la dette. Enquête sur les infortunes de l'État et la prospérité du marché* (La Découverte, 2016).

Noam Maggor is Senior Lecturer in American History at Queen Mary University of London. He is the author of *Brahmin Capitalism: Frontiers of Wealth and Populism in America's First Gilded Age* (Harvard University Press, 2017).

Stefanie Middendorf is Professor of Contemporary History at the University of Bremen and associate researcher at the Leibniz Centre for Contemporary History in Potsdam. She is the author of "Ökonomisierung des Regierens? Überlegungen zum Wandel 'moderner' Staatsfinanzierung in Deutschland und Frankreich (1920–1980)," *Archiv für Sozialgeschichte* 57 (2017), 281–311, and of *Ermächtigungen. Staatstechniken des Reichsministeriums der Finanzen seit 1919* (DeGruyter/Oldenbourg, in print).

Éric Monnet is Professor of Economic History at EHESS and PSE in Paris, and a research affiliate at the Centre for Economic Policy Research in London. He is the author of *Controlling Credit: Monetary Policy and the Planned Economy in France, 1945–1973* (Cambridge University Press, 2018).

Alexander Nützenadel is Professor of Social and Economic History at Humboldt University (Berlin). He is the coeditor of *The Political Economy of Public Finances: Taxation, State Spending and Debt since the 1970s* (Cambridge University Press, 2017).

Matthieu Rey is a research fellow at IFAS-Research and Wits History Workshop (Johannesburg). He is the author of *Histoire de la Syrie, XIXe-XXe siècle* (Fayard, 2018).

Stephen W. Sawyer is Professor of History at the American University of Paris. He is the author of *Demos Assembled: Democracy and the International Origins of the Modern State, 1840–1880* (University of Chicago Press, 2018).

Jérôme Sgard is Professor of Political Economy at Sciences Po (Paris). He is the coeditor of *Contractual Knowledge: A Hundred Years of Experimentation in Global Markets* (Cambridge University Press, 2016). His forthcoming book is an oral history of the 1980s' international debt crisis: *Debt, Sovereignty and the IMF* (Elgar).

Rebecca L. Spang is Professor of History at Indiana University, where she directs both the Center for Eighteenth-Century Studies and the Liberal Arts and Management Program. The author of *Stuff and Money in the Time of the French Revolution* (Harvard, 2015) and of *The Invention of the Restaurant* (new edition; Harvard, 2020), she has held visiting positions at the University of Minnesota, the University of Tübingen, and Yale School of Management.

David Todd is Senior Lecturer in World History at King's College London. He is the author of *Free Trade and its Enemies in France, 1814–1848* (Cambridge University Press, 2015), and his book *A Velvet Empire: French Informal Imperialism in the Nineteenth Century* will come out with Princeton University Press in 2021.

Adam Tooze is the Kathryn and Shelby Cullom Davis Professor of History at Columbia University. He is the author of *The Deluge: The Great War, America, and the Remaking of the Global Order, 1916–1931* (Penguin Books, 2014), and *Crashed: How a Decade of Financial Crises Changed the World* (Viking, 2018).

Blaise Truong-Loï is a PhD Candidate at Sciences Po (Paris), working on institutions of international financial control and public debt accounting in the late nineteenth century.

Ali Coşkun Tunçer is Associate Professor of Economic History at University College London. He is the author of *Sovereign Debt and International Financial Control: The Middle East and the Balkans, 1870–1914* (Palgrave Macmillan, 2015).

Patrik Winton is Senior Lecturer in History at Örebro University. He is the author of "The Political Economy of Strategic Default: Sweden and the International Capital Markets, 1810–1830," *European Review of Economic History* 20, no. 4 (2016), 410–28.

Dong Yan is a postdoctoral fellow at the Center for Chinese Studies in University of California, Berkeley. A historian of modern Chinese economy and ideas, he is currently preparing a book manuscript entitled "Sinews of Paper: Public Debt and Chinese Political Economy, 1850–1914," examining the adaptation of modern public debt in late-nineteenth and early-twentieth-century China.

Alexia Yates is Lecturer in Modern History at the University of Manchester. She is the author of *Selling Paris: Property and Commercial Culture in the Fin-de-Siècle Capital* (Harvard University Press, 2015).

PART I

Political Crises and the Legitimacy of Public Debts (1770s–1860s)

By the end of the eighteenth century, public debt became a major issue in many countries throughout Europe. The need to fund repeated wars, each more global in its reach than the previous one—what some historians called the "second hundred years war"—the mounting debt levels, but also the transformations of public discourse on what public debt actually *was*, all brought about a reconceptualization that is still influential in the ways we understand public debt today.

Yet, that understanding needs revising. Much of the scholarship has erected the conflicting experiences of Britain and France in the late eighteenth century as a lesson about good practices and good institutions, consecrating the British peculiar setup as a model of "successful" public debt. As this first part will show, however, there were a variety of viable ways of borrowing and managing debts for European states, and what really turned them into an issue had more to do with the political legitimacy of political institutions, and to whom they catered, than any measure of economic sustainability. The historical cases of Spanish America, France, and Sweden explored here thus suggest that we should revisit this period, and revise even well-known examples such as Britain, to better understand the reasons why, by the mid-nineteenth century, a liberal debt regime became dominant in Europe before being exported, sometimes forcefully, to other parts of the world. As we argue, those reasons were largely political.

As Regina Grafe underlines in Chap. 1, public financial institutions (including public debt) were themselves the result of political compromise, settlement, and pragmatism. Spanish American colonies had developed a very different system from the one the British were then consolidating. This decentralized, interconnected network of local Treasury chests, enmeshing religious institutions and merchant capital into its circuits, enabled the Spanish to sustain what was then the largest empire in the world while keeping the central government with little debt compared to other European powers. Yet this system rested on the political legitimacy of Church and Crown—precisely what the revolutionary wars in Europe, then the wars of independence in Spanish America, destroyed. The lessons liberal reformers tried to apply were, precisely, the wrong ones.

This question of political legitimacy and liberal reform going awry is where Rebecca Spang picks up in Chap. 2. As she argues, it was the political fight around public finance, rather than economic unsustainability, that made the French Monarchy's debt problematic in the 1780s and precipitated the French Revolution. In turn, the revolutionaries tied public debt (and honoring it) to the very legitimacy of the new regime and the financial instruments it wielded. The political centrality of public debt, thus, was a crucial engine in the radicalization of the Revolution; and, in turn, the partial default of 1797, while sealing the fate of the regime, also gave its successors the tools to rebuild a new political legitimacy.

Public debt and its management had thus become, in the eighteenth century, a key lever for the control of political power and the state. Sweden's example, Patrik Winton argues in Chap. 3, might be little known but is illuminating in that regard. Describing several key episodes from the mid-eighteenth century to the 1820s, he shows how public debt was intimately tied to the nature of the political regime, and who wielded power within the state structure. Decisions to borrow domestically or abroad, and between various lenders in Europe, all had an impact on the internal balance of power in Sweden, and the institutional makeup of a regime, that balanced between the absolutist power of the king and more divided power between the estates—until French Marshal Bernadotte turned king of Sweden could attach the new public debt of the country to his own person, thus definitely building his own political legitimacy.

The importance of public debt in building political legitimacy in post-revolutionary Europe is at the heart of David Todd and Alexia Yates's argument in Chap. 4. Returning to France, they show how the state, in spite of multiple changes of regimes, could rebuild a political legitimacy through debt in the post-Napoleonic years. It did it through intellectual and material innovations that produced a positive view of public debt as citizen democratic participation in the life of the state—and its foreign relations. That France could become so rapidly a financial powerhouse after the Revolution and the indemnities imposed on it in 1815 is a testament to this new system, that was compatible with the ascendant liberal debt regime that dominated the world in the second half of the nineteenth century, but represented a significant variation with long-term consequences—all the way to World War I.

CHAPTER 1

An Empire of Debts? Spain and Its Colonial Realm

Regina Grafe

Public debt is a fundamental part of the fiscal viability of any complex polity. In the early modern period, small city states, larger territorial states, and the largest overseas empire of the western hemisphere, the early modern *Españas* (Spains), needed access to credit for at least two reasons. First, revenue and expenditure streams do not follow the same cycle. Prior to the late nineteenth century, military spending was by far the largest item of expenditure. It was also particularly uneven. Money needed to be available up-front when campaigns started. Armies, whether regular, militia, or mercenaries, stopped fighting and started looting if their masters were too far behind on pay. Revenues, on the other hand, tended to flow in steadily over the year, and even if they came in as lump sum payments from tax farmers, those pay schedules hardly ever coincided with major expenditures. This was even more so in those fiscal regimes that relied overwhelmingly on trade and consumption taxes rather than direct land taxes as was the case in the early modern Spains.[1]

R. Grafe (✉)
Department of History and Civilization, European University Institute, Florence, Italy
e-mail: regina.grafe@eui.eu

© The Author(s) 2020
N. Barreyre, N. Delalande (eds.), *A World of Public Debts*, Palgrave Studies in the History of Finance,
https://doi.org/10.1007/978-3-030-48794-2_1

Second, revenue and expenditure are often spatially incongruent especially, though not only, in large empires. Taxes collected in a number of cities far from the frontier ended up financing the militias sent to defend the border. Much research has gone into the ability of early modern states to raise revenue, that is, their fiscal capacity, and their effectiveness and efficiency at providing the basic functions of political organizations such as internal and external protection, that is, their legal capacity.[2] Arguably the intertemporal and interspatial transfers that were at the heart of this state capacity were the internal plumbing of any fiscal system. But the shape of that system needed to be negotiated politically, financed usually by drawing on credit, and executed in practice. The purpose of this paper is to chart how that political negotiation of intertemporal and interspatial transfers emerged and evolved over time in Spanish America during the colonial period, and what its legacy was on the fiscal and financial systems of modern Spanish American republics.

In the literature on comparative empires the question of colonial legacy looms justifiably large. Economic historians of Latin America in the later nineteenth and twentieth centuries have searched the colonial past for explanations why, to paraphrase a famous book, "Latin America fell behind." They concluded that the late development of modern financial markets in most of the states after Independence (1808–25) explains at least some of the problems.[3] Even in the larger Latin American republics, banks, stock exchanges, and bond markets only became fully functional in the modern sense of those institutions relatively late in the nineteenth century. Narrow and shallow capital markets held back industrialization in particular, with long-term negative consequences for Latin Americans' economic opportunities.[4]

Historians of Latin American independence in turn viewed the poor financial infrastructure of the late colonial period as one of the reasons for the empire's collapse and the unfavorable starting conditions for the successor states. How else can one explain why the continent that produced by far the largest share of world bullion into the nineteenth century struggled to establish financial institutions? New Latin American republics turned to the most important international bond market, London, for the first time in the 1820s. The experience ended in the default of all loans, with the exception of those of Brazil, which had become independent as an Empire.[5] The civil wars of the first half of the nineteenth century in Latin America made a return to bond markets impossible. Latin American polities finally did raise money again, but the new wave of loans ended again in widespread defaults in 1873 and the Baring Crisis of the 1890. A bad start seemed to have turned into a pattern of financial, fiscal, and monetary instability that would shape Latin American economic and political developments up to our times, one that was driven by cyclical, excessive lending on the part of international investors, and over-borrowing on the Latin American side.[6]

We would do well, though, to heed Marc Bloch's famous warning against the "demon of origins."[7] Most of the historiography either argues explicitly or assumes implicitly that the weakness of both private and public finance in the nineteenth and twentieth centuries was the result of the colonial past. Notably, the colonial Spanish American treasury never developed the equivalent of modern sovereign bonds.[8] Private banking was considered to have existed only in rudimentary forms, and there were few examples of joint-stock companies. In the jargon of economic history, that meant that "impersonal sources of capital" to finance public and private activity had not emerged during the colonial period, or only to an insufficient degree. The colonial failure to create an institutional environment that would allow for the development of formal banks, publicly listed companies, and sovereign bond issues meant that private and public actors' need for capital had to be serviced through personal relationships, limiting access to capital. This seemed to be the sort of "origin [that] is a beginning that explains" against which Bloch warned us.

Why had the political economy of colonial Latin America been so uncongenial for "London-style" financial markets? In the conventional story of public debt, the institutional development of private and sovereign lending mechanisms is often seen as a canary in the mine for the strength of property rights regimes. Transparent and well-regulated lending mechanisms are unlikely to develop in political regimes that tend to abuse their executive and legislative power to prey upon private investors' bonds, or credits, or returns on investments. The same is true for polities that do not provide independent judicial means of defense against such more or less overt expropriations.

For many observers the colonial legacy which hampered pre- and post-Independence Spanish America was the rapacity of the state and of its entrenched elites.[9] This is viewed as the root cause of poorly developed financial institutions,[10] creating a "Spanish American predicament" characterized by excessive debt, with roots going back to expropriating colonial governance, and poor manageability of that debt, which was further complicated by poor public and private "modern," impersonal financial institutions.

There is no denying the dire financial history of Spanish America in the nineteenth and twentieth centuries (although, as Chap. 5 of this book shows, this story needs revisions). But this chapter challenges the view that it should be understood in terms of continuities. The first half of the chapter revisits the narrative that sought to establish the colonial origins of the Spanish American debt problem. Drawing on earlier research undertaken with M.A. Irigoin, I start by placing the Spanish and Spanish American colonial public debt situation in a comparative context, which raises the puzzle of seemingly small debt levels in the eighteenth century.[11] The chapter then discusses the degree of (de-)centralization of fiscal decision-making. What were the relevant spaces in which the negotiation over public debt met private creditors? How much colonial extraction was there? I argue that the lack of formal sovereignty of the colonial territories should not be mistaken for a lack of fiscal agency of colonial populations. Instead we observe a well-financed system in full expansion able to draw on capital at relatively modest rates of interest. The allegedly colonial origins of modern financial instability emerge as largely driven by presentist perspectives that sit uncomfortably with the historical data.

The second half of the paper argues that the existence of a well-functioning fiscal system in the almost entire absence of public bonds, private banks, and stock markets has gone largely unrecognized because historians were blinkered by not just a Eurocentric but a more restrictive Anglo-French master narrative of the development of modern financial markets. They simply looked for financial institutions in the wrong places. They should have gone to Church more often or visited the local merchant guild or the taxmen, because these were the backbones of credit. The argument put forward is that there were alternative paths to sophisticated financial systems and impersonal sources of capital, in which joint-stock companies, stock exchanges, and bond markets were largely unnecessary for the provision of credit. To put it another way, the particular institutions that we today identify as *conditiones* sine qua non for successful economic growth may have been considerably less important in the eighteenth or even nineteenth centuries. However, the alternative institutional path was upended by *political* events. Paradoxically, the Spanish American predicament of poor financial markets began not with colonial continuity but with a dramatic post-colonial rupture.

Polycentric Rule and Imperial Finance

The expansion of European and Asian Empires in the early modern period resulted in governance structures in the far-flung territories that were built on metropolitan institutional models. But in due course they adapted or assimilated to, or were complemented by the economic, political, social, and cultural institutions of the conquered societies. Spanish, French, or Chinese expansion thus carried differences in institutional structure with it. But it was also molded in different directions by the interaction with, and contestation of, conquered peoples and conditions in conquered spaces. In order to better understand the dynamics of fiscal and financial systems and their relation to debt in an imperial context, we therefore need to consider both where they came from and where they went to.[12]

Figure 1.1 illustrates some of the similarities and differences in the fiscal setup of three of the European colonial metropolises in the late eighteenth century, Spain, Britain, and France, on the eve of the French Revolution. Notwithstanding the commonalities in the proportion of military spending in the Spains and Britain, and civilian spending in France and the Spains, the one distinct feature of the Spanish case that stands out is the quasi-absence of debt. While France and Britain dedicated between 30

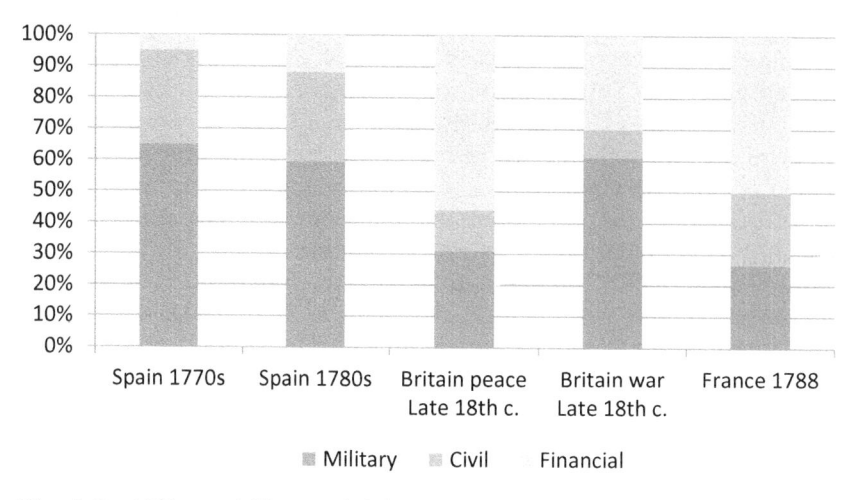

Fig. 1.1 Military, civilian, and debt service expenditure in European Britain, France, and Spain in the late eighteenth century. In percent of total. (Source: Grafe and Irigoin, "A Stakeholder Empire")

and 55 percent of all expenditure to debt service, the share never exceeded 15 percent on average in any decade before the 1780s in the Spains. The low outlays on debt suggest that the fiscal and financial governance of the peninsular Spains differed in some fundamental way from those of its British and French peers.

In the past two decades economic historians have rewritten the early modern fiscal history of the Spains. It is now well understood that the Hispanic reigns were anything but the fiscal basket-case they had previously been taken for. In the sixteenth century the central *hacienda* used cutting-edge financial structures to turn its substantial accumulated debt in the form of loans into a funded debt based on the issuance of redeemable bonds, known as *juros*. The treasury was highly leveraged by the standards of the time, but always solvent. The contracts it underwrote with the syndicates of its debtors contained ex ante clauses designed to manage the occasionally unavoidable liquidity crises caused by political stalemate between the monarchy and the estates, or simply the inconsistencies in time and space between revenue raising and (military) expenditure. What the historiography used to call bankruptcies were in fact renegotiations that took place along relatively well-established rules.[13]

As the sixteenth-century economic boom turned into seventeenth-century contraction accompanied by intensifying military engagements, clear signs of overleveraging of the public debt began to appear. Short-term measures such as the debasement of small coin (though not the silver currency), repeated attempts to lower the interest rate on existing bonds, and various other expedients finally gave way to a set of more profound reforms starting in the 1680s. In essence the sovereign debt was consolidated by applying a general haircut to investors, local treasuries who held most of the tax-raising powers, and the monarchy. The general write-down shared the burden, but was only possible because by then most of the debt was held domestically rather than by foreign bankers.[14] As the eighteenth century progressed, the picture seen in Fig. 1.1 emerged. The proportion of expenditure devoted to the military by the central treasury was at least as high as that of its European peers. But unlike them it did not resort to the issuance of large amounts of public debt to finance war until the 1780s. Military expenditure remained high in war and peacetime, and financial expenditure remained low by European standards.[15]

As one might expect, fiscal realities in the American territories did not neatly match those in the Peninsula. Figure 1.2 compares the two breakdowns of expenditure for the pensinsular Spains already shown in Fig. 1.1

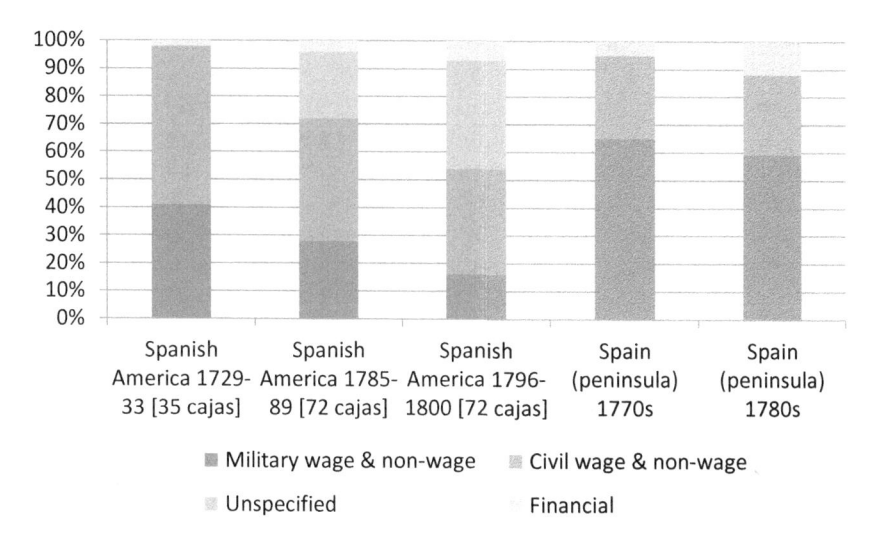

1 AN EMPIRE OF DEBTS? SPAIN AND ITS COLONIAL REALM

Fig. 1.2 Military, civilian, unspecified, and debt service expenditure in peninsular Spain and Spanish America in the eighteenth century. In percent of total. In the case of Spanish American districts, the share is of expenditure without transfers to Spain or intra-colonial transfers. (Source: Grafe and Irigoin, "A Stakeholder Empire")

with those for the Spanish American Treasuries across the eighteenth century. The lower military wage and nonwage expenditure in the latter stands out at once. So does the large civilian expenditure, again comprising both wage and nonwage payments. Colonial treasuries spent less on external defense and internal repression than European polities. Over the eighteenth century an increasing number of items of expenditure contained in the accounts of Spanish American Treasuries are hard to identify in terms of purpose. But registered debt service accounted for an equally small or even smaller proportion of total expenditure in the American reigns as in the European ones. Between the 1730s and the 1790s the share rose from 2 to 7 percent.

Was this an Empire without debt? If so, what accounts for this peculiarity and what were the consequences? After all neither parliamentary Britain nor the republican Netherlands nor monarchical France, all of them participants in the supposed colonial competition between European polities, relied as little on debt finance as seems to have been the case in the Hispanic reigns. What sort of political economy can explain this?

Two very different models to conceptualize the governance of the Spanish Empire have been put forward. One, which we could call the center-periphery model, stresses in particular an eighteenth-century tendency to increasing centralization and lack of political representation for colonial elites, let alone the great majority of indigenous subjects, mestizos, African Americans, and poor "Spaniards." In this view Madrid ordered, and the periphery executed, policies designed to achieve maximum extraction from the American territories. Latin American elites in turn took advantage of the poorly informed and often unworkable decrees emanating from the center to ignore them in a way epitomized by the famous phrase "the law will be obeyed but not complied with" (*la ley se acata pero no se cumple*).[16]

The center-periphery model argues that as a result, corruption and mismanagement were the norm. On the one hand, the center designed the system to guarantee maximum extraction of resources from the Americas toward the center; on the other hand, the resistance provoked by unworkable extractive institutions led to low fiscal and legal capacity. In the end colonial treasuries were marked by both insufficient funds and an inability to guarantee either public or private property rights. Since the system was thus neither financially viable nor perceived as legitimate by American subjects of the monarchy, it was caught in a vicious circle. Fiscal evasion and avoidance only served to reinforce extractive strategies imposed by the center. In this model—which has long been dominant in the literature—the absence of a public debt in the peninsular Spains and in particular in the Americas thus indicates the weakness of the property rights regime. The latter in turn held back the development of private and public financial institutions.

The second model of governance in the Spanish Empire has been developed under the label of polycentric or stakeholder empire.[17] The Spanish reigns in Europe and beyond consisted of a network structure that linked various centers, such as Madrid, Naples, Mexico City, and Lima. Proponents of this interpretation see policy-making as the outcome of negotiation between those centers and within them. This was particularly true for fiscal policies, which were largely designed and controlled either by the estates of European territories within the Spanish monarchy, or by towns within the Peninsula, or by regional elites who dominated within the local treasury district in the Americas. Local and regional decision-making served to make the monarchy the legitimate arbiter within the system. At the same time the cooperation of elites guaranteed the survival of the imperial structure.

In the polycentric or stakeholder model imperial rule is thus seen as both fiscally viable and politically legitimate, at least in the sense that challenges to rule targeted local elites rather than imperial rule. Extractive practices are seen not as a fundamental feature of the relationship between the European and the American parts of the empire, but instead largely as the outcome of political negotiations within each constituent part of the empire and the relative strength or weakness of local power groups vis-à-vis other local subjects. Polycentric rule was not the same as devolution. It is important to note that the location of power had never been centralized to begin with and therefore was not the monarchy's to devolve. Strong local and regional elite influence was at the same time a strength and a weakness. It reduced opposition to imperial rule, but it also resulted in lower degrees of integration of goods and capital markets. Coordination failures potentially resulted in lower growth.[18] But even if market size became a casualty of coordination failure the question arises why in a polycentric governance structure there should have been so little credit on offer to the public purse?

A closer look at the fiscal governance of Spanish America can provide a clue to this conundrum. To start with, the question of whether or not Spanish American governance was centralized or even over-centralized is in fact quite easy to document. Figures 1.3 and 1.4 map the treasury districts in Mexico/New Spain and Spanish South America toward the end of the eighteenth century. The multitude of regional treasury districts is clearly visible. As shown elsewhere, tax modalities differed significantly from one treasury district to another, demonstrating that the notion of an integrated and centralized fiscal system does not concur with historical evidence.[19]

On the contrary, the treasury system in the Americas was highly decentralized. By the late eighteenth century there were more than a hundred treasury districts, those visible in Figs. 1.3 and 1.4, as well as a significant number in the Caribbean. Revenue collection was mostly decided locally, and as a result tax rates differed across sectors of the economy, corporate groups of taxpayers, and products being taxed. This was responsive to local elite aspirations and their priorities for economic development. But by giving priority to their interests it also restricted market integration, as noted above.

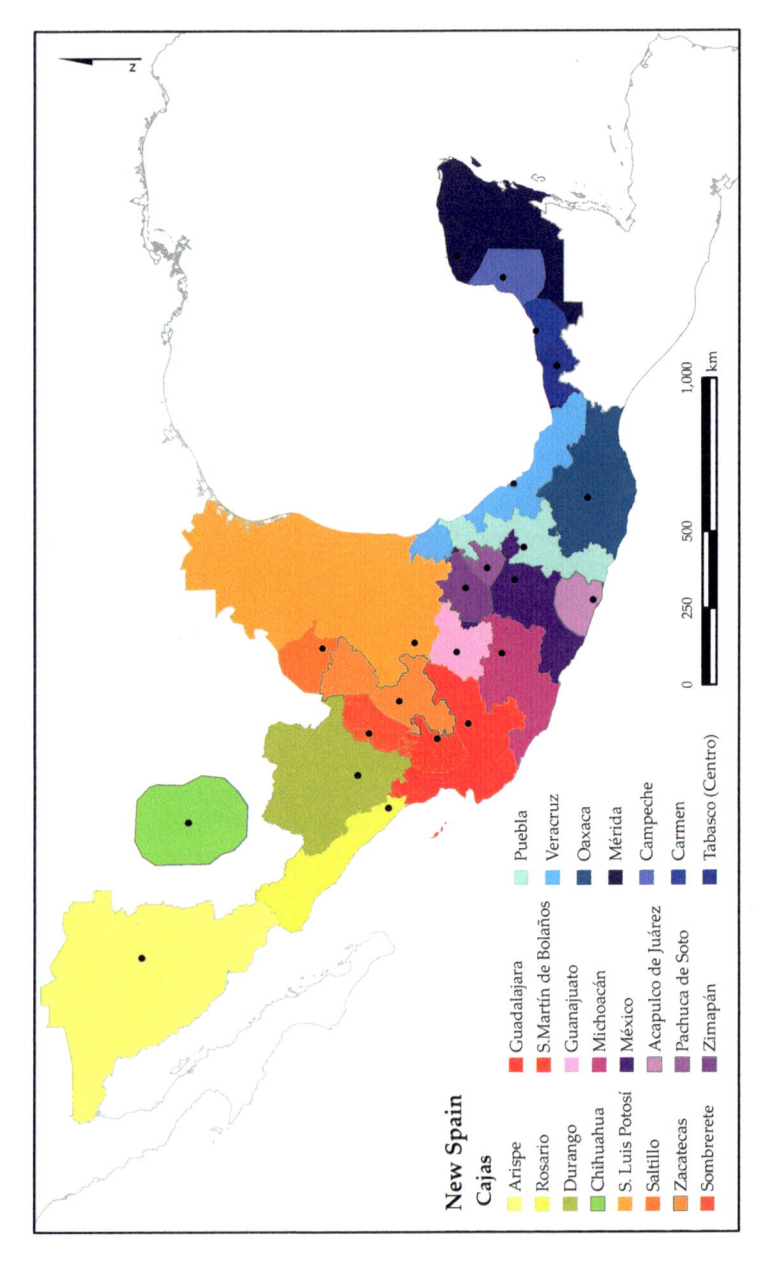

Fig. 1.3 Mapping governance structures: Treasury districts (*cajas*) in late eighteenth-century New Spain. (All the maps in this chapter were created with financial support from a British Academy Small Grant SG-113363. We thank Alejandra Castrodad for her assistance)

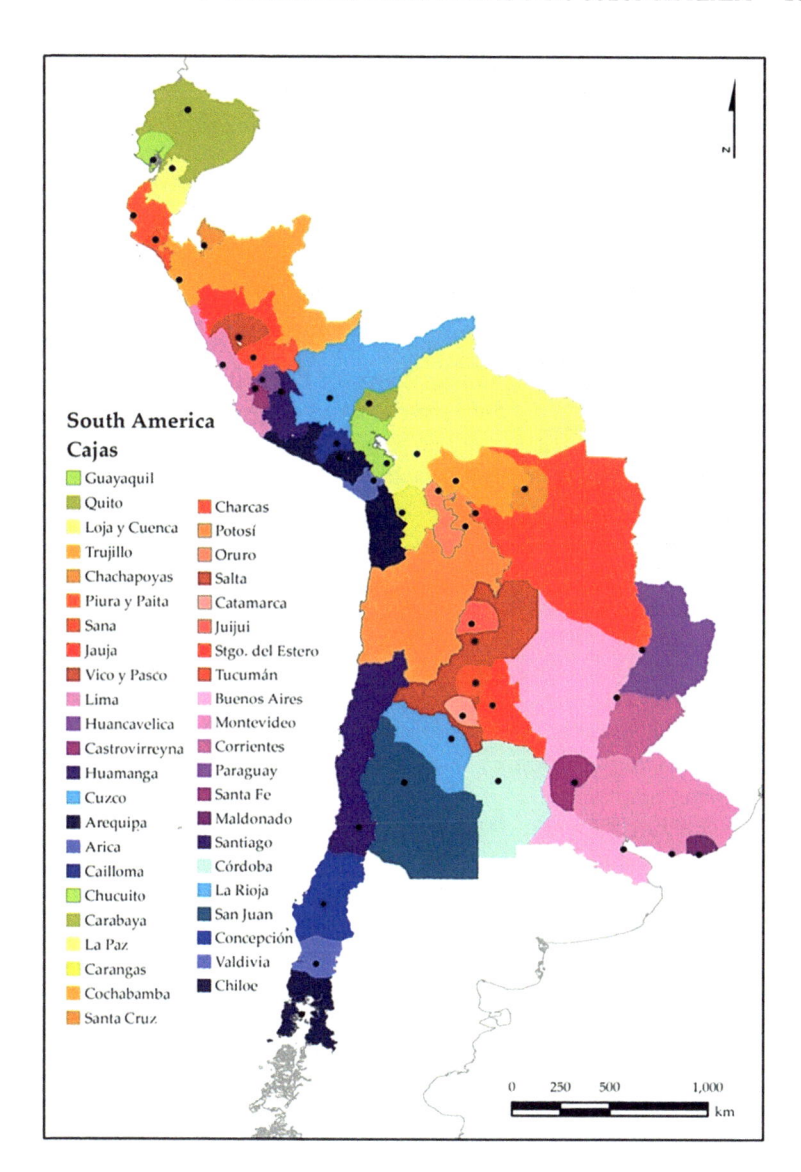

1 AN EMPIRE OF DEBTS? SPAIN AND ITS COLONIAL REALM   15

Fig. 1.4 Mapping governance structures: Treasury districts (*cajas*) in Ecuador, Peru, Upper Peru, Rio de la Plata, and Chile (late eighteenth century)

This was not a static system, but rather a snapshot of a network in constant flux. Imperial expansion was a continuous process that was still ongoing even after three centuries. The notion of a "conquest" that resulted in a stable established system of governance with a fixed set of institutions after an initial phase could not be more mistaken. Part of the process was that of extending the frontier similar to other imperial (and national) expansions in the Americas. But more important in the Spanish case was a continuous tendency for subdivision. As economic activity intensified, new subdivided treasury districts were established.

The mapped snapshot at the end of the eighteenth century illustrates already that in the core regions in terms of population density and economic activity, New Spain and Peru/Upper Peru, the average district was territorially much smaller than in regions that only very recently had become economically important such as the River Plate or indeed those that remained marginal such as the north of New Spain. This pattern was not only true for the treasury districts but also for the higher level of administration, the Viceroyalty. Over the course of the eighteenth century, two additional Viceroyalties, New Granada and Rio de la Plata, were cut out of an existing one, Peru. Figures 1.5 and 1.6 document the evolution of the network of fiscal districts in Spanish America from the sixteenth to the eighteenth centuries. Darker shades correspond to an earlier foundation date. The visualization traces the lighter shades, that is, new districts, not only to frontier regions. Instead the subdivision of existing historic districts was the norm.

The story of the creation of new districts has mostly been written as local history. New creations sometimes followed the emergence of new streams of potential revenue, for example a new mining area being opened up. In turn, when fortunes took a turn for the worse, *cajas* were sometimes closed.[20] But as in the case of the viceroyalties, local elite support for such new institutions was important. One of the better documented cases is the haphazard process that led to the creation of the viceroyalty of New Granada, which was created at least three times only to be abandoned twice.[21] The history of institutional reform in Spanish America is replete with cases of intense negotiation on the introduction of the new fiscal districts, intendancies, merchant guilds (*consulados*), or judicial districts. More often than not an up-and-coming elite of a previously smaller city established its own, independent institutions. Existing institutions shaped the practices of negotiation. Yet, at the end of those negotiations often stood new institutions that localized decision-making even further.

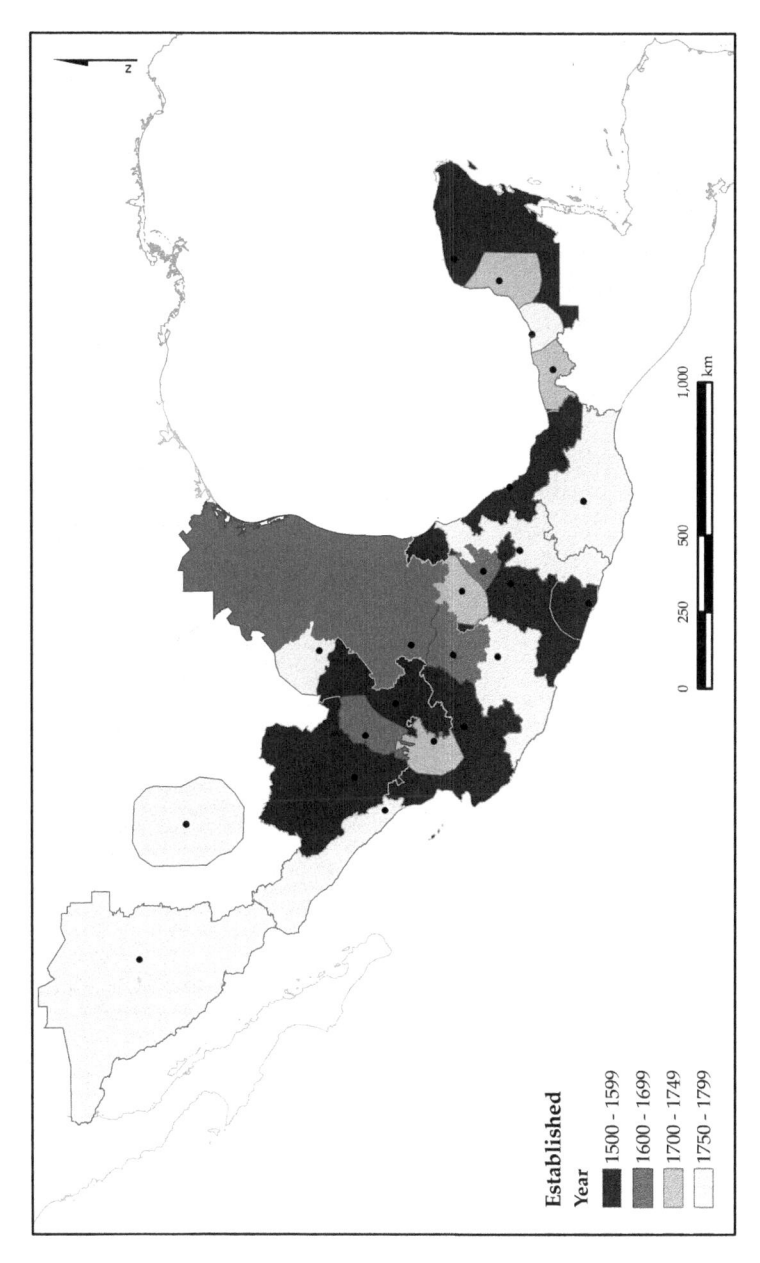

1 AN EMPIRE OF DEBTS? SPAIN AND ITS COLONIAL REALM

Fig. 1.5 The evolution of fiscal districts (sixteenth to eighteenth century): New Spain

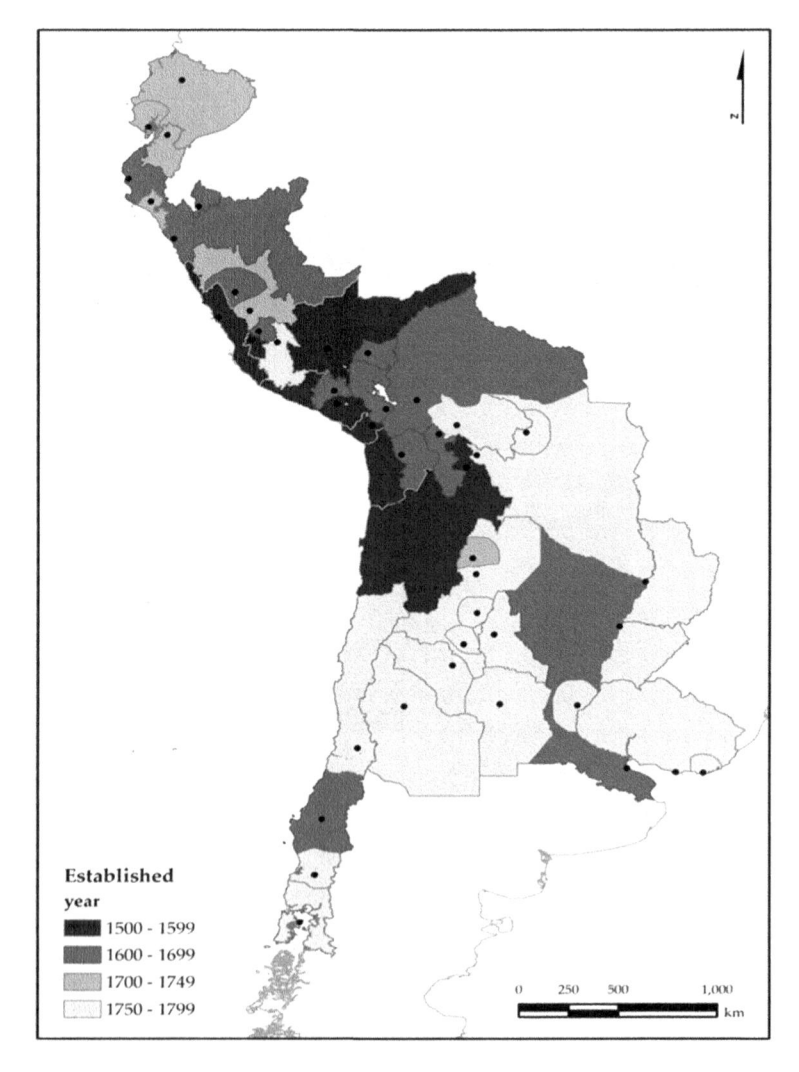

Fig. 1.6 The evolution of fiscal districts (sixteenth to eighteenth century): Spanish South America

Institutions provided positions, and sometimes politics was one of the best business opportunities.[22] Historians have often dismissed the political jostling for the establishment of new legal, fiscal, and political institutions as rent seeking. The term suggests something illegitimate, an attempt to use political power to cream off the benefits of private economic activity. However, such a notion presupposes the separation between the public and private sectors that did not exist before the nineteenth century. Within the logic of early modern society, the question was not whether private and public activity were enmeshed, they always were. Instead, the efficiency of social political and economic governance depended largely on how monopolized political power was. In that sense the subdivision of fiscal districts ensured not only proximity to the potential sources of revenue but also a healthy inter-institutional competition.

The fiscal state constructed in the Spanish Americas was organic rather than imposed from a central authority. This helps us to further debunk the center-periphery model. But the peculiar absence of sovereign debt still needs explaining. Theory and history would suggest that a locally embedded system of raising taxes should have been perceived as basically legitimate, and therefore should have benefited from what is known as "voluntary compliance."[23] If it is true that local elites had more than a little say in the management structure of the fiscal system created around the regional *caja*, one might expect an increased willingness to lend money to the treasury. Michael Kwass argued that the French Crown only lost elite support when it tried to force previously exempt elites to pay some of the new, universal direct taxes of the later eighteenth century, creating what he called an "oxymoronic creature," the privileged taxpayer.[24] In Spanish America, direct taxation was mostly restricted to indigenous subjects, via tribute. But the additional burden of direct taxes raised in the eighteenth century via the *repartimento de mercancias* benefited local office holders and local *cajas*, not the monarchy.[25] Meanwhile, "Spaniards," that is, whites, had always been subject to indirect taxation on consumption and trade, which as in the peninsular Spains meant that the de facto benefits of any existing tax privileges had always been modest. In the Spains the privileged taxpayer had never been an oxymoron.

The traditional model of colonial financial underdevelopment leaves room for only one explanation for the absence of lending: locals knew that a particular treasury was in an unsustainable situation, either because revenues were simply too low or because the revenue collected was extracted to the center of the Empire. By the late eighteenth century, the revenue raising capacity of different European polities in both European and overseas territories had begun to diverge substantially. Britain and the Netherlands in particular collected revenue per capita that was almost double that of most other European states (although there might be an accounting issue here, as suggested in Chap. 19 of this volume).[26] However, differences between France and the Spains, for instance, were not terribly large. The French and Spanish metropolitan values of revenue collection can thus serve as a yardstick for the American territories.

Given the fragmentation of the fiscal system in the Americas described above, it is surprising that Spanish American Treasuries collected amounts of revenue in line with the European Spains and France. Differences between Latin American macro-regions, reported in Fig. 1.7, were large however. Revenues per capita in out of the way Chile were less than one fifth of those in New Spain and one fourth of those in Peru or Upper Peru, today's Bolivia. While it is impossible to know what the GDP differences between those regions were, it is at least likely that higher revenue did reflect greater economic per capita production in the corresponding region. In sum, fiscal capacity in Spanish America was reasonably high and quite similar to that in the European Spains. This contrasts sharply with the situation in the British or Dutch colonies in the Atlantic. In both cases metropolitan revenue levels were multiples of those in the colonies, not

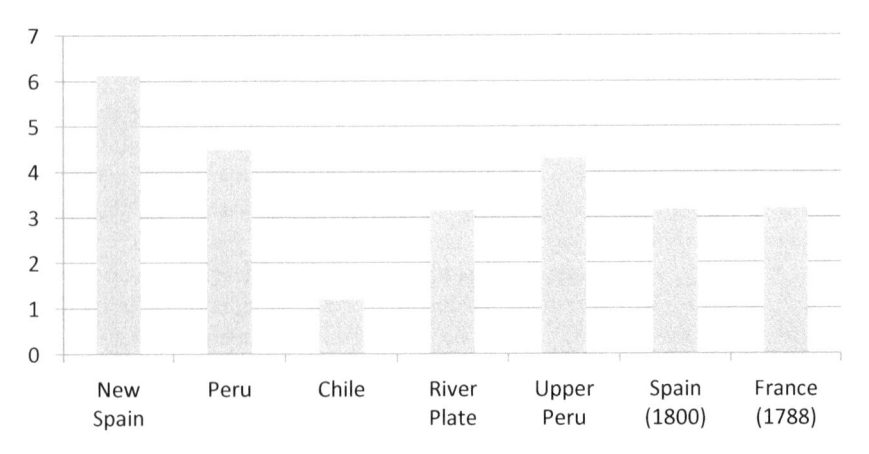

Fig. 1.7 Revenues per capita, 1785–89: France and the Spains. In pesos. Revenues are net of intra-colonial transfers and carry-overs in the case of Spanish America. (Source: Grafe and Irigoin, "A Stakeholder Empire")

only because metropolitan tax incidence was high, but also because colonial ones were very low. A comparison of colonial tax regimes suggests that the Spanish case stands out not in terms of overall state capacity but because the American territories were so similar to the European ones. Yet, that makes the lack of lending even more puzzling. The large differences between districts suggest that the need for borrowing of the local treasury districts was even more pronounced, at least in some of them.

That leaves the alleged extractive nature of the fiscal system as the last possible explanation for the low debt ratio within the conventional model of the relationship between fiscal and financial institutions. But as has been shown by various historians for individual *cajas*, and for the entire system by the work undertaken together with Irigoin, outright transfers of Spanish American revenue to the peninsular Spains were limited, certainly by the eighteenth century.[27] In the 1730s still about 12 percent of total revenue collected in the American treasury districts found its way into the central *Hacienda* in Madrid. That was not a negligible percentage, but importantly by the 1780s that ratio had fallen to 5 percent, and below 4 percent (of a much larger revenue) at the end of the eighteenth century.[28]

In the face of the substantial fiscal capacity in the Spanish Americas the limited extraction toward the Madrid treasury is worth discussing. Strong local and regional control over revenue collection and expenditure were responsible for the inability of the central treasury to get its hands on more revenue from the Americas. Documents related to the treasury district of Havana in the 1680s illustrate the sort of politics at play:

> .... And they [the *cajas*] report a surplus that should be remitted [to peninsular Spain] of 224,766 *reales*. But the governor issued an act *not* to remit but to keep the money in the *caja* except for the 117,852 *reales* that came from an investigation... and the 65,600 *reales* that belong to a deposit made of the properties of the Catalan Gil Carroso...[29]

The treasury official acknowledged that in theory the substantial surplus that resulted in the local *caja* should be remitted to the Peninsula. But he then went on to state that the governor had issued a legal provision that the money should remain in Havana except for those amounts present in the local treasury chest that were in fact the private property of individuals. That is what happened. De facto, governors and local treasury officials could and did regularly overrule notionally higher authorities.

A recent attempt to study the fiscal sustainability of nine important colonial treasury districts econometrically confirmed that most were sustainable most of the time. The argument that the Spanish American empire was on its last fiscal leg in the late eighteenth century is not supported. Given the fragmented nature of the system, trends were not uniform as Herbert Klein and John TePaske noted several decades ago.[30] But the primary balances, that is, revenues minus expenditures for the two most important *cajas* never became negative for a particularly long period and rarely did so at the same time.[31] Also, the less important districts often did better than the central ones.

The evidence presented thus far just serves to deepen the puzzle. It suggests that we can safely discard a number of possible explanations for the low debt ratio of Spanish American and peninsular Spanish treasuries. The system had grown quite organically over three centuries of imperial rule, illustrating responsiveness to changing economic fortunes at the regional level. There was no centralized system of extraction toward a supposed colonial center, but instead a network of *cajas* subject to very substantial local elite control. Nor was the system overall underfunded; indeed by the standards of European colonial expansion it was unusually similar in terms of fiscal capacity to its European equivalent.

As far as one can see, then, there was no obvious reason why investors would not lend to the Spanish treasuries in the Peninsula or in the Americas. Indeed, the yield on debt instruments circulating in the Peninsula, the only ones that were traded on secondary markets, indicates investors' willingness to provide credit. As I have shown elsewhere, the yield on old bonds, the so-called *juros*, was remarkably stable at around 4 percent throughout the eighteenth century.[32] The Spanish monarchy for the first time issued new bonds known as *vales reales* late in the century. Their yield not surprisingly hovered around 4 percent until 1793, when the French Revolutionary Wars started wreaking havoc on the public finances of most European polities (Fig. 1.8). If there were willing lenders, why was there apparently no interest on the part of the state to borrow more?

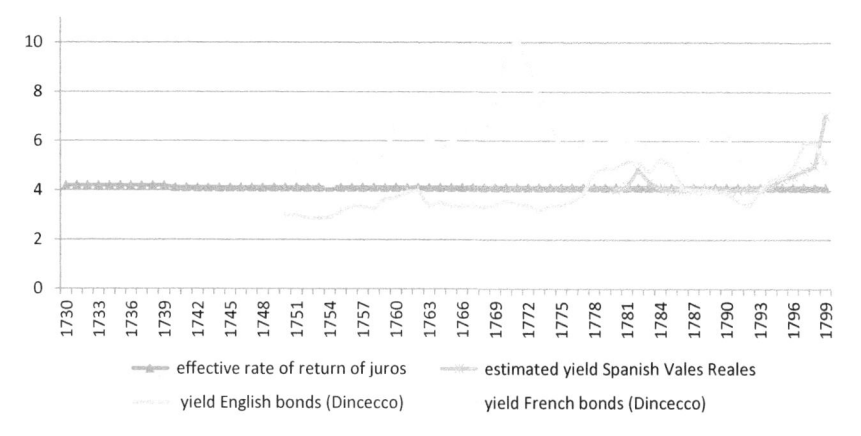

Fig. 1.8 Yields of old bonds in eighteenth-century peninsular Spain (*juros*), newly issued bonds (*vales*), English and French bonds. (Sources: Grafe, *Distant Tyranny*; Mark Dincecco, *Political Transformations and Public Finances: Europe, 1650–1913* (Cambridge: Cambridge University Press, 2011))

Monasteries, Guilds, and *Cajas*: The Local Actors of Financial Transfers

The obvious answer is that the public and private sector did borrow. Yet, credit in the Spanish political economy took forms that are unfamiliar to us and therefore harder to read. What we consider today modern banking and credit institutions in many ways are the result of scarcity, that is their development responded to the need to match potential lenders with potential borrowers under conditions of capital scarcity on the one hand, and a shortage of liquidity on the other. In this respect, Spanish America was notably different. It was hardly the Eldorado of European dreams, where streams of silver and gold flowed. But for most of the early modern period it was a place where liquidity was less restricted than almost anywhere else in a global economy that relied on specie money. High nominal wages and prices in much of Latin America attest to that reality notwithstanding the constant complaints of contemporaries regarding a supposed shortage of circulating medium and capital. Global historians, keen on stressing the role of Latin American silver in trade between Europe and Asia, often forget that the one place where liquidity was greatest was Latin America. That liquidity effect was reinforced by the existence of a common, very stable coinage across an enormous territory, which lowered transaction costs within the very large internal market.

I want to suggest that in these conditions a set of institutions developed in a co-evolutionary form that underpinned public and private lending institutions in Spanish America and served private and public needs successfully almost to the end. Banks, joint-stock companies, and bonds existed legally within this financial sector. But their importance was marginal, except in a few regions such as Venezuela, where the *Real Compañía Guipuzcoana*, a joint-stock company, was an important player.[33] Merchant banks came and went, but rarely developed into stable institutions. Some of them were very large, like that of Juan de Cuerva in Lima between 1615 and 1635. But its business model was based on a consortium that cornered the market and was susceptible to exogenous shocks that led to a fabled bankruptcy.[34] The old Spanish bonds (*juros*) had been for sale in the early seventeenth century, but then became insignificant.[35]

Instead of banks, shareholding companies, and bonds, pride of place in financial services belonged to another trio of institutions: religious institutions, guilds, and regional treasuries. The first turned into a de facto network of investment funds that provided local, regional, and increasingly super-regional credit. The second progressively took on financial intermediation. They bundled small, medium, and large investors' money into large loans to the public purse, often directly feeding those credits into the local *caja*. Finally, the local treasuries served as a source of liquidity and of a rudimentary system of *giro banco*, that is, an interspatial and sometimes intertemporal cashless transfer mechanism not unlike that developed by Italian bankers as early as the fifteenth century and turned into a dedicated institution by Venetian bankers in the early seventeenth century.[36]

That religious institutions played a crucial role in financial intermediation in the Spanish Americas and in the peninsular Spains is well known. I constructed the yield curve reported above for Spanish bonds on the basis of the returns received by the Cathedral Chapter of Zamora in the peninsula. For Spanish America, the historians Asunción Lavrín and Gisela von Wobeser have demonstrated the workings of the credit system in colonial New Spain, while the work of Kathryn Burns has offered insights into the same mechanisms in colonial Peru.[37] Religious foundations of all kinds received endowments dedicated to provide for alms, the upkeep of a church or hospital, or to pay for masses to be read for the salvation of the donor's soul. Convents received large amounts in the form of dowries of prospective nuns. The overwhelming majority of donations were not directly invested in altar pieces, that is consumption. Instead they were lent to the private and public sector.

The more or less standard interest rate on such loans was initially about 7 percent but lowered to 5 percent by the seventeenth century, where it remained until the late eighteenth century when it dropped to about 4 percent in some cases.[38] Religious institutions on the whole were conservative investors. They were rent-seekers in the very sense of the word, just as any pension fund today. Von Wobeser estimates that until the mid-eighteenth century they were the single most important source of credit in colonial Mexico.[39] Large convents in Peru such as the one studied by Burns were like most pension funds not really interested in the redemption of a loan but instead valued steady returns.[40] The financial instrument most in use, the *censo al quitar o consignativo*, catered to that need.

The *censo* was in theory a perpetual loan guaranteed by real property that the borrower could redeem at any time but did not have to redeem. This turned the donation or dowry that the convent had received de facto into an endowment which produced a steady annual return by means of extending mortgages. The advantage of the backing by real property was twofold. Convents were often patient lenders, in part because they could draw on rents from the mortgaged rural or urban properties or land before having to go through the legal trouble of pushing for bankruptcy proceeding, though they had few qualms in doing so if necessary. Even the treasuries benefited. In order to avoid any accusations of usury, loans were structured as sales contracts in legal terms, which meant that they paid the sales tax, *alcabala*.[41] Several historians have pointed out that the ease with which owners of *haciendas* or urban property could find credit they were never meant to repay led eventually in the late eighteenth century to substantial overleveraging.[42] Credit had become too easy.

Monasteries, charitable institutions, and other religious entities such as confraternities did differ to some extent in investment strategy. Table 1.1 illustrates the breakdown of the annual income of the Poor House of Mexico in 1811. Various endowments produced nice returns, as did investments in tax collection organized by the merchant guild, some of which was derived from rental properties. Less than 1000 of the 15,000 pesos of income came from alms-giving or payments by residents who could contribute to their care. Ninety-four percent of revenue came from endowments, that is, fairly diversified investments in private and public debt.

Table 1.1 Sources of income of Mexico City's Poor House, 1811

Sources of income (1823 for 1811)	Principal (pesos)	Annual interest/income
Tribunal del Consulado (Fondo de Averia)	250,000	11,250
Rental properties	?	800
Alms		468
Pensioners		504
Temporalidades	25,355	1268
Tribunal de Mineria	14,035	702
Private endowment Conde de Xala	6000	300
Tribunal del Consulado (Renta del Tabaco)	4740	237
Private endowment D. Jose P Cobian	2917	155
Obrapia D Juan Ruiz Aragon	2406	102
Capt Antonio Pineiro	1800	90
D.a Maria G Verdeja (Hacienda de Huizastitlan)	453	23
D. J. Ximenez Arenal	202	10
D.a Maria G. Villanueva (rancho de pulques, Zempaola)	178	9
Estate of D. Fernando Zorrilla	?	?

Source: Silvia Marina Arrom, *Containing the Poor: The Mexico City Poor House, 1774–1871* (Durham: Duke University Press, 2000)

Another big player in New Spain was the Inquisition.[43] In 1791 almost 40 percent of its income stream relied on such investments. Its operating profit for the year was a healthy 21 percent in part because the institution could defray half of its expenditures from its own endowments, and annual returns were destined toward further investments. Before a *censo* was offered, the value of potential borrowers' property was surveyed. But as capital began to chase investment opportunities in the late eighteenth century, the Inquisition's *Real Fisco* (treasury) changed strategy and began to offer shorter-term loans, secured by guarantors. They also, like the Poor House, began to subscribe to the public loans that the merchant guilds (*consulados*) were syndicating.

The merchant guilds became the second element in the Spanish American credit system. As argued elsewhere, they took over the function of merchant banks.[44] As such they pooled investments of large numbers of smaller and larger investors, such as individual widows, the Poor House, and the Inquisition, into large loans to the public purse. These large loans, "known under the euphemism of *donativos*," increasingly carried a similar interest rate to that of most other loans.[45] For the *consulados* they provided additional advantages since they usually came with the right to collect the taxes earmarked for the servicing of the debt and a modest fee of about 1 percent. The combination of providing tax collection services and financial intermediation became the Lima guild's main business.[46] It also guaranteed access to liquidity. In New Mexico the treasury of the Inquisition invested the staggering amount of 548,000 pesos in loans syndicated by the Merchant Guild on a total of seven occasions between the 1740s and 1811.[47] As in the case of the financial dealings of large religious institutions, these were sophisticated impersonal sources of capital.

The final piece in the puzzle of Spanish American financial development is the local treasuries. In a prescient piece published in 1969 Lohmann Villena pointed out that the three types of institutions, religious bodies, merchant guilds, and the *cajas*, likely were the backbone of public and private credit.[48] The American treasury districts in collaboration with merchant guilds served to mediate between local investors and the needs of the monarchy for money, especially in the wars of the late eighteenth century. More importantly for the workings of the financial and fiscal system within America were the extremely large amounts of money moved between the individual treasury districts in America. These intra-colonial transfers accounted for anywhere between a quarter and more than 40 percent of the total expenditure of all *cajas* in the eighteenth century (Fig. 1.9). Their role within the fiscal governance of Spanish America has been subject to much debate in the last decade.[49] It has been argued that the ability to move money from economically better off districts to poorer ones via these so-called *situados* was one reason why Spanish governance was rolled out successfully over three centuries.

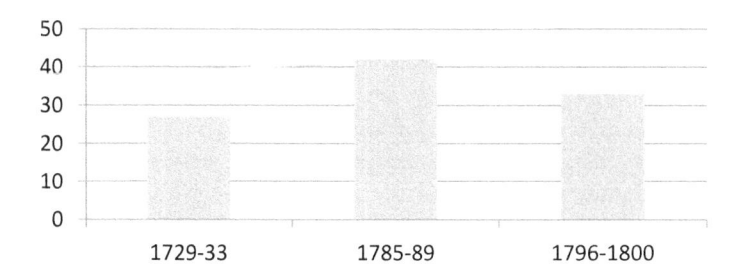

Fig. 1.9 Intra-colonial revenue transfers (ICTs), 1729–1800. In percent of net expenditure. (Source: Grafe and Irigoin, "A Stakeholder Empire")

The more interesting issue from the point of view of the present paper is that those transfers provided a system of *giro*, interspatial clearing. Local elites controlled much of the decision-making over these transfers. After the Intendant of New Orleans in 1781 complained to the viceroy of Mexico about the dire straits his *caja* faced, the reply from Mexico must have pleased its recipient.

> His Excellency the Viceroy [of New Spain] has issued a decree ... having seen your letter which describes the scarcity of funds that your Province suffers ... and *after having heard the officials of the cajas of Mexico to whom he forwarded the file* he has decided to send ... an additional 315,000 pesos [via Havana].[50]

It should be noted that the largesse of the Mexican *caja* was no more an act of Christian charity than the *censos* of Peruvian nuns. The New Orleans Intendant had wagered his ability to allow contraband into mainland New Spain to convince the New Spain treasury that sharing was in its own interest. And it was. Merchants from New Spain would take the funds to Havana likely in the form of goods purchased in New Spain. There they could exchange them for local goods, and Havana merchants would then take the goods and cash to New Orleans. In the process, the merchants involved would not only *not* pay interest for the de facto loan and interspatial transfer but also receive payments for their transfer services.

These financial networks involved a combination of local elite control and a very large Spanish American fiscal system. As we have seen the Spanish American treasuries managed amounts that as a percentage of GDP might have been similar to that in many European polities. This put control over an enormous amount of liquidity into the hands of local officials and merchants at practically zero interest. More importantly, it provided a mechanism to overcome the one potential problem of a financial system that relied on religious institutions and merchant guilds. Notwithstanding the enormous amounts of capital they moved, they rarely intermediated large sums of money across space. It is hard to say if they did not engage more in interspatial clearing because the *cajas* indirectly served that purpose or if the *cajas* became part of a *giro* system because the merchant guilds were unwilling to engage in this. The beauty of institutional co-evolution is that different organizational solutions begin to complement each other over time until it becomes impossible for one to function without the other.

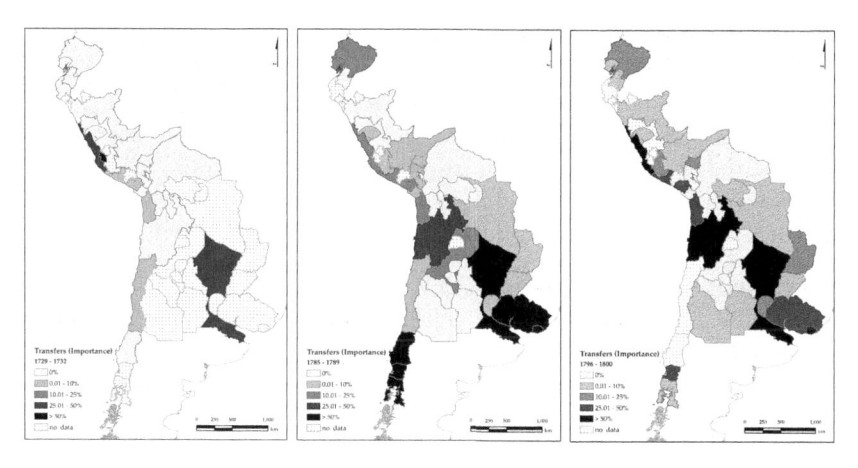

Fig. 1.10 Self-reinforcing polycentrism: ICTs as a share of total revenue for each district (1720s–1800)

This process is at least in part illustrated in Fig. 1.10. The maps show the South American *cajas* discussed above for the periods 1729–33, 1785–89, and 1796–1800 from left to right. Darker shades indicate a higher share of ICTs in total expenditure. Even without detailed analysis, the main trend is clearly visible, namely, that over time more districts had a higher share of intra-colonial transfers as part of their expenditure (and by extension as part of the revenue of other *cajas*). Put differently, larger and larger shares of local fiscal moneys in more places ended up in the great redistribution system. Contemporaries understood this only too well. Manuel Amat y Junyent, Viceroy of Peru from 1761 to 1776, suggested in his *Memoria de Gobierno* that the *cajas* should officially provide a service to send bills of exchange across the Americas and to Europe, earning a commission in the process.[51] Nothing came of that proposal. But as the above-cited quote from the Havana *caja* illustrates, individuals did deposit private funds with the local treasuries presumably for transfer. That explains why the treasury coffers contained more than 65,000 pesos of the Catalan Gil Carroso.

> * * *The Spanish Empire was not an empire without debt. But it was indebted to its stakeholders rather than to bondholders. Those stakeholders maintained the viability of public finances while also providing local and regional private credit. Larger interspatial transfers

went through the public treasuries which also guaranteed liquidity. The decentralization of the financial system is notable as is the complementarity of the elements that had developed over three centuries. The economy expanded and the public sector functioned because they could draw on a functioning financial system of interlocking institutions. Yet, the latter looked very different from the sort of financial system modern economic historians are familiar with.

It stands to reason that the relative abundance of coinable mineral in the Americas allowed for fewer constraints on the development of the financial system. Its purpose was less to overcome an overall shortage of capital and liquidity. Instead it had to mediate large distances while guaranteeing effective monitoring. Religious endowments proved as successful at providing investable capital as today's pension funds. Most economic historians have woefully underestimated their importance. Banking historians seem to find it hard to believe that a bunch of nuns and Inquisition officials made sound investment decisions and left the subject more often than not to historians of gender or religion. Yet, there is now overwhelming evidence that most of these religious institutions invested conservatively but successfully. Rent-seeking deserves a better press among economic historians. And their religious role helped to improve the monitoring of debtors, who were less likely to default on a loan from the gatekeepers of heaven.

The financial system was also decentralized, competitive, and provided impersonal sources of capital. Interest rates were clearly customary and did not change for long periods of time. But they did adapt when there was a capital glut in the late eighteenth century. Nor was this simply a contractor state.[52] The state farmed out military provision and much more as the contractor state model suggests. However, the collaboration and enmeshing of private and public was a feature on both sides of the accounts, revenue and expenditure. There was not a powerful central state, as in England, that could contract out.[53]

The system outlined above thus served as a sophisticated structure providing impersonal credit to the Spanish American economies that expanded rapidly over the eighteenth century. By the late eighteenth century, the private and the public sector were heavily indebted. But the system did not collapse under its own weight. Thus, it is hard to say if the debt was excessive or if there had been a credit bubble. Nevertheless, the financial system imploded over a relatively short period of two or three decades in the early nineteenth century. The cause was not the rapaciousness of the colonial state or poor manageability, at least not in the sense the historiography has suggested.

Instead, the Spanish American financial system sui generis became the collateral damage of two larger developments. First, the collapse of the Spanish empire and the political fragmentation during the wars of independence shut down the system of intra-colonial transfers and with it the *giro* mechanism. Second, the impact of war and destruction conspired with one of the greater economic crimes of the heroes of the Enlightenment in the Spanish territories. Starting in the late colonial period and accelerating with Independence, disentailment destroyed the economic basis of religious and charitable institutions. Being more familiar with French philosophy than Latin American economic realities, reformers unwittingly ruined the credit circuits of Spanish America.[54] This outsized act of expropriation did indeed shut down the banking system, causing a major rupture in Spanish America's financial history. The colonial legacy was largely that of a system that French and British enlightenment commentators simply did not care to try and understand.

Notes

1. Regina Grafe, *Distant Tyranny: Markets, Power and Backwardness in Spain, 1650–1800* (Princeton: Princeton University Press, 2012).
2. Timothy Besley and Torsten Persson, "The Origins of State Capacity: Property Rights, Taxation, and Politics," *American Economic Review* 99, no. 4 (2009); Bartolomé Yun Casalilla and Patrick K. O'Brien, *The Rise of Fiscal States: A Global History, 1500–1914* (Cambridge: Cambridge University Press, 2012).
3. Stephen H. Haber, ed., *How Latin America Fell Behind: Essays on the Economic Histories of Brazil and Mexico, 1800–1914* (Stanford: Stanford University Press, 1997).
4. Stephen Haber, "Financial Markets and Industrial Development: A Comparative Study of Governmental Regulation, Financial Innovation, and Industrial Structure in Brazil and Mexico, 1840–1930," in *How Latin America Fell Behind*, ed. Haber.
5. Frank Griffith Dawson, *The First Latin American Debt Crisis: The City of London and the 1822–25 Loan Bubble* (New Haven: Yale University Press, 1990).

6. Carlos Marichal, *A Century of Debt Crises in Latin America: From Independence to the Great Depression, 1820–1930* (Princeton: Princeton University Press, 1989).
7. Marc Bloch, *The Historian's Craft* (New York: Vintage Books, 1953), 25.
8. The *vales reales* issued in the late eighteenth century by the Madrid treasury circulated in Spanish America, but had not been issued by local treasuries.
9. Daron Acemoglu and James A. Robinson, *Why Nations Fail: The Origins of Power, Prosperity, and Poverty* (New York: Crown, 2012).
10. Jorge I. Domínguez, "Explaining Latin America's Lagging Development in the Second Half of the Twentieth Century: Growth Strategies, Inequality, and Economic Crises," in *Falling Behind. Explaining the Development Gap between Latin America and the United States*, ed. Francis Fukuyama (Oxford: Oxford University Press, 2011).
11. Regina Grafe and Alejandra Irigoin, "The Spanish Empire and Its Legacy: Fiscal Re-Distribution and Political Conflict in Colonial and Post-Colonial Spanish America," *Journal of Global History* 1, no. 2 (2006); Regina Grafe and Alejandra Irigoin, "A Stakeholder Empire: The Political Economy of Spanish Imperial Rule in America," *Economic History Review* 65, no. 2 (2012); Alejandra Irigoin and Regina Grafe, "Bargaining for Absolutism: A Spanish Path to Empire and Nation Building," *Hispanic American Historical Review* 88, no. 2 (2008); Regina Grafe and Alejandra Irigoin, "Negotiating Power: Fiscal Constraints and Financial Development in Early Modern Spain and the Spanish Empire," in *Questioning Credible Commitment*, eds. D'Maris Coffman, Adrian Leonard and Larry Neal (Cambridge: Cambridge University Press, 2013).
12. James Mahoney, *Colonialism and Postcolonial Development: Spanish America in Comparative Perspective* (Cambridge: Cambridge University Press, 2010).
13. Mauricio Drelichman and Hans-Joachim Voth, *Lending to the Borrower from Hell: Debt, Taxes, and Default in the Age of Philip II* (Princeton: Princeton University Press, 2014); Mía J. Rodríguez-Salgado, *The Changing Face of Empire: Charles V, Philip II and Habsburg Authority, 1551–1559* (Cambridge: Cambridge University Press, 1988); Carlos Álvarez-Nogal and Christophe Chamley, "Debt Policy under Constraints: Philip II, the Cortes, and Genoese Bankers," *Economic History Review* 67, no. 1 (2014).
14. Grafe, *Distant Tyranny*.
15. For a more detailed analysis of war finance, see Rafael Torres Sánchez, "The Triumph of the Fiscal-Military State in the Eighteenth Century: War and Mercantilism," in *War, State and Development: Fiscal-Military States*

in the Eighteenth Century, ed. Rafael Torres Sánchez (Pamplona: EUNSA, 2007).
16. Acemoglu and Robinson, *Why Nations Fail*; Mahoney, *Colonialism and Postcolonial Development*; Allan J. Kuethe and Kenneth J. Andrien, *The Spanish Atlantic World in the Eighteenth Century: War and the Bourbon Reforms, 1713–1796* (Cambridge: Cambridge University Press, 2014); Stanley J. Stein and Barbara H. Stein, *Silver, Trade, and War: Spain and America in the Making of Early Modern Europe* (Baltimore and London: Johns Hopkins University Press, 2000).
17. Pedro Cardim et al., *Polycentric Monarchies: How Did Early Modern Spain and Portugal Achieve and Maintain a Global Hegemony?* (Portland, Or.: Sussex Academic Press, 2012); Grafe and Irigoin, "Stakeholder"; Regina Grafe, "Tyrannie à distance. La construction de l'État polycentrique et les systèmes fiscaux en Espagne (1650–1800)," in *Ressources publiques et construction étatique en Europe*, ed. Katia Béguin (Paris: IGPDE, 2015).
18. Grafe, *Distant Tyranny*.
19. Grafe and Irigoin, "Stakeholder."
20. For a description of the system, see Herbert S. Klein, *The American Finances of the Spanish Empire: Royal Income and Expenditures in Colonial Mexico, Peru, and Bolivia, 1680–1809* (Albuquerque: University of New Mexico Press, 1998); Herbert S. Klein and John J. Tepaske, *The Royal Treasuries of the Spanish Empire in America* (Durham: Duke University Press, 1982), introduction; Irigoin and Grafe, "Bargaining for Absolutism."
21. Kuethe and Andrien, *Spanish Atlantic World*.
22. Cristina Ana Mazzeo, *El comercio libre en el Perú. Las estrategias de un comerciante criollo, José Antonio de Lavalle y Cortés, Conde de Premio Real, 1777–1815* (Lima: Pontificia Universidad Católica del Perú, Fondo Editorial, 1994).
23. Margaret Levi, *Of Rule and Revenue* (Berkeley: University of California Press, 1988).
24. Michael Kwass, "A Kingdom of Taxpayers: State Formation, Privilege, and Political Culture in Eighteenth-Century France," *Journal of Modern History* 70, no. 2 (1998).
25. Jürgen Golte, *Repartos y rebeliones: Túpac Amaru y las contradicciones de la economía colonial* (Lima: IEP, 2016).
26. Nuno Palma and Jaime Reis, "From Convergence to Divergence: Portuguese Demography and Economic Growth, 1500–1850," *Working paper, Groningen Growth and Development Centre* (2016).
27. Herbert S. Klein, "Origin and Volume of Remission of Royal Tax Revenues from the Viceroyalties of Peru and Nueva España," in *Dinero, moneda y crédito en la Monarquía hispánica*, ed. Antonio Miguel Bernal (Madrid: Marcial Pons, 2000).

28. Grafe and Irigoin, "A Stakeholder Empire," figure 1.
29. Archivo General de Indias (AGI), Contaduria, Legajo 1160.
30. Herbert S. Klein, "The Great Shift: The Rise of Mexico and the Decline of Peru in the Spanish American Colonial Empire, 1680–1809," *Revista de Historia Económica* 13, no. 1 (1995).
31. Javier Arnault, "Was Colonialism Fiscally Sustainable? An Empirical Examination of the Colonial Finances of Spanish America," *AEHE Working Paper 1703* (2017).
32. Grafe, *Distant Tyranny.*
33. Montserrat Gárate Ojanguren, *La Real Compañía Guipuzcoana de Caracas* (San Sebastián: Sociedad Guipuzcoana de Ediciones y Publicaciones, 1990).
34. Margarita Suarez, *Desafíos transatlánticos. Mercaderes, banqueros y el Estado en el Perú virreinal, 1600–1700* (Lima: Fondo de cultura económica, 2001).
35. Kenneth J. Andrien, "The Sale of Juros and the Politics of Reform in the Viceroyalty of Peru, 1608–1695," *Journal of Latin American Studies* 13, no. 1 (1981).
36. For a late-fifteenth-century example, see Richard A. Goldthwaite, *Economy of Renaissance Florence* (Baltimore: Johns Hopkins University Press, 2011), 435–36.
37. Asunción Lavrín, "The Role of Nunneries in the Economy of New Spain in the Eighteenth Century," *Hispanic American Historical Review* 46 (1966); Gisela von Wobeser, *El crédito eclesiástico en la Nueva España. Siglo XVIII* (Mexico: Fondo de cultura económica, 2010); Kathryn Burns, *Colonial Habits: Convents and the Spiritual Economy of Cuzco, Peru* (Durham: Duke University Press, 1999). For Spain, see Cyril Milhaud, "Interregional Flows of Long-Term Mortgage Credit in Eighteenth-Century Spain. To What Extent Was the Market Fragmented?" *Working Paper*, version 3 (2018), https://hal-pse.archives-ouvertes.fr/hal-01180682v3.
38. Gisela von Wobeser, "La inquisición como institución crediticia en el siglo XVIII," *Historia Mexicana* 39, no. 4 (1990): 864. Expressed as 14,000 or 20,000 al millar.
39. Gisela von Wobeser, "Las fundaciones piadosas como fuentes de crédito en la época colonial," *Historia Mexicana* 38, no. 4 (1989): 786.
40. Burns, *Colonial Habits.*
41. von Wobeser, "Inquisición."
42. Burns, *Colonial Habits*, 152–54.
43. von Wobeser, "Inquisición."
44. Grafe and Irigoin, "Stakeholder," 626–30. See Appendices II through IV for details. For Spain and the *Cinco Gremios*, see Guillermo Pérez Sarrión, "Gremios, gremios mayores, cinco gremios mayores: Madrid, 1680–1790.

Una interpretación y algunas preguntas," in *Recuperando el Norte: empresas, capitales y proyectos atlánticos en la economía imperial hispánica*, ed. Alberto Angulo Morales and Álvaro Aragón Ruano (Bilbao: Universidad del País Vasco, 2016).
45. Guillermo Lohmann Villena, "Banca y crédito en la América española. Notas sobre hipótesis de trabajo y fuentes informativas," *Historia* 8 (1969).
46. Suarez, *Desafíos -ransatlánticos*; Cristina Ana Mazzeo, *Gremios mercantiles en las guerras de la independencia: Perú y México en la transición de la Colonia a la República, 1740–1840* (Lima: Banco Central de Reserva del Perú, 2012).
47. von Wobeser, "Inquisición," cuadro 5.
48. Lohmann Villena, "Banca."
49. See the forum in *Hispanic American Historical Review* 88, no. 2 (2008): Carlos Marichal, "Rethinking Negotiation and Coercion in an Imperial State"; William R. Summerhill, "Fiscal Bargains, Political Institutions and Economic Performance"; Irigoin and Grafe, "Bargaining for Absolutism."
50. AGI Cuba legajo 604b, f453.
51. Lohmann Villena, "Banca," 304.
52. Rafael Torres Sánchez, *Military Entrepreneurs and the Spanish Contractor State in the Eighteenth Century* (Oxford: Oxford University Press, 2016).
53. Roger Knight and Martin Wilcox, *Sustaining the Fleet, 1793–1815: War, the British Navy and the Contractor State* (Woodbridge: Boydell & Brewer, 2010).
54. Gisela von Wobeser, "La Consolidación de Vales Reales como factor determinante de la lucha de independencia en México, 1804–1808," *Historia Mexicana* 56, no. 2 (2006).

CHAPTER 2

Publicity, Debt, and Politics: The Old Regime and the French Revolution

Rebecca L. Spang

It has often been said that the French revolutionaries of 1789 wanted to break completely with history. Bemoaned by Edmund Burke as showing woeful disregard for chivalrous tradition, the same gesture was later joyfully anthropomorphized by Jules Michelet when he depicted French liberty in 1789 as a smiling newborn in her cradle. In what follows, I reconsider the notorious French attempt "to break with the past…to create an unbridgeable gulf between all they had hitherto been and all they now aspired to be" (the words are Tocqueville's) from a new angle: the relation between public debt and modern politics.[1] Revolutionaries began by wanting to leave France's fiscal regime behind, but to do so they eventually created new monetary and political regimes as well.

Central to any political or social history of modern Europe, the French Revolution should also be foundational to our understanding of public debt. This chapter argues that revolutionaries' dedication to honoring past commitments—in other words, their *reluctance* to break with the

R. L. Spang (✉)
Department of History, Indiana University, Bloomington, IN, USA
e-mail: rlspang@indiana.edu

© The Author(s) 2020
N. Barreyre, N. Delalande (eds.), *A World of Public Debts*,
Palgrave Studies in the History of Finance,
https://doi.org/10.1007/978-3-030-48794-2_2

past—had the unintended effect of stimulating monetary innovation and that those changes then provoked further social and cultural unrest. Attempting to create a stable debt regime, in other words, led to political instability. The Revolution's growing radicalization was less the product of extreme ideology than it was of the contradictions between existing property relations and new models of citizenship and participation. This analysis hence poses a sharp contrast with accounts of Britain's eighteenth-century "Financial Revolution," which generally see property rights, political participation, and modern public debt as supporting and re-enforcing each other.[2] According to historians of Britain, the Glorious Revolution and the creation of the Bank of England lay the foundations for a new kind of debt: national borrowing, approved by Parliament (and funded by the tax legislation it passed), replaced the monarch's personal debt. As the holders of public debt and the authors of fiscal policy became largely one and the same, the state was able to borrow greater sums for longer periods of time and at lower rates of interest. An increasingly effective excise bureaucracy combined with the rule of law and sanctity of property rights fueled the growth of modern politics and the expansion of Britain's imperial power.[3] In the British case, that is, the growth of public debt and of the bourgeois public sphere apparently coincided.[4] By examining the very different case of France, this chapter shows that the elaboration of modern regimes of public debt depended on local political circumstances and forces us to reconsider what we think we know about the relation between political, monetary, and fiscal regimes.[5]

Making Finances Public

State debt ties current policy choices to past events. It does so through the medium of money, but other media contribute more to debt's political significance: in the eighteenth century, these media included manuscript correspondence, newsletters, print publications, even song and theatre. Though shrouded in official mystery, the finances of the French absolutist state were nonetheless subject to lively debate. As Michael Kwass has noted, secrecy invites speculation. In the case of farmed taxes on consumption, for instance, it was widely conjectured that the Farmers-General pocketed nearly as much as they passed to the royal treasury. Rumor and popular resistance (which extended to widespread sympathy for smugglers and their activities) identified the Farmers as villains, but—as Eugene

White has shown—politics and capital constraints limited the Crown's ability to negotiate more favorable terms or bring the Tax-Farmers to heel.[6]

Louis XVI's Controller-General of Finance, the Genevan banker Jacques Necker (father of that talented self-publicist Madame de Staël) hence showed himself an astute political strategist when he published the first open report on France's finances.[7] At a time when courtiers were attacking him as a foreigner, a Protestant, and a commoner, Necker's *Compte rendu au Roi* (literally, *Rendering of Accounts to the King*) made him nonetheless a popular favorite since it implied a surplus and—even more important—because it apparently established that the monarchy had nothing to hide. As if to anticipate Douglass North and Barry Weingast's analysis of two hundred years later, Necker began his report by noting that Great Britain's easy access to credit (its "greatest weapon in wartime") derived not only from the "nature" of its government but also, crucially, from "the public notoriety" to which British finances were subject. Thanks, he argued, to an annual, published report made to Parliament, Britain's lenders were no longer troubled by those "suspicions and fears" that invariably accompanied secrecy. Constitutions, Necker implied, might make commitments credible, but they could only do so if the public first knew what those commitments were.[8] His own *Compte rendu*, he asserted, would protect France's credibility from "shadowy authors [...] who cause trouble with their lies" and would—if made a routine publication—motivate future Finance Ministers to the highest levels of probity and energy.

The royal edict promulgating Necker's *Compte rendu* drew further direct links between public media and trust, knowledge and credibility. "We believe only benefits can arise from permitting this publication," it stated. "By allowing our faithful subjects to know the state of our finances, we expect to bring them closer to us and to make ever stronger that unity of interests and that affinity of trust that are the strength of states and the happiness of monarchs."[9] Sure enough, the Duc de Croÿ noted shortly thereafter:

> The booksellers have never seen such crowds…three thousand copies were printed, but they immediately disappeared, and soon 20,000 had been sold… Never before were all the Kingdom's finances revealed nor had the King, as it were, given an account—a very detailed account—to his people. It was a brilliant political stroke to show matters in such a good light at just the moment when M. Necker had opened [*venait de publier*] a new loan for sixty million livres.[10]

Two weeks after the *Compte rendu*'s publication, a local newspaper reported that a provincial book dealer had already sold all his copies and that reading it "fills the soul with enthusiasm and an indescribable sentiment of patriotism. There is no one who does not weep tears of happiness."[11] Marie Antoinette was reported to be among its many joyful readers, and within a few months the text had supposedly been "translated into all known languages." By the end of the year, journalists were asserting the *Compte rendu* had sold an extraordinary 100,000 copies and that it was being used as a primer to teach small children to read.[12]

Much as had happened with the Crown's appeals to patriotism during the Seven Years' and American Revolutionary Wars, however, making finances public unleashed forces which no one could fully control. In the first instance, having called on "the nation" and "the people" for mass support of its military actions, the monarchy found it could not demobilize those groups when the conflicts ended. Instead, *nation* and *patrie* became key categories of public debate in the 1780s and far beyond.[13] So too did "debt" and "credit." Representative institutions always represent the interests of *particular members* of the political public. When that public is vocal and divided, then a constitution and public commitments alone do not guarantee the state's behavior as a debtor.[14] Politics comes into play.

1780s France had neither written constitution nor representative institutions, but it had a deeply divided political elite. Those divisions were in part religio-cultural: they pitted Jansenist proponents of France's historic, "patriot" constitution (including many noble magistrates) against courtiers more supportive of absolutist royal power. The first, already well versed in using the Old Regime's limited public sphere to protest attempted administrative centralization, often cast their critique of court society in monetary or fiscal terms: they denounced the court's "credit' as insubstantial, based on patronage, and subject to abuse by women and dandies. Theirs were *political* demands (i.e., they had to do with how power was allocated in society), but they expressed them in a vocabulary that resonated with calls for sound money, balanced budgets, and financial accountability.[15] The elite was also divided in socio-economic and geographical terms: provincial aristocratic households continued to derive most of their wealth from landed property, while Paris- or Versailles-based noble families were much more likely to invest in banking, government debt, mining, or overseas trade. Though the distinction was far from hard and fast, John Shovlin has convincingly shown that "a loose dividing line… [separated]… a provincial nobility dependent on agriculture for its economic well-being, and a Paris nobility with a very much weaker relationship to land." While the first of these adamantly opposed any extension of taxes to their privileged holdings, the latter were especially concerned to ensure prompt payments on royal loans (in which they had heavily invested) and French competitiveness with the British and Dutch in international commerce. Necker's *Compte rendu* could only comfort both groups as long as it indicated revenue sources other than property taxes—in this case, further foreign loans.

The members of France's political class had distinct material interests. They expressed those divergent interests, however, in a shared vocabulary of "freedom" versus "despotism."[16] By voicing their own priorities as matters of *public* interest, members of the French elite attempted to use the rhetoric (and reality) of indebtedness to their own ends but instead inadvertently contributed to the expansion of France's political public.[17] Consider, for example, the steps that led to the calling of the Estates-General. When Charles Alexandre de Calonne became Controller-General in 1783, he followed largely in the footsteps of his predecessors. He extended two loans opened under Necker, continued to borrow heavily from foreign investors (in his case, the Dutch), and he went on restoring venal offices (as Necker's successor and his own immediate predecessor, Joly de Fleury, had done).[18] Yet his public pronouncements said little of this continuity. Instead, as a courtier with close ties to the Versailles-based elite that had been most critical of Necker, Calonne announced that current revenues fell 20 percent short of expenses and blamed the unexpected deficit on the Genevan banker's mismanagement. Wishing to tarnish Necker's reputation and locked in a power struggle with the judges of the Paris Parlement (the highest court in the land and the body responsible for registering any new taxes or loans), the Controller-General did not speak from a position of dispassionate objectivity. By insisting that the kingdom's finances were in a "critical state" and that the country was nearly bankrupt, Calonne was instead staging a crisis in order to circumvent the Parlement and achieve his own policy goals. So grave was the situation, he asserted, that a hand-picked Assembly of Notables would have to be convoked; Calonne expected that body to respond to the emergency by approving a series of reforms (including a new, universal tax) already rejected as "despotism" by the Parlement. When the Assembly convened in February 1787, Calonne therefore opened its meetings by painting a very dark picture of the recent past, asserting that upon assuming his position, he had found "all the coffers bare, public securities falling in value, wealth not circulating ... trust destroyed." Necker's *Compte rendu* had painted a much cheerier picture, but—so Calonne claimed—it had only been able to do so by "mixing the present with the future... what is real with what is hoped." Such confusion of temporalities and violation of bookkeeping norms had to end, Calonne continued. "We must liquidate the past and pay off what is due," he continued [*il faut liquider le passé, solder l'arriéré*], "in order to bring ourselves up to date."[19]

The assembled Notables, like the judges of the *parlements* and the French public itself, were in no position to verify any of the numbers produced by either Necker or Calonne. Numbers did not (and do not) "speak for themselves." Instead, figures and calculations were animated into political significance by nearly seventy distinct pamphlets published on the subject in 1787–1788.[20] While readers barely reacted to the budget for 1788 (which showed a dwindling deficit), they responded enthusiastically to defenses of Necker and criticisms of Calonne.[21] Necker's reputation for accountability mattered far more than did the numbers themselves; small wonder, then, that the Notables defended their own privileges by calling for greater openness and transparency in the state's accounts.[22] Refusing to endorse Calonne's proposals, they preferred the public acclaim of calling for a meeting of the Estates-General (France's quasi-parliamentary body, which had last met in 1614). Much as Calonne had thought to use an Assembly of Notables to confirm his own place in future histories, so the cardinals and princes of the blood anticipated dominating the Estates-General. They expected to be able to use its deliberations to defend their own position and fend off central administration. Debt and apparent fiscal necessity again provided the necessary pretense for this extraordinary political assembly: "The Nation, as represented by the Estates General, alone possesses the right to grant the King the necessary taxes."[23]

The French debt crisis of the late 1780s was political in making, economic and fiscal in its consequences. While the shortfall described by Calonne was real, it was not inherently excessive. Britain's debt had increased more quickly than had France's in the previous decades and the British Crown's subjects paid more in taxes than did the French. As economic historians Eugene White, François Velde, and David Weir have shown, there was nothing fore-ordained about the collapse of the French monarchy's finances in 1787–1789. Debt and deficit alone did not cause the outbreak of the Revolution.[24] Instead, growing politicization provoked the crisis of the late 1780s. French social elites and political pamphleteers on all sides gave added urgency to these debates because they felt confident they could use them to their own ends. They could not.

At any point, Louis XVI *might have* followed in his grandfather's or great-great-grandfather's footsteps and simply defaulted on the existing debt (or revalued the coinage, another way of doing the same thing). That he did not—and that the second edict issued by the National Assembly was a commitment *never* to declare bankruptcy (much as Louis XVI's own very first edict in 1774 had been a promise to honor inherited debt)—tells us a great deal about what happens to state debt once it is opened for public consideration and investment.[25] Public debt in the modern era owes something to constitutions and representative institutions, but it has been shaped much more by the volatile force of public opinion. A medieval city-state with a small and uniform elite could easily sustain considerable debt over decades because the merchants providing funds and the few individuals shaping politics were one and the same.[26] In a territorial state with overseas colonies and international investors, however, this identity no longer existed. Thrown into the public sphere of contestation and debate, debt in the modern era became first and foremost a matter of politics.

The Revolutionary Paradox: Tax Repudiation and Debt Commitment

Before it was a period in French history, the "old regime" was a way of collecting taxes. For much of the eighteenth century, the main connotations of the word *régime* were dietetic (as in a "regimen"), but the word also referred to administrative structures. While it might be used of any management and was especially common in describing that of monastic houses, the increasing popularity of physiological language in texts assessing the health of the body politic made "regime" an especially evocative term for political economy.[27] As the proper regimen ensured a regular flow of healthy blood, so a good regime kept money circulating. Likewise, critics used sanguinary imagery in diagnosing fiscality's ills: the monarchy's taxes were, in the words of feudal commissioner and future radical, François-Noël (Gracchus) Babeuf, just so many "leeches" sucking the nation's life away.[28]

When the term "ancien régime" was first used in the late summer and autumn of 1789, it therefore did not refer to the monarchy as a whole or even to divine-right absolutism. Rather, it referred to various components of ministerial administration, especially the taxation system.[29] Under absolutism, piecemeal efforts at tax reform had already led to the introduction of a "nouveau régime" for the salt tax in 1786.[30] In this pre-revolutionary context, "régime" referred to discrete administrative structures or personnel: there could be a "new regime" for Paris tax collectors without affecting those in Nantes, Nevers, or Montélimar.[31] In such usages, the word resonated as much with "régie" (used to describe the direction of the Indies Company) as it did with physicians' recommendations for living a long life or returning to perfect health.[32] In contrast, once the Estates-General had been convened, refused to meet as such, and instead took the name "National Assembly," even moderate revolutionaries used *régime* to refer to the entire structure of fiscal administration. In an extended discussion of the kingdom's prospects (October 1789), the baron d'Allarde insisted that the "return of confidence depends on a *new order of things*, a *new regime* of taxation" and maintained that everyone would happily make a few sacrifices now in order to "hasten the coming of a regime that will free people from the yoke of fiscality forever."[33]

D'Allarde was hardly alone in treating "fiscality" as a regime and that regime as the past's defining vice. Direct taxation—which knit together concerns about privilege and responsibility, publicness, and accountability—had become an especially charged issue over the previous century. By attempting to impose new "universal" taxes (i.e., taxes which had to be paid even by the Church and nobility), the monarchy undermined the very logics of difference and distinction on which its own existence rested. Jurists and noblemen led the opposition to these taxes, but they framed their resistance—as reformers did their proposals—in terms of "the public good," a vocabulary that of course resonated with other sectors of the population as well.[34] In contrast, rural commoners were far more exercised about indirect taxes (those added to the cost of goods and services) and expressed bitter resentment about the exemption from direct taxation for which the Church and nobility lobbied.[35] The two groups' concerns and demands were, in fact, diametrically opposed, but conceiving the fisc as a single "regime" made it possible for privileged and commoners alike to call for its dismantling. Regardless of their social position, the French king's subjects—when reconceived as French "public opinion"—were united in hostility to the former regimen of tax collecting.

Because it was subject both to elite resistance and to popular violence, taxation was at the forefront of revolutionary activity in the summer of

1789. On 17 June, in their first act after adopting the title "National Assembly," the members of that body declared all existing taxes to be illegal. Yet their seeming clear break with the "Old Regime" was immediately complicated by that same Assembly's next measures: emphatically insisting that they would honor all existing monetary obligations and therefore ordering the continued collection of existing (albeit illegal) taxes. On 13 July, the Assembly further underlined its commitment to the debt by resolving that "no power has the right to pronounce the infamous word *bankruptcy*" and that the monarchy's debt now belonged to the nation.[36] Since there could be no debt regime without a source of revenue, the old regime of fiscality and confiscation would have to be maintained until citizens agreed to pay off the nation's debts voluntarily (a prospect that many—in the heady days of summer 1789—actually envisioned).

When the members of the National Assembly declared the state's debts to be legitimate while its taxes were not, they took actions that had profound consequences for the course of the French Revolution. Declaring the debt to be "sacred" was, in a sense, an attempt to de-politicize it: to remove it from the realm of everyday conflict and insist that it somehow transcended disagreements about power, representation, and administration. Yet because payments had to be made on it, the debt's sanctity had almost the opposite actual effect. It lodged the "old regime" (existing taxes) squarely in the present, hence making a break—not with just the past but with the present as well—all the more imperative. The *Moniteur* reported Robespierre as saying "since the tax-collecting system has to subsist until it has been expressly revoked, the Assembly should declare there are no grounds for considering a motion that it be preserved," but another publication summarized his words in a different, more pointed, fashion: "Robespierre preferred—without positively stating that the old regime would continue for another year—that it last until a new regime had been established."[37] In short, because of the debts to be paid, the old regime would have to endure until—but only until—a new one was in place. There could be no transition period, no overlap, no gradual evolution. The regime would be new, or it would be nothing at all. As one petitioner wrote: "If we do not wipe out our debt in its entirety, we will be leaving traces of the former [old] regime and will have very good reasons to be anxious for the future one."[38]

While it might be burdensome, the debt also had significant political uses (as Necker's and Calonne's jockeying for public favor had shown). Lawmakers knew that without the debt, the Estates-General would probably never have been called. In the words of leading revolutionary journalist Camille Desmoulins, "In Rome, it took the death of Verginia to re-establish liberty … in France, the deficit will do so. O blessed deficit, o my dear Calonne!"[39] With typical rhetorical wit, Mirabeau announced "the deficit is a national treasure and the public debt was the seed of our liberty." In spring 1790, the Assembly repeated this assertion in a proclamation to the French people: "Look behind you for an instant: it was the disorder in our finances that brought us to the happy days of liberty."[40] Had they sanctioned a default, the King could have thanked the deputies for solving his financial problems and then sent them home. Suspicious of just such actions, some radicals argued that the Assembly should refuse to open the question of finances until after a constitution had been written and ratified.[41]

In the uncertainty of summer 1789, the political stakes of balancing the books were higher than ever before. Justice required both that the old taxes be abolished and that the old debts be paid. As if this logical conundrum were not enough, the National Assembly's members were simultaneously surrounded with rural unrest, urban violence, and royal indecision.[42] Groups and individuals in each of those contexts—villagers sacking a toll booth or a château, city-dwellers gathered at a café or in a city square, courtiers and Louis XVI himself—could and did claim to speak on behalf of France. In the early months of the Revolution, the "public" became increasingly vocal; since it spoke with more than one voice, its message was far from clear.

The political challenges posed by public debt in an era when the very definition of "the public" was up for grabs were intensified by the material fact of collapsing state credit. The political crisis of summer 1789 made it almost impossible for the monarchy to borrow and rendered its existing short-term notes nearly worthless. At the very moment when its revenue sources had been declared illegitimate, the state had to find cash to pay its military and import grain. Once again, numbers did not tell a clear story. Repeatedly confronted with financial statements and spending estimates that few could follow, members of the National Assembly mainly knew that they saw empty purses everywhere they looked. They were, as the marquis de Ferrières ruefully remarked, "like the man whose brilliant plans for the day are disrupted in the morning by the inopportune appearance of his creditors."[43] Necker (returned to the position of Finance Minister in 1788, briefly sacked in July 1789, and then recalled to renewed popular acclaim) issued grim words of warning in late September 1789: "Nothing will work, Gentlemen, nothing will get any better, if the payment of taxes is interrupted, if you do not ensure their collection." Acknowledging the difficulty of getting people to pay the current, desperately unpopular, taxes, he encouraged the Assembly to draft new legislation immediately. "You must do it all together," he concluded. "The future and the present, speculation and reality."[44] The old regime was failing. Debt and deficits made a new one all the more urgent.

THE POLITICAL ECONOMY OF THE *ASSIGNATS*

In the first year of the French Revolution, men we now think of as moderate revolutionaries tried repeatedly to use the threat of empty coffers and unpaid debts to achieve their own political goals. This strategy never succeeded as planned, however. For while it sanctified the general *idea* of debt, it simultaneously provoked acts of moral-historical bookkeeping that proved increasingly divisive. If debt were sacred, it was first imperative to know how much was due and to whom.[45] For instance, in autumn 1789, anti-clerical voices within the National Assembly juxtaposed the legitimate claims of investors in state debt with the (in their eyes) far less legitimate holding of vast properties by the Catholic Church; they then called for nationalizing the latter to secure the former. While John McManners has since demonstrated the complexity of the Church's holdings—in eighteenth-century France, its income was pieced together from complicated investments and renting out pews, from urban monuments and semi-feudal dues—contemporaries stereotyped the Church's wealth as consisting chiefly of fertile wheat fields and precious vineyards.[46] Characterizing the Church's possessions as agricultural estates had the effect of making them all the more attractive to the many who argued that the French nation (unlike the Old Regime's monarch) needed to borrow against solid, rather than reputational, assets. If the Church had no right to these properties, they reasoned, the nation had need of them. As long as the state took over the expenses funded by those properties (everything from upkeep on buildings to poor relief and salaries for the clergy), transferring them to a different balance sheet would not create any new debt.

While securing the inherited royal debt with the *biens nationaux* did not technically create new obligations, it did eventually result in the creation of a new monetary instrument. Changes in the debt regime, that is, affected the monetary regime—and those changes then had the unintended effect of further disrupting the political regime. Declared "at the

Nation's disposal" in early November 1789, the former Church properties (henceforth known as *biens nationaux* or "national properties") were in the following months to be inventoried, appraised, and auctioned. Since the state could not wait until the *biens* sold in order to pay its creditors, it issued large-denomination, interest-bearing bills backed by their value. Called *assignats* because they were "assigned to" the value of the *biens* for payment, these bills were to serve an interim, mediating function. The state could pay those it owed with them, and those creditors—or others to whom they then passed the bills—could then exchange them for some part of the *biens nationaux* (a few vineyard acres in Burgundy, an abolished monastery in Brittany, whatever) of equal value. As long as the total value of *assignats* issued did not exceed that of the *biens nationaux* to be privatized, and as long as the *assignats* were removed from circulation when they returned to the state in payment, it could plausibly be argued that the notes were not a monetary creation. Rather, they were, as their supporters often insisted, "land in a form that could circulate."

Within months, however, it became obvious that France also faced a severe money shortage. (This social problem was not the same as the state's fiscal woes, though it followed closely from them.) When public debt became a polarizing political issue, all private debts came due. The unparalleled situation of a state that could only borrow against real estate (and real estate that—in the eyes of roughly half of France—did not belong to it at all, but to the Catholic Church) brought much ordinary economic activity to a near standstill. Spread throughout society by the uncertainty and violence of 1788–1790, this political and emotional shortage of trust seriously undermined commercial networks based on credit. In a world without credit, cash became more necessary than ever before. The combination of the two crises—investors' lack of trust in the state and the collapse of customary credit arrangements in the private sector—in spring 1790 made a powerful argument for converting the *assignats* from interest-bearing bonds into a general-purpose currency.

Not initially intended as a new or permanent form of money, the *assignats* were nonetheless monetized. By honoring existing debt in the context of radically new political and cultural upheaval, the Assembly ended up making monetary policy that itself then had further social and political consequences. The *assignats* had been meant to stabilize state finances and reassure France's creditors, but their status as a solid asset rested on the nation's politically controversial claim to the *biens nationaux*. When the Assembly voted further changes to the French Catholic Church ("superfluous" churches to be sold, bishops and priests to be elected, all clergy required to take an oath of loyalty to the nation), the *assignats* became all the more sacrosanct in some minds and clearly sacrilegious in others.[47] Since no *assignat* was ever issued without at least the pretense of being backed by the *biens nationaux*, the question of public debt throughout the period of the bills' circulation (1790–summer 1796) was inextricably intertwined with the legitimacy of the Revolution itself. By monetizing the *assignats* (and eventually issuing them in very small denominations), the Assembly inadvertently guaranteed that debates about the public debt reached into all corners of France.

In late September 1790, the Assembly voted to honor another class of debt—that arising from the abolition of venal office—by issuing further *assignats*. Not on the books at the start of the Revolution, this debt was one the revolutionaries made for themselves. Having "abolished privilege" in a stirring, late night session on 4 August 1789, the National Assembly then spent months determining what this abolition would look like in actual practice. Some aristocratic privileges were declared obvious abuses that could and should be abolished outright: monopolies on pigeon coops and on hunting, for instance, clearly fell into this category. But the Assembly also concluded that many other Old Regime "privileges" were, in fact, forms of property. This latter category included purchased military titles and other venal offices (judgeships and notaryships, but also positions as bailiffs or even wigmakers): paid for in cash, these positions could be mortgaged and in many cases were heritable. By eighteenth-century logic and law, they were as much "real estate' as were the *biens nationaux*. While the Assembly denounced the principle of venality as an abuse, it nonetheless recognized venal officeholders (including many of its own members) as lawful owners of property. And since property was sacred (as stated in article 17 of the Declaration of the Rights of Man and Citizen), it could not be confiscated without compensation. The bill for abolishing venality—a brand new debt—hence came to the enormous sum of 1.4 billion livres. Reporting on behalf of the Finance Committee, the former marquis de Montesquiou suggested that paying off this "current debt" could be done without an additional issue of *assignats* if it were stretched over the next thirty-two years—but this would mean excessive delays (for instance, a fellow member of the Finance Committee, Jean-Baptiste Kytspotter, might not be reimbursed until 1821 for the judgeship he had purchased in 1782). Moreover, since a decree promulgated on 3 November 1789 distinctly specified that "those holding [venal] offices shall continue to exercise their functions ... until the Assembly has provided means to reimburse them," gradual reimbursement would mean only a partial abolition of venality.[48] For decades, there would be some judges and commanding officers who had bought their positions, others who had earned them. Such a slow, steady liquidation would also add millions in interest payments. "You see, gentlemen," Montesquiou concluded, "[if we were to pay off the current debt gradually], we would actually need to increase taxes [to cover interest payments] ... and our primary goal, the relief of the people, would prove only a chimerical fantasy." As he had done in earlier speeches on related fiscal topics, Montesquiou then contrasted the miseries wrought by gradualism with the happiness likely to result from a more abrupt and immediate financial settlement: "If we could trade some or all of the *biens nationaux* for the entire current debt in an instant... we would find ourselves more prosperous than we dare hope... and the work of half a century would be finished in a day."[49]

Montesquiou's promise of a debt paid off "in an instant," thanks to the value stored in former Church properties, proved enticing. For those who voted to issue more *assignats*, doing so seemed to provide a speedy and equitable solution to the otherwise intractable problem of how to pay for the old regime and clear space for the new. Categorizing venal offices as an abusive privilege rather than as legitimate property would have had the same effect, but that possibility was never seriously entertained. Instead, and after a year in which taxes had gone largely uncollected, the Assembly first took on new debt and then further antagonized many Catholics by the choice of how to pay it.

* * *

Revolutionaries expected that making a break with past fiscal and administrative regimes would help guarantee political stability. Combined with the continuity of the debt regime, however, this attempted break had the unexpected effect of necessitating a new monetary regime. This last did much to exacerbate social and cultural strife and, eventually, led to the creation of a new political regime.

For more than a generation, institutionally minded economic historians have described a positive feedback loop between the defense of property rights, the rule of law, and sustained economic growth in the modern era. In the case of eighteenth-century France, however, the rights of certain property holders (those who had invested in the monarchy's debts or purchased venal offices) proved *too* strong for the regime. Their right to property did not so much stabilize the "old regime" (as everything before summer 1789 eventually came to be called) as it radicalized the new. With the 1797 Bankruptcy of the Two-Thirds, the Jacobin republicans of the Second Directory gambled on a new debt structure as the best means of stabilizing monetary, fiscal, and political regimes. While, on the face of things, they lost their political bet (Bonaparte's 1799 coup put an end to the Directory and his crowning as Emperor Napoleon in 1804 marked the end of the First Republic), they did successfully introduce a new and enduring regime of public debt. Their so-called consolidation of the debt (two-thirds was written off and the remaining third consolidated into a single instrument) was the first and last state default in modern France's history. If revolutions are about breaking with past forms of public debt, we might date the French one not to 1789 but to 1797.

NOTES

1. Edmund Burke, *Reflections on the Revolution in France*, ed. Frank Turner ([1791] New Haven: Yale University Press, 2003); Jules Michelet, *History of the French Revolution*, trans. Charles Cocks (London: H.G. Bohn, 1847), 8–9; Alexis de Tocqueville, *The Old Regime and the French Revolution*, trans. Stuart Gilbert (New York: Doubleday Anchor, 1955), vii.
2. Peter George Muir Dickson, *The Financial Revolution in England: A Study in the Development of Public Credit, 1688–1756* (London: Macmillan, 1967); Bruce G. Carruthers, *Politics and Markets in the English Financial Revolution* (Princeton: Princeton University Press, 1996).
3. John Brewer, *The Sinews of Power: War, Money, and the English State, 1688–1783* (Cambridge, Mass.: Harvard University Press, 1989).
4. Though this argument has recently been challenged, see D'Maris Coffman, Adrian Leonard and Larry Neal, eds. *Questioning Credible Commitment* (Cambridge: Cambridge University Press, 2013).
5. For an excellent corrective to the idea that property rights were uniformly sacrosanct in Georgian Britain, see Julian Hoppit, "Compulsion, Compensation and Property Rights in Britain, 1688–1833," *Past & Present* 210 (Feb. 2011): 93–128.
6. Michael Kwass, "Court Capitalism, Illicit Markets, and Political Legitimacy in Eighteenth-Century France," in *Questioning Credible Commitment*, 228–250, especially 232, and *Contraband: Louis Mandrin and the Making of a Global Underground* (Cambridge, Mass.: Harvard University Press, 2014); Eugene N. White, "From Privatized to Government-Administered

Tax Collection: Tax Farming in Eighteenth-Century France," *Economic History Review* 57, no. 4 (2004): 636–63.
7. For overviews, see Jacob Soll, *The Reckoning: Financial Accountability and the Rise and Fall of Nations* (New York: Basic Books, 2014), chapter 9, and Gail Bossenga, "The Financial Origins of the French Revolution," in *From Deficit to Deluge: The Origins of the French Revolution*, ed. Dale Van Kley (Stanford: Stanford University Press, 2011), chapter 1.
8. Jacques Necker, *Compte rendu au Roi* (Paris: Imprimerie Royale, 1781), 2–3; Douglass North and Barry Weingast, "Constitutions and Commitment: The Evolution of Institutions Governing Public Choice in Seventeenth-Century England," *Journal of Economic History* 49 (1989): 803–32.
9. "Edit du roi... enregistré 13 février 1781," in *Affiches du Dauphiné* (23 Feb. 1781), 170–171.
10. Vicomte de Grouchy and Paul Cottin, eds., *Journal inédit du duc de Croÿ* (Paris: Flammarion, 1906–1921), vol. 4, 230.
11. *Affiches du Dauphiné* (9 March 1781), 178–179.
12. Louis Petit de Bachaumont, *Mémoires secrets pour servir à l'histoire de la république des lettres en France* (London: John Adamson, 1780–1789), 17:142–3 (27 April 1781); Michael Kwass, *Privilege and the Politics of Taxation* (Cambridge: Cambridge University Press, 2000), 214–5.
13. David A. Bell, *The Cult of the Nation in France* (Cambridge, Mass.: Harvard University Press, 2001).
14. David Stasavage, "Partisan Politics and Public Debt: The Importance of the 'Whig Supremacy' for Britain's Financial Revolution," *European Review of Economic History* 11 (2007): 123–53.
15. Dale Van Kley, *The Religious Origins of the French Revolution* (New Haven: Yale University Press, 1996); Sarah Maza, *Private Lives and Public Affairs: The Causes Célèbres of Pre-Revolutionary France* (Berkeley: University of California Press, 1993); Clare Crowston, *Credit, Fashion, Sex: Economies of Regard in Old Regime France* (Durham: Duke University Press, 2013).
16. John Shovlin, *The Political Economy of Virtue: Luxury, Patriotism, and the Origins of the French Revolution* (Ithaca: Cornell University Press, 2006), 71. See also Paul Cheney, *Revolutionary Commerce: Globalization and the French Monarchy* (Cambridge, Mass.: Harvard University Press, 2010); Kwass, *Privilege and the Politics of Taxation*; and Thomas E. Kaiser, "Money, Despotism, and Public Opinion in Early Eighteenth-Century France: John Law and the Debate on Royal Credit," *Journal of Modern History* 63 (1991): 1–28.
17. The following draws on the analysis in my *Stuff and Money in the Time of the French Revolution* (Cambridge, Mass.: Harvard University Press, 2015), chapter 1.

18. Eugene Nelson White, "Was There a Solution to the Ancien Régime's Financial Dilemma?" *Journal of Economic History* 49 (1989): 545–68, and Shovlin, *Political Economy of Virtue*.
19. *Discours du Roi, à l'assemblée des notables: tenue à Versailles, le 22 février 1787, avec le discours prononcé... par M. de Calonne* (Versailles: Imprimerie royale, 1787), 6.
20. For sustained consideration of how numbers were used as political weapons in eighteenth-century Britain, see William Deringer, *Calculated Values: Finance, Politics, and the Quantitative Age* (Cambridge, Mass.: Harvard University Press, 2018).
21. Vivian Gruder, *The Notables and the Nation: The Political Schooling of the French, 1787–1788* (Cambridge, Mass.: Harvard University Press, 2007), 184–85.
22. Vivian Gruder, "A Mutation in Elite Political Culture: The French Notables and the Defense of Property and Participation, 1787," *Journal of Modern History* 56 (1984): 598–634.
23. Parlement de Paris, "arrêté du 30 juillet 1787," cited in Kwass, *Privilege and the Politics of Taxation*, 274.
24. White, "Was There a Solution...?" As David Weir has observed, even Marcel Marion (the historian who was among the harshest critics of old-regime borrowing) recognized that Britain's debt was larger; see David R. Weir, "Tontine, Public Finance, and Revolution in France and England, 1688–1789," *Journal of Economic History* 49 (1989): 96, n.8 and Marcel Marion, *Histoire financière de la France depuis 1715* (Paris: 1914–1931), vol. 1, 460–61. Other economic historians have calculated that the debt, if measured in livres of constant silver value, actually shrank by 10 percent between 1715 and 1789; see Philip Hoffman, Gilles Postel-Vinay, and Jean-Laurent Rosenthal, *Priceless Markets: The Political Economy of Credit in Paris, 1660–1870* (Chicago: University of Chicago Press, 2000), 98–105.
25. *Edit du roi, portant remise du droit de Joyeux-avènement: Qui ordonne que toutes les rentes... continueront d'être payées comme par le passé...donné à la Muette au mois de mai 1774* (Paris: Imprimerie royale, 1774). On the consequences of the change of political discourse, see also Joël Félix, "'Ce maudit milliard qui deviendrait tôt ou tard la perte du royaume.' Banqueroutes et politique de la dette en France au XVIIIe siècle," in *Les crises de la dette publique: XVIIIe-XXIe siècle*, eds. Gérard Béaur and Laure Quennouëlle-Corre (Paris: IGPDE, 2019), 45–68, http://books.openedition.org/igpde/6092.
26. David Stasavage, *States of Credit: Size, Power, and the Development of European Polities* (Princeton: Princeton University Press, 2011).
27. For standard definitions, see *Dictionnaire universel françois et latin* (*Dictionnaire de Trévoux*) 5th ed. (1752), 6:754 and Diderot and

D'Alembert, eds., *Encyclopédie, ou Dictionnaire raisonné des sciences, des arts et des métiers* (1751–1765), 14:11–16. Diego Venturino traces the increasing use of "regime" for "administration" to the Physiocrats, but does not comment on the importance of physiological imagery; see his "La Naissance de 'l'Ancien Régime'", in *The Political Culture of the French Revolution*, ed. Colin Lucas, vol. 2 of *The French Revolution and the Creation of Modern Political Culture*, 4 vols. (Pergamon: Oxford, 1987–1994), 11–40.

28. Gracchus Babeuf, *Cadastre perpétuel* (Paris, 1789), xx–xxi.
29. As Venturino notes, "regime" in summer-autumn 1789 was still always prefaced with an adjective; there was a "constitutional regime," a "fiscal regime," etc. but no sense of an entire epoch. It is my contention that responses to the "fiscal regime"—because it was treated as a block, and because it brought the debt question along with it (see below)—served as a model for conceiving past experience as both omnipresent and something to be left behind.
30. *Déclaration ... qui établit un nouveau régime sur les frontières des provinces rédimées, limitrophes des pays de gabelle ...* (Paris: Knapen et fils, 1786).
31. *Édit... portant création de deux offices de receveurs généraux des finances de Paris et un nouveau régime pour les six receveurs particuliers des impositions de ladite ville ...* (Paris: P.-G. Simon, 1784).
32. "Régie," in *Encyclopédie*, 14:4.
33. *Archives parlementaires* (hereafter: *AP*) 9:278, 286 (2 Oct. 1789), emphasis added. D'Allarde, most famous for giving his name to one of the laws that abolished the guilds, was a liberal nobleman with a military background.
34. Kwass, *Privilege and the Politics of Taxation*; for an overview of the peasantry's perception of taxation, see Peter M. Jones, *The Peasantry in the French Revolution* (Cambridge: Cambridge University Press, 1988), 34–42.
35. For a careful dissection of peasant grievances, and a comparison with those of the Nobility and the urban Third Estate, see Gilbert Shapiro and John Markoff, *Revolutionary Demands: A Content Analysis of the Cahiers des doléances of 1789* (Stanford: Stanford University Press, 1998), especially chap. 20.
36. *AP* 8:128–129, 230 (17 June and 13 July 1789).
37. *Affiches du Dauphiné* (11 Feb. 1790), 69.
38. Archives Nationales (Paris) F[4] 1938 (Engren to Necker, 8 Dec. 1789).
39. *La France Libre* in *Œuvres de Camille Desmoulins*, ed. Jules Claretie (Paris: Charpentier, 1874), 79.
40. *AP* 8:499 (27 August 1789); 15:344 (30 April 1790).
41. See, for instance, the comments by Populus, *AP* 8:221 (11 July 1789) and by Duport and Brostaret, *AP* 9:232 (1 Oct. 1789).

42. For an excellent overview of the Revolution's first year from the perspective of the deputies, see Timothy Tackett, *Becoming a Revolutionary* (Princeton: Princeton University Press, 1996).
43. Charles Elie Ferrières-Marçay, *Correspondance inédite*, cited in Tackett, *Becoming a Revolutionary*, 261.
44. *AP* 9:145 (24 Sept. 1789).
45. The following draws on my *Stuff and Money*, chapters 2–4.
46. John McManners, *Church and Society in Eighteenth-Century France* (Oxford: Oxford University Press, 1998).
47. Nigel Ashton, *Religion and Revolution in France, 1780–1804* (Washington, D.C.: Catholic University of America Press, 2000); Timothy Tackett, *Religion, Revolution, and Regional Culture in Eighteenth-Century France: The Ecclesiastical Oath of 1791* (Princeton: Princeton University Press, 1986).
48. William Doyle, *Venality: The Sale of Offices in Eighteenth-Century France* (Oxford: Oxford University Press, 1996), 1–3 and 275–311.
49. *AP* 18:354–355 (27 Aug. 1790).

CHAPTER 3

Politics of Credit: Government Borrowing and Political Regimes in Sweden

Patrik Winton

European states' increasing reliance on public credit during the eighteenth century had fundamental consequences for the political order and for the distribution of power and resources in the continent's polities. Governments tried to attract capital to fund the debt and to allocate means to pay interests, while at the same time negotiate with influential political groups how existing deficits and debts should be funded.[1] Concurrently, the growing dependence on borrowing led to public discussion about the implications of this new arrangement. Although some argued that growing financial markets improved liquidity and strengthened state capacity, many others warned about the rising debt levels and the threat that the borrowing posed to the political status quo. In particular, the creditors' claims were seen as a force that could overturn the influence of established elites and give bondholders and opinions a greater political say.[2]

Governments created different borrowing arrangements. Some of the resources were sought internally by selling long-term bonds to the population, or by entering into tax farming agreements, or by issuing different

---

P. Winton (✉)
School of Humanities, Education, and Social Sciences, Örebro University, Örebro, Sweden
e-mail: patrik.winton@oru.se

© The Author(s) 2020
N. Barreyre, N. Delalande (eds.), *A World of Public Debts*, Palgrave Studies in the History of Finance,
https://doi.org/10.1007/978-3-030-48794-2_3

forms of paper money.[3] Other resources were borrowed externally in financial centers such as Amsterdam, Antwerp and Genoa.[4] All of these borrowing arrangements, as well as the decisions to either honor or default on the accrued debt, were associated with costs and benefits for governments which were both economic and political in nature. The arrangements were highly contingent upon the political context, especially the balance of power between ideas, interests and institutions. Thus, the specific set of borrowing techniques used by a state was closely linked to the existing political settlement. This in turn meant that alterations in the balance of political power tended to have consequences for the borrowing arrangements and for the choices governments made in the realm of fiscal affairs. However, the borrowing activities could also have the potential to alter the distribution of power and eventually lead to a new political settlement.[5]

Scholars who have worked on the financial and political developments in Europe during the eighteenth century have foremost concentrated on the two cases of Britain and France. They have been seen as opposites: one had a parliamentary political system which was able to raise sufficient tax revenue to service the mounting debts and subsequently be committed to honoring the state's debts. As a consequence, a growing number of citizens became creditors, which in turn strengthened the state's ability to fund its wars. France on the other hand has been characterized as an absolute state, which never managed to organize its borrowing as successfully as Britain or increase taxation to solve the issue of the deficit. This divergence in development between Britain and France has also been pivotal in generalized arguments about the superiority of parliamentary political systems and centralized states, and why absolute states were plagued by institutional weaknesses such as royal moral hazard and fiscal fragmentation.[6]

The problem of this largely institutional approach is twofold: first it tends to over generalize the two contrasting cases of Britain and France by neglecting historical contingency and turning historical hindsight into preordained outcomes. Second it overlooks the wide array of borrowing arrangements that existed in the eighteenth century. As Rebecca Spang shows in the previous chapter, public debt in France, for example, depended on local political circumstances. Thus, alternative fiscal solutions, which do not necessarily fit into simplistic absolute/parliamentary models, were prevalent, especially in smaller European states.[7] Smaller states faced similar economic and political challenges to those of the major powers, but there were also important differences. On the one hand, they were more vulnerable in the international states system since they had to abide by terms set by the major powers. The partitions of Poland in the second half of the eighteenth century are examples of the military and political muscle of the major powers and how this could affect minor powers.[8] On the other hand, smaller states could benefit from their position in the system by seeking subsidies from the major powers or by using a strategy of neutrality during wartime in order to strengthen the country's trade.[9] Thus, government borrowing was also affected by international relations.

In this chapter the case of Sweden—a middle-ranking power at the end of the eighteenth century—will be highlighted in order to clarify how the issue of government debt affected the balance of power and the political relationships between the different members of the elite and between the elite and the king. In other words, the chapter will analyze how government debt became a central object of political contestation and how this contestation framed the character and the direction of the state's activities.

The analysis will focus on two periods of crisis when existing borrowing arrangements were challenged. The first crisis circles around the Seven Years' War when the mobilization of resources created fiscal and monetary pressures, which led to the development of new relationships with both internal and external creditors. The second crisis occurred during the Napoleonic Wars when the existing fiscal arrangement was renegotiated and the public debt was eventually dismantled. These periods of crisis coincided with changes to the constitutional order, as well as the structure of the European states system. In the middle of the eighteenth century, a system of parliamentary rule was in place. This system was replaced in 1772 when the king Gustavus III strengthened the power of the monarchy by organizing a coup d'état. This order of royal absolutism survived until 1809 when the then king, Gustavus IV Adolphus, was overthrown by a coup organized by the elite. Subsequently, a new constitution was adopted, which guaranteed a division of power between the monarchy and the Diet. When the French Marshal Jean Baptiste Bernadotte was elected Crown Prince a year later, the establishment of a new political order was completed, which turned out to be relatively stable.[10]

The Seven Years' War and the Birth of a New Public Debt

In 1757, Sweden joined the anti-Prussian coalition and sent troops to the province of Western Pomerania. The Swedish Council of the Realm, which had been promised substantial subsidies by France if military action was taken, hoped that it would be a quick and victorious campaign and that Sweden would be rewarded for its support at a future peace conference. However, the Prussian military resistance soon shattered this hope. Sweden therefore had to maintain a troop presence in the province for several years, which put pressure on the government's finances and which led to the collapse of the existing system of relying on loans from the Bank of Sweden (Riksbanken) and subsidies from France. This in turn increased political tensions between the estates when the state had to find new ways of financing its deficits.[11]

The Swedish political settlement and the structure of borrowing that it rested on were based on the central role of the Diet with its four estates. The Diet convened every three years and decided on such matters as taxation, legislation and foreign policy. The Diet also controlled the Bank of Sweden, which was both a bank of exchange and a lending and deposit bank, by electing its governors and by providing them with instructions on how to operate the bank. Although the four estates were considered equal, the peasant estate was the weakest and the noble estate was the most influential in political terms. The political system was oligarchic in character since a number of leading noble officers and civil servants, merchants and bishops all held influential positions. They wielded influence through their seats on the powerful Secret Committee, which comprised members from the nobility, clergy and burghers. The committee dealt with issues such as foreign policy, government spending and the operations of the bank. The Council of the Realm functioned as the government, but its noble members were dependent on having the support of the Diet. Thus, the councilors could be dismissed from office by the Diet. The king participated in the meetings of the Council, but he could not pursue any independent policies.[12]

The ruling oligarchy depended on a combination of loans from the bank and subsidies from the French government to cover existing deficits. This arrangement provided the necessary resources without having to negotiate with other members of the estates about tax increases or having to share details about the state of fiscal affairs. The subsidies were paid by

France in order to prop up the Swedish state's military capacity. Sweden thereby became part of the French alliance system which also included states such as Denmark and Genoa.[13] In 1750, the subsidies contributed close to 20 percent of total revenue, and in 1755 around 7 percent. The loans from the bank could also be substantial: in 1752 nearly 23 percent of total revenues came from the bank, while in 1755 the bank provided around 2 percent to the total revenue.[14]

The bank's lending was arranged through the issue of notes, which became accepted as equivalent to coin. The notes were first backed by specie reserves, but this relationship between notes in circulation and reserves was abandoned in 1745. The bank increased liquidity by providing loans to the government and to private individuals, many of whom were members of the political elite. For instance, the volume of loans to individuals increased from 10.3 million in 1750 to 19.8 million silver dalers in 1755, while the loans to the government increased during the same time from 15.5 million to 17.8 million.[15] Although there was some apprehension about the close relationship between the state and the bank, many members of the elite approved the acceleration of lending. Using credit from the bank was an easy way to finance government expenditure, and the loans to owners of landed estates and ironworks were seen as contributing to the growth of the economy.[16]

The practice of combining loans from the bank and subsidies from France was utilized to fund the war against Prussia. During the conflict, loans from the bank accounted for 44 percent of the total resources that were mobilized for the war effort, while French subsidies amounted to 20 percent. The loans accelerated the issuance of bank notes from 13.8 million in 1755 to 33.2 million in 1760. This liquidity increase created inflation, but it also resulted in a fall in the value of the Swedish currency on international capital markets. When the French government was unable to continue paying the subsidies, the government's fiscal position became strained.[17]

A similar fiscal arrangement was also utilized in Denmark, where an absolute king and his advisors ruled without a representative assembly. Thus, the arrangement could be used both by an oligarchy in a parliamentary system and by a royal absolutist political order. The Danish Courant Bank, which had been founded in 1736 as a semi-public company with a royal charter, used notes to increase lending from 1.6 million rigsdaler in 1750 to 10.2 million at the end of 1762. The notes were first backed by specie reserves, but this guarantee had to be abandoned in 1757 when the government needed loans to prepare for war. Denmark also received subsidies from the French government to remain neutral in the European conflict, but the payments dwindled in 1760 since they only amounted to around 3 percent of Danish total revenues.[18]

The price increases in combination with a developing political dissatisfaction with the war led to a growing public debate in Sweden about the causes of the financial problems. The debates also affected the discussions at the meetings of the Diet. Many critics argued that the councillors should be punished for dragging the realm into the war and into debt. They also criticized the leading merchants, who were members of the political elite, for profiting from the falling exchange rate at everyone else's expense. Concurrently, it was argued that the number of bank loans had to be curtailed and transparency in public affairs increased in order to address the pressing financial difficulties. The defenders of the existing arrangement stressed that the councillors had promoted the realm's honor when entering into the conflict. They also argued that the price increases were imaginary and that the credit provided by the bank had helped to strengthen trade and manufacturing. However, a majority of the members of the Diet decided to dismiss two councillors from their duties and later to curtail the number of new bank loans.[19]

When the state could not rely on the bank or subsidies it was obvious that alternative sources of revenue had to be found. One avenue that was opened in 1761 was to get the citizens more actively involved in the financing of the war. Subsequently, a long-term bond issue was introduced and over 700 bonds were purchased from December 1761 to October 1762.[20] Another attempt at borrowing internally was introduced in 1770 after the war. The interest on the loan was set at 5 percent and the investor could choose a maturity date between one and ten years. The government also stressed that all inhabitants had an equal opportunity to participate in the loan. However, the minimum amount of 100 silver dalers was a substantial sum that only propertied groups could afford. Thus, it was primarily members of the elite who entrusted their savings to the government. Although some resources were mobilized through this offer, only 87 bonds had been issued at the end of 1770.[21]

While domestic long-term borrowing had limited success, the same cannot be said about the Swedish state's attempts to create links with international credit markets. Although the first attempt to borrow in Antwerp in 1761 failed mainly due to a ban by Empress Maria Theresia on loans to foreign states, the endeavor to borrow in Genoa in 1766 was more successful.[22] The contact with the Genoese was established by the Swedish envoy in Vienna, Nils Bark and was in response to the fiscal and monetary problems after the war. It was especially the volume of bank notes in circulation together with the poor exchange rate that were seen as serious difficulties. Many argued that an external loan would improve the lives of people by replacing more expensive loans and help to strengthen the exchange rate, while others stressed that it was adventurous to put the realm in the hands of foreigners and to burden the state's coffers with foreign loans. Despite these reservations, a majority agreed to start negotiating with the Genoese.[23]

Clearly, the Genoese elite saw the Swedish state's demand for resources as an opportunity to strengthen both economic and political ties to Sweden. Besides the obvious financial aspects, it was mainly trade in iron and tar from the Swedish kingdom to the Mediterranean and salt from the Mediterranean to the Swedish realm that affected the relations between the two states.[24] Furthermore, the Genoese Republic, which tried to find a balance between Austria, France and Spain, needed new benevolent allies. Like Sweden, Genoa had long been part of the French alliance system, but French support ceased in the 1760s.[25]

One of the key issues during the negotiations, which mostly took place in Vienna between Bark and diplomatic representatives from Genoa, was how to convince the broader public in Genoa that it was safe to lend money to a remote state in Northern Europe. The mechanism which was used to create the necessary guarantees consisted of two bonds signed by the Swedish king and representatives from the Agency for Public Management (*Statskontoret*), which administered the state's resources. These bonds, which were also guaranteed by the Bank of Sweden, were deposited in Genoa. To clarify that revenues, which were assigned to administer the debt, were not already mortgaged, the Council of the Realm sent copies of the Swedish government journal in which the announcements regarding the redemption of existing government bonds were printed. During the negotiations, it was reported by Bark that there were negative rumors circulating in Genoa about the Swedish state's ability to manage its debts. It was said that Sweden already had large loans in Hamburg and Holland and that the government had mishandled the payments. Another rumor claimed that it was unsafe to trade with Sweden because the Diet constantly changed its decisions. To counter these rumors, Bark was ordered to spread knowledge about the economic decisions taken at the last meeting of the Diet. He also sent a letter to Genoa, in which he elucidated how the Swedish political system functioned. By printing it in Genoa, it was hoped that it would influence public opinion.[26] These actions manifest that the contemporary views of the Swedish political system among some key groups in the port city was understood as an issue to be wary of.

The Council of the Realm's and Nils Bark's assertiveness in responding to the demands of the Genoese and the rumors circulating shows how important a successful outcome of the negotiation was deemed to be by the Swedish political elite. Success would not only lead to an inflow of essential resources but also strengthen the image and legitimacy of the political order. The fact that the negotiations dealt with a multiplicity of issues showed that gaining the trust of external creditors did not just circle around the political system, expressed commitments to pay or reputation, but also the concrete steps taken by the regime to prioritize the creditors' claims.

The political interest on both sides in reaching a deal resulted in a loan agreement, which limited the amount to 400,000 Hamburg Banco and set the interest rate at 5 percent. Furthermore, the loan would mature after 12 years and the banking house G. & C. Marchelli received a commission of 4 percent. When the loan offer was announced to the general public, investors began making deposits with the well-established *Casa di San Giorgio* with the documents from Sweden as collateral. Despite some time lags the loan was fully subscribed in 1767.[27]

Although the loan was eventually a success, the Diet was not willing to become too dependent, fiscally or diplomatically, on the Genoese. The members therefore decided that further loans could be sought elsewhere.[28] One of the alternative locations to Genoa was Amsterdam, which had long played an important role for trade in the Baltic Sea and which several Swedish merchants had close ties with. The Dutch city had also functioned as a financial center for the Swedish state since the seventeenth century.[29] Attempts to borrow in Amsterdam started in 1767 when the merchant Niclas Sahlgren in Gothenburg was asked by the President of the Chancellery, Carl Gustaf Löwenhielm, to broker a relationship with a Dutch banking firm. Sahlgren used his good connections in Amsterdam to recommend Hope & Co. to initiate negotiations with the Swedish state.[30]

After a relatively short negotiation process with Hope & Co., in which Löwenhielm, Sahlgren as well as the Swedish envoy in The Hague, Carl Johan Creutz, participated on the Swedish side, it was decided that the king and representatives from the Agency for Public Management would sign a number of bonds, which also had to be guaranteed by the Bank of Sweden. The authenticity of the bonds had to be certified by a notary in Amsterdam and then deposited in the city's bank. A total of 30 such bonds was issued, which were used as collateral for the sale of 750 bonds to the public. Furthermore, the interest rate was set at 5 percent, and the loan would mature after ten years. When the terms of the loan were agreed upon a prospectus was printed and published in several Dutch newspapers in order to spread information about the offer. The lending mechanism as well as the terms of the loan was similar to the negotiated deal in Genoa.[31]

The relatively quick negotiation process, as well as the successful sale of the issued bonds, was affected by the favorable market conditions. Although there were some negative rumors circulating in the Dutch Republic about the Swedish state's capability to handle its financial affairs, many Dutch capital holders wanted to find new and higher yielding objects of investment. Since the interest rate on local or British bonds was relatively low it was tempting for many investors to buy bonds issued by countries such as Denmark, Russia, Sweden and Austria, which promised a better return.[32] The willingness to buy Swedish bonds was also facilitated by the relatively close existing commercial relationship between Sweden and the Dutch Republic. These ties contributed greatly to keeping the Dutch public fairly well informed about the economic and political situation in Sweden. It was therefore not necessary for Creutz or other Swedish officials to explain the political system or highlight recent decisions taken by the Diet.[33]

The successful negotiations in Genoa and Amsterdam meant that the Swedish government gained access to new resources, but the outcome also led to the establishment of a new borrowing arrangement, which at least partly replaced the old practice of relying on subsidies and loans from the bank, and created a shift in the existing balance of power. The external creditors' demand for specie put pressure on the political representatives at the Diet to abandon the paper money system and supplant it with a more stable and convertible currency. It also meant that elite groups, which had benefited from the expansion of credit, would have more restricted access to these resources.

The bank had halted new liquidity in 1762, especially to private individuals, and the exchange rate had improved, but the number of bank notes in circulation was only slightly reduced from 33.2 million in 1760 to 31.8 million in 1769.[34] How this situation should be interpreted and what solutions should be implemented created heated exchanges in pamphlets and journals, and in formal political arenas. However, most actors agreed that it was necessary to reduce the volume of bank notes in circulation, and that the state could use additional external loans to achieve this goal. They had therefore accepted the new borrowing arrangement and what it entailed politically.[35]

A similar change occurred in Denmark during the 1760s when the Courant Bank reduced its total lending from 11.2 million rigsdaler in 1763 to 7.7 million in 1770, and the number of notes in circulation was cut from 5.5 million in 1762 to 4.4 million in 1770. The reliance on bank loans and on subsidies was replaced by external loans in Hamburg and the Dutch Republic, and by increasing borrowing from the realm's inhabitants.[36] The similar responses to the financial situation in Denmark and Sweden show that it was not formal political institutions which formed the shift in borrowing arrangements. Instead the crisis led to political realignments within the two political systems, which forced the governments to find new ways to prop up the regimes financially.

Information about the new borrowing arrangement in Sweden spread relatively quickly to various actors on the international credit markets. There the new practice was seen as an opportunity to make money. One of the firms that swiftly seized the opportunity was Horneca, Hogguer & Co in Amsterdam, who wrote a letter to the speaker of the noble estate offering their services to the Swedish state. A few months later a competing offer was presented by a Danish merchant, who argued that he was able to provide a better deal than the Dutch firm had presented.[37] Both of these competing offers included terms and conditions which were similar to the earlier loans, which shows that the practice of offering loans to Sweden had been relatively standardized, and that Sweden had established itself as a reliable actor on the international credit markets. Consequently, several new arrangements for loans were made in the Dutch Republic and in Genoa in 1770.[38]

The revenue that was received from these loans was primarily utilized to deal with various debts accrued in Swedish Pomerania during the Seven Years' War, and which had been used to fund the military campaign. Additionally, resources were allocated to the Bank of Sweden in order to stabilize the value of the Swedish currency on the international capital markets.[39] These priorities indicate that the Diet focused on the reestablishment of the Swedish state's authority in Pomerania after the war, and on the state's ability to handle the monetary situation. In other words, the Diet was ultimately dealing with the political legitimacy of the regime.

One of the challenges to the legitimacy was the recurring deficits during the 1760s and early 1770s. The Diet managed to agree on increases in taxes during the meetings of the Diet in 1760/62 and 1765/66, but the revenue fell in the latter part of the decade because of pressure to reduce taxation, from the peasant estate in particular. The revenue from the external loans could not solve the deficit, since those resources were directed at the monetary situation. Thus, there was pressure on the Diet to come up with new solutions, which led to tensions between the estates. Many commoners argued that there had to be cutbacks in the state apparatus, where many nobles were employed, in combination with a renegotiation of the privileges of the estates. The nobility on the other hand tried to protect their interests and political influence. Increasingly the three non-noble estates cooperated, which meant that they could determine the outcome of the political discussions and override objections made by the nobility. These tensions made it difficult to reach compromises, especially since the influence of the oligarchy had been reduced. Instead there was a real possibility that the commoners would present radical solutions which would lead to a sweeping redistribution of resources in society. In the early 1770s there were therefore many nobles and other members of the elite who started to question the political system and whether it was favoring their interests.[40]

Before the Diet could reach any solutions the young king Gustavus III intervened in the ongoing political struggles by organizing a bloodless coup in 1772. The new constitution, which instituted a change in the balance of power, granted the king influence over foreign policy and military affairs, and was backed by royal control over how government resources were spent. The estates retained their taxation and legislative prerogatives, and their control of the bank. The king was mostly supported by the nobility, but there were also other members of the elite who thought that the only solution to the economic and political problems was to strengthen the influence of the king. Crucially, the king also had the backing of France, which provided a total of 8.1 million silver dalers in subsidies during the period 1772–1776.[41]

The Royal Coup and the Transformation of the Borrowing Arrangement

Although the king had been granted greater powers by the constitution and the Diet had provided him with a broad mandate to deal with the monetary and fiscal situation in the way he saw fit, his autonomy was circumscribed by the government's bank loans and the elite's influence over the bank. If the arrangement was left intact, he would have to negotiate with the elite on a regular basis how the loans should be handled. In order to change this situation, and despite opposition from the bank's governors, he pushed through a currency reform in 1776 that entailed the introduction of a new currency which was convertible to silver as well as a write-off of the government's debt to the bank. New loans in Amsterdam and Genoa helped to finance the currency reform. The decisions led to a drastic reduction in the government's debt to the bank from 7,564,153 riksdaler (the new currency) in 1777 to 211,045 riksdaler in 1779. Thus, the bank's role in financing deficits and other major projects was drastically reduced, which curtailed the political elite's ability to influence the king's policies. Instead of borrowing from the bank, the king became increasingly dependent on external loans arranged by bankers in Amsterdam, Antwerp and Genoa.[42] In other words, the changes in the balance of political power led to a new borrowing arrangement for the state.

The availability of external credit helped the regime to consolidate its position, but the limitations of the system became clear during the war with Russia in 1788–1790. The silver-backed currency, which strengthened the government's ability to manage the interest payments on the external debt, made it difficult to increase liquidity during the war. Concurrently, the king was facing growing opposition from the elite against his policies. In order to mobilize more resources the king first turned to the bank and requested funds, but the governors declined to provide credit by referring to the importance of maintaining a stable currency. The king was then forced to summon the Diet in 1789, a few months before Louis XVI went ahead with a similar move to address France's fiscal problems. At the meeting of the estates, Gustavus III proposed a new political settlement that included a deal concerning the government's debt and a strengthening of his powers. A new National Debt Office would be created which would take over the administration of the government's existing debt and be assigned specific revenues to handle all transactions. The office would also issue new debt on domestic and international markets. Furthermore, it would be controlled by representatives from the four estates. By handing over the responsibility for the debt to the Diet the king agreed to a reduction in his fiscal autonomy in exchange for more resources. The plan was therefore adopted by the members of the Diet.[43] Similar measures to strengthen governments' abilities to administer the growing ties with both internal and external creditors were also initiated in other European states, such as Denmark and Spain, around this time.[44]

A key component of this new borrowing arrangement in Sweden was the introduction of non-interest-bearing promissory notes issued by the Debt Office. The volume of these notes increased quite dramatically to 8.4 million riksdaler in 1790 and to 14.6 million in 1795. As Rebecca Spang shows in the previous chapter, a similar increase of paper money occurred in France during the 1790s. Although they had initially been introduced to increase liquidity during the war, the continued expansion after the conflict shows that they played a more general role in financing the government's activities. The notes were issued in the same currency as the Bank of Sweden's notes, but while the silver standard was upheld by the bank the promissory notes soon lost their value in relation to the bank's notes.[45] Since taxes could be paid with the promissory notes the government's revenue was losing value, which made it more costly for the Debt Office to handle the external debt.[46]

The difficulties that the Debt Office was facing in order to uphold the state's external credit in combination with many inhabitants' criticism of the fluctuating value of the promissory notes put pressure on the regime to reduce the role of the notes.[47] The Diet was therefore summoned to agree on a new currency reform that would create a fixed exchange rate between the promissory notes and the bank's notes. This system was introduced in 1803 with the help of a new external loan negotiated in Leipzig the previous year.[48]

The currency reform, which exhibits some similarities with Napoleon's settlement of the French system of *assignats*, led to an improvement in the Debt Office's capacity to handle the external debt by drastically reducing the volume of notes in circulation.[49] As in the 1770s, this process increased the king's political autonomy. However, the reduction in liquidity made it more difficult to finance military operations, especially when the Napoleonic war made it difficult to get access to further external credit. When Sweden became involved in the coalition against Napoleon in 1805 the king relied largely on British subsidies to support the military activities, while trying to protect his political autonomy. When Russia attacked the Swedish realm in 1808 the king refused to summon the Diet despite the need to mobilize more domestic resources. Instead he continued to largely rely on British subsidies. Eventually the elite organized a coup in order to overthrow the king and to introduce a new constitution in 1809.[50] Thus, a combination of internal and external political circumstances fostered a situation, which made foreign subsidies rather than public debt the crucial source for funding the war and for maintaining royal rule. When the elite could not utilize the debt to influence the king's decisions, their only viable option was to use force to change the political status quo.

The Fiscal Consequences of the Napoleonic Wars

Ever since the 1760s the Swedish government had relied on external borrowing and it had paid external creditors even during difficult times. The bondholders in turn manifested their trust in the Swedish state by trading the issued bonds close to their nominal value. However, in 1808 the Swedish government decided to temporarily defer payments to the Netherlands and to Genoa following the outbreak of war.[51] The new regime continued to defer payments to external creditors, but in 1812 the government decided to unilaterally default on parts of the debt. The decision, which signaled a new borrowing arrangement after the existing balance of political power had shifted, was driven by the Swedish resolution to join a new anti-French coalition. The default was therefore presented as a retaliatory action against provocations by the French government. Since Genoa and the Low Countries were incorporated into the French realm, it was deemed acceptable to target bondholders there as objects of Swedish retaliation.[52] When the government's proposal was discussed at the Diet it was primarily a number of merchants who voiced their concern about the plan. They thought that a default would damage Sweden's good reputation and bring misfortune to the country. Many noblemen, clergymen and peasants argued against this standpoint by stressing the need to protect the interests of the state. The three estates therefore agreed that two-thirds of the external debt in Amsterdam, Antwerp and Genoa would be defaulted on and that the last part could later be recognized by the king.[53] Although it was not stated explicitly, the proportion chosen to default on clearly followed the principles introduced in France in 1797.[54]

By defaulting, the Diet could reallocate tax revenues from administering the debt to the preparations for war. The decision was also influenced by the perceived opportunity to receive large British subsidies. Although Sweden had not signed any agreements when the decision to default was taken, negotiations with Britain had started and they would result in an agreement guaranteeing £2.6 million for the period 1812–1814.[55] Thus, even if it was possible to uphold the Swedish state's external credit, considerations of the international political situation took precedence when the Diet and the government measured the different policy options in 1812.

The bondholders reacted very negatively to the default by either selling their assets or voicing their grievances to the bankers and the Swedish authorities. Although the information about the creditors' complaints was received in Stockholm, neither the government nor the Debt Office reacted to the demands.[56] Instead the government went ahead with liquidating the remaining external debt when the war was over. The liquidation was handled by the king and his adopted son, the former French marshal Jean Baptiste Bernadotte. Thus, the responsibility for the external debt was transferred from the Debt Office to the royals. The background to this decision was the supply of resources that Bernadotte had managed to secure from a number of foreign governments when the coalition against Napoleon was built. The payments can be seen as investments by Britain, Russia and Prussia in the loyalty of Bernadotte. The resources, which amounted to 12.5 million riksdaler or around three years of ordinary government revenue, were given to him personally and not to the Swedish state. In order to reduce internal criticism about this arrangement, the royals offered to use part of the money to liquidate the external debt in exchange for a yearly 200,000 riksdaler perpetual payment to the royal family from the Debt Office. The offer was accepted by the four estates without any debate.[57] This decision meant that the political autonomy of Bernadotte was strengthened since he could use the independently controlled resources to interact with the elite from a position of strength without getting involved in the struggles that his predecessors had been concerned with. The resources also meant that Bernadotte, unlike other European rulers such as the Danish king, did not have to rely on external credit to distribute resources. In other words, the new fiscal arrangement constituted a new balance of political power.

The Swedish officials involved in the liquidation process attempted to reach broad debt settlements with the bondholders in order to speed up the process. They were also purchasing bonds on the secondary markets at a discount. Agreements were reached with the Dutch and the Genoese rather quickly, but it still became a rather protracted process with holdouts in Saxony especially. By the early 1830s almost all bonds had been liquidated. At the same time, the Debt Office was involved in a slow process of reducing the number of long-term government bonds on the credit markets by redeeming the bonds at maturity while at the same time only selling a limited number of new ones. As a consequence, the Swedish state was practically debt-free in the 1830s.[58] The regime hailed this as a great achievement. Thus, as in the United States during the presidency of Andrew Jackson, the legitimacy of the political order became based on not having a public debt.[59]

* * *

Swedish fiscal developments from 1760 to 1830 clearly show how the different borrowing arrangements were closely connected to the balance of political power and the legitimacy of the state. When the existing political order was challenged, or when it was overthrown, the dominant borrowing arrangement was altered in order to serve the new rulers and their interests, and to distance the new regime from the previous balance of power. Government borrowing was therefore highly politicized, and it influenced the struggles between the estates and between the king and the estates in relation to the allocation of resources. The political matrix was also affected by alternative sources of revenue such as foreign subsidies.

These findings about the development of public credit in Sweden have ramifications for more general arguments about the role of formal political institutions in the creation of a functioning public debt. The Swedish Diet, which was an established representative assembly, did help to create trust in organizations such as the Bank of Sweden and the National Debt Office among investors, and in establishing a reputation for the Swedish state as a committed debtor on international credit markets. However, the institution did not function as a bulwark against defaults or other debt restructuring measures. Instead different domestic actors could utilize the institution to legitimize actions which targeted different creditor groups and their interests. International conflicts or internal upheavals, in particular, could be used strategically to make changes to the structure of the debt, which in turn changed the relative political strength of different actors. In other words, the outcome of these political processes was determined more by the mediation between different interests and the various resources which were available for redistribution than by the existence of a representative assembly or rules governing decision-making. Public credit therefore was, and still is, a highly political object.

Notes

1. Peter George Muir Dickson, *The Financial Revolution in England: A Study in the Development of Public Credit, 1688–1756* (London: Macmillan, 1967); John Brewer, *Sinews of Power: War, Money and the English State, 1688–1783* (London: Unwin Hyman, 1989); François R. Velde and David R. Weir, "The Financial Market and Government Debt Policy in France, 1746–1793," *Journal of Economic History* 52, no. 1 (1992); Hamish Scott, "The Fiscal-Military State and International Rivalry during the Long Eighteenth Century," in *The Fiscal-Military State in Eighteenth-Century Europe: Essays in Honour of P.G.M. Dickson*, ed. C. Storrs (Farnham: Ashgate, 2009); Rafael Torres Sánchez, *Constructing a Fiscal Military State in Eighteenth-Century Spain* (Houndmills: Palgrave Macmillan, 2015); William D. Godsey, *The Sinews of Habsburg Power: Lower Austria in a Fiscal-Military State 1650–1820* (Oxford: Oxford University Press, 2018).
2. Michael Sonenscher, *Before the Deluge: Public Debt, Inequality, and the Intellectual Origins of the French Revolution* (Princeton: Princeton University Press, 2007); Carl Wennerlind, *Casualties of Credit: The English Financial Revolution, 1620–1720* (Cambridge, Mass.: Harvard University Press, 2011).
3. For example, Dickson, *Financial Revolution*; Richard Bonney, "France and the First European Paper Money Experiment," *French History* 15, no. 3 (2001); Renate Pieper, "Financing an Empire: The Austrian Composite Monarchy, 1650–1848," in *The Rise of Fiscal States: A Global History, 1500–1914*, eds. Bartolomé Yun-Casalilla and Patrick K. O'Brien (Cambridge: Cambridge University Press, 2012).
4. Giuseppe Felloni, *Gli investimenti finanziari genovesi in Europa tra il seicento e la restaurazione* (Milan: A. Giuffrè, 1971); James C. Riley, *International Government Finance and the Amsterdam Capital Market, 1740–1815* (Cambridge: Cambridge University Press, 1980); Christiaan van Bochove, "External Debt and Commitment Mechanisms: Danish Borrowing in Holland, 1763–1825," *Economic History Review* 67, no. 3 (2014).
5. For the importance of politics, see Caroline Van Rijckeghem and Beatrice Weder, "Political Institutions and Debt Crises," *Public Choice* 138 (2009);

Nicolas Delalande, "Protecting the Credit of the State: Speculation, Trust, and Sovereignty in Interwar France," *Annales HSS* 71, no. 1 (2016); Anush Kapadia, "The Structure of State Borrowing: Towards a Political Theory of Control Mechanisms," *Cambridge Journal of Regions, Economy and Society* 10 (2017).

6. Douglass C. North and Barry R. Weingast, "Constitutions and Commitment: The Evolution of Institutions Governing Public Choice in Seventeenth-Century England," *Journal of Economic History* 49, no. 4 (1989); David Stasavage, *Public Debt and the Birth of the Democratic State: France and Great Britain, 1688–1789* (Cambridge: Cambridge University Press, 2003); Mark Dincecco, *Political Transformations and Public Finances: Europe, 1650–1913* (Cambridge: Cambridge University Press, 2011); Daron Acemoglu and James A. Robinson, *Why Nations Fail: The Origins of Power, Prosperity and Poverty* (London: Profile, 2012); Gary W. Cox, *Marketing Sovereign Promises: Monopoly Brokerage and the Growth of the English State* (Cambridge: Cambridge University Press, 2016).

7. For a critique of the institutional perspective, see D'Maris Coffman, "Credibility, Transparency, Accountability, and the Public Credit under the Long Parliament and Commonwealth, 1643–1653," and Alejandra Irigoin and Regina Grafe, "Bounded Leviathan: Fiscal Constraints and Financial Development in the Early Modern Hispanic World," in *Questioning Credible Commitment: Perspectives on the Rise of Financial Capitalism*, eds. D'Maris Coffman, Adrian Leonard and Larry Neal (Cambridge: Cambridge University Press, 2013). See also Julian Hoppit, *Britain's Political Economies: Parliament and Economic Life, 1660–1800* (Cambridge: Cambridge University Press, 2017), 28–34.

8. Hamish M. Scott, *The Emergence of the Eastern Powers, 1756–1775* (Cambridge: Cambridge University Press, 2001), 3–7, 249.

9. John M. Sherwig, *Guineas and Gunpowder: British Foreign Aid in the Wars with France 1793–1815* (Cambridge, Mass.: Harvard University Press, 1969), 34–53, 216–38, 294–314; Ole Feldbæk, "Eighteenth-Century Danish Neutrality: Its Diplomacy, Economics and Law," *Scandinavian Journal of History* 8 (1983); Leos Müller, "Swedish Merchant Shipping in Troubled Times: The French Revolutionary Wars and Sweden's Neutrality 1793–1801," *International Journal of Maritime History* 28, no. 1 (2016).

10. Arnold H. Barton, *Scandinavia in the Revolutionary Era, 1760–1815* (Minneapolis: University of Minnesota Press, 1986).

11. Franz A.J. Szabo, *The Seven Years War in Europe 1756–1763* (Harlow: Pearson Longman, 2008), 132–4; Patrik Winton, "Sweden and the Seven Years War, 1757–1762: War, Debt and Politics," *War in History* 19, no. 1 (2012).

12. Michael Roberts, *The Age of Liberty: Sweden 1719–1772* (Cambridge: Cambridge University Press, 1986), 6–9; Patrik Winton, "La hiérarchie contestée. La reconfiguration de l'équilibre des pouvoirs au sein et entre les ordres du Riksdag suédois, 1750–1772," *Revue d'histoire nordique* 10 (2010): 34–7.
13. Roberts, *Age of Liberty*, 26–7; Peter George Muir Dickson, *Finance and Government under Maria Theresia 1740–1780* (Oxford: Clarendon Press, 1987), 2:394.
14. Karl Åmark, *Sveriges statsfinanser 1719–1809* (Stockholm: Norstedt, 1961), 230, 609.
15. Carl Hallendorff, *Riksens ständers bank 1719–1766*, vol. II, *Sveriges Riksbank 1668–1918* (Stockholm: Sveriges Riksbank, 1919), 220–1, 238–9.
16. Sekreta utskottets protokoll 1751/52, 24–25 Oct., 8 Nov., 20 Dec. 1751, vol. R2956 and Sekreta utskottets protokoll 1755/56, 8 May 1756, vol. R3045, Swedish National Archives, Stockholm, (SNA).
17. Winton, "Sweden and the Seven Years War," 22–4.
18. Generalindtægtsbog 1760, Hovedbogholderikontoret, Rentekammeret, Danish National Archives, Copenhagen (DNA); Erik Rasmussen, *Kurantbankens forhold til staten 1737–73* (Copenhagen: Institutet for historie og samfundsøkonomi, 1955), 115–47 and appendix III; Szabo, *The Seven Years War*, 132.
19. Sekreta utskottets protokoll 1760/62, 4–6 Feb., vol. R3143, 28 Aug. and 2 Sep. 1761, vol. R3144; Pehr Niclas Christiernin, *Utdrag af föreläsningar angående den i Swea rike upstigne wexel-coursen, til desz beskaffenhet, orsaker och påfölgder, samt botemedel emot wexel-prisets ytterligare uplöpande* (Stockholm, 1761); Anders Nordencrantz, *Tankar om den höga wexel-coursen och dyrheten i Swerige* (Stockholm, 1761).
20. Statskontorets avräkningsböcker over inrikes lån, vol. 2406 and 2418, Kamrerarekontoret, Riksgäldsdirektionen, SNA.
21. Akter rörande särskilda lån, vol. 2262, Huvudarkivet, Riksgäldsdirektionen, SNA.
22. On the loan in Antwerp, see Sekreta utskottets protokoll 1760/62, 27 Feb., 17 Mar., 7 Apr., 8 Apr., 6 May and 22 Jun. 1761, vol. R3143, SNA.
23. Sekreta utskottets protokoll 1765/66, 12 Oct. 1765 and 12 Apr. 1766, vol. R3273, SNA.
24. Leos Müller, *Consuls, Corsairs, and Commerce: The Swedish Consular Service and Long-Distance Shipping, 1720–1815* (Uppsala: Acta Universitatis Upsaliensia, 2004), 134–44.
25. Dickson, *Finance and Government*, 119 and tables 5.4, 5.6.
26. Rådsprotokoll i utrikesärenden 1766, 3–4 Sep., 13 Oct., 10 Nov, vol. 3, Utrikesexpeditionen, SNA; Sekreta utskottets protokoll 1765/66, 8 Aug., 29 Aug., 4 Sep., 1 Oct. 1766, vol. R3274, SNA; Nils Bark to the President

of the Chancery 29 Dec. 1766, Genuesiska lånet 1762–78, vol. 2236, Räkenskaper och handlingar rörande upptagna lån, Huvudarkivet, Riksgäldsdirektionen, SNA.
27. Nils Bark to the President of the Chancery 29 Dec. 1766 and lists concerning interest payments 2 Oct. 1767 and 3 Oct. 1768, Genuesiska lånet 1762–78, vol. 2236, Räkenskaper och handlingar rörande upptagna lån, Huvudarkivet, Riksgäldsdirektionen, SNA.
28. Sekreta utskottets protokoll 1765/66, 1 Oct. 1766, vol. R3274, SNA.
29. See for example Leos Müller, *The Merchant Houses of Stockholm. c. 1640–1800: A Comparative Study of Early-Modern Entrepreneurial Behaviour* (Uppsala: Acta Universitatis Upsaliensia, 1998).
30. Rådsprotokoll i utrikesärenden 1767, 2 Mar., vol. 1, Utrikesexpeditionen, SNA. Sahlgren's name is mentioned 19 Nov.
31. Rådsprotokoll i utrikesärenden 1767, 17–19 Nov., vol. 2, Utrikesexpeditionen, SNA; Hope & Comp., Holländska lån 1767–1778, vol. 2238, Räkenskaper och handlingar rörande upptagna lån, Huvudarkivet, Riksgäldsdirektionen, SNA.
32. Riley, *International Government Finance*, 83–194; Christiaan van Bochove, "Configuring Financial Markets in Preindustrial Europe," *Journal of Economic History* 73, no. 1 (2013): 269.
33. Rådsprotokoll i utrikesärenden 1767, 17 Dec., vol. 2, Utrikesexpeditionen, SNA. See also 19 Nov.
34. Huvudböcker 1760–1772, vol. 1672–1684, Huvudbokföringen, Sveriges Riksbank, SNA; Arthur Montgomery, "Riksbanken och de valutapolitiska problemen 1719–1778," vol. III, *Sveriges riksbank 1668–1918* (Stockholm: Sveriges Riksbank, 1920), 122; Markus A. Denzel, *Handbook of World Exchange Rates, 1590–1914* (Farnham: Ashgate, 2010), 344.
35. See, for instance, Sekreta utskottets protokoll 1769/70, 7 Jul., 10 Jul., 14 Aug., 21–23 Aug., 27 Oct. and 30 Oct. 1769, vol. R3457, SNA; Jacob von Engeström, *Egne tankar om orsaken til wexel-coursens stigande samt sättet til des fällande och stadgande* (Stockholm, 1769); Anders Nordencrantz, *Sanningar som uplysa orsakerne til wäxel-coursens hastiga fall samt nu öfwerklagade wäxelbrist* (Stockholm, 1769).
36. Hovedbøger passive gæld ind- og udlandet 1763–1774, Overskattedirektionen, DNA; Rasmussen, *Kurantbankens forhold*, appendix III; Bochove, "External Debt," 673–4.
37. Sekreta utskottets protokoll 1769/70, 9 Oct. 1769, vol. R3457, SNA; Rådsprotokoll i utrikesärenden 1769, 7 Dec., vol. 2, Utrikesexpeditionen, SNA.
38. Åmark, *Sveriges statsfinanser*, 629.

39. Genuesiska lånet 1762–78, vol. 2236 and Holländska lån 1767–78, vol. 2238, Räkenskaper och handlingar rörande upptagna lån, Huvudarkivet, Riksgäldsdirektionen, SNA.
40. Åmark, *Sveriges statsfinanser*, 218–9, 230; Peter Hallberg, *Ages of Liberty: Social Upheaval, History Writing, and the New Public Sphere in Sweden, 1740–1792* (Stockholm: Statsvetenskapliga institutionen, 2003), 172–231; Winton, "La hiérarchie contestée," 41–4.
41. Georg Landberg, "Den svenska riksdagen under den gustavianska tiden," *Sveriges Riksdag*, vol. 7 (Stockholm: Sveriges Riksdag, 1932), 7–38; Åmark, *Sveriges statsfinanser*, 586; Henrika Tandefelt, *Konsten att härska: Gustaf III inför sina undersåtar* (Helsinki: Svenska litteratursällskapet i Finland, 2008), 52–113.
42. Åmark, *Sveriges statsfinanser*, 234–6, 626.
43. Landberg, "Den svenska riksdagen," 110–6; Bertil Dahlström, *Rikets gäld 1788–1792. Studier i den svenska riksförvaltningen jämte krigsfinansieringen 1788–1790* (Stockholm: Stockholms högskola, 1942), 36–143.
44. Hans C. Johansen, *Dansk økonomisk politik i årene efter 1784*, vol. I (Aarhus: Universitetsforlaget, 1968); Torres Sánchez, *Constructing a Fiscal Military State*.
45. Åmark, *Sveriges statsfinanser*, 644–5; Torbjörn Engdahl and Anders Ögren, "Multiple Paper Monies in Sweden 1789–1903: Substitution or Complementarity?," *Financial History Review* 15, no. 1 (2008): 76–81.
46. Patrik Winton, "The Political Economy of Swedish Absolutism, 1789–1809," *European Review of Economic History* 16, no. 4 (2012): 436–8.
47. See for example articles in the journal *Läsning i blandade ämnen*, vol. 32 (1799) and vol. 33–5 (1800).
48. Winton, "The Political Economy of Swedish Absolutism," 438.
49. Eugene N. White, "The French Revolution and the Politics of Government Finance, 1770–1815," *Journal of Economic History* 55, no. 2 (June 1995): 234–41; Winton, "The Political Economy of Swedish Absolutism," 438–9.
50. Winton, "The Political Economy of Swedish Absolutism," 440–3.
51. E.g. Fullmäktiges hemliga protokoll 1799, 11 Feb., 11 Mar., vol. 4379 and Fullmäktiges protokoll 1808, 29 Feb., vol. 4077, Huvudarkivet, Riksgäldskontoret, SNA; *Koninklijke courant* 15 Jan. (1807), 1 Feb. and 30 Jun. (1808), 5 Jan. (1809).
52. Statsrådsprotokoll i finansärenden 1812, vol. 1, 13 May, Handels- och finansexpeditionen, SNA. For the international context, see Sherwig, *Guineas and Gunpowder*, 275.
53. Hemliga utskottets protokoll 1812, 27 May, vol. R4521 and Statsutskottets riksgäldsavdelnings protokoll 1812, 30 Jun., vol. R4473, SNA. See also Patrik Winton, "The Political Economy of Strategic Default: Sweden and

the International Capital Markets, 1810–1830," *European Review of Economic History* 20, no. 4 (2016): 417–8.
54. See Chap. 2 in this volume.
55. Sherwig, *Guineas and Gunpowder*, 284–6.
56. Fullmäktiges protokoll 1814, 7 Jul., 15 Sep., vol. 4086, Huvudarkivet, Riksgäldskontoret, SNA.
57. Winton, "The Political Economy of Strategic Default," 421–2.
58. Avräkningsböcker över lånet på 100 år för Trollhätte-Slussverk och obligationer emot 5 procents ränta 1830–1831, vol. 8293 and Koncepthuvudböcker 1834, vol. 7035, Bokslutskontoret, Riksgäldskontoret, SNA.
59. See for instance the royal report to the Diet 23 Dec. 1817, Statsutskottets riksgäldsavdelning 1817/18, vol. R4479, SNA. On the American developments, see Max M. Edling, *A Hercules in the Cradle: War, Money, and the American State, 1783–1867* (Chicago: University of Chicago Press, 2014).

CHAPTER 4

Public Debt and Democratic Statecraft in Nineteenth-Century France

David Todd and Alexia Yates

That France would "set the fashion in finance" for nineteenth-century states would have surprised many observers of European public credit after the cataclysm of 1789 and near bankruptcy of the 1790s.[1] The resurrection of the country's credit, largely via a series of successful public loans required by the indemnities imposed by the Second Treaty of Paris in 1815, was nearly miraculous. Across the following decades the French state would develop the institutions capable of increasing its debt from the modest levels that existed in the wake of the Revolution to the world's largest by the end of the nineteenth century.[2] While the original revolutionaries failed to uphold the sacrality of public debt which they proclaimed, with the "Banqueroute des Deux Tiers" in Vendémiaire Year 6 (September 1797), successive political regimes after 1800 succeeded in

D. Todd
Department of History, King's College London, London, UK
e-mail: david.todd@kcl.ac.uk

A. Yates (✉)
History Department, University of Manchester, Manchester, UK
e-mail: alexia.yates@manchester.ac.uk

© The Author(s) 2020
N. Barreyre, N. Delalande (eds.), *A World of Public Debts*, Palgrave Studies in the History of Finance,
https://doi.org/10.1007/978-3-030-48794-2_4

maintaining it through the revolutionary upheavals of 1830, 1848, and 1871.[3] The solidity of French public credit was taken to manifest a new form of domestic stability and undergirded—as well as undermined—the development of French global ambitions; at the root of the rapid growth of public debt lay the considerable indemnities imposed with the military defeat of 1815 as well as that of 1870, and the enormous costs of the conquest and colonization of Algeria from 1830, of the frantic foreign interventionism of the Second Empire, and of rapid colonial expansion under the Third Republic. Nineteenth-century France proved to be a democratic reincarnation of the eighteenth-century fiscal-military state.[4]

Such a tremendous expansion of public debt required and effected transformations in the intellectual rationale and political signification of public credit, as well as in its social distribution and embeddedness. In the eighteenth century, concerns about the political and moral risks of public debt were as potent in France as elsewhere in the West. Echoes of David Hume's 1764 warning that "the nation must destroy public credit, or public credit will destroy the nation" abounded in the writings of Marquis de Mirabeau (*père*), perhaps the most widely read author of political economy at the time.[5] This anxiety responded to the rhapsody of public debt affected by mercantilist writers and ministers, and can even be construed, Michael Sonenscher has shown, as the lynchpin for the reconfiguring of sovereignty and political legitimacy during the Revolution.[6] At the end of the next century, however, conventional political economy such as Paul Leroy-Beaulieu's *Traité de la science des finances* (1877) breezily opined that "David Hume … was mistaken" about the dangers of public debt, presenting as evidence the formidable prosperity achieved by Europe and its colonial offshoots in spite of the unremitting growth of public indebtedness in the nineteenth century.[7] What explains that Leroy-Beaulieu and his fellow mainstream economists remained so cool before a phenomenon that had elicited such angst until the beginning of the nineteenth century? The significance of this turnaround of French political economy is compounded by the fact that in Britain, most economists, politicians, and public opinion had continued to take Hume's warning seriously, and to condemn public indebtedness as consistently noxious to the political and moral health of the nation as well as its economic growth.[8] The difference in outlooks was registered by savvy readers of national political economies; when Austria-Hungary proposed imposing taxes on foreign holders of its 1865 loan, letters justifying the decision from Chancellor Beust to his Austrian ambassador in Britain, Count Rudolph Apponyi, were filled with praise for British skepticism of public debt—"none have denounced the deadly system of public loans more powerfully than the British Parliament!"—while letters sent simultaneously to the ambassador to France, Richard von Metternich, tackled the allegedly questionable legality of the particular loan, taking as a given the validity of public borrowing as a general practice.[9]

Part of the answer to this question lies in changing perceptions of the relationship between public debt and political legitimacy in France, a country plagued by anxieties of political instability and geopolitical decline after 1815. In the national debt, the state and the *bourgeoisie rentière* found a durable terrain upon which to negotiate questions of representation and administration in rapidly changing political circumstances. Among the earliest European powers to establish universal male suffrage, France's assiduous development of a mass market for public debt is one of the distinctive features of its economic and political modernity, and was closely linked to efforts to make and *manage* a democratic (later republican) state. The state signaled its commitment to the establishment of this investing public from 1854, when it initiated direct subscription of its debt by substituting its network of local treasury officials for the private banking houses usually deployed as intermediaries in such affairs. By the time Leroy-Beaulieu came to be established as one of the country's preeminent economic authorities, the diffusion of multiple forms of public debt, foreign and domestic, had transformed the physical and social geography of French investment and capital markets. While there were only 200,000 holders of consols in Britain throughout the nineteenth century, in France the number of holders of *rentes* rose from 125,000 in 1830 to more than three million by 1914.[10]

Underscoring the political and geopolitical functions of public debt, we argue, helps account for the extensiveness of its commodification in France. As *la rente* and its cognates moved into "attics and cottages," Leroy-Beaulieu suggested, their residents learned "to trust a scrap of paper with certain signatures on it."[11] Among those scraps of paper, the debt of public entities like the city of Paris and the Crédit Foncier held privileged places, as did the public debt issued by foreign states and cities; these last represented 246 out of the 928 securities on the official Paris Exchange in 1891 and enjoyed a preferential tax status vis-à-vis other foreign securities from 1872 through to the early twentieth century.[12] Even in the portfolios of the richest investors, the debts of foreign states consistently outpaced the levels invested in foreign equity or foreign private bonds between

1870 and 1914, a period when overall investment in foreign ventures increased by nearly three times.[13] The dissemination of these bonds was ripe for interpretation by those in authority as an expression of public favor, while it also provided the material means of projecting power on a global scale. The predilection of French investors for foreign public bonds was intimately connected with—though not determined by—the vicissitudes of foreign policy.[14] In contrast to the claims of an earlier historiographical tradition, these investments were not economically irrational but rather enjoyed widespread appeal thanks to a combination of handsome returns and a myriad of legal, fiscal, or informal incentives in their favor adopted or tolerated by the French state.[15]

In order to reappraise the country's distinct engagement with public debt in this period, the chapter reconstructs the intellectual arguments that generated a striking and robust defense of public debt in the nineteenth century—striking in particular because it reversed earlier critiques of the desirability of state indebtedness. The articulation of this position took place in the corridors of legislative chambers as well as in the hallways of the Collège de France, and helped to shape the terrain upon which investors and policymakers engaged from mid-century onward. Yet public credit was more than a contested category of state finance, more than a tool to be deployed or avoided as political perspectives and pragmatic possibilities demanded. It had a consequential, material life outside the political and intellectual debates that shaped its palatability and dissemination. Thus, this chapter also examines particular instances and instruments of the marketization of public debt in order to show how it was being reworked with an eye to assembling a new public of investment consumers from the mid-nineteenth century. Looking particularly at the bonds issued to finance France's Mexican "adventure" in the early 1860s, we reveal significant contestation among legislators, as well as extensive popular mobilization, around the issue of state responsibility for its investing citizenry.[16] Following the deployment of debt instruments aimed chiefly at the lower classes allows us to open up the surprising range of publics envisioned and enacted by changing mechanisms of public debt. The story of France's public debt in the modern era, conventionally told as one of the more-or-less efficient operations of economic institutions, becomes a narrative of political interests whose action extends from the rarefied realms of policymakers to the everyday lives of ordinary individuals.

The Rehabilitation of Public Credit

The story of the successful issuance of large amounts of public debt by the Bourbon Restoration, to settle the harsh financial conditions of the peace of 1815 after Waterloo, is well known: thanks to the support of the Barings bank, Baron Louis and the Duc de Richelieu raised enough funds to bring forward the end of France's occupation by Allied forces. It has often been told as a tale of heroic determination and ingenuity, by both the ministers who carried out this resurrection and by later historians. A recent revision has even shown that a larger share of the loans was subscribed domestically than previously thought, suggesting that French investors already had a significant appetite for public bonds in the 1810s.[17] Yet the impact of this success on perceptions of public debt, especially on the liberal (left) side of the political spectrum, has received little attention. Public debt was anything but a new political and moral concern after 1815, and until the 1820s, liberals tended to remain faithful to the exhortations of Mirabeau *père* about its terrible noxiousness. Jean-Baptiste Say, France's leading political economist until his death in 1832, sternly maintained in the successive editions of his *Traité d'économie politique* that capital borrowed by the state was always "dissipated and wasted." He even expanded his critique in the fifth edition (1826), with a condemnatory description of the complex maneuvers devised by an imaginary Jewish firm, "Samuel Bernard," in order to raise loans for absolutist regimes (a none too subtle attack on the Rothschilds), and a commendation for Robert Hamilton's *Essay on the National Debt* (1813), a vitriolic attack on the expansion of British public borrowing and still "the best work written about public debt."[18]

Say's additions to his *Traité* in 1826 were almost certainly a response to the powerful and often scandalized reaction to the banker Jacques Laffitte's pamphlet in support of a conversion of the French national debt, *Réflexions sur la réduction de la rente*, published in 1824. The scandal was partly political, because Laffitte, an avowed liberal, endorsed a financial operation devised by the royalist President of the Council Joseph de Villèle, and it was partly venal, since the conversion, by reducing the interest owed on *rentes*, was perceived as inimical to the interests of debt-holders, who were more numerous among the liberal bourgeoisie than royalist landowners.[19] Yet it was also intellectual, because the *Réflexions* drew, explicitly and implicitly, on a strand of thought going back to the defense of John Law's system in the 1710s in order to rehabilitate public credit as a "system so simple, so grand, which displays so well the characteristics of a great progress in social machinery." Contradicting Say and most other liberals who continued to view Britain's enormous debt as a burden that would eventually cause its downfall, the text contended that the British government had successfully used public indebtedness to turn "this nation into the wealthiest, that is to say, the most powerful of the universe."[20] In effect, Laffitte's pamphlet was reviving an intellectual tradition which urged the old French monarchy to emulate the economic policies of Hanoverian Britain, represented by authors such as Jean-François Melon, Law's secretary, or René Louis Voyer d'Argenson, another eulogist of Law, who defended the expansion of public debt as a means of forging a "democratic monarchy" (or "royal democracy") reconciled with commerce and capable of dominating Europe.[21] In the language of modern historical analysis, the project resuscitated by Laffitte may be described as an attempt to found a fiscal-military state with financial resources comparable to Britain's and similarly able to project its power abroad, but with a deeper, more extensive, and more domestic base of investors in public debt.

Laffitte's *Réflexions* represented more than the banker's personal opinions. In reality, it was probably written by the young Adolphe Thiers.[22] Thiers's own views on public debt were in turn certainly influenced by the Prince of Talleyrand, his then patron. Tellingly, the first two volumes of Thiers's *Histoire de la Révolution française*, which made him famous in 1823, lavished praise on the financial wisdom demonstrated by the "bishop of Autun" in 1790–1791, when Talleyrand sponsored the nationalization of land owned by the Catholic Church in order to bolster France's credit, but opposed the transformation of the *assignats* into paper money as a bankruptcy in disguise.[23] Thiers also went on to publish a measured reappraisal of Law's system in 1826, and throughout his long career he repeatedly defended the commercial and financial pragmatism of eighteenth-century political economy against the abstract theorizing of nineteenth-century economists.[24] His authorship of the *Réflexions* is not certain, but his adhesion to the views it expounded cannot be questioned, since he privately praised the pamphlet as "a work of genius."[25] Thiers was therefore a major composer of a rejuvenated French rhapsody of public debt after 1820. Without doubt, at least, he became one of its main interpreters, from his first ministerial position as undersecretary of finance at the beginning of the July Monarchy until the success of the *emprunts de libération nationale* he launched as the first president of the Third Republic. Contemporaries even compared his masterful oratory on "abstruse financial problems" to the famous eloquence of the Liberal statesman William E. Gladstone, the incarnation of British sound finance.[26]

The resurrection of enthusiasm for public debt symbolized by the *Réflexions* was not only due to the success of the Bourbon Restoration's early loans. It also reflected a Europe-wide and, with the issuance of multiple loans by newly independent Latin American states in London after 1822, almost global frenzy for public borrowing in the early 1820s.[27] The emphasis placed by the *Réflexions* on the growing interconnectedness of financial places—"the funds of all the states belong to capitalists from all countries"—as a guarantee of a more stable valuation of state bonds was even one of the most original features of the revived rhapsody: "one lends to all the governments," Laffitte (or Thiers) marveled, "even to barbaric governments" (a probable allusion to Portugal, Spain, Greece and perhaps Russia) and "to those whose color has not yet been amnestied by the whites of Europe" (an allusion to the loans issued by fledging states in the New World).[28] The scholarly literature often describes this first boom in foreign public bonds as a chiefly British affair. Yet Latin American bonds were issued in London rather than Paris in part for political reasons, since France could not recognize the independence of Spain's rebel colonies out of solidarity with its Spanish ally.[29] French financiers had no such scruples. The contracts for most Latin American loans were even concluded in France and according to French law, in order to evade already heavier taxes on financial transactions in Britain and the stringency of English legislation on usury.[30] Tellingly, the first lawsuit concerning a Latin American loan, the one issued by Colombia in 1822, was brought in London by a (shady) French investor, Gabriel Doloret, and the suit incidentally mentioned that the bonds were "very generally circulated in London and Paris."[31]

This enthusiasm for public debt in the 1820s remained confined to a small section of French society. Besides the high face value of the smallest bonds (1000 francs in 1816, reduced to 200 francs in 1834 for French *rentes*; £100, or c. 2500 francs, for the Mexican bonds issued in 1825), investment remained held back by the high level of political risk attached to public debt in an age of seemingly endless revolutionary upheavals and intercontinental warfare.[32] Pierre-François Paravey, the manager of a new Parisian bank founded in 1818, considered speculation in "public funds" one of the most hazardous types of investment: "Not only can governments borrow too much, poorly administer their finances, face unforeseen wars, experience internal commotions, but the value of public bonds can be significantly altered by a mere accident or a personal misfortune, or even a mistake of the public, which lets itself be misled so easily, especially at the Bourse."[33] Paravey's judgment can also be read as a criticism addressed to his bank's two *commanditaires* (partners), the Prince de Talleyrand-Périgord and the latter's friend the Duc de Dalberg, who both indulged in the early 1820s in extensive speculation in public funds, partly because they felt themselves superiorly well informed in political matters. Yet at the urging of the two partners, Paravey, too, was eventually unable to resist the lure of public debt, and in 1825, he became the agent—alongside Laffitte's bank, Rothschild frères and the *syndicat des receveurs généraux*—for the loan raised by Haiti in order to pay for the indemnity imposed by France on its former colony. Unfortunately for Paravey, the loan was issued at the Bourse only a few days before the London and Paris markets experienced a catastrophic crash in November 1825, leaving him unable to sell most of the bonds he had underwritten. The Haitian loan was therefore a major cause of his bank's bankruptcy, shortly followed by his suicide, in 1828.[34] In subsequent years, Talleyrand frequently lamented "the Haity business," "this horrible business," which cost him dear because he and Dalberg had personally guaranteed Paravey's participation in the loan.[35]

The involvement of Talleyrand, whose name remains a byword for backstage maneuvering and inside knowledge, in the affair of the Haitian loan is suggestive of how restricted the public of public debt—especially foreign public debt—remained in Restoration France. Yet it also points to the early role played by geopolitical considerations in the resurrection of a discourse in defense of public indebtedness. While in exile in the United States in the 1790s, Talleyrand already noted how high levels of British lending had helped preserve Britain's commercial and political pre-eminence in its former colony, and in his memoirs he attributed Napoleon's eventual defeat to Britain to his abandonment of public credit.[36] His and Dalberg's speculations in foreign public funds were rarely unrelated to projects of reviving French dominance abroad. For instance, Dalberg's speculations on Spanish bonds were connected with the politics of French military intervention in the Iberian Peninsula to restore Ferdinand VII on the Spanish throne in 1823, and at the same time as he was purchasing Mexican bonds in the mid-1820s, he lobbied the French court with another project of intervention for turning Mexico into an independent monarchy under French protection. (The Mexican expedition under the Second Napoleonic Empire, which, as will be seen below, would play a significant part in the dissemination of foreign public debt in the French public, had deep roots.)[37] Talleyrand and Dalberg's interest in the Haitian loan also certainly reflected geopolitical calculations. The indemnity it served to finance was imposed upon Haiti by gunboat diplomacy, and the loan itself was designed as a means of restoring French predominance in what had been France's wealthiest colony before the Revolution, as well as healing a revolutionary wound by offering plantation owners compensation for their losses.[38]

In the long run, the main significance of the rehabilitation of public credit by Laffitte *et alii* in the mid-1820s probably lay in its impact on the financial ideas of the Saint-Simonians, the most fanatic advocates of modern capitalism in early nineteenth-century France. Their journal *Le Producteur*, launched in 1825 and subsidized by Laffitte, swarmed with articles on the merits of public credit, including a reappraisal of Law's system by Olinde Rodrigues, one of the sect's two supreme fathers, and a scheme by Prosper Enfantin, the other supreme father, for the complete replacement of taxation by public borrowing.[39] Such ideas, divested of their utopian garb, gained greater consideration and considerable influence with the rise to prominence of Michel Chevalier, Enfantin's closest disciple, under the July Monarchy and the Second Empire. Chevalier's ascent was itself facilitated by the patronage of Thiers, who as minister of commerce in 1833 had Chevalier released from prison—to which he, alongside other Saint-Simonians, had been sentenced for their critique of conventional sexual morality—before sending him to investigate the use of public loans to finance the construction of railways in the United States. It was almost certainly in part to bolster support for an increase in public borrowing that Thiers, while he was preparing a grand national scheme of railway construction as President of the Council in 1840, secured Chevalier's appointment as professor of political economy at the Collège de France.[40]

The elevation of Chevalier to the chair previously held by Jean-Baptiste Say scandalized the latter's disciples, not least due to Chevalier's heterodox views on public finances.[41] Chevalier's early lectures at the Collège de France focused on the development of credit (private and public) and the construction of infrastructures as the chief complementary means of promoting economic development. The distrust of public credit, Chevalier conceded, may have been legitimate under the bellicose and secretive Old Regime. Yet the Revolution of 1789, confirmed by that of 1830, made such suspicions groundless: the "hideous bankruptcy," "this monster against which Mirabeau [*fils*, who shared his father's views on public credit] formerly made his thunderous voice heard" in the Constituent Assembly, was "much less to be feared" now that France had a transparent budget subject to parliamentary scrutiny. Chevalier acknowledged the persistent hostility of British economists to public indebtedness but dismissed it as reflecting the efforts of Britain's aristocracy to maintain its pre-eminence against royal power. Such a consideration was inapplicable to France's "democratic" July Monarchy, which the development of public credit would even consolidate by encouraging saving and investment among all classes.[42] In other words, a different political regime entailed and enabled a different public debt regime.

Chevalier's vision of a monarchy bolstered by a widening investor class bore an unmistakable resemblance to the ideas of eighteenth-century defenders of Law's system. To be sure, his Saint-Simonian pacifism ensured that his lectures said little about the military advantages of public credit. But this difference with the eighteenth-century discourse of public credit was rhetorical, given the role played by public borrowing in facilitating the costly conquest of Algeria or the Second Empire's numerous and equally expensive wars against Russia, China, or Mexico. Such civilizing wars were justified in Chevalier's view because they were tantamount to public investment that would yield considerable benefits to France and mankind.[43]

THE MATERIAL LIFE OF BONDS

Chevalier's elegy of public debt served to legitimize its formidable expansion and democratization under Napoleon III, whom Chevalier served with gusto as Councillor of State in charge of economic legislation in 1852 and as Senator in 1860.[44] This era saw the initiation of public subscription of the *rente* via local treasury officials, instituting a direct transactional relationship between the state and its investing citizenry, as well as a dramatic increase in state-authorized issuances of municipal and departmental debt. Municipal debt in particular grew from the 1860s, rising to the unprecedented figure of 3.2 billion francs by 1890.[45] The para-public Crédit Foncier, founded in 1852, contributed an explosion of publicly backed mortgage debt and enjoyed the right to issue bonds for municipal and departmental loans from 1860. By 1887, this company had placed approximately three billion francs in mortgage and municipal bonds among a broad investing public.[46] The instruments that made up a growing public debt thus took multiple and complex forms in the nineteenth century.[47] While some, such as the perpetual *rente* that undergirded the fortunes of the country's middle classes, are well known, others await analysis. Appreciating the diverse mechanisms by which a saver became a public creditor offers crucial insights into the politics of public debt. Not only do they bring to light the broad range of debt arrangements employed to transfer private money to public hands, they also reveal the range of cultural and social concerns, operating from above and below, that shaped the construction of a distinct public debt regime in the nineteenth century.

Significant numbers of the new public securities described above, for instance, were issued in a form specifically designed to enhance the credit of issuing bodies by appealing not to existing investors but to new markets of small savers-cum-investors. Known as lottery bonds, these securities combined the conventional features of a bond (quarterly interest payments, right to repayment of the principal) with semi-annual drawings for significant cash prizes. Technically, they were assimilated to a public lottery, illegal in France from 1836 (and in Britain from 1826).[48] Yet France departed from its cross-Channel neighbor by permitting the use of lottery bonds with government authorization.[49] The Crédit Foncier enjoyed nearly unlimited ability to issue such bonds, and could even sell fractions as small as a tenth (e.g., 50 francs on a 500 franc issuance). The city of Paris was a pioneer, deploying lottery bonds in its loans of 1817 and 1832 and repeatedly thereafter, becoming one of the chief issuers of these instruments.[50] The cities of Lyon (1879), Marseille (1877), Bordeaux (1862), Lille (1859 and 1863), Amiens (1871), and, under slightly different conditions, Tourcoing and Roubaix (1860) followed the capital's example. But their use was not limited to domestic ventures. Lottery bonds were particularly deployed for ventures of international prestige and national interest, such as the Suez Canal (1868) and the Panama Canal (1888). Foreign state debt enjoyed privileges in this arena, with the French government extending authorization for lottery loans for the Mexican "adventure" (1864–1865) as well as to foreign states to which it granted "favored nation status," such as Belgium, Austria, the Congo Free State, and the Ottoman Empire.[51] By 1900, it was estimated that 10% of all French securities on the official exchange were lottery bonds. Between the official and curb markets, 57 different bonds, totaling approximately 37 million certificates worth nearly 8 billion francs, were available to investors.[52]

The national state, in its diverse nineteenth-century manifestations, never issued its debt in this form in this period. Lottery loans posed practical problems for debt conversion and were generally understood as better suited for reimbursable debt, rather than the perpetual debt favored by the state.[53] But the state's reticence was also informed by the serious legal and moral quandaries that the bonds inspired. While they had not been explicitly mentioned in the lottery prohibition of 1836, for many observers it was nevertheless clear that by partaking of the lottery form these bonds "depended on exciting a taste for gambling" and ought, therefore, to be forbidden.[54] Legal decisions on whether these instruments did or did not fall under the lottery ban were inconsistent through the 1870s. Nevertheless, the French state increasingly authorized lottery bonds for public purposes, ensuring via their distribution that increasing numbers of savers found their way into investment in public ventures and enterprises. The Crédit Foncier's bonds, for instance, were permitted to emulate the *rente* in important ways: they were brokered through the state's treasury agents, accepted as security for advances by the Bank of France, their capital and interest payments were unseizable, and they were designated as legal investments for the funds of minors and other legally incompetent individuals.[55] Such design features reinforced both the appearance of stability and practical utility of the bonds, all the while capitalizing on the enthusiasm generated by lottery drawings. Yet the way these bonds were linked, materially and procedurally, with the state was not without its problems. Critics of lottery bonds noted particularly the dangers associated with the fact that each issuance had to be authorized by the government. The phrase "authorized loan" plastered across a loan's advertisements was thought to greatly enhance its appeal, lending an aura of official guarantee that reassured novice investors and savers grown used to secure placement in *rente* or government-backed railroad bonds. Each authorization, therefore, occasioned heated debate about the protection owed French savings and the threat of government-backed *drainage du capital* into exotic ventures.[56]

The fact that these bonds became particularly popular with modest investors heightened the stakes of these debates. Studies carried out on investment portfolios in the Bank of France confirmed their popularity among more modest fortunes, noting that "investment begins invariably with lottery bonds" before moving into more sophisticated securities.[57] Their particular attraction for the lower classes generated reflection on unequal modes of participating in the market. As the Comte de Casablanca, attorney general at the Cour des Comptes (Court of Audit), reported to the Senate in 1870, the fact that "billions of francs of these bonds have penetrated all classes of society, and frequently form the larger part of the fortune of the most modest households" meant that defining their legal status was key to protecting the first steps of savers into financial investment.[58] Chevalier added his voice to their defense, reflecting on their capacity to generate useful habits of thrift, and observing that their low rates of return—low because investors accepted 3% rather than 4% in exchange for the chance to participate in lottery drawings—made them a cheaper way of raising capital for issuers, thus reducing the costs of public ventures.[59] Critics, in reply, decried them as predatory and poorly remunerative.

The issuance of lottery bonds for the support of national projects in Mexico during the Second Empire offers a case study of the legal and political complexity of these instruments and the markets they created. The Mexican enterprise had its origins in an 1861–1862 international military venture launched in response to President Benito Juárez's declaration of a temporary moratorium on the country's foreign debt repayment. In concert with the Spanish and British—both of whose investors had a higher financial stake in Mexican loans to that point—French forces sailed to Mexico in order to compel the country to meet its obligations.[60] France's intervention continued beyond that of Spain and Britain, partially on the basis of exaggerated financial claims and demands for compensation for the costs of the intervention. In 1864 and 1865, loans were authorized as part of agreements overseen by a Joint Commission on Mexican Finances that were intended to contribute to indemnifying French and British interests.[61] The first of the two loans, issued in Britain and France, generated an underwhelming response, prompting more aggressive conditions for the retailing of the second. In 1865, 500,000 bonds totaling 170 million francs were made available "in every town, even the smallest villages of France," and taken up "with an unprecedented excitement" thanks to their retailing through the Comptoir d'Escompte (recently permitted to open branches across the empire) and the state's treasury officials.[62]

This was no ordinary foreign loan, though the government tried hard to paint it as such once confronted with an onslaught of demands for satisfaction by ruined investors in the late 1860s. As these individuals and groups noted, the loan had offered no less than a new empire, linked with France's, as its security; ministers and government envoys had lyricized in the legislative chamber on the wealth of a regenerated Mexico, "the most favored country in the world," and of the necessity and glory of extending

France's zone of influence.[63] One of the Second Empire's most important officials, the Comte de Germiny, was placed in charge of the commission monitoring the situation of Mexican finances; money was literally handed to the state, in the person of its tax collectors.[64] "MM. the *receveurs-généraux*!," one pamphlet exclaimed, "That's the Ministry of Finance! That's the government! […] Everyone takes this to mean that there is no risk, that subscribers will be scrupulously repaid."[65] In 1868, disabused investors wrote to deputy and financier Isaac Péreire—whose Crédit Mobilier was a key intermediary for the issuance of the first series of bonds—to stress that it was the assurances of the government and the legislative chamber that encouraged their participation: "Do you think that if Emperor Maximilian had presented himself alone as borrower we would have contributed to the 274 million francs that flooded from private hands into the public treasury? […] They spoke to us of French honor, French interests, we heard only France, the call of her voice."[66] Banker and financial commentator André Cochut averred, in a contribution to *Le Temps* in 1865, that it was the "quasi-official pronouncements, issued the very evening before the subscription, which ensured that the family man and the shopkeeper, the assistant and the worker, ran, cash in hand, to take up 500 000 bonds in three days. This is how things are in France: the government spoke, it was done."[67]

In making the case for the worthiness of their claims, these pleas studiously avoided reference to what many deemed the most appealing part of the loan issuance: the lottery chances attached to the certificates. The lottery prizes were phenomenal—for a 340-franc bond, as much as 500,000 francs could be won at a time. These opportunities added a new popular character—in both senses of the word—to the loan issuance. Drawings, held in concert halls and other public venues in the first half of 1865, were widely advertised and well attended. A spate of operations sprang up to broker the Mexican bonds in fractions, capitalizing on promises of bonanzas and what many viewed as an implicit government guarantee to push portions as low as ten francs, or schemes that pooled the modest outlays of multiple buyers, onto interested purchasers.[68] Such practices were often illegal, because they distorted the balance of lottery and investment, transforming the economic hopes materialized in a piece of paper from respectable and prudent investment into a frivolous lottery ticket. So many dubious ventures clustered around the issuance, in fact, that Chevalier felt pressed in 1867 to offer guidance that aimed to prevent future lottery issuances from degrading into cheap and ephemeral commodities.[69]

Critics of the Mexican adventure were quick to seize on the debt's lottery aspect as a key component of their opposition. Deputy Ernest Picard labeled the loan "a flagrant violation of the law," referring to longstanding injunctions against the circulation of foreign lotteries on French soil.[70] Indeed, in April 1865, just as the second series of bonds was being released, a member of the Direction de la Sûreté Générale wrote to the Minister of the Interior to express concerns that the loan amounted to a foreign lottery, which should be prohibited not only on the basis of law but also because it constituted easy pickings for the government's opposition.[71] But hostility to the loan was expressed on moral as well as legal grounds. For opposition deputy Jules Favre, these bonds were a clear effort to manipulate the public into doing something it was otherwise inclined against. The lottery amounted to a form of coercion, its "irresistibility" obviating the voluntary character of investment and recalling longstanding distinctions between compulsive taxation and consensual lending. But the social aspect of this irresistibility was particularly concerning to this republican opponent of the regime. Lacking any "natural" means of attracting capital, he declared, the government instead opts to "enflame passions," "speculate on the credulity and eagerness of the lower classes." In the process, they unfairly distributed the weight of public costs, burdening the most vulnerable: "the lowliest passerby, the humblest citizen, the most modest, the poorest—that's who's being called on to give their 340 francs, 340 francs that would win them 500 000!"[72] Even as he asserted the injustice of a public finance regime that leaned over much on small savers, Favre's criticism betrayed concern that the spread of this kind of investment enrolled ever greater numbers of people into the projects of the imperial government, further entangling the populace and the imperial regime.

From the perspective of the politics of public debt, the Mexican adventure was both distinctive and consequential. Liberalization measures introduced under the Second Empire meant that it was one of the first significant foreign ventures opened for debate in the Corps Législatif, giving a unique platform to considerations on the legal and ethical parameters of public finance. Having acceded to innovative measures in order to transfer money from private into public hands and suborned, however tacitly, the generalization of an investing public, the state found itself obliged to accept responsibility and accede to partial repayment of investors in 1868—an unprecedented step that was not to be repeated.[73] These loans were thus "public" in several registers. This is not to say that investors uniformly understood themselves as partnering with the government in a national project. Geneviève Massa-Gille notes observations from contemporaries like those of the *procureur général* of Amiens in July 1865, who opined that "Capital has no opinion. The success of this operation lies entirely with the credit enjoyed by its promoters [the Comptoir d'Escompte] and with the growing fashion for these operations—cleverer than they are moral—that are reigniting the thrills and dangers of the lottery. How can anyone resist the appeal of 14% interest and the chance to win 500 000 francs?"[74] It was the lottery, redemption bonuses, and inordinately high returns rather than any feeling of imperial ambition that made the Ottoman loans—the estimated two billion *valeurs à turban* circulating in France in the 1870s—typical of *petits portefeuilles*.[75] The interventions of Chevalier and others ensured that the legality of these bonds was no longer contested from the 1870s. They were an important part of the broader endeavor of economic liberals, to which we now turn, to make public debt respectable by defending its economic utility and political virtues.

Domestic Legitimacy and Imperial Power

During the Third Republic, Chevalier's efforts in this arena were taken up by Paul Leroy-Beaulieu—Chevalier's material as well as intellectual heir, since he married Chevalier's daughter in 1870 and succeeded his father-in-law as professor of political economy at the Collège de France in 1879. Leroy-Beaulieu also spoke up in favor of lottery bonds, commending the way their elements of thrill and excitement "made saving attractive, turned it into a dream, appealing not only to the reason, but to the imagination."[76] In response to those who argued that reliance on fortune and chance undermined healthy economic behavior, Leroy-Beaulieu argued that luck was unavoidably central to the capitalist endeavor, linking the investment practices of the popular classes to those of more substantial *rentiers*. Lottery bonds ensured both financial and affective investment in the nation, strengthening *la petite épargne* as a discursive and material weapon against what Leroy-Beaulieu and his fellow economists viewed as the creep of "state socialism," with its ambitions for more aggressive wealth extraction through tax reform.[77]

This defense of public debt was far from a purely domestic issue. Leroy-Beaulieu distinctly sharpened the imperialist tone of the French rhapsody. In the *Traité* the economist spoke specifically to his fellow citizens' enthusiasm for investment in the debt of other sovereign states. In a chronicle of the numerous instances in which French capital ventured abroad had found itself jeopardized by default, Leroy-Beaulieu moved smoothly from targets of colonial ambition like Tunisia to semi-imperialized Egypt to Turkey, Greece, Spain, and Portugal, constructing a category of debtor polities defined by the inability to maturely manage their national finances. Faced with such counterparties, he asserted, "a powerful country whose lending citizens are dispossessed by a failing state should never hesitate to intervene officially and vigorously [...] It should not even hesitate to use force in order to subject the failing state's finances to its own control."[78]

Contemporary critics of such practices skewered them as coercive measures imposed by strong states against weaker ones.[79] For Leroy-Beaulieu, in contrast, such intervention "ought not to be considered a humiliation or a calamity by a failing country. To the contrary, it is a great boon, like legal guardianship for an inexperienced and spendthrift minor."[80] When "old countries [...] those immense factories of capital," he wrote elsewhere, extend their resources into other countries through investment, they are engaging in profitable behavior, yet also in "a humane act of solidarity." Countries that abused this credit, so generously offered, "banished themselves definitively from the community of civilized nations" and deserved harsh correctives.[81] In the work for which Leroy-Beaulieu is still more famous, *De la colonisation chez les peuples modernes* (1874), he suggested that the exportation of capital could indeed substitute for colonization by European settlers.[82] The second edition of his book emphasized that this *colonisation des capitaux* (investment colonization) was particularly suited to France; although devoid of emigrants as a result of demographic stagnation, "France has capital in abundance; she lets it travel willingly; her trusting hands disseminate it to the four corners of the universe." Another advantage of capital exports in a democratic age was the way in which it made empire accessible to a growing fraction of the population: "every person who saves some money, a small employee, a farmer, a worker, a spinster or a widow, can, while staying close to their fireplace and without any great knowledge of geography, powerfully contribute to colonization, to the exploitation of the globe."[83]

The connection drawn by Leroy-Beaulieu between the accessibility of financial instruments at home, which before 1880 would have most often taken the form of public bonds, and French projects of expansion or domination abroad illustrates well the political rather than economic significance of public debt in nineteenth-century France. Given the high and rising level of wealth concentration, the macroeconomic benefits of expanding the market for public debt, by permitting ever smaller levels of subscription or by tolerating the resort to morally dubious methods of commercialization such as lottery bonds, were limited: the bulk of investment in public debt continued to be provided by a narrow, extremely wealthy section of society.[84] Yet making public debt appear accessible helped render it acceptable and enhanced its sacrality in an age of mass political participation. It also helped secure consent for foreign activism, as a means of opening new markets for investment or of enforcing the payment of existing debts, and to justify a major cause of national public indebtedness. The eventual fiasco of the Mexican bonds was soon superseded by the success of the loans issued by the fledgling Third Republic to settle the disastrous war of 1870–1871 against Prussia, a second alleged financial miracle after that of the 1810s, which consolidated the regime's legitimacy and reinforced the belief in the political virtues of the dissemination of public debt.

Hence the paradox that although French republicans of the early nineteenth century abhorred public debt, the Third Republic after 1870 became the golden age of the *rentiers*. Rather than disown the politics of public debt elaborated under the Bourbon Restoration, the July Monarchy, and above all the Second Empire, the new regime maintained and refurbished a complex array of legal and commercial mechanisms that turned public debt into a commodity at least apparently within the reach of every purse. The only lesson drawn from the Mexican fiasco was a greater prudence in the endorsement by the French state of public debt issued even by friendly foreign states, or at least a tendency to reduce, without extinguishing, the impression given to the public that the state implicitly guaranteed such debt. According to its *rapporteur*, the law of 25 May 1872 that repealed restrictions on the issuance of foreign public debt was precisely intended to absolve the French state of "moral responsibility" in case of default. However, the French government could still influence the success or failure of such operations, since even after foreign bonds were legally issued the ministers of finance and foreign affairs retained the right to authorize their quotation on the Paris stock exchange—a procedure that ensured that the offices of these ministries received thousands of demands for compensation and protection from bondholders throughout the final decades of the nineteenth century.[85] Skillful statecraft often relies on complex ambiguities, and the Third Republic used public indebtedness very skillfully indeed, domestically to consolidate its legitimacy, and internationally as a pretext for colonial expansion (Tunisia, 1881) or to secure geopolitical advantages (*emprunts russes* from 1888).

* * *

The rehabilitation of public debt in France after 1815 was indeed a rhapsody—a single movement with disconnected parts, exuberant and rooted or affecting to be rooted in popular sentiments, and evoking a distant past—rather than a harmonious economic theory or unified economic practice. Echoing anxieties about the political implications of the rise of commerce before 1789, it remained informed throughout the period by a common concern with the financial means of reconciling politics—in the sense of a powerful state, domestically and internationally—with modern capitalism. Yet it experienced substantial and consequential variations, not least an increasing emphasis on the dissemination of public debt, national and later foreign, across French society. This diffusion served pragmatic and political ends, enhancing the capacities of the French state while enrolling ever larger numbers of the country's residents materially (and perhaps ideologically) in the fortunes of successive regimes. Placing commodification at the heart of the story of the success of French public finance, as well, perhaps, as at the heart of a process of turning peasants into Frenchmen, is of both historical and historiographical significance for the study of public debt, emphasizing the importance of being attentive to the multiple publics it constituted and the material practices involved in their construction, as well as the ways that the packaging and merchandising of that debt mattered to both investment, its regulation, and its politicization.

A desire to democratize the possession of public debt should not, however, be equated with an embrace of republican egalitarianism. Indeed, as the anxieties that surrounded the development and distribution of lottery bonds indicate, the diversification of the bondholding class—the promise that for steady payments of five francs a month, or with only a tenth of a City of Paris bond, anyone could be a *rentier*—could perpetuate rather than level structural inequalities. From Talleyrand to Leroy-Beaulieu, the composers of the rhapsody of public debt favored an enlightened monarchical solution to the French constitutional quandary, even if they occasionally tolerated (Talleyrand in the 1790s, Thiers and Leroy-Beaulieu after 1870) formally republican institutions. The tune continued to be played, amplified even, under the democratic Third Republic, but it suggests that the latter's economic culture was far from exclusively republican. Approaching the political economy and political culture of Third Republic France from the perspective of public debt reveals potent continuities in the capacity to imagine and construct debt's publics, even as those publics undergo significant transformation. The Abbé Sieyès's intuition in the 1790s that the solution of the public debt conundrum lay in either "a republican monarchy or a monarchical republic," rather than in a virtuous republic, proved prescient.[86]

Notes

1. R. Dudley Baxter, *National Debts* (London: R. J. Bush, 1871), 81.
2. Eugene N. White, "Making the French Pay: The Cost and Consequences of the Napoleonic Reparations," *European Review of Economic History* 5, no. 3 (2001): 337–65; Ayla Aglan, Michel Margairaz and Philippe Verheyde, *1816, ou la genèse de la foi publique. La fondation de la Caisse des dépôts et consignations* (Geneva: Droz, 2006); Zheng Kang, "L'État constructeur du marché financier," in *Le marché financier français au XIXe siècle*, eds. Pierre-Cyrille Hautcœur and Georges Gallais-Hamonno (Paris: Publications de la Sorbonne, 2007), 1:159–93 and Jacques-Marie Vaslin, "Le siècle d'or de la rente perpétuelle française," in *Le marché financier français*, 2:117–208; Richard Bonney, "The Apogee and Fall of the French Rentier Regime, 1801–1914," in *Paying for the Liberal State: The Rise of Public Finance in Nineteenth-Century Europe*, eds. José-Luis Cardoso and Pedro Lains (Cambridge: Cambridge University Press, 2010); Michel Lutfalla, "La rente, de Waterloo à Sedan," in *Histoire de la dette publique en France*, ed. Michel Lutfalla (Paris: Garnier, 2017), 81–104; Jerome Greenfield, "Public Finance and the Making of the Modern French State, 1799–1853," (PhD diss., University of Cambridge, 2017), esp. chapters 2 and 3.
3. See Rebecca Spang, Chap. 2, this volume.
4. On the concept of fiscal-military state, see John Brewer, *The Sinews of Power: War, Money and the English State, 1688–1783* (London: Routledge, 1989) and Aaron Graham and Patrick Walsh, eds., *The British Fiscal Military States, 1660–c.1783* (London: Routledge, 2016); on the model's applicability to France after 1789, see Jerome Greenfield, *The Making of a Fiscal-Military State in Post-Revolutionary France* (Cambridge: Cambridge University Press, forthcoming).
5. Istvan Hont, "The Rhapsody of Public Debt: David Hume and Voluntary State Bankruptcy," in *Political Discourse in Early Modern Britain*, eds.

Nicholas Phillipson and Quentin Skinner (Cambridge: Cambridge University Press, 1993), 321–48; Michael Sonenscher, "The Nation's Debt and the Birth of the Modern Republic: The French Fiscal Deficit and the Politics of the Revolution of 1789," *History of Political Thought* 18, no. 1 (1997): 64–103.
6. Michael Sonenscher, *Before the Deluge: Public Debt, Inequality, and the Intellectual Origins of the French Revolution* (Princeton: Princeton University Press, 2009).
7. Paul Leroy-Beaulieu, *Traité de la science des finances* (Paris: Guillaumin et Cie, 1877), 2:470. On Leroy-Beaulieu, see Dan Warshaw, *Paul Leroy-Beaulieu and Established Liberalism in France* (DeKalb: Northern Illinois University Press, 1991).
8. On the persistent prevalence of negative views on public debt among British classical economists, see Nancy Churchman, *David Ricardo on Public Debt* (Basingstoke: Palgrave, 2001) and Takuo Dome, *The Political Economy of Public Finance in Britain 1767–1873* (London: Routledge, 2004); on the unpopularity of public debt, see Boyd Hilton, *The Age of Atonement: The Influence of Evangelicalism on Social and Economic Thought* (Oxford: Oxford University Press, 1991) and Eugenio Biagini, *Liberty, Retrenchment and Reform: Popular Liberalism in the Age of Gladstone* (Cambridge: Cambridge University Press, 1992).
9. Archives Diplomatiques, La Courneuve, 752SUP/144: Valeurs étrangères, impôts, loteries: Letter from Baron de Beust to Comte Apponyi, 9 June 1868; Letter from Duc de Gramont, Ambassador in Vienna, to Ministry of Foreign Affairs, 18 June 1868. On these rhetorical strategies, see Nicolas Barreyre and Nicolas Delalande, Chap. 20, this volume.
10. "État indiquant le classement par catégories des propriétaires des rentes françaises à 5% subsistantes au 1er janvier 1830," Centre des Archives Économiques et Financières [hereafter CAEF], B 49463. See also Vaslin, "Le Siècle d'or de la rente," and Zheng Kang and Thierno Seck, "Les épargnants et le marché financier," in *Le Marché financier français*, 2:314–53. Pierre-Cyrille Hautcoeur, "Les transformations du crédit en France au XIXe siècle," *Romantisme*, no. 151 (2011): 23–38, 36.
11. Leroy-Beaulieu, *Traité de la science des finances*, 2:137.
12. Alfred Neymarck, "La répartition et la diffusion de l'épargne française sur les valeurs mobilières françaises et étrangères," *Bulletin de l'Institut international de statistique* 6, no. 1 (1892): 205–223, 208–210. See also Adeline Daumard, "Les placements étrangers dans les patrimoines français au XIXe siècle," *Revue d'histoire économique et sociale* 52, no.4 (1974): 526–46.
13. Figures from Thomas Piketty, Gilles Postel-Vinay, Jean-Laurent Rosenthal, "Inherited vs. Self-Made Wealth: Theory and Evidence from a Rentier

Society (Paris, 1872–1937)," *Explorations in Economic History* 51 (2014): 21–40.

14. The magnitude of Britain's capital exports was comparable to France's until the 1870s, and superior after that date until 1914, but the bulk of British exports of capital took the form of private securities, rather than foreign public bonds or investment in a steadily decreasing national debt; see Albert H. Imlah, "British Balance of Payments and Capital Exports," *Economic History Review* 5, no. 2 (1952): 208–39 and Maurice Lévy-Leboyer, "La balance des paiements et l'exportation des capitaux français," in *La position internationale de la France. Aspects économiques et financiers, XIXe-XXe siècles*, ed. Maurice Lévy-Leboyer (Paris: EHESS, 1977), 75–142 on the level of capital exports, and Brinley Thomas, "The Historical Record of International Capital Movements to 1913," in *Capital Movements and Economic Development*, ed. John H. Adler (London: Palgrave, 1967), 3–32, on the preference of British investors for private securities.

15. Influential statements of this traditional view include Herbert Feis, *Europe, the World's Banker, 1870–1914: An Account of European Foreign Investment and the Connection of World Finance with Diplomacy before the War* (New Haven: Yale University Press, 1930), 33–59, 118–59 and Rondo Cameron, *France and the Economic Development of Europe, 1800–1914* (London: Routledge, 2000 [1961]), 64–88, 404–24; for work undercutting the narrative of *dirigisme* in French foreign investments, see René Girault, *Emprunts russes et investissements français en Russie* (Paris: Publications de la Sorbonne, 1973); Jessica Siegel, *For Peace and Money: French and British Finance in the Service of Tsars and Commissars* (Oxford: Oxford University Press, 2012); Antoine Parent and Christophe Rault, "The Influences Affecting French Assets Abroad Prior to 1914," *Journal of Economic History* 64, no.2 (2004): 328–62; Rui Esteves, "The Belle Époque of International Finance. French Capital Exports 1880–1914," Department of Economics Discussion Paper Series 534 (University of Oxford, 2011); David Le Bris and Amir Rezaee, "French Foreign Investment in the Late 19th Century: A Modern Portfolio Theory Analysis," https://pdfs.semanticscholar.org/c98a/b3110164942465e601126b3c2ce9d66fc586.pdf [accessed November 16, 2019].

16. On the Mexican side of this "adventure," see Juan Flores, Chap. 5, this volume.

17. Jerome Greenfield, "Financing a New Order: The Payment of Reparations by Restoration France, 1817–1818," *French History* 30, no. 3 (2016): 376–400.

18. Jean-Baptise Say, *Traité d'économie politique* (Paris, 1803), 2:514 and *Traité d'économie politique* (Paris, 1826), 3:242–3, 251; on the Rothschilds'

role in the development of public credit after 1815 and the antisemitic responses it elicited, see Niall Ferguson, *The House of Rothschild*, 2 vols (New York: Penguin, 1998), 1:111–38.

19. See for instance James [Jean-Jacob] Fazy, "Examen et réfutation de l'ouvrage de M. Laffitte," in *Opuscules financiers sur l'effet des privilèges, des emprunts publics et des conversions sur le crédit de l'industrie en France* (Paris: J. J. Naudin, 1826), 109–268.
20. Jacques Laffitte, *Réflexions sur la réduction de la rente* (Paris: Bossange, 1824), 20–1.
21. Sonenscher, "The Nation's Debt," 75–8.
22. Bertrand Gille, *La banque en France au 19e siècle. Recherches historiques* (Geneva: Droz, 1970), 111.
23. Adolphe Thiers, *Histoire de la Révolution française* (Paris: Lecointe et Duret, 1823–1827), 1:211, 278; on the national debt and the *assignats*, see Rebecca Spang, *Stuff and Money in the Time of the French Revolution* (Cambridge, Mass.: Harvard University Press, 2015), esp. chs 1 and 2, and Chap. 2 of this volume.
24. Adolphe Thiers, *Law* (1826), which he later expanded into a *Histoire de Law* (Paris: J. Hetzel et Cie, 1858); on Thiers's economic culture and ideas, see David Todd, *Free Trade and its Enemies in France, 1814–1851* (Cambridge: Cambridge University Press, 2015), 125–9.
25. Thiers to Johann Friedrich Cotta, 1 Aug. 1824, in Robert Marquant, *Thiers et le baron Cotta. Étude sur la collaboration de Thiers à la Gazette d'Augsbourg* (Paris: Presses Universitaires de France, 1959), 157–60.
26. Edward Blount, *Memoirs*, ed. Stuart J. Reid (London: Longmans, Green, and Co, 1902), 252; on budgetary orthodoxy among British liberals, see Biagini, *Liberty, Retrenchment and Reform*.
27. Marc Flandreau and Juan Flores, "Bonds and Brands: Foundations of Sovereign Debt Markets, 1820–1830," *Journal of Economic History* 69, no. 3 (2009): 646–84; on Latin American bonds, see Frank G. Dawson, *The First Latin American Debt Crisis: The City of London and the 1822–25 Loan Bubble* (New Haven: Yale University Press, 1990).
28. Laffitte, *Réflexions*, 40, 155–6.
29. Rafe Blaufarb, "The Western Question: The Geopolitics of Latin American Independence," *American Historical Review* 112, no. 3 (2007): 742–63.
30. Michael P. Costleloe, *Bonds and Bondholders: British Investors and Mexico's Foreign Debt, 1824–1888* (Westport: Greenwood Press, 2003), 14–16.
31. Chancery Court Pleadings for Gabriel Marie Doloret vs Charles Herring, William Graham, John Diston Powles [the agents for the loan], and Simon Bolivar [president of Gran Columbia], 16 and 17 January 1823, Kew (London), The National Archives, C 13/2173/15 and C 13/2175/28. Doloret was a notorious swindler, who had been revoked from his position

as *receveur général* in the Somme after he embezzled public monies in 1818; see Pierre-François Pinaud, *Les receveurs généraux des finances, 1790–1865* (Geneva: Droz, 1990), 117.
32. Costleloe, *Bonds and Bondholders*, 12.
33. Paravey to Dalberg, 4 Nov 1824, Worms Stadtarchiv [hereafter WS], Dalberg MSS, 159/376/7.
34. Karl-Georg Faber, "Aristokratie und Finanz. Das Pariser Bankhaus Paravey et Compagnie (1819–1828)," *Vierteljahrschrift für Sozial- und Wirtschaftsgeschichte* 57, no.2 (1970): 145–230.
35. Talleyrand to Dalberg, 30 June and 13 Sep. 1829, *Talleyrand und der Herzog von Dalberg: unveröffentlichte Briefe 1816–1832*, ed. Erberhard Ernst (Frankfort: Peter Lang, 1987), 68, 80; on Talleyrand and Dalberg's losses arising out of the Haitian loan, see documents on the liquidation of the Banque Paravey in Roubaix, Centre des Archives du Monde du Travail [hereafter CAMT], 132 AQ 73, file 1.
36. Charles-Maurice de Talleyrand-Périgord, *Mémoire sur les relations commerciales des États-Unis avec l'Angleterre* (London, 1808), 20–1; Charles-Maurice de Talleyrand-Périgord, *Mémoires: 1754–1815*, eds. Paul-Louis Couchoud and Jean-Paul Couchoud (Paris: Plon, 1982), 90–91.
37. See correspondence on Spanish bonds, 1820–1821, in WS, Dalberg MSS 159/376/2, and "Emprunt mexicain," 16 June 1826, on the purchase of seven Mexican bonds for a nominal value of £1000, in WS, Dalberg MSS, 159/382/7 and Paravey to Rothschild, 7 Apr. 1827, on the use of 21 Mexican coupons to settle Dalberg's account, in London, The Rothschild Archive, XI/38/200; and Duc de Dalberg, "Le Mexique vu du Cabinet des Tuileries," [1828], SW, Dalberg MSS, 159/748.
38. Jean-François Brière, *Haïti et la France, 1804–1848. Le rêve brisé* (Paris: Karthala, 2008), esp. 161–6.
39. *Le Producteur*, 3 (1826), 221–52 and 4 (1826), 5–19.
40. Jean Walch, *Michel Chevalier, économiste saint-simonien* (Paris: Vrin, 1975), 33, 51; see also Michael Drolet, "Industry, Class and Society: A Historiographic Reinterpretation of Michel Chevalier," *English Historical Review* 123, no. 504 (2008): 1229–71.
41. Adolphe Blaise, "Cours d'économie politique du Collège de France par M. Michel Chevalier," *Journal des économistes* 1 (1842): 204–8.
42. Michel Chevalier, "Discours d'ouverture de l'année 1842–43," in *Cours d'économie politique* (Paris: Capelle, 1842–1850), 2:1–24 (esp. 13–17); Michel Chevalier "Discours d'ouverture de l'année 1843–44" and "Discours d'ouverture de l'année 1844–45," in *Cours d'économie politique* (Paris: Capelle, 1855–1866), 1:63–107 (esp. 65, 95).
43. Edward Shawcross, *France, Mexico and Informal Empire in Latin America, 1820–1867* (Basingstoke: Palgrave Macmillan, 2018), esp. 119–31.

44. It may also have contributed to inspiring the spirited defence of public debt by Lorenz von Stein, who had studied in Paris in the 1840s and expressed a preference for the "French literature" over "English" works about public debt in his *Lehrbuch der Finanzwissenchaft* (Leipzig, 1860), 460–2; on favorable views of public indebtedness and the proliferation of treatises on public finance in Germany, which may in turn have inspired Leroy-Beaulieu's *Traité*, see Carl-Ludwig Holtfrerich, "Public Debt in Post-1850 German Economic Thought vis-a-vis the Pre-1850 British Classical School," *German Economic Review* 15, no. 1 (2013): 62–83.
45. "Les dettes communales," *Bulletin de statistique et de législation comparée* 32 (1892): 275–300. On the significance of municipal debt, see Noam Maggor and Stephen W. Sawyer, Chap. 10, this volume.
46. CAMT 2001 026 649: Rapports annuels du Crédit Foncier, Exercice 1887.
47. See Éric Monnet and Blaise Truong-Loï, Chap. 19, this volume.
48. Archives de Paris, Chambre de Commerce et d'Industrie, 2ETP/3/6/12 3: Étude sur la question des loteries commerciales, Lettre à M. le Garde des Sceaux, 31 décembre 1835.
49. Henri Levy-Ullmann, "Lottery Bonds in France and in the Principal Countries of Europe," *Harvard Law Review* 9, no. 6 (Jan. 25, 1896): 386–405, drawn from his longer study: *Traité des obligations à primes et à lots* (Paris: Larose, 1895). Other key works include Georges-Marie-René Frèrejouan Du Saint, *Jeu et pari, au point de vue civil, pénal et réglementaire: loteries et valeurs à lots, jeux de bourse, marchés à terme* (Paris: Larose, 1893); A. Goda, *De l'aléa. Jeux, opérations de bourse, loteries et tombolas, valeurs à lots, Crédit Foncier* (Paris: Delamotte Fils & Cie, 1882).
50. Geneviève Massa-Gille, *Histoire des emprunts de la ville de Paris, 1814–1875* (Paris: Commission des travaux historiques de la Ville de Paris, 1973); see also Georges Gallais-Hamanno, "La création d'un marché obligataire moderne. Les emprunts de la ville de Paris au XIXe siècle," in *Le marché financier français*, 2:263–362.
51. Lottery bonds for the Congo Free State were permitted on the Paris Bourse in 1888 as part of a land exchange in Africa between France and Belgium in 1885. See the question and answer in the *Journal Officiel*, Chambre des Députés, 17 juillet 1888, 2129–31.
52. Alfred Neymarck, "Rapport," *Congrès international des valeurs mobilières*, 5 vols. (Paris: Paul Dupont, 1901), 1:361–2. These included loans for Austria, Egypt, Serbia, Russia, and others, as well as several European cities. See also Lucien Louvet, *Code des valeurs à lots. Notice sur les procédés de tirages* (Paris: A. Durand et Pedone-Lauriel, 1891).
53. J. Durant de Saint-André, "La loterie et ses applications les plus remarquables," *Revue générale d'administration* 39 (octobre 1890): 129–51.

54. "Discussion, mercredi 6 juin. Émission et négociation des valeurs à lots, publication des tirages," *Congrès international des valeurs mobilières* (1901), 1:129–36, 130.
55. Jean-Baptiste Josseau, *Traité du crédit foncier* (Paris: Cosse, Marchal et Billard, 1872).
56. See the debate on the issuance of lottery bonds for the Panama Canal: *Journal officiel*, Chambre des Députés, 27 April 1888, 1349–75. Summaries of diverse positions and legislation on lottery bonds can be found in the contributions of Alfred Neymarck, Eugène Lacombe, and Emmanuel Vidal in *Congrès international des va-leurs mobilières*, vols. 3 and 5 (1901).
57. The study was carried out by Pierre des Essars, head of the Bank of France's economic services division; cited by Edmond Théry, "Les Valeurs mobilières en France," *Congrès international des valeurs mobilières*, 2 (1901): 40.
58. Procureur Général Comte de Casablanca, Rapport au Sénat, séance du 15 février 1870, *Journal officiel*, 16 February 1870, 317.
59. See, for example, Michel Chevalier, Rapport au Sénat, séance du 28 juin 1870, *Journal officiel*, 29 June 1870, 1120.
60. Steven Topik, "When Mexico Had the Blues: A Transatlantic Tale of Bonds, Bankers, and Nationalists, 1862–1910," *American Historical Review* 105, no. 3 (2000): 714–38; Michele Cunningham, *Mexico and the Foreign Policy of Napoléon III* (Basingstoke: Palgrave, 2001).
61. Albert Gigot, *Consultation sur les bases et le mode de répartition de l'indemnité due aux Français établis au Mexique, en vertu des traités du 10 avril 1864 et du 27 septembre 1865* (Paris: Bourdier, 1867); Gustave Niox, *Expédition du Mexique, 1861–1867. Récit politique et militaire* (Paris: Libraire Militaire de J. Dumaine, 1874). On foreign oversight of state finances by European financial commissions in this period, see Ali Coşkun Tunçer, Chap. 6, and Malak Labib, Chap. 7, this volume.
62. Brunement, *À Messieurs les Députés au Corps Législatif* (Paris: A. Chaix, 1868), 3. The Comptoir d'Escompte led a consortium of more than 35 French and foreign banking houses charged with rolling out the loan: Adolphe Pinard, *Lettre à Messieurs les Députés au Corps Législatif* (Paris: Chaix, 1867); *Exposé des faits concernant le traité conclu le 28 septembre 1865 pour la vente des obligations mexicaines du Trésor entre M. le Ministre des Finances et M. Pinard* (Paris: Chaix, 1867); Conseil d'État, Section du Contentieux, *Mémoire pour M. Alphonse-Louis Pinard… contre le Ministre des Finances* (Paris: Chaix, 1868).
63. Account of the speeches of Corta and Rouher, 9 and 10 April 1865, in Niox, *Expédition du Mexique, 1861–1867*, 494. See also C. Menut, *Réflexions sur le sort des valeurs mexicaines* (Évreux: A. Hérissey, 1868); Jules Forfelier, *Consultation pour les souscripteurs aux emprunts mexicains* (Paris: Chez l'auteur, 1866), 10.

64. Points raised by A. Picard, *Lettre à son excellence M. Rouher, Ministre d'État, pour les porteurs d'obligations mexicaines* (Paris: Charles Schiller, 1868), 3.
65. Forfelier, *Consultation pour les souscripteurs*, 20.
66. *Les obligataires de l'emprunt mexicain dans les Pyrénées-Orientales à M. Isaac Péreire, le 27 mars 1868* (Perpignan: Imprimerie de Tastu, 1868).
67. André Cochut, *Le Temps*, 14 June 1865.
68. The journalist Timothée Trimm ran one such operation from the pages of *Le Petit Journal* (see "Partageons-nous les cinq cent mille francs," *Le Petit Journal*, June 20, 1865). Trimm was colluding with one Millaud in the profitable, but ultimately illegal, scheme. Both were fined at the end of 1865. See *Bulletin de la Cour Impériale de Paris* (1865) 2:896–907.
69. "Note," Apr. 1867, Paris, Archives Nationales 44 AP 20.
70. "Corps Législatif," *Le Temps*, 11 June 1865.
71. "Emprunt Mexicain. Note transmise au Ministère de l'Intérieur par la Direction Générale de la Sûreté Publique," *Documents pour servir à l'histoire du Second Empire* (Paris: E. Lachaud, 1872), 278–80.
72. "Corps Législatif," *Le Moniteur universel*, 9 June 1865, 768. Favre stuck to these arguments when considering issuances for the Suez Canal later in the empire as well: "Corps Législatif," *Le Moniteur universel*, 17 June 1868, 858.
73. See Papiers de la Commission de l'emprunt contracté par Maximilien empereur du Mexique (1864–1869): F30 1594–1599, now in CAEF.
74. Geneviève Massa-Gille, "Les capitaux français et l'expédition du Mexique," *Revue d'histoire diplomatique* 79 (1965): 194–253.
75. Comte de Vogüé to Minister of Foreign Affairs, 1873, CAEF, F30 356.
76. Paul Leroy-Beaulieu, *Traité de la science des finances* (Paris: Guillaumin et Cie., 1906), 2:369–70.
77. Nicolas Delalande, *Les Batailles de l'impôt. Consentement et résistances de 1789 à nos jours* (Paris: Seuil, 2011); Stephen Sawyer, "A Fiscal Revolution: Statecraft in France's Early Third Republic," *American Historical Review* 121, no. 4 (2016): 1141–66.
78. Leroy-Beaulieu, *Traité de la science des finances*, 2:569.
79. Lawyer Michel Kebedgy described international financial control commissions as violations of sovereignty "always taken against weak states, never against strong ones." ("De la protection des créanciers d'un État étranger," *Journal du droit international* 21 (1894): 59–72, 65). Remarks by Arthur Raffalovich at the International Congress on Securities in 1900 that "state intervention beyond the diplomatic has only been taken against small countries—in other words, when there wasn't much danger" provoked laughter from the assembly ("D'une entente internationale pour l'émission et la négociation des valeurs internationales," *Congrès international des valeurs mobilières*, 1:203).

80. Leroy-Beaulieu, *Traité de la science des finances*, 2:569.
81. Leroy-Beaulieu, préface, in Maurice Lewandowski, *De la protection des capitaux empruntés en France par les États étrangers ou les sociétés* (Paris: Guillaumin et Cie, 1896), viii, x.
82. Minutes of the Section d'économie politique, 19 Mar. 1870, Paris, Archives de l'Institut, Académie des Sciences Morales et Politiques, 2D5, fos 35–8.
83. Paul Leroy-Beaulieu, *De la colonisation chez les peuples modernes* (Paris: Guillaumin et Cie, 1882), 536–41.
84. The share of national wealth owned by the richest 10 percent rose from c. 80 percent in 1870 to c. 90 percent in 1910; in Thomas Piketty, *Capital in the Twenty-First Century*, trans. Arthur Goldhammer (Cambridge, Mass.: Harvard University Press, 2014), 314.
85. The need for an administrative authorization to quote foreign public debt and other financial instruments had been introduced by Villèle during the negotiation of Haiti's loan in November 1825; see Folder "Admission à la cote officielle des titres des emprunts étrangers, 1873–1890," in Archives Diplomatiques, La Courneuve, 752SUP/145.
86. Sonenscher, "The Nation's Debt," 307.

PART II

Global Capital, Imperial Expansions, and Changing Sovereignties (1860s–1914)

By the mid-nineteenth century, Europe had become a financial powerhouse ready—and eager—to export capital throughout the world. The period from the 1860s to the 1910s has been identified in the historiography as the "first globalization," a liberal regime imposed on the world by trade, finance, and military imperialism. It was characterized by the legal protection of property rights, the gold standard, soon its international financial controls, and threats of "supersanctions."

Yet this aerial view does little to account for the *liberal debt regime* that became hegemonic during those years—or its sudden collapse with World War I. Part II proposes to dig deeper, and the historical cases explored here allow us to make a few key points. First, the local embeddedness of political power relations and debates were crucial in shaping the imposition of a particular debt within the larger debt regime. This entails the necessary attention to the different interest groups, within debtor countries and within creditor countries, to explain the particular fate of a public debt, and whether European financial markets were accessible and at what conditions. This also gave importance to a new class of intermediaries—soon to be an interest group in themselves: experts, indispensable to make particular countries "readable" for European financial markets and imperial governments. Their actions are also a good place to examine the gap between the liberal discourses and the actual practices of the debt regime. Finally, public debt had powerful redistributing effects, spatially across regions and socially among classes; and those effects had a powerful impact on the legitimacy of political regimes—as even France and Britain would realize during World War I.

Chapter 5, on Latin America, picks up the story where Chap. 1 ended, after independence left the former Spanish colonies without the financial institutions that had sustained them. Their rocky introduction in international financial markets led to many defaults. Yet this never prevented access to European credit. As Juan Flores argues from the cases of Mexico and Peru, the explanation lies in interest-group politics.

In Chap. 6, Ali Coşkun Tunçer goes further in identifying the politics of those interest groups, but also the geopolitics of great-powers rivalries in the type of financial control and debt settlement strictures imposed on the Ottoman Empire during that period. He shows how international control could be leveraged for domestic reasons. Yet this proved a dangerous game, invisibly undermining the very political legitimacy of the regime.

The building of knowledge, and of a group of experts able to wield it, was at the heart of that kind of political wrangling, at the intersection of geopolitical games and local practices. Chapter 7, on Egypt, revisits one of the seed cases for institutions of international financial control by focusing on the experts, and how they attempted to impose competing processes on a very different accounting tradition they did not understand—often against their own liberal discourses. As Malak Labib shows, Egypt boosted a new kind of experts, who would act as a new interest group and influence the elaboration of international law.

Leigh Gardner's Chap. 8 lies at the intersection of expertise and sovereignty. Focusing on four Western African countries—one independent state and three British colonies—she reexamines the question of an "empire effect" on access to capital, and shows the crucial role of under-the-radar intermediaries (here, the Crown agents). The incestuous relations between financial actors and government officials go a long way to explain access to credit and the strings attached to it.

In Chap. 9, Dong Yan looks at some of the same groups, but from inside Imperial China. There too, competing political and economic interests both leveraged, and suffered from, recourse to international capital at some key political and military junctures. Access to foreign capital, but also the conditions that came with it created a radical redistribution of wealth and power across the country, sapping the legitimacy of the Emperor.

Such spatial redistribution through public debt was as much true in the "core" as in the "periphery," as Noam Maggor and Stephen Sawyer show for France and the United States. Chapter 10 brings our attention to municipal debts—public but not "sovereign"—and describes a vibrant use of public borrowing to transform cities, with robust public debates around the means and ends of such borrowing. Public debt could reshape the spatial and social distribution of wealth and growth, and everywhere its legitimacy could be contested because of that.

Thus, although public debts (even local, regional, or semi-private railroad debts) could and did put the sovereignty of states at unprecedented risk, they also came with an enlarged sense of the opportunities they could foster. What mattered were its precise modalities, and they had often more to do with politics than finance. What appears throughout the period is the need to constantly renew the legitimacy of public debt and of the political regime attached to it—something that even the great financial centers of the world, London and Paris, would shockingly discover in World War I.

CHAPTER 5

The Entanglements of Domestic Polities: Public Debt and European Interventions in Latin America

Juan H. Flores Zendejas

During the last decades of the nineteenth century, one of the vectors of imperialism, either formal or informal, was external debt, especially when local government defaulted. Middle Eastern and North African cases have been well documented, with diplomatic and military interventions by British and French governments, after which political control could promptly involve a wide range of economic policies, including those related to trade, fiscal and monetary issues, with the active participation of bondholders.[1] Well-known examples include the defaults of Tunisia in 1867, Egypt in 1876 and Morocco in 1903.[2] Other cases did not lead to full political takeover, but involved other forms of quasi-colonial regimes, with creditor countries taking direct control of aspects related to repayment capacity, such as fiscal monitoring or fund management, but also imposing trade liberalization. These cases include the defaults of the

J. H. Flores Zendejas (✉)
Paul Bairoch Institute of Economic History, University of Geneva, Geneva, Switzerland
e-mail: juan.flores@unige.ch

Ottoman Empire in 1875, Greece in 1893, Serbia in 1895 and Liberia in 1912.[3] In the early twentieth century, US military interventions on behalf of its bondholders in Central America echoed these European precedents.[4]

The different mechanisms through which finance and imperialism interacted have long been at the heart of academic debate. For some, finance was a prominent part of what has been termed "informal imperialism" or the "imperialism of free trade."[5] Some scholars have claimed that the British government pursued a preconceived strategy of economic expansion in which banks and investors played a key role.[6] Others have questioned this approach and argued that the British government adopted a mostly pragmatic stance, defined on a case-by-case basis depending on geopolitical interests.[7]

However, this literature has barely analyzed sovereign debt on its own. As a result, we do not know the reasons why certain defaults led to military interventions, or why other coercive actions such as the control of customs receipts or the establishment of foreign control were undertaken in other cases.[8] Answering these questions requires comparing distinct narratives on how default could lead to different types of foreign control or to other types of "direct" or "indirect" rule.[9] An additional complication concerns the fact that even when defaults may have been at the origin of territorial annexation or colonization, this could take place only after several years or even decades, relegating the original debt disputes to a secondary role.[10]

Latin America, often considered as an essential part of the British informal empire, is a good place to explore those issues, as the nexus between debt default and military intervention was mostly absent there—a striking historical fact when we consider that Latin American governments were both frequent borrowers and often "serial defaulters" (to use today's terminology). A short and potentially incomplete explanation suggests that Latin America was not at the center of the political international scene as was, for instance, China.[11] The Middle Eastern region had been a crucial arena in which imperial rivalries contended for supremacy.[12] However, imperial rivalries were more important in Latin America than has been previously acknowledged, particularly between European powers and the US.[13] Already during the closing years of the Spanish Empire, the British navy intervened on a number of fronts, particularly in the Southern cone. Historians have often suggested that in the aftermath of independence, contemporary British policymakers considered the subcontinent as part of their empire, while rivalries with other European countries—and to a certain extent with the US—led to isolated episodes of military intervention. By the late 1820s, the supremacy of Great Britain was implicitly recognized and accepted, even though this status quo remained fragile and was rapidly challenged by internal and external threats.[14]

In this paper I argue that a closer look at the mid-nineteenth-century foreign loans to Latin American governments—the same time span in which cases of defaults leading to foreign interventions prospered—suggests that during this period, different forms of financial control were exerted through private agents. In particular, merchant banks adopted a relevant role in maintaining a certain equilibrium between the defense of British interests—not necessarily compatible with one another—and preserving a close relation with successive local governments to secure collaboration. Merchant banks also interacted with their home governments and with bondholders. While the literature on informal empire in Latin America mainly focuses on Argentina, I will analyze two contrasting cases: Mexico and Peru. In the case of Mexico, the French experience of quasi-colonial control over the country failed largely because French political aims were not aligned with British economic interests, preventing British merchant banks from collaborating with the new political regime established in Mexico. Most Mexican political actors questioned the new loans contracted during that period, as they served mainly to finance the permanence of French troops in Mexico, further fragilizing the political regime imposed by the French government. The loans were thereafter repudiated and Mexico would remain in default during almost two decades.

In Peru, British merchant banks were more effective in channeling the claims of bondholders to defaulting governments whose effect was to mitigate their pressure vis-à-vis the British government. Peru's model succeeded in allowing trade to expand while confining the resolution of default disputes to banks and private investors, though it imposed a harsh limit on Peru's sovereignty, mainly because the government was obliged to cede the management of its natural resources. This solution also explains why, contrary to other regions, governments were able to enjoy a wider margin of maneuver regarding commercial policy. Highlighting the role of private agents in the resolution of default disputes further allows us to revise the literature on gunboat diplomacy and "supersanctions," which argues that the persistent permanent threat of intervention prompted governments to repay their debts, thereby expanding the market for sovereign debt. I conclude that cases of foreign control in Latin America existed—albeit in different forms than in other regions—but that their consequences triggered uncertain results that rather depended upon a complex set of economic and political factors.

Missing "Supersanctions"

Economic history has largely focused on the existence of an "imperial component" that exerted an overwhelming influence on the development of sovereign debt markets, particularly at the end of the nineteenth century. In this vein, borrowing governments perceived the usefulness of gunboat diplomacy and the imposition of "supersanctions"—defined as extreme sanctions of a military, economic or political nature—as an effective threat that served to avert sovereign defaults.[15] The expansion of sovereign debt markets and the fall of risk premia of government bonds in secondary markets are two features attributed to this policy.

However, these claims have been questioned on several fronts. Cases of gunboat diplomacy were rare events in which geopolitical interests largely explain the decision of governments from creditor countries to intervene.[16] These governments were reluctant to use military intervention, while morally the risk of lending was supposed to be the creditor's.[17] British and US governments based their decision to grant diplomatic and official support on political and financial considerations. They could nevertheless have recourse to the use of force to secure payment once all other enforcement mechanisms had been exhausted. A major problem with this procedure was its opposition to the basic principle of arbitration, defined as "the peaceful settlement of international disputes." In this regard, the Drago doctrine of 1907 inaugurated an age in which arbitration mechanisms became the preferred option in sovereign debt disputes and the recourse to force remained as the option to be used as a very last resort.[18]

Given the high frequency of defaults in Latin America during the whole nineteenth century, it is puzzling that governments in creditor countries were less active in defending their bondholders than in other regions. In the case of Great Britain, two explanations have been proposed by Alan Knight.[19] On the one hand, Knight puts forward the "negative" metropolitan argument that the British government lacked geopolitical interests in the region, coupled with the rising hegemony of the United States mainly in Mexico and Central America. On the other hand, he asserts that by the 1900s, local elites were in line with British commercial interests, assuming governing functions while Britain supplied credit and goods.

While the first argument may explain why the dominant British position did not translate into formal colonization, it does not tell us why no other form of foreign control was considered as an intermediate solution to the bondholders' recurrent disputes with Latin American governments. As we shall see, the levels of international investment, trade and public debt were not very different from those in other regions in which foreign control was established. Moreover, after the creation of the Corporation of Foreign Bondholders in 1868 (and similar bodies in other countries such as France, Belgium or Holland), official recognition served to consolidate the bondholders' political voice, which lobbied for interventionism in countries unwilling to settle their debt disputes in terms acceptable to investors. In previous cases in which governments from creditor countries intervened, agents were placed in the ports and at the official money-issuing agencies—such as during the second Anglo-French blockade of Buenos Aires in 1852[20]—or new governments were established (such as the French intervention of 1862–1863 in Mexico). But such extreme solutions differ considerably from the intermediate cases mentioned above and found in other regions.

Furthermore, while most elites had been favorable to trade since the mid-nineteenth century, continual political instability and struggle among different political and ideological positions did not guarantee that governments would always favor trade openness. The interests of Latin American elites were dynamic and conflicted with those of British and European subjects as their presence in different economic sectors expanded. As was shown for Argentina, certain socioeconomic groups favored protectionism and local state intervention and developed negative attitudes toward foreign competition in sectors such as banking and public utilities.[21] Peru also experienced several periods of protectionism from the 1820s on.[22] The level of protectionism reached such a high level that Latin America can be seen as the most protectionist region in the world.[23] In some cases, decisions to resort to protectionist measures were even supported by foreign diplomats and bankers. This is in sharp contrast to the limited autonomy in terms of commercial policy determination experienced in countries in other regions that would later be colonized or in those having undergone external control. In fact, this tolerance can be interpreted as an implicit recognition that customs revenues were the bulk of most governments' fiscal revenues and the ultimate resources with which debt could be repaid.

This may not mean, nevertheless, that protectionist policies did not lead to diplomatic tensions, or that European powers did not react to events affecting their interests.[24] On the contrary, we may safely assert that the disconnection between sovereign defaults and open intervention was not predetermined. European and US governments reserved their right to intervene, and in certain cases, they did. France and Britain were active in Argentina, Brazil and Uruguay; the United States intervened in Mexico in 1846, as did France in 1838 and 1861. By the turn of the century, the United States was active in Central America, while Britain, Germany and Italy intervened in Venezuela in 1902. Even if sovereign debt disputes rarely triggered these interventions, they could nevertheless figure prominently as *casus belli*.

Debt Defaults and Economic Relations Since Independence

Following independence, building new nation-states proved challenging. The fiscal and monetary bases of the former Spanish colonies had been destroyed,[25] and rebuilding a productive economy required financial resources. British merchant banks became important as underwriters of the first foreign loans to Latin American governments, but also as key actors in the export-import markets.[26] Most countries with a strong mining sector, such as Mexico, Peru or Bolivia, received high levels of British private investment that aimed to resume the production of gold and silver. However, a disappointing performance, largely related to political instability, deterred investors for several decades.[27] The fall in British investment, along with a relatively modest trade growth, led to limited diplomatic efforts by the British government to support bondholders.

In other countries, however, foreign trade had begun to expand even before independence, such as British trade with Argentina, Brazil or Chile.[28] Perhaps strikingly, in many cases the growth in bilateral trade occurred despite the debt defaults that took place as early as 1825, and despite the persistent political instability. Certain merchant banks, while developing permanent relations with local agents and commercial houses, also intervened on behalf of bondholders to support their claims.[29] These mostly successful efforts, along with the expansion of commercial activity, led to a second and major increase in private investments and government loans in the 1860s, a cycle more or less driven by global economic factors, but also by favorable political regimes and by the region's abundant natural resources.[30] Again, commercial and financial expansion was not accompanied by armed interventions, despite the high levels of macroeconomic volatility and, in some cases, institutional and political uncertainty.

If we assume that economic incentives strongly motivated European expansionism, then the first countries to be colonized should be precisely those with which bilateral trade and European investment expanded the most. While we do not have precise figures on foreign investment for the years prior to 1865, estimates exist regarding the amounts of capital borrowed from the main financial centers of Europe and the United States, as well as the volume of bilateral trade.[31] In the case of foreign investment, the 1860s lending boom from Britain to the rest of the world benefited Latin America and the Middle East similarly. Most Latin American countries defaulted on their external debts, as did other countries in the Middle East. Yet, while the British and French governments supported bondholders of Middle Eastern governments, this was not the case for investors in Latin American public debts. This is at odds with the fact that the most relevant default in terms of total volume of loans was that of Peru (£24.6 million), which exceeded those of Egypt (£11.5 million) and of the Ottoman Empire (£7 million).[32]

Trade, however, was a different matter. In 1870, Peru's bilateral trade with Britain reached around £6.5 million (the figure for Argentina, Britain's most important trade partner in Latin America, was £12.5 million). For Egypt, it was £22.8 million, and for the Ottoman Empire £12.3 million. In exports per capita terms, nevertheless, Peru and Argentina presented higher figures than their counterparts in the Middle East (2.29 and 1.6 versus 0.51 and 0.66 in 1860, respectively).[33] But this openness also meant that there was ample room for reversal, and in fact, the degree of protectionism increased from at least 1865 and remained the highest in the world.[34]

Economic relations between Latin America and Europe by the late nineteenth century were so close that some scholars saw them as the sign of some sort of foreign control, mostly exercised in the private sphere. In Argentina, for instance, the British presence was dominant in most sectors, including finance. By then, the role of merchant banks had become important even in the determination of fiscal and monetary policies. In this sense, Argentina's relationship with Britain was characterized by the secondary role played by the British government, as compared to private agents, in assuming control over economic policy and activity. This feature also implied that, while the absence of territorial ambitions may have deterred (colonial) interventionism, foreign control in fiscal and monetary issues permitted the expansion of investment and trade. The management of the Baring crisis of 1890 by the British banks, with the support of the Bank of England, exemplified this. In this regard, the final outcome stemming from a blurring of the borderline between public and private actors also had a colonial flavor.[35]

This could also be true for Central America. The resolution of Santo Domingo's debt in 1888 was called by one scholar "a case of neo-colonial financial solution, much applauded by European bankers," since a private agent, Western Corporation, assumed control over tax collection.[36] These types of control over tax collection were later replicated in the region. In South America, Brazil was portrayed as a bankers' colony, given the imposition of a painful monetary regime, which has been interpreted as the demonstration of external financial power.[37] This situation was possible given the financial dependence of the central government upon London (and upon the merchant bank Rothschild in particular) since at least 1855.[38] Rothschild provided short-term loans and successfully issued long-term bonds even during downward business cycles. In exchange, Brazil avoided defaulting until 1898, and accepted the conditions attached to the bailout loan, which affected the monetary and fiscal policies of the country despite their contractionary effects on the economy, including a banking crisis after the funding loan was signed.[39] This solution, which largely replicated Argentina's agreement of 1891, had also been attempted in Greece in 1893 by the Hambros Bank.[40] But contrary to Argentina and Brazil, the government there failed to comply with the conditions attached and defaulted, paving the way for the establishment of the International Financial Commission in 1898.

Foreign Control in Latin America: Two Case Studies

The resolutions of debt disputes varied considerably across Latin America. This diversity affected the recovery rates of bondholders, but also the fiscal capacity of governments, their access to financial markets and the terms of new loans. In more extreme cases, these resolutions included conditions on economic policies, such as commercial, monetary or fiscal policies, or the cession of control over customs receipts. Here I focus on two contrasting cases during a period in which debt negotiations were far from being institutionalized when European governments were acting actively in debt disputes in other countries.

These two cases are Mexico and Peru. Mexico is interesting as a case in Latin America —the only one during the mid-nineteenth century—in which a debt dispute led to a military intervention. Analyzing the case of Mexico serves to qualify previous claims on the relevance of geopolitics in Latin America. In Peru, while the real possibility for intervention is still disputed by historians, the case shows how foreign control could be exerted by private agents. Debt disputes were a relevant point of entry that permitted European merchant banks to dominate the extraction and distribution of Peru's most relevant natural resource. The fragile initial conditions in both cases were similar, and reflect to a large extent the same situation as that in other Latin American countries. Both governments were obliged to face internal and external threats, prompting them to increase their military expenditure and often resort to expensive internal loans, further weakening their fiscal position. Furthermore, as was the case in most other countries, exports and public revenues were highly dependent upon a reduced set of commodities, mainly silver in the case of Mexico and guano in the case of Peru. Both cases show how private and public factors were porous, but also the relevance of specific actors in understanding the process and resolution of debt defaults.

Mexico

Even if it is difficult to draw a strict frontier between geopolitical and economic reasons for the French intervention in Mexico, the historiography concurs that the former was largely dominant. This episode highlighted the existence of a French informal empire, as the government sought to expand trade between the two countries while, until then, the economic connections had been relatively unimportant. Nevertheless, it occurred at a time when bondholders in London and Paris were aggressively lobbying for a more active attitude from their governments. The French government's incursion led to the establishment of a monarchical regime that turned out to be short-lived, but showed that the possibility of a debt default leading to foreign intervention was also plausible in Latin America.[41]

Given that Mexico was the first country in which this type of intervention was used, a deeper analysis seems in order. Two points need investigation: the role of merchant banks and the reasons why this experience failed. The US-Mexican War of 1846 resulted in large territorial losses for Mexico, but also in the perceived threat of a complete conquest by the United States. Proposals were even made in the British Parliament to establish a European protectorate to counter it: British investments were deemed sufficiently high for the US territorial expansion to be considered as injurious to British interests, while subsequent internal conflicts considerably weakened Mexico's successive governments and public finances.[42] In fact, the British government had even evoked a guaranteed loan on behalf of Mexico as early as 1824 (as would later be the case in other, "foreign-controlled" cases, such as Greece in 1833 and Turkey in 1855), but the British government refused precisely because of the "political complications" that such a solution would have involved.[43] These proposals to establish a more permanent and institutional presence in the country temper the idea of Britain's disinterest in the region.

A different issue is whether bondholders and financial intermediaries favored intervention, and whether political considerations were alien to such interests. It seems that bondholders and the British press had favored the intervention of the British government since at least 1856. However, the British government was more reluctant. As in most other cases, while Lord Palmerston admitted that the bondholders were acting within their rights to claim repayment, the government wanted to avoid creating a precedent that could induce investors to assume that the Foreign Office would act as debt collector.[44]

Nevertheless, from a Mexican perspective, the possibility of a British or European invasion for non-payment seemed very real. This perceived threat included the defaulted debts incurred by the government toward British citizens and merchants established in Mexico.[45] This could even motivate Mexican creditors to become nationals of Britain (or of another European country) so they could ask for the support of those governments. The acceptance of these claims often became diplomatic conventions.[46] Under such new contracts, the Mexican government acknowledged these debts under especially onerous conditions, while increasing its commitment to an international compromise. Given the continuously precarious state of Mexican finances, local loans were expensive and very often went into default. As a result, these conventions prompted European governments to actively intervene on behalf of their creditors.

There were reasons for the British government to monitor the Mexican problem in the early 1860s, first and foremost, due to the political and economic consequences of French territorial ambitions which led to a permanent French presence under the monarchy of Maximilian. The financial outcome of a new political regime in Mexico was uncertain, partly due to increased pressure on Mexican public resources. About 70% of customs revenues were mortgaged to British claimants from the previous agreements and conventions referred to above.[47] From an overall indebtedness of 13.4 million pesos, only 0.19 were owed to the French conventions. Furthermore, the "London debt," which comprised Mexican loans that had been issued on the London capital market, amounted to 64.2 million pesos.[48] It is therefore illuminating to analyze the relationship that was forged between the British government and Baring Brothers. This bank had been the Mexican government's agent in London since 1826, at the moment when the country entered a period of successive defaults combined with temporary agreements.[49] The bank persisted in its position as a defendant of bondholders' interests, and during the French invasion in 1862 Barings sent a permanent agent to the country—George Henry White—to negotiate the resumption of debt service and report on the events related to the conflict.[50] White was in permanent communication with Charles L. Wyke, the British Minister in Mexico, who was in turn in contact with the Foreign Office.

Both agents took a pragmatic stand, focusing on the administration of the customhouses at Veracruz and Tampico, the most important ones in the country over which the French military had assumed control. This was not a minor item, since the key element that triggered military intervention was not directly linked with British financial claims, but, rather, with a default of an internal issue of Mexican Treasury bonds acquired by a local banking house, J.B. Jecker, whose owner was a Swiss citizen later naturalized French.[51] Jecker's claims concerned a much smaller amount than previous external loans issued in London. However, bondholders were put on the same footing as other creditors from Spain, Mexico and the French government's own claims for military expenses.

Overall, the economic interests of the French intervention were relatively negligible compared with those of Britain. It is therefore unsurprising that the main concern recurrently expressed by White was the effects of the war on trade, which had been either reduced or deviated to minor ports, like Matamoros, in which contraband trade had been increasing. One solution, according to White, was either effective control over those ports or a general reduction in the level of tariffs of the ports under French control. But this was only part of a major set of reforms that, White reported, were to be set up by the French government. In a letter dated 8

December 1862, White notified Barings about a project in which a Mr. Davidson, Rothschild's agent in Mexico, had been in contact with the French government regarding the issue of a new loan on behalf of Mexico, aimed at consolidating the government's external debt, and which, it was claimed, was part of a strategy for "putting Mexican finances in order."[52] In June of the following year, White updated Barings about these plans, which now included a guarantee by the French government and "other powers if they will join."[53]

Indeed, Napoleon III needed to achieve some institutional stability in Mexico to attract international capital (i.e. merchant bank support), a condition for the sustainability of the new political regime, and he expected Barings and Rothschild to participate in the issue of a new loan. But they desisted, given the remaining political uncertainties in Mexico, the lack of confidence in the new financial structure of the Maximilian government—whose sustainability was partly weakened by France's own demands for war indemnities—and the lack of support within the French government for guaranteeing the planned Mexican loan. This lack of banking support arose despite the establishment of the Financial Commission in Paris in 1864 (with three members from Mexico, France and Britain), and the fact that Maximilian's government had agreed to let French agents collect and manage the country's customs.[54]

Nevertheless, one of the reasons for the failure of this experience in Mexico was the sudden reluctance of the French government to support the Maximilian regime after May 1866. Some attributed this shift in French policy to the lack of confidence in the rapid reestablishment of financial stability and fiscal sustainability, to which the absence of banking support certainly contributed. In a sense, the fate of regime established in Mexico was also largely dependent upon its popular support but also upon key private actors from different nationalities, in particular British, whose interests did not necessarily diverge from those from the French government. This explains why, after the failure of the Maximilian regime and the consequent repudiation of the loans contracted during his term, the fate of the bonds remained a bone of contention between the two countries, affecting their economic and political relations during several decades.[55] Mexico's government remained in default until 1886, at the time when under the Porfirian regime, the fiscal framework was reinforced, the country was pacified and trade began to expand.

Peru

Comparatively speaking, European geopolitical interests in Peru were minor. However, Britain witnessed a major rise in its economic interests over the country as shown mainly by its imports of guano, a natural fertilizer from the accumulated excrement of seabirds and bats, which had been increasingly in demand in Europe since the 1840s. By the 1860s, one contemporary financial publication was able to state that "a cargo of guano is the ready equivalent for so much gold."[56] Peru's government did not exploit this resource directly, but delegated its extraction, loading, transport and sale to private agents. Since 1849 until 1861, the British merchant house Antony Gibbs & Sons held the monopoly of these activities and was thus the main intermediary between Peru and Europe.[57]

Peru's commercial expansion was not unproblematic. The Peruvian government had been in default since the 1825 crisis and British bondholders had persistently appealed for official support. However, the involvement of the British government remained secondary throughout the negotiations.[58] The rise of guano as a relevant commodity for the agricultural sector further complicated the position of the British government, which had to deal with the conflicting interests of the agricultural community and of investors.[59] Since the late 1840s, farmers had lobbied the government for coercive action to push the Peruvian government to lower the price of guano. They considered that this price, which was due to the nationalized ownership of guano deposits and the monopolistic position of Antony Gibbs, was too high. On the other hand, investors opposed any change in the system given the profits to be obtained from this trade by Peru's government, a factor which, bondholders expected, would favor the resumption of debt service.

The settlement of Peru's first default took place in 1849, coinciding with a sharp increase in the price of guano. Under this agreement, Antony Gibbs was instructed to retain the necessary proceeds from the sale of guano in Britain to meet the service of the debt. In the 1850s, however, the need for guano prompted farmers to look for alternative sources of guano or close substitutes. In 1857, the British press called the situation the "guano crisis," as prices continued to climb and the supply of guano was not sufficient for the existing demand in Britain and Europe.[60] Despite these claims, the British government did not intervene in Peru.

Nevertheless, a second and brief default took place in 1855, when the Peruvian government repudiated a loan incurred two years earlier by the previous government. Interestingly, this loan was a partial conversion of an internal debt into an external one.[61] As a result, it was British merchants in Peru who mainly called for intervention.[62] This repudiation led to the contemplation of military action by the British and French governments. However, no such intervention seems to have occurred and Peru's government eventually recognized the debt in 1857. The British government's active attitude and bondholders' support has generated a huge debate within the historiography of Peru. On the one hand, the British government did not threaten the Peruvian government, and certainly recognized its own military limitations in the region. It also knew that bondholders asking for intervention had bought the bonds in the secondary market at depressed prices, but claimed repayment in a collective action under the umbrella of the Corporation of Foreign Bondholders, whose position to exploit insider information was occasionally reported in the press.[63] On the other hand, there were British and French navy activities off Peru in 1857, which probably pressured the government of Peru to settle its remaining disputes with its bondholders.[64] The main target of the British and French governments, however, was the Chincha Islands, where guano was extracted. It may be no wonder, therefore, that Peru's government ended up accepting all the bondholders' demands.

More recently, scholars have emphasized the positive incentives that the government of Peru had to settle its disputes with bondholders.[65] Its desire to exploit its resources and increase its export capacity was certainly at the center of this. Furthermore, the British government encouraged the involvement of a private firm to manage the competing interests of agriculture and finance. As a result, the government agreed with a British merchant house, Antony Gibbs & Sons, to manage the income from guano exports (as consignee) and service its foreign debt (the funds were handed to underwriting banks in London and Paris), in practice withdrawing control of the Peruvian government over a substantial portion of fiscal revenues. But this merchant house was also in a position to condition short-term credit to the government and support long-term loans, a fact that led historians of Peru to highlight the dependence of Peru's economy upon a small number of foreign merchant houses, which controlled the government's own credit and the sales of its only staple in Europe.[66]

During the 1860s, the increase in guano prices and total production raised public revenues, allowing the government to lower import tariffs.[67] After 1862, guano management was assumed by the house of Dreyfus from Paris, which also became the agent in charge of negotiating the external loans of the Peruvian government with British and French merchant houses. Dreyfus had been a recurrent lender to Peru's national government, and after 1869 some of the advances made by these banks were to be repaid through the sale of specific amounts of guano at an agreed price. Thereby, Dreyfus became the exclusive seller of Peru's guano, a fact that led to internal political disputes with domestic capitalists and attempts by the government to cancel the agreement. Quiroz provides evidence of the concerns raised by French diplomacy regarding the potential conflict between Dreyfus and the Peruvian government, and the possible need for official intervention.[68] The fall in guano prices after 1873 and the failure by underwriting banks to place new loans led to financial distress and default.[69]

The attitude of the British government in the aftermath of this default was not to intervene in favor of the bondholders, and several scholars have demonstrated that the government consistently favored the principle of non-intervention as laid down in Palmerston's 1848 circular.[70] By that time, the relevance of guano had declined as reflected in the fall of guano prices, mostly due to competition and to the increased use of substituting fertilizers. Exports to Britain had peaked in 1858 and remained irregular though a declining trend was evident. By 1875, exports in terms of total volume had fallen to about a third of that peak. Furthermore, the contracts signed with Dreyfus show that each of the loans in the 1860s was secured through explicit permission to access the resources in the islands in which it was produced, which in practical terms implied the cession of Peru's sovereignty over the management of these resources.[71]

Along with the decline of guano's relevance to the British economy, the British government continued to refrain from intervening in the negotiations between the government of Peru and the bondholders. These negotiations were further complicated after the Pacific war in which Chile defeated Peru and annexed some of the territories in which guano was produced and that served as a pledge for loans to Peru. The peace treaty provided no information regarding the responsibility for the loans, and Chile's governments refused to assume responsibility for the debts. However, the Chilean government finally opted for a negotiation with bondholders after diplomatic intervention through an official letter of protest jointly signed by France, Britain and five other European governments. For Felipe Ford Cole, this was a diplomatic procedure that had preceded military intervention in Mexico (and that would also precede the one in Venezuela in 1902).[72]

Conclusions

The absence of a causal link between sovereign default and foreign control can lead to two different interpretations. One is the idea of foreign control as a prior step to formal colonialism. This historical presupposition is appropriate in cases such as Egypt or Tunisia, or those that were also applied by the United States in Central America. However, this interpretation offers a limited perspective to analyze other cases such as the Ottoman Empire, Greece or Serbia in the later nineteenth century, and even less so the new forms of external control developed in the interwar period by the League of Nations or in Germany under the Dawes plan.

An alternative explanation, as provided in this paper, suggests that foreign control as exerted by states' representatives, while politically motivated, mainly served to secure economic targets, particularly the development of trade. In cases in which the market had been unable to reach a permanent, favorable framework to achieve this primary purpose, the intervention of European governments became unavoidable, particularly in those countries with which trade prospects appeared attractive. Nevertheless, to the extent that sovereign debt entered the field of private capital markets, European governments preferred to restrain from a more proactive intervention.

Such a compromise could also be affected in cases of geopolitical competition, regardless of the economic interests. The French intervention in Mexico can hardly be attributed to debt disputes, but it demonstrated that the establishment of friendly, political regimes did not suffice to attract investment and develop bilateral trade without the participation and support of private agents, particularly merchant banks. While other permanent interventions were absent in Latin America, the commissions and debt management devices already established in Mexico were revised in other, subsequent cases in other regions. These Financial Commissions, while adopting different legal forms, were founded to manage and collect the fiscal revenues pledged for the service of external debt. After the first commission established in Mexico in 1864 (Franco-British Financial Commission), others were founded in Tunisia (Commission financière, 1869), in Egypt (International commission of liquidation of 1880 and the Caisse de la dette publique) and in Greece (International Financial Commission of 1898). The installation of a similar commission was discussed in Venezuela at the turn of the nineteenth century.[73] They are all referred to as "international financial control" cases, to the extent that representatives of various states sat on those commissions, and, while some of them were preceded by bodies that operated as branches within each government's administration (such as the Caisse de la dette publique in Egypt), they later became international organs.[74] These Commissions would later develop different tasks also related to fund management (from the specific public revenues that were pledged as loan guarantees) and sometimes even revenue collection.[75] Their emergence would be accompanied by a debt restructuring agreed upon with bondholders' participation, and often also the issue of a new private loan (occasionally guaranteed by the colonial power) to support the regime during transition.

Finally, the case of Peru demonstrated that effective, fiscal management could be delegated to private entities, while the fall of guano exports and the shift to other more lucrative markets by British merchants contributed to the abandonment of Peru as the main destiny of foreign capital. However, this period also marked the trend to a new period in which other, more active and powerful merchant banks took the lead in a different form of foreign control without the state.

Acknowledgment I am particularly grateful to Nicolas Barreyre, Nicolas Delalande, Étienne Forestier-Peyrat and participants at the public debt workshop held in Paris in June 2016 for comments on previous versions of this paper, and to Rafael Dobado, Alejandra Irigoin, Leonardo Weller and Ali Coşkun Tunçer for fruitful discussions. All remaining errors are my own responsibility. I also thank the archivists at ING Baring, London, for their kind cooperation. Financial support from the SNF is gratefully acknowledged.

Notes

1. While the typology of debt defaults is complex, a typical external debt default concerned the debt issued by national governments in international financial markets, mainly London and Paris, which interrupted debt service in either sinking fund or interest payments. These defaults led to disputes with bondholders, which had to be settled before a government could be allowed to issue new bonds. The London Stock Exchange developed a strict regulatory framework which served to protect the rights of bondholders and to prevent holdouts. See Larry Neal and Lance Davis, "The Evolution of the Structure and Performance of the London Stock Exchange in the First Global Financial Market, 1812–1914," *European Review of Economic History* 10, no. 3 (2006): 279–300; Marc Flandreau, "Sovereign States, Bondholders Committees, and the London Stock Exchange in the

Nineteenth Century (1827–68): New Facts and Old Fictions," *Oxford Review of Economic Policy* 29, no. 4 (2013): 668–96. An analogue type of regulation emerged in Paris. See Pierre-Cyrille Hautcoeur and Angelo Riva, "The Paris Financial Market in the Nineteenth Century: Complementarities and Competition in Microstructures," *Economic History Review* 65, no. 4 (2012): 1326–53.
2. On Egypt, see Herbert Feis, *Europe, the World's Banker, 1870–1914: An Account of European Foreign Investment and the Connection of World Finance with Diplomacy before the War* (New Haven: Yale University Press, 1931); William H. Wynne, *State Insolvency and Foreign Bondholders: Selected Case Histories of Governmental Foreign Bond Defaults and Debt Readjustments* (Washington, DC: Beard Books, 1951); on Morocco, see Adam Barbe, "Public Debt and European Expansionism in Morocco from 1860 to 1956" (Master's thesis, Paris School of Economics, 2016).
3. See Chaps. 6 and 8 in this volume. See also Donald C. Blaisdell, *European Financial Control in the Ottoman Empire: A Study of the Establishment, Activities, and Significance of the Administration of the Ottoman Public Debt* (New York: AMS Press, 1966); Wynne, *State Insolvency and Foreign Bondholders*; Ali Coşkun Tunçer, *Sovereign Debt and International Financial Control: The Middle East and the Balkans, 1870–1914*, (Basingstoke: Palgrave Macmillan, 2015); Leigh Gardner, "Colonialism or Supersanctions: Sovereignty and Debt in West Africa, 1871–1914," *European Review of Economic History* 21, no. 2 (2017): 236–57.
4. See Emily S. Rosenberg, *Financial Missionaries to the World: The Politics and Culture of Dollar Diplomacy, 1900–1930* (Cambridge, Mass.: Harvard University Press, 1999).
5. John Gallagher and Ronald Robinson, "The Imperialism of Free Trade," *Economic History Review* 6, no. 1 (1953): 1–15.
6. On categorizations and different theoretical perspectives, see Jürgen Osterhammel, "Semi-Colonialism and Informal Empire in Twentieth-Century China: Towards a Framework of Analysis," in *Imperialism and After: Continuities and Discontinuities*, ed. Wolfgang J. Mommsen (London: Allen & Unwin, 1986), 290–314.
7. Henry Stanley Ferns, *Britain and Argentina in the Nineteenth Century* (Oxford: Clarendon Press, 1960); William Mitchell Mathew, "The Imperialism of Free Trade: Peru, 1820–70," *Economic History Review* 21, no. 3 (1968): 562–79; Desmond Christopher Martin Platt, *Finance, Trade, and Politics in British Foreign Policy: 1815–1914* (Oxford: Clarendon Press, 1968). Peter J. Cain and Antony G. Hopkins, *British Imperialism: 1688–2000* (London: Routledge, 2014), underline the importance of the financial sector as the main driver of British imperial expansionism.

8. Matthew Brown, ed., *Informal Empire in Latin America: Culture, Commerce and Capital* (Oxford: Blackwell, 2008).
9. This categorization was laid out by Alan Knight, "Rethinking British Informal Empire in Latin America (Especially Argentina)," *Bulletin of Latin American Research* 27, no. 1 (2008): 23–48.
10. This assertion needs to be qualified. In their seminal article, Gallagher and Robinson, "The Imperialism of Free Trade," suggest, based on Lenin's "Imperialism, the Highest Stage of Capitalism," that there are two sub-periods in which mid-Victorian "indifference" toward formal imperialism shifted into late-Victorian "enthusiasm" for formal imperialism, resulting from the previous growth in foreign investment and international trade, the watershed taking place around 1880. However, Gallagher and Robinson further argue that British colonial expansion remained important throughout both periods. On the other hand, the prominent rise of France into a capital exporting country was accompanied by the expansion of its colonial territories. See Catherine Coquery-Vidrovitch, "De l'impérialisme britannique à l'impérialisme contemporain: l'avatar colonial," *L'Homme et la société* 18, no. 1 (1970): 61–90.
11. Gallagher and Robinson, "The Imperialism of Free Trade," 312; Platt, *Finance, Trade, and Politics*; Carlos Marichal, *A Century of Debt Crises in Latin America: From Independence to the Great Depression, 1820–1930* (Princeton: Princeton University Press, 1989).
12. Şevket Pamuk, *The Ottoman Empire and European Capitalism, 1820–1913: Trade, Investment and Production* (Cambridge: Cambridge University Press, 1987).
13. Edward Shawcross, *France, Mexico and Informal Empire in Latin America, 1820–1867: Equilibrium in the New World* (London: Palgrave Macmillan, 2018).
14. Rafe Blaufarb, "The Western Question: The Geopolitics of Latin American Independence," *American Historical Review* 112, no. 3 (2007): 742–63.
15. Kris James Mitchener and Marc D. Weidenmier, "Supersanctions and Sovereign Debt Repayment," *Journal of International Money and Finance* 29, no. 1 (2010): 19–36.
16. See Michael Tomz, *Reputation and International Cooperation: Sovereign Debt Across Three Centuries* (Princeton: Princeton University Press, 2007); Marc Flandreau and Juan H. Flores, "Bonds and Brands: Foundations of Sovereign Debt Markets, 1820–1830," *Journal of Economic History* 69, no.3 (2009): 646–84; Marc Flandreau and Juan H. Flores, "The Peaceful Conspiracy: Bond Markets and International Relations During the Pax Britannica," *International Organization* 66, no. 2 (2012): 211–41; Juan H. Flores, "Crying on Lombard Street: Fixing Sovereign Defaults in the 1890s," *European Review of History/Revue Europeenne d'histoire* 19, no. 6

(2012): 979–97; Juan Flores Zendejas, "Financial Markets, International Organizations and Conditional Lending: A Long-Term Perspective," in *Contractual Knowledge: One Hundred Years of Legal Experimentation in Global Markets*, eds. Grégoire Mallard and Jérôme Sgard (Cambridge: Cambridge University Press, 2016), 61–91.

17. See Mauro Megliani, *Sovereign Debt: Genesis-Restructuring-Litigation* (New York: Springer, 2014).
18. Michael Waibel, *Sovereign Defaults before International Courts and Tribunals* (Cambridge: Cambridge University Press, 2011).
19. Alan Knight, "Britain and Latin America," in *The Oxford History of the British Empire* (Oxford: Oxford University Press, 1999), vol. III, ch. 7.
20. During wars and political unrest, British soldiers took control of the Customs House and the National Bank in Buenos Aires in the mid-nineteenth century. See Maria Alejandra Irigoin, "Finance, Politics and Economics in Buenos Aires, 1820s-1860s: The Political Economy of Currency Stabilisation" (PhD diss., London School of Economics, 2000).
21. Charles Jones, "'Business Imperialism' and Argentina, 1875–1900: A Theoretical Note," *Journal of Latin American Studies* 12, no. 2 (1980): 437–44.
22. Paul Gootenberg, "The Social Origins of Protectionism and Free Trade in Nineteenth-Century Lima," *Journal of Latin American Studies* 14, no. 2 (1982): 329–58.
23. John Coatsworth and Jeffrey Williamson, "Always Protectionist? Latin American Tariffs from Independence to Great Depression," *Journal of Latin American Studies* 36 (2004): 205–32.
24. Tenenbaum evokes the protests of the British government to protectionist measures in Mexico. See Barbara A. Tenenbaum, "Merchants, Money, and Mischief, The British in Mexico, 1821–1862," *The Americas* 3, no. 3 (1979): 317–39.
25. See Chap. 1 of this volume. See also Regina Grafe and Maria Alejandra Irigoin, "The Spanish Empire and Its Legacy: Fiscal Redistribution and Political Conflict in Colonial and Post-Colonial Spanish America," *Journal of Global History* 1, no. 2 (2006): 241–67.
26. Frank Griffith Dawson, *The First Latin American Debt Crisis: The City of London and the 1822–25 Loan Bubble* (New Haven: Yale University Press, 1990).
27. James Fred Rippy, *British Investments in Latin America, 1822–1949* (London: Routledge, 2000).
28. Manuel Llorca-Jaña, *The British Textile Trade in South America in the Nineteenth Century* (Cambridge: Cambridge University Press, 2012).
29. See, for instance, Stanley David Chapman, *The Rise of Merchant Banking* (London: G. Allen and Unwin, 1984); Marc Flandreau and Juan H. Flores,

"Bondholders versus Bond-Sellers? Investment Banks and Conditionality Lending in the London Market for Foreign Government Debt, 1815–1913," *European Review of Economic History* 16, no. 4 (2012): 356–83.
30. Carlos Diaz Alejandro, "Stories of the 1930s for the 1980s," in *Financial Policies and the World Capital Market: The Problem of Latin American Countries*, eds. Pedro Aspe Armella, Rudiger Dornbusch, and Maurice Obstfeld (Chicago: University of Chicago Press, 1983), 5–40.
31. Post-1865 figures for the British capital markets can be found in Irving Stone, *The Global Export of Capital from Great Britain, 1865–1914: A Statistical Survey* (New York: St. Martin's Press, 1999).
32. Figures are from Stone, *The Global Export of Capital*. They include governments' capital calls between 1865 and 1873.
33. Pamuk, *The Ottoman Empire*, 141.
34. Coatsworth and Williamson, "Always Protectionist?"
35. Charles Jones, "'Business Imperialism' and Argentina"; Antony G. Hopkins, "Informal Empire in Argentina: An Alternative View," *Journal of Latin American Studies* 26, no. 2 (1994): 469–84.
36. Marichal, *A Century of Debt Crises*, 123.
37. Gustavo Barroso, *Brasil, colonia de banqueiros; história dos emprestimos de 1824 a 1934.*, 6th ed. (Rio de Janeiro, Civilização brasileira, sa, 1937); Steven C. Topik, "Brazil's Bourgeois Revolution?" *The Americas* 48, no. 2 (1991): 245–71.
38. Marc Flandreau and Juan H. Flores, "Bondholders versus Bond-Sellers?"
39. Winston Fritsch, *External Constraints on Economic Policy in Brazil, 1889–1930* (Pittsburgh: University of Pittsburgh Press, 1988).
40. See Wynne, *State Insolvency and Foreign Bondholders*.
41. Shawcross, *France, Mexico and Informal Empire*; Steven C. Topik, "When Mexico Had the Blues: A Transatlantic Tale of Bonds, Bankers, and Nationalists, 1862–1910," *American Historical Review* 105, no. 3 (2000): 714–38; Richard J. Salvucci, *Politics, Markets, and Mexico's "London Debt," 1823–1887* (Cambridge: Cambridge University Press, 2009).
42. Intervention by George Bentinck in the Commons Sitting of Monday, August 24, 1846. British Parliamentary Papers, Third Series, Volume 88.
43. Platt, *Finance, Trade and Politics*, 318.
44. Salvucci, *Politics, Markets*, 230.
45. Tenenbaum, "Merchants, Money, and Mischief."
46. Jan Bazant, *Historia de la deuda exterior de México: 1823–1946* (Mexico City: Colegio de Mexico, 1968).
47. Yusuf Abdulrahman Nzibo, "Relations between Great Britain and Mexico 1820–1870," (PhD diss., University of Glasgow, 1979).
48. Figures from Bazant, *Historia de la deuda exterior de México*, 97.

49. See Philip Ziegler, *The Sixth Great Power: A History of One of the Greatest of All Banking Families, the House of Barings, 1762–1929* (New York: A. A. Knopf, 1988); Michael P. Costeloe, *Bonds and Bondholders: British Investors and Mexico's Foreign Debt, 1824–1888* (Westport: Praeger, 2003).
50. ING Baring Archive, correspondence HC4.5.31–33.
51. Nancy N. Barker, "The Duke of Morny and the Affair of the Jecker Bonds," *French Historical Studies* 6, no. 4 (1970): 555–61.
52. ING Baring Archive, correspondence HC4.5.31–33, White to Barings, 8 December 1862. We may safely assume that it was Nathaniel Davidson, who was active in the business of mining (particularly quicksilver) in different places in South and North America; he retired from Mexico after the French invasion, and Rothschild closed its agency in that country. On the Rothschilds in Mexico, see Geneviève Massa-Gille, *Les capitaux français et l'expédition du Mexique* (Paris: Éditions A. Pedone, 1965); Alma Parra, "Mercury's Agent: Lionel Davidson and the Rothschilds in Mexico," *The Rothschild Archive Annual Review* 9 (2007): 27–34.
53. ING Baring Archive, HC4.5.33 Part 2. Letter from George White to Baring Brothers, 15 August 1863.
54. Geneviève Gille, "Los capitales franceses y la expedición a México," in *Un siglo de deuda pública en México*, eds. Leonor Ludlow and Carlos Marichal (Mexico City: Colegio de México, 1998), 125–51.
55. Topik, "When Mexico Had the Blues," 737.
56. Charles Fenn, *Fenn's Compendium of the English and Foreign Funds, Debts and Revenues of All Nations: Banks, Railways, Mines.*, 10th ed., (London: E. Wilson, 1869), 372.
57. Wynne, *State Insolvency and Foreign Bondholders.*
58. William M. Mathew, "The First Anglo-Peruvian Debt and Its Settlement, 1822–49," *Journal of Latin American Studies* 2, no. 1 (1970): 81–98.
59. See Mathew, "The Imperialism of Free Trade."
60. See *The Farmer's Magazine* (London: Rogerson and Tuxford, 1857), or *Perthshire Advertiser*, 16 April 1857.
61. Mathew, "The Imperialism of Free Trade."
62. This default is not listed in the historical records of the CFB. See the list of defaults between 1823 and 1876 in Corporation of Foreign Bondholders, *Annual Report of the Council of the Corporation of Foreign Bondholders* (London: 1877).
63. Mathew, "The First Anglo-Peruvian Debt"; Flandreau, "Sovereign States."
64. Javier Tantaleán Arbulú, "Tesis y contratesis. Debate sobre la era del guano (avances de una investigación)," in *Guerra, finanzas y regiones en la historia económica del Perú* eds. Carlos Contreras, Cristine A. Mazzeo and Francisco Quiroz (Lima: Banco Central de Reserva del Perú, 2010), 323–72; Jorge Basadre, *Introducción a las bases documentales para la historia de la*

República del Perú con algunas reflexiones (Ediciones P. L. V., 1971); Barbara Stallings, "Incumplimiento de pagos vs refinanciación: crisis de la deuda externa peruana 1826–1985," *Hisla, Revista Latinoamericana de Historia Económica y Social* 6 (1985): 59–86.

65. Catalina Vizcarra, "Guano, Credible Commitments, and Sovereign Debt Repayment in Nineteenth-Century Peru," *Journal of Economic History*, 69, no. 2 (2009): 358–87.
66. William M. Mathew, *La firma inglesa Gibbs y el monopolio del guano en el Perú* (Lima: Banco Central de Reserva del Perú, 2009).
67. Catalina Vizcarra, "Guano, Credible Commitments."
68. Alfonso W. Quiroz, *Historia de la corrupción en el Perú* (Lima: Instituto de Estudios Peruanos, 2013).
69. Marichal, *A Century of Debt Crises*.
70. Platt, *Finance, Trade, and Politics in British Foreign Policy*, 339.
71. Wynne, *State Insolvency and Foreign Bondholders*, 116–120.
72. Felipe Ford Cole, "Debt, Bondholders and the Peruvian Corporation, 1820–1955," conference paper, Business History Conference, Baltimore, April 5–7, 2018.
73. See François Deville, *Les contrôles financiers internationaux et la souveraineté. de l'État.* (Saint-Nicolas: V. Arsant, 1912); Michel Fior, *Institution globale et marchés financiers. La Société des Nations face à la reconstruction de l'Europe, 1918–1931* (Bern: P. Lang, 2008). A comparison of the commissions established in South Eastern Europe and the Middle East is included in Tunçer, *Sovereign Debt*.
74. Karl Strupp, *L'intervention en matière financière*, 1926.
75. Tunçer, *Sovereign Debt*.

CHAPTER 6

Leveraging Foreign Control: Reform in the Ottoman Empire

Ali Coşkun Tunçer

Comparative studies in economic history label international financial control organizations as "fiscal house arrest" and discuss them in the context of other "supersanctions" which helped reduce the cost of borrowing for the defaulting countries and restored access to international financial markets.[1] The Ottoman case is usually referred to as one of the most successful cases of supersanctions. Following the default of the Ottoman Empire in 1876 and the subsequent foundation of the Council for the Administration of the Ottoman Public Debt (hereafter the Council), the representatives of foreign bondholders were assigned the task of administering and collecting certain tax revenues to compensate for the unpaid interest and capital of the debt and they enabled the Ottoman government to carry on funding mounting military expenditure until World War I.[2]

Yet opinions differ in the Ottoman historiography on the role of the Council and its contribution to the Ottoman Empire's economic and financial development. Traditional views argue that the Council was a

A. C. Tunçer (✉)
Department of History, University College London, London, UK
e-mail: a.tuncer@ucl.ac.uk

© The Author(s) 2020
N. Barreyre, N. Delalande (eds.), *A World of Public Debts*, Palgrave Studies in the History of Finance,
https://doi.org/10.1007/978-3-030-48794-2_6

symbol and instrument of European imperialism, which led the Empire to economic destruction, whereas revisionist views emphasize the fact that the Council restored the creditworthiness of the Ottoman government, contributed to the modernization of its fiscal system, and acted as a third party that was independent of European powers.[3] Besides Ottoman historiography, the role of the Council is also debated in the broader historical literature on pre-1914 international financial control. These studies outline the major functions and legal-administrative structure of international financial control organizations and analyze them in the context of international law and enforcement of loan contracts.[4]

This chapter aims to elaborate on the political economy dimension of the question by focusing on the relationship between the Ottoman government and the executive organ of the Council from the 1880s to the start of World War I. To provide historical context and identify some key actors, I first document the process which led to the default of the Ottoman government in 1876 and the emergence and formation of the Council in 1881. I then elaborate on the activities of the Council, its relationship with the Ottoman government, and its fiscal performance. I aim to show that in the short term the Council had a positive impact on the Ottoman state finances as it restored the trust of foreign bondholders and reinstated creditworthiness successfully—more significantly than other instances of international financial control (IFC) in the region. Unlike the previous line of historiography, however, I attribute this success primarily to the fact that the Ottoman government was *willing* and *able* to cooperate with its foreign creditors, and that it complied with the policies of the Council. I maintain that the willingness of the Ottoman government to cooperate with its foreign creditors was mainly driven by the high costs of tax collection as the Ottoman fiscal system relied heavily on direct taxes from the agricultural sector collected by tax farmers. The Ottoman government was also able to cooperate with its foreign creditors thanks to the absence of political pressure from taxpayers. Thus, it transferred the economically and politically costly tax collection business partly into the hands of foreign creditors in exchange for future creditworthiness. On the negative side, the low cost of borrowing in international financial markets delayed the reforms in Ottoman fiscal institutions and improvements in fiscal capacity, as the government managed to meet its increasing spending with the help of the Council and without entering negotiations with its taxpayers. These findings are consistent with one of the main threads of this book that the interactions between global and domestic politics of public debt played an important role in the modernization of political and fiscal institutions in the peripheries of the global economy before 1914.

The rest of the chapter is structured as follows. Section "State Modernization, International Credit, and the Road to Default" provides a brief overview of the history of sovereign debt of the Ottoman Empire from its beginning to the establishment of the Council. Section "The Council at Work" is an overview of the Council and its activities, introducing its administrative structure and organization as well as key turning points in its history. Section "Control or Cooperation?" presents the evidence on the performance and extent of the control in terms of administering revenues and restoring the creditworthiness in international financial markets. It also puts forward a framework to interpret the interaction between fiscal-political institutions of the Ottoman Empire and the Council. A brief conclusion follows.

State Modernization, International Credit, and the Road to Default

Until the late eighteenth and early nineteenth centuries, the Ottoman Empire relied on two traditional sources of revenue like other states: taxation and seigniorage. The idea of borrowing to finance budget deficits emerged for the first time in the late eighteenth century when the government was urgently in need of funds due to the Russo-Turkish War of 1787–92. However, only after the start of the Crimean War, in 1854, did the Ottoman government sign its first foreign loan agreement. For the next 60 years, this would become the most important means of dealing with budgetary difficulties. In the early stages of this process, the Ottoman government issued loans in London and relied on financial intermediaries such as Dent Palmer and Rothschild. In the following two decades Paris also became a popular destination and the Ottoman government contracted loans with the Imperial Ottoman Bank (IOB),[5] Crédit Mobilier and Comptoir d'Escompte. From 1854 to 1881, the Ottoman government issued 18 loans with a total face value of £219 million and an average effective interest rate of 8.6 percent.

These loans were secured on a wide range of direct and indirect tax revenues including the Egyptian tribute; customs revenues from Istanbul, Izmir, and Syria; tithes of several provinces; and revenues from tobacco, salt, silk, fisheries, olive oil, sheep tax, and stamp duty. Although most of these pledges were quite valuable, creditors were aware that the securing of future revenues for the payment of a loan did not mean that the Ottoman government would, in fact, use them for this purpose or manage them in a way that was beneficial to the lenders.[6] Financial markets were aware of the unsustainability of the rapid increase in debt, especially after the Franco-Prussian war in 1870, when a new Russo-Turkish war was only seen as a matter of time. Moreover, on the supply side, with the crisis of 1873, surplus capital started to deplete, and it became almost impossible for the Ottoman government to contract a new loan.[7] In October 1875, the Ottoman government partially suspended the interest payments; from January to March 1876, the suspension was extended and the government defaulted on all its outstanding debt, which then stood at around £191 million.[8] This was a "long-predicted catastrophe,"[9] but what made it exceptional was the scale of it, as it was the biggest sovereign default to date.[10]

The international financial markets remained closed to the Ottoman Empire until the government reached a reasonable deal with the bondholders. The successful settlement of the debt, however, was not achieved until 1881 due to a series of domestic and international crises. In March 1876, the uprisings in the Balkans started and this was followed by the deposition of the existing Sultan Abdülaziz. In December 1876, Sultan Abdülhamid II acceded to the throne and introduced the first constitution of the Ottoman Empire. This was, however, a short-lived experiment as both the constitution and the parliament were suspended due to the war with Russia, which started in April 1877 and came to an end with the Congress of Berlin in June 1878. It was also during the Berlin Congress that the claims of the bondholders first received official acknowledgement by the Powers, leading to formal negotiations with the Porte.[11] Yet, progress was slow due to the conflicting interests of the creditors and the Ottoman government.

By the time of the Ottoman default, British and French bondholders jointly held almost 90 percent of the Ottoman debt; and their representatives were keen to introduce a strong international control over Ottoman finances with their joint representation. The Ottoman government, however, wary of what was going on in Egypt at the time, was determined not to hand too much sovereignty over to its foreign creditors.[12] As the frequent meetings between French and British bondholders were taking place to agree on a solution, a group of domestic bankers based in the Galata district of Istanbul took the first steps to reach a deal with the Porte in November 1879.[13] The Galata bankers had provided vital financial support with short-term advances to the Ottoman government during the Russo-Turkish war when the European markets were entirely closed to it. Most of these loans were concluded by using taxes from certain indirect revenues and monopolies as collateral. These revenues formed the basis of the agreement between the Ottoman government and the Galata bankers. The deal gave the Galata bankers the right to administer indirect revenues from stamps, spirits, fisheries, and silk, as well as the monopolies of salt and tobacco for ten years.[14] The Porte also reserved the right to denounce the agreement to make it more advantageous to the other bondholders.

From the perspective of the government, the deal was an attempt to reassure its foreign creditors while safeguarding the rights of local bankers and avoiding official European intervention. Through interlocking directories, Galata bankers were represented in important financial institutions such as Crédit Général Ottoman, Banque de Constantinople, and the IOB. At the time, the total debt of the government to the Galata bankers and the IOB was around 8.7 million liras, three-quarters of which was held by the IOB. Other holders of the debt were George Zarifi (600,000 liras) and Solomon Fernandez and Alfred Barker (1.8 million liras).[15] The annual payment of this debt, 1.1 million liras, was to be met from the revenues from six indirect taxes. It was also expected that the revenues of the Administration would exceed the interest payments, and in that case, they would be used for the claims of foreign bondholders. The management of the Administration consisted of three representatives of the IOB and a group of Galata bankers.[16] The bankers appointed Robert Hamilton Lang as the director of the Administration. This was a strategic move, as Lang was a well-known and credible name among the European bondholders, and he had a success record of reforming Romanian state finances. Despite the attempts of the Ottoman government and the Galata bankers to increase the credibility of the deal, European bondholders were not favorable to this agreement. First, Galata bankers had acted on their own without consulting them, and second, the arrangement was considered unfair to foreign bondholders as it gave seniority to the domestic debt over the foreign debt. While European bondholders started making counterproposals to avert the arrangement, the Administration started its operations and started acting as a modern tax administration for the first time in the history of the empire. Its first year in operation was a great success, which led European bondholders to put even more pressure on the Ottoman government to transfer the Administration to them.[17]

Following a series of exchanges, in October 1880, the Great Powers and the Porte agreed on the provisions of the debt settlement. In January 1881, the bondholders finally chose their representatives and sent them to Istanbul. In the meantime, the Porte turned to Germany, which held no more than 8 percent of the Ottoman debt, and hired German advisors to help the government with the negotiations. During the talks, while Britain and France were pushing for a harsher deal, the German bondholders' representative was keener on finding a compromise. Eventually, in December 1881, the Decree of Muharrem was signed between bondholder representatives and the government. Thanks to German support, the Ottoman government secured an advantageous deal involving a 50 percent write-down of its outstanding debt and more than 80 percent of its interest arrears. Furthermore, the international financial control was shared between the representatives of all European creditor nations, large and small: Britain, France, Germany, the Netherlands, Italy, and Austria-Hungary. In the meantime, the previous arrangement with the Galata bankers was denounced and the bankers were to be paid 590,000 liras per annum for the outstanding debt of 8.1 million liras. This payment was granted with seniority from the revenues of the Council. The IOB also bought the debt of the other Galata bankers and became the sole holder of the domestic debt.[18] The settlement of the claims of the Galata bankers resulted in limiting the opportunities of this strong domestic financial group at the expense of granting power to European financial groups. Unlike the initial era of borrowing (1854 to 1881), as a result of this arrangement, the domestic bankers now lost their influence on the public debt management of the Ottoman government.

As part of the Decree of Muharrem, the Ottoman government agreed that an administrative council (the Ottoman Public Debt Administration) was to be established in Istanbul to represent the bondholders and to act in their interests. The Council consisted of bondholder representatives from each creditor country plus a member of the Ottoman government. The government transferred its right to administer revenues from the monopolies of tobacco and salt, stamp duty, duties on spirits and on fishing, and the silk tithe of several provinces, which were shown as a guarantee for the payment of previously contracted loans. The Council held the right to decide upon all modifications and improvements that might be introduced in the taxes of these monopolies and revenue items, and it had the direct administration, collection, and encashment of them. The net gains from these revenue sources were to be used for the payment of interest and the sinking fund of the Ottoman debt. Thus, in return for a drastic reduction in the debt stock and interest service, the Ottoman government agreed to consign almost one-fifth of the state's revenues to the Council until the complete settlement of the outstanding debt.

The Council at Work

Starting from 1883, building upon the previous Administration of the Galata bankers, the Council established more than 20 offices in various provinces of the Empire extending from Yemen to Salonica. These offices were administered from the central headquarters in Istanbul. This was an extensive tax collection network employing around 4500–5000 officers (including inspectors, collectors, security guards, etc.), a majority of whom were employed in the provinces and represented a bigger network than the Ministry of Finance. This was not the first example of foreign control of finances of a sovereign state in the region and it would not be the last. However, unlike the other cases of international financial control in the region, such as Greece, Serbia, Bulgaria, and Egypt, the Council operated without the intermediation of the political representatives of the creditor states involved. Bondholder representatives, having complete autonomy in the way that they managed hypothecated revenues, implemented both short- and long-term solutions to compensate for their losses and to increase the ceded revenues. The lessons derived from the Egyptian experience and the fear of resistance from the local population made the representatives of bondholders choose a gradual method of replacing the existing local staff, introducing new techniques of production, and reforming the existing collection system for the ceded revenues. From the perspective of the Ottoman government, dealing directly with the private bondholders was also a more acceptable and legitimate solution to the problem of foreign debt as it enabled a partial separation of fiscal/financial matters from broader diplomatic affairs.[19]

The foremost priority of the Council was to increase the revenues under its control. This could be achieved by introducing improvements in the collection methods of tax revenues and/or creating incentives to increase the production of underlying revenue sources. In the first decade of its operation, the Council established new trade links and reinforced the existing ones for this purpose by using the financial and commercial network of bondholders. This was accompanied by importing new production methods from Europe. The Council assigned some of its members the task of transplanting the existing system of monopoly administration for salt and silk. The Council also acted at a micro level to address revenue specific problems, which included establishing several schools and institutions to train local producers with the objective of increasing the quality and the number of goods. To enter the French wine market, it established a nursery in Istanbul to carry out experiments to combat vine diseases. Although to begin with the government hesitated to join in these efforts, the Ministry of Agriculture later actively cooperated with the Council. Similarly, for silk production, in Bursa, European experts started to offer a consultancy service to the producers. This service was later offered under the School of Sericulture, which was established jointly by the government and the Council in 1889. The Council chose to develop the salt monopoly under its own direction, whereas the tobacco revenue was farmed to the Régie Company[20] according to an agreement in May 1883 between the Council and the government. The concessionaires were the Credit-Anstalt of Vienna, Bleichröder of Berlin, and the IOB, which held 74 percent of the shares. The proposal of this syndicate had the support of the Council, as these three banks were also involved in the Ottoman debt as issuing houses. Moreover, the previous director of the Administration of the Galata bankers, R. Hamilton Lang, was made the managing director of the Régie. According to the terms of the contract, the Régie paid the Council an annual rent of 750,000 liras for a period of 30 years. The Council and the government were also to benefit according to a fixed scale in the profits above this sum. Although, in theory, the Company had incentives to promote agricultural production and to provide credit to the producers, the unlicensed production of tobacco continued until 1914. As a result, the disputes between the Régie and the producers were numerous. In some cases, local powerholders were also involved in these disputes. Local governors, as the representatives of the central government, could either side with the producers or not depending on their relationship with the Régie.[21] As for the Porte, it adopted a pragmatic approach to avoid widespread social unrest and at the same time direct confrontation with the Régie. To fight against "armed banditry" and smuggling, the Council put pressure on the government to organize "corps de surveillance" with the proper powers to use arms when necessary. These efforts were endorsed by the government and the volume of smuggling and trade in contraband declined over time.[22]

As detailed further below, the activities of the Council reshuffled the existing coalitions among producers, merchants, local governors, tax farmers, and the Porte. The new alliance created a change in domestic balance of power and gave way to the cooperation of the Porte and the Council at the expense of local powerholders. Thanks to this political cooperation, the Council worked efficiently in its management of the resources for which it was responsible (see Fig. 6.1). Both the revenues from indirect contributions (silk, salt, spirits, stamps, and fisheries) and from the Régie increased significantly.

The mutually beneficial relationship between the Council and the Ottoman government led to the extension of the rights of the Council in September 1888 upon the request of the Ottoman government. This new arrangement transferred the management of revenues assigned to railway bonds and kilometric guarantees to the Council. These revenues were mainly tithes from the provinces through which the railways ran. Additionally, the Council was asked to collect the surtax of one-and-a-half

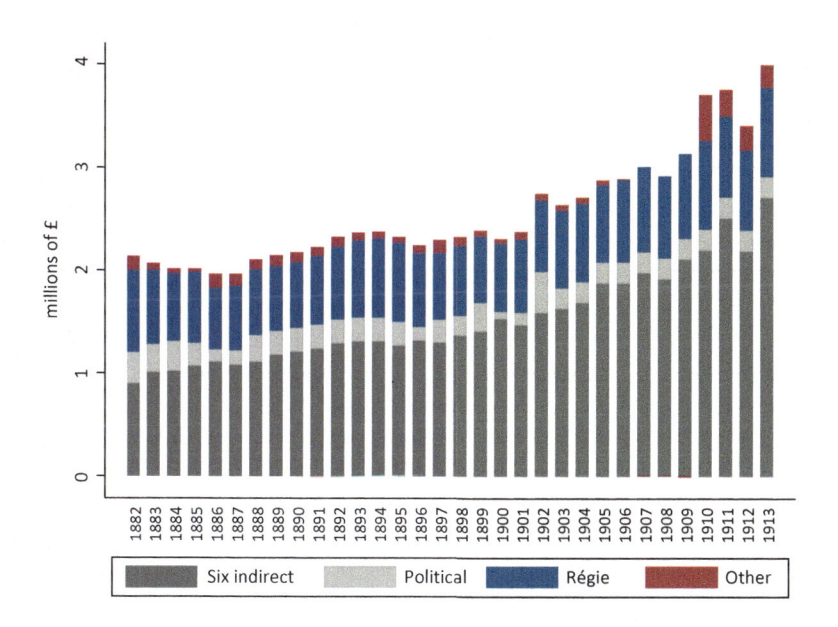

Fig. 6.1 Revenues controlled by the Council, 1882–1913 (Source and notes: Tuncer, *Sovereign Debt*, 73. Six indirect revenues were from silk, salt, spirits, tobacco, stamps, and fisheries. Political revenues refer to the annual taxes from the tributary states (Egypt and Cyprus) of the Ottoman Empire)

percent on the silk and tobacco tithes on behalf of the government. The Council, after collecting and deducting the collection expenses, was then to transfer the entire net revenue to the government. Therefore, the expenses of administration and collection of these revenues were borne by the revenues themselves and did not fall upon the revenues ceded to the bondholders. Given the close link between the railway companies and the Council, this arrangement was in line with the Ottoman government's desire to extend its railway network. Moreover, it reflected the fact that, in the eyes of the Ottoman government, creditors had been shown to be more successful in collecting and administering the revenues. For the creditors, the extension of transfer of fiscal sovereignty was a sign of trust between them and the government, which in return secured the position of the Council in the overall fiscal system of the Empire.[23] As the extension of the Council's duties proved to be successful, similar agreements were concluded in the following years. In 1890 the collection of valonia and opium tithes was handed over to the Council. In 1898 a new one-half percent surtax was introduced by the government on all tithes assigned as pledges for kilometric guarantees and for the service on the 1890 and 1896 loans. The collection of this surtax was likewise entrusted to the Council.[24] Overall, the ceded revenues, that is, revenues transferred to the bondholders to compensate for the unpaid interest and capital of the debt in default, were on average 15 percent of the total revenues of the state. However, counting the revenues administered on behalf of the government, the extent of the Council's power over state finances reached almost one-third of overall revenues of the Ottoman government.[25]

As the confidence of the bondholders increased, first in 1903 and then in 1907, the Ottoman government and the Council agreed to modifications on the 1881 deal with supplementary decrees. In September 1903, a new debt consolidation and further reduction in the outstanding debt and the interest rate was concluded. The nominal value of the new issue was around 32 million liras. The rate of interest was 4 percent; the rate of redemption was 0.45 percent per annum. Anything over the fixed sum of two million liras, which represented the charges on the new issue, was to be divided between the government and the Council to the ratio of 75 and 25 percent, respectively. In other words, the government could now participate in the distribution of profits from the ceded revenues. Another significant change concerned the increase in customs surtax. Negotiations between the government and the European powers to raise import tariffs from 8 to 11 percent were started as early as the 1880s but they were finally concluded in 1907. This 3 percent increase in the customs surtax contributed positively to the Council's revenues, but the government also profited from the balance over the fixed charges. In both 1903 and 1907, the management of several other public bond issues of the Ottoman government was also transferred to the Council as a third party, further reinforcing its role in the Ottoman state finances.[26]

Right after the agreement on the customs surtax, in 1908 the Young Turk revolution took place. The new government revised the text of the 1876 constitution and reinstated it. From that year onward, the representative assembly had the power to pass legislation over the Sultan's authority, and the dominant political force was the nationalist Committee of Union and Progress, which eventually led the Empire to the World War I. In line with the progressive principles voiced by the leaders of the Young Turk movement, the new regime supported free trade and foreign direct investment until 1912 when protectionism was adopted as the main economic policy. Moreover, in ensuring fiscal discipline and reorganizing the administration, the government applied to foreign experts and expertise of the Council for assistance. British, French, and German experts were appointed as inspector-generals, customs advisors, judicial consultants, and military trainers to the different departments of the Ottoman government.[27] In a similar vein, the new government continued to cooperate with the Council. As far as the Council was concerned, the change from autocracy to constitutional government had few drawbacks, as long as their policies were aligned.[28] In the post-1908 period, one of the most notable changes was the increase in the number of issues of railway bonds with greater involvement of German intermediary banks.[29] This shift had already been underway since 1881 in parallel to diplomatic changes. In 1881, following the Decree of Muharrem, the percentage of Ottoman bonds held by German bondholders increased from 4.7 to 12.2 percent in 1898, and to 20.1 percent in 1913. During the same period, France had a share of 40–49 percent. The significant decline was in the share of British bondholders, which fell from 29 percent in 1881 to 6.9 percent in 1913. Other bondholders were from Belgium, Austria, Holland, and Italy; each had a share of 4–6 percent in 1881 which had not changed significantly by the end of the period.[30]

Control or Cooperation?

The mutually beneficial relationship between the Council and the Ottoman government can also be observed by looking into the changes in the cost of borrowing following the default. Using monthly prices of the Ottoman government bonds in the London Stock Exchange and comparing them with those of other peripheries suggests that the Ottoman Empire made a significant recovery following the foundation of the Council and the debt settlement in 1881. Moreover, the steady decline in bond spreads continued and the Ottoman Empire benefited from low borrowing costs in the longer term, performing significantly better than the Latin American periphery, and closely trailing the European periphery (see Fig. 6.2).[31] The improvement was not only on the "price" of bonds issued under the control of the Council. The Ottoman government managed to contract a significant number of loans under the control of the Council and did not have any problem in securing new loans until 1914. From 1882 to 1914, it issued 23 loans with a face value of £90 million and an average effective interest rate of 4.7 percent. Compared to the period before 1882, the initial cost borrowing declined by almost 40 percent, and the debt per capita went down from £8.9 to £6.2. This success was partly due to the revenues assigned as security. In this regard, an important difference was the fact that the Council acted as a trustee by using the surplus funds under its control or acquiring the control of further future revenues to secure each issue. Finally, during this period, the Ottoman Empire managed to benefit from two debt conversions in 1903 and in 1906 with the intermediation of the Council.

How do we account for this striking international performance despite the bad fiscal record and default history of the Ottoman Empire? A possible explanation for this recovery is the degree of control exercised by the bondholder representatives over the Ottoman state finances. As summarized above, the Council established an extensive network in the Ottoman Empire and worked in harmony with the Ottoman government, which was willing to extend its privileges. In this regard, the Council even made explicit and direct invitations to the bondholders to reward such cooperative behavior. In 1891, two years after the agreement between the Ottoman government and creditors regarding the extension of the Council's rights on state finances, the director and the British representative of the Council made the following remarks in his annual report to the bondholders:

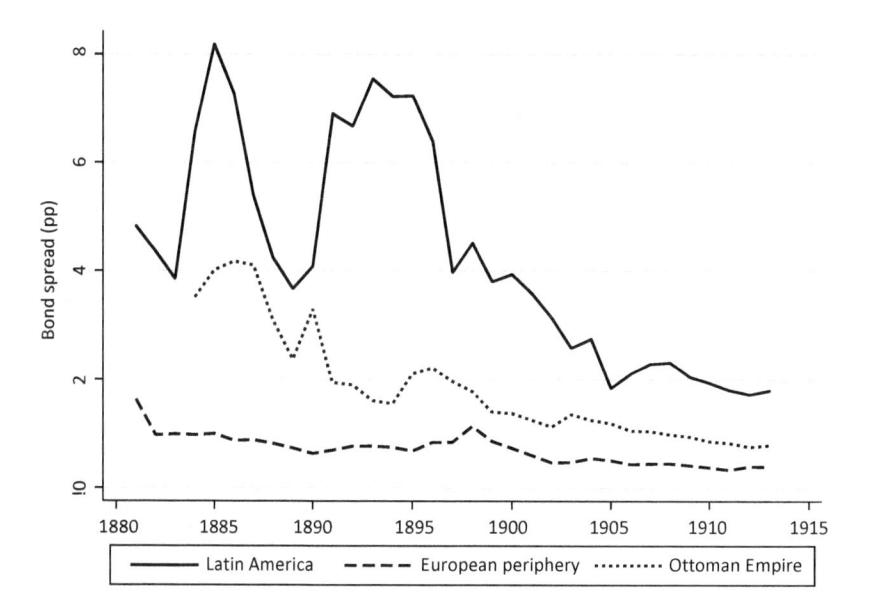

Fig. 6.2 Bond spreads, 1880–1913 (Source and notes: Latin America represents the average of Brazil, Chile, Colombia, Uruguay and Mexico. European periphery is the average of Greece, Hungary, Portugal and Spain. Calculated from Tuncer, *Sovereign Debt*, 187; P. Mauro, N. Sussman and Y. Yishay *Emerging Markets and Financial Globalisation Sovereign Bond Spreads in 1870–1913 and Today*. (Oxford: Oxford University Press, 2006); N. Ferguson and M. Schularik, "The empire effect: the determinants of country risk in the first age of globalization," *Journal of Economic History*, Vol. 66, No. 2, (2006), 283–312)

I venture here to suggest that it is surely time that English capitalists should forget old sores, and begin to turn their eyes once more to a country so interesting as Turkey, so full of possibilities and lying so close to their doors… It is true that years ago Turkey was overtaken by bankruptcy and in this she did not lead the way. Where she did lead the way, was in honestly recognising her sins and making an arrangement as good as possible and as secure as possible for the creditors whom she had previously wronged. Since that time she has shown complete good faith and has set an example which more than one other country would do well to follow. She surely then is once more to be trusted and believed. Frenchmen think so, Germans think so and they have proved it. Why should Englishman be behindhand in the appreciation of honest action and slow to assist in promoting the prosperity of a well-deserving and naturally favoured country?[32]

The significant decline in bond spreads suggests that the Council's call for "English capitalists" to invest in Ottoman bonds found a response. Despite the fact that the Ottoman Empire had failed to pay its debts just 20 years before the above remarks, the bond spreads remained at quite low levels with lower volatility. It should be underlined that from the second half of the nineteenth century to World War I, the Ottoman Empire was in political crisis, characterized by territorial losses, and costly military campaigns against its minority groups and neighboring countries. It was an export-oriented agrarian economy with a continuous budget deficit and a "chaotic" monetary system. The figures, however, suggest that for the creditors investing in Ottoman loans, these factors were of secondary importance.

These findings together with the preceding discussion to some extent challenge the conventional perception of the Council in the literature as a "sanction" imposed on the government. There were clearly times when the Ottoman government cooperated with the Council in its reform efforts and willingly expanded the extent of its control, as there were also times when the Council was not willing to be deeply involved in the country's financial matters. One way to interpret this relationship is to consider the political and fiscal conditions under which the Council operated. For most of the nineteenth century, the Ottoman Empire remained an authoritarian monarchy despite several reforms aimed at modernizing the state apparatus. An Ottoman parliament and the constitution for the first time emerged in 1876, which aimed to introduce accountability over fiscal matters and regularize the authority of the Sultan. However, in practice the only group it empowered was the existing Ottoman political elite and moreover it was suspended a few months later by the Sultan because of the war with Russia. A representative assembly was not successfully established again until after the Young Turk Revolution of 1908.[33] As for the tax revenues, they mostly relied on the traditional tithe collected almost exclusively with the help of tax farmers. In order to finance the costly reforms and shift the tax burden from the countryside to the urban centers, the government repeatedly but ultimately unsuccessfully attempted to replace tax farming with salaried tax collectors. While customs duties had the potential to be a significant revenue source, due to the capitulations and bilateral trade treaties, the Ottoman government was not able to modify the rates unilaterally. Finally, the personal tax, a symbol of transition to the modern tax state, was only introduced in 1903.[34] Overall, most of the revenues of the Ottoman government were based on direct taxes levied mainly upon the land, despite an increase in the share of indirect taxes throughout the period. Moreover, the Ottoman Empire struggled to introduce a centralized tax collection system and had to share most of the tax revenues with other intermediaries such as local notables and tax farmers. Given its lack of monopoly over taxation, the Ottoman government was willing to cooperate with foreign creditors in transferring revenues. It is, however, important to note that the Council in the Ottoman Empire represented an unusual case of taxation *without* representation and negotiation with taxpayers, and with a "foreign" and semi-autonomous character. Unlike many European countries during the same period, representation and negotiation with local elites played a very minor role in the evolution of fiscal institutions in the Ottoman Empire.[35] The ability of the Ottoman government to borrow was determined exogenously with no links to its monetary system and fiscal regime, and the Council acted as a mechanism of a "good housekeeping seal of approval" and credible commitment in the eyes of foreign creditors. This greater access to the international financial markets meant a loss of incentive to tax.

Thus, the Council was an effective tool in improving the creditworthiness of the Ottoman government. It achieved this by regularly transferring the surplus from assigned revenues to the bondholders in order to compensate for their losses, and by the close collaboration of the Ottoman government with the Council. In political terms, the existing system of tax farming supported by the provincial powers was challenged by the Council's tax collection efforts. The interference of the Council in fiscal affairs disturbed the old alliances in the Ottoman fiscal system. The Ottoman government had historically struggled to introduce a centralized tax collection system and had to share most of the tax revenues with local powerholders. At the time the Ottoman Empire defaulted on its foreign debt, it had a limited ability to levy taxes. Given its lack of monopoly over taxation, the Ottoman government was willing to cooperate with the foreign creditors in transferring revenues at the expense of local powerholders. In this context, the cooperation with the Council and the accompanying low costs of borrowing delayed the process of fiscal consolidation even further, as the Ottoman government could now borrow without going through the costly route of negotiation with local elites and producers.

* * *

The Ottoman Empire joined the international financial markets during the Crimean war in 1854 as part of the Great Power rivalry of the time. From this year onward, both financial and political factors determined the ability of the Ottoman government to borrow publicly in European financial centers. The availability of surplus capital in London, Paris, and Berlin and the official encouragement of the respective European governments combined with the continuous budget deficits of the Ottoman government resulted in one of the biggest debtors and defaults of the time. In the process of debt settlement, the rivalry among the Great Powers, and domestic and foreign bondholder groups helped the Ottoman government to reach a relatively favorable deal in 1881. The Ottoman government managed to secure a considerable reduction in its outstanding debt and interest payments, but in return agreed to the foundation of the Council of the Ottoman Public Debt Administration, a foreign-led control over its state finances. The establishment of international financial control over state finances meant a partial loss of fiscal sovereignty in the Ottoman case.

This chapter has highlighted the multi-dimensional character of this pre-1914 sovereign debt enforcement mechanism implemented by foreign bondholders. The extent and the success of foreign control were driven by the interaction between global politics and domestic political/fiscal institutions. The enforcement of creditors was effective in improving the creditworthiness of the Ottoman government, primarily because the Ottoman government was willing and able to cooperate with its foreign creditors. The lack of fiscal centralization in the Ottoman Empire created an incentive for the central authority to cooperate with its foreign bondholders instead of leaving the control of taxable revenues to the tax farmers and/or local elites. This cooperation helped to contain local powerholders and provide access to cheap foreign capital at the same time. Although the Ottoman Empire was able to borrow during this period on a long-term basis at a very low cost, the speed of transformation of political institutions and fiscal centralization remained slow compared to the other debtors of the region. Reinforced creditworthiness combined with the lack of well-developed political institutions slowed down the fiscal centralization even further, as the government was more willing to choose the less costly path of borrowing. These findings point out that the local political conditions of debtor countries, especially the balance of domestic power and the interaction among interest groups, may act as a constraint over the economic impact of public debt and shape its management.

Notes

1. Kris J. Mitchener and Marc D. Weidenmier, "Supersanctions and sovereign debt repayment," *Journal of International Money and Finance* 29, no. 1 (2010): 19–36.
2. The method of establishing foreign control over state finances following defaults was not unique to the Ottoman Empire. Similar international financial control organizations became the dominant form of dealing with defaults in the Middle East and the Balkans from the 1870s to 1914 including Tunisia, Egypt, Serbia, Bulgaria and Greece. For a comparative study of international financial control in the Ottoman Empire, Egypt, Greece and Serbia see Ali Coşkun Tunçer, *Sovereign Debt and International Financial Control: The Middle East and the Balkans, 1870–1913* (Basingstoke: Palgrave Macmillan, 2015). For Bulgaria see Roumen Avramov, "Advising, Conditionality, Culture: Money Doctors in Bulgaria, 1900–2000," in *Money Doctors: The Experience of International Financial Advising 1850–2000*, ed. Marc Flandreau (London: Routledge, 2003), 190–215; Adam Tooze and Martin Ivanov, "Disciplining the 'Black Sheep of the Balkans': Financial Supervision and Sovereignty in Bulgaria, 1902–1938," *Economic History Review* 64 (2011): 30–51.
3. Some of the seminal works in this literature are Parvus Efendi, *Türkiye'nin Mali Tutsaklığı* (İstanbul: May Yayınları, 1977); Donald C. Blaisdell, *European Financial Control in the Ottoman Empire* (New York: AMS Press, 1966); Emine Zeynep Kiray, "Foreign Debt and Structural Change in 'The Sick Man of Europe': The Ottoman Empire, 1850–1875" (PhD diss., MIT, 1988). For a more recent contribution see Murat Birdal, *The Political Economy of Ottoman Public Debt Insolvency and European Financial Control in the Late Nineteenth Century* (London: Tauris Academic Studies, 2010).
4. François Deville, *Les contrôles financiers internationaux et la souveraineté de l'État* (Saint-Nicolas: V. Arsant, 1912); André Andreades, *Les contrôles financiers internationaux* (Athens, 1925); Edwin Borchard and William Wynne, *State Insolvency and Foreign Bondholders* (New Haven: Yale University Press, 1951); Herbert Feis, *Europe, the World's Banker, 1870–1914* (New York: Kelley, 1974). Michael Waibel, *Sovereign Defaults before International Courts and Tribunals* (Cambridge: Cambridge University Press, 2011) is a recent contribution on the subject.
5. This bank, originally named the Ottoman Bank, was founded by British capital in 1856. Following its merger with a French capital group in 1863, it was renamed the Imperial Ottoman Bank (IOB). In addition to acting as the major intermediary between the Ottoman government and the European financial markets, the IOB held the monopoly of issuing gold

convertible bank notes across the Ottoman Empire—acting as a central bank of issue. Edhem Eldem, *A History of the Ottoman Bank* (Istanbul: Ottoman Bank Historical Research Centre, 1999).

6. Although some of the initial bond issues in 1855 and 1858 stipulated the formation of special commissions composed of foreign delegates to monitor the spending of the funds and collection of pledged revenues, these efforts were eventually ineffective. Şevket Kâmil Akar and Hüseyin Al, *Osmanlı Dış Borçları ve Gözetim Komisyonları, 1854–1856* (İstanbul: Osmanlı Bankası Arşiv ve Araştırma Merkezi, 2004).
7. Kiray, *Foreign Debt*; Şevket Pamuk, "Foreign Trade, Foreign Capital and the Peripheralization of the Ottoman Empire 1830–1913" (PhD diss., University of California, Berkeley, 1978).
8. Şevket Pamuk, *A Monetary History of the Ottoman Empire* (Cambridge: Cambridge University Press, 2000), 213–4; Edhem Eldem "Ottoman Financial Integration with Europe: Foreign Loans, the Ottoman Bank and the Ottoman Public Debt," *European Review* 13, no. 3 (2005): 431–445.
9. "The Turkish Repudiation," *The Economist*, 9 October 1875, 1190.
10. The other two significant cases were Spain, which defaulted on an outstanding debt of £170 million, and Egypt on around £100 million. Christian Suter, *Debt Cycles in the World Economy: Foreign Loans, Financial Crises and Debt Settlements, 1820–1990* (Boulder: Westview Press, 1992), 67–69.
11. This was mainly because private bondholder organizations such as the London-based Corporation of Foreign Bondholders had little leverage with the Ottoman government in reaching a deal. Moreover, the Porte during these years was occupied with a range of domestic and international crises. Joseph Yackley, "Bankrupt: Financial Diplomacy in the Late Nineteenth-Century Middle East" (PhD diss., University of Chicago, 2013), 134 and Blaisdell, *European Financial Control*, 84–85.
12. On debt imperialism in Egypt see Chap. 7, this volume.
13. On the importance of domestic interest groups in the context of Latin America, see Chap. 5, this volume.
14. The official name of this administration was *Rüsum-ı Sitte*, hereafter the Administration.
15. Haydar Kazgan, "Düyun-i Umumiye" in *Tanzimat'tan Cumhuriyet'e Türkiye Ansiklopedisi*, vol. 4, (İstanbul, İletişim Yayınları, 1985), 701.
16. On behalf of the IOB, Morgan H. Foster, Émile Deveaux, Johan von Haas; and on behalf of the Galata bankers, George Zarifi, Solomon Fernandez, Bernard Tubini, Eustace Eugenidis, Theodore Mavrocordato, A. Vlasto, Alfred Barker, Z. Stefanovitch, Leonidas Zarifi, George Coronio, Ulysses Negropontis, and Paul Stefanovitch Schilizzi took seats on the managing council.

17. Blaisdell, *European Financial Control*, 88; Kazgan, "Düyun-i Umumiye," 701.
18. Pamuk, *Foreign Trade*; Christopher Clay, *Gold for the Sultan. Western Bankers and Ottoman Finance 1856–1881* (New York: I. B. Tauris, 2000); Yackley, *Bankrupt*, 125–181.
19. Tunçer, *Sovereign Debt*, 53–78.
20. The full name of the company was *Société de la régie cointéressée des tabacs de l'empire Ottoman*, hereafter the Régie.
21. Filiz Dığıroğlu, *Memalik-i Osmaniye Duhanları Müşterekü'l-Menfaa Reji Şirketi* (İstanbul: Osmanlı Bankası Arşiv ve Araştırma Merkezi, 2007), 87–90.
22. *Council of Ottoman Public Debt Administration*, Annual Reports (London, 1882), 21–22; Donald Quataert, *Social Disintegration and Popular Resistance in the Ottoman Empire, 1881–1908: Reactions to European Economic Penetration* (New York: New York University Press, 1983); Tunçer, *Sovereign Debt*, 53–78.
23. Blaisdell, *European Financial Control*, 128–130.
24. Blaisdell, *European Financial Control*, 150.
25. Tunçer, *Sovereign Debt*, 75.
26. Vedat Eldem, *Osmanlı İmparatorluğu'nun İktisadi Şartları Hakkında Bir Tetkik* (Türkiye İş Bankası Kültür Yayınları: Istanbul, 1970), 263; Blaisdell, *European Financial Control*, 93–118.
27. Mika Suonpää, "Foreign Advisers and Modernisation before the First World War: British Diplomacy, Sir Richard Crawford, and the Reform of the Ottoman Empire's Customs Service, 1906–1911," *International History Review* 37, no. 2 (2015): 386–404. Zafer Toprak, *Türkiyede Milli İktisat, 1908–1918* (İstanbul: Doğan Kitap, 2012).
28. *Council of Ottoman Public Debt Administration*, Annual Reports (London, 1909); Feroz Ahmad "Vanguard of a Nascent Bourgeoisie: The Social and Economic Policy of the Young Turks, 1908–1918," in *From Empire to Republic: Essays on the Late Ottoman Empire and Modern Turkey*, vol. 1, ed. Feroz Ahmad (Istanbul: Istanbul Bilgi University Press, 2008), 23–61.
29. On the links between foreign debt and diplomacy see Chap. 3 in this volume.
30. Eldem, *Osmanlı İmparatorluğu*'nun, 256; Pamuk, *Foreign Trade*, 105–112.
31. Elsewhere, I statistically analyze bond spreads by implementing a structural break test and compare the results with other countries which experienced similar forms of international financial control. The findings point out the significance of international financial control in restoring creditworthiness. See Tunçer, *Sovereign Debt*, 123–51.

32. *Council of Ottoman Public Debt Administration*, Annual Reports (London, 1893), 88.
33. Nathan J. Brown, *Constitutions in a Nonconstitutionalist World* (Albany: State University of New York Press, 2002), 23–26; Kemal Karpat, "The Transformation of the Ottoman State, 1789–1908," *International Journal of Middle East Studies* 3 (1972): 243–81.
34. Kıvanç Karaman and Şevket Pamuk "Ottoman State Finances in European Perspective, 1500–1914," *Journal of Economic History* 70, no. 3 (2010): 598; Nadir Özbek "Osmanlı İmparatorluğu'nda Gelir Vergisi: 1903–1907 Tarihli Vergi-i Şahsi Uygulaması," *Tarih ve Toplum Yeni Yaklaşımlar* no. 10 (2010): 43–80; Stanford J. Shaw, "The Nineteenth-Century Ottoman Tax Reforms and Revenue System 1517–1798," *International Journal of Middle East Studies* 6, no. 4 (1975): 421–59.
35. On the links between legitimacy of the political regime and the nature of public debt see the contributions in Part 1 of this volume.

CHAPTER 7

The Unforeseen Path of Debt Imperialism: Local Struggles, Transnational Knowledge, and Colonialism in Egypt

Malak Labib

In the mid-1870s, Egypt witnessed a severe financial crisis, and its government suspended the payment of its foreign debt interest. The crisis—the outcome of two decades of heavy indebtedness—marked the beginning of a sweeping European involvement in the country's finances and administration, and ultimately led to British occupation in 1882.

The Egyptian debt liquidation has been regarded, by legal scholars, as a key step in the construction of international financial controls (IFCs): The discussion focused, in particular, on debt liquidation in relation to public international law and the enforcement of debt contracts.[1] Historical scholarship has equally extensively discussed the Egyptian case: The landmark studies by David Landes, Jacques Thobie, and Samir Saul examined sovereign debt within the larger history of banking and finance in Egypt and the Middle East,[2] while the two studies by Jean Bouvier and Richard Atkins shed light on the interplay between political and financial interests

M. Labib (✉)
Free University of Berlin/Forum Transregionale Studien, Berlin, Germany

© The Author(s) 2020
N. Barreyre, N. Delalande (eds.), *A World of Public Debts*, Palgrave Studies in the History of Finance,
https://doi.org/10.1007/978-3-030-48794-2_7

in the years leading to the British occupation.[3] The Egyptian case has also figured in the literature on the British Empire, where it contributed to economic theories of imperialism, from Hobson's and Lenin's writings in the early twentieth century to Cain and Hopkins' concept of "gentlemanly capitalism."[4]

While Egyptian sovereign debt has thus been regarded as a classical case-study of IFC or debt imperialism, this chapter proposes to revisit this trajectory by examining, in contrast, the specific and locally embedded power dynamics that shaped Egypt's debt regime in the 1870s and early 1880s. It investigates, in particular, the place of experts and expertise in the political wranglings over debt.

The success of IFC in Egypt was partly contingent, I argue, on the ability of Europeans to establish a network of information, and the consolidation of financial control involved, in turn, the reorganization of the state's statistical and accounting apparatus. The few studies that discuss the reform of public finance and accounting practices during that period tend to describe it as a process of the substitution of rational principles of administration for the arbitrariness and disorder of the pre-colonial order.[5] In contrast, this chapter shows that information gathering and statistical production was a contested terrain, where political struggles, opposing local and international actors, intersected with "technical" debates about fiscal and financial issues. In the following pages, I follow the actors involved and the type of expertise mobilized in the negotiations about the settlement of the Egyptian debt crisis, in the years preceding the British occupation. In doing so, my study seeks to connect the political history of public debt with a history of knowledge approach. In particular, I highlight the fractured and heterogeneous nature of information gathering in the context of the debt crisis, and I pay attention to the political and power dynamics that underlie the choice of, and the controversies over, accounting and statistical procedures.[6] In other words, I both attend to "instruments and ideas of calculation"[7] and look at the ways in which these instruments relate to discourses about "good government."[8]

Finally, this chapter moves beyond an exclusively national perspective, by paying attention to the flows of expertise that shaped debt negotiations. Egypt presents a privileged site, in fact, for examining the invention and routinization of IFCs in the late nineteenth and early twentieth century. The liquidation of Egyptian debt was informed by earlier experiences of financial control, and the Egyptian experience itself later operated as a model or anti-model for other countries. By the turn of the twentieth century, and with the rise of public international law as a legal order, Egypt was becoming a key case-study within the emerging body of writings on IFCs.[9] By examining the transnational circulation of actors, discourses, and techniques, I thus look at the early precursors of the international structures of economic governance that emerged in the interwar period.[10]

The Debt Crisis and Its Actors: What Models of Financial Control?

Egypt contracted its first foreign loans in the 1860s, and for the next two decades, this would become the principal means of dealing with the government's chronic budget deficits. The local government first went into debt to fund the development of infrastructures. The growing specialization of the Egyptian economy in the production of cotton and the expansion of trade with Europe led to significant public works, whose cost could not be covered by state revenues. Starting from the late 1850s, the government began issuing short-term bonds and this soon gave way to long-term borrowing. Between 1862 and 1873, Egypt contracted eight loans on European capital markets, loans that were secured with specific state revenues, as well as the revenues of the private estates of the ruler and his family (*Dā'iras*).[11] The 1873 crisis in the international markets put a brake on the export of European capital to Egypt, however. The government found itself progressively reduced to seeking short-term advances in order to cover its administrative expenses and the interest payments on earlier loans. The public debt crisis came only a few months after the Ottoman default.

It was in this context of imminent bankruptcy and growing pressure from European creditors that, in the fall of 1875, the Khedive Ismāʿīl[12] asked the British government to send two advisers to help put state finances in order.[13] The Egyptian request came only a few weeks after Great Britain's purchase of the Khedive's shares in the Suez Canal Company, and resulted in the establishment of a British mission of inquiry, led by the Paymaster-General and Member of Parliament, Stephen Cave. The British fact-finding mission triggered, in turn, French intervention, with the dispatch of France's former consul in Alexandria, Maxime Outrey.[14] These financial missions were the starting point of intricate negotiations. While London banks, in particular Frühling & Goschen, mainly held bonds in long-term Egyptian loans, Paris-based ones, represented by the Crédit Foncier and the Crédit Agricole, held most of Egypt's short-term (floating) debt.[15] Financial discussions also involved, to various degrees, the Foreign Office and the Quai d'Orsay.[16]

While the details of these competing debt-settlement schemes—in terms of amount, maturity, interest rates, and so on—have been extensively analyzed, the way in which the instruments of foreign financial supervision were devised and negotiated is less well-known. These instruments were, I argue, not created *ex nihilo* but were part of an emerging body of transnational practical expertise relating to financial controls, in a period marked by the multiplication of defaults in many debtor countries.[17] The first country where an international debt administration was established was Tunisia, following the suspension of payment on foreign debt (1866–1867).[18] This early experiment in foreign financial control constituted a reference point for French plans in Egypt. The case of the Ottoman Empire, which defaulted in 1875, following various ineffective attempts at establishing mechanisms of financial control, was also constantly invoked in the discussions on the Egyptian debt liquidation. In fact, many of the French banking houses involved in Egyptian finance were also present in Constantinople.

A brief analysis of the creation of the Caisse de la Dette Publique (Caisse) in 1876 sheds light on the dynamics and stakes related to the transfer and appropriation of financial control instruments. The first official foreign mission on Egyptian finances, the Cave mission, suggested among its main recommendations the setting up of a Control department which would receive certain branches of Egyptian revenue, and exercise control over public indebtedness. The creation of such a body was seen as a key condition for the success of any debt-settlement scheme.[19] On the other hand, on the French side, the Parisian bankers Jules Pastré and Louis Frémy[20] supported the establishment of a state bank, with the object of effecting the conversion and gradual payment of the very large floating debt, which was mostly held by French banks. The proposed bank was to collect all state revenues, to ensure the payment of the coupons of the loans, in addition to being allowed, as a state bank, to issue bank notes. The French project was modeled after the Imperial Ottoman Bank (IOB), established by a group of French and British capitalists in Constantinople, and operating both as a state bank and as a "financial broker of the Empire."[21] Yet, the French negotiators did not wish to reproduce in Cairo the exact model of the IOB. They insisted on the bank's inability to set effective limits over public indebtedness, and they blamed this failure on the absence of any diplomatic connection that would have allowed this institution to exercise more rigorous control over its client.[22] Acting with the support of the French Ministry of Foreign Affairs, Pastré thus advocated the creation, as part of the proposed bank, of a commission of control entrusted with the surveillance of state accounts,[23] a suggestion that was rejected by Egyptian negotiators as a violation of sovereignty.

Ultimately, the French proposal failed, due to Egyptian and British opposition, and it gave way to the idea of a special body for the service of state debts (Caisse de la Dette Publique). Yet, disagreements surfaced again over the precise attributions of the new body. While the khedival government sought to limit the role of the Caisse to the reception of the assigned funds, French negotiators insisted that it has a more active role in the collection of revenues.[24] One of the main actors in these discussions was Victor Villet, the former vice-president of the International financial commission in Tunisia. [25] Villet, dispatched to Cairo in March 1876, hoped to use Tunisia as a model for Egypt.[26] In particular, he insisted that the Caisse be allowed to receive assigned revenues without any interference from the financial administration, and that it be provided with a right of investigation and surveillance over public accounts and over the collection of revenues.[27] However, the French expert was systematically marginalized by the Khedive, who refused to "be treated like the Bey of Tunisia," asserting both his sovereign rights as well as Ottoman sovereignty over Egypt. And ultimately, the institutional framework established in Cairo differed in significant ways. The Caisse, created in May 1876, was placed under the direction of foreign commissioners, selected by their respective governments.[28] These commissioners were allowed to receive the revenues assigned to debt directly from the collection officials, and not through the Treasury. However, the May decree did not provide the Caisse with a right of investigation and surveillance over public accounts and the budget. The power balance between the khedival government and the creditors, during these early stages of the financial crisis, still allowed the government to limit the extent of European encroachment upon local autonomy.

Financial Illegibility and Early Failures of Financial Control

Less than a year elapsed between the beginning of the financial discussions and the creation of the Caisse. Yet, from the moment of its creation, this body faced numerous difficulties. French and British banks had divergent interests in Egypt—as in the Ottoman Empire—and these disagreements led to a renegotiation of the debt consolidation scheme only a few months after its adoption. The new arrangement, concluded in November 1876 following the Goschen-Joubert mission,[29] also proved unworkable soon after its implementation. Similarly, the international financial commission, established two years later, admitted its inability to produce a precise and reliable estimate of the normal revenues of the country, drafting instead a temporary plan for debt repayment.

The internal disagreements among creditors, their unwillingness to reduce debt, as well as the lack of local political cooperation have often been invoked as the main factors explaining these repeated failures. A closer analysis also reveals, however, the extent to which the success of financial control also depended on the ability of Europeans to develop a network of information and communication. In practice, this task proved difficult owing to the lack of knowledge of local conditions as well as to the resistance that foreign experts and diplomats met on the ground.

In their attempt to settle the debt question, Europeans faced obvious problems in engaging with the local "information order."[30] There was first a problem of trust, which made the production of reliable estimates regarding the state of Egyptian finances a difficult task. In fact, the main source of information for Europeans was the Khedive himself and his close associates, a fact that raised continuous suspicion as to the veracity and accuracy of the statistics and other data provided by the local administration. And due to the language barrier, bankers, diplomats, and financial experts had to rely on translators and other informants, who, given their status as local intermediaries, also raised suspicions about their loyalty.[31]

In addition, a key obstacle resided in the Europeans' lack of familiarity with the indigenous fiscal and accounting systems. An analysis of the backgrounds and trajectories of the high-ranking civil servants who were sent to Cairo on short-term fact-finding missions, or as employees of the financial control institutions, shows that very few of them had prior experience with Egyptian finances. Unlike other sectors of the Egyptian bureaucracy, where the expertise of foreigners was actively solicited, public finance was traditionally closed to Europeans. In addition, while foreign advisors often claimed a special expertise, there were no well-defined requirements for what an "expert" should be, and the selection of these high-ranking officials was not determined according to a set of homogeneous criteria. Some of them were simply diplomats, with no prior experience in the field of public finance.[32] Others came from colonial administrations, such as

British officials who had earlier served in India.[33] Evelyn Baring, for example, worked as the secretary of the Viceroy in India before being selected as a member of the Caisse.[34] Similarly, Auckland Colvin began his career in India, before traveling to Egypt in 1878, to serve as the head of the cadastral survey, then as the British commissioner of the debt.[35] There were some experts who had formal training in public finance, like Charles Rivers Wilson, a former Controller-General of the British National Debt Office, or Ernest de Blignères and Baravelli, respectively, inspectors of Finance in France and in Italy. Yet their previous experiences within European financial administrations proved of little help to their work in Egypt, which involved dealing with an idiosyncratic accounting system combining elements from the Ottoman, Coptic, and European traditions.

The difficulties Europeans faced in engaging with the local "information order" can be seen, for instance, by examining how they dealt with the question of land taxation, which was the principal source of public revenue. According to the November 1876 decree, the land revenue of a number of provinces was to service the debt, but very quickly deficits started to appear in the Caisse accounts and the debt administration suspected the khedival government of embezzlement. Faced with the growing pressure of the creditors, local officials—whether at the central or provincial levels—did not, in fact, hesitate to divert funds assigned to debt, by creating special funds outside the State treasury,[36] or by marginalizing the collection agents who were under the authority of the Control institutions.[37]

In addition, while European creditors sought to establish special fact-finding missions to investigate the causes of deficits in debt revenues, these missions often failed to reach any decisive conclusions. For instance, when an international financial commission was formed in April 1878, one of its key objects of investigation was the question of taxation. The Commission of Inquiry on the Finances of Egypt (CIFE) tried to explore the causes of the great irregularity—both temporal and spatial—in land tax receipts. Some of these variations had to do with the difference between the taxation of the *ʿushr* lands—a class of privileged lands paying the tithe (*ʿushr*, literally "tenth")—and that of the other lands known as *kharāj*. But within each of these two categories, numerous variations were observed, which could not be accounted for. While the commission accumulated a large number of documents, and conducted interviews with a number of state officials, a significant gap existed between the expectations of investigators and the actual information provided by the various sources. Among the key witnesses interviewed by the commission were the two inspectors of Upper and Lower Egypt, ʿUmar Lutfi Pasha and Shahīn Pasha. In the words of the British consul-general in Cairo, "no men in the country are better acquainted with the state of affairs in the provinces, none are more powerful or influential for good or for evil."[38] The two inspectors were questioned on the way in which the land tax was determined and collected in the various localities; other questions focused on the mode of collection of tax arrears and on the nature and extent of the surveillance exercised by the central authority on village *shaykhs*, who were granted extensive prerogatives in the tax collection process.[39] The interview, however, was marked by mutual suspicion and the investigators' questioning tactics resembled the methods of a court interrogation.[40] The inspectors, meanwhile, gave laconic replies and refrained from answering certain questions. Unsurprisingly, the commissioners appeared disappointed by the final outcome of the encounter, pointing out that the two Egyptian officials "lied with utmost effrontery."[41] Similarly, when a few weeks later, the investigators visited the headquarters of the Jīza province, near Cairo, in order to observe the functioning of the financial administration on a local level, the commission's vice-president, Wilson, noted with irony:

> The day before yesterday all the Commissioners and Secretaries drove out to Guizeh and put the unhappy Receiver-General of the Province to the torture (mental) of an uncommonly sharp examination; all his words [were] taken down by a shorthand writer whom he must have thought to be an emissary of the devil! He lied, poor wretch, with persistency and thoroughness, and so I think will most, if not all, of the fellows we interrogate.[42]

The available archives do not give us access, however, to the manner in which local officials perceived the interviewers.

The problem, for the commission, was not only one of trust. When its members attempted to check the books and accounts of this *mudīriyya*, as well as those of other provinces, they were faced with "insurmountable difficulties."[43] They quickly realized that the nomenclature of accounts used by the financial administration at the provincial level was different from the classification adopted in the monthly statements of revenue and expenditure submitted by the khedival government to debt administration. In addition, the examination of accounts could only be done through local interpreters or *drogmans*, whose loyalty was also suspect.[44]

The Debt Liquidation and "Administrative Reform"

These early difficulties to a large extent shaped the evolution of financial control, which gradually came to encompass the broader question of "administrative reform." While Europeans initially sought to establish a set of enforcement mechanisms, through the creation of bodies representing foreign creditors and the assignment of specific revenues to debt repayment, these arrangements soon came to be seen as inadequate. Rather, it was the wholesale "reform" of the financial administration, entrusted to a body of European agents, that gradually came to be viewed as the guarantee for Egypt's repayment of its debts. The extension of European control over Egypt was based, on the one hand, on a "liberal" discourse highlighting the lack of transparency and legitimacy of the khedival government and, on the other, on a program of institutional reform, which effectively impeded the development of constitutional politics.

In fact, by 1878–1879, the "reform" of public finances, which involved the reorganization of taxation and of public accounts, was becoming a key element of creditor states' policy in Egypt. And the financial question was increasingly inscribed in a discourse of political reform. If, as noted by Ann Stoler, state-sponsored commissions of inquiry are privileged sites for reorganizing knowledge, the language used by the CIFE in its first report clearly illustrates the politicization of the discourse on debt.[45] The report established a direct link between the state of Egyptian finances and the existing political regime. Criticizing the "limitless" powers of the head of state in financial matters, the report proposed the necessary limitation of these powers as a condition for exiting the crisis.[46] To be sure, the notion of a "spendthrift" and "extravagant" oriental ruler, applied to the Khedive Ismaʿīl, was not in itself new. What was new, however, was how this set of representations came to constitute the dominant framework within which the financial crisis would be analyzed. The crisis was increasingly discussed in terms of the extreme concentration of power in the hands of the Khedive and his immediate entourage, as well as the absence of checks and balances, in the form of independent legislative and judicial bodies. Traces of this discourse can also be found in the British press, such as the articles by the influential public commentator and journalist Edward Dicey, who castigated the prodigality of the Khedive, pointing to his and his family's large private estates.[47] In fact, with the growing deterioration of the financial situation in the years 1877 and 1878, European creditor groups started campaigning for dispossessing the Khedive and his family of their properties. The growing focalization on the figure of the Khedive Ismāʿīl, in European financial and political circles, is to be understood in this context.

In practical terms, the program of "administrative and financial reform" meant an extension of the debt administration at the expense of khedival authority, rather than the reinforcement of the checks and balances. In 1878, following the publication of the CIFE's preliminary report, the Khedive was made to accept the cession of his private properties to the state, and these properties subsequently served as a security on which the Domains Loan was raised. In addition, the Khedive's Privy Council (*al-Majlis al-khusūsī*) was dismantled, to be replaced by a Council of Ministers (*Majlis al-nuzzār*) which became in charge of formulating and implementing administrative policies. This meant that the Khedive could no longer direct the government's daily affairs.[48] In the cabinet formed in August 1878, Wilson was appointed Minister of Finance, while the French member of the Caisse, Blignères, became Minister of Public Works.

The years 1878 and 1879 also marked the beginning of a process of reorganization of state accounts, under Anglo-French leadership. Yet, rather than being understood in terms of the transfer of a single Western model of rationality to an "oriental" country, the reform of public finance was in reality a contested political matter, and a terrain of inter-imperial rivalry. While European controllers aimed at reinforcing their control over the accounts of the various provinces and administrations, they faced resistance from the Egyptian bureaucracy. In addition, the French and the British disagreed over the details of the reorganization of state accounts and, in particular, over the structure and attributions of the new audit authority. While the French sought to create a commission of audit, upon the model of the French Cour des Comptes, the British objected to such a proposal. As noted by the British diplomat Lord Lyons, political control and financial control were highly contingent on the nature of the accounting language adopted:

> It is not to be doubted that French officials in Egypt will seek to introduce in that country the French complicated and theoretical system of finance and the French financial phraseology. […] it has in their eyes the great merit—that it will be hardly possible to work it there by other than French hands.
>
> It may be necessary for the Englishmen employed in Egypt, and especially for those who have any part in directing or inspecting the finances of

that country, to be very watchful on this point, and to resist any French encroachments of the kind at the outset.

I am told that M. de Blignères, for his intimate acquaintance with what the French call "comptabilité," is well adapted to the task of imposing the French system upon Egypt.[49]

Government accounts were thus becoming a prominent arena of competition and comparison between various European models. Ultimately, Wilson, who held the key portfolio of Finance within the new Egyptian cabinet, was able to impose British views. The decree of December 14, 1878, established the new position of Auditor-General of Receipts and Expenditure, on the British model of the Comptroller and Auditor-General.[50] Selected among the members of the Caisse, the Auditor-General was to ensure that "the revenues comply with existing laws and that expenditure complies with the budget."[51] He was to exercise preventive control and continuous monitoring over financial operations. In parallel, Wilson nominated the sub-Controller of Revenues, Fitzgerald, to the newly created position of Controller-General of Accounts. Before arriving in Egypt, Fitzgerald had worked as Assistant Comptroller-General of India, then as Accountant-General of Madras, and of Burma, and he took part in the reorganization of the Indian accounting system.[52] Once in Egypt, Fitzgerald established the Directorate-General of State Accounts, which absorbed the earlier accounting administration, and he selected a number of British, French, and Italians to fill key positions.[53] The new body was responsible for preparing the budget as well as the statements of receipts and expenditure, and it later also became in charge of auditing state accounts.[54]

At the same time, the European-led "administrative revolution" made no room for an independent parliamentary institution. As noted earlier, European critique of khedival rule was made in reference to the liberal political model, and the discourse of financial controllers and advisors such as Cromer, Wilson, and Blignères strongly emphasized the link between the financial crisis and the "despotic" nature of the government. The idea that countries with constitutional governments were more likely to repay their debt was, in reality, relatively commonplace, and it informed some of the Rothschilds' attempts to impose a similar type of conditionality on several of their loans.[55] Yet, in practice, it was a very different model that European administrators ultimately sought to implement in the context of Egypt. Here, the language of "character" operated as the main justification for excluding any local representative institutions.[56] Egyptians were portrayed as lacking the moral and mental discipline necessary for establishing an orderly and sound financial system, and thus as being incapable of self-government. The European response to the growing number of defaults in non-European countries was thus producing its own vocabulary and justifications for the type of austerity program to be carried out in debt-ridden countries of the periphery: a policy based on the collaboration of a small circle of local politicians, identified by their Western financial advisors as "reformers."[57] Public debt was also becoming a crucial terrain for the production of discourses about "backwardness" and "civilization." It constituted, in this sense, an important site where the tensions and paradoxes of liberal imperialism were played out.[58]

It is to be noted, however, that the implementation of the European "reform" program was far from a linear process: It was challenged by a wide protest movement that culminated with the 'Urabi revolt (1879–1882). Historians have shown how the 'Urabi movement was made of a multitude of mobilizations by various social groups (the big landlords, moderately wealthy and rich peasants, the intelligentsia, army officers, urban merchants, and artisan guilds), whose interests sometimes coincided and sometimes diverged.[59] Within this broad nationalist movement, the question of budget control and consultative government remained a key claim, first raised by the indigenous semi-legislative body, *Majlis Shūrā al-Nuwwāb* (the Chamber of Delegates). The "National Program" drafted by the Chamber in 1879 was based, on the one hand, on a debt settlement scheme that would permit property-owning elites to maintain their economic privileges, which were directly threatened by European control, and, on the other, on extending the powers of the Chamber, with regard to budget control and parliamentary monitoring of public finance.[60] Yet, the debate around the financial question also went beyond official instances, to include a wider public, whose demands were expressed via newspapers, petitions, and so on. Some of these writings did not limit their critique to the "exactions" of European controllers, but extended to the "corruption" of the Khedive and his close associates. In this context, the very definition of notions such as "public interest" (*al-maslaha al-ᶜumūmiyya*) and "reform" (*islāh*) became subject to debate and contestation, not only between Europeans and Egyptians but also within the national movement itself.[61]

An Egyptian Model of International Financial Control?

In his *longue-durée* history of international financial advising, Marc Flandreau argues that the financial crises of the second half of the nineteenth century contributed in important ways to the development of "money doctoring": Money doctors traveled from Western Europe and the United States to crisis-ridden countries in Latin America, Eastern Europe, and the Mediterranean; and international flows of expertise operated, he argues, as complements of international capital flows.[62] Yet, a closer attention to the transnational circulation of actors, ideas, and instruments shows that non-Western countries were more than simple recipients of ready-made expertise.[63] I have examined, above, how financial discussions in Egypt were informed by the Tunisian and Ottoman experiences. I would like to conclude this chapter by examining how the Egyptian experience in turn informed later cases of IFC and how, in the process, it contributed to the development of a body of practical expertise on financial controls.

The late 1870s and early 1880s were marked by a gradual extension of financial control instruments in Egypt and these shifts had consequences beyond the national level. The Egyptian and the Ottoman debt liquidations were in fact negotiated in parallel, and the developments in Cairo had a direct influence on the discussions between the Ottoman government and its creditors.[64] While the setting up of an international financial commission in Cairo in 1878 opened the way to a period of increased foreign intervention in Egyptian finance and administration, a number of actors sought to replicate this experiment in Constantinople. The establishment of an international commission was suggested for the first time during the 1878 Berlin Congress, but the proposal met with opposition from the Porte. And the growing European pressures on the Khedive Ismāʿīl to abdicate, in the summer of 1879, only hardened Ottoman resistance to any encroachment on its financial sovereignty.[65] As for the major European powers, especially Great Britain and France, their main concerns focused on the maintenance of the balance of power in Europe and the stabilization of the Ottoman Empire; financial questions were thus relegated to a secondary position. The project of an international financial commission was put back on the agenda, in the spring of 1880, with the visit of one of the main actors of Egyptian negotiations, Goschen, as a special ambassador to the Porte. The British banker elaborated a plan, which included the launching of a financial enquiry, coupled with an extensive reform program, on the Egyptian model. Yet the proposal did not get the support of the IOB, which remained committed to the 1879 convention that framed its relations with the Ottoman government. The Goschen project was also frustrated by the general agreement among the Powers that the priority issue upon which Ottoman assent had to be secured was the surrender of Dulcingo to Montenegro; as a consequence, no immediate action was taken on the financial question.[66]

Ultimately, the creditor states were not directly involved in the lengthy negotiation that led to the adoption of the Decree of Muharrem (1881), which remained in essence a private arrangement between the Imperial government and its creditors.[67] In addition, the lessons derived from the Egyptian experience led the newly created Ottoman Public Debt Administration (OPDA) to keep the number of foreign officials as small as possible. The provincial executive was thus left entirely in the hands of the locals, while foreign officials only held positions of supervision and control.[68] In the words of Vincent Caillard, the president of the OPDA, who also had previous experience in Egyptian affairs,

> it is vain to import numbers of highly trained Frenchmen or Englishmen and set them down to apply the methods they have been taught to regard as perfect upon a population alien by race, antagonistic in religion and perhaps naturally more averse from change than even the most conservative in the European world [...]. We have seen an example of this in Egypt: the reasons which gave popularity to the late rising there, would operate with far greater force in Turkey.[69]

Here again, we see how racial notions occupied a key place in foreign advisors' thinking about financial control. Yet, rather than serving as a model of financial control, the Egyptian experiment appears, in this particular case, to have operated as an anti-model.

While it would be possible to further extend this analysis by investigating the ways in which the Egyptian experience influenced other cases of financial control in the 1880s and 1890s, one also needs to pay attention to the narratives that were constructed around it. By the turn of the twentieth century, in fact, the Egyptian debt liquidation was becoming a key case-study within the nascent literature on IFCs. International lawyers started mentioning specific institutions and instruments used in state practice, such as the Caisse, as examples in their writings on "international commissions." Public international law was then a young legal discipline, and lawyers attempted to expand its scope.[70] In this context, the Egyptian debt administration, as well as the Ottoman one, operated as a "justification narrative," to legitimize the use of international commissions in public international law.[71] In other words, the ad hoc arrangements devised for the liquidation of Egyptian bankruptcy, arrangements which resulted from complex power relations involving a multiplicity of actors, were gradually becoming formalized in the language of international law and integrated in Geneva's international organization of the interwar period.[72]

NOTES

1. See, for instance, Nicolas Politis, *Les Emprunts d'État en droit international* (Paris: A Durand et Pedone-Lauriel, 1894); François Deville, *Les contrôles financiers internationaux et la souveraineté de l'État* (Saint-Nicolas: V. Arsant, 1912); Edwin Borchard and William Wynne, *State Insolvency and Foreign Bondholders* (New Haven: Yale University Press, 1951).
2. David Landes, *Bankers and Pashas: International Finance and Economic Imperialism in Egypt* (London: Heinemann, 1858); Samir Saul, *La France et l'Égypte de 1882 à 1914. Intérêts économiques et implications politiques* (Paris: Comité pour l'histoire économique et financière de la France, 1997); Jacques Thobie, "Banques européennes. Finances et industrie au Moyen-Orient, 1870–1914," *Annales du Levant*, no. 2 (1987): 177–86.
3. Jean Bouvier, "Les intérêts financiers et la question d'Égypte (1875–1876)," *Revue historique*, no. 224 (1960): 75–104; Richard Atkins, "The Origins of the Anglo-French Condominium in Egypt, 1875–1876," *The Historian* 36, no. 2 (1974): 264–82.
4. Peter J. Cain and Anthony G. Hopkins, *British Imperialism: Innovation and Expansion* (London: Longman, 2000).
5. See Robert Tignor, "The 'Indianization' of the Egyptian Administration under British Rule," *American Historical Review* 68, no. 3, (1963): 636–61. On khedival finances, see Robert Hunter, *Egypt under the Khedives, 1805–1879: From Household Government to Modern Bureaucracy* (Cairo: The American University in Cairo Press, 1999), 60–66.
6. See Alain Desrosières, *Pour une sociologie historique de la quantification. L'argument statistique I* (Paris: Presses de l'École des mines, 2008); Pierre Lascoumes and Patrick Le Galès, *Gouverner par les instruments* (Paris: Presses de Sciences Po, 2004).
7. Andrea Mennicken, Peter Miller, "Accounting, Territorialization and Power," *Foucault Studies*, no. 13 (2012): 6.
8. On the relationship between public debt and discourses about "good government," see also Chap. 20 in this volume.

9. Lea Heimbeck, "Discovering Legal Silence: Global Legal History and the Liquidation of State Bankruptcies (1854–1907)," in *Entanglements in Legal History: Conceptual Approaches*, ed. Thomas Duve (Frankfurt am Main: Max Planck Institute for European Legal History, 2014), 475.
10. On this period, see Juan Flores and Yann Decorzant, "Going multilateral? Financial markets' access and the League of Nations loans, 1923–1928," *Economic History Review* 69, no. 2 (2016): 653–78; Patricia Clavin and Jens-Wilhelm Wessel, "Transnationalism and the League of Nations: Understanding the Work of Its Economic and Financial Organisation," *Contemporary European History* 14, no. 4 (2005): 465–492; Susan Pedersen, *The Guardians: The League of Nations and the Crisis of Empire* (Oxford: Oxford University Press, 2015).
11. Annual charges on these loans, including interest and amortization, ranged between 10 and 15 percent. AbdelAziz Ezzelarab, *European Control and Egypt's Traditional Elites: A Case Study in Elite Economic Nationalism* (Lewiston: Edwin Ellen Press, 2002), 11.
12. The Khedive Ismāʿīl was the ruler of Egypt from 1863 to 1879. Egypt was at the time a semi-autonomous province of the Ottoman Empire.
13. British National Archives, Foreign Office (hereafter FO), FO 407/7, no. 1, Stanton to Derby, 30 October 1875; FO 407/7, no. 3, Stanton to Derby, 6 November 1875.
14. French Ministry of Foreign Affairs (hereafter MAE), Political Correspondence (hereafter CP), Égypte, vol. 57, no. 1, Outrey to Decazes, 12 January 1876.
15. Bouvier, "Les intérêts financiers," 75–104.
16. Authors have noted the significant involvement of French diplomacy in defense of Parisian banks, a policy attributed in part to the close relationship tying political and financial interests in this country. On the British side, the literature has also highlighted how, despite "more covert" techniques of intervention, the British government was able to maintain sufficient control over the course of negotiations, and to achieve ascendency over the French. Atkins, "The Origins of the Anglo-French," 264–82; Bouvier, "Les intérêts financiers," 75–104.
17. The Egyptian default was preceded by defaults in Tunisia, Honduras, Saint-Domingue, Spain, Guatemala, Costa-Rica, Bolivia, Paraguay, Uruguay and Peru. Saul, *La France et l'Égypte*, 234.
18. The International financial commission was made up of representatives of French, British and Italian bondholders, in addition to a French official and two Tunisian officials. As the hegemonic power in North Africa, France played a major role in the establishment of the commission. Jean Ganiage, *Les origines du protectorat français en Tunisie 1861–1881* (Paris: Presses Universitaires de France, 1959), 367–68. For an analysis of

European interventions in Latin America, during the same period, see Chap. 5 in this volume.
19. British Parliamentary Papers (hereafter PP), Egypt, no. 7 (1876), Report by Mr. Cave on the Financial Condition of Egypt, 9.
20. Respectively, the directors of the Anglo-Egyptian bank and the Crédit Foncier. Jules Pastré was also the brother of Jean-Baptiste Pastré who was the founder of Pastré frères, one of the largest banking and commercial houses in Egypt. Landes, *Bankers and Pashas*, 195–96.
21. Edhem Eldem, "The Imperial Ottoman Bank: Actor or Instrument of Ottoman Modernization," in *Modern Banking in the Balkans and West-European Capital in the Nineteenth and Twentieth Centuries*, ed. Kostas Kostis (Aldershot: Ashgate, 1999), 52.
22. FO 407/7, no. 108, Lord Lyons to Derby, 14 February 1876.
23. MAE, CP, Égypte, vol. 57, no. 23, Outrey to Decazes, 27 February 1876.
24. MAE, CP, Égypte, vol. 57, no. 39, Projet de décret pour la création d'une Caisse de la dette publique, 29 April 1876.
25. On the work of Villet in Tunisia, see Ganiage, *Les origines du protectorat*, 370–80; Abdel-Jawed Zouari, "European Capitalist Penetration of Tunisia, 1860–1881: A Case-Study of the Regency's Debt Crisis and the Establishment of the International Financial Commission," (PhD diss., University of Washington, 1998), 262–71.
26. In Tunisia, the financial commission was endowed with extensive attributions, which included investigating the country's financial resources, receiving the entirety of state revenues, and drawing up a debt liquidation plan. Ganiage, *Les origines du protectorat*, 367–68.
27. MAE, CP, Égypte, vol. 57, no. 39, Victor Villet, Observations sur le projet de création d'une Caisse d'amortissement, 29 April 1876.
28. The decree was issued following the agreement concluded between the khedival administration and the "Grand Syndicat," a banking consortium mainly formed by the Comptoir d'Escompte, the Crédit Foncier, the Crédit Agricole, and the Anglo-Egyptian bank. Bouvier, "Les intérêts financiers," 93–94.
29. Named after the two bankers who conducted the mission, namely George Goschen, from the Frühling and Goschen bank, and Edmond Joubert, from the Banque de Paris et des Pays-Bas.
30. Christopher Alan Bayly, *Empire and Information: Intelligence Gathering and Social Communication in India, 1780–1870* (Cambridge: Cambridge University Press, 1996), 3.
31. Rapport préliminaire de la commission supérieure d'enquête, in *Règlement de la situation financière du gouvernement égyptien, 1876–1885* (Le Caire: Imprimerie Nationale, 1897), 253.

32. For instance, when a Franco-British financial inspection body (the Dual Control) was established, the French foreign service selected its ex-ambassador in Rome, the Baron de Malaret, as the French member.
33. On the circulation of British colonial administrators between India and Egypt, see Tignor, "The 'Indianization' of the Egyptian Administration."
34. Baring would later become the British consul-general in Egypt and the *de facto* ruler of the country. Roger Owen, *Lord Cromer: Victorian Imperialist, Edwardian Proconsul* (Oxford: Oxford University Press, 2004).
35. William Ferguson and Beatson Laurie, *Sketches of Some Distinguished Anglo-Indians* (Delhi: Asian Educational Series, 1999), 125–36.
36. Dār al-wathā'iq al-qawmiyya (Egypt, hereafter DWQ), *al-Majlis al-khusūsī* (hereafter MK), 0019-02008, no. 28, Daftar qayd al-qarārāt bi l-majlis al-khusūsī, 18 jumādā al- ūlā 1294 (31 May 1877).
37. FO 633/2, Baring to Goschen, 22 February 1878. See also Jirjis Hunayn, *al-Atyān wa l-darā'ib fī l-qutr al-misrī* (Cairo: al-Matbaʻa al-amīriyya, 1904), 27.
38. FO 407/10, no. 174, Vivian to Salisbury, 17 May 1878.
39. DWQ, *Majlis al-wuzarā'* (hereafter MW), 0075-022775 and 0075-022777, Commission supérieure d'enquête. Interrogatoire de ʻUmar Lutfi pacha et Shahīn pacha, 13 and 14 May 1878.
40. In his study of official commissions of inquiry in nineteenth century Britain, Oz Frankel noted that these bodies followed investigation procedures very similar to common law methods and court practices. Oz Frankel, *States of Inquiry: Social Investigations and Print Culture in Nineteenth Century Britain and the United States* (Baltimore: Johns Hopkins University Press, 2006), 13–14.
41. FO 407/10, no. 174, Vivian to Salisbury, 17 May 1878.
42. Charles Rivers Wilson, *Chapters from My Official Life* (London: Edward Arnold, 1916), 121.
43. Rapport préliminaire, in *Règlement de la situation financière*, 253.
44. For a more detailed analysis of the work of this commission, see Malak Labib, "Crise de la dette publique et missions financières européennes en Égypte, 1878–1879," *Monde(s). Histoire, Espaces, Relations* 2, no. 4 (2013): 23–43.
45. Ann Laura Stoler, *Along the Archival Grain: Epistemic Anxieties and Colonial Common Sense* (Princeton: Princeton University Press, 2008), 29.
46. Rapport préliminaire, in *Règlement de la situation financière*, 259.
47. See for instance, Edward Dicey, "Egypt and the Khedive," *The Nineteenth Century and After: A Monthly Review* 2 (Dec. 1877): 854–67.
48. Hunter, *Egypt under the Khedives*, 201.
49. FO 407/13, n°103, Lyons to Salisbury, 9 August 1879.

50. In the United Kingdom, the office of the Comptroller and Auditor-General was created in 1866 to carry out the examination, certification and reporting on government accounts. The Comptroller and Auditor-General combined the functions of the Comptroller-General of the Exchequer with those of the Commissioners of Audit. This new office was created in the context of the reforms of government accounting initiated by William Gladstone, who was the Chancellor of the Exchequer from 1859 to 1866. Marie-Laure Legay et al., eds., *Dictionnaire historique de la comptabilité publique 1500–1850* (Rennes: Presses Universitaires de Rennes, 2010), 16–26.
51. FO 407/10, no. 424, Nubar to the Khedive, 17 December 1878.
52. On the reorganization of Indian government accounts, see Manu Goswami, *Producing India: From Colonial Economy to National Space* (Chicago: University of Chicago Press, 2004), 76–78.
53. DWQ, *Dīwān al-māliyya* (hereafter DM), 3003-019231, *Jarīdat istihqāqāt qism ʿumūm al-hisābāt bi l-māliyya*, 1882; FO 407/19, no. 342, Malet to Granville, 27 February 1882.
54. For more details on the reorganization of state accounts, see Malak Labib, "La Statistique d'État en Égypte à l'ère coloniale. Finances, espace public et représentation (1875–1922)" (PhD diss., Aix-Marseille Université, 2015).
55. Owen, *Lord Cromer*, 109; Niall Ferguson, *The World's Banker: The History of the House of Rothschild* (London: Weidenfeld & Nicolson, 2000).
56. On the centrality of the language of "character" in the discourse of British officials in Egypt, see Peter Cain, "Character and Imperialism: The British Financial Administration of Egypt, 1878–1913," *Journal of Imperial and Commonwealth History* 34, no. 2 (2006): 132. Yet, Cain surprisingly argues that the British "tried to encourage the development of a constitutional monarchy and liberal political institutions in Egypt that would provide, under British guidance, disciplines necessary to long-term financial control and stability." Ibid., 184.
57. Owen, *Lord Cromer*, 136.
58. On liberal imperialism and the notion of race, see Jennifer Pitts, *A Turn to Empire: The Rise of Imperial Liberalism in Britain and France* (Princeton: Princeton University Press, 2005), 19–21.
59. There is a substantial literature on the 'Urabi revolt. See Juan Cole, *Colonialism and Revolution in the Middle East: Social and Cultural Origins of Egypt's 'Urabi Movement* (Princeton: Princeton University Press, 1993); Latīfa Sālim, *al-Quwā al-ijtimāʿiyya fī l-thawra al-ʿurābiyya* (Cairo: al-Hayʾa al-ʿāmma li l- kitāb, 1981).
60. See AbdelAziz Ezzelarab, "The Fiscal and Constitutional Program of Egypt's Traditional Elites in 1879: A Documentary and Contextual

Analysis of 'al- La'iha al-Wataniyya' (The National Program)," *Journal of the Economic and Social History of the Orient* 52, no. 2 (2009): 301–24.
61. Labib, "La Statistique d'État en Égypte," 139–42.
62. Marc Flandreau, "Introduction: Money and Doctors," in *Money Doctors: The Experience of Financial Advising, 1850–2000,* ed. Marc Flandreau (New York: Routledge, 2003), 1–9.
63. Blaise Truong-Loï, "La dette publique chinoise à la fin de la dynastie Qing (1874–1913)" (MA thesis, Institut d'Études Politiques de Paris, 2015), 157–67.
64. On this point, see Chap. 6 in this volume.
65. Christopher Clay, *Gold for the Sultan: Western Bankers and Ottoman Finance, 1856–1881* (London: I. B. Tauris, 2000), 383–84, 441–42.
66. Ibid., 473–75.
67. Edhem Eldem, "Ottoman Financial Integration with Europe: Foreign Loans, the Ottoman Bank and the Ottoman Public Debt," *European Review* 13, no. 3 (2005).
68. See Chap. 6 in this volume. See also, Murat Birdal, *The Political Economy of Ottoman Public Debt: Insolvency and European Financial Control in the Late Nineteenth Century* (London: Tauris Academic Studies, 2010), 105.
69. Cited in Ali Coşkun Tunçer, *Sovereign Debt and International Financial Control: the Middle East and the Balkans, 1870–1913* (Basingstoke: Palgrave Macmillan, 2015), 67.
70. Lea Heimbeck, "Liquidation of State Bankruptcies in Public International Law. Juridification and Legal Avoidance between 1824 and 1907," *Journal of the History of International Law* 15 (2013): 10–13.
71. Lea Heimbeck, "Discovering Legal Silence," 475.
72. On this point, see also Chap. 20 in this volume.

Trading Sovereignty for Capital? Public Debt in West Africa, 1871–1914

Leigh Gardner

The period from around 1880 until 1914, described as the "first large experiment in financial globalisation," also saw the first entry of African governments into the London market for sovereign debt.[1] African governments were not major players in these markets before 1914. Apart from the Cape Colony and Natal, incorporated as South Africa in 1912, the governments of sub-Saharan Africa were relatively small players on the global capital market, attracting a minute share of investment.[2] They also borrowed relatively late in the period. Apart from two small bond issues by Liberia and Sierra Leone in 1871, the first West African loan was not marketed in London until 1902. Still, the history of borrowing by African countries represents an important gap in our understanding of the relationship between sovereignty and creditworthiness in the first era of financial globalization.

Around the world, this period saw both a proliferation of newly recognized states as well as the colonial conquest of significant portions of Asia

L. Gardner (✉)
Department of Economic History, London School of Economics, London, UK
e-mail: l.a.gardner@lse.ac.uk

© The Author(s) 2020
N. Barreyre, N. Delalande (eds.), *A World of Public Debts*,
Palgrave Studies in the History of Finance,
https://doi.org/10.1007/978-3-030-48794-2_8

and Africa. Economic development, often defined at the time by the construction of infrastructure and the promotion of export industries, was an important part of nation-building for new governments on the periphery, whether independent or colonial administrations, and usually required foreign capital. However, access to capital was frequently linked to some limitation on the sovereignty of borrowers, to the point where some have speculated about an explicit "trade-off for poor countries between political sovereignty and creditworthiness."[3]

Sovereignty is a complicated concept, with no universally agreed definition.[4] It can be defined both internally, in terms of the state's superiority over other institutions within its territorial realm, or externally, reflecting its relationship to other states. In some cases, both external and internal sovereignty can be further divided into constituent functions. This divisibility of sovereignty was central to imperial relations, both formal and informal, during the period. In their study of empires as a political system, Burbank and Cooper describe a system of "layered" sovereignty.[5] Protectorates and systems of indirect rule imagined, at least in theory, that indigenous rulers had ceded control over external sovereignty while retaining internal sovereignty.[6]

The notion of an exchange of sovereignty for capital also raises problems of agency. A number of different actors played a part in this system, and each had their own interests. This was as true in African countries as in the two Latin American countries compared in Chap. 5 of this volume. These included the governments of both lending and borrowing countries, financial intermediaries, investors in lending countries, and taxpayers in borrowing counties. How these groups interacted across this period varied depending on specific circumstances, but shaped the ways in which countries could access capital. In many cases, limitations on sovereignty were imposed by force, through colonial conquest or gunboat diplomacy.

Colonies in particular were able to borrow at reduced costs, referred to in financial history literature as the "empire effect."[7] Whether or not this was a benefit to the colonies seems to be a matter of perspective. Davis and Huttenback, in their accounting of the costs and benefits of empire, argue that reduced costs of borrowing represented "the second largest component of the imperial subsidy," the first being imperial defense spending.[8] Others take a more circumspect view. Kesner, for example, argues that the ability to borrow more was "at best a mixed blessing" for colonies.[9] At the other end of the spectrum, anthropologist and activist David Graeber writes of Madagascar under French rule that "one of the first things

General Gallieni did after 'pacification,' as they liked to call it then, was to impose heavy taxes on the Malagasy population, in part so they could reimburse the costs of having been invaded, but also, since French colonies were supposed to be fiscally self-supporting, to defray the costs of building the railroads, highways, bridges, plantations and so forth that the French regime wished to build."[10]

Conquest was not the only way in which sovereignty was sacrificed, however. At times, elites in borrowing countries agreed to concede some sovereign rights in exchange for access to capital or reduced borrowing costs.[11] Such concessions took different forms, but perhaps the most common were known as international financial control regimes in which foreign officials had some degree of control over the public finances of the borrower. These could be imposed by coercion or invitation, and at times had a destabilizing effect on domestic politics, as illustrated in this volume by the studies of the Ottoman Empire (Chap. 6) and Egypt (Chap. 7).[12]

Borrowing by African countries represents a historically interesting test of how well such sacrifices in sovereignty satisfied investor appetites for risk. Even with much of the continent under colonial rule, contemporaries remained wary about lending to Africa.[13] No less a figure than John Maynard Keynes complained in 1924 that "perhaps the limit of the absurdity, to which the Trustee Acts can lead, was reached early this year when £2,000,000 was borrowed by Southern Rhodesia on about the same terms as a large English borough would have to pay." Southern Rhodesia, he continued, "is a place somewhere in the middle of Africa with a handful of white inhabitants and not even so many, I believe, as one million savage black ones."[14] In the minds of many investors, African countries remained marginal and the subject of considerable doubt regarding their economic prospects. How they still managed to borrow, to pay for the construction of public works or shore up budget shortfalls, provides an important lens into the political implications of sovereign borrowing. What were the political hazards and opportunities of lending to Africa for both borrowers and lenders? What motivated different groups to act as they did and how did this change over time?

This chapter uses the case of four countries in West Africa which raised loans on the London market before 1914 to examine the relationship between sovereignty and debt in an African context. Three (the Gold Coast, Nigeria, and Sierra Leone) were formal colonies of Britain. The fourth (Liberia) had political independence at the start of the period but came under increasingly stringent international financial controls linked to its efforts to borrow. Though all four struggled to attract investors, the three formally colonized territories were able to borrow more and on better terms than Liberia, even after Liberian elites had ceded important sovereign privileges to foreign interests. This chapter examines the different networks of private and public interests in which the four countries were embedded to explain this difference.

A Brief History of West African Borrowing[15]

This section offers a brief history of the borrowing patterns of four West African governments up to 1914.[16] These were part of a larger group of "emerging market" countries, with underdeveloped domestic financial markets and relatively low per capita incomes.[17] Limited access to domestic financing meant that, in practice, any significant government borrowing in all four countries had to be done on foreign markets. This section therefore focuses on foreign loans undertaken by these four governments in order to outline the problem to be addressed later in the chapter, namely the different conditions under which colonies and independent states borrowed. Subsequent sections consider the interaction of foreign debt with other types of liabilities.[18]

For most of this era of financial globalization, none of the four West African governments looked like likely candidates for investment. Trade taxes remained the most important revenue source, and budgets were therefore vulnerable to any sudden decline in the prices of a few key exports. The volume of those exports was increasing rapidly, but from a low level. On the expenditure side, there were frequent shocks linked to the still-ongoing process of colonial conquest. All four of the governments considered here spent most years in deficit rather than surplus, raising the potential risks of default during years when the budget did not add up. In this context it is perhaps not surprising that, as an underwriter in London put it in 1911, West African stocks "have never been a popular investment among the outside public."[19]

Nevertheless, they were able to borrow, sometimes in considerable sums. Table 8.1 provides a list of loans raised in London by all four West African governments over the period 1871–1914. Liberia and Sierra Leone were the first West African governments to borrow in this way, both in 1871. Sierra Leone borrowed a total of £50,000 in two installments of £25,000 at 6 percent interest. Liberia raised a loan of £100,000 at 7 percent. An interest rate of above 5–6 percent signaled limited confidence; in

Table 8.1 Loan issues to sub-Saharan Africa, 1871–1913

Date	Country	Amount	Rate	Price
May 1871	Sierra Leone	£25,000	6%	100
Aug 1871	Liberia	£100,000	7%	85
Jun 1873	Sierra Leone	£25,000	6%	100
March 1902	Gold Coast	£1,035,000	3%	91
June 1904	Sierra Leone	£1,250,000	4%	98
March 1905	S Nigeria	£2,000,000	3.5%	97
1906	Liberia	£100,000	6%	NA
May 1908	S Nigeria	£3,000,000	4%	99
May 1909	Gold Coast	£1,000,000	3.5%	99.5
Nov 1911	S Nigeria	£5,000,000	4%	99.5
Jan 1913	Liberia	$1,700,000	5%	97
Dec 1913	Sierra Leone	£1,000,000	4%	97

Source: Gardner, "Colonialism or supersanctions."

the period up to 1914, according to one account, only "2 percent of government debentures and 5 percent of company debentures returned over 6.5 percent."[20] In addition, 3 years' interest payments were deducted from the proceeds. This meant that, at best, the most money Liberia could hope to receive for £100,000 in bonds was just under £50,000. Owing in part to the rather ruinous terms of its loan, the Liberian government defaulted in 1874, joining a number of other countries which defaulted or rescheduled their debts in the 1870s.[21]

Interest arrears on the loan accumulated until the Liberian government agreed to a renegotiation with the Corporation of Foreign Bondholders in 1898, the same year that Sierra Leone finished repaying its 1871 loan. The new agreement reduced the interest rate to 3 percent for 3 years, rising half a percent every 3 years to a maximum of 5 percent. Certificates were also issued for the arrears of interest which, by that point, exceeded the principal of the loan. These were to be redeemed after the principal had been paid. As security for the renegotiated loan, the government offered the proceeds of export duty on rubber and half of the revenue from duties paid on tobacco and gunpowder.[22]

It is perhaps worth asking why the Liberian government agreed to renegotiate at that time, after such a long period in default. One clue can be found in the context. The final decades of the nineteenth century saw the division by European powers of much of Africa into formal colonies. There was considerable fear within the Liberian government that the long-standing default on the 1871 loans would provide a justification for colonial conquest from either the British or one of their competitors in the region (France or Germany). As early as 1876, an article in the African Repository, the newsletter of the American Colonization Society, remarked that Liberia "lies at the mercy of her bondholders. England, with her lion's paw on the trade of the world, would, and perhaps will eventually, assume the debt for the trifling consideration of possession."[23] Negotiating with the CFB allowed the government to avoid perhaps more precarious dealings with imperial agents of various powers, a strategy also pursued by other independent governments such as Peru (Chap. 5) and the Ottoman Empire (Chap. 6).

Just as Liberia began its repayments under the amended agreement, the two larger British West African territories began to enter the market, following the passage of the Colonial Stock Act in 1900, which granted trustee status to colonial bond issues.[24] Like Sierra Leone's 1871 loan, these loan issues were managed by the Crown Agents for the Colonies and a standard set of underwriters.[25] In 1902 the Gold Coast issued £1,035,000 in bonds at a rate of 3 percent and an issue price of 91. The loan was intended to fund the construction of the Sekondi-Kumasi railway and was secured with the revenues of the colony.[26] Sierra Leone returned to the market 2 years later, in June 1904, raising £1,250,000 at 4 percent interest, again secured with the revenues of the colony.[27] The next year it was Southern Nigeria's turn in what was to date the largest West African bond issue, £2,000,000 at 3.5 percent, to "provide funds for railway construction."[28]

Liberia raised a further loan of £100,000 in 1906 at 6 percent. The 1906 bonds were purchased by Emile Erlanger and Co. in partnership with a concession company, the Liberian Development Company, established by Harry Johnston. Johnston was a well-known figure in British Africa who developed an interest in Liberia.[29] Johnston's company was to manage the proceeds of the loan, ostensibly for the purposes of road construction and the establishment of a national bank.[30] The most important legacy of the 1906 loan for Liberia was the precedent set by its conditions. As in the case of the 1871 issue, the 1906 bonds were secured by the revenue from customs tariffs, along with an export duty on rubber.[31] However, in this case, enforcement of the terms of the loan was made by means of two British officials placed in charge of customs collection.[32] This was the first in a series of concessions of sovereignty by the Liberian government, in which local control over customs revenue and eventually defense was also given over to foreign officials.

These concessions deepened in 1913 when a loan of $1,700,000, known as the "refunding loan," was raised primarily in New York at 5 percent. The proceeds of the loan were "entirely used to consolidate existing internal and external debts."[33] The loan followed the recommendations of a commission appointed in 1909 by the American government to investigate conditions in Liberia. The commission advised "the establishment of some system of collection and control of the revenues of the country for the benefit alike of the Government and its creditors, modeled in some respects upon the plan which has been of such practical success in Santo Domingo."[34] In Liberia's case, this involved the establishment of a Customs Receivership under the leadership of the American receiver general and placed American officials in charge of the Liberian Frontier force.

Even in the narrative accounts of these loans, differences between the experience of Liberia and the three colonized territories are apparent. Colonial loans were issued at lower interest rates and more frequently at or near par value. They were also used more effectively for the construction of the railways instead of the redemption of previous obligations, an important factor in facilitating repayment.[35] Further colonial loans were serviced on time while Liberia carried a heavy financial burden from its early default. This difference becomes readily apparent if we look at the secondary market for West African bonds.

Figure 8.1 gives monthly spreads over British consols for West African bonds from 1902 until 1914. Spreads are a common measure of how investors perceived the risk of default for particular countries. In this case, Liberian spreads are much higher than those for the three colonized territories. While they do decline after the establishment of foreign control over customs collection and the military, they do not decline to the same level as the three colonies. Second, there is little difference between the spreads of the three colonies, suggesting that investors did not view any one as substantially riskier than the others. Figure 8.2 compares these spreads to countries outside Africa, making the contrast even more apparent.

How can these differences be explained? In part, the wide gap between the experiences of the British colonies and that of an independent country is what the "empire effect" literature would lead us to expect. However, that literature also predicts that concessions of sovereignty like those made by Liberia should have the same effect as formal membership of an empire,

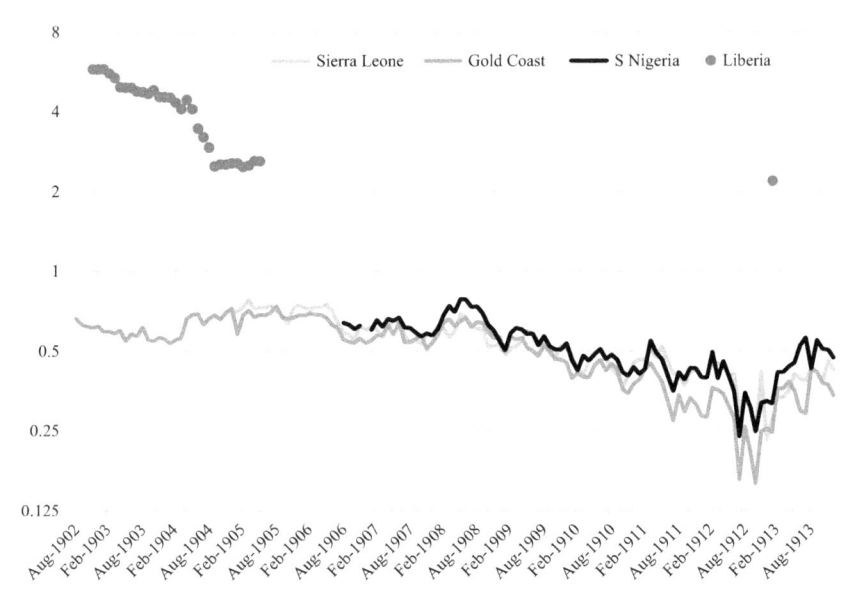

Fig. 8.1 West African bond spreads. (Source: Gardner, "Colonialism or supersanctions")

which in this case at least, they do not. Explaining this requires a more detailed consideration of the mechanisms by which colonies and independent states raised loans and, in particular, the role of imperial networks in reducing borrowing costs for British colonies.

West African Sovereignties Before 1914

The previous section has suggested that the nature of the political institutions raising West African loans influenced the terms of access to capital. This section examines how those institutions came into being in the second half of the nineteenth century. In the middle of the century, when European presence in Africa remained restricted to a few coastal outposts, political sovereignty resided in a number of indigenous African polities. These ranged from highly centralized and complex bureaucratic states such as the Asante in present day Ghana or the Sokoto Caliphate in what is now Nigeria to more fragmented political units.[36] Rulers of these states depended to varying degrees on the control of external trades and

a. British colonies

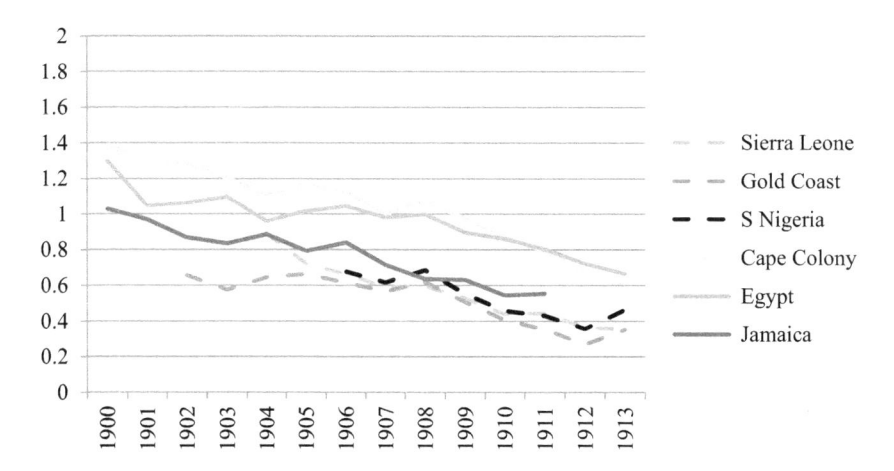

b. Sovereign states

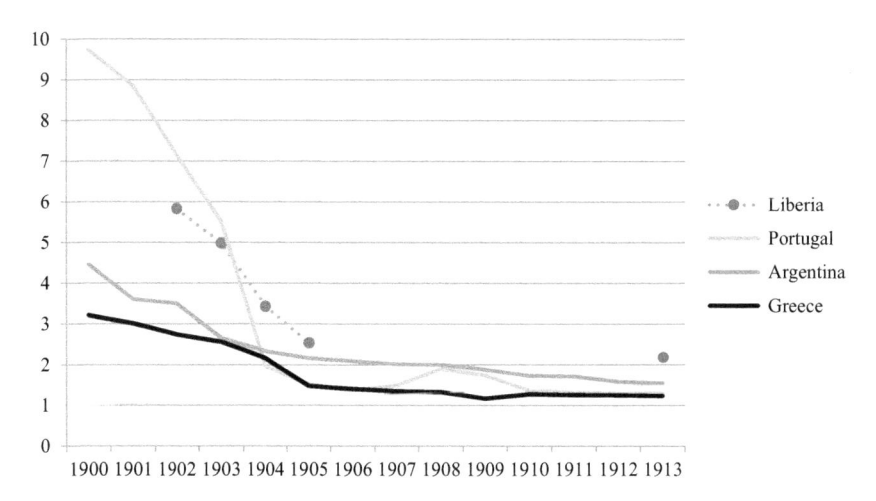

Fig. 8.2 West African bond spreads in comparative perspective, 1900–1914. (Source: Gardner, "Colonialism or supersanctions.")

relationships for revenue. This dependence has various names, from "extraversion" to "gatekeeper states," and continued into the colonial period.[37]

By the beginning of World War I, however, external sovereignty had been stripped by various means from indigenous rulers through treaty or conquest and instead rested in the hands of foreigners. In most of West Africa, colonial conquest meant that sovereignty rested in the governments of the relevant imperial power. For the purposes of three of the countries to be discussed in this chapter, this was the British government in London. This is not to say that the colonial powers were sovereign according to all possible definitions. They faced frequent and continuing challenges from Africans. In these three colonies alone, this included the Hut Tax War in Sierra Leone in 1898, the Asante uprising in 1900, and ongoing campaigns in Northern Nigeria. It was not until 1905 that, as Hargreaves puts it, "although there were still remote districts in the rainforest and the desert where no effective "pacification" had yet taken place—the fact of colonial rule had generally been accepted."[38]

Even where this was the case, however, internal sovereignty in many cases continued to be exercised by African elites, sometimes though not always the heirs to pre-colonial institutions. Resource constraints and lack of political capital often forced imperial powers to integrate Africans into the machinery of colonial administration, and the extension of internal sovereignty remained a challenge for colonial administrations until decolonization.

In Liberia, foreign rule took a different form. Liberia as a state was the creation of the American Society for the Colonization of Free People of Color (ACS), an organization founded with the express purpose of removing free African-Americans from the United States to West Africa.[39] Settlers began to arrive in 1820, and established an initially tenuous series of communities along what had been formerly known as the "Grain Coast" for its production of pepper. Governance of Liberia was initially in the hands of an official appointed by the ACS. However, a dispute over trade taxes in the 1840s prompted the British government to press the American government to declare whether it claimed Liberia as a colony or not. When the American government declined to do so, Liberia declared independence in 1847 and swiftly received recognition from a variety of European governments (though not, initially, from the American government, which feared the racial politics of a black ambassador).[40]

In extending its authority over the interior of what is today Liberia, the new government moved slowly, often constrained by limited resources as well as conflict with indigenous groups. Only when territorial acquisitions by European colonizers began to encroach did the Liberian government take steps to extend its hegemony in any practical way. When it did, that rule took a similar form to the "indirect rule" of British colonial administrations, with chiefs appointed to govern the interior. The structure of the Liberian state has led some to label it "black imperialism."[41]

External recognition of political hegemony, colonial or independent, was what allowed West African governments to borrow on the London market. It was difficult for indigenous states to do the same. For example, a proposal by the Asantehene in the 1890s to raise European capital to build a railway was eventually halted by British military action.[42] However, both types of government had to contend with limited local legitimacy, and banked on development interventions funded by external borrowing to help support development and build local support. However, not all external recognition was equal. Subsequent sections argue that European colonial rule created an encompassing interest which encouraged cooperation among a variety of actors and, ultimately, allowed the three colonized territories access to capital at a much lower cost than Liberia.

Imperial Institutions and Colonial Borrowing

If foreign financial control was insufficient to inspire confidence in Liberian debt as an investment, why was formal colonial rule more effective? This section examines the process by which British colonies raised loans and the role of various actors in reducing their costs. It argues that colonial rule provided an "encompassing interest" which facilitated cooperation between actors and institutions with different interests. It is this cooperation which helps explain why West African colonies were able to borrow.

As noted above, loan issues by the three West African colonies were managed by a semi-autonomous organization called the Crown Agents for the Colonies, just like all crown colony loan issues since the 1860s. The Crown Agents for the Colonies acted as a general commissary service for all colonial administrations, managing their finances as well as government purchasing.[43] The origins of the Crown Agents date to the eighteenth century, when colonies receiving parliamentary grants appointed agents to account for funds issued from the British Treasury.[44] Research on the determinants of borrowing costs has stressed that "prestige" intermediaries could lower the cost of borrowing because investors trusted them to help overcome information asymmetries.[45] The experience of the West African colonies suggests that the Crown Agents may have also played such a role. They did so partly by providing an initial screening of requests for loans by colonial administrations, ensuring, for example, that they had sufficient revenue to service a proposed loan as well as contribute to a sinking fund for the repayment of the principal.

The British government and Crown Agents not only monitored the state of colonial administration finances but also intervened to mitigate sudden fiscal crises. While the Liberian government had to resort to short-term cash advances at high cost, the three colonial administrations all received interest-free advances and loans from imperial institutions. The colonial administration of Lagos, for example, received an interest-free loan of £20,000 in 1873 to repay several loans advanced from local merchants to "meet the current expense of the government."[46] In 1879, Sierra Leone received a loan of £38,000 at zero interest from the imperial government "in aid of the local revenue of the settlement."[47] This was repaid in uneven installments by 1890. A further concessionary loan was issued to assist with the costs of the 1898 Hut Tax War, an uprising against the extension of British authority over the interior.[48] These funds—a total of £45,000—were advanced from the Treasury Chest, described as "a fund of several hundred thousand pounds spread through the Empire for public services and emergencies."[49] The colonial administration of the Gold Coast received several concessionary loans through the 1890s to cope with the costs of the Ashanti Wars.[50]

The Crown Agents also advanced funds to support the construction of infrastructure which would later be repaid through bond issues. The prospectuses for the West African loans announced prominently that the railways for which the colonies were borrowing had already been at least partly constructed. In the prospectus for the Gold Coast loan, it was stated that "the first section (39¼ miles) from Sekondi to Tarkwa is already open to public traffic, although some stations and other works at the Port still require completion. A further section of 9¾ miles from Tarkwa to Cinnamon Bippo is now approaching completion."[51] The announcement for the Sierra Leone issue also noted with regard to the railway that the "greater part" was "already completed and open for traffic."[52] In all three West African colonies, railway construction had actually begun in the 1890s, proceeding sporadically with frequent interruptions due to conflicts with the African population, the difficulty of continuing surveys and construction during the wet season, insufficient labor supplies, and high turnover among the European staff.[53]

Financing for this early construction came from the Crown Agents as well as the Imperial Treasury and the private sector. In Lagos, £725,000 of the £2,000,000 raised through the issue of the 1906 loan was used to repay the Treasury for earlier railway loans.[54] In Sierra Leone, the advances which paid for the early construction of the railway came from the Crown Agents, who later recovered the money with the proceeds of the loan issue.[55] In other cases, favorable arrangements were made with private companies to generate the necessary capital. In the Gold Coast, for example, the Ashanti Goldfield Corporation paid half the annual interest and sinking fund charges on the Tarkwa-Kumassi line and agreed to supplement the earnings of the railway if they fell below a certain level. In return, they received a share of the profits and guaranteed rates for the use of the railway.[56]

Fiscal stabilization efforts and the advance construction of the railways were, however, not enough to ensure demand for West African bonds. Like other intermediaries of the period, the agents also relied on a range of "market-making" activities to keep prices high. This included the purchase of bonds by the Crown Agents as well as by individuals and corporations with a stake in the success of the West African colonies. In their report on the Nigeria 1911 loan, the underwriters noted that "in ordinary times there is very little market in the stocks of Southern Nigeria, Gold Coast and Sierra Leone, and it is only the heavy purchases made from time to time by your good selves which has kept the prices of these stocks at their comparatively high level."[57] They made these purchases using funds they held on behalf of other colonies. They also negotiated with other financial institutions to arrange the informal underwriting of the bonds. For the 1911 issue, for example, Scrimgoer noted that half of the bonds were purchased by "certain of the larger underwriters with our active co-operation in order to strengthen the position." Such purchases were not systematically documented in the records, but some snapshots can be found. For example, a listing of the holders of the Sierra Leone 3½ percent bonds in 1933 showed that £467,668 in bonds were held by imperial and colonial institutions of various types, including reserve funds of both colonial administrations and local-level "native" administrations, colonial savings banks, note reserve funds, etc.[58]

In short, the ability of West African colonies to borrow at such comparatively low rates was linked to pro-active interventions by a variety of imperial institutions and actors which ranged from the British government itself to quasi-independent entities like the Crown Agents to private-sector companies. While their overall impact of this alignment of interests on the costs of African borrowing is difficult to measure, contemporaries found it to be important. But why were their interests so aligned? West Africa remained an economically marginal region of the British Empire in this period, and the economic fundamentals of the three West African colonies did not seem to inspire much confidence among investors.

One possible answer might lie outside individual colonies and in the fact that imperial institutions had interests which cut across multiple colonies. One contribution to the "empire effect" literature argues that colonies were able to borrow at lower cost because investors saw colonial administrations as subsidiary units of the British government, and thus assessed the risk of default as that of the British government. If this is true, then any sign of greater risk from any one colony could potentially undermine the system as a whole. This gave further urgency to the success or failure even of bond issues from relatively small and unimportant parts of the empire. To address the problem of limited demand for bonds issued by West African colonies, the Crown Agents made use of the often substantial funds they managed on behalf of other colonial governments. This deepened interconnections between colonial administrations by linking the financial health of a wide range of colonial institutions to the prompt servicing and repayment of colonial loans. The involvement of private companies is potentially more difficult to understand. However, as noted above, many of the private companies involved also had lucrative relationships with colonial administrations. The Ashanti Goldfields company received valuable monopoly privileges in return for their support of the Gold Coast Railway.[59] The Bank of British West Africa, another investor in West African bonds, served as government banker for the colonial administrations in their respective capitals, and thus stood to gain from financial transfers they would help manage.[60] It was perhaps also in the interest of such organizations to be helpful to the Crown Agents and Colonial Office.

The management of West African colonial debt therefore reflects an empire that, as John Darwin puts it, "embraced an extraordinary range of constitutional, diplomatic, political, commercial and cultural relationships."[61] Jane Burbank and Frederick Cooper echo this point, arguing that, for people at the time, "empire was the political reality with which they lived. People labored in enterprises sustaining imperial economies, participated in a network nurtured by imperial contacts, and sought power, fulfillment, or simply survival in settings configured by imperial rule and by imperial rivalries."[62] Colonial conquest had served to enmesh West African societies in this network of imperial interests, and it was through this network that the "empire effect" operated, rather than through the impartial workings of the market.

Trading Sovereignty for Capital?

The importance and unique structure of these networks of interested parties becomes clearer when the experience of the three colonies is placed alongside that of an independent country. Ceding control over customs collection and the military was supposed to reduce the costs of borrowing in London after Liberia's initial default. Some have argued that such arrangements should be equivalent to formal colonial rule.[63] Figure 8.1 showed that while the costs of borrowing did come down, they did not reach the same level as those of colonial administrations in West Africa. Responses from the financial press at the time support this impression. *The Financial Times* stated that "under the international control now established the bonds seem fairly well secured, though they can hardly be described as a gilt-edged investment."[64] The verdict of *The Economist* was even less enthusiastic, noting "the revenue depends very largely on Customs duties and the condition of trade and the stability of the state administration are not satisfactory enough to make the present offer attractive."[65] This section examines the choices made by the Liberian government to make partial concessions of its sovereignty to foreign officials as a condition of the 1906 and 1913 loans.

The loan of 1871 set the stage for a long and often antagonistic relationship between the Liberian government and international capital markets, and for long-standing debates in Liberia about the benefits and risks of trying to attract foreign capital.[66] President Roye was deposed and died shortly thereafter in mysterious circumstances. In December 1871, *The Times* reported that "it now appears that the little community is in a state of political anarchy, and that while the contending factions would each be willing to handle the proceeds of the loan, they are equally prepared to denounce as illegal any appropriation that might be made by their opponents."[67] A manifesto authored by the Secretary of State, Hilary Johnson, argued that among other transgressions Roye had "contracted a foreign loan contrary to the law made and provided; and without an Act of

Appropriation by the Legislature, he has, without his officers, been receiving the proceeds of that loan."[68]

Though Roye remained the object of criticism, later presidents would cast a wider net in attributing blame for the Liberian government's default. The same Hilary Johnson, in his annual message to the legislature in 1890, argued that the default was

> due not alone to the condition of the finances of the country, but also to the fact that the Republic was actually defrauded out of three fourths of the nominal sum, or two thirds of the sum at which the bonds were placed on the market. This instance of the Liberian seven per cent loan is not unique—similar cases occur with other nations—the smaller states. And the same principle, or rather non-principle, underlies them all: the money is squandered or consumed by the so-called foreign friends of these smaller states under the pretense of developing their alleged untold and inexhaustible resources.[69]

Other observers were more prepared to blame Liberia's finances: in particular, the short-term measures to which it resorted to cover recurrent deficits. These included both resorting to the printing press, leading to a depreciation of Liberian currency, as well as taking on high-interest cash advances from merchant firms. In 1896, Governor Cardew of Sierra Leone reported to the British Foreign Office that Liberia's customs revenue was "deeply mortgaged, principally to two firms, one a Dutch and the other a German." Cardew concluded that "it is quite hopeless to expect that Liberia will ever be in a position to pay any interest to the bondholders, much less the capital debt."[70]

Anecdotal evidence suggests that some in Liberia feared that foreign indebtedness would threaten its new sovereignty. A proposal to raise a loan in 1885 was scrapped by the Liberian government itself over fears that Liberia would become "another Sierra Leone."[71] Similar sentiments were also expressed abroad. In 1891, a Colonial Office memorandum addressed "a possible request from the Government of Liberia that the country should be taken under British protection." The memorandum noted that "there can be little doubt that the French have in view the ultimate acquisition of Liberia, and that, unless it is taken under the protection of Great Britain, this will be the fate of the Republic." Such an extension of French territory would, it said, have dire consequences for British interests in the region.[72]

The foreign control introduced under the 1906 loan had a mixed reception. A number of observers indicated that the customs revenue improved after control was passed to British officials as a condition of the loan. Ernest Lyon, the American Consul-General, reported to the State Department that the job of these officials was to "develop the customs resources, to punish smugglers, to enforce the laws against smuggling, and with the approval of the Liberian Secretary of the Treasury to make such rules and regulations that will place the customs on a better and more paying basis." He added that "the increase of revenue from this source has been gratifying to the authorities."[73] At the same time, however, this step generated uncertainty about Liberia's political future, particularly among people living in the contested borderlands. A letter from the officer commanding the Sierra Leone Battalion of the West African Frontier Force to the Collector of Customs from 1908 observed that "the country is at present in a very unsettled state, chiefly owing to the fact that the natives are uncertain whether they are eventually to come under the British or the Liberian government."[74]

Liberia's final loan of the period before World War I, the so-called refunding loan, extended foreign control through the creation of a Customs Receivership with representatives from four of the leading nations of the world at the time: the United States, Britain, France, and Germany. Though largely an American project, the inclusion of the three European powers reflected an uneasy truce. All three feared that the others were seeking greater political involvement in Liberia, and the Liberians themselves feared that owing too much to any one power would threaten their sovereignty still further. In 1896, for example, the Governor of Sierra Leone had reported to the British government that the German consul "is doing all he can to take advantage of the indebtedness of the Liberian government, by advancing it money and advising it to raise a loan in Germany to bring it under obligation to that Power."[75] It was not only foreign bond issues which caused such worries. Liberia also carried considerable domestic debt, largely in the form of high-interest cash advances. With regard to the 1912 loan, the Liberian president noted in his annual remarks to the Legislature that "it has been no easy task on the part of those responsible for the launching of the loan to harmonize the various interests to whom the Government has been obligated. This task has been rendered the more delicate in view of the fact that these interests were more or less supported by their governments."[76]

In sum, while the refunding loan required some concession of Liberian sovereignty, it was a smaller concession than the outright conquest feared by the Liberian government. The Customs Receivership had a very specific remit, namely to pay the interest on the refunding loan with Liberian customs revenue, over which it had control. Any balance of the revenue should be paid to the Liberian government for its own purposes, which were not controlled by the Receivership. It was therefore only a partial panacea for the same kinds of financial problems which had contributed to Liberia's default on the 1871 loan, which continued beyond 1912. Similar arrangements were in place in a number of countries around the world at the same time, and had limited success in improving fiscal outcomes or preventing suspensions of debt payments.[77]

In Liberia and elsewhere, such arrangements were also controversial, and debt and sovereignty remained the subject of debate in Liberian politics.[78] In the 1930s, a leading outlet for such opposition published a number of articles on the link between Liberia's relative poverty and the predations of foreign financial interests. One editorial, published in 1930, proclaimed that "one hundred and seven years have passed and yet we can scarcely feed ourselves; say nothing of providing ourselves with the other necessities of life. The reason is plain. We have always depended upon foreign loans and foreign capitalists and therefore we have been compelled to give them a free hand in our affairs making sacrifices indeed of our sovereign rights."[79] Another, published the next year, drew comparisons between Liberia and Mexico. "If a country is to be truly independent, a large proportion of its citizens must be so economically. Mexico under the dictatorship of Diaz, is a case in point. Diaz, supported by a clique of self-centered autocrats bent on enriching themselves, gave foreign concessionaires the land and mineral resources of the Mexican people, reducing them to a state of peonage in the land from which their fathers had driven the Spaniards at the cost of so much blood and suffering, and thereby vitiating their political autonomy."[80]

The second editorial drew explicit comparisons between the Americo-Liberian elite and the "self-centered autocrats" of Mexico. Arguably, the settlements of 1906 and 1911 suited the interests of these same elites, allowing them to retain some autonomy over the country's other resources and avoiding wholesale colonial conquest. The cost was continued international doubt about investments in Liberia, which kept borrowing costs high. Limiting the degree of foreign interest in Liberia also had the perhaps paradoxical effect that the country saw little benefit in terms of infrastructure from the expenditure of the loans. However, they did manage to retain national sovereignty by strategically allowing erosions of it. From a political standpoint, a total loss of sovereignty was perhaps too high a price to pay for access to capital.

* * *

In his landmark study of capital investment in sub-Saharan Africa, S. Herbert Frankel argued that "African economic development is governed by numerous monopolistic and sectional interests, by particular fiscal policies and by exceptional social techniques and institutions. Diverse politico-economic policies have in the past influenced, and continue to affect, the flow of resources."[81] This chapter has used the case of borrowing by four West African countries before 1914 to illustrate the ways in which sovereignty and the need for capital interacted under different conditions of foreign influence.

Recent work on the determinants of borrowing costs has speculated that countries faced a "trade-off" between sovereignty and access to capital. The history of borrowing by the governments of emerging economies suggests that for many countries there was a link, though often complex and multi-directional, between borrowing and political vulnerability. However, not all infringements into the sovereign rights of poor governments were equal in the eyes of investors. This chapter has compared the experience of three African governments under formal colonial rule with that of an independent country, Liberia, to understand the different ways in which foreign conquest influenced borrowing patterns.

The three British colonies were able to borrow at costs very close to those of much wealthier and better-established borrowers like the Cape Colony or Canada. This was not merely because they were colonies but rather because a variety of institutions, both public and private, cooperated to help reduce the costs of borrowing for colonies which did not otherwise seem attractive to investors. Their incentives to do this were, in turn, connected to the financial structure of the empire and the interdependence of different colonies.

After struggling initially to borrow on competitive terms, the Liberian government agreed as a condition of further borrowing to cede certain areas of governance—customs collection and the military—to foreign control. While this did allow them to borrow, it did not replicate the effects of colonial rule in terms of either reducing the cost of borrowing or influencing the uses of the funds. This arrangement, however, suited Liberian elites.

This comparison highlights the complex ways in which the "trade-off" between capital and sovereignty could interact, depending on a range of contingent factors. One was the extent to which interests in recipient and borrowing countries aligned. In the case of the three British colonies, colonial policies which linked the financial fate of the poorest colony to the wealthiest provided a number of actors with an incentive to cooperate. This same set of incentives did not exist in independent Liberia, even under foreign financial controls. Another is the interactive nature of the relationship between debt and sovereignty. While sacrifices in political sovereignty may have been necessary to borrow, the proceeds of that borrowing could help strengthen and solidify tenuous territorial control. As noted in the introduction, Africa has been largely neglected in debates about sovereign risk and financial globalization. The aim of this chapter has been to show that the borrowing of countries "in the middle of Africa," as Keynes put it, can still reveal much about the ways in which politics and economics interacted in the financial globalization of the nineteenth century.

NOTES

1. Marc Flandreau and Frederic Zumer, *The Making of Global Finance, 1880–1913* (Paris: OECD, 2004), 12.
2. S. Herbert Frankel, *Capital Investment in Africa* (Oxford: Oxford University Press, 1938); Irving Stone, *The Global Export of Capital, 1865–1914: A Statistical Survey* (Basingstoke: Macmillan, 1999).
3. Niall Ferguson and Moritz Schularick, "The Empire Effect: The Determinants of Country Risk in the First Age of Globalization, 1880–1913," *Journal of Economic History* 66 (2006): 308.
4. Alan James, *Sovereign Statehood: The Basis of International Society* (London: Allen & Unwin, 1986), ch. 1.
5. Jane Burbank and Frederick Cooper, *Empires in World History: Power and the Politics of Difference* (Princeton: Princeton University Press, 2010), 17.
6. Isabelle Surun, "Writing Sovereignty in Invisible Ink? Autochthonous Sovereignty and Territorial Appropriations in Nineteenth-Century Franco-African Treaties," *Annales. Histoire, Sciences Sociales (English Edition)* 69 (2014): 313–48.
7. Recent contributions to the "empire effect" literature include Olivier Accominotti, Marc Flandreau and Riad Rezzik, "The Spread of Empire:

Clio and the Measurement of Colonial Borrowing Costs," *Economic History Review* 64 (2011): 385–407; Ferguson and Schularick, "Empire effect"; A. G. Hopkins, "Accounting for the British Empire," *Journal of Imperial and Commonwealth History* 16 (1988); Maurice Obstfeld and Alan M. Taylor, "Sovereign Risk, Credibility and the Gold Standard: 1870–1913 versus 1925–31," *Economic Journal* 113 (2003): 241–75. For a historical take, see Andrew Smith, "Patriotism, Self-interest and the 'Empire Effect': Britishness and British Decisions to Invest in Canada, 1867–1914," *Journal of Imperial and Commonwealth History* 41 (2013): 59–80.
8. Lance E. Davis and Robert A. Huttenback, *Mammon and the Pursuit of Empire: The Political Economy of British Imperialism, 1860–1912* (Cambridge: Cambridge University Press, 1986), 167.
9. Richard M. Kesner, *Economic Control and Colonial Development: Crown Colony Financial Management in the Age of Joseph Chamberlain* (Westport. Conn.: Greenwood Press, 1981), 84.
10. David Graeber, *Debt: The First 5,000 years* (New York: Melville House, 2011), 5.
11. Andreea-Alexandra Maerean and Paul Sharp, "Sovereign Debt and Supersanctions in Emerging Markets: Evidence from Four Southeast European Countries, 1878–1913," mimeo (2014); Kris Mitchener and Marc Weidenmier, "Supersanctions and Sovereign Debt Repayment," *Journal of International Money and Finance* 29 (2010): 19–36.
12. Emily S. Rosenberg, *Financial Missionaries to the World: The Politics and Culture of Dollar Diplomacy, 1900–1930* (Durham: Duke University Press, 2007), 55, 77; Adam Tooze and Martin Ivanov, "Disciplining the 'Black Sheep of the Balkans': Financial Supervision and Sovereignty in Bulgaria, 1902–38," *Economic History Review* 64 (2011): 30–51.
13. Leigh Gardner, "Colonialism or Supersanctions: Sovereignty and Debt in West Africa, 1871–1914," *European Review of Economic History* 21 (2017): 236–57.
14. John Maynard Keynes, "Foreign Investment and the National Advantage," in *The Collected Writings of John Maynard Keynes. Volume 19, Activities 1922–1929: The Return to Gold and Industrial Policy Part 1*, eds. Elizabeth S. Johnson and Donald E. Moggridge (Cambridge: Cambridge University Press 1981), 291–2.
15. This section summarizes more detailed analysis in Gardner, "Colonialism or Supersanctions."
16. The fourth British territory in West Africa, The Gambia, did not borrow in this period and has therefore been excluded.

17. Paulo Mauro, Nathan Sussman and Yishay Yafeh, *Emerging Markets and Financial Globalization: Sovereign Bond Spreads in 1870–1913 and Today* (Oxford: Oxford University Press, 2006), 10–11.
18. For debates about the measurement of public debt, see Chap. 19 in this volume.
19. A. Scrimgoer to Crown Agents, 16 November 1911, TNA CAOG 9/37.
20. Stone, *Global Export of Capital*, 26.
21. These included Honduras, Costa Rica, Santo Domingo, Paraguay, Spain, Bolivia, Guatemala, Uruguay, Egypt, Peru, and the Ottoman Empire. See Sevket Pamuk, *The Ottoman Empire and European Capitalism, 1820–1913: Trade, Investment and Production* (Cambridge: Cambridge University Press, 1987), 61, n. 16.
22. Corporation of Foreign Bondholders, *Annual Report 1899*, 239.
23. "Liberia and the American Flag," *African Repository* 1876, 109.
24. Kesner, *Economic Control*, 70–88.
25. David Sunderland, *Managing the British Empire: The Crown Agents 1833–1914* (London: Royal Historical Society, 2004), ch. 6.
26. "Gold Coast Government 3 Per Cent," *The Financial Times*, 20 March 1902, 8.
27. "A Sierra Leone issue," *The Financial Times*, 3 June 1904.
28. "Lagos Loan," *The Financial Times*, 25 February 1905.
29. He had been the first commissioner of British Nyasaland in the 1890s and was a widely published naturalist and explorer. Just before the loan was issued, Johnston published what remained for many years a widely cited study of the country. See Judson M. Lyon, "The Education of Sir Harry Johnston in Liberia, 1900–1910," *The Historian* 51 (1989): 627–43 and Harry Johnston, *Liberia* (London: Hutchinson & Co, 1906).
30. George W. Brown, *Economic History of Liberia* (Washington, DC: Associated Publishers, 1941), 165–6.
31. Corporation of Foreign Bondholders, *Annual Report 1913*, 211.
32. Brown, *Economic History of Liberia*.
33. Christian Suter, *Debt Cycles in the World Economy: Foreign Loans, Financial Crises and Debt Settlements 1820–1990* (Boulder: Westview Press, 1992), 149.
34. US Senate, *Affairs in Liberia* (Washington, DC: Government Printing Office, 1910), 11.
35. Albert Fishlow, "Lessons from the Past: Capital Markets during the 19th Century and the Interwar Period," *International Organization* 39 (1985): 383–49; Trish Kelly, "Ability and Willingness to Pay in the Age of Pax Britannica, 1890–1914," *Explorations in Economic History* 35 (1998): 31–58.

36. Walter Hawthorne, "States and Statelessness," in *The Oxford Handbook of Modern African History*, eds. John Parker and Richard Reid (Oxford: Oxford University Press, 2013), 79.
37. Jean-Francois Bayart, *The State in Africa: The Politics of the Belly* (Cambridge: Polity Press, 2009), 20–32; Frederick Cooper, *Africa Since 1940: The Past of the Present* (Cambridge: Cambridge University Press, 2002), 156–7.
38. John Hargreaves, "Western Africa 1886–1905," in *The Cambridge History of Africa*, vol. 6: *From 1870 to 1905*, eds. George N. Sanderson and Roland A. Oliver (Cambridge: Cambridge University Press, 1985), 257–97.
39. P. J. Staudenraus, *The African Colonization Movement 1816–1865* (New York: Columbia University Press, 1961), ch. 3.
40. Christopher Clapham, *Liberia and Sierra Leone: An Essay in Comparative Politics* (Cambridge: Cambridge University Press, 1976), 6–16.
41. Monday B. Akpan, "Black Imperialism: Americo-Liberian Rule over the African Peoples of Liberia, 1841–1964," *Canadian Journal of African Studies* 7 (1973): 217–36.
42. Isaias Chaves, Stanley L. Engerman and James A. Robinson, "Reinventing the Wheel: The Economic Benefits of Wheeled Transportation in Early Colonial British West Africa," in *Africa's Development in Historical Perspective*, eds. Emmanuel Akyeampong, Robert H. Bates, Nathan Nunn and James A. Robinson (Cambridge: Cambridge University Press, 2014), 349.
43. Kesner, *Economic Control and Colonial Development*.
44. Arthur William Abbot, *A Short History of the Crown Agents and their Office* (London: The Grosvenor Press, 1971), 12.
45. Marc Flandreau and Juan H. Flores, "Bonds and Brands: Foundations of Sovereign Debt Markets, 1820–1830," *Journal of Economic History* 69 (2009): 646–84.
46. Lagos, *Blue Book* for 1873.
47. Sierra Leone, *Blue Book* for 1879.
48. John Hargreaves, "The Establishment of the Sierra Leone Protectorate and the Insurrection of 1898," *Cambridge Historical Journal* 12 (1956): 56–89.
49. Davis and Huttenback, *Mammon*, 149.
50. Gold Coast, *Blue Book for 1901*; Kesner, *Economic Control and Colonial Development*, 44.
51. "Gold Coast Government 3 per cent inscribed stock," *Financial Times*, 20 March 1902.
52. "A Sierra Leone issue," *Financial Times*, 3 June 1904.
53. House of Commons, *Papers Relating the Construction of Railways in Sierra Leone, Lagos and the Gold Coast* (London: HMSO, 1905).

54. Lagos, *Blue Book for 1905*.
55. Sierra Leone, *Blue Book for 1903*.
56. Sunderland, *Managing the British Empire*, 215.
57. A. Scrimgoer to Crown Agents, 16 November 1911, TNA CAOG 9/37.
58. See TNA CAOG 9/63. As some share of the bonds had been redeemed by 1933 it is difficult to give a total amount of those outstanding.
59. Sunderland, *Managing the British Empire*, 215.
60. Leigh Gardner, "The Rise and Fall of Sterling in Liberia, 1847–1943," *Economic History Review* 67 (2014): 1099.
61. John Darwin, *The Empire Project: The Rise and Fall of the British World-system 1830–1970* (Cambridge: Cambridge University Press, 2009), 1.
62. Burbank and Cooper, *Empires in World History*, 2.
63. Accominotti et al., "Spread of Empire"; Pamuk, *Ottoman Empire*, 56; Nnamdi Azikiwe, *Liberia in World Politics* (London: Arthur H Stockwell, Ltd., 1934).
64. "Liberia five per cent bonds," *Financial Times*, 4 January 1913, 6.
65. "New capital issues," *The Economist*, 4 January 1913, 28.
66. Ibrahim Sundiata, *Brothers and Strangers: Black Zion, Black Slavery, 1914–40* (Durham: Duke University Press, 2003), 30.
67. *The Times*, 25 December 1871, 7.
68. Johnson, "Manifesto," IUARA Liberia collection.
69. "Message of the President of Liberia to the second session of the twenty-second legislature, 15 December 1890," IUARA Liberia collection.
70. Cardew to Salisbury, 3 November 1896, in TNA FO 881/6835.
71. Monday B. Akpan, "The Liberian Economy in the Nineteenth Century: Government Finances," *Liberian Studies Journal* 6 (1975): 129–61, here 158.
72. Colonial Office memorandum, November 1891, in TNA CO 879/35.
73. "Report of the Commercial, Financial and Industrial Conditions in the Republic of Liberia for the Year 1906," December 31, 1906, in NARA RG 84 UD 584 Volume 7.
74. Officer commanding Sierra Leone Battalion, WAFF to Collector of Customs, 29 Sept 1908, IUARA Svend Holsoe collection.
75. Cardew to Salisbury, 3 November 1896, in TNA FO 881/6835.
76. "Message of the President to the Legislature," December 1912, reprinted in *Foreign Relations of the United States 1912*, 651
77. See Chap. 9 in this volume, or Noel Maurer, *The Empire Trap: The Rise and Fall of U.S. Intervention to Protect American Property Overseas, 1893–2013* (Princeton: Princeton University Press, 2013), 91.
78. For other examples, see Tooze and Ivanov, "Disciplining," on Bulgaria or Juan J. Cruces and Christoph Trebesch, "Sovereign Defaults: The Price of

Haircuts," *American Economic Journal: Macroeconomics* 5 (2013): 85–117 on Greece.
79. "Liberia—A Democracy," *Crozierville Observer* February 1930, from *Daily Observer* Library, Monrovia.
80. George Best, "The Economic Aspects of Political Independence," *Crozierville Observer* May 1931, from *Daily Observer* Library, Monrovia.
81. Frankel, *Capital Investment in Africa*, 15.

CHAPTER 9

The Domestic Effects of Foreign Capital: Public Debt and Regional Inequalities in Late Qing China

Dong Yan

The introduction of modern public debt into late nineteenth-century China has been a goldmine for historians of Sino-Western diplomatic relations, but its impact extends well beyond that of great-power rivalry over China. In particular, how modern public debt interacted with the existing framework of fiscal redistribution in late Qing China has been mostly overlooked.[1]

Compared to nineteenth-century Europe and the Middle East, modern public debt was late on arrival in China, with most of its features gradually introduced between the 1850s and 1890s. The established framework of fiscal redistribution before the 1850s was one that in principle eschewed intertemporal transfers in favor of spatial transfers, and managed to function for almost two centuries over a vast geographic area without long-term public debt or bond markets. It was buttressed by ongoing discussions on public spending that emphasized a light fiscal footprint on the peasantry, as well as legitimizing projects of spatial redistribution by

D. Yan (✉)
Center for Chinese Studies, University of California, Berkeley, CA, USA

© The Author(s) 2020
N. Barreyre, N. Delalande (eds.), *A World of Public Debts*, Palgrave Studies in the History of Finance,
https://doi.org/10.1007/978-3-030-48794-2_9

mid-eighteenth-century officials. The first section briefly introduces key elements of this earlier fiscal framework, its relationship with credit instruments, and political considerations behind its focus on spatial and social redistribution. When we remember that public debt is in essence an intertemporal transfer, the magnitude of the transition between the two regimes of financing public expenditure becomes clearer.

However, the transition was by no means a simple switch of fiscal instruments, as some Chinese-language historiography would lead us to believe. Rather, the displacement of the existing framework of fiscal redistribution after the 1850s by a debt-financed regime was fraught with renegotiations between political actors, resulting in a shift of governing priorities by the late Qing bureaucracy. The second and third sections look into the imposition of modern debt, which came at a pivotal moment of political and fiscal disarray, and how it became embedded in renegotiation over fiscal resources between central and provincial authorities. Official ambivalence over foreign debt in the late nineteenth century can also be viewed through the prisms of political autonomy and legitimacy, as Qing officials grappled with the reconfiguration of power dynamics that resulted from foreign debt. For Qing China, modern public debt was not simply an instrument of foreign domination, although it did accomplish some of the latter's goals, but a new lever that propelled a new fiscal and political relationship between different regions and classes within the empire.

As with earlier frameworks of fiscal redistribution, modern public debt came with its own evolving set of ideas on political economy, particularly over the role of the state in deploying public debt as competing strands of late nineteenth-century liberalism were adapted by Chinese intellectuals. These links between public debt and the diffusion of ideas on political economy form the final part of this discussion, as the impact of these ideas both corresponded to the increasing scale of China's indebtedness, and was magnified by the rebalance of regional and social priorities that took place through debt. At the same time, we should examine the politics of wielding these ideas on public debt; different discursive framings of public debt reflected competing political interests, and as the imperial rhetoric of benevolence gave way to nationalist representation in debt, public debt in early twentieth-century China acquired new political sponsors who enforced its repayment.

Public Finance Before the 1850s: A Precarious Balancing Act?

The framework of public finance that modern public debt supplanted in the late nineteenth century was designed to sustain the political legitimacy of a large, agrarian-based empire with significant regional and social imbalances. It was the result of sustained negotiations and recalibrations between key interest groups throughout the eighteenth and early nineteenth centuries, but compared to its European contemporaries, it was a framework with limited space for credit instruments and participation by private merchants. Instead, an intricate and often unwieldy system of intra-provincial transfer was used to partially address glaring disparities between regions and social groups.

Take the spatial mismatch between where revenue was collected and spent as an example: land taxes, which formed about 60 percent of official revenue sources in the mid-eighteenth century, were weighted toward the Yangtze region, with taxes per unit around Suzhou almost 20 times higher than in borderland provinces.[2] These regions were also assigned much higher rice tribute quotas to Beijing. Jiangsu region alone was required to send almost 25 percent of the nationwide quota in 1753, about 21 times more than Hebei province.[3] Yet throughout the eighteenth and early nineteenth century, it was Qing's borderland expeditions and river management projects that soaked up its funds.[4] Even the straitened court in the early nineteenth century managed to spend approximately 200 million silver taels (tls.) in suppressing rebellious religious sects, while maintaining an annual expenditure of 4.9 million tls. for the Yellow River and the Grand Canal.[5]

A similar phenomenon existed if these discrepancies are considered from a social angle. Grain and salt merchants from the Yangtze delta and Canton were the chief subscribers to the sale of public offices and honors, which brought in about 2 million tls. annually between 1796 and 1850.[6] An equivalent of office sales consisted in extracting "contributions" from salt merchants and overseas trade in Canton; an incomplete source puts contributions made by Canton merchants between 1773 and 1832 at 5.4 million tls.[7] On the other hand, regular flood prevention projects employed between 200,000 and 400,000 laborers at any one time, disproportionately beneficial to peasants and seasonal laborers in North and Central China. Intermittent tax breaks, dispensed under the rhetoric of imperial largesse, were also mainly aimed toward the peasantry.[8]

In response to the spatial and social mismatches in public spending, the treasury in Beijing constructed a fiscal framework by sequestering fiscal resources from provincial revenues. Between 1734 and 1820, about 10–30 percent of total provincial revenues were retained by the provinces, with the remainder controlled by, if not actually transported to, the treasury in Beijing.[9] Provincial treasuries were required to submit revenue figures twice a year, and these treasuries were divided into ones that generally ran surpluses (mainly coastal and southern provinces), remained even (Canton and Fukien), and those requiring fiscal subsidies (Sichuan and other western and frontier regions). Provinces with surpluses were required to deliver a portion to Beijing, and another portion generally to the nearest province in deficit. In 1744, for example, five western provinces were scheduled to receive 4.17 million tls. in subsidies from six coastal provinces.[10] Military spending in northwestern and southwestern China in the eighteenth century was generally funded through the same principles, that is, a combination of reserves from the treasury in Beijing and "contributions" from provincial sources.

What is remarkable about this framework of public finance is the absence of public debt and secondary markets. State borrowing did not feature prominently, if at all, in the maintenance of this framework. Small, stop-gap borrowings by local officials from merchants to cover emergency outlays did exist, but these loans were usually made in the name of the official, and rarely featured any collaterals. The "contributions" levied upon Canton merchants were more regular, but they should be seen more as fees for entering into overseas trade with official sanction. This is not to say that Qing officials were unfamiliar with the world of credit; on the contrary, officials managing the privy purse had long relied on large-scale lending to private merchants, with monthly interest rates usually ranging between 0.5 percent and 1 percent.[11] At times, the court even pressed loans on reluctant salt merchants, with interest proceeds of up to 1.4 million tls. per year.[12] But they were highly personalized interactions, sometimes with the emperor personally dictating the interest rates, or waiving them altogether for long-serving merchant families. The intertemporal aspect of public debt was not deployed in the planning of public finances, as military campaigns or infrastructural projects tended to rely on existing pools of funding, even if regional merchant groups (such as Shanxi merchants) were involved in the remittance of these funds to borderlands.

This system of inter-provincial fiscal transfers, as with the focus on peripheral provinces and peasantry, was based on strategic and political considerations. The pacification of borderland regions was a priority carried over from the late Ming, and regular expeditions in Xinjiang and outer Mongolia in the eighteenth century only increased this fiscal demand, while the management of major waterworks was not only a technical problem but a political one, that is, of providing the court in Beijing with grain from the south, keeping northern peasants from periodic unrest.[13] That the previous Ming dynasty had failed on both counts was recognized by Qing officials as a key reason for its downfall, and coming from a minority ethnic group, Mid-Qing rulers further responded by freezing the poll tax headcount in 1711 and merging it into land taxes, so population increases after 1711 were no longer reflected in official tax receipts. This was meant to alleviate peasant tax burdens, but had the effect of adding extra-budgetary fees and levies onto the now-static land taxes.[14]

To justify these political considerations, Qing officials espoused a range of ideas on political economy that endorsed the primacy of agricultural pursuits, while remaining ambivalent about commercial enterprises. This ambivalence was perhaps most profound in the field of financial innovation: major financiers and merchant groups were excluded from direct political participation (although their influence was detectable in laws relating to these groups), while financial developments such as the use of private-backed commercial papers for inter-provincial trade were kept at arm's length from public finances, despite frequent use of these services by officials in their private capacity. This is both a reflection of the asymmetrical yet symbiotic power relations between officials and merchant groups and an understanding of commerce-based revenue by Qing officials as supplementary to their revenue estimates. It also reflects an acceptance of long-term fluctuations (rather than sustained upward growth) in its agricultural-based land taxes when gains from population growth were fiscally neutralized by the abolition of poll tax.

But for treasury surpluses to accumulate, the Qing court needed long periods of peace, and steady supplies of liquidity at reasonable rates, in this case silver from Spanish America.[15] Especially in terms of liquidity, as even in the decades of comparative plenty in the late eighteenth century, commercial interest rates remained much higher than their counterparts in Spanish America, with monthly interest rates usually ranging between 0.5 percent and 1 percent.[16] The interest differential here is an important one, since supposing that Qing officials even entertained the idea of issuing public bonds, the interest rates they needed to offer would have had to be in reasonable proximity with private credit, yet to achieve an annual return of between 7 percent and 12 percent prior to the industrial revolution, the structure of its public finances and economy would have had to be radically revised in order to avoid bankruptcy.

By the early nineteenth century, although a tenuous peace was kept, China was faced with a liquidity problem as silver grew scarcer between 1820 and 1855, while giving up the demographic gains of the poll tax did not absolve Qing rulers from the consequences of population growth. Official anxieties about overpopulation, resource scarcity, and social instability took on Malthusian undertones during this period.[17] Intermittent remissions of land taxes, despite diminishing state revenue, were losing their effectiveness, as the copper-to-silver ratio was stacked against the peasantry.[18] Chronic deficits were partially financed through residuals of surpluses accumulated through "contributions" by merchant groups, sale of offices, and increases in salt levies, but the court was already in a straitened state when the Taiping rebellion broke out in 1851.[19]

GRAFTING PUBLIC DEBT ONTO THE QING STATE: 1865–1895

With the Qing state heavily reliant on revenues from the lower Yangtze delta, the Taiping Rebellions (1851–1864) dealt a second blow to its attempts at maintaining fiscal stability. The treasury surpluses, from which past military expenditure were largely financed, dwindled rapidly; by 1853, it could only locate 227,000 tls., compared to an estimated peak of 78 million tls. in the late eighteenth century.[20] Although these figures recovered somewhat in the 1880s, depleted treasury reserves and weakened central control in Southeast China resulted in two major changes to the fiscal framework: provincial officials were permitted to raise transit levies on commodities to fund local militias, and foreign powers wrested control over Shanghai customs from Qing officials.

The imposition of transit levies (*likin*) by provincial governments was crucial in reconfiguring state-merchant relations: for the first time in Qing history, the commercial vitality of a broad range of commodities became directly relevant to state finances.[21] With the rise of foreign trade after the Opium Wars, *likin* taxed the increasing global demand for Chinese goods, as well as the growing capacities for consumption domestically.[22] Domestic merchants also became much more involved in the setting and collection of *likin*, both bargaining with provincial officials through petitions and strikes, and organizing internally to facilitate its collection. Local financiers became particularly entwined with provincial finances as they arranged larger stop-gap loans for provincial officials, with the proceeds of local *likin* collection posts as security. Their social and political status also rose accordingly as they funded local militias through purchasing official posts and honors, including the posts of *likin* commissioners.

The foreign take-over of Shanghai customs, which by the mid-1860s mutated and expanded into foreign management of maritime customs throughout Chinese coastal and littoral ports had a similar impact on reshaping power dynamics between central and provincial governments. With little effective oversight over the assessment and collection of *likin* by provincial governments, the Board of Revenue in Beijing was careful to maintain control over maritime customs proceeds collected by its foreign staff; indeed, the efficient collection and transferal of customs revenue to the central government was an argument used by foreign staff and diplomats to justify foreign management in the 1860s and 1870s. At the same time, provincial governors viewed encroachments of maritime customs into transit taxes with growing alarm, and jealously guarded their newly retained control over *likin*.

These new commerce-based tax revenues, as well as the changed political dynamics, formed the basis for foreign loans, which began with small-scale borrowings by provincial governors from foreign trading firms in the 1850s.[23] These loans, which were used for suppressing the Taiping rebels and for reconstruction, quickly grew in scale as the Qing state was successively faced with Muslim rebellions in Xinjiang, famine, and war with France, all of which required major multi-year expenditures. These burdens went hand in hand with the expansion of state investment in armament production and modern industries, as seen below (Table 9.1):

These long-term investments usually involved exorbitant start-up expenses amortized over decades of operation. For example, initial investments in Hanyang Ironworks in Hubei in the late 1880s came to 5.83 million tls. prior to its operation.[24] It was not a model that would readily integrate with pre-1850s public finances, and provincial officials were often criticized by the treasury for the immense sunk cost with little to show for it in the first few years.[25] Still, with liquidity in short supply in private Chinese markets, investments on this scale required either concerted efforts from both central and provincial governments or foreign capital via public debts.[26]

Table 9.1 Public investment in Chinese state-owned industries, 1863–1894

Category	Number	Capital
Armament production	19	69,943,461
Mining	7	2,716,228
Ironworks	9	6,637,250
Textiles	5	6,103,803
Transport & communications	7	12,508,702

Unit: Silver Taels., at approx. 1 tls. = £ 0.27 (1885)

Source: Huang Rutong, *Zhongguo Shehui Jingjishi Luncong* (Taiyuan: Shanxi People's Press, 1982), 510.

This set the scene for the second stage of foreign lending. From 1874 to 1894, the average size of each loan jumped from around 120,000 tls. in the 1850s and 1860s to around 1.5 million tls. The duration of these loans also lengthened, although average rates remained stable at around 9.5 percent per annum, higher than European sovereign debt, but around the same range as the major Ottoman loans before its first default.[27] Compared to the first series of loans, negotiated between foreign trading firms and provincial officials as short-term commercial loans, this period saw the first public offerings of Chinese government bonds on London and Hong Kong markets, and the establishment of foreign financial institutions, the Hongkong and Shanghai Bank being the most famous example.

The injection of foreign funds alleviated center-provincial disputes over the funding of the Xinjiang campaign, mediated by foreign banking institutions. The first issuance of Chinese bonds made available for trading in London was rather small compared to those of the Ottomans and Egypt, but guaranteed by the foreign-managed customs service, it enabled provincial treasuries to regularly remit installments to service these debts. In amortizing the lump sum over a time span of 6 to 8 years, the burden of finding irregularly large sums at short notice by the provincial authorities was reduced, while the security of foreign lenders was still maintained by the guarantee of customs duties.[28] By embedding a commitment device in the shape of implicit foreign intervention, the central government was able to more readily persuade provincial officials to contribute promptly, and it retained sufficient authority at this stage to successfully enforce these outcomes.

This political and technical compromise worked between 1874 and 1894 because of China's low levels of indebtedness; it was small enough for the provincial authorities to find the sums through the growing *likin* and customs duties, and to effectively limit the likelihood of foreign fiscal supervision, the examples of the Ottomans and Egypt being known to Chinese diplomats. Yet, much to the dissatisfaction of Chinese officials, the terms of these loans enhanced the political and fiscal importance of the customs service, which in the person of Robert Hart worked relentlessly at making Chinese loan demands understandable to London bankers. This involved making information on Chinese trade and the Chinese economy publicly available and reformatted, including the publication of trade and customs duty figures, extensive surveys on local trading conditions and market fluctuations, as well as the first overall estimates of official revenues.[29]

It was precisely the fear of introducing new (moreover, foreign) political actors onto the fiscal landscape, tenuously patched up following the Taiping rebellion, that caused Chinese officials, both at the central and provincial level, to limit their borrowing for industrial development, despite the urging of reformist pamphlets and foreign advisers. Although some literature has attributed this to a conservative backlash against failed experiments in fiat money during the 1850s, reflecting the long-held ambivalence on financial innovation, political concerns over further involvement of foreign powers in Chinese finances seemed a more urgent concern.[30] Of course, adherence to older discourses of political economy persisted among Chinese officials during this period, but it would be difficult to divorce these discourses from a distrust of new political actors by the officials, whether it be the rapacious foreigners or presumptuous merchants, and an urge to preserve and restore past frameworks of public finances.

Public Debt as Catalyst and Enforcer, 1895–1911

China's defeats in the Sino-Japanese War of 1894–1895 and the Boxer Rebellion of 1900 forced the Mandarins' hand. The Japanese required a payment of 204 million tls., with annual interest of 5 percent, while the Boxer Indemnities totaled at 982.23 million tls. to be paid over 39 years.[31] As a framework of comparison, annual government revenue for 1890–1894 hovered between 81 and 86 million tls.[32] Enticed by Japanese promises of interest remission if payment could be expedited within 3 years, Chinese officials sought three major foreign loans from Anglo-German and Franco-Russian consortia, each at par value of 16 million pounds sterling (the

Franco-Russian loan was for 400 million Fr.), with a discount of 6 percent for the first two loans (offered at 94), and an expensive rate of 16 percent discount (effectively offered to the banks at 83) for the last Anglo-German loan of 1898.[33] In view of these usurious rates, the Qing government was allowed to issue Boxer Indemnity debt directly to foreign powers at 4 percent, with interior customs and salt levy as collateral, and monitored through the customs service.

The imposition of these foreign debts on the Qing government dramatically altered the status of public debt in its system of public finances. Between 1885 and 1894, annual debt service payments fluctuated between 4.3 percent and around 6.0 percent (1892) of Qing government spending as a result of its cautious policy of foreign borrowing. This shot up to around 22.8 percent for 1899, even after significant increases in government revenue, and reached around 31 percent by 1905, when state spending had reached 134.92 million tls., over 65.9 percent higher than its nominal equivalent in 1894. By 1911, when the first national budget was drawn up, around 56.41 million tls., or 16.65 percent of that year's expenditure, was spent on servicing public debt, both foreign and provincial.[34] Thus, for the first 10 years between 1895 and 1905, the growth of foreign and provincial debt outstripped that of government revenue, while between 1905 and 1911, public debt growth stabilized somewhat, with the single largest loan of Hubei—Canton Railway Loans in 1911 at 48.82 million tls.[35] At the provincial level, servicing foreign debt took up on average between 13.7 percent and 24.2 percent of their annual revenues, with certain provinces reaching well over 30 percent. Furthermore, the figures below were unclear as to whether provincial debts issued by provincial governments in the 1900s were included in the figure; the surprisingly low figures for Zhili Province, incorporating both Beijing and Tianjin, suggests that it might not have been included, since Zhili was documented as having issued provincial bonds during this decade (Table 9.2).

Through searching for means to service these major foreign debts, the gradual evolution of central-provincial fiscal relations, which could be detected in earlier introductions of public debt, quickened into a major decentralization of fiscal resources and authority in the last decades of Qing rule. Prior to the major indemnities, the annual amount that provincial treasuries were required to transfer to Beijing was based on an assessment of the province's revenues submitted to and approved by the central government. With the introduction of *likin*, provincial governments invariably under-reported the actual amount received, which led to

Table 9.2 Provincial revenue and foreign debt service, 1910

Province	Annual revenue	Foreign debt service	Percentage
Zhili (Hebei)	25,335,170	1,036,559	4.1
Henan	9,741,000	1,865,655	19.2
Shaanxi	4,213,510	996,592	23.7
Gansu	3,805,956	355,637	9.3
Shanxi	8,188,561	1,327,421	16.2
Jiangsu (Suzhou)	9,834,751	3,424,991	34.8
Jiangsu (Nanjing)	25,741,937	4,444,697	17.3
Zhejiang	14,289,452	3,451,590	24.2
Anhui	4,997,800	1,805,930	36.1
Hubei	13,545,147	2,567,739	19.0
Hunan	7,661,153	1,430,651	18.7
Jiangxi	7,432,925	2,955,967	39.8
Guangdong (Canton)	23,201,957	4,771,768	20.6
Fujian	5,061,163	1,611,854	31.8
Sichuan	23,676,100	3,885,972	16.4
Guangxi	4,470,000	610,250	13.7

Unit: Silver Taels., at approx. 1 tls. = £ 0.1323 (1910)

Source: Memorandum by Feng Rukui, Xuantong 3, 6th Month, 12th Day, No. 1 Historical Archives, Beijing.

perennial complaints from treasury officials in Beijing. In 1899, officials were sent to the key provinces of Jiangsu, Zhejiang, and Guangdong to further ferret out undeclared sources of provincial funds, with limited success.[36] It is important to note that this drive toward investigating and incorporating under-reported sources of local revenue was part of a long-standing tendency on the part of the central government since the mid-eighteenth century, thus firmly entrenched in the existing fiscal arrangements of the Qing state.

The need to serve the Boxer Indemnities speedily prompted the treasury in 1901 to allocate annual provincial quotas for foreign debt service. In the directive issued to provincial governors, treasury officials were explicit about the need to "adapt according to local circumstances and allow for expediencies; (provincial officials) are permitted to improvise on the spot to extract and collect (revenue)."[37] This effectively legitimized a practice that was already in place after the Japanese indemnities, whereby the central government acknowledged the existence of undeclared revenue by the provinces, and gave provincial authorities *carte blanche* to raise further revenue as they saw fit. The semi-annual quotas, once filled, were to be directly transferred to foreign banks based in Shanghai, without interference from the central government. This framework of debt services essentially permitted the expansion of provincial fiscal autonomy, a feature of late Qing public finance that the central government had attempted to eradicate since its earliest formation in the 1850s.

The expansion of provincial fiscal autonomy went hand in hand with official efforts at promoting revenue growth. As mentioned earlier, the mid-Qing framework of public finance possessed an ambivalent relationship with interest and revenue growth, which could also be detected in its handling of *likin*, a rapidly growing commercial tax that was criticized as being too extractive. Although the influence of these ideas gradually diminished in the late nineteenth century, as major industrializing projects demanded state-directed intervention, it was not until the aftermath of Japanese indemnities that revenue growth became central to the Qing government's fiscal agenda. The issue of fiscal management (*licai*) dominated official discussions on political economy during this period, and even in training manuals for expectant officials. Although cost-cutting measures were advocated, attention was paid to policies and projects that would "increase interest" (*zengli shiye*), such as the minting of copper coins, investment in state-owned industries, and issuing provincial debts.[38]

Since both foreign and provincial public debts required significant land tax, salt levy, and *likin* as collateral or direct sources of payment, the system of inter-provincial fiscal transfers under the coordination of the treasury in Beijing ran into serious difficulty. By 1908, despite an annual government revenue reaching over 200 million tls. by most estimates, the amount actually deposited to the treasury stood at around 24.5 million tls., barely enough to cover the operational costs of the court, much less to allow for redistributing fiscal revenues.[39] This effect was most evident in the frontier provinces of Xinjiang and Gansu, which witnessed a decline in fiscal transfers following the end of conflicts in the 1880s. Between 1900 and 1902 alone, over 3.53 million tls. were owed by various provinces to Xinjiang and Gansu.[40] Similarly, state subsidies to Mongolian and Manchu banners were also slashed through successive rounds of austerity, resulting in higher records of indebtedness to Han merchants in Mongolia, a focus of ethnic grievances later on. Peripheral provinces such as Yunnan and Guizhou, which depended on fiscal transfers from richer provinces, were owed over 1.95 and around 5 million tls. between 1895 and 1899 by other provinces.[41] Most significantly, state agencies for major water management projects, most notably those of the Grand Canal and the Yellow

River, were reduced to a mere fraction of their previous levels, before being partially abolished in order to pay for the Boxer Indemnities of 1901.[42] Although this also had to do with the rise of steamship transportation, which reduced the cost and time of transporting grain, the collapse in fiscal support for regions in Central and Northern China that had long enjoyed unparalleled levels of subsidies caused significant upheaval in the local economy. This was also accompanied by a reduction in state intervention in the field of disaster relief as it began to delegate the work to non-state agents (local gentry and foreign missionaries) while dismantling the institutions of official granaries.

On the other hand, the benefits of modern public debts began to accumulate within the provinces that funded them. Provincial centers and major cities along the Yangtze River were already beneficiaries of state-led efforts of industrialization before the Sino-Japanese War of 1894–1895, with the construction of major steelworks and factories in Nanjing, Fujian, and Wuhan. At the time, funding for these state-owned projects came mostly from the growing customs duties, with a minority from provincial revenue sources. Following the appropriation of customs duties to service foreign debts in the late 1890s and 1900s, provincial authorities began to borrow from foreign banks to continue funding these enterprises, while the central government embarked on major foreign debt negotiations for national railway projects. Although this meant that the proceeds of public debt were being used for revenue-generating purposes, it also hastened the process of fiscal decentralization, as the governor of Jiangsu argued in 1898: "it stands to reason that provincial proceeds should be used for provincial purposes,"[43] which in his case entailed the appropriation of funds allocated for the central government. At the same time, ongoing investments in railway services, mostly funded through the major railway loans of the late 1890s, connected major cities along the eastern provinces, resulting in increasing freight revenues for the central and provincial governments, as well as greater market and price integration between major urban areas (Table 9.3).[44]

Similarly, the establishment of new governmental departments, systems of modern schooling, and increased spending on Western-trained armies meant that provincial governments were forced to incur foreign debts. For example, of the nine loans undertaken by the Hubei provincial treasury between 1900 and 1911, four were spent on armament purchases and the expansion of cadet schools, three were used for investments in local industries and education, while two later loans were intended to ensure liquidity

Table 9.3 Railway revenue, 1907–1909

Year	Total	Passenger	Freight
1907	21,299,858	9,108,040	11,744,933
1908	24,938,811	9,737,426	14,625,490
1909	28,182,678	105,281,146	16,649,268

Unit: Silver Taels, at approx. 1 tls. = £ 0.1323 (1910)

Source: Yan Zhongping, ed., *Zhongguo Jindai Jingjishi Tongji Ziliao Xuanji* (Reprint, Beijing: Social Sciences Press, 2012), 209.

Note: Miscellaneous incomes from railway property etc. were omitted.

on the Hankow financial market, as well as restructuring previous loans.[45] The location of major educational establishments and industries in Hubei, as well as the purchase of Western armaments, lends credence to the argument that urban populations were by far the most direct beneficiaries of the proceeds of public debt during this era. A more general effect of public debt concerned financial centers such as Shanghai and Tianjin, which benefited from the negotiation of debts and the liquidity it provided, since for major indemnities such as the Sino-Japanese War debts, each province was assigned a seasonal quota in silver, which they had to transfer to foreign banks such as HSBC in Shanghai for conversion into pound sterling. Because of the time gap that often existed between provincial transfers and coupon payments in London, this interest-free loan to foreign banks was in turn lent to Chinese money-brokers as short-term loans (also called "chop-loans"), thus boosting market liquidity and attracting further speculation from rural gentry and merchants, eager to flee from the economic stagnation and instability of their regions.

However, if we examine the sources of debt repayments, then another picture of regional and social inequality emerges. After exercising relative restraint on land tax and salt levy surcharges through the 1870s and 1880s, the Qing government increasingly relied on land taxes and levies on mass-consumption materials as means of servicing new debts. For the Boxer Indemnities, over 49.5 percent of newly raised revenue sources came from surcharges on salt, opium, tobacco and alcohol, rice, tea, and sugar levies, while another 20.5 percent came from land tax increases.[46] For Changlu Salt Mines near Tianjin, the surcharges levied between 1895 and 1909 for the purposes of debt repayment and railway construction were twice as much as all previous surcharges since 1809 put together.[47] In comparison, increases in stamp taxes and various business taxes comprised only 14.5 percent of Boxer Indemnities payments. Given the mass consumption nature of salt, rice, and the particular inelasticity of opium, the recessive qualities of these debt payment sources are quite clear. Furthermore, improved administration of the salt taxes on the Western model in the 1900s and 1910s did not necessarily result in a lightening of the burden for consumers, since the wholesale price of salt did not decline significantly; rather, the aim was for it to become a sustainable and monitored stream of revenue for debt payments. The flat structure of tariffs prior to the 1930s also weighed against the consumers of mass commodities such as kerosene oil and cheap cotton yarn, two of the largest imports for China during this period. Interestingly, it was also during this period (1902) that the sale of offices was finally halted, while enforced contributions by merchant groups also declined as a source of revenue, thus effectively ending one of the key ways of revenue extraction from major merchants and the gentry.

Beyond successfully directing the flow of public debt to particular regional and urban projects, provincial officials, local gentry, merchants, and intellectuals also demanded greater participation and accountability over public debt negotiations and budget planning.[48] The decentralization of public finances in the early 1900s gave provincial officials the scope to incorporate elements of Western accounting standards into provincial budgets, as they attempted to plan for the amortization of foreign debt payments.[49] As greater clarity and standardization were introduced into provincial fiscal management, the state of provincial finances became a matter of public debate among the elites of those regions, especially in the more prosperous areas of Hubei, Jiangsu, and Hunan, where foreign debt usually came with ceding commercial rights and privileges to foreign lenders. The formation of provincial legislatures between 1906 and 1910 gave these elites the venue and means to monitor provincial borrowing, which in the case of Hubei and Jiangsu in 1910, shifted the outcomes of government negotiations with foreign creditors. The right to monitor and approve provincial borrowing also became a significant bone of contention between provincial legislators, the provincial governments, and their respective superiors in the national legislature and imperial court.

At the national level, the increasing proportion of public debt to state revenue in the 1900s prompted the expansion of surveys on revenue bases by the central government, the first step in its attempts to rein in provincial borrowing. With earlier estimates by foreign observers and staff at the customs service as blueprints, the newly constituted Ministry of Finance issued a series of directives in 1908 that demanded provincial governors to set up bureaus for fiscal reform, staffed by officials who reported directly to the Ministry of Finance.[50] These bureaus were given the task of listing and detailing the proportion of provincial revenue that was not reported or listed in their reports to the central government (Table 9.4).

Despite various clerical errors and inaccuracies, this nationwide effort formed the basis for the first national budget of 1910, where annual revenue was estimated at around 296.96 million tls.[51] Although this figure does not represent the amount actually remitted to the central government, it was almost four times the amount for 1894. Since the drive toward accountability and integrating undeclared revenue was an integral feature of Qing public finance, then the question became: why were the reforms of 1908 so much more successful at divulging information? One of the causes, I suggest, is the influence of foreign debt as a "supersanction" in prompting provincial accountability toward the central government during this era as the memory of foreign discussions on joint foreign management of Chinese public finances during the Boxer Rebellion remained very fresh in the minds of Chinese officials and elites alike.[52] The Qing government, at various levels, remained wary of potential disputes with foreign creditors that could lead to military intervention, and as such,

Table 9.4 Official and undeclared sources of revenue for Guangdong, 1908–1910

Revenue source	Total no. of items	Official	Undeclared	Percentage of undeclared
Land taxes	91	51	40	44
Salt levies	100	35	66	66
Customs (inland)	31	23	8	26
Misc. commercial taxes	42	32	10	24
Opium levies	1	1	0	0
Likin	24	15	9	36
Business taxes	58	30	28	48
Contributions	11	6	5	45
State-owned properties	14	6	8	57
Misc.	438	148	290	66
Total	**810**	**347**	**464**	**57**

Source: Bureau of Fiscal Reform, ed., *Guangdong Caizheng Shuomingshu (Guidebook on Guangdong Public Finances)* (1910), 1:39.

it gave the central government a reasonably effective tool for enforcing debt quotas throughout the 1900s, as well as extracting useful information on provincial public finances.

By 1910, earnings from state-owned industries, railways, banks, and properties had overtaken land taxes and *likin* as the single largest source of revenue for the Qing state. Even discounting potential inaccuracies (Table 9.5), this meant that almost half of government revenue came from sources that were not listed or were extant before 1850, all of which were contingent upon the growth of commercial enterprises and domestic consumption.

Given that foreign and public borrowing were major sources of funding for these state-directed efforts at industrialization, and that the sources of repayment came from prosperous and peripheral regions and social groups alike, one could argue that beyond hastening the process of fiscal decentralization, which forms a key part of this chapter's argument, public debt as an institution in late Qing also served as a lever to extract resources from peripheral regions and disadvantaged groups, which were then used

Table 9.5 Revenue forecast for the 1911 budget

Tax/Revenue source	Amount	Percentage	Notes
Land taxes	46,165,000	17.1	Temp. income 1,937,000
Salt, tea, sugar levies	46,312,000	17.2	
Customs (foreign)	35,140,000	13.0	
Customs (domestic)	6,991,000	2.6	Temp. income 8000
Stamp duties and other commercial taxes	26,164,000	9.7	
Likin	43,188,000	16.0	
State property earnings	46,601,000	17.3	
Miscellaneous earnings	19,194,000	7.1	Temp. income 16,051,000
Total	269,755,000	100	

Unit: Silver Taels, at approx. 1 tls. = £ 0.1323 (1910).

Source: *Qingchao Xuwenxian Tongkao*, 68:8245.

Note: Income from sale of offices (5,652,000 tls.) and public debt (3,560,000 tls.) was omitted in the original source.

to propel industrializing and modernizing projects in key coastal and urban areas into self-sustaining trajectories of growth.

Another point on public debt and its application in non-Western settings refers to the relationship between public debt and growth; through the multiplier effect of interest rates, the integration of public debt in public finances necessitates continuous growth in state revenue. As one has seen in the case of nineteenth-century China, the greater the proportion of public debt to state revenue, the greater the demand that revenue sources be linked to economic growth. For agrarian societies or those with a public finance system based on agrarian sources, it was not enough simply to adopt the mechanisms and institutions of public debt; it was also necessary to adopt the particular relationship between tax revenue and growth mandated by public debt, and furthermore, the prevailing idea on political economy that prioritized economic growth above concerns of distribution and inequality among regions and classes.

DISMANTLING IMPERIAL BENEVOLENCE: PUBLIC DEBT AND DISCOURSES ON POLITICAL ECONOMY

The debate over accountability and legislative monitoring of public debt was part of a larger framework of ideas on public finance and political economy introduced into China around this time, beginning with missionaries' translations of political economy textbooks in the 1870s and 1880s; the author of *Political Economy for Use in Schools* was a noted biographer of Hume, one-time secretary to the Scottish Prison Board, and distrustful of socialist doctrines.[53] His book was loosely translated into Chinese in 1885, and next to a brief description of public debt was a lengthy refutation of wealth redistribution among the poor, variously translated as *fen chan* (dividing properties) or *ping chan* (equalizing properties).[54] Similarly, a partial translation of Henry Fawcett's *Manual of Political Economy*, itself a summary of J.S. Mill's *Principles of Political Economy*, was published in 1883, where the section on distinguishing between productive and unproductive public debt was followed by a warning against the raising of taxes on capital.[55]

Given the selective nature of early translations on political economy, the weaving of public debt with fiscal redistribution probably reflected more the anxieties of Anglo-American missionaries than those of their Chinese readership. Chinese acquaintance with Gladstonian liberalism in public welfare was at the time limited to positive, but fleeting, impressions of British workhouses by Chinese diplomats, and in the summaries of public debt written by Chinese authors during this period (1870–1905), it was rare to encounter arguments that directly linked public debt with fiscal redistribution and social welfare.[56] Instead, it was the distinction between productive and unproductive uses of public debt that caught the attention of Chinese readers.

This theoretical distinction, which contributed to the mid-Victorian reduction in British public debt, was particularly appealing to Chinese intellectuals with links to private enterprises, such as Wang Tao (1828–1897) and Zheng Guanying (1842–1922), because it both justified the raising of public debt by the state, which was seen as useful in attracting foreign and domestic investment, and critiquing its deployment by the state and state-owned enterprises on the grounds of misuse, inefficiency, and waste. In his reformist treatise *Shengshi Weiyan* (read and praised by a young Mao Zedong), Zheng spoke through a Chinese diplomat stationed in Britain that "when borrowing to construct railways, telegraphs, mines, waterworks and other wealth-enhancing projects, the bonds will perform well and accrue good earnings. No one likes to lend money to wasteful and useless projects, least of all borrowing for armaments."[57] This line of argument, with the implication that private enterprises are better placed to deploy public debt for reasons of efficiency,[58] became entrenched in the rhetorical repertoire of Chinese industrialists and bankers regarding debt.[59] However, a discourse of productivity and efficiency in using public debt is also one that implicitly viewed many redistribution schemes – including subsidies for frontier provinces in the 1870s—with dismay.

These arguments of efficiency and productivity in public debt formed part of a new discourse on economic governance that questioned and displaced the older rhetoric of benevolent rule, with its emphasis on agriculture and peasant welfare. The rhetoric of benevolent rule underpinned the pre-Taiping era patterns of fiscal distribution and governance, and even during the post-Taiping period, a significant portion of the mandarinate still heeded the rhetoric's usefulness to stabilizing rural areas.[60] Reformist officials and intellectuals did not begin by questioning the premises of benevolent rule; to do so would have invited accusations of sedition to a dynasty that clung to memories of such governance in the eighteenth century as a source of political legitimacy. Instead, Wang Tao and others pointed to easily observable corruption and inefficiencies in everyday administration as a way to displace the older rhetoric, characterizing those who argued for agricultural primacy as merely "knowing how to survey land for taxes, barraging and pestering for fees and levies, setting rapacious officials to ruin the people […] possessing the form but not the substance, yet shamelessly holding forth, such are contemporary intellectuals' common weaknesses."[61]

Such distinctions became more explicit and subversive by the late 1890s as the Qing court's political legitimacy was further eroded through military defeats. In refuting arguments for benevolent rule (and, by extension, loyalty to the court) by senior Chinese officials, Kai Ho, a barrister and member of the legislative council of Hong Kong, pointed out that "to call for light taxes and offer alms is indeed benevolent […] but from what I've seen during the reigns of Tongzhi and Guangxu (1860–1908), great officials enforced contributions while the rich hid themselves, politicians were enriched while the poor were left unsupported; so much so that in areas of disaster and famine, the people rather prefer the Court not to dispense such alms. The recent *Zhaoxin* bonds also serve to demonstrate how concessions made by the top could not benefit the bottom, and only famine relief by prosperous citizens could achieve a certain effect … is this benevolent or not benevolent?"[62] In contrast, Ho and others supported the use of public debt on commercial and industrial enterprises, arguing that these were effective routes to national salvation and prosperity.[63] The use of efficiency and productivity as discursive devices to delegitimize the existing practices of economic governance was hardly unique to China, of course; their British contemporaries in Egypt made similar claims as they took over rural administration and surveys. However, instead of explicitly linking the mercantilist promotion of commerce and industry to improvements in peasant welfare, the peasantry as a category, under intense scrutiny in older discussions of benevolent rule, was subsumed under a larger category of the nation-state. The newer set of discourses on economic governance did not refer to liberal concepts of the "deserving poor" eagerly proffered by British translators; rather, peasant welfare and agricultural improvements were recognized but relegated to a subsidiary position in relation to the more urgent tasks of nation-saving (*jiu guo*).

That said, while it was one thing to dismantle older ideas on economic governance, another set of discourses was still needed to persuade and justify individual (and at times compulsory) subscriptions to public debt in late nineteenth and early twentieth-century China. To this one must return to Chinese accounts of public debt during this period.

A key feature of Chinese accounts of public debt between 1870 and 1900 was the downplaying of the need for financial intermediaries. Of course, translations made by British missionaries were quite vague about the role of merchant banks in mediating capital flows through successful public debt issuances, and allowances could be made for translators' lack of technical knowledge on this matter, but even in writings by leading compradors and officials who were much better acquainted with international trade and finance, the absence and indeed the distaste for financial intermediaries was remarkable. Zheng Guanying, whose main work was as comprador to Swire and Co. (a prominent British shipping company) asked: "Would Chinese and foreign investors have less trust in the Treasury than in banks, less trust in Chinese than in foreign institutions?" He counseled that "even if one must borrow from foreigners ... one should not ask banks based in China to handle them, so to avoid discounts ... but the Chinese ambassador in London should negotiate directly with Lloyds, Schroders, Barings and other major banks, where interest rates are no more than 4-5%."[64] If the comprador-commentator had at least heard of major London banks, the directives for *Zhaoxin* bonds by the Treasury in 1898 left almost no room for the involvement of modern banks or traditional brokerages, except to handle coupon repayments.[65]

What might explain this lack of interest in getting modern banks involved in public debt issuance and management? The experience of dealing with foreign banks in issuing foreign debts between 1874 and 1898 was certainly unpleasant for Chinese officials as they resented the layers of fees and discounts provided to intermediaries such as the Hongkong and Shanghai Bank (HSBC). Furthermore, they suspected that foreign bankers were also speculating in silver prices around the time of each debt repayment, which involved converting silver taels into gold sterling.[66] On the other hand, this reaction also stemmed from a deliberate reading of foreign sources on public debt. Commenting on Japanese issuance of domestic public debt in 1887, Chinese diplomat Huang Zunxian praised how public subscription came from a keen awareness of individual stakes in national prosperity: "furthermore, with frequent contributions to the public purse by rich merchants and gentry, they could withstand adversity together, and deepen ties of mutual dependence, thus solidifying national interest."[67] Similarly, for Yen Fu, one of the most sophisticated thinkers and translators of the time, Adam Smith's admonitions against incurring national debt only sparked his admiration at the patriotism that Yen believed to have partly motivated the British to subscribe in public debt.[68]

Thus a direct relationship between the state and bond subscribers was envisaged, unencumbered by financial intermediaries, and linked through the rhetoric of self-interest and patriotism. When compared with contemporary French policies of promoting bond subscriptions through lotteries and branches of local government, we might detect a common impulse to respond to the intermediary-dominated regime of public debt issuance seen in late nineteenth-century Britain.

This emphasis placed on patriotism as a motive for debt issuances was popular in part due to its resonance with the older rhetoric of public-spiritedness, a significant component in the neo-Confucian discourses of rural gentry leadership. By the mid-eighteenth century, this rhetoric of public-spiritedness was extended to provisioning of public goods, such as urban infrastructure and education, as well as maintenance of market order.[69] However, these discourses and the acts that they entailed were usually confined to the local village or township level, and in issuing domestic public debt, late Qing officials and intellectuals were faced with the problem of updating and expanding the geographical reach of this concept; could purses that opened for a village or county be opened for an empire?

Late Qing officials in the 1890s first began by weaving the rhetoric of public-spiritedness with that of dynastic loyalties, partly by referring to past records of benevolent rule in the eighteenth century, and also by appealing to residual family and historical links between the imperial court and its Manchu and Mongol nobilities. In edicts proclaiming *Zhaoxin* bonds of 1898, officials "who were deeply favored by the court should at this moment of fiscal difficulty … offer familial deposits for public usage,"[70] while senior princes, Mongolian lamas, and key officials petitioned the Court to view their subscriptions as "loyal offerings, and dare not ask for compensation."[71]

This framing of public debt as a semi-personalized exchange of loyalties, more akin to borrowings by early modern European monarchs, was not well received by intellectuals and merchants based around treaty-port areas, most significantly in Shanghai, its financial center. Editorials emphasized the need to "gain trust from people … as (they) expect productive uses for the silver lent (to the government) … even if it is used for infrastructural and other wealth-enhancing purposes … cost-saving measures and careful management will be necessary … so that profits earned by the Court will be enough to cover interest payments to the people, just like those who borrowed money to run trading ventures."[72] Ultimately, the liberal distinctions of productive and unproductive public debt swayed the opinions of potential subscribers as *Zhaoxin* bonds were dismally undersold in Shanghai, while municipal improvement bonds issued by Shanghai's foreign concession zones enjoyed a brisk subscription. The contrast in subscription tallies stood witness to the power of new ideas on political economy and debt as it validated authorities with arguably fewer claims to political legitimacy than the Qing court.

With the failure of *Zhaoxin* bonds and diminished legitimacy of the court following the Boxer Rebellion, the identification of public-spiritedness with dynastic loyalty began to be transferred to that of the nation-state in the early 1900s. Much has been written on the reconceptualization of the Chinese state during this era, and for the purposes of this chapter, what is interesting here is the appropriation of concepts of public-spiritedness and nationalist patriotism to at times justify enforced subscription to public debt by the peasantry.[73] This appropriation of patriotic discourse in public debt was apparent in the case of the Sichuan-Hankow railways in 1904 where Sichuan merchants and intellectuals began agitating for local ownership through public subscription. In broadsheets written by students for popular audiences, the specter of "Sichuan becoming another Manchuria (and) India" through railway monopolies by "big foreign capitalists" was raised to justify the imposition of land and salt surtaxes. Both of these surtaxes were disproportionately borne by Sichuanese peasantry, who were in theory given chits to claim interest payments once the railway had been completed, and the method of enforcing surtax collection was broadly similar to other surtax charges.[74] Although contemporary commentaries deplored some of the extreme measures used to extract "subscriptions" for public debt, the appeal of a nation in peril from foreign interlopers was used by the debt's advocates to overlook these individual cases. This surge of rural taxation in the 1900s, as many have noted, represented the demise of imperial benevolence and restraint as a governing discourse, with the Qing court quickly collapsing in its wake in 1911.[75]

* * *

Although by no means an exhaustive account, this chapter has sketched out the redistributive effects from the imposition of modern public debt on late Qing China. Because the fiscal regime that public debt displaced was both institutionally and intellectually structured to support the Qing court's political legitimacy through spatial and social redistribution, the imposition of a new debt regime—with its emphasis on intertemporal transfers—not only reshaped how fiscal resources were distributed in China but also demanded new institutions and ideologies to legitimize this shift in priorities.

Yet, the embeddedness of established discourses on political economy mean that although the debt regime reigned throughout early twentieth-century China, it was accompanied by a discourse on public debt that viewed financial intermediaries with at best ambivalence, preferring to stress direct links between the people and the state through patriotic appeals, even at the expense of tolerating extractive and coercive methods to sustain bond subscriptions.[76] Ripples from this line of thinking could be found in how Communist authorities dealt with public debt in the post-1949 era, including its repudiation of public debt (both domestic and foreign) as a form of state financing in the 1960s, and preference for other forms of "silent financing" over debt to this day.

Notes

1. English-language discussions of Chinese public debt have featured in histories of the customs service (Hans van de Ven, *Breaking with the Past: The Maritime Customs Service and the Global Origins of Modernity in China* (New York: Columbia University Press, 2014) is the latest study that began with Stanley Wright's chronicles in 1927), as well as banking and business histories of the period, such as Frank H.H. King's *History of the Hongkong and Shanghai Bank* (Cambridge: Cambridge University Press, 1991), and Brett Sheehan's *Trust in Troubled Times* (Cambridge, Mass.: Harvard University Press, 2003) for the Republican banks. There also exists an extensive literature on British and Japanese informal empire and "gentlemanly capitalism," where the subject of Chinese public debt regularly appeared, while late Qing political history also discussed foreign debt in light of great power diplomacy. Two good examples in English are Wolfgang J. Mommsen and Jürgen Osterhammel, eds., *Imperialism and after: Continuities and Discontinuities* (London: Allen & Unwin, 1986); Robert A. Bickers and Isabella Jackson, eds., *Treaty Ports in Modern China: Law, Land and Power* (New York: Routledge, 2016).
2. Xu Ke, "Jiading Fufu Sandayu," *Qingbai Leichao* (Reprint, Beijing, 2010).
3. Ye-chien Wang, *Land Taxation in Imperial China, 1750–1911* (Cambridge Mass.: Harvard University Press, 1974), 92–93.
4. Estimates from Wang Qingyun, *Shihe Yuji* (Beijing, 1985), vol. 3. Stipends for the Civil Service in 1812 came to around 6.16 million tls. per annum.

5. Zhao Erxun et al., *Draft History of the Qing* (Reprint, Beijing, 1998), vol. 125, section 6.
6. Tang Xianglong, *Zhongguo Jindai Caizheng Jingjishi Lunwenxuan* (Chengdu, 1987), 188–90.
7. Chen Feng, *Qingdai Yanzheng yu Yanshui* (Zhengzhou, 1998), 220.
8. Nationwide tax breaks were implemented approximately every 10 years during the Qianlong era, reducing the tax burden by around 27 million tls. per break. Estimates from Wu Qingdi, *Jiaolang Cuolu* (Beijing, 1990), vol. 1. However, due to backlogs of provincial fiscal deficits, a significant portion of the tax remissions were simply unpaid tax claims from previous years that were struck off.
9. Liang Fangzhong, *Zhongguo Lidai Hukou Tiandi Tianfu Tongji* (Shanghai, 1980), 426–27.
10. "*Wei Qinfeng Shangyu Shi,*" 14th Day 12th Month, Ninth Year of Qianlong, First Historical Archive, Beijing.
11. Wei Qingyuan, *Mingqingshi Bianxi* (Beijing: China Social Sciences Press, 1989).
12. "Re-transport and Loans," *Lianghuai Yanfazhi,* Jiaqing Era, vol. 17.
13. Scholarship on the history of regions surrounding the waterways in Southwest Shandong attests to the importance of government investment and oversight of major waterworks in maintaining local stability. See Kenneth Pomeranz, *The Making of a Hinterland: State, Society, and Economy in Inland North China, 1853–1937* (Berkeley: University of California Press, 1993).
14. See Madeleine Zelin, *The Magistrate's Tael: Rationalizing Fiscal Reform in Eighteenth-Century Ch'ing China* (Berkeley: University of California Press, 1984).
15. This is harder than it looks, since arguably neither conditions were quite in the hands of Qing officials, rendering Lord McCartney's comment "fortunate succession of able and vigilant officers" a prescient one.
16. Qingyuan, *Mingqingshi Bianxi.*
17. For a short summary of key positions in early nineteenth-century thinkers, see Wang Fansen, *Zhongguo Jindai Sixiang yu Xueshu de Xipu (The Genealogies of Modern Chinese Ideas and Learning)* (Taipei: Linking Publishing, 2003), 81.
18. See Lin Man-houng, *China Upside Down: Currency, Society, and Ideologies, 1808–1856* (Cambridge, Mass.: Harvard University Press, 2007) for a more detailed discussion of the silver crisis.
19. Estimates put the amount of salt merchant contributions to military campaigns between 1734 and 1820 at 41 million tls., excluding contributions of traders in Canton.

20. *Qing Wenzong Shilu (Veritable Records of the Xianfeng Emperor of Qing)*, vol. 97, 33. One should note that the mid-eighteenth-century figure was an estimate made by the Board of Revenue of reserve under its management; actual deposits of silver sycees are likely to be smaller, though still much larger than the amount found in 1853.
21. Import figures from the western-managed maritime services indicated a fourfold rise in value for commodities imported between 1864 and 1894 from 46.21 million to 162.1 million tls. Yao Xiangao ed., *Zhongguo Jindai Duiwai Maoyishi Ziliao (Materials on the History of Chinese Foreign Trade in Recent Years)* (Beijing: Zhonghua Book Co. 1962), 3:1591.
22. Commodity value for tea, silkworms, cotton, opium, and grains traded domestically increased by roughly 180 percent between 1840 and 1894, forming a progressively growing tax base for *likin*. See Xu Dixin and Wu Chengming eds., *Zhongguo Ziben Zhuyi Fazhanshi (History of the Development of Chinese Capitalism)* (Beijing: People's Press, 1990), 2:302.
23. Around 150,000 tls. per loan. People's Bank of China, *Zhongguo Qingdai Waizhaishi Ziliao (Materials on Qing-era Foreign Loans)* (Beijing: China Financial Press, 1991), 2.
24. Wang Jingyu, *Zhongguo Jindai Gongyeshi Ziliao (Materials on History of Modern Chinese Industries)* (Beijing: Science Press, 1957), 2:103.
25. Association of Chinese Historians, ed., *Yangyu Yundong Zilao Congkan (Compiled Materials on the Self-Strengthening Movement)* (Shanghai: Shanghai People's Press, 2000), 4:340–46.
26. Most domestic brokerages, with an average capital of around 200,000 to 300,000 tls., were also deeply leveraged.
27. See Christopher Clay, *Gold for the Sultan: Western Bankers and Ottoman Finance, 1856–1881* (London: I. B. Tauris, 2001) for further discussion. The predicaments faced by the Porte in sufficiently accounting for its governmental budget are particularly comparable to the late Qing.
28. And indeed, these were the actual reasons cited by the proponents of Xinjiang loans in the late 1870s. See People's Bank of China, ed., *Zhongguo Qingdai Waizhaishi Ziliao (Materials on Qing-Era Foreign Debts)* (Beijing: China Financial Press, 1991), 25, 48.
29. Some of these figures were first used by French credit rating agencies. See Marc Flandreau, "Caveat Emptor: Coping with Sovereign Risk without the Multilaterals," Centre for Economic Policy Research Discussion Paper Series No. 2004, 1998, http://ssrn.com/abstract=141392
30. He Wenkai, *Paths toward the Modern Fiscal State* (Cambridge, Mass.: Harvard University Press, 2012), chap. 3–4.
31. People's Bank of China, ed., *Zhongguo Qingdai Waizhaishi Ziliao*, 890.
32. Liu Jinzao, ed., *Qingchao Xuwenxian Tongkao* (Reprint, Hangzhou: Zhejiang Guji Press, 1988), vol. 68.

33. All of which were enormously lucrative for the banks concerned; most of HSBC's annual profit for 1897–1898 came from the issuance of Anglo-German Loans. See Frank H.H. King, *The Hongkong Bank in Late Imperial China, 1864–1902: On an Even Keel* (Cambridge: Cambridge University Press, 1987).
34. Even factoring in the devaluation of silver vis-à-vis gold-standard currencies, when the silver tael depreciated around 21 percent between 1894 and 1910, the amount used to service foreign debt in 1911 would still have represented over 52 percent of total government spending in 1894.
35. Figures from *Qingchao Xuwenxian Tongkao*, vol. 65–68.
36. Zhu Shouming ed., *Guangxuchao Donghua Lu (Court Memorials of the Guangxu Era)* (Reprint, Shanghai: 2007), 4:4370–94.
37. "Memorial by the Treasury on the need for collective effort at indemnity repayment," *Beijing Xinwen Huibao*, vol. 6, Guangxu 27, 9th Month, 3546.
38. "Guangdong Keliguan Zhangcheng (Curriculum for Guangdong Official Training Institute)," in Deng Shi, ed., *Zhengyi Congshu* (Reprint, Taipei: Wenhai Press), 513.
39. Wei Guangqi, "Qingdai Houqi Zhongyang Jiquan Caizheng de Wajie (The Disintegration of Centralized Fiscal System in Late Qing)," *Jindaishi Yanjiu (Research in Modern History)* 1 (1986): 223–24.
40. Memorial by Song Fan, Viceroy of Shaanxi and Gansu, Guangxu 31, 3rd Month, 24th Day. In *Guangxuchao Donghua Lu*.
41. Memorial by Wang Yuzao, Governor of Guizhou, Guangxu 24, 3rd Month, 29th Day. In *Guangxuchao Donghua Lu*.
42. Water management expenses for the Shandong stretch of the Yellow River declined from over 2 million tls. in the 1810s to around 500,000 tls. per annum in 1907, even without discounting for inflation during this period. See Shen Bing, *Huanghe Tongkao (General Survey of the Yellow River)* (Taipei: Zhonghua Congshu Bianshen Weiyuanhui, 1960).
43. Memorial by Liu Kunyi, Guangxu 24, 7th Month, 23rd Day. In *Guangxuchao Donghua Lu*, vol. 147, 8–19.
44. See Zhang Ruide, *Pinghan Tielu yu Huabei de Jingji Fazhan, 1905–1937 (Peking-Hankow Railroad and Economic Development in North China, 1905–1937)* (Taipei: Institute of Modern History Academia Sinica, 1987).
45. People's Bank of China eds., *Qingdai Waizhaishi Ziliao*, vol. 2, 224–226, 294–95, 508.
46. Wang Shuhuai, *Gengzi Peikuan (The Boxer Indemnities)* (Taipei: Institute of Modern History, Academia Sinica, 1974), 163.
47. *Qing Yanfa Zhi*, vol. 23–24.
48. In this, the history of Chinese public debt between 1906 and 1914 almost consciously parallels the Whiggish interpretations of public spending and representation offered by late nineteenth-century Western commentators,

which were faithfully reprinted in Japanese and Chinese textbooks and pamphlets on public finance in the early 1900s.
49. See Liu Zenghe, "Xifang Yusuan Zhidu yu Qingji Caizheng Gaizhi (Western Budget systems and late Qing fiscal reforms)," *Lishi Yanjiu (Historical Research)* 2 (2009): 82–105, especially in the case of Hubei province, where Japanese elements of budget planning were adopted as early as 1902.
50. Figures submitted to the occupying powers during the Boxer Indemnity negotiations by the Customs Service put annual revenue at around 88.2 million tls. around 1899, while H. B. Morse estimates for 1904 were around 102.92 million tls.
51. Given that provincial officials possessed incentives to under-report their revenue (since foreign debt service quotas were assigned accordingly), the figure was almost certainly an underestimate of the actual figures.
52. In Michael Tomz, *Reputation and International Cooperation: Sovereign Debt across Three Centuries* (Princeton: Princeton University Press, 2007); although the author qualified his positive empirical findings on enforcement through gunboats with case studies that emphasized his original argument on reputational concerns, he allowed for the likelihood that some debtors probably feared military intervention (p. 151). Secondly, his figures indicated that Britain, the largest lender to the Chinese government at the time, "evince[d] statistically significant patterns of militarized action against defaulters" (p. 125). Thirdly, the author failed to include figures for Japan in his studies, which became a creditor country to China following the Sino-Japanese War of 1894–1895. All this is not to discount the general application of his argument against the "gunboat theory," but the case of late Qing China deserves a second look.
53. The author (John Hill Burton) was perhaps more widely read in Meiji Japan than Qing China, where his writings were publicized by Fukuzawa Yukichi (1835–1901). See Albert M. Craig, *Civilization and Enlightenment: The Early Thought of Fukuzawa Yukichi* (Cambridge, Mass.: Harvard University Press, 2009), chap. 3.
54. Fu Lanya [John Fryer], Ying Zuxi (trans.), *Zuozhi Chuyan (Humble Words in Aid of Governance)* (Shanghai: Shanghai Shudian Chubanshe, 2002).
55. Interestingly, although the original discussion referred specifically to income tax, the Chinese translation did not distinguish this, since income tax as a specific category was not implemented until the 1930s. Ding Weiliang [William Martin], Wang Fengzao (trans.), *Fuguo Ce (Strategies for National Wealth)* (Peking: Tongwen Guan, 1880).
56. Guo Songtao et al., *Guo Songtao deng Shixiji Liuzhong (Six Excerpts of Diplomatic Journals by Guo Songtao and others)* (Beijing: Sanlian Shudian, 1998). Kang Youwei (1858–1927) did propose institutions similar to

British workhouses in his utopian tract *Datong Shu*, but his proposal seemed to be in the minority in late Qing discourses, and unrelated to public debt.

57. Zheng Guanying, *Shengshi Weiyan (Words of Warning in Times of Prosperity)* (Zhengzhou: Zhongzhou Guji Chubanshe, 1998), 290.
58. Indeed, prominent gentry-industrialists such as Zhang Jian (1853–1926) petitioned the imperial court to transfer trusteeship of bond proceeds to gentry-led chambers of commerce for investment purposes. Zhang Jian, *Dai Niqing Liu Gesheng Gukuan Zhenxing Nonggong Shangwu Shu (代拟请留各省股款振兴农工商务疏)*, in Nantong Municipal Library, ed., *Zhang Jian Quanji (Collected Works of Zhang Jian)* (Nanjing: Jiangsu Guji Chubanshe, 1994), vol. 2.
59. Similar arguments could later be seen in editorials on *Zhaoxin* bond issues for 1898, and later public debt crises in the early 1920s, as Chinese bankers and merchants sought to restrain public spending on armaments. For a general, English-language discussion on the 1920s, see Marie-Claire Bergère, *The Golden Age of the Chinese Bourgeoisie, 1911–1937* (Cambridge: Cambridge University Press, 1989), 217–27.
60. See Mary C. Wright, *The Last Stand of Chinese Conservatism: The T'ung-Chih Restoration, 1862–1874* (Stanford: Stanford University Press, 1957) for a classic account of the period.
61. Wang Tao, *Taoyuan Wenlu Waibian (Further Articles from Tao Gardens)* (Shanghai: Shanghai Shudian Chubanshe, 2002), 36.
62. Kai Ho, *Quan Xue Pian Shuhou (Comments on "Exhortation to Learning")*, in Kai Ho and Hu Liyuan, *Xinzheng Zhenquan (True Explanations to New Policies)* (Hong Kong: Zhongguo Baoguan, 1900), vol. 6.
63. Zhu Huashou, "Zhaoxin Piao Kaitong Youyi Zhongguo Lun (Issuing Zhaoxin bonds will benefit China)," *Shuxue Bao*, 7 (1898): 34–41.
64. Guanying, *Shengshi Weiyan*, 292.
65. Board of Revenues, "*Niding Geifa Zhaoxin Gupiao Xiangxi Zhangcheng Shu (Petition for Draft Articles to Zhaoxin Bond Issuance)*," in Qian Jiaju ed., *Jiu Zhongguo Gongzhai Shi Ziliao (Materials on the History of Public Debt in pre-1949 China)* (Beijing: Zhonghua Shuju, 1984), 14–16.
66. And they were partially right about this; senior managers within HSBC discussed ways to persuade Chinese officials to borrow for longer periods as bank managers foresaw arbitrage opportunities from a long-term decline in global prices of silver. McLean to Jackson, 29 September 1885, David McLean Papers, MS 380401, SOAS Library.
67. Huang Zunxian, *Ribenguo Zhi (Account of the State of Japan)* (Shanghai: Shanghai Guji Chubanshe, 2001), 18:10–12.
68. See Benjamin Schwartz, *In Search of Wealth and Power: Yen Fu and the West* (Cambridge, Mass.: Belknap Press, 1964), chap. 5.

69. See William T. Rowe, *Hankow: Conflict and Community in a Chinese City, 1796–1895* (Stanford: Stanford University Press, 1989), chap. 4.
70. Board of Revenues, "*Niding Geifa Zhaoxin Gupiao Xiangxi Zhangcheng Shu,*" 15.
71. Emperor Guangxu sent to the Bogd Lama (later Bogd Khan of Mongolia) for his subscription/offering of 200,000 tls.: "*...one processional canopy in bright yellow, embroidered with dragons; one set of seat cushions in yellow silk brocade with dragon patterns...,*" which would not have looked out of place in an eighteenth-century exchange of gifts between the Qing court and Tibetan-Mongolian lamas. See Zhu Shoupeng, *Donghua Xulu (Records of Donghua Gate: Guangxu Era)* (Beijing: Zhonghua Shuju, 1959), vol. 143.
72. Editorial, "Da Guanwen Yinzao Gupiao Shi (In Answer to Inquiries on the Printing of Bonds)," *Shenbao*, 8 February 1898.
73. For a recent summary of this field, see Peter Zarrow, *After Empire: The Conceptual Transformation of the Chinese State, 1885–1924* (Stanford: Stanford University Press, 2012).
74. The last stretch of the Sichuan-Hankow railway was completed on July 1, 2012. Xinhua News Agency, "Chuanhan Railways in Full Service; Fulfilling a Century-Long Dream," *Xinhua News*, July 1, 2012. http://news.xinhuanet.com/local/2012-07/01/c_112328727.htm
75. Taisu Zhang, "Fiscal Policy and Institutions in Imperial China," *Oxford Research Encyclopedia: Asian History*, December 12, 2019. https://papers.ssrn.com/sol3/papers.cfm?abstract_id=3503055
76. For an interpretation of the new fiscal framework in early twentieth-century China, see Debin Ma, "Financial Revolution in Republican China During 1900–1937: A Survey and a New Interpretation," *Australian Economic History Review* 2 (2019): 1–21.

CHAPTER 10

Fiscal Federalism: Local Debt and the Construction of the Modern State in the United States and France

Noam Maggor and Stephen W. Sawyer

In the latter decades of the nineteenth century, the volume of local and municipal debt exploded in both the United States and France. Megametropolises, rapidly growing cities, and ambitious provincial towns borrowed (and spent) ever increasing amounts that, in cumulative terms, rivaled and in some ways surpassed the fiscal prowess of national governments around the world. In this so-called first age of globalization, public borrowing by local authorities thus became a primary technology for mobilizing resources, enhancing state power, spurring economic development, and translating political priorities into government policy. Away from the lofty domain of national sovereigns, empire builders, and global

N. Maggor (✉)
School of History, Queen Mary University, London, UK
e-mail: n.maggor@qmul.ac.uk

S. W. Sawyer
Department of History, American University of Paris, Paris, France
e-mail: ssawyer@aup.edu

© The Author(s) 2020
N. Barreyre, N. Delalande (eds.), *A World of Public Debts*, Palgrave Studies in the History of Finance, https://doi.org/10.1007/978-3-030-48794-2_10

bankers, public debt in this context often assumed a more mundane quality. It nevertheless had profound redistributive—and thus politically contested—effects on the allocation of wealth and power across geographical regions, metropolitan space, and social classes.

The transatlantic trajectory of municipal debt in the late nineteenth century runs askew of existing accounts of public debt that have emphasized the tight-knit relationship between state-building, public borrowing, and territorial sovereignty. One body of literature has interrogated public debt with a set of institutional questions in mind. Guided by the work of Douglass North and Barry Weingast, this scholarship has focused on the constitutional rules that began to constrain and bind sovereigns in the early modern era.[1] Another body of social scientific literature has explored the disruptive forces of twenty-first century globalization, which ostensibly fractured a longstanding symmetry between territory, sovereignty, and public credit.[2] The massive accumulation of municipal debt in the nineteenth-century United States and France instead demonstrates that public borrowing was never the privileged domain of territorial nation-states. It was, rather, a more flexible mode of governance that linked local politics, regional development, and global flows of capital. This perspective moves away from the conventional institutionalist focus and instead inscribes public debt in relationships of power between social groups, regions, financial markets, and a multi-scalar state. Indeed, there was a politics—oftentimes a highly contested politics—to the accumulation of public debt that played an essential role in modern state-building but which had little to do with territorial sovereignty. The emphasis on subnational public debt, furthermore, strains easy dichotomies that separate "the West" from other regions around the world. Subnational public debt, much like public debt elsewhere around the world, raised deeply political questions about the relationship between access to financial resources and political jurisdiction, and, by implication, the tension between regional homogenization and differentiation that was typical of this phase of globalization.[3] By focusing on local and regional debt practices, this history thus "provincializes" the United States and France, situating the two countries on a similar plane of analysis, and even more broadly, in a comparative framework with other locales—China, West Africa, Latin America, and the Middle East—in the world economy (examined in the other chapters of this section).

A shared examined of subnational public debt in the United States and in France may at first sight appear odd. Rarely have two countries' relationships to the distribution of power and the forms of state necessary for such distribution been so opposed as in the United States and France. At the heart of the distinctions between the two governmental systems has been the allegedly insurmountable difference between American decentralization and French centralization. The United States, we are told, embodied the possibilities of a formal federalism, cultivating a broad distribution of sovereign power across its territory. In so doing, it limited the power of a central government, and for some, even hindered the construction of a modern "state" in the sense proposed by traditional (European) social science.[4] France, on the other hand, has symbolized an ideal type of state centralization. From the reign of absolutism through the extraordinary state consolidation of the Revolution and Napoleon, the power of the central state, we are told, slowly chipped away at any trace of local or regional sovereignty as well as at the very possibilities of a vibrant civil society that could check elephantine Gallic statism.

The stakes of such interpretations are particularly high as they have deep roots in our most prized conceptions of political modernization and liberalism, as well as in the myths and stories of national exceptionalisms they have fostered. Nonetheless, such stark oppositions have gradually come under attack. As the pendulum has slowly swung away from nationalist histories inspired by the successes (Hartz) and failures (Furet) of liberalism in these respective national contexts and toward new questions about political economy, and primarily the relationship between capitalism and democratic politics, some of these tired oppositions have begun to unravel.[5] The challenge to such oppositions has also come from a change in the scale of our political economic analyses. Indeed, when one examines the construction of these capitalist and democratic states at the subnational scale one increasingly breaks out of oppositions that have fetishized "national" difference.

What follows reconsiders these oppositions through an examination of American and French subnational debt in the second half of the nineteenth century. Our approach traces the process of debt accumulation on municipal and regional levels as a state-building strategy that allowed local polities to accelerate development, build infrastructure, and provide crucial services. It is our contention that this mode of fiscal federalism did not evolve as a challenge to central government authority. Rather, we propose a more pragmatic conception of federalism which may be understood as a process of building up local state capacity. By pragmatic, or anti-formalist, we mean that these municipalities were not attempting to enact some federalist ideal, or engage in some institutional process of accumulating local sovereignty at the expense of national sovereignty, but were rather attempting to find fiscal solutions to complex challenges and opportunities on the ground.

Such an anti-formalist fiscal federalism provides a new perspective on a comparative history of public debt, revising some of our basic assumptions of state construction. When we set aside a story about the successes or failures of liberalism, or the peculiarities of republicanism, a new transnational history emerges. In the American case, it suggests that the accumulation of debt and fiscal resources on the local level was not simply a process of limiting the central government's reach, but a more complex and often contradictory process of ameliorating the modern state's infrastructural power. The American state grew through territorial expansion, resource extraction, and the enhanced authority of state and local actors. In the case of France, the accumulation of municipal debt provides proof that in spite of the supposed "Jacobin centralization" of the French state, some of the most important economic and political decisions—which would affect France and its world Empire—were made on the local level and were designed precisely to overcome resistance that might be generated through the reach, or overreach, of national institutions. From this perspective, fiscal federalism was not so much a process of decentralization or limiting of the state—let alone a marker of state "weakness"—but a technology of modern governance that was essential to the construction of a democratic state across the tremendous territories that imperial nation-states occupied.[6] We suggest then that from the perspective of local debt and fiscal federalism, the United States and France are hardly as opposed as our common stories of political and economic modernization have suggested.

NATIONAL CONSOLIDATION? THE RISE OF LOCAL DEBT IN THE UNITED STATES AND FRANCE

More than any other period, historians of the United States and France conventionally associate the end of the nineteenth century with the process of national consolidation. Leaning more or less explicitly on modernization templates, they often narrate the integration of a national market as a sweeping, almost automatic process that was triumphantly carried forward by such transformative technologies as the railroad and telegraph.

Thereafter, as this story goes, economic activity gained a national and imperial scale, "making necessary" the rise of centralized government power, on the Federal level in the case of the United States, and the national scale in the case of the French Third Republic.[7]

Exactly how such a state materialized in the American and French cases has been a preoccupation for historians of both countries in recent decades.[8] In both cases, revisionist literature on the state has forced social scientists to reconsider the relationship between the scales of the state and non-state actors, the deployment of power both horizontally and vertically, and the capacity to govern through "infrastructural" power.[9] A focus on subnational public debt continues this revisionist trajectory, telling an equally complex story. The formation of a national economy, it suggests, proceeded not via the transcendence of local and state institutions but rather through increases in their capacities. While there are obvious differences between France and the United States, it is possible to uncover some important underlying trends in the accumulation of debt that shaped capitalist development as a political project in these two countries.

Indeed, the immense rise in public indebtedness financed a rapid acceleration in American and French state capacity in the last decades of the nineteenth century. Debt, however, did not only consolidate on the national level. On the contrary, it proliferated. Local governments, jostling to improve their position in a rapidly changing economic landscape, leveraged access to immense financial resources that far exceeded their existing assets and revenues. They invested in an array of local improvements that had a substantial, yet long underappreciated, impact on the overall trajectories of the American and French political economies. In the United States after the Civil War, for example, the growing number of local polities—many hundreds and even thousands of them—became the most active borrowers within the structure of the American state. While the Federal government retrenched and redeemed the bonds that funded the war effort, the total debt of local governments grew by leaps and bounds. This debt roughly quadrupled in size between 1870 and 1902 and then doubled again by World War I, reaching $4 billion in total (compared to roughly $380 million of state level debts and $1.2 billion in national debt). At that point, the total liabilities of all local governments accounted for 72 percent of all public debt in the United States (see Table 10.1). Not all municipalities became equally indebted, of course. Large cities, especially in the East, led the way. They borrowed more per capita (and spent and taxed more) than other municipalities. Cities in the

Table 10.1 Government debt by level of government in levels and shares in the United States (1838–1992)

Year	State debt	Local debt	National debt	State share	Local share	National share
1838	172	25	3	86.0%	12.5%	1.5%
1841	193	25	5	86.4%	11.4%	2.3%
1870	352	516	2436	10.7%	15.6%	73.7%
1880	297	826	2090	9.2%	25.7%	65.0%
1890	228	905	1122	10.2%	40.1%	49.8%
1902	230	1877	1178	7.0%	57.1%	35.9%
1913	379	4035	1193	6.8%	72.0%	21.3%
1922	1131	8978	22,963	3.4%	27.1%	69.4%

Source: John Joseph Wallis, "American Government Finance in the Long Run: 1790 to 1990," *Journal of Economic Perspectives* 14, no. 1 (2000): 61–82

Midwest and the trans-Mississippi West soon followed suit, while cities in the South did not.[10]

The French state was not fundamentally different, revealing a similar tendency toward large subnational debt accumulation. While the case of Paris was no doubt one of the most extraordinary, local debt in France was hardly limited to the capital city. As one observer noted in the 1860s, creative use of bond issues on the local scale "is the only way to continue the regenerative movement not only in Paris, but in Lyon, Bordeaux, Marseille, Nantes, Lille, Strasbourg, and Rouen and anywhere else where life and health must be supported and developed." And indeed, the popularity of these schemes in the provinces was one of the issues that political opponents in the 1860s, such as the Republican Jules Ferry, railed against with the most vehemence: "Marseille, Besançon, Bourges, Bergerac, Blaye, Vienne, Rive-de-Gier, Pithiviers have borrowed at will in the form of long-term public works."[11]

And, in one sense, Ferry was right to be alarmed. Like cities across the United States at the same time, the total amount of municipal debt during the last third of the nineteenth century soared as cities sought to rebuild their infrastructures, provide new municipal services, or participate in the construction of new railroad lines. The figures were startling. Despite a massive national debt following the Franco-Prussian War, compounded by the cost of France's own civil war in 1871 and the tremendous increase in national state debt for war reparations to Germany, local debt also rose to over 3 billion in the first decades of the Third Republic (Table 10.2).[12]

Table 10.2 France's Public Debts from 1852 to 1897

Year	Public debt servicing	Consolidated public debt (nominal capital)	Communal debt	Departmental debt
1852		5.5		
1871	681	12,500		
1872	1100			
1873	1300			
1874	1200			
1875	1200			
1876	1100	20,000		
1877	1200		2700	
1878		19,900		
1879				
1880	1200			
1881	1200			
1882				
1883				
1884				
1885			3000	465
1886				496
1887				523
1888	1100	21,200		
1889				
1890	1300		3200	
1891	1300		3200	
1892			3200	
1893			3300	544
1894			3300	
1895			3500	418
1896	1200		3500	
1897	1200			

In million francs

Sources: *Annuaire Statistique de la France* (Paris: Imprimerie Nationale, 1878–1894) and "Les dettes communales," *Bulletin de statistique et de législation comparée* 32 (September 1892), 275–300. It is worth noting that the *Annuaire Statistique* did not present systematic figures from year to year

The steady accumulation of debt, especially in larger cities of over 20,000 inhabitants, was pursued throughout France, although, like in the United States, this debt was distributed unevenly across the country. By the beginning of the Third Republic, municipal debt was almost half as much as the national debt had been at the beginning of the Second Empire. In the 1880s, Paris accounted for a little over half the municipal debt in France (New York City's municipal debt was valued at about one-half of the total debt of all states in the Union). In 1885, Paris still had over 1.7 billion in debt compared to the next highest, Marseille's 109 million.

Heavy borrowing by large cities like Paris and New York, however, was not necessarily the most remarkable aspect of municipal debt. In these large cities, heavy borrowing was offset by a large revenue base. This was not the case in the provinces, where the ratio of debt to revenue was much larger. Take, for example, the total for French cities of 20,000 inhabitants in 1885 which amounted to 7.4 million in debt to 1.6 million francs in (ordinary) revenues or a ratio of approximately 4.5 to 1. Some of the cities cited by Ferry had in fact far outstretched that ratio. Marseille had racked up 109 million in debt with only 13.5 million in ordinary revenues, a ratio of about 8 to 1, slightly higher than the 7.5 to 1 ratio for the French capital. In contrast, Bordeaux had amassed only 37.2 million in debt with over 9 million in revenues, a ratio of about 4 to 1. Besançon had accumulated 4.7 million in debt but it also had a revenue in 1885 of a little over 1.5 million, which meant a ratio of a little over 3 to 1. Other cities listed by Ferry such as Bourges (6 to 1) or Vienne (5 to 1) did have substantial debt ratios, even if they remained under that of the capital or Marseille. Overall, these debt loads appeared relatively reasonable compared to some of the northern industrial cities such as Lille with a 9 to 1 revenue to debt ratio or Dunkerque with 1.4 million in revenues and 37.3 million in debt or an almost 27 to 1 ratio!

The case of Dunkerque merits special mention. Like many cities that accumulated unprecedented debt levels during this period in France and the United States, the main driver of debt accumulation seems to have been bound to the issue of infrastructural investment. Such extraordinary debt in the case of Dunkerque was no doubt the product of the massive investments in the reconstruction of the city's port and the municipality's contribution to the construction of the railways launched in 1879 to distribute and ship the goods running through the port. Moreover, it seems clear that these new opportunities for municipal debt were tied to the ambitions of local investment throughout the department of the Nord since the cities of the department had the highest debt of any in France outside of the department of the Seine in 1893 with 127 million, while, for example, the communes of the Bouches-du-Rhône with Marseille had 111 million.[13] Clearly, subnational bodies were accumulating unprecedented debt in France and the United States at precisely the moment that their national economies were supposedly consolidating. Pierre-Joseph Proudhon lamented in his treatise on speculation that "Departmental and municipal budgets, like those of the State, grow worse every year without ever balancing with their revenues."[14]

Beyond the actual numbers, however, what is striking in this age of skyrocketing local and subnational public debt is the relative lack of supervision that seemed to be coming from the national scale. There is indeed an extraordinary level of variation in local debt and investment strategies and ranges of what the municipalities spent money on, in each case leading to extensive local political debates. Indeed, Jules Ferry's alarm in France was spurred by the fact that he considered there to be almost no oversight: "The law has been violated, it is the law that places limits, traces the rules of the communes that seek to borrow. In a great number of cities, these rules have been entirely forgotten. In some cases loans are disguised by a pre-approval; in others an authorized loan is employed toward other ends."[15] In the case of France there were certainly cities which sought to emulate Paris, like Marseille, while others pursued an extremely conservative investment agenda. Thus even while concern developed about the potential dangers of such debt, the national government did not seem to have consistent statistics or even a consistent policy about how municipalities could and should leverage their local resources. At the very least, the question of oversight was vague enough that it could be mobilized politically by the opposition against the government.

The American case shows a similar development, with subnational debt ballooning outside of the purview of national authorities. Subnational public borrowing was not new in this period; American states earlier in the century used their newfound sovereign powers to borrow in European bond markets. State borrowing in support of infrastructure projects—canals, then railroads—became widespread as a way to nurture economic development.[16] After the Civil War, local governments surpassed states as the largest borrowers. Locked in competition against other locales (Galena vs. Chicago, Leavenworth vs. Kansas City, Sandusky vs. Cleveland—the stakes were high!), municipalities were moved to become extraordinarily proactive. They borrowed to subsidize railroad construction and secure strategic railroad links.[17] Controversially, they borrowed to support local manufacturing and other industries. They borrowed to provide services and amenities to growing populations, including thousands of miles of paved streets, water and sewage systems, police and fire stations, schools, parks, and public libraries.[18]

More than any legal or political oversight, what regulated the movement of these resources was the willingness of large financial institutions on the US east coast to gobble up this debt, which they generally proved all too eager to do. Always pressed to find remunerative investment outlets for their growing reserves, they embraced subnational public debt, which was considered relatively safe and also lent itself to easy diversification. Insurance Companies, whose resources ballooned in those decades, happily added these securities to their hefty portfolios. As a percentage of the total assets of American insurance companies, state and local bonds grew from 8.1 percent in 1860 to 21.6 percent in 1870 and 37.7 percent in 1880 (Federal debt added up to only 3.1, 9.1 and 8.7 in the same years).[19] In 1890, for example, the New England Mutual Life Insurance Company of Boston held the bonds of more than forty different municipalities from all regions of the US. The Mutual Life Insurance Company of New York held more than seventy. The Aetna Life Insurance Company of Connecticut far outpaced the others. It held roughly 350 different bonds issued by states, counties, cities, and school districts in the United States (and Canada). Trust companies, savings banks, and other financial institutions joined the fray.[20] In an age of rapid growth and volatility, these institutions became increasingly reliant on public debt as a prudent place to park large portions of their immense financial resources.[21] This debt greatly enhanced the power and capacity of local governments. The conventional wisdom about the period notwithstanding, the usurpation of their power by national authorities was nowhere on the horizon.

The Local Politics of Public Debt

Not surprisingly, the relationship between the urban state, bond markets, and national economic development was at the core of American and French politics in the closing decades of the nineteenth century, triggering a fierce debate over who could borrow, how much, and for what purposes. All states and cities faced similar dilemmas and contradictory demands. Should local governments borrow aggressively to forge a foundation for the future or stay fiscally sound to gain favor with "the investing public"? Which projects and initiatives deserved the support of public credit? Would government subsidies to corporations help secure necessary advantages, or were they nothing but extortions that jeopardized the future of the community? Inevitably, these issues expanded to a broader set of questions, each prompting a spectrum of responses: Could democratic majorities be trusted with sensitive fiscal decisions? Should fiscal decisions be made by property owners alone ("taxpayers") or by the voting public at large? Could these questions be left to the discretion of the elected bodies, which were subject to intense lobbying, or were external constitutional limits necessary? Could privately owned ventures like railroads and canals be considered *public* enterprises and thus deserving of subsidies from government treasury? Most fundamentally, since access to bond markets came very much with strings attached, how should local governments negotiate the relationship with their lenders? Was that relationship perfectly harmonious or necessarily antagonistic? How much of a say should outside lenders have in setting priorities for government action? How much leverage did municipalities have in pushing back against the power of national financial institutions? These questions were debated in the public sphere, within government, and, endlessly, in the courts.[22]

The issue of public debt became politically poignant precisely because it stood at the crux of the relationship between local institutions and the larger political economies of the United States and France. Public debt helped regulate the nexus between national financial institutions and locally based political authority, social relations, and economic activity. It became, in essence, a mechanism for mediating the relationship between subnational governments who simultaneously surrendered part of their autonomy, becoming more compatible nodes in a larger integrated system, even as they mobilized unprecedented resources to stimulate economic development and provide urban services. Public debt could therefore encourage municipalities to privilege national infrastructure (e.g., railroad branch lines, terminals, central stations) at the same time that it enabled investment in local improvements (water, streets, sewers, schools, etc.). Large-scale, highly capitalized industries (mining, stockyards, railroads) were often prioritized over local markets and producers. Thorny questions of distribution were often suppressed in favor of the pursuit of subjectively defined notions of "public good." Overall, however, local governments, under the pressures of local business interests or, alternatively, the demands of mass constituencies, invested at a scale that was previously unimaginable.

Public debt, as a political issue, thus emerged as a prime site for a high stakes and, at times, surprisingly open-ended struggle over the fundamental *terms* of market formation and integration.[23] National elites struggled to impose discipline on this unwieldy, decentralized apparatus. They tried to set priorities for borrowing, taxing, and spending through constitutional restrictions, legal decisions, market incentives like low interest rates, and, most importantly, direct and indirect political lobbying. Their power in a democratic political system, however, was ultimately limited, leaving them in many ways vulnerable to an unpredictable deliberative process. The results of these many ongoing confrontations were not elegant and consistent public policy resolutions as envisioned by experts, but mixed bags of allowances, prohibitions, overarching and specific restrictions. They bore the mark of political triumphs, concessions, and compromises that shaped the relationship between local authorities and national governments.

The confluence of historical actors, political wrangling, and state institutions came into sharp relief whenever public borrowing moved from scholarly discourse to the public sphere, for example, as frontier settlers on the far reaches of the United States gathered to write constitutions for new western states. The issue of public debt greatly preoccupied delegates in Olympia, Washington in the summer of 1889 as they drafted their state constitution. "We take the liberty to address you upon the subject of municipal indebtedness," Illinois banker N.W. Harris announced to the rugged Washingtonians. The matter was as follows: Harris and his colleagues in the Windy City had recently acquired bonds issued by a county and a city in Washington. Having gained "confidence in the growth and prosperity" of the territory, which had initially developed under the tutelage of the national government but was about to become an independent state in the Union, the bankers "contemplated" large additional purchases from other local authorities in the new Commonwealth. With this in mind, and with the goal of securing the continued financial backing of "eastern capitalists," the Chicagoans proposed that the new constitution include a special provision strictly limiting city debt to 5 percent of a municipality's taxable property. Such a constitutional limit would not only promote "economical management" of public affairs and prevent municipal bankruptcies but also allow local governments to borrow at much lower rates of interest. This was clearly evident in the premium prices of city and county bonds in states like Illinois, Iowa, Missouri, Indiana, and Wisconsin that had adopted such constitutional limits, thereby bolstering the "confidence of the investing public," relative to those of Minnesota that had not.[24]

The insinuation of "foreign" bankers and their preferences into the democratic deliberations in Olympia, Washington, drew resistance from a variety of sources. Members of the City Council of Seattle declared themselves opposed to the debt ceiling as it threatened plans to float 1 million dollars in municipal bonds to construct much-needed urban improvements. The expense for water works, sewers, roads, lighting, and other amenities would have unquestionably exceeded 5 percent of the assessed valuation of the city.[25] The residents of Spokane similarly opposed "this notion of paternity or guardianship over the people," an "arbitrary law prohibiting indebtedness for public improvements, regardless of all local conditions."[26] Representatives from the municipality of Colfax joined the chorus and pointed out that debt limits could be highly detrimental. Their town had twice burned down and recovery could not have taken place without extensive borrowing. Finally, the local assembly of the Knights of Labor called upon the state to explicitly authorize municipalities to "own and control such industries and public conveniences as the people may choose to own or control." Seeking radical expansion of public authority, they certainly had little patience for such a priori restrictions on government borrowing.[27]

The most impassioned opposition to the debt ceiling, in a notable departure from their more routine emphasis on prudence and economy, came from the business leadership of several counties in the rural parts of the state, which were desperate to attract outside investment in railroads and canals. They reasoned that without the ability to float bonds that could be used to subsidize private enterprise, their communities would be hard pressed to lure outside investors and initiate large construction projects. Members of the Board of Trade of the budding city of Ellensburg argued that "it is for the best interest of our state that counties should be allowed to float a bonded indebtedness to aid and assist public improvements, either railroad or irrigation, when the public improvement intends to develop the resources of our country... we should in every way encourage the speedy development of our resources by either domestic or foreign capital." Another petition from the Board of Trade of Montesano announced that "Whereas, great capital is necessary to the development of our enormous resources; And whereas, the building of new lines of transportation, requiring the investment of capital from other states, is a necessity to our industrial progress; And whereas, we believe in self local government, the liberty of contract, and that fair open competition is the safest regulator in commercial affairs... wisdom dictated a liberal policy in regard to common carriers [i.e. railroads], and that encouragement and not restraint, will contribute most to our local and state government."[28] The notion of "fair competition" included not only freedom from regulatory oversight but also the mustering of public resources to gain a competitive advantage over less generous districts.

The uneven results of these constitutional scuffles were evident in the final draft of the constitution, which was—in quite typical fashion—somewhat combative in its relationship with financial markets. The constitution limited borrowing on the state level but allowed for a majority of voters to authorize "special indebtedness" for some single work or object."[29] Municipal indebtedness would be usually limited to 5 percent of the value of taxable property. However, against the wishes of the bankers of Chicago, the approval of three-fifths of the voters was necessary to allow *further* indebtedness, not to exceed an additional 5 percent, "for supplying such city or town with water, artificial light, and sewers."[30] Finally, in what was considered a "black eye" to the residents of Walla Walla, "for she more than any other county" sought to subsidize railroad construction, the convention determined that "no county, city, town, or other municipal corporation shall give money or property, or loan its money, or credits to or in aid of any individual, association, company or corporation."[31] Other Western states ended up with different bargains and compromises.

Passing from the deep periphery of the US territories to the heart of Europe, it is striking how the politics of local public debt in France was no less ambitious or conflictual. In fact, it is surprising how often the attempts to limit the accumulation of local debt by central or state governments consistently ran into similar difficulties. In the national/imperial capital, regional centers, and other cities throughout France, the ambition to build infrastructures and invest in urban projects grew steadily, generating new levels of municipal debt but also creating a new autonomy and field for local financial decisions. From this perspective, the overwhelming example of Paris should not be misread as a form of centralization or inevitable urban modernization, any more than the equally massive investment in the rest of the country should be ignored. Indeed, while the figures of Parisian borrowing dwarf even the largest of the provincial cities, the tendency toward fiscal and local debt independence on the part of municipalities is confirmed as much by the Parisian case as any other.

In the midst of the Second Empire, the city of Paris was famously undergoing a reconstruction that has become emblematic of the very processes of modern life. The cost of building this capital of modernity, however, was not negligible. While the figures remained something of a mystery for the better part of the first decade and a half of the city's reconstruction, by the mid-1860s, the colossal scale of Parisian municipal debt burst onto the French and European political scene. On December 11, 1864, the City's Prefect, Georges-Eugène Haussmann, explained in the official newspaper, *Le Moniteur*, that "contrary to the opinion of many local governments (départements) in France, the State had not given Paris preferential treatment when it offered a subsidy from the Treasury of approximately 77 million" because "the city of Paris had already engaged in an enormous set of measures totaling investment of more than 650 million."[32]

But even with these impressive figures, Haussmann undersold the extent of municipal investment in the city and the debt required to pay for it. Indeed, devoting between 50 and 80 million francs per year, Haussmann's reconstruction of the capital over seventeen years ultimately cost something in the neighborhood of 2.5 billion francs, exploding the already gigantic original estimates of 1.1 billion. This of course required consistent recourse to debt, including three major loans that were approved by the national legislature. The first loan came in 1855 for 600 million and was approved by the assembly without any opposition. The second came just a few years later in 1858 for 120 million. When he returned two years later asking for the approval of 120 million more, the legislature began to balk, but it was not until he then returned for approval for a fourth loan of 400 million that the opposition soared and Haussmann's unprecedented accumulation of debt became deeply politicized.[33]

This massive borrowing had consequences far beyond the city's reconstruction, drawing in a series of economic actors who had previously been estranged from the quiet world of municipal finance. The scale of this borrowing also generated unique new tools of debt accumulation. One of the most original responses to this increasing opposition did not come from the state or the municipal administration, however, but from a little-known notary who claimed to have invented a system for the accumulation of massive floating debt in the early 1860s, E. Baronnet. Arguing for the importance of continuing the reconstruction of Paris and the necessity of freeing up capital for doing so, Baronnet elaborated a system that allowed the municipality to continue its work through a system that he referred to as "delegation bonds" (*bons de délégation*). "The municipal administration has been abandoned [by the state] and therefore has no choice but to go out in search of loans," he argued. The problem, to his mind, was the fact that speculators had a far more accurate conception of the city's debt capacity than the legislative body and the Minister of Finance who tended to obscure Paris's real fiscal resources behind a cloud of political gamesmanship. Members of the central government simply did not have enough faith in the tremendous resources of the city's finances and its collection of taxes: "this timidity has generated the difficulties faced by the Prefect of the Seine and the insufficiency of the loan of 1865," he argued.[34]

Baronnet was of course not alone in insisting on the city's capacity to fulfill whatever financial obligations were necessary to complete its massive reconstruction. Indeed, there was tremendous support, not just within the municipal government but among local lenders as well. Baronnet therefore proposed an alternative system which would overcome, or rather avoid, any resistance on the part of the legislature: "It is a question of finding a financial system that makes it possible to complete the major reconstruction of Paris without depending on loans."[35] Baronnet's system did so by creating a kind of floating debt triangle. The city accepted to transfer the sum equivalent to the value of the lands that were purchased before work was completed. This money was transferred in regular payments as soon as the city became owner of the land. The contractor then took on the risk of expropriation and eviction as they demolished and sold the materials and lots. The contractor's profit came from the difference between the initial price and what they were able to sell it for after initial work had been done. So the contractor first had to pay for the expropriations and clearance before receiving anything from the city. In this case, what the contractor lacked was the capital to begin the second phase of construction. This money was to come from the bank—*Caisse des travaux* of the city—which advanced the money to the contractor through regular payments. These funds were reimbursed by "delegation bonds" that were then given by the city to the contractor who could use them to pay off the bank. The bank could then collect interest on the bond (5 percent) or sell them to another bank or its clientele.[36]

This system was extraordinarily successful and its implications vast. First of all, it allowed the city of Paris to expand its debt far beyond its previous efforts, totaling more than 400 million in a few short years by 1867. Second, and perhaps more importantly, it introduced a level of informal fiscal independence into the city's organization that was unprecedented. The city was now effectively raising its own taxes—largely through the tax wall (*octroi*)—to manage a budget that was larger than some smaller European countries and contracting unprecedented amounts of debt from banks without working through the central government. From this perspective, Baronnet's pamphlet, "The Great Works of Paris and the

Delegation Bonds," may as well have been called a *Declaration of Parisian Independence*, for it effectively sealed the liberation of the city's capital from any oversight on the part of the national government. In light of the Commune that would break out a few years later, such extraordinary fiscal independence requires deeper consideration.

The problem with such a massive accumulation of occult debt in under three years was that it was of course just a matter of time before such extraordinary borrowing combined with the fiscal freedom that made it possible became a deeply political issue. Indeed, in spite of its extraordinary revenues, the city was not in a position to reimburse the colossal sums it had borrowed in such a short time. It therefore renegotiated its agreement with the banks that were managing the bonds for a massive buy-out in exchange for a 400-million-franc loan at a rate of 5 percent to be paid out over sixty years. While this solved the problem of municipal solvency, it also threw the city back into the arms of the legislative body, since all official loans required its approval. The debate over this loan turned into one of the most important political battles of the 1860s.

The charge against Haussmann's financing was led by Jules Ferry and his famous *Les Comptes fantastiques d' Haussmann*. Ferry was one of the leaders of the Republican opposition in the final years of the Second Empire. Haussmann's reconstruction and its massive debt therefore provided him with a prized opportunity to show the irresponsibility and massive financial dangers of the imperial regime. Equating Haussmann with the Emperor, Ferry insisted that a government without accountability would necessarily lead the country and its capital to fiscal ruin. "The city has silently borrowed 398 million that it cannot pay back which it now wants to spread over 60 years," Ferry clamored, asking "How was it possible for the city to borrow 398 million without the Legislative Body ever even being made aware of the fact?"[37] For Ferry the issue was above all political: "for the last fifteen years, there has been an administration without any controls, without any accountability."[38]

In presenting Haussmann as a single-minded, unaccountable, and authoritarian city manager, Ferry captured what has become a central leitmotif in political histories of nineteenth-century France. French historians have overwhelmingly insisted upon the centralization of the nineteenth-century French polity, especially under the Napoleonic regimes. Trapped within an account of French history in which construction in Paris was necessarily the product of a top-down imposition of a centralized nation-state that ignored the needs of local populations (associated with the provinces), it has been assumed that Haussmann acted alone through the silent support of the Emperor at the expense of the interests of the French nation. Moreover, it has been assumed that Haussmann's reconstruction of Paris actually reinforced French centralization by pouring massive resources into the nation's capital at the expense of the country's other cities and regions.

The problem with such an account however is that it misses the extent to which Haussmann's reconstruction was accomplished largely outside the concerned arms of the central state. Rather it was pursued on a local level that interacted directly with local and international financial markets. Moreover, it also misses what might be referred to as the "democratic" politics of this massive municipal debt. Louis Girard concluded a brief article from 1951 on the finances of the Second Empire's public works projects by noting the "democratic" features of the massive accumulation of debt during this period: "Ultimately, if these processes were possible over the long-term it is because the Empire operated outside the control of the parliament, submitting itself instead to a daily plebiscite of capital; not the capital of a few isolated financiers, but the democracy of bond markets that constantly spread and followed it."[39] Girard's passing (and rarely, if ever, noted) conclusion actually offers an important insight into the functioning of Haussmann's debt, as well as the debt that was accumulated in the years to come under the Third Republic in the last decades of the nineteenth century. Indeed, Haussmann's project was rooted in what Ernest Renan would refer to a few years later as a "daily plebiscite." This daily plebiscite was made through the choice of speculators and other small and large investors who believed in the solidity of Parisian finances. They expressed their support with every opportunity they had to buy a bond or a share of Paris's debt. This is not to say that Haussmann's construction was a deeply "democratic" project in any traditional political sense. It does however suggest that the ways that a massive new group of people participated in urban construction required a kind of popular "investment" in the local state that was previously unimaginable. It also suggests that the emergence of a massive and independently accumulated municipal debt, the fiscal self-sufficiency of the capital, and its roots in a financial "democratization" were setting the stage for a profoundly new relationship between financial markets, local power, and the nation.

The case of Paris was replicated in big American cities that similarly accumulated massive debts during this period. As in France, the numerous reports, studies, and statistical compendiums, including those by the

Federal Census Bureau, were themselves evidence of invigorated elite efforts to combat the costs of urban democracy, which indeed grew, as one observer put it, "out of all proportion."[40] In 1884, New York City, which had gained the reputation for being "the most expensively governed [city] in the world," spent and borrowed at a rate that alarmed observers. The city's gross indebtedness had doubled between 1850 and 1860, hitting $19 million, only to then quintuple, exceeding $100 million by 1880. As tax-paying elites were quick to point out, this was the equivalent of one-nineteenth of the entire national debt, about one-half of the public debt of all states in the Union, and roughly one-sixth of all municipal debt in the United States. Boston's net funded debt had greatly distressed observers in 1860 when it reached $7.5 million. By 1880, it neared $28 million, which in per capita terms surpassed that of New York. Chicago quickly followed suit. Whereas its population grew by an astounding 260 percent between 1860 and 1875, its debt rose by almost twice as much, increasing by a total of 487 percent.[41]

These ballooning debts generated a contentious debate that shaped local politics as well as their relationships to state governments and financial markets. Class animosities pitting the urban masses against creditors and propertied taxpayers never lurked far below the surface.[42] The city's standing in financial markets came up, for example, when Bostonians contemplated the annexation of vast new suburban lands into the municipality, a popular measure that promised to alleviate a housing crisis in the inner city but was bound to massively increase spending. Opponents were quick to point out that this policy would severely diminish Boston's superb credit and reputation, which allowed the city to borrow at low cost in London. "Should the proposed change of the city government lead to an increase of city debt, as it would be likely to do," elite commentators pointed out, "it would naturally reduce the market rate of the securities," with disastrous long-term consequences.[43] When voters appeared unmoved by this reasoning, elite opponents took their case to court, arguing that the change in status unconstitutionally impaired the property rights of municipal bond holders, whose securities would thereby be rendered less secure. Although the judge rejected the reasoning of the petitioners in this particular case, the political message of these legal challenges was crystal clear. A city that failed to cultivate harmonious relations with creditors did so at its peril. Needless to say, the same objections were not raised when elite cultural institutions (Harvard College, the Museum of Fine Arts, the fashionable Back-Bay Churches, to name three) received hefty tax exemptions or when downtown business interests lobbied for railroad subsidies, harbor improvements, and other beautification schemes. With these tensions always ongoing, the massive expansion in local borrowing thus proceeded, not smoothly in accordance with hard-and-fast institutional arrangements but through charged political confrontations.

Viewed in light of the rapid expansion in public borrowing on the municipal level, the integration of places far afield into a national market clearly did not obliterate the fiscal or governing capacity of local political institutions. Nor did it render municipal governments obsolete or somehow irrelevant. Rather, the process energized—and proceeded through—state formation on the local level. It nurtured a rapid increase in the number of subnational political units and greatly enhanced their fiscal capacity. The national market gradually emerged not merely via the inexorable growth of national institutions but through the explosion of literally hundreds of local units, each one jostling to facilitate development, negotiate between competing social groups, and secure a share of outside investment. This was as true for New York and Boston as it was out West, where the Federal government parceled out its vast domain, creating an array of new states that provided the primary political frameworks for development. But it was also true in France where cities as different as Paris, Marseille, and Dunkerque accumulated an extraordinary degree of debt even as they stood under the nose of the national government.

Many of these subnational and urban sites in France and the United States had virtually no banking resources of their own but were endowed with various forms of authority ranging from chartering corporations and opening or exploiting natural resources and waterways to building new, sometimes massive, infrastructure projects. In the case of the western United States, they also escalated the dotting of the landscape with countless new cities, towns, and counties, while in the French case they generated one of the emblematic urban reconstructions of the modern world and solidified France's place as a leader in global capitalism. The same was true, albeit in a different way, in the eastern United States, where the governments of densely populated metropolises embraced ambitious public agendas. They taxed, spent, and borrowed at an accelerating pace.[44] Much of the drama around government finance unfolded, not in Congress or any other unitary national site but, rather, in a proliferating number of locales where the proper use of public borrowing became the subject of intense controversy.

* * *

In this sense, the accumulation of municipal debt paved the way for a new role for local governments, which, in both countries, were far from becoming obsolete or somehow irrelevant to the story of public debt. To the contrary, the vast accumulation of debt by local authorities contributed to the shifting of important financial decisions to local figures beyond or regardless of the watchful eye of national political authorities. Such opportunities would emerge in the municipal political movements that became the backbone of French politics in the Third Republic as well as in the "New Federalism" of the United States.[45]

Thus, at first glance, the growing consolidation of national markets in the wake of the Civil War in the United States and on either side of war and the Commune of 1870–1871 in France had a somewhat contradictory nature. It did not merely lead to the inexorable growth of national institutions and their consequent sway over the countries' finances. Instead, national integration also generated a parallel movement in the opposite direction: that is, the explosion of a new, sometimes informal, capacity within local units as they vied to facilitate improvements, negotiate financial pressures on multiple scales, and secure new levels of resources.

The lesson to be drawn from this comparative study, however, is that such developments only appear contradictory when one considers the development of local and national capacity within the integrating forces of the modern state as a zero-sum game. As long as processes of national integration are understood to be in opposition to local autonomy it is impossible to understand the simultaneous development of peripheral local and central national power. And yet, the construction of the modern state was never reserved to the national scale any more than it depended on the opposition between the national and the local. State infrastructural capacity effectively developed on the local and the national scale simultaneously.

The fact that such municipal borrowing took place in the context of civil war in both countries, wars fought over the question of national unity and the limits and possibilities of local power, is not insignificant. While literature on the French Commune as well as the American Civil War has overwhelmingly focused on the questions of national sovereignty, and the consolidation of national power in the wake of the conflict, what emerges in this comparative study of local debt is that even if the bid for the "idea" of greater local sovereignty was lost, a capacity to solve local problems and shape economic change actually increased during the second half of the nineteenth century. This new capacity, which we have referred to as an informal fiscal federalism, has remained largely hidden from view.

It has been hidden largely for two reasons. First, that it was informal and attempted to operate outside the prying eyes of a national government with other priorities was precisely one of its defining characteristics. Indeed, the accumulation of municipal debt hid itself from national authorities so successfully that historians have missed it as well. But it has also been hidden for another, more profound reason that has its roots in the methodological nationalism of studies of national market and political integration. As we have continued to reify national boundaries and considered them the fundamental container for state capacity, we have missed the ways in which the accumulation of state power and the transformative impact in local areas was not necessarily a means of challenging "national" sovereignty but was also a means for building state capacity locally or on the periphery. Indeed, the extraordinary fiscal autonomy of these local bodies in nineteenth-century France and the US was one of the most important factors in integrating their nations into a vast web of international finance, just as it was one of the most important ways for building national state infrastructural capacity far beyond what the central state would have been able to do on its own. Indeed, in the story told here, increased fiscal independence inaugurated by the massive accumulation of municipal debt in local and international markets participated in a broader revolution in the construction of the modern nation-state.

Notes

1. David Stasavage, *Public Debt and the Birth of the Democratic State* (Cambridge: Cambridge University Press, 2003); Michael Sonenscher, *Before the Deluge: Public Debt, Inequality, and the Intellectual Origins of the French Revolution* (Princeton: Princeton University Press, 2009); Douglass C. North and Barry R. Weingast, "Constitutions and Commitment: The Evolution of Institutions Governing Public Choice in Seventeenth-Century England," *Journal of Economic History* XLIX (1989): 803–32.
2. Odette Lienau, *Rethinking Sovereign Debt : Politics, Reputation, and Legitimacy in Modern Finance* (Cambridge, Mass.: Harvard University Press, 2014); Saskia Sassen, *The Global City: New York, London, Tokyo* (Princeton: Princeton University Press, 1991); Neil Brenner, *New State Spaces : Urban Governance and the Rescaling of Statehood* (Oxford: Oxford University Press, 2006).

3. Christopher A. Bayly, *The Birth of the Modern World, 1780-1914: Global Connections and Comparisons* (Malden, Mass.: Blackwell, 2004); Sven Beckert, *Empire of Cotton: A Global History* (New York: Knopf, 2014); Eric J. Hobsbawm, *The Age of Empire, 1875-1914* (New York: Vintage Books, 1989).
4. On this point, see Stephen W. Sawyer, William J. Novak and James T. Sparrow, "Beyond Stateless Democracy," *The Tocqueville Review/La Revue Tocqueville* 36, no. 1 (2015): 43–91.
5. Louis Hartz, *The Liberal Tradition in America; An Interpretation of American Political Thought Since the Revolution* (New York: Harcourt, Brace, 1955). François Furet, *Revolutionary France, 1770-1880* (Cambridge: Blackwell, 1992).
6. On local power as a technology, see William J. Novak, "The Myth of the 'Weak' American State," *American Historical Review* 113, no. 3 (2008): 752–72; William J. Novak, "Beyond Max Weber: The Need for a Democratic (Not Aristocratic) Theory of the Modern State," *The Tocqueville Review/La Revue Tocqueville* 36, no. 1 (2015): 43–91.
7. Alfred D. Chandler, *The Visible Hand: The Managerial Revolution in American Business* (Cambridge, Mass.: Belknap Press, 1977); Alfred D. Chandler, *Scale and Scope: The Dynamics of Industrial Capitalism* (Cambridge, Mass.: Belknap Press, 1994); Robert H. Wiebe, *The Search for Order, 1877-1920* (New York: Hill and Wang, 1967). More recently, see Steven Hahn, *A Nation without Borders: The United States and Its World in an Age of Civil Wars, 1830-1910* (New York: Viking, 2016); Charles S. Maier, *Once Within Borders: Territories of Power, Wealth, and Belonging since 1500* (Cambridge, Mass.: Harvard Belknap Press, 2016). For the classic statement of this argument, see Eugen Weber, *Peasants into Frenchmen: The Modernization of Rural France* (Stanford University Press, 1976).
8. On convergences between social science literature on the French and American states, see the articles and the introductory essay "Toward a History of the Democratic State" in the special issue on the French and American States in *The Tocqueville Review/La Review Tocqueville* 33, no. 2 (2012).
9. See, most notably, Richard Hofstadter, *The Age of Reform: From Bryan to F. D. R.* (New York: Knopf, 1955); Martin J. Sklar, *The Corporate Reconstruction of American Capitalism, 1890-1916: The Market, the Law, and Politics* (Cambridge: Cambridge University Press, 1988). For the "American Political Development" (APD) field, see Stephen Skowronek, *Building a New American State: The Expansion of National Administrative Capacities, 1877-1920* (Cambridge: Cambridge University Press, 1982); Peter B. Evans, Dietrich Rueschemeyer, and Theda Skocpol, eds., *Bringing the State Back In* (Cambridge: Cambridge University Press, 1985). The

formation of a national economy as a political project has been most productively problematized in Richard Franklin Bensel, *The Political Economy of American Industrialization, 1877-1900* (Cambridge: Cambridge University Press, 2000); Nicolas Barreyre, *Gold and Freedom: The Political Economy of Reconstruction*, trans. Arthur Goldhammer (Charlottesville: University of Virginia Press, 2015). The concept of "infrastructural power" comes from Michael Mann, "The Autonomous Power of the State: Its Origins, Mechanisms, and Results," in *States in History*, ed. John A. Hall (Oxford: Oxford University Press, 1986), 109–36.

10. Local debt continued to rise in absolute terms in the twentieth century but was thereafter greatly overshadowed by borrowing on the Federal level. Compiling numbers for countless local governments in the United States is notoriously difficult. We are relying here on the best available estimates provided in John B. Legler, Richard Sylla, and John J. Wallis, "U.S. City Finances and the Growth of Government, 1850-1902," *Journal of Economic History* 48, no. 2 (1988): 66; John Joseph Wallis, "American Government Finance in the Long Run: 1790 to 1990," *Journal of Economic Perspectives* 14, no. 1 (2000): 61–82.

11. Jules Ferry, *Les comptes fantastiques d'Haussmann. Lettre adressée à MM. les membres de la commission du Corps législatif chargés d'examiner le nouveau projet d'emprunt de la ville de Paris* (Paris: A. Le Chevalier, 1868), 42-43.

12. *Annuaire Statistique de la France* (Paris: Imprimerie Nationale, 1878-1894).

13. *Annuaire Statistique de la France*, vol. XVI, 1895-1896, 495.

14. Pierre-Joseph Proudhon, *Manuel du spéculateur à la bourse* (Paris: Garnier, 1857), 194.

15. Ferry, *Comptes fantastiques*, 42-43.

16. Alfred Chandler observed that "Federal aid assisted in the building of only 8 percent of the nation's railroad system. State, municipal, and county aid was in the long run more significant than federal assistance," Alfred D. Chandler, *The Railroads, the Nation's First Big Business: Sources and Readings* (New York: Harcourt, Brace & World, 1965), 43–44. For a detailed examination of state-level promotion, particularly in the pre-Civil War era, see Harry N. Scheiber, *Ohio Canal Era: A Case Study of Government and the Economy, 1820-1861* (Athens: Ohio University Press, 1969); Carter Goodrich, *Government Promotion of American Canals and Railroads, 1800-1890* (New York: Columbia University Press, 1960). For a transatlantic comparison, see Colleen A. Dunlavy, *Politics and Industrialization: Early Railroads in the United States and Prussia* (Princeton: Princeton University Press, 1994).

17. In the years 1866–1873 alone, twenty-nine states granted over eight hundred authorizations for aid by local governments to railroad projects. See Goodrich, *Government Promotion of American Canals*, 241.
18. Alberta M. Sbragia, *Debt Wish: Entrepreneurial Cities, U.S. Federalism, and Economic Development* (Pittsburgh: University of Pittsburgh Press, 1996), 44–56; Jon C. Teaford, *The Unheralded Triumph, City Government in America, 1870-1900* (Baltimore: Johns Hopkins University Press, 1984). The scholarship on the American state has generally focused more on the failings of the local fiscal state, not on its remarkable accomplishments. See Clifton K. Yearley, *Money Machines: The Breakdown and Reform of Governmental and Party Finance in the North, 1860-1920* (Albany: State University of New York Press, 1970); Ajay K. Mehrotra, *Making the Modern American Fiscal State: Law, Politics, and the Rise of Progressive Taxation, 1877-1929* (New York: Cambridge University Press, 2013). Comparative studies, by contrast, have demonstrated the crucial economic role of subnational state actors, see Stanley L. Engerman and Kenneth Lee Sokoloff, eds., *Economic Development in the Americas since 1500: Endowments and Institutions* (Cambridge: Cambridge University Press, 2012).
19. They were rivaled only by mortgage loans until the rise of railroad bonds in the 1880s and 1890s, see Lester W. Zartman, *The Investments of Life Insurance Companies* (New York: H. Holt, 1906), 14. See also Bruce Michael Pritchett, *A Study of Capital Mobilization: The Life Insurance Industry of the Nineteenth Century* (New York: Arno Press, 1977).
20. *Annual Report of the Insurance Commissioner of the Commonwealth of Massachusetts*, vol. 36 (Boston: Wright and Potter, 1891), 22–30, 100–113, 41–53. Insurance companies and savings banks were more strictly regulated than other banking institutions. Laws of different states were gradually liberalized to allow them to acquire the bonds of out-of-state municipalities.
21. Foreign investors held large portions of American public debt in the first half of the nineteenth century (46 percent in 1853) but this debt was popular with American banking institutions and was therefore increasingly held domestically, see Mira Wilkins, *The History of Foreign Investment in the United States to 1914* (Cambridge, Mass.: Harvard University Press, 1989), 54, 184–89. As one British economist explained in 1893 in regard to local debt, "if the municipality is little known it is distrusted. If it is widely known and well established, the rate of interest paid is not sufficient to attract the British investor," quoted in ibid., 187.
22. In the US, between 1864 and 1888, the Supreme Court alone dealt with *100 cases* dealing with "railway-assistance securities." Justice Fields, who served between 1863 and 1897 heard over *300 municipal bond cases*:

"There is hardly any question connected with this species of securities that has not been discussed and decided by the Court," see Charles Warren, *The Supreme Court in United States History*, rev. ed. (Boston: Little, Brown, and Company, 1926), 532. See Charles W. McCurdy, "Justice Field and the Jurisprudence of Government-Business Relations: Some Parameters of Laissez-Faire Constitutionalism, 1863-1897," *Journal of American History* 61, no. 4 (1975): 970–1005.

23. We are drawing here on the work of Michael Geyer and Charles Bright, particularly their discerning analysis of how the history of globalization, rather than displacing local and regional histories, in fact reveals the full significance of all regions to world history as "actors and participants in the very processes being narrated," see Michael Geyer and Charles Bright, "World History in a Global Age," *American Historical Review* 100, no. 4 (1995): 1044–45. See also Noam Maggor, "To 'Coddle and Caress These Great Capitalists': Eastern Money and the Politics of Market Integration in the American West," *American Historical Review* 122, no. 1 (2017): 55–84.
24. *The Journal of the Washington State Constitutional Convention, 1889* (Seattle, Washington: Book Publishing Company, 1962), 44–46.
25. "Seattle's Water Bonds," *Tacoma Morning Globe*, July 13, 1889, 1. Washington's cities grew very rapidly in the 1880s: Seattle from 3500 to about 42,000, Tacoma from 1000 to 36,000, and Spokane from 356 to almost 20,000.
26. *The Seattle Times*, August 2, 1889, 4.
27. *The Journal of the Washington State Constitutional Convention*, 149.
28. *Tacoma Morning Globe*, August 3, 1889.
29. *Journal of the Washington State*, 672.
30. *Journal of the Washington State*, 676. "Provided the infrastructure remained under the ownership and control of the municipality."
31. *Journal of the Washington State*, 680.
32. Baron Haussmann, Mémoire de M. le préfet de la Seine, *Le Moniteur* (11 decembre 1864).
33. See G. Cadoux, *Les finances de la ville de Paris de 1798 à 1900* (Paris: Berger-Levrault, 1900); Geneviève Massa-Gille, *Histoire des emprunts de la Ville de Paris, 1814-1875* (Paris: Ville de Paris, Commission des travaux historiques, 1973); Bernard Marchand, "Le financement des travaux d'Haussmann: un exemple pour les pays emergent?" working paper, 2011, https://halshs.archives-ouvertes.fr/halshs-00583457
34. E. Baronnet, "Les grands travaux de la ville de Paris et les bons de délégation. Mémoire présenté à M. le Baron Haussmann, Sénateur, Préfet de la Seine le 15 janvier 1863." (Paris: Dentu, 1867): "L'administration municipale, réduite en quelque sorte à l'isolement, se voit contrainte et forcée de se lancer dans la voie des emprunts … M. Foule n'a pas voulu croire à la

puissance des revenus municipaux ni à l'accroissement annuel du budget de la Ville; cette timidité dégénérant en tracasseries a impose au Préfet de la Seine l'emprunt insuffisant de 1865."

35. Baronnet, "Les grands travaux de la ville de Paris et les bons de delegation," 18–19.
36. Georges Gallais-Hamonno, "La création d'un marché obligataire moderne," in *Le marché financier français au XIXe siècle. Vol 2: Aspects quantitatifs des acteurs et des instruments à la Bourse de Paris* (Paris: Publications de la Sorbonne, 2007), 269.
37. Ferry, *Comptes fantastiques*, 9.
38. Ferry, *Comptes fantastiques*, 17.
39. Louis-P. Girard, "Le financement des grands travaux du second Empire," *Revue économique* 2, n°3 (1951): 343–55.
40. William M. Irvins, "Municipal Finance," *Harper's New Monthly Magazine*, June 1, 1884, 779.
41. Yearley, *Money Machines*, 7–10. Yearley's canonical study has drawn attention and dramatized this fiscal trend, influencing generations of urban historians in the US. Our own view is that reform was primarily driven not by what reformers labeled a "breakdown" of government machinery (a view Yearley uncritically accepted) but rather by the fiscal machinery's great effectiveness in raising the much-needed public resources.
42. Yearley, *Money Machines*, 11.
43. George R. Minot & Others, Petitioners vs. City of Boston and Others, Brief for the Petitioners, Minot Business Papers, Carton 40, folder 1873, Massachusetts Historical Society. See also Theophilus P. Chandler v. Boston, 112 Mass. 200 (1873).
44. See Sven Beckert, *The Monied Metropolis: New York City and the Consolidation of the American Bourgeoisie, 1850–1896* (Cambridge: Cambridge University Press, 2001); Noam Maggor, *Brahmin Capitalism: Frontiers of Wealth and Populism in America's First Gilded Age* (Cambridge, Mass.: Harvard University Press, 2017).
45. For the US, see Kimberley S. Johnson, *Governing the American State: Congress and the New Federalism, 1877-1929* (Princeton: Princeton University Press, 2007); Gary Gerstle, "The Resilient Power of the States across the Long Nineteenth Century," in *The Unsustainable American State*, eds. Lawrence Jacobs and Desmond King (New York: Oxford University Press, 2009), 61; Gary Gerstle, *Liberty and Coercion: The Paradox of American Government from the Founding to the Present* (Princeton University Press, 2015). For France, see Paolo Capuzzo and Mathieu Cloarec, "Municipalisme et construction de l'hégémonie politique. Les transports collectifs à Vienne, 1896-1914," *Genèses* 24 (1996); Patrizia Dogliani, "Un laboratoire de socialisme municipal: France

(1880-1920)" (PhD diss., Paris VIII, 1991); Alexandre Fernandez, "La création en 1919 de la Régie municipale du gaz et de l'électricité de Bordeaux," *Revue historique* 294, no. 1 (1995): 595; Jean Lojkine, "Politique urbaine et pouvoir local," *Revue française de sociologie* 21, no. 4 (1980); Joana Jean, "L'action publique municipale sous la IIIe République (1884-1939). Bilan et perspectives de recherches," *Politix* 11, no. 42 (1998): 151–78; Bernard Meuret, *Le socialisme municipal. Villeurbanne 1880-1982* (Lyon: Presses Universitaires de Lyon, 1982); Jean-Yves Nevers, "Système politico-administratif communal et pouvoir local. Étude d'un cas: la municipalité radicale socialiste de Toulouse, 1888-1906" (PhD diss., Toulouse II, 1975); Michel Offerlé, "Les socialistes et Paris (1881-1900). Des communards aux conseillers municipaux" (PhD diss., Paris I, 1979); Gilles Pollet, "La construction de l'État social à la française: entre local et national (XIXe et XXe siècle)," *Lien social et politique* 33 (1995); Joan Wallach Scott, "Social History and the History of Socialism: French Socialist Municipalities in the 1890's," *Mouvement social* 111 (1980).

PART III

The Great Transformation of Public Debts (1914–1970s)

The *liberal debt regime* of the nineteenth century, with its supposedly clear delineation between credible borrowers and serial defaulters, and the imperial impulse it gave to European capital, experienced massive challenges and transformations in the two world wars and the Great Depression. The dramatic rise in public indebtedness for all the belligerent countries, which had to print money, sell bonds, and attract foreign credit on an unprecedented scale, led to the total mobilization of the populations' resources. The massification of public debts, now owned by millions of people, created new constraints for sovereign borrowers to secure political legitimacy: they had to honor their commitments not only toward big financial institutions and foreign creditors but also toward the many "citizen-investors" who had joined the war effort, as Nicolas Delalande shows in Chap. 11. The two biggest financial powers of the pre-1914 world, Great Britain and France, while struggling to repay their huge public debts and cope with popular unrest in the metropolis and the empire in the 1920s, lost their position as the world's creditor nations to the benefit of the United States. Domestic life and international relations were then deeply impacted by debt relations in a new economic environment marked by inflation and austerity measures in the 1920s, the global financial crisis of 1929, and the end of free trade and the gold standard that followed.

Debtor countries like Germany, Stefanie Middendorf argues in Chap. 12, developed new "depoliticized" techniques of state financing, relying on intermediary institutions to channel resources and blurring the lines between the state and the market. This example, which transcends the political break of 1933, illustrates how a new *dirigiste debt regime* emerged from the wreckage of wars and crisis, and expanded across very different types of political regimes until the late 1960s, on a global scale. State administrative power and economic expertise proved much more essential than parliamentary rules or liberal values to sustain rising public debts in these turbulent times. With the rise of a new Keynesian macroeconomic approach to public finance in the late 1930s and the need to tap all available resources in World War II, market regulations and "financial repression" became legitimate tools in the hands of interventionist public authorities. When debts seemed unbearable, states could even default or suspend without sanction. Indeed, the Bolshevik repudiation of 1918 gave new political legitimacy to this practice, while the legal doctrine of "odious debt" gained intellectual support in the following decade. But communist regimes soon proceeded to accumulate substantial debts anew, both foreign and domestic, as Étienne Forestier-Peyrat and Kristy Ironside show in Chap. 13. Even in the "anticapitalist" world, public debt played a key role for state-building and economic expansion, at least until the 1970s, when it severely endangered the communist regimes' political legitimacy, eventually precipitating their demise in the late 1980s.

At the same time, new nation-states were born out of the crisis of European empires, especially after 1945. In Chap. 14, Matthieu Rey recounts the cases of Iraq and Syria to demonstrate how these recently independent nations succeeded in attracting foreign capital for development purpose, without implementing full parliamentary representation. The Cold War, regional tensions, and the growing intervention of international institutions authorized local elites to build state institutions without taxation, and secure their domination over the people. The Bretton Woods system set up in 1944 and the global competition between the United States and the USSR allowed many countries to bolster political legitimacy at home while protecting themselves from financial pressure. In this newly dominant *dirigiste debt regime*, much less globalized than the previous one, only a few public debts remained at the mercy of markets.

CHAPTER 11

The Financial Challenges of Total War: Britain, France, and Their Empires in the First World War

Nicolas Delalande

All the states involved in the First World War had to levy taxes, issue loans (internal or external), print money, and call on their citizens' patriotism. The war opened a global financial competition, in which states had to innovate if they wanted to keep up with the unprecedented pace of war expenditure. It also marked the end of the era of nineteenth-century "liberal finance," grounded in budget equilibrium, the gold standard, price stability, and elite-based parliamentarism, even if few contemporaries could foresee the dramatic and enduring consequences it would have for the twentieth century. Public finances would now have to cope with new challenges, in terms of state power, democratic participation, and monetary practices.[1]

This article focuses on a particular aspect of the subject, namely internal war loans, which were issued in all belligerent countries. They had clear domestic objectives, from a financial but also a political perspective, since

N. Delalande (✉)
Centre d'Histoire, Sciences Po, Paris, France
e-mail: nicolas.delalande@sciencespo.fr

they were a means for political authorities to collect resources, mobilize civil societies, and strengthen their infrastructural power. But they also had international and imperial implications, a point that has often been overlooked in the literature. Their success or failure was under close scrutiny on a global scale, for they gave indications about the population's support of the war effort and the financial vigor of the states. Collecting savings was at the same time a domestic, an international, and an imperial issue, especially for France and Great Britain, which had been the two dominant financial powers before 1914 and hoped to benefit from their international reputation. Even if each financial system had its own peculiarities at the outbreak of war, it became more necessary than ever to look at foreign experiences to consider how the war could be dealt with from a political and financial point of view. The transnational sphere of expertise may have been disrupted during these years, but there was still room for some transfers of knowledge and practices, particularly in the financial domain.[2]

In most countries, financing war through debt and direct credits from the central bank seemed more appropriate than triggering harsh political disputes about tax reforms and tax hikes. Thus all countries mostly relied on their public credit and money creation to finance the war, albeit in various proportions. It is a well-established fact that Great Britain and the United States were able to cover up to 25–28 percent of their war spending through taxation, a ratio that was utterly unattainable for other countries (taxation amounted to 15 percent of the war effort in France, and even less in Germany, Austria, Italy, and Russia). At first, political and financial elites thought that short-term debt (treasury bonds and obligations) and advances from the central bank would provide enough money to fund what was expected to be a short war. In France, the *bons de la Défense nationale* introduced in September 1914 were sold to banks, corporations, and the general public. In Britain, the Treasury started to issue treasury bills and exchequer bonds, for short-term credit purposes, in the summer of 1914.[3] War loans were then issued to consolidate the vast amounts of short-term credits that had piled up since the beginning of the war, while additional funds also came from foreign credits (especially for the *Entente* countries, given that the central powers had no real possibilities of receiving external aid, except from some neutral countries such as Switzerland).[4] Almost all the belligerent powers had to launch war loans, as early as 1914 for some of them, later for the others. France joined the move belatedly, in fall 1915, while Germany issued its first loan one year before. Organizing large war loans and collecting money through savings banks, postal accounts, and commercial banks became common practice in France, Great Britain, Germany, Austria-Hungary, Italy, Russia, and the United States. These financial operations were a tool for mobilizing the Home Front and measuring the population's support in favor of the conduct of the war.[5]

This chapter aims at highlighting why British and French political authorities were so obsessed with the success of war loans, in both the metropolis and the empire, and how they continuously observed and emulated each other (as well as other countries) during the war years. Apart from their economic and financial aims, war loans were designed to display national unity and enshrine new conceptions of citizenship and patriotic duties. While they created new opportunities for mass participation in public finances, they also brought about new risks, given that so many people were now involved in the business of funding the state, a matter that would become socially explosive in the late 1910s and 1920s. Modernization and massification came together, opening up potential contradictions and disillusions.

THE POPULARIZATION OF WAR FINANCE

The First World War was at the same time the result and the climax of a tremendous change in political practices at the turn of the twentieth century. Political legitimacy was no longer based on restricted suffrage but implied mass participation and popular consent, as well as powerful (and at times coercive) state institutions. The nationalization of the masses, originating in the nineteenth century, made the total mobilization of men and women in the war effort possible.[6] It also greatly increased the power of states to levy resources, through taxation or public credit, ushering in a new age for public finances.[7]

Raising money through war loans had both an economic and a political purpose. On the economic side, these long-term loans aimed at consolidating the floating debt, restraining consumption, and curbing inflation. In the absence of other alternatives (stock markets were disrupted and capital exports tightly controlled), public bonds were the only remaining and safe investment opportunities for private capital. On the political side, the amount of money collected was also meant to demonstrate mass support from savers, and to show the world how strongly united a nation was. While direct elections were suspended in most countries, war loans were interpreted as expressing the populations' wishes and trust. They were as much *techniques of government* as *financial devices*, intended to mobilize the Home Front, repress potential dissenters, and promote supposedly "spontaneous" forms of patriotism. In each country, financial plebiscites were presented as rituals binding citizens together and attaching them to the nation's interests. Propaganda stressed that subscriptions to war loans would lead to final victory and help shorten the war. Andrew Bonar Law, the British Chancellor of the Exchequer from December 1916 to January 1919, argued that mass subscriptions mirrored the population's total involvement in the war effort. Savings practices, restrained consumption, and a significant investment in war loans had a great role to play in the global war opposing nations and empires. For Britain and France, who were eager to present themselves as bulwarks of liberty, democracy, and civilization, only democratic regimes could rely on the total participation of investors and savers. The 1917 British Victory Loan was thus conceived as "a sort of general election in which the candidates are Justice and Injustice, and the principles at issue those of life and death. Everyone who buys stocks or buys more than usual of War Saving Certificates is casting a vote which may be decisive (…) In a democratic country it is the individual vote that counts."[8]

This justification in the name of democracy, which assumed that only democracies could raise considerable funds,[9] quickly came to be refuted by a fact that no observer could seriously overlook. Even supposedly undemocratic countries could levy huge resources through war loans and stimulate or manipulate their populations' enthusiasm. In Germany and Russia, war loans were also meant to demonstrate how popular the war was. The mass mobilization of civil society in Germany was a source of astonishment for British and French officials, who were convinced that the country they depicted as an authoritarian regime would never succeed in raising mass war loans. In Russia, conversely, liberals thought that the demise of the Tsarist regime in February 1917 and the issuance of a Liberty Loan would be warmly welcomed by the population, with the advent of a more pluralistic regime. These hopes were soon to be disillusioned. The workers and middle classes did not subscribe to the new loan, leading to its complete failure. The liberal creed of the new Russian government was of no help in countering the population's distrust.[10]

The First World War was a critical juncture, in that it promoted increased practices of observation and comparisons between countries and their financial practices. The transnational movement in favor of savings institutions and practices, which had its roots in the nineteenth century, reached its climax during the war years. Savings were judged to be critical for a nation's financial strength and independence. Not that they solved all problems, but they limited the dependence on foreign credits, while strengthening the links between governments and their bondholders.[11] France, for instance, took pride in its capacity to collect vast amounts of savings and invest them all around the world. Its public debt, totaling around 60 percent of its Gross Domestic Product in 1914, was the heaviest in the world, but that fact was not considered alarming. On the contrary, political elites and economic experts hailed it as a national strength, a chance for the nation's independence, deriving from its ability to overcome the 1870–1871 defeat against Prussia. Above all, French politicians were eager to insist on the supposedly "democratic" nature of the French public debt. Attempts at popularizing public debt dated back to the Second Empire and the 1870–1871 trauma.[12] The French imperial regime was one of the first in the world to try and finance itself directly from the public by launching public offerings while trying to lessen the role and power of big financial institutions. However costly it may have been, this way of levying resources was presented as a French specificity, deeply embedded in the bonapartist vision of plebiscites (war loan operations were labeled "financial plebiscites," as if political lessons should and could be drawn from their success or failure).

The American political economist, Henry C. Adams, who wrote a comprehensive essay on the political and social effects of public debts in the 1880s, recognized the singularity of this model, but expressed mixed feelings about its results. The language of democracy could also be understood as the power given to a class of *rentiers* who were now strong enough to resist the policy reforms they resented, especially when the state was willing to convert old loans to new ones with lower interest rates in the 1880s.[13] France had between 2 and 3 million bondholders in 1914 (for a total of 4.4 million inscriptions to the *Grand Livre*), a number without any equivalent in the world at the time. These old links between the French state and its bondholders led the authorities to think that financing war through credit would be an easy business. For them, France's public credit could only be compared with Britain's financial reputation. The success of the National Defence bonds and the number of subscribers to the first war loan (3.13 million) seemingly confirmed this impression.

Despite all this, it soon became obvious that France wasn't the only power that could boast this kind of popular success. French and British observers soon became aware that the German war loans also had tremendous results, favored by a strong mobilization of civil, military and religious authorities.[14] This popular mobilization, that was hard to deny and partly spontaneous, contradicted the old stereotypes depicting the German regime as authoritarian and unable to gain support from its people. In fact, Germany had been experiencing democratic practices since the late 1860s, with mass participation in general elections.[15] There too, men, women, pupils, bankers, priests, journalists, and others joined the war effort from the very first weeks of the war. Campaigns for gold collection started in fall 1914, with calls launched by public authorities and clergymen; schoolchildren could even earn extra holidays if they collected enough money. The *Kriegsanleihen* were launched every six months in the winter and fall; by the end of the conflict, nine loan drives had been launched, against merely four in France. As elsewhere, propaganda—coordinated by the Reichsbank—used various means and techniques, with press articles, leaflets, posters, church sermons, and so on. The war bonds, sold by commercial banks, savings banks, and postal offices, were widespread. 98 billion marks were subscribed during the war, with a total of 7.1 million signatures in spring 1917 for the sixth loan, and still 6.9 million in spring 1918 (after the Brest-Litovsk treaty).[16] Of course, subscriptions were unevenly distributed, since only a tiny minority of subscribers contributed most of the money collected.[17] Moral suasion and coercion were at play, as they were in more democratic countries. Corporations created withholding mechanisms so that workers and employers would subscribe automatically on their salaries. Savings banks massively invested their deposits in war bonds, which meant that savers were simply unaware that they were taking part in a war loan.[18] Later in the war, especially after 1917, bureaucratization and militarization weakened civil society's enthusiasm. Inflation and money depreciation significantly altered the attractiveness of state bonds, with increasing doubts about the state's ability to pay back such a huge amount of debt, even if Germany were to receive financial reparations after the war.[19] Despite all these difficulties and uncertainties, it was only in the last year of the war that public trust entirely collapsed.

The British configuration was, in comparison, very different at the outbreak of the war. The British public debt had been the most secure and admired long-term asset in the world since the eighteenth century, but it was organized on very different grounds.[20] There were far fewer bondholders than in France (around 185,000 at the end of the nineteenth century), while the Bank of England and the city played a critical role in state financing. Financial elites were not really interested in promoting what the French called the "democratization of the *rente*." However, the war of attrition forced Treasury and city officials to change their mind. The results obtained by the first British war loan could not compete with German ones. Hardly 1 million subscribers took part in the first British war loan—which was perceived as a failure, all the more so since few workers and employees had participated. The Treasury looked carefully at the figures announced by the German Minister of Finance, Karl Helferrich, during the third *Kriegsanleihe* in 1915, which had been subscribed by more than 4 million people. A Treasury official complained that "in Germany practically everyone has subscribed something to the war loan. This is not the case here. The reason for this is not, as the Germans wrongly imagine, that the Briton is less patriotic than the Boche, but so far we have not been very emotional about our investment."[21] For all its reputation and efficiency, the British system of public indebtedness had to be amended to keep up with the pace of war.

Beyond propaganda discourses opposing democracies versus authoritarian regimes, it was the states' capacity to mobilize the masses that made the difference. What changed over the war, and from one country to the other, was the mix between freedom and coercion, but nowhere was it possible to rely solely on pure and spontaneous feelings of patriotic sacrifice. Financial mobilization had to be carefully organized and sustained if states wanted to consolidate their debts.[22]

Cross-Observations, Reform Processes, and Infrastructural Power

The posters and words used during bond campaigns are well-known subjects for cultural historians of the Great War. Their similarity across countries, in spite of national variations, conveys the impression of a spontaneous process of homogenization. Practices and administrative settings did actually vary, but what really accounts for these converging trends in mobilization techniques is the continuous efforts made by belligerent states to observe and emulate each other. Modernizing the infrastructural powers of the state to collect money from civil society and markets constituted one of the major stakes of the period. Cross-observations and policy transfers played a major role, which does not mean that all practices and techniques could circulate. In spite of their long-standing prestige and domination, Britain and France had to reform their practices and systems in order to win the war. Their early reaction, based on their instinctive feeling of superiority, was no longer appropriate for the situation. To compete with German financial mobilization, it was necessary to observe what the other countries were doing and implement a set of reforms.

British authorities launched a reform process in 1915 in order to compensate for the lack of emotion and organization previously mentioned. Their main goal was to increase the number of "small investors," both from a financial and political perspective. Wooing the middle classes and workers became a major aim of the Treasury, which was willing to restrain consumption and limit inflationary pressures. A committee set up in 1915, presided by Sir Edwin Montagu, recommended the creation of a national organization, the War Savings Committee, which would be in charge of coordinating thousands of local committees and associations devoted to collecting the population's savings. The short-term goal was to compete with the legendary thrifty habits of the French peasants and with the apparently efficient mobilization of the Germans. References to foreign experiences played a critical role in the reform process. British propaganda called on citizens to emulate the French, the Germans, or the Japanese, who were known to invest their savings in the public debt. The result was a curious mix between the professionalization and centralization implemented by the National War Savings Committee (headed by Sir Robert Kindersley, a businessman and a director of the Bank of England)—which developed its own organization chart, a proper budget, and a national action plan—and the numerous (between 250,000 and 300,000) voluntary associations, in which many women and children were involved (they were in charge of more than 40,000 war savings associations, organized on a local basis). All these committees took part in the war effort by promoting food controls, savings certificates, and subscriptions to war loans.

The British example illustrates how centralized measures and local voluntarism could be successfully combined. In only a few months, the British invented a policy of "continuous borrowing," with a view to making savings practices and their connection with public debt commonplace and routine. The goal was not only to increase the number of war loan subscribers but also to develop permanent savings practices, whose funds would be directly invested in public bonds. This policy achieved good results in 1917. The war loan was now subscribed by more than 2 million people (1 million at the Bank of England, 1 million through the postal network), and more than 3 million people were buying war savings certificates from local associations. An official report thus estimated that there were now 5.289 million subscribers to war loans, a figure five times higher than two years earlier.[23] Banks and credit institutions, though still important, played a lesser role than before.

British authorities grew confident as their country no longer lagged behind as far as its ability to collect resources from the general public was concerned. Just after the war, *The Times* triumphantly announced that the National War Savings Committee had succeeded in debunking all the criticisms formerly addressed to the supposed lack of thrift and spirit of sacrifice of the British.[24] The Chancellor of the Exchequer even received spontaneous gifts from the population, for instance, from women who offered their jewels to be melted down and added to the Bank of England's gold reserves. In 1917, official discourses insisted that it was no longer enough to invest money in the public debt; subscribers were now invited to over-subscribe, so that their gesture would not only represent a profitable calculation but a genuine sacrifice. The long-term objective was to transform the working classes' economic behaviors so that the war effort would pave the way for the birth of a true society of capitalists and *rentiers*.

Whereas it had been commonplace to celebrate France's limitless saving power, the war called for new modes of thinking. The highly popular *bons de la Défense nationale* dangerously increased short-term debt.[25] Meanwhile, French authorities were reluctant to impose heavy tax increases for fear that it would trigger social tensions and reopen old disputes. Direct income tax was not implemented until 1916, with poor results during its first years of existence.[26] In 1915, it became urgent to increase the gold reserves of the Bank of France (whose advances to the state had been increased several times) and convert short-term debts into consolidated public bonds. The gold campaign and the first war loan were thus launched in the fall. Even if big war loans weren't a new thing for French investors, the authorities knew that major efforts would be required to compete with other countries' results. The British example became a source of inspiration and emulation once the action of the National War Savings Committee came to be known.[27]

The classical opposition between a Jacobine and centralized France, on the one hand, and a decentralized and liberal Great Britain, on the other, needs to be qualified in this case. Up until 1917, French financial mobilization certainly benefited from the Bank of France's network, the state apparatus, and a dense web of commercial banks and savings institutions. However, it lacked a national organization in charge of coordinating propaganda and local actions all over the country. Local initiatives, from chambers of commerce, banks, and other actors continued to play a major role in 1915–1916. The national committee for gold collection, created in 1916, was originally proposed by the chamber of commerce of Marseille, not by the central state. The Bank of France tried to coordinate local actions, but there was no clear centralization such as the one set up in Britain.[28]

From 1917 onwards, however, the level of mobilization seemed to wane. The French minister of finance, Louis-Lucien Klotz, now called for the creation of a national committee, the *Commissariat National à l'Emprunt*, whose task would be to rationalize and professionalize propaganda. This body was created in the summer of 1918, a few months before the fourth war loan was issued. This national organization was thus put into place three years after the British had set up their National War Savings Committee. This lack of central coordination was now considered a weakness, which prompted curiosity and envy for what the British and Americans had experimented during the war. The role of the *Commissariat National* was then to "popularize techniques used in other allied countries, which have proven so useful and efficient." As in Britain, the minister of finance expressed his willingness to widen the circle of bondholders. The US example became a driver for reform: "Our American allies owe their financial success to their propaganda methods; even if there are differences in cultures between our two peoples, these methods should be a source of inspiration and information for us."[29] The financier Octave Homberg, who had traveled to the United States and Britain to negotiate foreign loans during the previous years, was nominated the head of the new commissariat. He was in charge of coordinating propaganda, while leaving room for local initiatives.[30]

The way the British and the French campaigned for their war loans was indeed significantly altered once the United States entered the war. On the other side of the Atlantic, bond drives were tremendously successful.[31] American officials benefited from their past experience (going back to Jay Cooke's role during the Civil War)[32] but also from the example offered by the British since 1915. In July 1917, the representative of the British Treasury to the United States, Sir Basil Blackett, gave a talk on the means employed by the National War Savings Committee to promote savings and thrift.[33] As in Britain, centralized organizations were soon set up in order to coordinate action (a War Loan Organization was created, as was a National Committee for War Savings Stamps, presided by Frank

A. Vanderlip, the head of the National City Bank of New York).[34] Four Liberty Loans, a Victory Loan, and millions of war savings stamps were issued in less than two years. Whereas only half a million Americans had owned financial assets before the war, more than 34 million people had a share in the national debt after the war, be they war bonds, war certificates, or savings stamps.[35] This mass mobilization included 1 million women who voluntarily joined the campaign.[36] Coercive measures were also widely implemented, since dissenters were silenced and put into jail, while recent immigrants were submitted to intense pressure to subscribe.[37] As in Germany, the workers whose employers had set up automatic payroll deductions had no real voice in the process. This had more to do with "compulsory voluntarism," fraught with discourses of fear and shame, than with purely disinterested patriotism, as several historians have noted.[38]

Nonetheless, European observers were struck by the commercial inventiveness displayed by American bankers, public authorities, and local associations to sell bonds to the public. Commercial banks played a crucial role in war financing by buying certificates of indebtedness issued by the Treasury to anticipate the yield of war loans and taxes.[39] Modern advertising techniques and marketing, such as movies and parades, were used on a wide scale. The attention paid to material culture soon inspired European practices in return. In Britain and the United States, there was a clear attempt at trivializing the war by resorting to concrete material objects so that it would enter the daily life of the population. Britain innovated when it launched famous operations such as the "feed the gun" or "tank weeks" campaigns, during which people were invited to buy war bonds or certificates to contribute to bomb and arms production. These techniques were used to create chains of emotions and solidarity between the givers and the soldiers, a classical technique also used in the philanthropic sphere to shape "emotional communities." Hence, the war would no longer be a distant and abstract phenomenon but a direct consequence of the day-to-day activities of anonymous people. Only a few months later, the French *inspection des finances* also turned its attention toward these new practices, which it found particularly appropriate to revive popular enthusiasm.[40] Germany and Austria-Hungary, too, had implemented quite surprising and innovative techniques, for example, with the giant figures set up in public spaces, on which people could hammer nails they had paid for.[41]

The use of American propaganda techniques prompted debate among the French and British financial elites, who were not always at ease with the mercantile and popular touch given to war loans in the United States.

The French minister of finance mentioned the fact that there were differences in temperament and customs between the American and French populations, so that it would be necessary to adapt American innovations to the national character. Alfred Neymarck, the spokesman of the *rentiers* class in France, added that French investors were fundamentally conservative and disliked any eccentric way of selling bonds. Financial *milieux* despised "American propaganda," which they deemed too prosaic and imbued with consumerism.[42] Playing on emotions was unnecessary to their mind, given that a wise investor would always be able to evaluate the risk and interest of buying public bonds, without requiring any other explanation or element of seduction. But for all their feeling of superiority, France and Britain had to acknowledge that the United States succeeded in selling their bonds to the public on an unprecedented scale. Addressing millions of people, the American propaganda managed to include workers, peasants, and popular classes within the war effort, thus strengthening social and financial mobilization. Conversely, the British knew from the very beginning of the war that they needed to make a special effort to attract working-class people:

> The failure of the working class to participate in the recent loan would appear to have been largely due not only to the fact that they are unaccustomed to invest money, but to the somewhat abstract and colourless form in which the loan was presented to them. The employment of some new device, peculiarly adapted to their mental outlook, appears to be necessary in order to arouse a sufficient degree of enthusiasm.[43]

This report, written in 1915, already argued for the introduction of lottery bonds, a system that was very popular in Germany, Italy, and Austria. The perspective of improving the war loans' appeal with promises of extra gains was thought to be compatible with the British working classes' love of gambling. The same kinds of proposals were made in France as well, especially in 1917 and 1918, when it became harder to convince new potential subscribers. Attaching lottery games to public bonds was highly contested. For numerous officials and experts, Britain and France could not adopt such measures without severely downgrading their credit. Their public bonds had been first-grade investments for decades, owing their reputation to their financial and moral record. Lottery schemes, on the contrary, were said to characterize low-credit countries which had to compensate for the low value of their public bonds.

In spite of the British Treasury's interest in premium bonds, a select committee set up in 1918 concluded that there were no valid grounds, nor any necessity, to introduce them in the system of British public finance.[44] Furthermore, the people in charge of the savings campaign, such as Robert Kindersley, feared that lottery bonds would compete with the moral rigor they were trying to inculcate into the British working class. The committee observed that there was strong opposition "to any state action which might be held to introduce an element of chance in our National Finance."

The latter example shows that not all financial and propaganda techniques would cross borders during the war years. International comparisons were instrumental in triggering reforms, but Britain and France remained attached to some of the peculiarities that had made their financial reputation before the war. Among them was their possession of the two largest colonial empires of the time.

THE IMPERIAL POLITICS OF WAR LOANS

Beyond their national realm and population, countries also tried to sell their war bonds abroad. Alongside huge foreign loans negotiated in the United States,[45] war loans were issued in neutral countries and, to some extent, in colonial territories, so that money in foreign currencies could be raised and used for import payments, thereby limiting exchange risks and preserving the central bank gold reserves. It explains why war loans were not only seen as domestic enterprises but also as major international issues, bound to reinforce a nation's credit and how it was perceived by the whole world. Fundraising and capital mobilization were indeed a matter of international competition, all the more so as global flows of capital were much harder to channel since the outbreak of the war. France and Great Britain thought they could benefit from their dominant financial positions, while Germany and other central powers would be deprived of any access to foreign capital. Neutral countries, even if they had lower investment capacities than the belligerent powers, were actively courted. In 1916, the British set up a committee, headed by the banker Charles Addis, to propose measures that would facilitate foreign subscriptions to British war loans in neutral countries and within the Empire.[46]

Whatever the amounts collected, it was important to attract all the resources that could be invested in the war effort, while making sure that Germany and its allies would not tap into foreign resources.[47] French and British public bonds were in competition on the London market (French war loans were sold in London), for instance, but also in other countries. War loans therefore had a twofold dimension, one domestic, the other on the international scene. By publishing leaflets and brochures advertising the high quality of their credit, French financial authorities endeavored to ensure that all investors would be convinced by the strength and vitality of the nation's economy.[48] French war loans were issued and sold in neutral countries, namely Europe and Latin America, where they were in competition with other loans.[49] However, this policy of raising money abroad was curtailed by the tendency of each nation to protect its savings, without any clear vision of what the economic future would hold in the aftermath of war. In some places, such as Spain, French officials and bankers had to be extremely careful when advertising in favor of French war loans, since the Spanish government officially refused to back one side or the other. Discreet action was needed to sell bonds without damaging the principle of neutrality.

This global competition for gold and money triggered rumors, attacks, and false information about the financial position of each nation. Misinformation was a weapon the powers could use to denigrate their opponents' creditworthiness. The Bank of France, for instance, compiled hundreds of articles from the German press, in search of negative rumors and information.[50] Germany was accused of organizing conspiratorial campaigns aimed at weakening French public credit, both in the eyes of its citizens and of the outside world.[51] In Britain as well, the language used during war loan campaigns was designed to oppose German propaganda and display popular support to counter rumors of faltering loyalty.[52]

France and Britain tried to collect resources in territories where they exerted financial influence or direct political power. All the financial ties developed before 1914 were used to strengthen their credit. This was particularly the case in Egypt, where both the British and the French wanted to divert local savings toward their public bonds. A British report written in 1916 stated that all Egyptian savings were already invested in Allied bonds and obligations.[53] French authorities nevertheless published multilingual propaganda to convince Egyptian savers and investors to buy French war bonds.[54] This global competition for money between the two allies and the other belligerent powers even reached Asia, for instance in some European concessions in China, where each power tried to mobilize its merchant and banking networks to collect money.

Colonial empires contributed with troops, raw materials, and manufactured goods to the war effort.[55] But they also had a role to play in the financial mobilization. In absolute terms, money coming from the colonies was hardly comparable to the sums raised in the metropole.[56] However, the funds collected were proportionally speaking significant when compared with the colonies' economic resources. Moreover, there were also political reasons why the imperial powers were willing to popularize war loans in some of their colonial realms. In India and Indochina, particularly, the imperial powers hoped that the war would help develop savings and investment practices, and temper nationalist claims.

In the British Empire, financial policies varied greatly according to the political and economic status of the colonized territories.[57] The British authorities were not in favor of collecting funds and subscriptions all over the empire; the best way for colonies to help the metropole was to promote financial self-sufficiency, without asking too much from the imperial center.[58] Reducing money flows from London to the colonies was a first step, before it could be envisioned that colonial subjects would lend the few savings they had to the imperial power. This is exactly what was expected from the Dominions and the West Indies territories. They had to raise money locally, thus developing their financial autonomy and relieving the metropole of costly financial transfers. Local self-sufficiency was privileged over imperial transfers, even if it implied curbing the colonies' desire to take part in the war effort. The British authorities thus had to decline offers made by local people who wanted to contribute to war loans. The Chancellor of the Exchequer Reginald McKenna proclaimed his preference in a speech given in the House of Commons in June 1915: "While I am anxious to give residents in the Dominions every opportunity for subscribing to the War Loan, I trust they will not lose sight of the fact that they can do perhaps an even greater service to the Empire by lending their resources to the governments of their own dominions and so reducing the calls by those governments on the resources of the United Kingdom."[59] Encouraging local loans, rather than direct imperial solidarity, ensured that London would not be burdened with extra liabilities toward its colonies after the war. Some dependent territories sent gifts, such as Ceylon, Hong Kong, Jamaica, or Barbados. These streams of "colonial generosity" were not directly solicited but could not be decently declined by the metropolitan authorities.[60] As for the West Indies, Treasury officials also favored local loans rather than transfers from the colonies to the metropole.[61]

India's economic and political situation was somewhat different. There, two imperial war loans were issued in 1917 and 1918 in order to increase the number of subscribers, be they of British or Indian origins. As in the metropole, the authorities strove to woo small investors from urban and rural areas, despite the fact that local interest rates were far higher than what the state could offer. They hoped that loan subscriptions would strengthen political ties between the colony and London, and hasten the spread of new "Western" economic practices in India. War, however, needed to be made concrete for imperial solidarity to be felt and put into practice. War loan operations thus offered an opportunity to overcome indifference and passivity from the local populations, according to the Governor of Bombay: "There are thousands of our countrymen here who hardly realise that their country is taking a great part in a conflict the greatest that history has ever recorded, which has convulsed nearly the whole world, and to whom it has never been brought home that it is owing to the very fact that they belong to the British empire and have had the protection of our Empire's navy, that they have been able to live their normal lives and carry on their avocations without any fear or anxiety of the depredations of the enemy."[62] Campaigning for the war effort was all the more necessary as nationalist claims and protest were threatening colonial loyalty.[63] The Governor-General invited Indians to take part in the war effort and distance themselves from Indian nationalists, pledging that their participation would be later rewarded with autonomy. The politicization of financial mobilization was clearly called for by colonial officials, who used both propaganda and censorship to secure subscriptions.[64]

For this political objective to be fulfilled, a strong and coherent organization had to be set up, as in the metropole. From London to rural India, British authorities aimed at "combining decentralization with effective coordination," so that local fundraising initiatives would be efficiently coordinated.[65] British agents were in charge of this policy in the provinces under colonial rule, while local princes were asked to galvanize their subjects in native states. Modern techniques were implemented, such as assigning quantitative objectives to local constituencies, taking into account the amount of taxes usually collected and the estimated wealth of the population. Withholding schemes were applied to the colonial agents' salaries, who could be rewarded if they had shown enough efficiency and enthusiasm in their participation in the war savings campaign. The goal was to create a political atmosphere in which nobody would ignore the war and the duties it created: "Our programme was so arranged that for some days the War Loan and the War Loan alone would be the sole subject of conversation amongst the people here," said one official from the

Poona district, near Bombay. However, excessive propaganda could produce backlash effects. Moral suasion was useful but only to a certain extent: "Last year there were indications that in certain districts there had been some excess of zeal in the matter of persuading people to invest in the loan. From this year's provincial reports it is clear that special measures were taken to ensure that there should be no foundation for any belief that improper official pressure was being exercised."[66]

It is striking to note that the way Indian subscribers were depicted did not differ much from discourse on the working classes in England.[67] War loans were conceived as a means to promote thrift and moderation among those who were judged unable to curb their immediate passions.[68] Nowhere more than in India can we observe the desire of colonial authorities to change economic behavior and build stronger financial and political ties between the savers and the metropolis. From an anthropological perspective, loan subscriptions were seen as a perfect opportunity to popularize new economic habits and concepts among supposedly "backward people." One commissioner from the Southern Division of India complained that "the idea of investment is entirely foreign to the cultivator." A classical colonial trope assumed that local populations could not understand what thrift and investment meant, thereby missing some of the key values of British "gentlemanly capitalism." This attitude also derived from the inability of colonial officials to understand how local credit networks operated. To overcome these barriers, imperial authorities translated their official propaganda into several vernacular languages. They also tried to adapt their language and schemes to the religious and cultural backgrounds of the population. Muslim people, for instance, were offered a specific scheme, a loan without interest, that was designed to comply with their religious rejection of interest-bearing loans: "In order to meet the wishes of Mahomedans and others who desire to subscribe to the Indian War Loan but for religious and other reasons are averse to receiving interest, arrangements have been made for the issue of 'No interest' cash certificates to those who apply for them. Purchasers of these 'No interest' certificates will, on applying for their repayment, receive only the amount actually paid for them."[69]

Material culture was also important in popularizing the war effort in India. War loan trains and tanks were displayed in several places, in Burma, as they were in English towns. Lotteries and horse races were organized to increase participation, contrary to what was done in the metropole. Specific attention was paid to the various groups and classes taking part in the loan campaign, with a view to knowing precisely which arguments and messages should be used to convince them to participate. All these efforts were aimed at consolidating the imperial rule, insofar as bondholders would be financially tied to the regime's fate. Savings certificates, sold to students and children, were meant to transform Indian subjects into British capitalists so that they became accustomed to thrift, moderation, and self-help.

British colonial authorities rejoiced at the results produced by the two campaigns launched in 1917 and 1918. The imperial war loans were subscribed by 77,000 persons in 1917, and around 100,000 in 1918, whereas hardly a thousand people had ever invested money in public bonds in pre-war India. This increased number of Indian bondholders, be they colonial or colonized, was hailed as a success in the attempt to develop a *rentier* class in British India: "It is perhaps not too much to hope that we have now in existence the germ of a large class of rentiers, the investment of whose savings in public loans should, in future years, be of almost incalculable value in furthering the development of the country."[70] As is often the case, however, most of the money collected came from a small number of subscribers, since 60 percent of all the money raised was contributed by only 1 percent of the bondholders: there was no process of democratization at all but an attempt at widening the circle of small bondholders and displaying political loyalty in a context of imperial tensions.

By comparison, the financial contribution of the empire to the French war effort was lower than the British one. Various estimates have been proposed by historians. It is plausible that between 1.5 and 2 billion francs were contributed by the colonies. Through loans and donations, the colonial territories only contributed 2.7 percent of the money collected during the war.[71] But these aggregated results hide contrasting situations. Half of the funds were provided by Algeria and Indochina. Elsewhere, the sums invested in war loans always remained very limited, for instance in West and East French Africa.

As in Britain, the many incentives given to savers and investors from Indochina were expected to demonstrate the economic potential of the colony. If the state could levy local resources for its war effort, it would then be able to use these resources for economic purposes, such as rural development, industrialization, or public works. This economic aim went alongside an attempt at "civilizing" the indigenous populations by spreading new economic and financial behaviors.[72] Albert Sarraut, the Governor-General in Indochina, praised the feelings of belonging and solidarity expressed by local populations toward their imperial power, as if subscribing to a loan was tantamount to a declaration of loyalty and consent.[73] Sarraut surely exaggerated the success of his propaganda. He nonetheless took pride in the fact that 47,000 indigenous people had subscribed to the loans. They accounted for 77 percent of all subscriptions, but theirs represented only a tiny part of the money raised. As in India, the absolute number of subscribers remained limited, but was ten times higher than in the pre-war period.[74]

Sarraut drew on anthropological arguments to describe how local populations reacted to financial mobilization. He thought that indigenous people were unable to differentiate between loan and gift practices. Some people were even said to have subscribed because they thought they were forced to do so. Official propaganda blurred the boundaries between loans and taxes, especially on the colonial ground.[75] This confusion also existed in the metropole, where the limits between free subscription and forced loan were not so clear. Whether true or not, the stories told by Sarraut and other colonial administrators cast light on their wishes to use war loans to provide indigenous populations with economic education, as if investing in public bonds would make them belong to the wider nation of *rentiers*. The imperial power's hope was to inject so-called Western practices and values into Asian societies to improve the colony's economic development. Sarraut thought that "this campaign (would) have two positive results, one financial, for the loan, the other on a long-term perspective, on the *mentalité indigène*, now open to Western financial practices." Colonial authorities were blind enough to consider loan results as markers of colonial assimilation. To their minds, colonial people were expressing recognition for the liberal policies they had been implementing. The good news was above all that the empire would no longer cost money in the near future, but would bring some money in. This was expected to open prospects for a self-sufficient empire, with a strengthened economic organization. This fallacy would soon clash with the colonial subjects' desires for emancipation and their refusal of such paternalistic discourses.[76]

* * *

The selling of war bonds gave way to mass public and marketing campaigns all over the world during the First World War, even in some distant parts of European empires. Each nation had its own model and traditions, but everywhere a combination of public and private actors, local initiatives and central coordination, local practices and global purposes was at play. Some of the transformations triggered by war finance (the increasing share of central banks in state financing, the weight of foreign credits, and stricter regulations) were to deeply impact international and domestic politics in the interwar period. Millions of people had been invited, willingly or not, consciously or not, to become small bondholders, whose destiny was more than ever tied to their nation's economic strength and creditworthiness. Propaganda and other official discourses claimed that it would be for the best, the war being an opportunity to spread bondholding practices and create wider classes of *rentiers* in the metropolis and in some of the most advanced parts of empires. The Bolshevik repudiation, German hyperinflation, the deadlock over allied credits and war reparations, and colonial demands for emancipation would soon prove how deceptive these hopes were. Mass participation in state funding would still be a great source of legitimation for warfare states until the Second World War[77] in conjunction with an ever-increasing sophistication of the less visible infrastructural techniques used by states to channel money flows that would characterize the new "dirigist" regime of public debts.[78] Therefore, the First World War ushered in a much more unstable world, while dramatically increasing the power of states to penetrate civil societies and regulate markets.

Notes

1. Most of the recent comparative and global historical studies on public finances end around 1900/1913 on the eve of the war: José Luis Cardoso and Pedro Lains, eds., *Paying for the Liberal State: The Rise of Public Finance in Nineteenth Century Europe* (Cambridge: Cambridge University Press, 2010); Mark Dincecco, *Political Transformations and Public Finances: Europe, 1650–1913* (Cambridge: Cambridge University Press, 2011); Bartolomé Yun-Casallila, Patrick K. O'Brien, and Francisco Comín Comín, eds., *The Rise of Fiscal States: A Global History, 1500–1914* (Cambridge: Cambridge University Press, 2012); Wenkai He, *Paths Towards the Modern Fiscal State. England, Japan, and China* (Cambridge, Mass.: Harvard University Press, 2013).
2. Emily Rosenberg, ed., *A World Connecting: 1870–1945* (Cambridge, Mass.: Harvard University Press, 2012); Davide Rodogno, Bernhard Struck, and Jakob Vogel, eds., *Shaping the Transnational Sphere. Experts, Networks, and Issues from the 1840s to the 1930s* (London: Berghahn Books, 2014).

3. Richard Roberts, *Saving the City: The Great Financial Crisis of 1914* (Oxford: Oxford University Press, 2013).
4. Martin Horn, *Britain, France, and the Financing of the First World War* (Montreal: McGill-Queen's University Press, 2002); Hans-Peter Ullmann, "Finance," in *The Cambridge History of the First World War*, vol. 2, ed. Jay Winter (Cambridge: Cambridge University Press, 2014), 408–433. By the end of the war, Britain and France owed 7.1 billion dollars to the United States. However, as Ullmann puts it, "domestic loans played the dominant role" (420).
5. In this sense, these financial operations were part and parcel of a larger process of political, economic, and cultural mobilization during the war. See John Horne, ed., *State, Society, and Mobilization in Europe during the First World War* (Cambridge: Cambridge University Press, 1997); Niall Ferguson, *The Pity of War. Explaining World War 1* (London: Basic Books, 2000); Hew Strachan, *The First World War*, vol. 1 (Oxford: Oxford University Press, 2003).
6. George L. Mosse, *The Nationalization of the Masses. Political Symbolism and Mass Movements in Germany from the Napoleonic Wars Through the Third Reich* (New York: Howard Fertig, 1975).
7. Thomas Piketty, *Capital in the Twenty-First Century* (Cambridge, Mass.: Harvard University Press, 2014); Kenneth Scheve and David Stasavage, *Taxing the Rich: A History of Fiscal Fairness in the United States and Europe* (Princeton: Princeton University Press, 2016).
8. The National Archives (Kew, UK), T 172/744, Victory Loan, 1917.
9. James McDonald, *A Free Nation Deep in Debt: The Financial Roots of Democracy* (New York: Farrar, Straus and Giroux, 2003).
10. Peter Gatrell, *Russia's World War: A Social and Economic History* (London: Pearson Longman, 2005), 132–153; V. V. Strakhov, "Vnutrennie zaimy v Rossii v pervuiu mirovuiu voinu," *Voprosy Istorii* 9 (2003): 38–43; http://encyclopedia.1914-1918-online.net/article/war_bonds
11. Sheldon Garon, *Beyond Our Means: Why America Spends While the World Saves* (Princeton: Princeton University Press, 2011).
12. In this volume, see Chap. 4 by David Todd and Alexia Yates.
13. Henry C. Adams, *Public Debts: An Essay in the Science of Finance* (New York: Appleton, 1887).
14. French authorities and observers were impressed by the ability of their German counterparts to mobilize priests and ministers for their propaganda, as shown in several conferences given in 1915 by people involved in the gold campaign.
15. Margaret Lavinia Anderson, *Practicing Democracy: Elections and Political Culture in Imperial Germany* (Princeton: Princeton University Press, 2000); Andreas Biefang, "La mobilisation politique dans l'Empire autori-

taire. Le spectacle des élections au Reichstag (1871–1912)," *Revue d'histoire du XIXe siècle*, no. 46 (2013): 95–117.
16. Alexander Watson, *Ring of Steel: Germany and Austria-Hungary at War, 1914–1918* (London: Allen Lane/Penguin Books, 2014), 487–490. There were 14 million households in Germany at the time. Gerd Hardach, "La mobilisation financière de l'Allemagne entre 1914 et 1918," in *La Mobilisation Financière Pendant la Guerre: Le Front Financier, un Troisième Front*, eds. Florence Descamps and Laure Quennouëlle-Corre (Paris: CHEFF, 2015), 88. In France, the four war loans raised only 24 billion francs (Ullmann, "Finance," 420). See also, in this volume, Chap. 12 by Stefanie Middendorf.
17. Strachan, *The First World War*, 913. Hardach mentions that the number of subscriptions below 1000 marks represented 81 percent of all the subscriptions, but only 10 percent of the money raised. Mass participation in the war loans did not mean at all that financial investments were more equally distributed (Hardach, "La mobilisation financière," 89).
18. Hardach, "La mobilisation financière," 89.
19. Roger Chickering, *The Great War and Urban Life in Germany: Freiburg, 1914–1918* (Cambridge: Cambridge University Press, 2007); Watson, *Ring of Steel*, 220–222; Konrad Roesler, *Die Finanzpolitik des deutschen Reiches im Ersten Weltkrieg* (Berlin: Duncker & Humblot, 1967); Reinhold Zich, "Kriegsanleihen," in *Enzyklopädie Erster Weltkrieg*, eds. Gerhard Hirschfeld, Gerd Krumeich, and Irina Renz (Paderborn: Schöning, 2003), 627–628; Stephen Gross, "Confidence and Gold: German War Finance 1914–1918," *Central European History* 42 (2009): 223–252.
20. Jeremy Wormell, *The Management of the National Debt of the United Kingdom, 1900–1932* (London: Routledge, 2000).
21. The National Archives, T172/144.
22. On the blurred boundaries between voluntary and forced saving in the interwar period, see in this volume Stefanie Middendorf's chapter (Chap. 12) on Germany, and Kristy Ironside and Étienne Forestier-Peyrat's chapter (Chap. 13) on Soviet Russia.
23. The National Archives, T 172/696, War Loan, 1917.
24. Archives of the Bank of France (Paris, France), 1069199014/21, *The Times* (April 3, 1920).
25. The French government raised 130 billion francs through credit between 1914 and 1918. Of this total, 42 percent came from short- and medium-term treasury bonds, 19 percent from war loans, 25 percent from foreign credit, and 13 percent from central bank credit. Therefore, short-term certificates far exceeded long-term debts, in spite of all the propaganda displayed to sell perpetual war loans (Ullmann, "Finance," 420).

26. Nicolas Delalande, *Les Batailles de l'impôt. Consentement et résistances de 1789 à nos jours* (Paris: Seuil, 2011).
27. Bank of England (London, UK), AC30/360, Loans office wallet, 4 percent French *rentes*, 1917 and 1918.
28. Here my point differs from John Horne, who describes a centralized effort starting as early as 1914. The state was responsible for advertising war bonds, but did not have a centralized organization of propaganda. See Horne, "Accepter la guerre. Les mobilisations de la bienfaisance et de l'épargne en France, 1914–1918," in *Dans la guerre 1914–1918: Accepter, endurer, refuser*, eds. Nicolas Beaupré, Heather Jones, and Anne Rasmussen (Paris: Les Belles Lettres, 2015), 81–103.
29. Official report from the minister of finances to the president of the Republic, July 1918.
30. Centre des Archives Economiques et Financières (Savigny-le-Temple, France), B68470, Official Directions to Prefects, September 6, 1918.
31. Julia Ott, *When Wall Street Met Main Street: The Quest for an Investors' Democracy* (Cambridge, Mass.: Harvard University Press, 2011), 55–100; Christopher Capozzola, *Uncle Sam Wants You: World War One and the Making of the Modern American Citizen* (Oxford: Oxford University Press, 2010).
32. Nicolas Barreyre, *Gold and Freedom: The Political Economy of Reconstruction* (Charlottesville: University of Virginia Press, 2015).
33. *Chronicle*, July 28, 1917.
34. Archives of the Bank of France, 1069199014/21.
35. Julia Ott, *When Wall Street*, 56.
36. Julia Ott, *When Wall Street*, 87.
37. Julia Ott, *When Wall Street*, 95–100; Adam Tooze, *The Deluge: The Great War and the Remaking of the Global Order, 1916–1931* (New York: Viking, 2014).
38. Olivier Zunz, *Philanthropy in America: A History* (Princeton: Princeton University Press, 2012), 64–66.
39. Jacob H. Hollander, "Certificates of indebtedness in our war financing," *Journal of Political Economy* 26, no. 9 (November 1918): 901–908, quoted by Tooze, *The Deluge*.
40. Centre des Archives Economiques et Financières, B68470, note by Finance Inspector Léon-Dufour.
41. Alexander Watson, *Ring of Steel*, 221–226.
42. On consumer culture and fears of "Americanization," see Frank Trentmann, *Empire of Things. How We Became a World of Consumers, from the Fifteenth Century to the Twenty-First* (London: Allen Lane, 2016), 348–354, who develops a critical approach to the "Americanization" thesis, to be compared with Victoria de Grazia, *Irresistible Empire: America's Advance*

Through Twentieth-Century Europe (Cambridge, Mass.: Harvard University Press, 2005).
43. The National Archives, T 172/1312, "Working Classes and War Loans. Object and Nature of Proposal," 1915.
44. *Report from the Select Committee on Premium Bonds, Together with the Proceedings of the Committee, Minutes of Evidence and Appendices, Ordered by the House of Commons to be Printed, January 16, 1918*, London, published by his Majesty's Stationery Office, 1918 (ref. Bank of England, 336.3).
45. Adam Tooze, *The Deluge*.
46. The National Archives, CO 323/719/41, Subscriptions to Government Bonds and War Savings from Overseas, Commission Appointed on August 21, 1916.
47. Avner Offer, "The British Empire, 1870–1914: a waste of money?," *Economic History Review* XLVI, no. 2 (1993): 235.
48. Archives of the Bank of France, leaflet entitled *French Economic Vitality* (1916): "French people have always put national credit before all other considerations, thus contributing themselves to the general confidence, which has never been shaken by the fact that France had a national debt."
49. On Latin American countries' participation in the European war effort, see Olivier Compagnon, *L'Adieu à l'Europe. L'Amérique latine et la Grande Guerre* (Paris: Fayard, 2013).
50. Gerd Hardach, "La mobilisation financière."
51. Archives of the Bank of France, "Pallain" Series, Box 13.
52. The National Archives, Note on "Points for speakers," 1917.
53. The National Archives, FO 141/817/33: "It may therefore be assumed that the great bulk of the capital which has become available for investment in Egypt during the war has been lent, directly or indirectly, to the Allied governments," 1916 Report.
54. Centre des Archives Economiques et Financières, B61785.
55. Offer, "The British Empire,": 235–236; Bouda Etemad, *De l'utilité des empires: Colonisation et prospérité de l'Europe, XVIe-XXe siècle* (Paris: Armand Colin, 2005); John Darwin, *The Empire Project: The Rise and Fall of the British World-System, 1830–1970* (Cambridge: Cambridge University Press, 2009); Robert Gerwarth and Erez Manela, eds., *Empires at War, 1911–1923* (Oxford: Oxford University Press, 2016).
56. Canada, Australia, and India contributed for £1 billion (Stephen Garton, "The Dominions, Ireland, and India," in *Empires at War, 1911–1923*, 155. The French Empire raised between 1.5 and 2 billion francs.
57. "British Empire was not a centre and peripheries polity, where authority flowed from the heart of Empire out to the colonies and dependencies, but a polymorphous entity, necessitating the deployment of diverse strategies ranging from imperial authority, military command, political enticements,

sentiment, and bonds of ethnicity, culture, and religion to mobilize for war," Garton, "The Dominions, Ireland, and India," 154. See also, on India, DeWitt C. Ellinwood and Satyendra Dev Pradhan, eds., *India and World War I* (New Delhi: Manohar, 1978).
58. Leigh A. Gardner, *Taxing Colonial Africa: The Political Economy of British Imperialism* (Oxford: Oxford University Press, 2012). In his 1993 article, Offer contradicts the idea of the empire as a "financial burden," demonstrating, for instance, how military and defense costs were also held by colonies. For a similar argument on France, see Elise Huillery, "The Black Man's Burden. The Cost of Colonization of French West Africa," *Journal of Economic History* 74, no. 1 (March 2014): 1–38.
59. The National Archives, CO 323/633/7, "Opportunity of Colonial Subjects to Invest in the War Loan," June 28, 1915.
60. The National Archives, 323/663/7, Gifts from the Colonies (1917 or 1918): "Generally speaking, it may be said that the liabilities which the Colonies have undertaken for the purposes of the War have been larger than prudent finance would allow, but His Majesty's Government have not considered it desirable to check the desire of the local legislatures and inhabitants to bear their full share of the common burden of the War."
61. The National Archives, CO 295/502/77, War Loans, Trinidad, December 1915.
62. British Library, India Office Record, IOR/R/20/A/3969, File 6/1 War Loans India, Speech of His Excellency the Governor Delivered on March 5, 1917 at the Town Hall Bombay.
63. Garton, "The Dominions, Ireland, and India," 158–160.
64. N. Gerald Barrier, "Ruling India: Coercion and Propaganda in British India during the First World War," in *India and World War I*, 75–108.
65. British Library, IOR/R/20/A/3969, File 6/1 War Loans India, Conference, Town Hall, Bombay, June 10, 1918.
66. The National Archives, T 1/12281, E.M. Cook to the Secretary of the Government of India, Controller of Currency, 10.
67. Garton highlights the numerous "commonalities in Home Front experiences across diverse parts of the empire," in "The Dominions, Ireland, and India," 165.
68. Whether these attempts were successful or not (all the more so in the colonies) is debatable. For a skeptical view on the power of propaganda and official campaigns to promote "enduring cultures of thrift," see Trentmann, *Empire of Things*, 417–419.
69. British Library, IOR/R/20/A/3969, File 6/1, Department of Commerce and Industry, Simla, May 10, 1917, Press communiqué.

70. The National Archives, T1/12281, Letter from the Controller of Currency to the Secretary of the Government of India, Finance Department, December 12, 1918.
71. Jacques Thobie, Gilbert Meynier, Catherine Coquery-Vidrovitch, and Charles-Robert Ageron, *Histoire de la France coloniale, 1914–1990* (Paris: Armand Colin, 1990), 75–76; Richard S. Fogarty, "The French Empire," in *Empires at War*, 109–129.
72. Alice S. Conklin, *A Mission to Civilize: The Republican Idea of Empire in West Africa, 1895–1930* (Stanford: Stanford University Press, 1997).
73. Centre des Archives Economiques et Financières, B61785, Minister of Colonies to the Minister of Finance, March 23, 1918; *Gouvernement Général de l'Indochine, Instructions Relatives à l'Emprunt National 4% 1917*, (Saigon: Imprimerie Nouvelle Albert Portail, 1917).
74. Albert Sarraut, *La Mise en Valeur des Colonies Françaises* (Paris: Payot, 1923), 45; André Touzet, *L'Emprunt National de 1918 en Indochine* (Hanoï-Haïphong: Imprimerie d'Extrême Orient, 1919).
75. Centre des Archives Economiques et Financières, B61785, report on the 1917 war loan, by Albert Sarraut, January 16, 1918.
76. Erez Manela, *The Wilsonian Moment: Self-Determination and the International Origins of Anticolonial Nationalism* (Oxford: Oxford University Press, 2007); Michael Goebel, *Anti-Imperial Metropolis: Interwar Paris and the Seeds of Third World Nationalism* (Cambridge: Cambridge University Press, 2015).
77. James T. Sparrow, *Warfare State: World War II Americans and the Age of Big Government* (Oxford: Oxford University Press, 2011).
78. On these later transformations and the development of "silent financing" techniques, see in this volume Chap. 12 by Stefanie Middendorf, as well as Chap. 15 by Anush Kapadia and Benjamin Lemoine.

CHAPTER 12

Beyond Democracy or Dictatorship: Structuring Sovereign Debt in Germany from Weimar to the Postwar Period

Stefanie Middendorf

"The whole civilized world," wrote Kurt Heinig, the Social Democratic chairman of the German Reichstag's budget commission, in spring 1931, "is made of debt obligations whose counter value no longer exists." In an article for the journal *Der Staat seid Ihr* ("you are the state"), he pleaded for an international solution to the debt problem caused by the First World War and called upon his fellow citizens to not put their trust in unilateral decisions or one-sided attacks against "America."[1] Only a few months after this, the democratic government introduced administrative controls on capital movements. This decision marked an important step toward the establishment of an authoritarian debt policy and financial autarky, further developed under National Socialist rule after 1933. Subsequently, this move was communicated to the public as a political strategy to enhance national autonomy and state power as well as to protect the country against international capitalism. Critics even bought into this rhetoric

S. Middendorf (✉)
Leibniz Centre for Contemporary History Potsdam, Potsdam, Germany
e-mail: middendorf@zzf-potsdam.de

when they denounced it as a "planned economic" transformation of state finance. Yet, these regulatory measures were strategically linked to the Hoover moratorium on inter-governmental loans in order to secure the interests of American capital and to a standstill agreement with commercial investors, negotiated by international experts and bankers in autumn 1931. The German Foreign Office hoped, in fact, that if Germany temporarily stopped transferring reparations it would be seen as a more trustworthy debtor in the eyes of possible private bondholders in the future.[2]

The history of German sovereign debt throughout the first half of the twentieth century cannot be understood without taking the intermingling logics of national politics and international finance into account. In coping with the socioeconomic legacies of the First World War, the German nation-state underwent profound transformation. The attempts of the Weimar Republic at democratic crisis management turned into the dictatorship of the Third Reich. The role of public finance within this process has often been discussed, mainly in regard to the effects of austerity under the Reich's Chancellor, Heinrich Brüning, during the last few years of the republic.[3] This chapter argues, however, that instead of continuing to discuss the political "mistakes" made by individual actors or the possible relevance of fixed "models" of financial governance for the advent of National Socialism, more attention should be given to the structural effects that practices of debt management had in regard to state power in Germany, under democratic as well as under dictatorial rule—and within a global political context that was defined by international financial interdependency.

In contrast to other European countries, sovereign debt and its relevance for state-building were topics that had not greatly featured on the political agenda in Germany before the war, even though some respected intellectuals such as Adolph Wagner, Karl Dietzel, Lorenz von Stein or Georg von Schanz had made attempts to address the issue in the second half of the nineteenth century.[4] Neighboring nations—especially the French and the British—had experienced the functionality of central state credit for centuries; in these countries, the systemic role of sovereign debt therefore figured more prominently within economic, philosophical and sociological imaginations of the modern state.[5] In light of this, Douglass C. North and Barry R. Weingast have famously referred to the historical connection between parliamentarism and public creditworthiness in seventeenth-century England in order to argue that the establishment of institutions of representative government enhances the ability of the sovereign to credibly commit to the repayment of debts and, by this, to borrow large sums for state purposes.[6] Later, this argument was extended to other early democracies in modern Europe and beyond in studies carried out by David Stasavage and James MacDonald.[7]

As the German case is historically different to the above, it can be used to widen the perspective set out by these scholars. Investigating the transformative period between democratic and dictatorial rule in the Reich from Weimar to the postwar period helps to question the narratives of ever-growing economic rationality and institutional progress and to stress the continuing importance of other, more informal and sometimes dubious elements of a state's power to mobilize resources, including personal relations, political bargaining, communicative tactics and coercion.[8] What is more, it brings the importance of war finance and related crisis management for the contemporary history of debt and sovereignty back into the picture. Cut off from Wall Street and other sources of external money supply, the Reich had managed to self-fund its war effort by internal loans, supported by large propaganda campaigns, with considerable success until 1916. Yet, from this time on, the results of bond drives began to lag behind the accumulated short-term debts. By December 1918, the Reich's debt amounted to 135 billion marks, 27 billion of which were placed in the Reichsbank's portfolio. This fostered inflationary effects that extended into the postwar period.[9]

With this, financing the war not only had an economic impact, it also altered the political and social system in Germany more visibly than in other countries. As different emergency policies had been implemented in order to accelerate material and financial war supply chains, the executive had gained importance. Thereby the likelihood that it would consolidate this powerful position throughout the early years of the Weimar Republic increased. The state, as a managing apparatus, had moved into the center of financial relations. The fact that the Reich actually defaulted on its internal debt by inflationary methods until stabilization was reached after 1923 led to social tensions in Germany. A lack of trust grew in the German population toward the government due to doubts surrounding the young democracy's creditworthiness.[10] In addition to the war debt, revenues dwindled as a consequence of the process of transformation from a military to a civic economy and the conditions imposed by the Treaty of Versailles, the transfer of payments to victims and the costs of demobilization. The reparation regime, in particular, came to represent the problem of "state credit" in Germany, turning financial data, as debt statistics or budget information, into a political weapon within international relations as well as into a main source of state power.[11]

Thus, sovereign creditworthiness in Germany after 1918 was a result of diverse political conflicts, material conditions and cultural schemes, within both national and international frameworks. Especially in the interwar years, German sovereign debt depended not only on internal conditions but on a state's reputation among global circles of experts and investors: a country that was judged to have defaulted without a legitimate excuse was branded a willful defaulter by this investment community and no longer received loans. In contrast, a nation that suspended payments due to "uncontrollable circumstances" was not blacklisted as long as it provided acceptable settlements after the bankruptcy.[12] The financial fate of debtor nations like Germany therefore relied on an efficient management of these contextual variables and on the state's capacity to control circumstances in ways that made them seem sufficiently uncontrollable. After 1933, the Hitler regime tried to change the rules of this game by force and, for a certain time period, with some financial success, but had to deal with capital market logics and investor interests within dynamic national and transnational spaces nonetheless.

Based on these observations, this chapter seeks to understand the "structuration" of sovereign debt in Germany as a social practice within the history of state-building, not—as in financial literature[13]—as a policy tool to improve the economic value of investments. This approach is based on Anthony Giddens' and William H. Sewell's theoretical reflections on the constitution of societies, addressing the changing modes in which social systems (here, the sovereign state and its public finance) are produced and reproduced through structured actions.[14] In doing so, it integrates the experiences of the Weimar Republic and National Socialism into an argument that focuses on qualitative changes in the relations between debt governance and state power. The continuities and discontinuities between democratic and dictatorial rule will be reconsidered—as their ambivalences question normative narratives that connect parliamentarian representation, economic liberalism and sustainable debt.[15]

Two analytical axes will be central to this chapter's argument. *First*, the blurring lines between the state and the market, especially during the interwar years, need to be put into focus. The underlying transformation had already begun in the nineteenth century, but intensified after the First World War. It brought about an effect of what Michel Foucault has called *étatisation*, but also the discovery of "the economy" (and *die Finanz* as one of its central parts) as an entity of its own.[16] Both the Weimar and the National Socialist governments relied on capital market logics in order to finance state activities—while at the same time regulating and changing markets according to their political aims. This transformation transcended the political caesura of 1933 and continued after 1945. It had lasting effects on the conception of state sovereignty. *Second*, the growing importance of intermediary institutions and financial mediators for the constitution of national statehood will be highlighted. In the German case, this was intensified by strong international dependencies in the financial realm at least until 1933. As an effect of this, the concept of state power changed. A sovereign state could no longer solely rely on its formal monopoly on the use of violence within one territory, but had to integrate a diverse number of actor interests through procedural practices, beyond borders and by non-formal means.[17] Historically, this development partly contradicted with, yet ultimately transcended the short-term effects of nationalist politics in the interwar period and the war years.

THE QUEST FOR SOVEREIGNTY: STATE AGENCY AND VESTED INTERESTS BEFORE THE SLUMP

Throughout most of its existence, the Weimar democracy was not able to receive credit from German investors and depositors, but relied heavily on external investments. Due to this, the development of public debt in Germany after the First World War was part of larger transformations in foreign policy and world economic relations. As already mentioned, the German state of the early twentieth century lacked the positive tradition of public debt so influential in other nations. Germany had been an important exporter of capital before 1918, deeply involved in international efforts to institutionalize sanctions and financial control over defaulting states like Greece or Venezuela. The tone prevailing in public debates as well as among experts before the outbreak of the war was therefore dominated by creditor interests, and was highly critical of excessive state debts. Over-indebtedness and insolvency were considered to be morally dubious and indicative of political failure seen as typical of "exotic" or "inferior" people.[18]

Yet, already in the prelude to the First World War, Germany had depended on external creditors much more than France or Great Britain. In 1913, almost 20 percent of the German public debt had been foreign in origin. While experts such as Wagner, business figures, financiers and politicians considered this dependency on international creditors as well as German investments abroad a useful means to the Reich's world political integration, it fueled controversy and distrust regarding public debt among larger segments of the population.[19] Nonetheless, driven by patriotic enthusiasm, the domestic German loan drives during the First World War proved successful in terms of popular participation. There were around 1.2 million subscribers to the first war loan in autumn 1914 and 5.3 million to the fourth, before the number of signatures went down to 3.8 million with the fifth loan in autumn 1916. Propaganda was then intensified, and the sixth loan in spring 1917 reached almost 7.1 million signatures. This was considered a financial plebiscite in favor of German policy and, by foreign observers, an example of "Teutonic efficiency" in public borrowing. But weaknesses soon started to show. The bond drives in autumn 1917 and spring 1918 mobilized about 5.5 million and 6.9 million subscribers, but participation decreased heavily in autumn 1918 to 2.7 million signatures.[20] The floating debt was beginning to expand and the Reichsbank had to purchase government bonds. Moreover, the huge success of German war loans cannot be explained without looking at "certain measures of promotion" beyond patriotic propaganda, for example, secretive information politics and the placement of bonds among savings banks. In 1914, the *Sparkassen* subscribed to 884 million mark of bonds, making up 19.8 percent of the loan's nominal amount; one-third of this was held by the banks themselves, two-thirds by their clients. This revealed the opportunities offered by public borrowing during the war to mediators such as savings banks; for example, the fact that by subscribing to and selling public loans they took a big step forward in becoming universal banks.[21]

The idea, uttered by the German minister of finance, Karl Helfferich, in 1915, that "the enemy must foot the bill" failed with Germany's defeat—at least at first sight. For the German population, the experience of participating in national finance schemes proved to be a devastating experiment when the postwar inflation destroyed their assets and fueled, as indicated above, a long-lasting disengagement of the population from subscribing to loans. For the German government, the management of such large amounts of debt was uncharted territory, as was a democratic and centralized regime in public finance in general.[22] This uncharted territory proved to be one defined by international frontlines, codified by the Versailles Treaty in 1919 (which made the newly established democratic government in Germany accept the old monarchy's debt[23]) and delineated by the Allies' vested interests regarding the reparations policy. The political function of sovereign debt took on a previously unknown complexity, threatening the existence of the Weimar state and alluding to the challenges of the German position within a new international order in the making after the war.[24] By its openly inflationary policies, the German government did not only disown those parts of its own population that held war loans.[25] These policies also caused foreign creditors and speculative investors to lose their money and forced them to pay for German reparation transfers. External creditors were excluded from revaluation measures undertaken by the German government in 1924/25 in order to partly compensate the domestic public for losses during the time of inflation.[26]

Inflationary politics were consequently perceived and discussed in relation to sovereign default. National bankruptcy was considered by political forces on the left as well as on the right as a legitimate element of state policy. Legal scientists endeavored to depict default as a historical normality rather than an exception—and as a sovereign right in order to "save" and "reanimate" the state. Yet, default as a specific instrument of state emergency law or as a revolutionary program against the power of capital (in the way the Bolsheviks repudiated the Tsarist debt, both internal and external) was widely discredited.[27] Instead, moderate observers like the sociologist Rudolf Goldscheid argued that the state should socialize assets more systematically in order to avoid a complete default.[28] Not surprisingly, holders of public bonds and others facing financial hardship due to devaluation argued that sovereign default resulted from governmental failure and should be overcome by tax reforms and monetary measures.[29]

Beyond such internal debates, the Reich as a former creditor state knew about the quasi-impossibility of forcing debtor states by military or diplomatic means into repaying their debts.[30] The German government's strategy of resistance to reparations that led to the French and Belgian occupation of the Ruhr in 1923 profited from this experience, albeit this time from the perspective of a nation unwilling to repay its own debt. On the other hand, leading German politicians of the 1920s, in particular, Foreign Minister Gustav Stresemann, realized that high amounts of external debt guaranteed foreign support of the Weimar state and constituted a strategic means to re-integrate Germany into the world economy through the interests of financial investors from abroad.[31] Consequently, the Dawes Plan of 1924 made German creditworthiness dependent on external private investments and on the implementation of an anti-inflationary budget balancing policy by the Reich's government. It was supervised by international institutions and interpreted as a vote in favor of "America" and its financial markets upon whose profit mentality Weimar politicians hoped to gamble. The German Foreign Office accordingly rejected French plans to commercialize reparation debts on a bilateral level in 1926 and opted for a close cooperation with the United States, "under whose creditor interests we fled deliberately by accepting the Dawes plan."[32] Tellingly, this policy was presented by the experts involved as a purely "economic" and decidedly "non-political" program. It was put into practice by politicians such as the Reich's Chancellor Hans Luther and his minister of finance Otto von Schlieben, both former civil servants who endeavored to embody the "neutrality" of technocratic governance.[33]

Framed in this way, German debt politics became structured by the logics of global finance. International networks of "money doctors" and civil servants took over quasi-public functions in negotiating the terms of financial interdependency between nations.[34] This implied not only the tactical de-politicization of debt management but also a certain limitation of the political autonomy of the nation-state. In order to secure this reordering of state power within the conditions of the reparation regime, guardian institutions like the Reichsbank were enforced, legitimized by international law, steered partly by international experts and committed to controlling public credit as well as the stability of the German currency.[35] This configuration fueled a perception among many leading Weimar politicians (even those from democratic parties) that regarded financial policy as a foreign policy first and foremost, discounting the need to actively legitimize statehood through public finance on the domestic level. Political debates at home, especially debates taking place at the German Reichstag, were dismissed as irrational and party-political "palaver."[36] At the same time, international organizations such as the League of Nations and their conferences evolved into platforms of strategic communication. Freelance economists such as John Maynard Keynes or Gustav Cassel who were involved in the production of knowledge under the auspices of the League of Nations, yet critical of the Versailles system, were read widely in Germany throughout the 1920s. The financial intelligence produced within this framework of international institutions left its mark on how the German government structured public debt as well as on how it represented related problems in public even though the League's efforts to effectively coordinate monetary policy and stimulate innovative governance ultimately failed.[37]

As a result, economic rationality increasingly challenged and transformed political argumentation. This was, of course, not simply the result of external influences but also had origins in the emerging Weimar welfare state's attempts at self-legitimation. The international rhetoric of financial politics presented by experts was entangled, yet also collided with the growing expectations of the German public vis-à-vis the social and economic capacities of the state. Here lies a decisive point in understanding the meaning of public debt for the history of German statehood after 1918. If simply considered a "financial plebiscite" in the classic sense of liberal state finance, the young republic's attempts to place bond issues among investors within Germany in 1927 and in 1929 must be seen as failures. The Reinhold Loan of 1927 (named after the Liberal Democratic minister of finance), with a yield of 5 percent, managed to fund 450 million RM of the 500 million RM nominal warrant—yet, the largest part of this amount was subscribed to by public or semi-public institutions. Two hundred million RM were taken up directly by public authorities, the remaining 300 million RM being bought by a consortium led by the Reichsbank in order to be placed among the public. Over 200 million RM of this sum were again placed among savings banks, pension funds, health insurance funds, etc. In the end, only 100 million RM remained open for public subscription—and had to be converted and finally bought back by the Reich. All in all, the Reinhold Loan was not a complete disaster, but depended heavily on intermediary institutions to be successful. After this, contemporary critics considered the German capital market to be exhausted.[38]

Moreover, this triggered a general discussion on the state of democratic finance, headed by Hjalmar Schacht as the President of the Reichsbank. Highly critical of the Reinhold Loan, he argued against the *Kreditwut* (the furor in accumulating debt) displayed by public authorities and in favor of a general "roll back of the social and interventionist state" in order to strengthen German private credit among foreign investors. Schacht considered state loans an inappropriate means of public funding and confronted the government's quest to gain political legitimacy by way of bonds with economic logic. He demanded the rationalization of government structures and a disentanglement of the interests of state, para-state and non-state institutions.[39] This contemporary critique has influenced historiographical accounts of Weimar financial politics ever since. Yet, the strategy of involving national intermediary actors in public bond drives, chosen by the Reich's government, cannot simply be considered as a political failure in mobilizing public support. It needs to be seen as a structural move to counter the interests of international creditors as codified by the reparation regime and to remodel sovereign finance under the auspices of a democratic welfare state.

This also became obvious in the wake of the second attempt of the Weimar Republic to issue public bonds in 1929, the so-called Hilferding Loan that was intended to end the Reich's cash flow problems. Even though it was equipped with a true yield of up to 9 percent (depending on the holder's marginal tax rate) and a short duration (15 years, as compared to the French state loan of 1928 that offered a duration of 75 years), only about 180 million of the expected 500 million RM were subscribed to.[40] To fill the gap, the Social Democratic minister of finance, Rudolf Hilferding, started to make arrangements—bypassing the Reichsbank— for two short-term foreign bridging credits from Dillon Read, a New York investment bank. Hilferding also negotiated a 12 to 42-year loan with the Swedish corporation Kreuger & Toll conditional on the ratification of the Young Plan and the concession of a monopoly on match sales in Germany to the corporation. Kreuger was considered a dubious connection at the time. Nicknamed the "Saviour of Europe" he had specialized in the 1920s, together with the Boston-based investment bank Lee Higginson, in funding weak states on the margins of Europe, in return for the highly lucrative privileges of match monopoly. The beneficiaries of Kreuger's interventions in the 1920s and early 1930s included—apart from Germany—Greece, Hungary, Poland, Romania, Turkey, Yugoslavia and France. Kreuger was an outsider, excluded from the closed circles of interwar financial advisers. Yet, in 1932, the *Economist* retrospectively celebrated his idea of wedding the acquisition of markets to the provision of capital for borrowing governments as an "inspired notion" and as having the potential to complement the programs proposed by the League of Nations Financial Committee.[41]

Contrary to such seemingly problematic alliances based on "odious debt," loan negotiations with J. P. Morgan conferred a positive branding upon European states. Representatives of this bank were involved in the Dawes and the Young plans. In regard to German creditworthiness, however, Morgan delivered a devastating judgment, calling the Germans a "second-rate people" whose business should be done "by somebody else."[42] Similarly, the Agent General for Reparation Payments, Seymour

Parker Gilbert, sharply criticized Hilferding's policy as hazardous, hindering the assignment of the Young Plan loan on the American capital market.[43] Again, the President of the Reichsbank, Schacht, initiated a campaign against the government's credit policy, forcing an amortization fund in respect of the floating debt onto the government in exchange for a short-term credit by the Reichsbank. Ultimately, Hilferding resigned together with his Conservative State Secretary, Johannes Popitz.[44]

As the cash crisis of 1929 shows, the international agreements of the early 1920s had shorn the central bank of its function as the final government failsafe in order to strengthen its international custodianship of the currency.[45] The public interest embodied by the German state was now negotiated under the conditions of the profitability of investments from abroad. Yet, this global rhetoric of "sound" finance has also to be placed within the context of political conflicts between nations. This can be illustrated by the fact that not only Parker Gilbert or Schacht but also the French government insisted on deflationary politics in Germany. It actually demanded the Germans to implement balanced budgets and austerity by transparent procedures. This caused a dilemma that fueled the final crisis of the Weimar Republic when the Chancellor Brüning, together with the Finance Ministry, attempted to force the Reichstag into accepting the budget—a move that in the end led to the dissolution of the parliament, followed by a National Socialist landslide victory and a period of authoritarian governance by emergency law until Hitler came to power in 1933.[46]

In regard to the governmental practices applied in order to finance the state, the 1929 experience had another important effect. Although having proved incapable of mobilizing individual public credit in "the liberal way," the Reich's government effectively probed new strategies of state funding by forcing public bonds on intermediary institutions. At the beginning of the year, non-rediscountable and non-interest bearing treasury certificates with terms of between 6 and 12 months had only been sold to private banks after a long succession of negotiations. By early May, the same banks would agree to take further treasury certificates only on better conditions of liquidity, inacceptable to the Reich.[47] Looking for other institutions to meet the state's financial requirements, the government increased pressure on parafiscal bodies and organizations under public governance. The 1929 budget law obliged social insurance funds to invest parts of their liquidity into state loans and to accept the Reich's subsidy in the form of treasury bills instead of cash money. At the same time, Hilferding expressed his resolution to resort to savings banks "that in case of need should be forced to accept state loans."[48] In fact, throughout the months that followed, the government managed to transfer large parts of its own illiquidity to intermediary organizations, prompting much criticism from interested parties.[49] Nevertheless, these strategies also created new spaces of negotiation and communication about the needs and limits of state power on a national level. Within these communicative spaces—that could be exploited not only by representatives of the state but also by the interlocutors on the side of the insurance funds or banks— economic and political logics further intertwined.

NAZI RULE? STATE POWER AND ORGANIZED CREDIT AFTER 1933

Such state structuring effects of debt management became ever more obvious during and after the Great Depression. This was at a time when international surveillance over the Reichsbank started to loosen its grip due to the agreements of the Young Plan and was replaced by the idea of central bank cooperation at the Bank for International Settlements (BIS), established in May 1930. In a similar way to the currency controls mentioned above, the installation of a Reich Commissioner for the banking sector in 1931 did not result from a one-sided and authoritarian intervention by the state but was preceded by intense consultations between state representatives, experts and bankers. The passing of the Credit Supervisory Law (*Kreditwesengesetz*) in 1934, much in the same vein, was the outcome of negotiations and established long-lasting structures of capital market regulation and corporatist governance. These measures aimed at reforming the weakened capital market under the auspices of the state, while at the same time helping to re-stabilize business-relevant resources such as public trust in the financial market.[50] Most relevant parties interpreted these measures as necessary interventions within modern statehood, not as deformations or unhealthy dirigisme.[51] Similar strategies appeared in the realm of debt management in regard to pension and health insurance funds; these funds played an ever-increasing role within the Reich's crisis management. By 1930, pressure on these parafiscal bodies had grown to such an extent that the Labor Ministry was prompted to call upon the Finance Ministry to loosen its grip. Yet, in 1931, the Reich's supervisory rights were again extended, much to the appreciation of the insurance industry that had requested the state guarantee its own economic "health."[52] At the same time, international attempts at establishing a solid financial and political architecture to manage the war's legacies failed. Technically, the BIS did help to buy time and organize loans, but it proved to be incapable of assessing the situation adequately due to conditioned economic analysis and the weight of international interests.[53]

It is against the backdrop of such experiences that the history of public debt in the Third Reich should be reconsidered. What has been dubbed "silent financing" and interpreted as Hitler's secretive strategy to avoid financial plebiscites among an allegedly skeptical German population,[54] reveals itself to be a rather consequential step toward the *étatisation* of German sovereign debt management, albeit radicalized under the autarkical conditions of forced rearmament and strategic preparation for war. Combining "liberal" and "illiberal" means, National Socialist debt policy appears as a decidedly tactical organization of state power through various instruments of borrowing, accompanied by internal and external negotiations. The National Socialist regime was bent on exploiting the divisions between its creditors to its own benefit in all areas and starting with the external debt service.

While attempts at international cooperation once again failed at the World Monetary and Economic Conference in July 1933,[55] German authorities had already taken steps to negotiate German external liabilities with the creditors independently. On 8 May 1933, the German Finance Ministry had notified the BIS that the service of the US Dawes bonds as well as the US, Swedish and UK issues of the Young Loan would henceforth be settled at the current exchange rate and would no longer be protected by the original gold clause. Soon afterward, the Reichsbank called a meeting in Berlin of Germany's foreign creditors to discuss the question of transfer of foreign exchange. The BIS was not invited, yet Schacht informed the BIS board personally about German plans to continue full service of the Dawes Plan, though not of the Young Loan. On 9 June 1933, a law was promulgated suspending transfers in foreign exchange with respect to most external liabilities and placing private external debt under tight control by the German Clearing Office. Shortly afterward, the Reichsbank convened long-term creditors on the fringes of the World Conference to discuss possible exemptions to the new transfer law. The BIS protested formally, yet abstained from legal action.[56]

Cracks emerged, therefore, in the German creditors' front. In the background, a parallel diplomacy developed that included secret talks between Montagu Norman from the Bank of England and the Reichsbank over the settlement of German debt. A transfer conference in Berlin was called by the Reichsbank in spring 1934, chaired by the BIS and prepared by private talks between Schacht, Norman, BIS president Leon Fraser and the creditors' representatives. In the end, no agreement could be reached. While the conference was still in session, the Germans informed the BIS that the Reich would not continue its service of the Dawes and Young loans after June 1934; after the end of the conference, a complete transfer moratorium was declared on all long-term government bonds. This step had been discussed within the ministerial bureaucracy for years.[57] The BIS complained, yet again without any practical effect. The German government then started to negotiate bilateral agreements with individual states; delegations to these meetings included civil servants who had already been involved in reparation diplomacy under Weimar's democratic governments.[58] Actually, bondholders in different markets saw their demands partially satisfied. Britain, for example, managed to secure preferential treatment from Germany by threatening to impose a clearing arrangement in 1934; as a result, British creditors were privileged over American bondholders by the Germans in the years that followed.[59] By resuming debt service on existing trade credit, the German state managed to regain some degree of creditworthiness, especially in London, benefiting from a general mood in British politics that has been described as "economic appeasement."[60] The BIS could no longer monitor the service of the Reich's loans, yet communication with German officials continued. Good relations were guaranteed by a group of high-ranking Reichsbank employees who acted as intermediaries in Basel and had an eye to the future, especially after the Reichsbank was put under tight government control in the late 1930s and then again from 1942 onward, as Germany's defeat became palpable. In June 1943, BIS economic adviser, Per Jacobsson, visited Berlin in order to talk informally to a select group of Reichsbank officials and commercial bankers about the Keynes and White plans on a postwar monetary system.[61]

In 1934, the National Socialist government not only defaulted on foreign loans but also initiated a coordinated strategy to place a domestic loan of 500 million RM. A law passed in December 1934 capped corporate dividends at 6 to 8 percent. This cap increased corporate taxes, and the compulsion of businesses to buy public bonds discouraged enterprises from placing new issues of stocks and bonds on the market. When the government floated a public bond issue in 1935, the sale was—compared to 1927 and 1929—a success.[62] At the end of the year, almost 2 billion

RM in long-term bonds had been mobilized. In the following years, state loans and treasury certificates were emitted for institutional and public subscription on a regular basis. The resulting investment in bonds amounted to a total of 1.35 billion RM in 1936, 2.57 billion in 1937 and 7.23 billion in 1938—an "unexpected success," as the minister of finance, Lutz Graf Schwerin von Krosigk, confessed at the time.[63] Until 1938, this strategy of handling the capital market for state needs proved relatively successful, even though it had to be accompanied by manipulative methods of capital market control. In effect, large parts of the loans were held not by individual investors but by banks, insurance companies and giro centers. By 1938, 81.9 percent of the public debt was credited by institutional investors, and 18.1 percent by the public.[64]

Archival sources from the Finance Ministry convey the level of intervention that was necessary in order to place large portions of public bonds into the hands of financial institutions. Negotiating the amounts to be subscribed to by the savings banks in 1935, the government official responsible informed his minister that one would have to offer moments of "rentability," that is, pay provisions to the giro centers and allow treasury certificates to be traded on the stock market. Two years later, the State Secretary of Finance and fierce National Socialist Fritz Reinhardt asked Hitler's Deputy Rudolf Heß to stop direct pressure being exerted on the private economy to subscribe; measures of coercion should be avoided because they could provoke these creditors into distancing themselves from the state and into selling their bonds to the market.[65] Instead of resorting to authoritarian power alone, the state bodies also tried to redefine the rules of the financial market. They gambled on economic interests and competitive market relations in order to maximize the amounts they could steer and to minimize the interest costs for the state.[66]

In 1938, the complex system of public bond finance suffered a serious setback as subscriptions decreased despite capital market regulation. Due to this, the Reichsbank had to purchase bonds. Debates on the inflationary effects and the general limits of public credit intensified among high-ranking politicians, the central bank, experts and the ministerial bureaucracy.[67] As a first measure, state control over institutional investments was intensified. In August 1938, the Reich prohibited any mortgage credits from being given by insurance funds and savings banks in order to further channel their liquidity into public bonds. March 1939 brought a further tightening of regulation; insurance funds were now required to place two-thirds of their assets into government securities and the remaining third into investments necessary for the military economy. Such dirigisme was "sold" to insurers by a law that forced all self-employed craftsmen who did not have life insurance to sign up to the employee's insurance, making 1939 a highly profitable year for the business.[68]

The National Socialist regime made no more attempts to issue public bonds as the capital market proved exhausted by government interventions and was from then on to be kept free for private bond issues. Instead, the regime modified its strategy under the auspices of forced mobilization for war, resulting in the so-called *Neue Finanzplan* (a rather short-lived experiment in the reorganization of the capital market). Moreover, unseen efforts were undertaken to channel the flow of private savings into state hands without public subscription and with the help of the central bank, now placed firmly under government rule.[69] In the course of this revision, not only was the propagandistic effort to mobilize the Germans for *Eisernes Sparen* (a forced savings program) intensified but also the grip on "the large reservoir of organized credit."[70] The regime further developed the strategic use of intermediary institutions. In the case of insurers, governmental tactics relied on the structural conflict between private and public institutions within the insurance market; this strategy actually proved successful and generated high rates of subscription by private companies (private and public insurance companies together invested 205 million RM in 1935, over 400 million RM in 1940 and 1.4 billion RM in 1941). In exchange, insurance companies were allowed by the Reich Price Commissioner to raise interest rates on their policies in 1942. By paying provisions to the representative bodies of the private insurance sector as a reward for their engagement in bond distribution, the Finance Ministry also fueled the competition between private insurers and traditional banking institutions.[71]

This hard-to-grasp dirigisme was related to changes in the public discourse on debt management. With the preparation for the Second World War, the discursive representation of public debt assumed a radicalized technocratic character, presented by leading politicians and bureaucrats in terms of strategic "flexibility" rather than in terms of consistency. Both the minister of finance, Schwerin von Krosigk, and the minister of economics, Walther Funk, argued in such a manner, seconded by military leaders: an OKW secret memorandum stated in October 1938 that methods of debt management and state financing should not be "dogmatic" or "systematic" but "efficient" and "dynamic."[72] Psychological aspects—especially the growing fear of inflation—were not ignored but countered by stressing the ever-transitory character of the state and public finance. Contemporary German experts accordingly rationalized debt management strategies under National Socialism as a modernizing attempt, intended to raise German public finance to the level of that of other countries. The fact that public debts now relied heavily on intermediary financial institutions was not considered a dysfunction but a necessary state reaction to altered strategies of consumption and saving in mass societies—and much in line with the contemporary development of public credit on a worldwide level. In 1944, the BIS reported that not only Germany but also Japan, Great Britain and the United States had intensively "tapped" monetary collection tanks such as insurance funds and saving banks.[73] Two years earlier, the BIS had already praised German innovations in cashless payments as making public borrowing more "effective."[74]

* * *

In order to mobilize financial and human resources for a "total war," the Nazi state not only relied on political propaganda and force but also on intermediary institutions, private interests and an image of functionality. This image could be maintained until 1943 with the help of concerted taxation and the constant renegotiation of control mechanisms that dated back to at least 1930/31. Within these strategies, credible commitment or popular legitimation were not considered to be of prime importance as long as the government managed to steer capital flows by other instruments. The necessary encounters between market rationality and state agency had already increased during the Weimar years and were then refined after 1933. National Socialist debt management needed and utilized these interactions in order to maximize mobilization and integrate the interests of diverse actors within an allegedly "organic," de facto "organized" system of state finance.[75]

Yet, these structural developments do not represent an episode of German financial history alone but a relevant chapter within a more global history of sovereign debt in the first half of the twentieth century; they are comparable to solutions of the debt problem in other countries at the time, related to their respective experiences of war and crisis.[76] The history of public debt in some postcolonial states, for instance, shows a predominance of foreign capital flows and international relations over national institution building that is comparable to the situation in the Weimar Republic.[77] And a historical investigation of communist debt practices makes clear that despite all radical rhetoric the bloc's integration into an "international-capitalist order of public debt" outlived claims for alternative systems of domestic financing based on alleged "mutual assistance," self-sacrification or coercion.[78] In this regard, the period from the First World War to the 1960s saw many "lights that failed" (Zara Steiner) but also an enduring restructuration of sovereign debt management between state agency and market logics. Experiments in financial dirigisme and organized competition that had initially been related to war finance or crisis relief were modified, de-politicized and turned into regular techniques of state funding, helped by transnational networks of state representatives, bankers and experts that survived the changes in political regimes. Within this framework, the genuinely controversial and contingent character of state sovereignty became more visible than before—as did the vision of the market as its necessary co-operator and counterpart. This was a global phenomenon, but it continued to be molded and diversified within national frameworks.

After 1945, the German Federal Republic, helped by the allied authorities and former war finance experts, defaulted on internal debts (except for equalization claims held by credit institutions, insurances and home loan banks) through the 1948 currency reform and started to re-build itself as a creditor nation.[79] Until the mid-1960s, German public debt was no big topic. Yet, the German state tried to steer capital flows even under the conditions of a growing market economy, again combining political and economic logic. The first state loan, launched in December 1952 and equipped with a short duration (5 years) and tax advantages, was promoted by the minister of finance, Fritz Schäffer, by stating that "the credit of the state is also the credit of the economy." A tranche of 400 million DM was guaranteed by a banking consortium, leaving only 100 million open for public subscription, but insurance funds as well as private households hesitated to invest.[80] The same year, high-ranking representatives of the insurance business argued against plans to use their assets for economic policy "by order or instruction from above, i.e. by coercion" and compared this to "the methods of the Hitler regime." Ultimately, insurance businesses declared themselves ready to invest in certain credits "voluntarily" as they otherwise feared a more rigid dirigisme by investment laws. Such corporatist bargaining once again proved to be profitable not only for the state.[81] In the following years, the importance of social insurance funds as national creditors of the state declined. Instead, it were the commercial banks that now resumed the leadership in financing the state and coordinating international monetary flows.[82] The later growth in public debts brought along new, astonishing ambivalences: in the early 1980s, a German economist proclaimed that the re-transformation of the state from a creditor to a debtor after the 1960s had not subordinated state policies to the rules of financial markets. On the contrary, it had made the state "mightier than the mightiest among equals," as the immense scope of the state's indebtedness enabled it to control capital market rules through public debt management.[83]

The development of sovereign debt management in Germany after the First World War makes it obvious that the power of the state was measured decreasingly by the amount of subscriptions of individual citizens to public bonds but rather by the capacity and autonomy of the state to direct and steer the capital market. The most powerful asset of the state became its differential impact on the capacity of (national as well as international) market forces to pursue their strategies and to realize their goals.[84] This even applies to the dirigiste approach of Nazi war finance. "Competition" and "indirect rule" were among the key words used by contemporary German financial experts in the final phase of the war; an ambivalent lesson in market economics learned during this period.[85] Offensive strategies of capital regulation according to political aims, however, were discredited in Germany after 1945—here it differs from other countries in the West, for example, France, where state rule over capital flow (the famous *circuit du Trésor*) was strengthened programmatically in the postwar period.[86]

It was not until the 1960s that the question of financial dirigisme was officially raised again in West Germany, now within the framework of a transnational debate on "Keynesian" reforms. This debate combined the rhetoric of emergency (referring to the Great Depression) with that of efficiency (the so-called *Globalsteuerung*), integrating the experiences of both the Weimar and, less explicitly, the National Socialist period. Even before this, in the 1950s, technocratic attitudes and regulatory ideas were being developed behind the ordoliberal façade of the 1950s—but their possible impact on sovereign debt management has yet to be scrutinized from a historical perspective.[87] In any case, the study of German sovereign debt until 1945 reveals that its structural effects on the powerful system of the state transcended established boundaries between "democratic" and "dictatorial," "liberal" or "authoritarian" regimes. Practices of public borrowing brought about a transformation of the principles of sovereignty that was rooted in the constant redefinition of the relationship between economic logic and state agency on an international scale rather than in national political institutions alone.

Notes

1. Kurt Heinig, "Revision der Kriegsschulden," *Der Staat seid Ihr*, March 16, 1931, 38.
2. Sören Dengg, *Deutschlands Austritt aus dem Völkerbund und Schachts 'Neuer Plan'. Zum Verhältnis von Außen- und Außenwirtschaftspolitik in der Übergangsphase von der Weimarer Republik zum Dritten Reich (1929–1934)* (Frankfurt: Peter Lang, 1986), 140–161; Niels P. Petersson, *Anarchie und Weltrecht. Das Deutsche Reich und die Institutionen der Weltwirtschaft 1890–1930* (Göttingen: Vandenhoeck & Ruprecht, 2009), 142–143; Susanne Wegerhoff, *Die Stillhalteabkommen 1931–1933* (Ph. diss., University of Munich, 1982), 11–15.
3. See Albrecht Ritschl, "Knut Borchardts Interpretation der Weimarer Wirtschaft. Zur Geschichte und Wirkung einer wirtschaftsgeschichtlichen Kontroverse," in *Historische Debatten und Kontroversen im 19. und 20. Jahrhundert. Jubiläumstagung der Ranke-Gesellschaft in Essen, 2001*, eds. Jürgen Elvert and Susanne Krauß (Stuttgart: Steiner, 2003), 234–244; Theo Balderston, *Economics and Politics in the Weimar Republic* (Cambridge: Cambridge University Press, 2002), 77–99; for a recent renewal of this discussion, see the contributions by Paul Köppen, Knut Borchardt and Roman Köster to *Vierteljahrshefte für Zeitgeschichte* 62 (2014): 349–375 and 63 (2015): 229–257, 569–578.
4. Karl Dietzel, *Das System der Staatsanleihen im Zusammenhang der Volkswirthschaft betrachtet* (Heidelberg: Mohr, 1855); Adolph Wagner, *Finanzwissenschaft. Erster Theil (Lehrbuch der politischen Ökonomie 5)* (Leipzig/Heidelberg: Winter, 1883), 130–183. For further examples, see Wilhelmine Dreißig, "Ausgewählte Fragen zur öffentlichen Verschuldung," *Finanzarchiv* 42 (1984): 577–612, 582; David Howart and Charlotte Rommerskirchen, "A Panacea for all Times? The German Stability Culture as Strategic Political Resource," *West European Politics* 36, no. 4, (2013): 750–770; Carl-Ludwig Holtfrerich, *Government Debt in Economic Thought of the Long 19th Century* (School of Business & Economics, Discussion Paper: Economics, Free University Berlin, N° 2013/4); Kenneth H.F. Dyson, *States, Debt, and Power. 'Saints' and 'Sinners' in European History and Integration* (Oxford: Oxford University Press, 2014), 3–5, 214.
5. See Michael Sonenscher, *Before the Deluge. Public Debt, Inequality, and the Intellectual Origins of the French Revolution* (Princeton, NJ: Princeton University Press, 2009); Jean Andreau, Gérard Béaur and Jean-Yves

Grenier, eds., *La dette publique dans l'histoire. Les journées du Centre de Recherches Historiques des 26, 27 et 28 novembre 2001* (Paris: CHEFF, 2006); for the period after the First World War see Nicolas Delalande, "Protéger le crédit de l'État. Spéculation, confiance et souveraineté dans la France de l'entre-deux-guerres," *Annales HSS* 71, no. 1 (2016): 129–161.

6. Douglass C. North and Barry R. Weingast, "Constitutions and Commitment: The Evolution of Institutions Governing Public Choice in Seventeenth-Century England," *The Journal of Economic History* 49, no. 4 (1989): 803–832.

7. David Stasavage, "Credible Commitment in Early Modern Europe: North and Weingast Revisited," *The Journal of Law, Economics, and Organization* 18, no. 1 (2002): 155–186; idem, *Public Debt and the Birth of the Democratic State: France and Great Britain, 1688–1789* (Cambridge: Cambridge University Press, 2003); idem, *States of Credit: Size, Power, and the Development of European Polities* (Princeton, NJ: Princeton Univ. Press, 2011); James McDonald, *A Free Nation Deep in Debt: The Financial Roots of Democracy* (New York: Farrar, Straus and Giroux, 2003).

8. For the relevance of such informal elements in modern debt relations, see also Nicolas Delalande's Chap. 11 in this volume, as well as Claire Lemercier and Claire Zalc, "Pour une nouvelle approche de la relation de crédit en histoire contemporaine," *Annales HSS* 67, no. 4 (2012): 979–1009; Mischa Suter, "Jenseits des 'cash nexus'. Sozialgeschichte des Kredits zwischen kulturanthropologischen und informationsökonomischen Zugängen," *WerkstattGeschichte* 53 (2009): 89–99.

9. Gerd Hardach, "Die finanzielle Mobilmachung in Deutschland 1914-1918," *Jahrbuch für Wirtschaftsgeschichte* 56, no. 2 (2015): 373-374; for a critical discussion, see Albrecht Ritschl, *Sustainability of High Public Debt: What the Historical Record Shows* (Centre for Economic Policy Research, Discussion Paper Series No. 1357, 1996): 13–14; idem, "The Pity of Peace: Germany's Economy at War, 1914–1918 and beyond," in *The Economics of World War I*, eds. Stephen Broadberry and Mark Harrison (Cambridge: Cambridge University Press, 2005), 61–63.

10. See Martin Geyer, *Verkehrte Welt. Revolution, Inflation und Moderne. München 1914–1924* (Göttingen: Vandenhoeck & Ruprecht, 1998); Gerald D. Feldman, ed., *Die Nachwirkungen der Inflation auf die deutsche Geschichte 1924–1933* (Munich: Oldenbourg. 1985).

11. Hans-Peter Ullmann, "Finance," in *The Cambridge History of the First World War*, ed. Jay Winter (Cambridge: Cambridge University Press, 2014); Adam Tooze, *Statistics and the German State, 1900–1945: The Making of Modern Economic Knowledge* (Cambridge: Cambridge University Press, 2001).

12. Michael Tomz, *Reputation and International Cooperation. Sovereign Debt across Three Centuries* (Princeton: Princeton University Press, 2007), 83.
13. For example, see, Patrick Bolton and Olivier Jeanne, *Structuring and Restructuring Sovereign Debt: The Role of a Bankruptcy Regime* (IMF Working Paper 07/192, 2007).
14. See Anthony Giddens, *The Constitution of Society. Outline of the Theory of Structuration* (Cambridge: Polity Press, 1984), esp. 15 and 25; William H. Sewell Jr., *Logics of History. Social Theory and Social Transformation* (Chicago/London: University of Chicago Press, 2005), esp. 143. For comments on some of the lacunae in Giddens' theory, see David Held and John B. Thompson, eds., *Social Theory of Modern Societies: Anthony Giddens and his critics* (Cambridge: Cambridge University Press, 1989).
15. See also, D'Maris Coffman, Adrian Leonhard, and Larry Neal, eds., *Questioning Credible Commitment: Perspectives on the Rise of Financial Capitalism* (Cambridge: Cambridge University Press, 2013).
16. Stephen W. Sawyer, "Foucault and the State," *La Revue Tocqueville* 36, no. 1 (2015): 135–164; Timothy Mitchell, "Society, Economy, and the State Effect," in *State / Culture. State-Formation After the Cultural Turn*, ed. George Steinmetz (Ithaca: Cornell University Press, 1999), 93; for a contemporary perception, see Carl Schmitt, "Demokratie und Finanz," in Idem, *Positionen und Begriffe im Kampf mit Weimar – Genf – Versailles 1923–1939* (Berlin: Duncker & Humblot, 1988 [1940]), 85–87.
17. For the theoretical discussion, see Anthony Giddens, *The Nation-State and Violence. Volume Two of a Contemporary Critique of Historical Materialism* (Berkeley/Los Angeles: University of California Press, 1987), 120; Colin Hay, "Neither Real nor Fictitious but 'as if Real'? A Political Ontology of the State," *The British Journal of Sociology* 65, no. 3 (2014): 459–480; Aradhana Sharma and Akhil Gupta, eds., *The Anthropology of the State. A Reader* (Oxford: Blackwell, 2006).
18. Petersson, *Anarchie*, 105–107.
19. Niall Ferguson, *The Pity of War* (London: Penguin, 1999), 128–135; Rudolf Kroboth, *Die Finanzpolitik des Deutschen Reiches während der Reichskanzlerschaft Bethmann Hollwegs und die Geld- und Kapitalmarktverhältnisse (1909–1913)* (Frankfurt: Peter Lang, 1986), 89–95.
20. Konrad Roesler, *Die Finanzpolitik des Deutschen Reiches im Ersten Weltkrieg* (Berlin: Duncker & Humblot, 1967), 207; Klaus Lapp, *Die Finanzierung der Weltkriege 1914/18 und 1939/45 in Deutschland. Eine wirtschafts- und finanzpolitische Untersuchung* (Ph. diss., University of Nuremberg 1957), 102; Gerd Hardach, "Die finanzielle Mobilmachung in Deutschland 1914–1918," *Jahrbuch für Wirtschaftsgeschichte* 56, no. 2 (2017): 367, 371–373; MacDonald, *Free Nation*, 407–413.

21. Roesler, *Finanzpolitik*, 56, 77, 133–134, 144–145.
22. Peter-Christian Witt, "Finanzpolitik und sozialer Wandel in Krieg und Inflation 1918–1924," in *Industrielles System und politische Entwicklung in der Weimarer Republik*, vol. 1, eds. Hans Mommsen, Dietmar Petzina and Bernd Weisbrod (Düsseldorf: Droste, 1977), 395–426.
23. See Art. 254, 255, 257 reg. state succession, In *Wörterbuch des Völkerrechts*, vol. 1, ed. Hans-Jürgen Schlochauer (Berlin: de Gruyter, 1960), 112.
24. See Adam Tooze, *The Deluge. The Great War, America and the Remaking of Global Order 1916–1931* (New York: Viking, 2014), 271–304; Mark Mazower, *Governing the World. The Rise and Fall of an Idea, 1815 to the Present* (New York: Penguin, 2012), chap. 5.
25. Gerald D. Feldman, *The Great Disorder. Politics, Economics, and Society in the German Inflation 1914–1924* (New York: Oxford University Press, 1997); Carl-Ludwig Holtfrerich, *Die deutsche Inflation 1914–1923. Ursachen und Folgen in internationaler Perspektive* (Berlin: de Gruyter, 1980); Niall Ferguson, "Constraints and Room for Manœuvre in the German Inflation of the Early 20s," *The Economic History Review* 49, no. 4 (1996): 636–666.
26. Stephen A. Schuker, *American "Reparations" to Germany, 1919–1933. Implications for the Third-World Debt Crisis* (Internat. Finance Sect., Dep. of Economics, Princeton University, 1988); Carl-Ludwig Holtfrerich, "Amerikanischer Kapitalexport und Wiederaufbau der deutschen Wirtschaft 1919–1923 im Vergleich zu 1924–1929," in *Die Weimarer Republik, belagerte civitas*, ed. Michael Stürmer (Königstein: Athenäum, 1985), 131–157.
27. Alfred Manes, *Staatsbankrotte. Wirtschaftliche und rechtliche Betrachtungen*, rev. ed. (Berlin: Siegismund, 1919), 22, 143–144, 159; Otto Schwarz, "Vermeidung des Staatsbankrotts," in *Handbuch der Politik, vol. 4*, ed. Gerhard Anschütz (Berlin: Rothschild, 1921), 49–54. For related debates see Odette Lienau, *Rethinking Sovereign Debt. Politics, Reputation, and Legitimacy in Modern Finance* (Cambridge, Mass.: Harvard University Press, 2014), chap. 3; for the Soviet case Lyndon Moore and Jakub Kaluzny, "Regime Change and Debt Default: The Case of Russia, Austro-Hungary, and the Ottoman Empire following World War One," *Explorations in Economic History* 42, no. 2 (2005): 237–258; Hassan Malik, *Bankers and Bolsheviks: International Finance and the Russian Revolution, 1892–1922* (Princeton: Princeton University Press, 2018), 162–207; Jennifer Siegel, *For Peace and Money: French and British Finance in the Service of the Tsars and Commissars* (Oxford: Oxford University Press, 2014), chap. 5; Kim Oosterlinck, *Hope Springs Eternal: French Bondholders and the Repudiation of Russian Sovereign Debt* (New Haven: Yale University Press, 2016).

28. Rudolf Goldscheid, *Sozialisierung der Wirtschaft oder Staatsbankerott. Ein Sanierungsprogramm* (Leipzig: Anzengruber,1919).
29. Georg Bresin, *Zum kommenden Staatsbankrott! Finanzreform oder Finanzrevolution? Wege zum Wiederaufbau* (Berlin: Verl. Volkspolitik, 1919); Wilhelm Albert Gatzen, *Deutscher Staatsbankerott. Die Maßnahmen zu seiner Verhütung und zur Hebung der Valuta* (Munich: Ante Portas, 1920); Otto Maaß, *Wie schützen wir uns vor dem Staatsbankrott?* (Erfurt: Freiland-Freigeld-Verlag, [1922]); Paul Beusch, "Deutschlands Verschuldung an das Ausland," in *Handbuch der Politik*, 7–13.
30. Petersson, *Anarchie*, 65–66.
31. The economic relevance of foreign debt is depicted by Albrecht Ritschl, *Deutschlands Krise und Konjunktur 1924–1934. Binnenkonjunktur, Auslandsverschuldung und Reparationsproblem zwischen Dawes-Plan und Transfersperre* (Berlin: Akademie, 2002); William C. McNeil, *American Money and the Weimar Republic. Economics and Politics on the Eve of the Great Depression* (New York: Columbia University Press, 1986).
32. Foreign Office Note "Empfiehlt sich ein Zusammengehen mit Frankreich in der Reparationspolitik bzw. in der Politik zur Liquidierung des Dawes-Plans?," cf. Petersson, *Anarchie*, 121; Peter Krüger, *Die Außenpolitik der Republik von Weimar* (Darmstadt: Wiss. Buchgesellschaft, 1993), 356–360; Manfred Berg, *Gustav Stresemann und die Vereinigten Staaten von Amerika. Weltwirtschaftliche Verflechtung und Revisionspolitik, 1909–1929* (Baden-Baden: Nomos, 1990).
33. *Die Sachverständigen-Gutachten. Die Berichte der von der Reparationskommission eingesetzten beiden Sachverständigenkomitees vom 9. April 1924 nebst allen Anlagen* (Berlin: Dt. Verlagsges. f. Pol. u. Gesch., 1924), 3; Michael L. Hughes, *Paying for the German Inflation* (Chapel Hill, NC: University of North Carolina Press, 1988), 119.
34. Stephen A. Schuker, "Money Doctors Between the Wars: The Competition between Central Banks, Private Financial Advisers and Multilateral Agencies, 1919–1939," in *Money Doctors. The Experience of International Financial Advising 1850–2000*, ed. Marc Flandreau (London: Routledge, 2003), 49–77; idem, "Europe's Bankers. The American Banking Community and European Reconstruction, 1918–1922," in *A Missed Opportunity? 1922: The Reconstruction of Europe*, eds. Marta Petricioli and Massimiliano Guderzo (Bern: Peter Lang, 1995), 47–59; Liaquat Ahamed, *Lords of Finance. The Bankers Who Broke the World* (New York: Penguin, 2009).
35. Petersson, *Anarchie*, 148; Rudolf Stucken, "Schaffung der Reichsmark, Reparationsregelungen und Auslandsanleihen, Konjunkturen (1924–1930)," in *Währung und Wirtschaft in Deutschland 1876–1975*, ed. Deutsche Bundesbank (Frankfurt: Knapp, 1976), 253.

36. Thomas Mergel, *Parlamentarische Kultur in der Weimarer Republik. Politische Kommunikation, symbolische Politik und Öffentlichkeit im Reichstag* (Düsseldorf: Droste, 2012), 399–408.
37. Patricia Clavin, "'Money Talks': Competition and Cooperation with the League of Nations, 1929–1940," in Flandreau, *Money Doctors*, 291–248; Zara Steiner, *The Lights that Failed. European International History 1919–1933* (Oxford: Oxford University Press, 2005), 369–371; Roman Köster, *Die Wissenschaft der Außenseiter. Die Krise der Nationalökonomie in der Weimarer Republik* (Göttingen: Vandenhoeck & Ruprecht, 2011), 101–112.
38. Ursula Bachmann, *Reichskasse und öffentlicher Kredit in der Weimarer Republik, 1924–1932* (Frankfurt: Peter Lang, 1996), 101–103.
39. Bericht des Reichsbankpräsidenten über währungs- und finanzpolitische Fragen, March 7, 1927, Akten der Reichskanzlei, Kabinett Marx III/IV, vol. 1, doc. no. 195, http://www.bundesarchiv.de/aktenreichskanzlei/1919-1933/0000/ma3/ma31p/kap1_2/para2_195.html
40. Theo Balderston, *The Origins and Course of the German Economic Crisis, November 1923 to May 1932* (Berlin: Haude & Spener, 1993), 271–277.
41. Dyson, *States*, 104; Frank Partnoy, *The Match King. Ivar Kreuger, the Financial Genius behind a Century of Wall Street Scandals* (London: Profile, 2009); "The Kreuger Tragedy," *The Economist*, March 19, 1932, cf. Schuker, *Money Doctors*, 54.
42. Cf. Harold James, *The Reichsbank and Public Finance in Germany 1924–1933. A Study of the Politics of Economics during the Great Depression* (Frankfurt: Knapp, 1985), 111; Ron Chernow, *House of Morgan. An American Banking Dynasty and the Rise of Modern Finance* (New York: Atlantic Monthly Press, 1990). See also Yvonne Wong, *Sovereign Finance and the Poverty of Nations. Odious Debt in International Law* (Cheltenham/Northampton, MA: Edward Elgar, 2012).
43. Ritschl, *Krise*, 133–135.
44. See James, *Reichsbank*, 95–118.
45. See Helmut Müller, *Die Zentralbank – eine Nebenregierung. Reichsbankpräsident Hjalmar Schacht als Politiker der Weimarer Republik* (Opladen: Westdt. Verlag, 1973), 38–43; Jürgen Flaskamp, *Aufgaben und Wirkungen der Reichsbank in der Zeit des Dawes-Planes* (Bergisch-Gladbach: Eul, 1986), 20–24.
46. Ritschl, *Krise*, 135; Dieter Hertz-Eichenrode, *Wirtschaftskrise und Arbeitsbeschaffung. Konjunkturpolitik 1925/26 und die Grundlagen der Krisenpolitik Brünings* (Frankfurt: Campus, 1982), 235–246; Stefanie Middendorf, "Finanzpolitische Fundamente der Demokratie? Haushaltsordnung, Ministerialbürokratie und Staatsdenken in der Weimarer Republik," in *Normalität und Fragilität. Demokratie nach dem*

Ersten Weltkrieg, eds. Tim B. Müller and Adam Tooze (Hamburg: Hamburger Edition, 2015), 315–343.
47. Balderston, *Origins*, 275–276.
48. Ministerbesprechung, April 22, 1929, Akten der Reichskanzlei, Kabinett Müller II, vol. 1, doc. no. 179, http://www.bundesarchiv.de/aktenreichskanzlei/1919-1933/0000/mu2/mu21p/kap1_2/kap2_179/para3_4.html
49. Bachmann, *Reichskasse*, 154–155, 182; Peter-Christian Witt, "Die Auswirkungen der Inflation auf die Finanzpolitik des Deutschen Reiches 1924–1933," in Feldman, *Nachwirkungen*, 43–95.
50. Christoph Müller, *Die Entstehung des Reichsgesetzes über das Kreditwesen vom 5. Dezember 1934* (Berlin: Duncker & Humblot, 2003), 442; Susanne Lütz, *Der Staat und die Globalisierung von Finanzmärkten. Regulative Politik in Deutschland, Großbritannien und den USA* (Frankfurt: Campus, 2002), 121–122.
51. Johannes Bähr, "Modernes Bankrecht und dirigistische Kapitallenkung. Die Ebenen der Steuerung im Finanzsektor des 'Dritten Reichs,'" in *Wirtschaftskontrolle und Recht in der nationalsozialistischen Diktatur*, ed. Dieter Gosewinkel (Frankfurt: Klostermann, 2005), 199–223; Christopher Kopper, "Kreditlenkung im nationalsozialistischen Deutschland," in *Banken, Konjunktur und Politik. Beiträge zur Geschichte deutscher Banken im 19. und 20. Jahrhundert*, eds. Manfred Köhler and Keith Ulrich (Essen: Klartext, 1995), 117–128.
52. Gerald D. Feldman, *Allianz and the German Insurance Business, 1933–1945* (Cambridge: Cambridge University Press, 2001), 39–40.
53. Patrick O. Cohrs, *The Unfinished Peace after World War I. America, Britain and the Stabilisation of Europe, 1919–1932* (Cambridge: Cambridge University Press, 2006), 573, 578–79; Gianni Toniolo, *Central Bank Cooperation at the Bank for International Settlements, 1930–1973* (Cambridge: Cambridge University Press, 2005), 114.
54. Willi A. Boelcke, *Die Kosten von Hitlers Krieg. Kriegsfinanzierung und finanzielles Kriegserbe in Deutschland, 1933–1948* (Paderborn: Schöningh, 1985), 24.
55. Patricia Clavin, *The Failure of Economic Diplomacy. Britain, Germany, France and the United States, 1931–1936* (Basingstoke: Palgrave Macmillan, 1996); idem, *Securing the World Economy. The Reinvention of the League of Nations, 1920–1946* (Oxford: Oxford University Press, 2013), chap. 3.
56. Toniolo, *Central Bank Cooperation*, 150–157.
57. Ibid, 154; Peter Berger, *Im Schatten der Diktatur. Die Finanzdiplomatie des Vertreters des Völkerbundes in Österreich, Meinoud Marinus Rost van Tonningen 1931–1936* (Vienna: Böhlau, 2000), 356–368; see also the dia-

ries of the former state secretary Hans Schaeffer, held at Institut für Zeitgeschichte Munich, ED 93-11.
58. Letter from Brüning to Norman Ebutt, June 11, 1946, cf. *Heinrich Brüning. Briefe und Gespräche 1934–1945*, ed. Claire Nix (Stuttgart: DVA, 1974), 39; related reports in the Hugo Fritz Berger Papers, Bundesarchiv (BArch) N 1181/60 and N 1181/77.
59. Tomz, *Reputation*, 182–190.
60. Albrecht Ritschl, *The German Transfer Problem, 1920–1933. A Sovereign Debt Perspective* (CEP Discussion Paper 1155, 2012).
61. Toniolo, *Central Bank Cooperation*, 228–231, 381: Karl Blessing, who had served on the BIS staff in the early 1930s, would become president of the German Bundesbank in 1958.
62. C. Edmund Clingan, *Finance from Kaiser to Führer. Budget Politics in Germany 1912–1934* (Westport, Conn.: Greenwood Press, 2001), 224.
63. Boelcke, *Kosten*, 24–25; Lutz Graf Schwerin von Krosigk, *Nationalsozialistische Finanzpolitik* [typescript, s.d.], 17, BArch R 2 / 24176.
64. Boelcke, *Kosten*, 25; Siegfried Schulze, *Wandlungen in der staatlichen Kreditpolitik der Großmächte* (Jena: G. Fischer, 1940), 115.
65. Bayrhoffer to Minister, January 19, 1935, BArch R 2 / 3402; Reinhardt to Hess, June 28,1937, BArch R 2 / 3248.
66. Karl-Heinrich Hansmeyer and Rolf Caesar, "Kriegswirtschaft und Inflation (1936–1948)," in Bundesbank, *Währung*, 380–386; Joachim Beer, *Der Funktionswandel der deutschen Wertpapierbörsen in der Zwischenkriegszeit (1924–1939)* (Frankfurt: Peter Lang, 1999).
67. Thorsten Beckers, *Kapitalmarktpolitik im Wiederaufbau. Der westdeutsche Wertpapiermarkt zwischen Staat und Wirtschaft 1945–1957* (Stuttgart: Steiner, 2014), 48; *Die Verschuldung Deutschlands*, ed. Reichswirtschaftskammer (Berlin: no publ., 1939).
68. André Botur, *Privatversicherung im Dritten Reich. Zur Schadensabwicklung nach der Reichskristallnacht unter dem Einfluß nationalsozialistischer Rassen- und Versicherungspolitik* (Berlin: Spitz, 1995), 66–67; Dieter Stiefel, *Die österreichischen Lebensversicherungen und die NS-Zeit. Wirtschaftliche Entwicklung – politischer Einfluss – jüdische Polizzen* (Vienna: Böhlau, 2001), 153–154; Peter Borscheid, *Mit Sicherheit leben. Die Geschichte der deutschen Lebensversicherungswirtschaft und der Provinzial-Lebensversicherungsanstalt von Westfalen*, vol. 1 (Münster: Westfäl. Provinzial, 1989), 142.
69. Michiyoshi Oshima, "Von der Rüstungsfinanzierung zum Reichsbankgesetz 1939," *Economic History Yearbook* 47 (2006): 177–217.
70. Geheime Reichssache, Richtlinien für die künftige Rüstungsfinanzierung, March 10, 1938, BArch R 2 / 3845.

71. Stefanie Middendorf and Kim Christian Priemel, "Jenseits des Primats. Kontinuitäten der nationalsozialistischen Finanz- und Wirtschaftspolitik," in *Kontinuitäten und Diskontinuitäten. Der Nationalsozialismus in der Geschichte des 20. Jahrhunderts*, eds. Birthe Kundrus and Sybille Steinbacher (Göttingen: Wallstein, 2013), 106–108.
72. Oberkommando der Wehrmacht, Der gegenwärtige Stand der Reichsfinanzen, October 14, 1938, 9, BArch RW 19 / 1582.
73. Schulze, *Wandlungen*, 163–167; Bank für Internationalen Zahlungsausgleich, *Jahresbericht* 14 (1943/44), Basel 1944, 182.
74. Bank für Internationalen Zahlungsausgleich, *Jahresbericht* 12 (1941/42), Basel 1942, 202.
75. Günter Schmölders, *Wirtschaftslenkung als angewandte Wirtschaftswissenschaft. Festrede, gehalten bei der Feier des Tages der nationalsozialistischen Erhebung, 29. Januar 1941* (Köln: O. Müller, 1941), 23.
76. Relevant data for comparative approaches can be found in S. M. Ali Abbas et al., *Sovereign Debt Composition in Advanced Economies: A Historical Perspective* (IMF Working Papers 14/162, 2014); Moritz Schularick, "Public Debt and Financial Crises in the Twentieth Century," *European Review of History/Revue européene d'histoire* 19, no. 6 (2012): 881–897.
77. See Chap. 14 on Iraq and Syria by Matthieu Rey in this volume.
78. See Chap. 13 by Etienne Forestier-Peyrat and Kristy Ironside in this volume.
79. Hans Möller, ed., *Die Vorgeschichte der deutschen Mark. Die Währungsreformpläne 1945–1948. Eine Dokumentation* (Basel: Kyklos, 1961); Michael Brackmann, *Vom totalen Krieg zum Wirtschaftswunder. Die Vorgeschichte der westdeutschen Währungsreform 1948* (Essen: Klartext, 1993), 191–200, 231–283.
80. "Die erste Bundesanleihe am Start," *Die ZEIT*, November 27, 1952; Wilhelmine Dreißig, "Zur Entwicklung der öffentlichen Finanzwirtschaft seit dem Jahre 1950," in Bundesbank, *Währung*, 728–733; G. Bruns and Karl Häuser, eds., *30 Jahre Kapitalmarkt in der Bundesrepublik Deutschland* (Frankfurt: Knapp, 1981), 188, 191.
81. Gerd Müller, "Unterstützung der Gesamtwirtschaft und Sicherung des Sparers," *Versicherungswirtschaft* 6, no. 12 (1951): 249.
82. Friederike Sattler, "Das Geschäft mit den Staatsschulden. Banken, Staatsschulden und die Securization of Debt nach der Ölpreiskrise von 1973/1974," *Geschichte und Gesellschaft* 41, no. 3 (2015): 422. For similar developments in France, yet with different temporalities, see Benjamin Lemoine, "Les 'dealers' de la dette souveraine. Politique des transactions entre banques et État dans la grande distribution des emprunts français," *Sociétés contemporaines* 92, no. 4 (2013): 59–88.
83. Karl Häuser, "Die Rolle des Staates auf dem Kapitalmarkt," in *30 Jahre Kapitalmarkt*, 105.

84. Bob Jessop, *State Theory. Putting the Capitalist State in its Place* (Cambridge: Polity, 1990), 9–10.
85. Brackmann, *Krieg*, 88–102.
86. See Chap. 15 by Benjamin Lemoine and Anush Kapadia in this volume as well as Benjamin Lemoine, "The Politics of Public Debt Financialisation: (Re)Inventing the Market for French Sovereign Bonds and Shaping the Public Debt Problem (1966–2012)," in *The Political Economy of Public Finance. Taxation, State Spending and Debt since the 1970s*, eds. Marc Buggeln, Martin Daunton and Alexander Nützenadel (Cambridge: Cambridge University Press, 2017), 240–261; idem, *L'ordre de la dette. Enquête sur les infortunes de l'État et la prospérité du marché* (Paris: La Découverte, 2016).
87. Alexander Nützenadel, *Die Stunde der Ökonomen. Wissenschaft, Politik und Expertenkultur in der Bundesrepublik 1949–1974* (Göttingen: Vandenhoeck & Ruprecht, 2005), 18–19, 357–360; Hans-Peter Ullmann, *Das Abgleiten in den Schuldenstaat. Öffentliche Finanzen in der Bundesrepublik von den sechziger bis zu den achtziger Jahren* (Göttingen: Vandenhoeck & Ruprecht, 2017), 50–64.

CHAPTER 13

The Communist World of Public Debt (1917–1991): The Failure of a Countermodel?

Étienne Forestier-Peyrat and Kristy Ironside

Communists were among public debt's most vehement critics. Under capitalism, public debt purportedly offered opportunities for profit and necessitated increasing taxes for the poorest categories of the population in order for "bourgeois" states to repay it, while external debt was an instrument of exploitation in the hands of imperial powers.[1] Engels' prediction that the state would "wither away" also called into question what precisely qualified as state debt: should it be redefined to take into account

---

The original version of this chapter was revised. Correction to this chapter can be found at DOI https://doi.org/10.1007/978-3-030-48794-2_21

É. Forestier-Peyrat (✉)
Sciences Po Lille, Lille, France
e-mail: etienne.peyrat@sciencespo-lille.eu

K. Ironside
Department of History and Classical Studies, McGill University, Montreal, QC, Canada
e-mail: kristy.ironside@mcgill.ca

© The Author(s) 2020, corrected publication 2020
N. Barreyre, N. Delalande (eds.), *A World of Public Debts*, Palgrave Studies in the History of Finance,
https://doi.org/10.1007/978-3-030-48794-2_13

an expanded public sphere that was not limited to the state per se, but could encompass state-run companies, social organizations, trade unions, and other institutions that blurred the boundary between public and private debts? In January 1918, the Bolsheviks repudiated the Tsar's debts—a seemingly new and audacious but, in fact, not unprecedented measure that became known as the doctrine of "odious debt," or the argument that debts incurred by a fallen regime should not be transferred to a subsequent regime if the debt did not benefit nor was authorized by the population.[2] Public debt, it would seem, had no place in the communist world.

Over the course of the twentieth century, however, communist regimes proceeded to accumulate substantial debts, both foreign and domestic. Shortly after the repudiation, the Bolsheviks began aggressively pursuing foreign credit. When this was not forthcoming, they turned inward and, by the Stalin era, had devised a highly coercive system of domestic borrowing, accumulating billions of rubles in debt to the population on state loans with returns so questionable that the contemporary American economist and Sovietologist Franklyn D. Holzman labeled them a "hoax."[3] Other communist governments, notably China and Yugoslavia, implemented similarly aggressive domestic bond programs. After the Second World War, the Soviet Union became a foreign creditor itself, lending billions of rubles in money and in-kind to the so-called People's Democracies of Central and Eastern Europe who, in turn, joined it in becoming creditors to budding socialist countries in the postcolonial world. External debts helped build an interdependent communist economic bloc, but also bound together a shaky alliance dominated by Soviet interests.

Foreign and domestic debts, furthermore, proved to be important causes of communist regimes' undoing in the late twentieth century. Though many countries, notably the Soviet Union, were considered creditworthy by foreign lenders until the 1980s, declining economic growth, coupled with unsustainable promises of rising living standards, led them to go on borrowing sprees and develop massive unsustainable debts in the last two decades of their existence. Growing public awareness of long top-secret debts in the late 1980s, along with painful austerity measures, undermined the already tenuous legitimacy of these regimes, many of which had been installed and stayed in power through rigged elections and the repression of their opponents. Their gamble that borrowing from the West to pay for technological improvements would spur production and ultimately raise living standards was a bust; instead, they found themselves stuck with massive loans in currencies other than their own that they could not pay, and the increased hard-currency revenues that were expected from exports never materialized. As Stephen Kotkin writes, "the capitalists had sold the bloc the rope with which to hang itself."[4]

Addressing the relationship between communism and public debt in the twentieth century, as this chapter aims to do, allows for a mutual reassessment. Though early communists were deeply critical of the international-capitalist order of public debt and, by the postwar period, claimed to have created an alternative system of self-sacrificing domestic financing and brotherly "mutual assistance," they made relatively conventional use of public debts to further their political and economic agendas. Moreover, although they would repeatedly disappoint domestic creditors, another radical repudiation of their foreign debts, as had occurred in 1918, did not take place. Mature communist regimes proved unwilling to reject the international order of public debt when they ran into economic trouble, accepting technical solutions to their financial woes and avoiding confrontations with Western lenders. As the anthropologist Katherine Verdery observed, far from teaming up to collectively default in the late 1980s, their willingness to repay their debts revealed "how vital a thing was capitalists' monopoly on the definition of social reality."[5]

Public Debt Between Political Control and War Mobilization

In the immediate wake of the Russian Revolution, public debt seemed as if it would go the way of other relics of capitalism including profit, private property, and money, but the new authorities quickly sensed its value as a bargaining chip with the former Tsarist regime's creditors; furthermore, the new socialist regime was broke. During the Russian Civil War, foreign lenders did not abandon hope of getting at least some of their money back, as demonstrated by the relative optimism of the markets: in 1920, 1906 bonds were traded with a 20 percent yield to maturity.[6] Though they were in default, Tsarist bonds were not entirely worthless. In September 1921, Georgy Chicherin, the Commissar of Foreign Affairs, pushed the Politburo to tie resumption of payments to a political settlement with the Allies. An expert commission was created to develop concrete proposals on the debt issue. At the Genoa conference in April–May 1922, Soviet delegates proposed to resume paying some of the Tsar's debts, but also demanded an immediate large loan in exchange. France insisted that the Bolsheviks assume responsibility for Russia's debts. As negotiations broke down, Chicherin and his German counterpart, Walter Rathenau, signed a treaty at Rapallo canceling all financial claims against one another. For the remainder of the interwar period, the Bolsheviks continued to offer partial debt repayment in exchange for new credit and, in the context of the Great Depression, boasted of being a credible debtor at a time when many other countries were defaulting on their foreign debt.[7] They held out hope that they might receive funds from the United States into the 1930s.[8] These efforts proved unsuccessful: no one had forgotten about the repudiation, nor did they trust the communists.

This forced the Soviet Union to turn inward. During the New Economic Policy, the government floated several internal lottery loans which it promoted as a means of protecting the value of money against the problem of hyperinflation, which they inherited from the Tsar and exacerbated through continued excessive currency printing.[9] In 1926, at the dawn of the industrialization drive, citizens' incomes and savings were targeted as internal resources to be better exploited.[10] In 1927, the Soviet government successfully experimented with selling its State Internal 10 percent lottery bond directly to workers in Soviet workplaces, and the so-called "mass subscription bond" was born. Unlike so-called "market" or "free-circulating" bonds—lottery bonds which continued to be sold under socialism primarily to wealthier elites on a voluntary basis and which were fully liquid—mass subscription bonds were subject to strict quotas, participation was virtually compulsory, and cashing them in was virtually impossible. Ideally, workers subscribed for at least 100 percent of one month's average wage to be deducted in ten installments with a short reprieve before the next year's campaign began. Collective farmers, by contrast, were expected to contribute minimum lump sums based on their expected cash earnings from private agricultural production.

Removing bond sales from the marketplace allowed the government to exert considerable "moral pressure" upon subscribers.[11] Unlike Nazi Germany, a famous example of the use of "silent financing," as Middendorf's contribution in this volume (Chap. 12) discusses, the Soviet Union resorted to more explicitly coercive strategies to ensure citizens' compliance. Activists embedded in the workplace, known as the Commissions for Contributions to State Credit and Savings (*Komissiia sodeistviia goskreditu i sberegatel'nomu delu,* better known as *komsody*) lectured their peers on the bonds' vital contributions to socialist construction, and often threatened a subscriber with social and economic retaliation when he or she offered less than what was expected or less than everyone else. Although the bonds' purchase was never officially portrayed as anything but voluntary, secret police reports paid close attention to expressions of discontent related to their purchase, aware that many citizens were less than thrilled to subscribe.[12] The coercion involved in meeting subscription quotas, coupled with the bonds' low returns and repeated conversions in 1930, 1936, 1938, and 1947 that extended their terms and reduced interest rates, led the economist Holzman to conclude that they were taxes in all but name.[13]

During the Second World War, the tradition of mass mobilization prevented a collapse of the economy in its first months.[14] The Soviet government turned to war bonds as a source of war financing, as many other belligerents did, at this time. War bonds were sold on the existing mass-subscription model, and the Soviet press expatiated on the enormous sums workers and peasants contributed to defend the Motherland.[15] Issues rose to unprecedented levels: 10.3 billion rubles in 1942, 13.5 billion in 1943, 25.12 billion in 1944, and 25 billion in 1945. The war marked a culmination of the coercive social dynamics driving the mass-subscription campaigns: with the exception of the last, each bond was oversubscribed within about a week of its announcement. While before 1942, subscriptions among workers never reached the ideal sum of the average monthly wage, usually not surpassing two-thirds, in 1945, subscriptions reached 120 percent and even peasants met steep subscription expectations. Between 1940 and the end of 1944, state debt to the population on the bonds more than doubled, from over 39 billion to over 94 billion rubles.[16]

The Second World War also saw the Soviet Union engage more directly with foreign states in the field of public debt. On the eve of the war, in March 1938, the USSR financed the Guomindang's war against Japan with a substantial dollar loan.[17] During the war, the Soviet government finally received foreign loans in the form of credit in-kind from the United States through the Lend-Lease program.[18] After the war, Soviet diplomats were instructed to obtain more credit from the Americans. In a letter to State Secretary Byrnes on 15 March 1946, the *chargé d'affaires* Nikolai Novikov explained that the Soviet government was eager to receive long-term credit to finance reconstruction and suggested tying it to the conclusion of a trade agreement.[19] That the United States and their allies should provide loans to the Soviet Union was perceived by Soviet leaders as part of a moral compact acknowledging the wartime sacrifices of the Soviet people. Similar arguments were made by the Central European countries that soon fell into the Soviet sphere of influence when they asked for credit from the Bretton Woods institutions. Poland, Yugoslavia, and Czechoslovakia were among the first members of the International Monetary Fund (IMF) and the International Bank for Reconstruction and Development (IBRD) to express such claims. The reluctance of these institutions to provide the amounts demanded by Central European countries merely accelerated the rift between East and West in the burgeoning Cold War.

A Communist World of Public Debt?

As communist regimes sprang up across Europe and Asia in the late 1940s, a new communist world of public debt began to take shape. Accepting, rather than repudiating, the previous regimes' debts was one way the new Soviet-backed authorities in Central and Eastern Europe positioned themselves as legitimate heirs to the national state tradition immediately after the war. These debts, both internal and external, were largely contracted for the needs of state-building and some as early as the nineteenth century.[20] At the same time, these states resorted to conversions and monetary reforms designed, in part, to reduce domestic debts. For example, the 1947 currency reform in the USSR reduced state debt on mass subscription bonds from 158.8 billion to 58.8 billion rubles with additional billions in debt de facto canceled because the paper bonds were not turned in for conversion by the deadline.[21] Across Eastern Europe, communist regimes sought to renegotiate their foreign debts and, after 1948, became more assertive and antagonistic toward the West. After the Prague coup in February 1948, financial negotiations between communist Czechoslovakia and the United Kingdom were suspended but resumed a few months later as Czechoslovak leaders conceded a debt settlement in exchange for a trade agreement.[22]

Postwar communist regimes' emulation of the Soviet model of public debt is reflected in their aggressive use of domestic loans to finance reconstruction.[23] The Soviet government floated several "reconstruction and development" bonds and by 1951 a record-sized issue of 30 billion rubles was launched. Within just four years, the Soviet Union's domestic debt had risen to 146 billion rubles, up from 28.7 billion rubles in the wake of the currency reform.[24] After the communist victory in China, the financial mastermind of the regime, Chen Yun, initiated a similar mass loan that called upon citizens' patriotism and emphasized the bonds' stabilizing effect on the economy in an effort to gain support from economic elites on the coast.[25] In Yugoslavia, slogans for its 1948 loan ranged from "Subscribing to the loan is the best patriotic act of every individual" to "Subscription to the national loan is the best way to invest your savings, since it pays 10 percent interest a year and lasts only four years."[26] A second National Loan followed in August–September 1950 with an intensified propaganda campaign and increased canvassing in the countryside. However, popular "enthusiasm" for the bonds proved elusive; the population complained about arrears on the first loan and about the economic difficulties their purchase entailed.

The consolidation of communist regimes in the late 1940s generated increasing tensions between them and international financial institutions (IFIs). In 1947, the political imbroglio surrounding the Polish and Czechoslovak Soviet-influenced rejection of the Marshall Plan revealed strong disagreements between communist politicians and other coalition members. The two states repeatedly complained of unfair treatment from IMF and the IBRD, despite being founding members of both institutions. Poland walked out of negotiations in March 1950 and Czechoslovakia refused to pay its share of capital, which led to its eventual expulsion in 1954.[27] The only exception to this was Yugoslavia. After the Tito-Stalin split in the spring of 1948, Western countries and IFIs took it upon themselves to "keep Tito afloat."[28] Yugoslav leaders pressured American diplomats for loans, which were necessary for the country's survival; at the same time, they tried to keep a low profile as they knew the Cominform would undoubtedly hold these loans against them.[29] The Yugoslav Politburo also never abandoned its distrust toward Western lenders, who sought to obtain political influence incommensurate with the relatively small amounts of credit they were ready to provide.[30] Yugoslav financial stakes with the West nonetheless contrasted with the communist bloc's drift toward an alternative communist community of credit.

Although the Soviet Union, in many respects, behaved like an "imperial scavenger" in Central Europe, it also became a major lender to other communist countries after the war.[31] Having forced its allies to refuse Marshall Plan aid, providing credit to rebuild their economies was necessary to bolster its legitimacy within the emerging Eastern bloc. Much of this debt was offered and expected to be repaid in-kind, in equipment, and in consumer goods. In January 1948, the USSR gave Poland 450 million rubles in credit in industrial equipment in order to create the steel complex of Nowa Huta, for example.[32] Simultaneously, Central European financial systems were refashioned along Soviet lines, and experts were sent to

Moscow to be trained by the State Bank and Ministry of Finance.[33] The People's Democracies were eager to exchange views and experience in dealing with debt issues with the West, as exemplified by Bulgarian solicitations to Yugoslavia, Hungary, Romania, and Poland to coordinate their behavior against Western creditors. Credit was also needed to prevent the natural trend toward autarky, a consequence of imitating the Soviet economic model. As a result, foreign debt to the Soviet Union grew rapidly between January 1951 and January 1956, by around 11.9 billion rubles, the vast majority of which constituted money loans and credit to the Peoples' Democracies in Central Europe. Poland alone owed 528 million rubles to the Soviet Union by 1955.[34]

Communist leaders and theoreticians emphasized that their practice of public debt fundamentally differed from Western conceptions of public debt, constituting fraternal "aid" and "mutual assistance." The absence of "surplus capital" in socialist economies supposedly changed the meaning of foreign credit.[35] Concrete differences between capitalist and socialist credits revolved more around technical details, however, such as lower interest rates and longer terms.[36] Advantageous conditions were particularly useful when courting Third World countries the Soviet government hoped would go communist, such as Sukarno's Indonesia, which obtained particularly low interest rates in the late 1950s.[37] Smaller, economically weaker countries in the Eastern bloc often emphasized their "backwardness" when attempting to reduce their debt burdens; for example, Albania and Mongolia regularly petitioned to reschedule or cancel outright their trade-related debt. At the end of 1957, the German Democratic Republic (GDR) conceded to the Albanian request to cancel the 61 million rubles in debt the republic had accumulated by 1955, but downplayed it publicly, as the write-off occurred simultaneously as it was asking East Germans to make great material sacrifices in the name of socialism. When the Albanian newspaper *Zeri i Popullit* published a letter of thanks to the GDR government, East German diplomats were embarrassed and tried to cover it up.[38] Similarly, Gomułka expressed his impatience with frequent demands by Mongolia to write off its debt during Comecon meetings, viewing it as a matter-of-fact necessity to honor one's debts.[39]

The solidarity supposedly underwriting communist mutual assistance within the Comecon was tested by the Hungarian revolt in the fall of 1956. Sizable deficits in its balance of payments had made Hungary dependent on Western credit by the 1950s; Imre Nagy and Mátyás Rákosi wanted to reduce this dependence through Soviet loans.[40] After the "counterrevolution" was crushed, the new Hungarian leadership asked all "friendly countries" for economic help through state and commercial credits in goods and currencies to the tune of 455 million dollars.[41] All communist countries offered help in the form of credit, as their contribution to the fight against counterrevolutionary forces. Zhou Enlai, who was on a tour of Central European countries in early 1956, made grandiose announcements about the Chinese government's support for Kádár's government in an effort to prop up his own country's importance within the bloc.[42] However, this channeling of socialist aid to Hungary also revealed its deepening rifts.

The Problem with Western Loans

The increasing use of foreign loans in communist countries was directly linked to their attempts to reform socialist economic systems and correct imbalances through market mechanisms in the 1960s. An alarming decline in growth rates in 1960–1962 prompted communist leaders to pay more attention to the limits of the Stalinist model of industrialization and collectivization. Reform programs were articulated in several countries. International institutions such as the UN's Economic Commission for Europe and the Bank for International Settlements (BIS) also played important roles in East-West policy and intellectual transfers.[43] These reform programs shifted economies toward external sources of growth. Foreign credit was sought in an attempt to secure much-needed technologies and licenses from the West. Under Khrushchev, the development of new sectors, such as chemical and car industries, was boosted by foreign inputs, financed in part by borrowing.[44] Foreign borrowing was particularly important in countries like Bulgaria and Romania, who wanted to overcome economic "backwardness" and develop full-fledged modern industries. Furthermore, the failure of economic integration within the Comecon and increasing assertion of "national sovereignty" made the pursuit of Western credit particularly important, a fact emphasized by the Romanian leadership in its famous declaration of independence in April 1964 when it refused to become the Comecon's agricultural base.[45] Lack of integration led to the replication of productive capacities throughout the bloc, accelerating indebtedness in the mid-1960s.

Acquiring foreign debt was seen as a painless process that would repay itself thanks to exports generated by industrial investments and licenses. It appeared to be a miracle solution for communist regimes trying to achieve stabilization and fight growing social unrest caused, in part, by their populations' mounting economic grievances. While the USSR could finance a more generous social welfare policy with revenues from oil and raw commodity exports until the mid-1970s, other countries developed dependence upon foreign lenders to finance their welfare agendas. This was not yet seen as worrying. Economic planners often saw foreign trade and financial obligations as a beneficial form of external discipline imposed on domestic actors, recreating a lacking market constraint. In Czechoslovakia, the reforms of the late 1960s emphasized the need to relaunch industrial competitiveness thanks to the external constraint of trade with the West.[46] External debt was perceived across the bloc as a way to defuse tensions and engineer a new wave of industrialization without requiring material deprivation and sacrifices on the part of their citizens.

Yugoslavia enjoyed rapid growth based on IBRD and IMF credit due to its closeness with the West and, unlike in other communist societies, where borrowing practices were concealed from the public and figures strictly classified, foreign credit was openly discussed there. Concerns about financial transfers and inequality between Yugoslavia's constituent units were mediated by discussions of foreign loans. In the summer of 1969, a major crisis emerged between the federal government and Slovenia over loans the IBRD had postponed, an action the Slovenes attributed to federal maneuvering. This crisis, known as the "road affair" because the funds were originally earmarked for the construction of two highways, sparked demonstrations in Slovenia and attacks on the federal government by Slovene authorities.[47] This debt-induced crisis was a landmark event in Yugoslav history, for it resulted in a constitutional revision which considerably extended the prerogatives of the republics and self-managing organizations.[48] This, in turn, facilitated a significant rise in public debt, disseminating it across a vast array of public and semi-public organizations. Until then, it was the federal government and Central Bank that had contracted the overwhelming majority of foreign loans; from 1968 to 1981, the share of federally endorsed external debt fell from 95.1 percent to 34.1 percent.[49]

Post-1969 Yugoslavia was an example, albeit an extreme one, of the manner in which external credit hunger was fueled by internal structural transformations, whereby the communist state's traditional monopoly on foreign trade and external financial relations was weakened. While intergovernmental or government-backed trade credits had made up the bulk of communist external debt in the 1960s, private debt contracted with

European, American, and Japanese banks went up in the 1970s. Foreign trade banks expanded their competency against central banks, as well as other investment, industrial, and agricultural banks, and an ever wider array of foreign trade actors.[50] This multiplication of actors coincided with intensified contacts in financial marketplaces and Eastern European countries' growing presence in the emerging Euromarkets. The international networks established by Soviet-controlled banks such as the Moscow Narodny Bank and the Eurobank illustrate the increasing integration which facilitated financing in Western currencies.[51] The status of external debt was therefore progressively changed in nature. It was contracted by actors who were often only remotely controlled by central-state decision makers. If this debt could be considered public, it partially defied the notion of central planning and ratification at the highest level, a situation some criticized as dangerous.

Foreign debt became a key issue for communist regimes during the period 1969–1972. By then, taking out foreign credit was a well-established practice, but Soviet leaders, in particular, were discomfited by how quickly their debts were rising. On 27 April 1971, the East German general secretary Walter Ulbricht was dismissed by the SED Politburo and the new leadership committed itself to reestablishing the primacy of economic relations with the Eastern bloc, disavowing Ulbricht's strong dependence upon Western credit and technology.[52] Debt was the recurring subject of top-secret central reports. In an August 1973 report to the Politburo, Konstantin Katushev, secretary of the Soviet Central Committee for relations with communist countries, emphasized the burden of foreign debts for all Central European countries. Anatoly Chernyaev remarked in his diary: "Everywhere the economy is going down. All these countries hold a considerable debt in Western currencies (in particular Bulgaria and Romania)."[53] This concern was expressed in private meetings with Central European leaders as early as 1970, and Brezhnev routinely emphasized the Soviet Union's inability to come to the rescue of failing debtors due to the burden it had already taken upon itself in the name of socialism.[54]

Attempts were made to rejuvenate the Comecon and, in turn, foster greater bloc integration.[55] Two banks were created to facilitate trade and international investments, but they failed to prevent further financial dependence upon the West. The most illustrative example was the Romanian decision to seek financial support in the Bretton Woods institutions that seemed to provide cheaper means for development. Interest in the IBRD and IMF grew in all communist countries at the end of the

1960s, with the creation of the Special Drawing Rights (SDRs) in 1969 but also with the renewed credit activism of the World Bank group. Reports were produced within the Comecon and in national institutions about them, and the temptation to use them as new sources to resolve balance of payment problems and finance investment grew. In January 1970, a report by the Romanian Bank for Foreign Trade emphasized the advantages of the SDRs and suspected that the USSR, Hungary, and Poland might be interested by joining the IMF.[56] Communist countries indeed seemed caught between different imperatives. On the one hand, Comecon reports criticized the IMF and the IBRD as "tools of imperialism" and tried to create their own financial institutions. On the other hand, several states were tempted to branch out on their own. In late 1971 and October 1972, Romania blocked attempts by Comecon organs to adopt a joint position toward the Bretton Woods organs as they were in the midst of negotiations with them.[57] Although Romania made its project known to other Comecon countries in May 1972, its adhesion to both organs in December 1972 came as a thunderbolt.[58]

Silent Financing and Its Discontents

While some Communist leaders began to worry about the growth of foreign loans, domestic debt was also becoming a cause for concern. Following Stalin's death in March 1953, the quasi-compulsory mass subscription bonds came under increased scrutiny as contradicting the new emphasis on raising living standards. Expected subscription amounts for low-earning citizens were scaled down and republic authorities were informed during the 1955 campaign that "observance of the voluntary principle" was now expected of them—in other words, to reduce the emphasis on coercive mobilizational tactics that helped to ratchet up subscriptions and the state's debt on the bonds.[59] The Ministry of Finance also began to warn that payments on the bonds for interest and prizes could not continue at current levels due to the burden on state finances and the inflationary risks associated with introducing billions of rubles into circulation in the form of interest, prizes, and redemption payments, money that could not be matched by consumer supply. In 1956, Minister of Finance Arseny Zverev predicted that, by 1960, state payments would reach 37.7 billion rubles, up from 30.2 rubles in 1955, or a rise of 25 percent. The government, by then, owed 228 billion on the bonds. By the end of the sixth Five-Year Plan, that would rise to an estimated 350 billion and, by 1960, the Soviet government would have to make 21.5 billion rubles in payments, he emphasized. Bondholders were poised to "recapture a real nest egg, possibly worth two or three times what [they] had paid for it," in the words of long-time critic of the bonds, Franklyn D. Holzman.[60]

In March 1957, the presidium of the Party Central Committee decided to abolish the bonds, leaving them "in the hands of the bondholders (as a symbol of their investment in the common project of building socialism)."[61] That April, in meetings with workers and peasants in Gorkii, Khrushchev came clean about the size of the state's debt—by then, around 260 billion rubles.[62] Though they had played a crucial role in financing socialist development, Khrushchev explained, the mass bonds had become a drain on state finances. The government was stuck in a "vicious cycle" because payments rose with each passing year: he estimated that in 1957, around 16–17 billion rubles would be spent on prizes and redemption payments, while in 1958, the government would pay 18 billion rubles and, by 1967, 25 billion rubles—almost the entire sum that would be obtained from planned proceeds of the bonds in 1957.[63] As a result, the government planned to halt all future issues as of 1 January, 1958 and freeze payments on existing bonds for 20 years. A "light bond" of 12 billion rubles was issued in 1957 instead of the planned bond of 26 billion. Despite the massive unpopularity of the move and accusations that the Soviet government had stolen "our only savings," a recurring line in letters of complaint, the last mass subscription bond was significantly oversubscribed.

The abolition of mass domestic loan programs was progressively implemented by all communist regimes. The aforementioned rise of external debt as the major source of economic and technological investment reduced the importance of such domestic borrowing, and socio-political stabilization diminished the need for and advantages of Stalinist mobilization methods. This paralleled a broader shift ongoing elsewhere, as illustrated by Matthieu Rey in his chapter on Iraq and Syria (Chap. 14), which increasingly turned to international organizations like the IBRD for loans to finance their development. The only country that continued to rely upon domestic mass-mobilization methods was China, now in open conflict with the Soviet Union. Mao emphasized the need for domestic debt to ensure popular support for the Great Leap Forward and because "the Soviets wanted their money back," a slogan that played upon popular rhetoric about usurers.[64] The end of these mass loans did not mean the end of domestic debt in communist countries, but a turn toward forms of silent financing, at a time when other non-communist nations did the same thing.[65] The phrase is particularly apt as all countries featured high levels of secrecy and dissimulation in official publications about the economy and the size of their public debts.[66] Financial experts in communist countries generally denied the existence of macroeconomic imbalances that justified deficits in capitalist economies. The existence of a budget deficit was never officially recognized by communist governments; instead, deficits were financed by direct transfers from the State banks and savings banks.[67] Savings steadily increased in these countries: in the USSR, they rose from 10 billion rubles in 1959 to 131 billion rubles in 1978.[68] This system was far from uncommon in post-1945 Western Europe, but was progressively abandoned in the 1970s, at a time when communist regimes increasingly relied upon it.

Internally, communist central bankers voiced criticism not dissimilar to what led to major reforms in Western countries. In the Soviet Union, the State Bank complained in November 1966 about the "insincerity" of the state budget for 1967, which featured an official deficit of 2.9 billion rubles, "whereas the actual budget deficit would be much higher," due to the manipulation of financial data. The short-term resources of the State Bank were used to finance long-term state investment, a policy opposed by the State Bank, to no avail.[69] A similar case was made by Nikola Lazarov, head of the research unit at the National Bank of Bulgaria, in July 1969. He reminded the government that the state budget had been replenished for several years by resources coming from the two main savings banks of the country, the DSK and the DZI. The state owed 1.1 billion levas to the DSK alone, since the DSK had transferred between 1954 and 1966 61 percent of all new savings to finance the hidden deficit of the state. The problem, Lazarov insisted, was that the Ministry of Finance did not intend in the least to pay this money back and only paid interest to the savings banks.[70]

This form of "silent financing," not dissimilar from the methods implemented in Nazi Germany, was facilitated by direct state control over intermediary financial institutions, such as savings banks and insurers. The major difference, however, lay in the absence of a context of mass mobilization through war, since silent financing was here a direct result of the transformations communist regimes had undergone since the 1950s: the rhetoric of material sacrifice inherent to domestic borrowing campaigns became incompatible with the promise of rising living standards and the population's savings had to be dealt with more carefully in order to avoid exacerbating inflationary pressures and depressing consumption.[71] The government had to accept the creation of a secondary market for state bonds in order to satisfy popular requests, although savings banks enjoyed advantageous conditions for buying back the bonds.[72] In the wake of the 1957 de facto default, the Soviet government enthusiastically promoted investing in "market bonds," that is, the 3 percent lottery bonds that were fully voluntary and liquid. A new 3 percent lottery bond was launched in 1966, converting the 1947 issue and reducing interest and prize payments; that issue was, in turn, converted in 1982. Repeatedly converting the bonds was unpopular: older citizens, in particular, lamented perpetually postponed repayment, complaining about low living standards and criticizing the younger generation for lacking their political consciousness when it came to making investments in socialism.[73] The Ministry of Finance diligently answered their letters, but held onto their investments, for now. The mass subscription bonds were not repaid until the mid-1970s, at which point inflation had undermined their value and many older bondholders had died without seeing the state's debt repaid.

TENSIONS AND DIVISIONS IN THE BLOC

The mounting contradictions of communist economies became obvious as Poland, Romania, Yugoslavia, and the GDR found themselves trapped in severe debt predicaments in the early 1980s. It is worth recalling, however, that the unity of the communist bloc was first tested in the mid-1970s. In September 1974, North Korea was the first communist country to suspend service on its debt, which was estimated at 400–700 million dollars, taking aback its creditors in the West and Asia.[74] They expected other communist countries to help the failing state, but no such solution was offered, since both China and the Soviet Union had grown impatient with the quirks of the North Korean regime by then. Western bankers who had lent money to North Korea were surprised by the lack of solidarity between communist countries, in contradiction with the basic assumption they had made until then. This forgotten debt crisis had the short-term effect of turning North Korea once again into a political and economic "Hermit Kingdom" after a decade of expanding contacts with the noncommunist world.

North Korea may have been odd enough a country to be discarded as an exception by Western financiers, but its default coincided with a growing awareness that foreign debt in the communist world was reaching perilous levels. Leading economists and planners in several countries criticized the debt accumulation that had made possible generous social programs, or the "unity of social and economic policies," as proclaimed by Erich Honecker and Edward Gierek.[75] In 1976, the heads of two East German research institutes submitted a report outlining the perils of a continued increase in external debt for the regime.[76] The Planning Commission was a stronghold for opponents to external indebtedness and its chairman, Gerhard Schürer, convinced the Central Committee secretary for economic affairs, Günter Mittag, to sign in March 1977 a joint letter to Honecker, pointing out the already tense situation on foreign currencies, exports, and debt.[77] The Kremlin had also become concerned regarding these countries' debt accumulation and the social instability it could create. Events such as the June 1976 unrest in Poland led Soviet leaders to discuss the issue with a reluctant Polish government, further increasing Moscow's qualms.[78] Some national leaders also realized that they could leverage this situation to their advantage with Moscow. Debt was routinely mentioned as a reason for Moscow not to reduce subsidies on oil and raw materials. Moscow had to save its allies from falling into the hands of Western capitalists, claimed the Bulgarian Communist Party leader Todor Zhivkov in April 1978 when he came asking for more aid.[79]

Moscow did provide some help, but remained in a situation significantly different from its allies—despite being forced to import food, for the time being, it maintained a relatively low level of foreign debt and the rising price on oil products replenished its coffers.[80] Its foreign debt nevertheless rose over the course of the 1970s. Estimates vary on the exact level of Soviet foreign debt, with the US Directorate of Intelligence putting it at 1.8 billion dollars in 1970 and 17.8 in 1980.[81] By the mid-1970s, the Soviet government was still considered a first-class borrower because of its centralized control over export revenue and commodities-based currency flows and, as a result, Western lenders were eager to give them seemingly "riskless" loans; however, they were unaware of the exact extent of its external debt due to statistical manipulations, the peculiarities of Soviet accounting practices, and price distortions.[82] Meanwhile, the Central and Eastern European countries plunged into unprecedented levels of indebtedness in Western currencies, in part due to the oil crisis and declining export revenues. Yugoslavia's debt jumped from 3.4 billion dollars to 20.6 billion during the 1970s and the reduction of remittances from Western Europe only sharpened the crisis.[83] In 1981, the overall debt of communist countries stood at around 90 billion dollars. The Soviet Union was also largely responsible for the debt crisis that erupted after its invasion of Afghanistan because of the restrictions on credit imposed by the Reagan administration in retaliation.

The debt crisis that unfolded was remarkable for the relative passiveness that characterized communist states' responses. Outright attacks on foreign debt as tools of global imperialism were largely absent from the discussion. The first reason for this silence was internal divisions within the bloc. Faced with financial difficulties, each country tried to defend its own case with little concern for others. If anything, they wanted to assure Western creditors that they were not just another communist country in trouble. In March 1980, the managers of the East German Bank for Foreign Trade met with their Czechoslovak counterparts, who informed them that they were trying to obtain credit from the West and insisted that they were far less indebted than other communist countries and were "first-class borrowers."[84] For GDR leaders who felt the pinch of the credit crunch, such an attitude was anything but cooperative. They used their own connections to get an exclusive loan from the Federal Republic of Germany (FRG) in the summer of 1983, the infamous *Milliardenkredit* negotiated by Bavarian politician Franz-Joseph Strauss. Romania soon followed a course of isolation and attempted to mobilize political allies in a rhetoric that avoided any reference to communism whatsoever. Asking for French support in their dealings with the banks and the IMF, the Minister of Foreign Affairs, Ștefan Andrei, suggested to Mitterrand that he could become a new Napoleon III and save Romania from the lenders, preventing it from falling back into the arms of the Soviets who had purportedly offered several billion dollars in loans.[85] The allusion to French help in creating Romania in the twentieth century was well in line with the new rhetoric of Ceaușescu's regime but not with the rhetoric of communist solidarity.

Western lenders and IFIs contributed to this division by adopting a conciliatory position. The IMF played a facilitating role in the negotiations pursued by the Club of Paris and the Club of London. The first rescheduling agreement was signed between the Club of Paris and Poland in April 1981 for 2.2 billion dollars.[86] The IMF expressed its support for a rescheduling of Romanian debt in 1981–1982 and maintained communication channels with the Romanian leadership amid rising distrust toward other lenders. The Reagan administration encouraged a policy of "differentiation" between communist countries and, although they criticized this policy, their leaderships were quite conscious that Western partners were ready to make concessions and no one was tempted to follow a confrontational course.[87]

A second reason for the absence of joint struggle was that the debt crisis could serve the interests of political actors engaged in power struggles. Although the Soviet Union provided some financial help to Poland at the peak of the crisis, observers speculated that Soviet leaders might find in the debt crisis a convenient way to bring the Poles back into the communist fold. Media coverage of debt problems became a vehicle for indictments of former rulers in several countries.[88] More figures were disclosed to IFIs and lenders and popular support was sought after to give credibility to structural reforms. In Yugoslavia, a new group of politicians embraced reform plans prepared with the IMF in an attempt to evict the old guard. Federal Prime Minister Milka Planinc shielded her actions behind the demands of the IMF and pushed through several new laws in July 1983. In East Germany, Günter Mittag and Erich Honecker strengthened their political control through managing external debt but their compromises with the West infuriated the "Moscow fraction," whose members secured the dismissal of Pro-West figures in the 1980s and sent incendiary reports to Moscow.[89]

A third reason had to do with the fact that several communist states saw themselves not only as debtors but also as lenders to the Third World.[90] By November 1979, the Soviet government had adopted stricter guidelines for credit to Third World countries and had taken measures to reduce its exposure to various risks of credit. This explains the difficulty involved in canceling the debt of underdeveloped countries: indeed, Fidel Castro and his associates found it difficult to mobilize communist leaders beyond private statements of solidarity. Outright criticism of the order of debt was limited to those communist countries that leaned toward the non-aligned movement. Yugoslavia and Romania shared sympathy for the group of 77 pursuing their objective of new economic relations with developed countries.[91] But even these countries had contradictory interests. As it pleaded for a comprehensive remaking of the international financial system and a debt write-off for Third World countries, the Romanian leadership reminded the same countries that "Romania, being still a developing country itself, needed all external resources and could not accept a cancellation or reduction of debts."[92] Similarly, the Soviet Union refused to side openly with Latin American countries in their struggle against Western creditors and the American Treasury.[93] At Fidel Castro's request, the

Soviet Central Committee created an ad hoc commission that concluded in June–July 1985 that developing countries owed 26 billion dollars to the USSR and should repay this debt.[94] However, after 1984, Castro was left alone in the Cartagena Process group, convoking a Latin American conference to denounce debt.[95]

Policies implemented in response to mounting debt in the 1980s diverged in significant ways across the bloc. A majority of Central European countries adopted austerity measures. While they varied in their severity, one common feature was the erosion of political legitimacy they caused. Jonathan R. Zatlin has convincingly demonstrated that East German leaders undermined their own legitimacy by multiplying concessions to the capitalist system in the 1980s. Mittag's policy to cut costs and increase exports demonstrated the failure of socialist ideology and practice: "The political imperative of staving off insolvency deepened the very reversal of means and ends the socialist ideology promised to rectify."[96] While Mittag condoned clandestine operations to obtain Western currencies through the infamous *Kommerzielle Koordinierung*, and diluted the unity of state action by creating parallel accounting systems, Hungary could sell itself as a "Swiss-style banking center" to investors.[97] Communist regimes did not manage either to use debt repayment as a way to improve their domestic legitimacy or to increase accountability. While their financial creditworthiness was progressively repaired by the mid-1980s, internal tensions increased. In Romania, the endeavor to pay back the entire external debt at an accelerated rhythm led to considerable suffering among the population, but also discontent among high-ranking officials and technocrats who criticized the very economic legitimacy of a move they blamed upon Ceaușescu's wounded pride.[98]

* * *

On 12 April 1989, Ceaușescu triumphantly declared to the Central Committee that Romania had repaid its external debt in full: "For the first time in her long history, Romania has no more external debt, pays tribute to nobody and is truly independent, economically and politically!"[99] This delirious expression of national pride illustrated the wide gap that had emerged between him and the Romanian people, who had by then hardened against him because of the painful material sacrifices this had required, but also the equally puzzling situation of a Communist leader who had been squarely focused on repaying foreign capitalist lenders for a decade.

Far from trying to remake or challenge the rules, Communist leaders of the 1980s had fully accepted the capitalist order of public debt. This undoubtedly factored into the demise of these regimes at the turn of the decade.

By the early 1990s, the countries of Central and Eastern Europe had come full circle on the issue of public debt, confronted once more with the question of who should inherit the burden of the previous regimes' debts. Here too, their responses are telling. The argument that "odious debts" need not be repaid was not seriously revisited—although communist states' questionable popular mandates to contract such massive debts could have made for a legitimate argument. Managing their debts figured prominently in the new regimes' capitalist transition agendas. Debt write-offs were also offered as an incentive to avoid the temptation to fall back upon socialist planning habits and fully transition to capitalism by Western governments, especially to heavily indebted countries such as Poland.

Ironically, perhaps no post-communist country's response was as diametrically opposed to debt repudiation as that of Russia. As the successor state to the Soviet Union, the Russian government assumed much of its estimated 85 billion dollars debt, and viewed repaying it as an important strategy for regaining Russia's geopolitical status. Russia became a member of the Club of Paris in 1997, repaying its debts to the group 14 years ahead of schedule in 2006. Of late, Russia has once again positioned itself as a benevolent creditor to its economically weaker allies. Vladimir Putin has used debt cancellations as a political tool, and official sources put these as high as 140 billion dollars over the last 15 years. For example, in early 2016, Russia allowed Mongolia to write off 97 percent of its debt to Russia acquired during the Soviet period, which, as of 2010, totaled 174.2 million dollars.[100] On the domestic debt front, the results are more mixed. While most of the former Soviet republics defaulted on their domestic debts upon breaking away from the Union, Yeltsin promised to repay "lost Soviet savings" to the Russian people, a process that has repeatedly stalled.[101]

The financial crisis of 2008, which resulted in a violent economic downturn and a massive withdrawal of capital in much of Central and Eastern Europe, saw some countries looking for lessons for how to deal with external debt in the communist past. In Bulgaria, the "secret bankrupts of communism" were associated with the corruption and incompetence of contemporary political elites.[102] In Romania, journalists revisited Ceaușescu's claim to have fully liquidated external debt. In Poland, these discussions were tightly linked with controversial memories of communism, and the announcement in 2012 that "Gierek's debt" to the Club of London had been liquidated renewed debates about the dismantling of welfare benefits that was supposed to pay for it. This lasting fascination with communist-era debt can, perhaps, be linked to the secrecy that long surrounded it. The truth is, however, that the fall of communism did not reveal any major discrepancies between official and "real" figures, contrary to what some expected.[103] The mystery of public debt, in a sense, became a metaphor for regimes that made secrecy a fact of life to the point that it became detrimental to their own interests.

Notes

1. P. Ia. Dmitrichev, ed., *Gosudarstvennye zajmy v SSSR* (Moscow: Gosizdat, 1956), 20–21; Martin Heilmann, "Zur politischen Ökonomie des Staates und der Staatsfinanzen bei Karl Marx," in *Staat, Steuern und Finanzausgleich*, eds.Walter A.S. Koch and Hans-Georg Petersen (Berlin: Duncker & Humblot, 1984), 15–53.
2. "Dekret ob annulirovanii gosudarstvennykh zaimov," 21 January 1918, in *Sbornik dekretov 1917–1918 gg.*, Moscow, Gosudarstvennoe Izdatel'stvo, 1920, 19. The Bolsheviks' repudiation caused a surge in public discussion of the issue, best exemplified by the Russian emigré Alexander Sack's treatise *Les effets des transformations des Etats sur leurs dettes publiques et autres obligations financières* (Paris: Recueil Sirey, 1927); however, a similar move had, in fact, been earlier contemplated after the Spanish-American war of 1898. On the emergence of the doctrine of "odious debts," see Odette Lienau, *Rethinking Sovereign Debt. Politics, Reputation, and Legitimacy in Modern Finance* (Cambridge, Mass.: Harvard University Press, 2014).
3. Franklyn D. Holzman, "The Soviet Bond Hoax," *Problems of Communism* 6, no. 5 (1957): 47–49.
4. Stephen Kotkin, "The Kiss of Debt. The East Bloc Goes Borrowing," in *The Shock of the Global. The 1970s in Perspective*, eds. Niall Ferguson, Charles S. Maier, Erez Manela, and Daniel S. Sargent (Cambridge, Mass.: The Belknap Press of Harvard University Press, 2010), 80–93.
5. Katherine Verdery, *What Was Socialism and What Comes Next?* (Princeton: Princeton University Press, 1996), 37.
6. Kim Oosterlinck, *Hope Springs Eternal. French Bondholders and the Repudiation of Russian Sovereign Debt* (New Haven: Yale University Press, 2016), 24, 30–31.

7. Karl Mannzen, *Sowjetunion und Völkerrecht. Die Fragen der Anerkennung der Schulden, und der Auslandspropaganda und des Aussenhandelsmonopols* (Berlin: Verlag Georg Stilke, 1932), 30; Richard B. Day, *Cold War Capitalism. The View from Moscow, 1945–1975* (Armonk: M.E. Sharpe, 1995), 73.
8. R. W. Davies et al., eds., *The Stalin-Kaganovich correspondence, 1931–36* (New Haven: Yale University Press, 2003), 111–112.
9. Kristy Ironside, "Khrushchev's Cash-and-Goods Lotteries and the Turn to Positive Incentives," *The Soviet and Post-Soviet Review* 41, no. 3 (2014): 303.
10. Dmitrichev, *Gosudarstvennye zajmy v SSSR*, 27; "Konferentsiia VKP(b). Khoziastvennoe polozhenie strany i zadachi partii. Doklad tov. A. I. Rykova; Nakopleniia, ego istochniki i temp khoziaistvennogo razvitiia," *Izvestiia*, October 30, 1926, 1.
11. James R. Millar, "History and Analysis of Soviet Domestic Bond Policy," *Soviet Studies* 27, no. 4 (1975): 609–610.
12. Sarah Davies, *Popular Opinion in Stalin's Russia. Terror, Propaganda and Dissent, 1934–1941* (Cambridge, Cambridge University Press, 1997), 35–36.
13. Franklyn D. Holzman, "An Estimate of the Tax Element in Soviet Bonds," *The American Economic Review* 47, no. 3 (June 1957): 390–393; *Soviet Taxation: The Fiscal and Monetary Problems of a Planned Economy* (Cambridge, Mass.: Harvard University Press, 1955), 200–208.
14. Mark Harrison, "The Soviet Union: The Defeated Victor," in *The Economics of World War II. Six Great Powers in International Comparison*, ed. Mark Harrison (Cambridge: Cambridge University Press, 1998), 272–273.
15. Kristy Ironside, "Rubles for Victory: The Social Dynamics of State Fundraising on the Soviet Home Front," *Kritika: Explorations in Russian and Eurasian History* 15, no. 4 (Fall 2014): 804–805.
16. "Dannye o gosudarstvennom dol'ge za 1940–1944," *Sovetskaia povsednevnost' i massovoe soznanie, 1939–1945*, eds. A. Ia. Livshin and I. B Orlov (Moscow: ROSSPEN, 2003), 239.
17. Lǐ Jiāgǔ, "Kàngrì zhànzhēng shíqī Sūlián duì Huá dàikuǎn yǔ jūnhuǒ wùzī yuánzhù," *Jìndàishǐ yánjiū* 45, no. 3 (1988): 214.
18. Albert L. Weeks, *Russia's Life-Saver: Lend-Lease Aid to the U.S.S.R. in World War II* (Lanham-Plymouth: Lexington Books, 2010).
19. Iu. V. Ivanov, ed., *Sovetsko-amerikanskie otnosheniia 1945–1948* (Moscow: Mezhdunarodnyi Fond "Demokratiia"-Materik, 2004), 176–177.
20. Daniel Vachkov, "Bŭlgarskijat vŭnshen dŭlg v godinite na sledvoennoto vŭzstanovjavane (1947–1953)," *Izvestija na dŭrzhavnite arkhivi*, no. 93 (2007): 32–51.

21. Report by Zverev to Stalin, 3 January 1948, in L.N. Dobrokhtov et al., eds., *Denezhnaia reforma v SSSR 1947 goda*. Dokumenty i materialy (Moscow: ROSSPEN, 2010), 346–358.
22. Jan Kuklík, *Do poslední pence. Československo-britská jednání o majetkoprávních a finančnich otázkách 1938–1982* (Prague: Nakladatelství Karolinum, 2007), 250–251.
23. Andrzej Drwiłło, *Konstrukcje prawne wewnętrznych pożyczek publicznych* (Gdansk: Wydawnictwo Uniwersytetu Gdańskiego, 1989).
24. I. Iu. Kashin and T. V. Kozlova, eds., *Po stranitsam arkhivnyh fondov tsentral'nogo banka Rossiskoi federatsii, vypusk 13* (Moscow: Tsentral'nyi bank Rossisskoi federatsii, 2012), 85. Hereafter *PSAF 13*.
25. Gāo Xiǎolín, "Shànghǎi sīyíng gōngshāngyè yǔ rénmín shènglì zhéshí gōngzhài," *Dāngdài Zhōngguóshǐ Yánjiū* 12, no. 6 (Nov. 2005): 49–55.
26. AJ (Archives of Yugoslavia, Belgrade), fonds 41, fasc. 119, a.je. 89.
27. Joanna Janus, *Polska i Czechosłowacja wobec planu Marshalla* (Kracow: Wydawnictwo Naukowe Akademii Pedagogicznej, 2001); Valerie J. Assetto, *The Soviet Bloc in the IMF and the BIRD* (Boulder-London: Westview Press, 1988), 73–74, 81–87; Jana Marková, "Postavení České republiky v Mezinárodním měnovém fondem," *Český finanční a účetni časopis* 9, no. 3 (2014): 96.
28. Lorraine M. Lees, *Keeping Tito Afloat. The United States, Yugoslavia, and the Cold War* (University Park: Pennsylvania State University Press, 1997); Vladimir Unkovski-Korica, *The Economic Struggle for Power in Tito's Yugoslavia* (London: I.B. Tauris, 2016).
29. William Z. Slany, ed., *FRUS, 1949. Vol. V. Eastern Europe; The Soviet Union* (Washington: United States Government Printing Office, 1976), 896–897; "Titov ekspoze na četvrtom vanrednom zasedanju Narodne Skupštine," *Borba*, 28 December 1948, quoted by Predrag J. Marković, *Beograd između Istoka i Zapada, 1948–1965* (Belgrade: Novinskoizdavačka ustanova, 1996), 124.
30. AJ, f. 507, a.je. III/48.
31. Austin Jersild, "The Soviet State as Imperial Scavenger: 'Catch up and Surpass' in the Transnational Socialist Bloc, 1950–1960," *The American Historical Review* 116, no. 1 (2011): 109–132.
32. Janusz Kaliński, "Nierównowaga zewnętrzna gospodarki Polski ludowej," *Kwartalnik Kolegium Ekonomiczno-Społecznego. Studia i Prace*, no. 3 (2011): 43.
33. Oleg Khlevniuk et al., eds, *Politbiuro TsK VKP(b) i Sovet Ministrov SSSR 1945–1953* (Moscow: ROSSPEN, 2002), 112.
34. RGANI (Russian Archives of Contemporary History, Moscow), f. 5, op. 30, d. 149, ll. 38–40.

35. A.M. Smirnov, "Mezhdunarodnye valjutnye i finansovye otnoshenija SSSR," in *Finansy i sotsialisticheskoe stroitel'stvo*, ed. A.G. Zverev (Moscow: Gosfinizdat, 1957), 328.
36. Viktor Rymalov, *SSSR i ekonomicheski-slaborazvitye strany. Ekonomicheskoe sotrudnichestvo i pomoshch'* (Moscow: Izdatel'stvo Sotsial'no-Ekonomicheskoj Literatury, 1963), 56–60; BArch-SAPMO (German Federal Archives, Berlin), DN 1/27846, f. 34.
37. Ragna Boden, *Die Grenzen der Weltmacht. Sowjetische Indonesienspolitik von Stalin bis Brežnev* (Stuttgart: Franz Steiner Verlag, 2006), 179–181.
38. PA AA (Archives of the German Ministry of Foreign Affairs, Berlin), MfAA, A 4392, ff. 1–2.
39. Jerzy Waszczuk, *Biografia niezlustrowana. Świadek historii w "Białym Domu"* (Torun: Wydawnictwo Adam Marszałek, 2013), 10.
40. A.N. Artizov et al., eds., *Sovetsko-vengerskie ekonomicheskie otnoshenija 1948–1973* (Moscow: Mezhdunarodnyi Fond Demokratiia, 2012), 86–89.
41. Artizov et al., *Sovetsko-vengerskie*, 120–121; Honvári János, *XX. Századi Magyar Gazdaságtörténet* (Budapest: Universitas-Győr, 2013), 310–316.
42. Austin Jersild, *The Sino-Soviet Alliance. An International History* (Chapel Hill: University of North Carolina Press, 2014), 110; Lì Píng and Mǎ Zhīsūn, eds., *Zhōu Ēnlái niánpǔ, 1949–1976*, Vol. 2 (Beijing: Zhōngyāng Wénxiàn Chūbǎnshè, 1997), 15.
43. Only the Soviet Gosbank and the GDR Staatsbank were not members of the BIS. See Gianni Toniolo and Piet Clement, *Central Bank Cooperation at the Bank for International Settlements, 1930–1973* (Cambridge, New York: Cambridge University Press, 2005), 346–347; Mira Šuvar, *Vladimir Velebit. Svjedok Historije* (Zagreb, Razlog, 2001); Johanna Bockman, *Markets in the Name of Socialism. The Left-Wing Origins of Neoliberalism* (Stanford: Stanford University Press, 2011), 62–63 and 84–86.
44. Sari Autio-Sarasmo and Katalin Miklóssy, eds., *Reassessing Cold War Europe* (London; New York: Routledge, 2011).
45. Stenographic report of the plenum of the Romanian Central Committee, 15–22 April 1964, in Dan Cătănuș, ed., *Între Beijing și Moscova. România și conflictul Sovieto-Chinez, Vol. I. 1957–1965* (Bucarest: Institutul Național Pentru Studiul Totalitarismului, 2004), 355; Vladimir Tismaneanu, *Stalinism for all Seasons: A Political History of Romanian Communism* (Berkeley: University of California Press, 2003), 178–179.
46. Lee Kendall Metcalf, "The Impact of Foreign Trade on the Czechoslovak Economic Reforms of the 1960s," *Europe-Asia Studies* 45, no. 6 (1993): 1071–1090.

13 THE COMMUNIST WORLD OF PUBLIC DEBT (1917–1991): THE FAILURE... 341

47. AJ, f. 507, a.je. 78 and 79; Steven L. Burg, *Conflict and Cohesion in Socialist Yugoslavia. Political Decision Making Since 1966* (Princeton: Princeton University Press, 1983), 88–100.
48. W.N. Dunn, "Communal Federalism: Dialectics of Decentralization in Socialist Yugoslavia," *Publius* 5, no. 2 (1975): 127–150; Dejan Jović, *Jugoslavija. Država koja je odumrla. Uspon, kriza i pad četvrte Jugoslavije (1974–1990)* (Zagreb-Belgrade: Prometej-Samizdat92, 2003), 14–15.
49. David A. Dyker, *Yugoslavia. Socialism, Development and Debt* (London; New York: Routledge, 1990), 114–116.
50. Cecylia Leszczyńska, *Zarys Historii Polskiej Bankowości Centralnej* (Warsaw: Narodowy Bank Polski, 2010), 45; Vladimír Wacker and Jan Kalvoda, *Mezinárodní platební a úvěrové vztahy ČSSR* (Praha: Nakladatelství Technické Literatury, 1987), 8–10.
51. Sophie Lambroschini, "La genèse du *bankir*: la valorisation de l'expérience du capitalisme au sein de l'élite soviétique (1974–1991)," in *Les élites en question*, eds. Bernd Zielinski and Jean-Robert Raviot (Bern: Peter Lang, 2015), 111–139.
52. Protocol of the Politburo of the SED, 27 April 1971, BArch, SAPMO, DY 30/J IV 2/2/1336, f. 3.
53. Entry of 4 August 1973, Anatolii Cherniaev, *Sovmestnyi iskhod. Dnevnik dvukh epokh, 1972–1991 gody*, (Moscow: ROSSPEN, 2008), 65.
54. Paweł Domański, ed., *Tajne dokumenty Biura Politycznego: Grudzień 1970* (London: Aneks, 1991), 128–130.
55. Giuseppe Schiavone, *Il Comecon. Cooperazione e integrazione fra le economie dei paesi socialisti* (Padua: CEDAM, 1979).
56. Report of the Romanian Bank for Foreign Trade, 22 January 1970, ABNR (Archives of the Romanian Central Bank, Bucarest), f. DVMP, ds. 25/1972, f. 7.
57. Note by Florea Dumitrescu, Romanian minister of Finances, about the session of the Comecon commission for monetary and financial issues held in Varna, 10–13 October 1972, ABNR, f. DVMP, ds. 21/1972, ff. 209–212.
58. Ion Alexandrescu, *România între Est și Vest: Aderarea la FMI și BIRD, I* (Târgoviște: Cetatea de Scaun, 2012).
59. RGANI, f. 5, op. 20, d. 136, l. 3.
60. Holzman, "The Soviet Bond Hoax," 49.
61. "Protokol no. 83 zasedanija 19 marta 1957," in *Prezidium TsK KPSS 1954–1964, tom 1: chernovye protokoly, zapisi zasedanii, stenogrammy*, ed. A. A. Fursenko (Moscow: ROSSPEN, 2004), 234–235.
62. "Rech' tov. N. S. Khrushcheva na soveshchanii rabotnikov sel'skogo khoziastva Gor'kovskoi, Arzamasskoi, Kirovskoi oblastei, Mariiskoi,

Mordovskoi i Chuvashskoi ASSR 8 aprelia 1957 goda v gorode Gor'kom," *Pravda*, April 10, 1957, 2.
63. "Iz stenogrammy vystupleniia N. S. Khrushcheva na soveshchanii rabotnikov sel'skogo khoziaistva v gor. Gor'kom," in *Nikita Sergeevich Khrushchev: Dva tsveta vremeni; dokumenty*, ed. N. G. Tomilina (Moscow: Mezhdunarodnyi fond "Demokratiia," 2009), 341.
64. Balázs Szalontai, *Kim Il Sung in the Khrushchev Era: Soviet-DPRK Relations and the Roots of North Korean Despotism, 1953–1964* (Washington: Woodrow Wilson Center Press, 2005), 154; Ralph A. Thaxton Jr., *Catastrophe and Contention in Rural China: Mao's Great Leap Forward–Famine and the Origins of Righteous Resistance in Da Fo Village* (Cambridge: Cambridge University Press, 2008), 119–120.
65. On postwar French and Indian forms of non-market financing, see Kapadia and Lemoine's contribution to this book (Chap. 15).
66. János Kornai, *The Political Economy of Communism* (Princeton: Princeton University Press, 1992), 138; Igor Birman, "The Financial Crisis in the USSR," *Soviet Studies* 32, no. 1 (Jan. 1980): 96.
67. Nikolai Barkovskii, *Memuary bankira 1930–1990* (Moscow: Finansy i Statistika, 1998), 136. For a rare contemporary acknowledgment of this mechanism, Jan Głuchowski, *Wewnętrzny kredyt publiczny w budżetach europejskich państw socjalistycznych* (Torun: Uniwersytet Mikołaja Kopernika, 1970), 98–99.
68. Igor Birman, *Secret Incomes of the Soviet State Budget* (The Hague; Boston; London: Martinus Nijhoff Publishers, 1981), 129–131, 142.
69. Memorandum of V. Vorob'ev, vice-chairman of the Gosbank, to the Council of Ministers of USSR, 16 November 1966, *PSAF*, Vyp. 16, 144–147.
70. Rumen Avramov, *Pari i de/stabilizatsija v Bǐlgarija 1948–1989* (Sofia: Institut za izsledvane na blizkoto minalo, 2008), 109–115.
71. Philippe Heldmann, *Herrschaft, Wirtschaft, Anoraks. Konsumpolitik in der DDR der Sechzigerjahre* (Göttingen: Vandenhoeck & Ruprecht, 2004), 177–179.
72. N.O. Voskresenskaia et al., *Istoriia Ministerstva Finansov Rossii, T. 31,933–1985* (Moscow: INFRA-M, 2002), 179–180.
73. See the letters for 1977 collected in RGAE (Russian State Economic Archives, Moscow), f. 7733, op. 64, d. 1243 and 1244.
74. Report of the French Ministry of Foreign Affairs, 11 August 1976, AMAE (Archives of the French Ministry of Foreign Affairs), Political Affairs, Asia-Oceania, North Korea, 1973–1980; Erik Cornell, *North Korea under Communism: Report of an Envoy to Paradise* (London; New York: Routledge, 2002), 5–6.

75. Piotr Olszański, *Historia polskiego zadłużenia międzynarodowego na tle wydarzeń społecznych i politycznych* (Warsaw: Szkoła Główna Handlowa w Warszawie, 2002), 27–28.
76. Rainer Weinert, "Die Wirtschaftsführer der SED: Die Abteilungsleiter im ZK im Spannungsfeld von politischer Loyalität und ökonomischer Rationalität," in *Sozialistische Eliten. Horizontale und vertikale Differenzierungsmuster in der DDR*, ed. Stefan Hornbostel (Opladen: Leske+Budrich, 1999), 65.
77. Letter of Mittag and Schürer to Honecker, 14 March 1977, BArch-SAPMO, DE 1/56323.
78. Piotr Kostikow and Bohdan Roliński, *Widziane z Kremla: Moskwa-Warszawa; Gra o Polskę* (Warsaw: BGW, 1992), 181–183.
79. Diary note, 16 April 1978, Cherniaev, *Sovmestnyi iskhod*, 318.
80. Jean-Charles Asselain, "Les économies socialistes européennes aujourd'hui: crises, adaptations, blocages," *Revue économique* 37, no. 2 (1986): 353.
81. Klaus Schröder, *Die Kredit- und Verschuldungspolitik der Sowjetunion gegenüber dem Westen* (Baden-Baden: Nomos Verlagsgesellschaft, 1987), 13–14. For diverging estimates, putting it at 4.7 billion dollars in 1980, see Vladimir Tikhomirov, "Russian Debt Problems in the 1990s," *Post-Soviet Affairs* 17, no. 3 (July–September, 2001): 263.
82. Andrei Vavilov, *The Russian Public Debt and Financial Meltdowns* (Basingstoke: Palgrave Macmillan, 2010), 13–14.
83. Vladimir Unkovski-Korica, "Self-Management, Development and Debt: The Rise and Fall of the 'Yugoslav Experiment,'" in *Welcome to the Desert of Post-Socialism. Radical Politics after Yugoslavia*, eds. Srećko Horvat and Igor Štiks (London; New York: Verso, 2015), 38–39.
84. Report by Kaminsky and Polze to Mittag, 25 March 1980, BArch-SAPMO, DY 3023/1094, p. 154.
85. Ştefan Andrei and Lavinia Betea, *Stăpânul secretelor lui Ceauşescu. I se spunea Machiavelli* (Bucarest: Adevărul, 2011), 370.
86. James M. Boughton, *Silent Revolution. The International Monetary Fund, 1979–1989* (Washington: IMF, 2001), 321–323.
87. Report of the East German Ministry of Foreign Affairs on financial and debt issues, 3 February 1984, BStU-Zentral Archiv (Archives of the former East German Ministry of State Security, Berlin), MfS – HA Aufklärung, 451.
88. Iliana Zloch-Christy, *Debt Problems of Eastern Europe* (Cambridge: Cambridge University Press, 1987), 85; the Grabski Commission in Poland was the most significant example of such indictments: Zbigniew Błażyński, *Towarzysze zeznają* (London: Polska Fundacja Kulturalna,

1987); Waldemar Kuczyński, *Po wielkim skoku* (Warszawa: Wydawnictwo Poltext, 2012).
89. See the personal notes of Werner Krolikowski, BArch-SAPMO, DY 30/25758 and 30/25759; Detlef Nakath and Gerd Rüdiger Stephan, eds., *Die Häber-Protokolle. Schlaglichter der SED-Westpolitik 1973–1985* (Berlin: Karl Dietz Verlag, 1999).
90. Sara Lorenzini, "Comecon and the South in the years of détente: a study on East-South economic relations," *European Review of History* 21, no. 2 (2014): 183–199.
91. Meeting between Erich Honecker and Raúl Ruiz Castro, 8 April 1985, BArch-SAPMO, DY 30/2462, ff. 256–269; note of the Yugoslav secretariat for Foreign Affairs to the Presidency, 29 September 1982, AJ, f. 803, fasc. 579.
92. Memorandum on Romania's position in the negotiations at the IMF and BIRD, 26 March 1989, ANIC (National Archives of Romania, Bucarest), F. CC al PCR, Secția Economică, Inv. 3294, ds. 367/1989, f. 34.
93. Duccio Basosi, "The 'missing Cold War': reflections on the Latin American debt crisis, 1979–1989," in *The End of the Cold War and the Third World. New Perspectives on Regional Conflict*, eds. Artemy M. Kalinovsky and Sergey Radchenko (London; New York: Routledge, 2011), 211.
94. Entries on 17 May, 9 June and 5 July 1985, Cherniaev, *Sovmestnyi iskhod*, 630, 638.
95. Fidel Castro, *Encuentro sobre la deuda externa de América Latina y el Caribe. Discurso, 3 de agosto de 1985* (Havana: Editora Política, 1985); Valerii Bushuev, *Latinskaja Amerika-SShA: Revoljutsija i kontrrevoljutsija* (Moscow: Mezhdunarodnye Otnosheniia, 1987), 251–253.
96. Jonathan R. Zatlin, *The Currency of Socialism. Money and Political Culture in East Germany* (Washington: German Historical Institute, 2007), 106.
97. William Engdahl and Laurent Murawiec, "East Bloc bankers setting their sights on the Euromarket," *EIR* 11, no. 36 (18 September 1984): 7; Matthias Judt, *KoKo – Mythos und Realität. Das Imperium des Alexander Schalck-Golodkowski* (Berlin: Berolina, 2015).
98. Thomas Kunze, *Nicolae Ceaușescu: Eine Biographie* (Berlin: Ch. Links Verlag, 2000), 304; Silviu Curticeanu, *Mărturia unei istorii trăite* (Bucarest: Historia, 2008), 42; Katherine Verdery, *National Ideology Under Socialism: Identity and Cultural Politics in Ceaușescu Romania* (Berkeley: University of California Press, 1991), 130.
99. *Scînteia*, 13 April 1989, *in* Ilarion Țiu, "Achitarea datoriei externe. Ultimul proiect grandios al lui Ceaușescu," *Sfera Politicii* XXII, no. 3 (May–June 2014): 103.

100. "Vladimir Putin spisal dolg Mongolii," 1 Feburary 2016, *Lenta.ru*, https://lenta.ru/news/2016/01/31/tugriki/
101. Under the Savings Protection Act of 1995, the Russian state recognized its liabilities to citizens of the former Russian socialist republic and promised that outstanding debts would be paid in special promissory notes in accordance with a new law, which was eventually written in 1996. The law has been repeatedly suspended by the Russian government since. In 2013, Russian lawmakers proposed a new law, canceling the Savings Protection Act and setting a firm deadline for paying all pre-reform savings as of 25 December 2020. See "Sovetskie obligatsii bol'she ne vyigraiut," *Kommersant*, 22 May 2013, http://www.kommersant.ru/doc/2194452. In 2018, the Russian Duma proposed a moratorium on paying back lost Soviet savings, delaying payments to no earlier than January 1, 2022. See "Gosduma prodlila do 2022 goda priostanovku vyplat kompensatsii po sovetskim vkladam," *Parliamenskaia gazeta*, November 13, 2018, https://www.pnp.ru/social/gosduma-prodlila-do-2022-goda-priostanovku-vyplat-kompensaciy-po-sovetskim-vkladam.html
102. Khristo Khristov, *Tajnite faliti na komunizma. Istinata za krakha na bilgarskija sotsializim v sekretnite arkhivi na delo No. 4/1990 za ikonomicheskata katastrofa* (Sofia: Ciela, 2007).
103. Armin Volze, "Ein grosser Bluff? Die Westverschuldung der DDR," *Deutschland Archiv* 29, no. 5 (September–October 1996): 701–713.

Open Access This chapter is licensed under the terms of the Creative Commons Attribution 4.0 International License (http://creativecommons.org/licenses/by/4.0/), which permits use, sharing, adaptation, distribution and reproduction in any medium or format, as long as you give appropriate credit to the original author(s) and the source, provide a link to the Creative Commons licence and indicate if changes were made.

The images or other third party material in this chapter are included in the chapter's Creative Commons licence, unless indicated otherwise in a credit line to the material. If material is not included in the chapter's Creative Commons licence and your intended use is not permitted by statutory regulation or exceeds the permitted use, you will need to obtain permission directly from the copyright holder.

CHAPTER 14

Debt Without Taxation: Iraq, Syria, and the Crisis of Empires from the Mandates to the Cold War Era

Matthieu Rey

In July 1946, *Alif Bā'*, one of the main Syrian newspapers, assigned the government a clear mission: "the budget has to be revolutionary."[1] This injunction continued to echo for two years after independence when the state announced its new goals. Admittedly, its interests encompassed ordinary sovereign functions such as the police, the military, and so forth, but in a new independent republic, the authorities also needed to attend to the social and economic conditions of the citizens in order to guarantee a situation in which they could practice their rights and duties as members of political bodies. Similarly in Iraq, although the government regained its budgetary capabilities in the wake of the second British occupation (1941–1943), successive governments used their bulletins to highlight their serious concerns regarding social and economic improvement.[2] While expenditure increased and expanded in scope, none of these

M. Rey (✉)
IFAS-Research, Johannesburg, South Africa
e-mail: matthieu.rey@ifas.org.za

© The Author(s) 2020
N. Barreyre, N. Delalande (eds.), *A World of Public Debts*, Palgrave Studies in the History of Finance,
https://doi.org/10.1007/978-3-030-48794-2_14

announcements clearly indicated how the authorities would levy the appropriate resources and revenue to cover these expenses. In the aftermath of World War II, developments in Iraq and Syria in many ways exemplified the evolution of states in the postcolonial period during which new authorities faced a number of challenges, mostly in regard to the increase in state intervention.

The advent of independent states in the second half of the twentieth century triggered a series of questions regarding their budgets and finances. When the mandate powers devolved power to local authorities, state resources remained limited. How could the new leaders secure adequate resources in the face of low-level taxation? Moreover, how and why should they create debt when Western powers had used this tool during the nineteenth century to take control over sovereign departments of the Ottoman Empire and its Egyptian province? These questions highlight the dilemma that confronted independent states dealing with post-imperial and colonial legacies, and which framed developments in both Iraq and Syria. These two states launched a wide range of experiments that explored what it meant to be sovereign and they were able to sustain state practices to this end. In this matter, the issue of debt was related to other problems: did a particular set of institutions mirror financial solutions, in other words, would representation mean taxation? How would the new states benefit or be harmed on the international stage by requests for funding? Eventually, how and why did the authorities find resources by creating tolerable debt in terms of sovereignty and legitimacy?

This chapter will explore how the authorities chose to externalize debt, considered the correct way to retain their financial capabilities and avoid harsh criticism from public opinion. Contrary to the ideas derived from commonly cited American revolutionary slogans, the establishment of a representative parliamentary system was accompanied neither by a new fiscal equity model, nor by an increase in resources through the levying of tariffs and taxes in the Middle East. These options would have required intense negotiation between the elites in power and the various components of society. Therefore, looking for loans seemed to be the best solution. Debt resulted from the intertwined processes of constituting a new elite and the refusal of the elite to encroach on its social and economic bases. Following a state/society approach,[3] this chapter examines the beginning of external debt in both countries on the domestic and the international stage. Both socio-economic forces and new international actors paved the way for this solution to the state's needs.

This study tackles several issues as yet not fully explored in the historiography of the period. The states' finances have not constituted a proper field of research that might enable us to understand the different routes by which taxation and debt were adopted or rejected. From Karl Wittfogel to Nazih Ayubi,[4] scholars have highlighted the patrimonial nature of the state without questioning the different stages and disruptions on its path. More precisely, they have looked at the way in which resources were extracted without questioning the relationship between this system on the one hand, and the institutional set-up and the main actors on the other. Contrary to these approaches, a close examination of the parliamentary records shows how politicians put debts and finance on the agenda as budgetary discussions remained at the core of annual debate and how actors interacted with different foreign partners to find financial and material supplies. A clear break occurred in the post-World War II period on the international stage. Odd Arne Westad has pinpointed the intertwined processes of decolonization and the development of the Cold War.[5] Henry Laurens has shown how the Eastern question, which connected local and foreign partners, framed conflict in the 1950s.[6] Both underline the international dimension of national and institutional conflict. In this matter, studying the issue of debt sheds new light on these conflicts during the period of sovereignty. Finally, this chapter identifies a new chronology for the rentier state,[7] considering that the rentier mechanism—the search for resources without accountability—pre-existed the oil boom of the 1970s. Researchers and writers have argued that this new wealth created the conditions whereby states could avoid public pressure regarding their conduct. Contrary to these conclusions, I would like to highlight the functioning and mindsets that led to this situation. All these issues form the general background for the present chapter which focuses on how the state built resources through the accumulation of credible debt.

To understand the nature of debt in Iraq and Syria, we need to take a closer look at modern history. Both countries shared a common history from the nineteenth century onward, as part of the Ottoman Empire, and their urban elites experimented with the late reforms (the tanzimat). At the beginning of the twentieth century, some of the younger generation, such as the future Prime Minister Nuri al-Said, were educated in Constantinople. In the aftermath of World War I, both territories fell under European control. Great Britain and France ruled these new states through an imported constitutional regime within which parliaments became the central place for debating policy. World War II eventually reframed the political game when the Allies forced France to recognize the independence of Syria and the British reoccupied and then left Iraq. All these different stages affected the discourse and practices concerning sovereignty, debt and state goals. This investigation will address three main topics: the institutions and their members; debates on revenues; and expenditure. The Syrian and Iraqi states shared this common fiscal history. After clarifying the nature of the imperial legacy and the mandate experiment, this chapter will demonstrate the progressive externalization of debt during the 1950s.

The Imperial and Mandate Legacies: In Search of Budgetary Self-Sufficiency

In the aftermath of World War I, France and Great Britain carved up the Arab provinces of the Ottoman Empire and created mandatory states, whose legislative apparatus was primarily based on Ottoman laws. Neither of the European powers planned their occupation of Iraq or Syria. However, a general pattern for ruling the country emerged due to the constraints of the post-war period. The budget maintained a fragile equilibrium but this situation was sustainable in an ordinary context, in which two main impulses animated a contradictory dynamic. Firstly, the authorities did not seek to develop either their resources or their administration. As the two countries were supposed to become independent, the Mandate powers refused to finance political development.[8] Secondly, financial exchanges, loans and financial reserves remained mostly outside the market. The local economy was not properly organized as a market since the elite families—the notables—monopolized these tools and directed them toward highly profitable rural short-term loans.[9] French authorities refused all requests on the international market as they feared encroachment on their control. In both countries, the Mandate budget aimed to cover administrative expenditure while responding to the international commitments of these countries, such as honoring their share of the Ottoman debts, protecting their population and consequently forming an army.

Both Mandate powers faced a serious dilemma when they entered the country. In Iraq, struggles between the Indian Office and the Arab Bureau undermined any concerted political program, at a time when a massive uprising threatened the forthcoming occupation. In 1921, the British suppressed the protest. From 1918 onward, the British spent 2.7 million pounds per month on ruling the country.[10] This met with strong criticism from public opinion which denounced a needless occupation. Similarly, the French settled in Syria, and the French authorities subsequently decreased the expenditure allowed to the Syrian states. A major uprising in 1925 forced the French to revise their approach. From this moment on, both Mandate powers proposed similar solutions: they aimed to reduce their expenditure and govern their new territory according to the guidelines of financial orthodoxy. European representatives balanced the budget.

The British and French adopted a common attitude to budgetary issues, even if they did not follow the same path toward building the institutional apparatus needed to implement their policies. They both simultaneously affirmed their role as Mandate representatives during the international negotiations with the Republic of Turkey[11] (between 1920 and 1932). While discussing with the Kemalist authorities, they had to settle Ottoman issues, such as those relating to territorial boundaries and the financial legacy. From this perspective, both recognized a share of the Ottoman debt. Paying back this share was a way to legitimize their new Mandate. It was finally decided that Iraq, Lebanon and Syria (no distinction was made between the latter two) had to make annual payments, approximately 428,000 gold Turkish lira for Iraq, 726,000 for Syria and Lebanon. The amount depended on the share of the imperial revenue in 1910–1911 for these territories.[12] This new step imposed a new way of conceiving of the relations between local authorities and the Mandate powers. The 1920s witnessed the setting-up of twin processes in terms of state-building, one to control the new territory and another to respond to international demands. In Iraq, the British quickly established a constitutional kingdom under Faysal I.[13] In 1925, Iraq formally became a constitutional monarchy in which the parliament exercised its prerogative in matters of decision-making.[14] However, at the same time, the Iraqi authorities had to make their first payment. They refused, arguing that their revenue would not cover the cost of the Ottoman debt and the salaries of civil servants. Indeed, between 1921 and 1924 revenue and expenditure remained low.[15] The surplus remained small. The British sent a mission directed by E. Hilton Young and Roland V. Vernon to reach an agreement.[16] The former had begun his career at *The Economist* then *The Morning Post*. After serving in the Royal Navy and being elected to Parliament in 1915, he became Chief Whip for Lloyd George in 1922. When he lost his seat in the 1923 general election, he devoted himself to journalism (at the *Financial Times*), business, and between 1926 and 1927 to various League of Nations assessments. He later became a civil servant at the colonial office before being appointed to the League of Nations. The British mission rescheduled Iraq's payment.[17] Nevertheless, the payment reduced state capacities. It became an element of Great Britain's tutelage over Iraq.

In Syria, the process was different. The country's total share of the Ottoman debt was 10.8 million Turkish gold lira. In 1923, the donation in favor of the Governor General—which remained overall the main resource in Syria and Lebanon—was suddenly reduced. The French representatives argued that the new Mandate would have to cover the expenditure for defense and administration. At the same time, the French implemented divisions in five different states (Lebanon, State of Damascus, State of Aleppo, Territory of the Alawites, the Druze Territory). However, these divisions prevented some resources from being shared, such as tariffs, and some expenditure from being paid, such as the Ottoman debt.[18] In this context, a massive upheaval occurred, forcing the French to manage different expenditures and resources through a single administrative body dedicated to "common interests," which remained active until 1950, aside from the other budgets (which disappeared in 1936 and 1946). Some resources were specifically assigned to the institution, such as tariffs on salt, alcohol, imports, tobacco, and so on. The legacy of the Ottoman Public Debt framed the procedure.[19] Therefore, contrary to Iraq, the debt burden of this new institution did not lead to the implementation of a new central and unified state apparatus but rather to negotiations between two sets of elites brought together in this supra-territorial organization for the "common interest."

At the beginning of the 1930s, public debt in Iraq and Syria resulted mostly from the budgetary deficit and the remaining Ottoman debts. The latter issue was solved by new agreements in 1932 (for Iraq) and 1933 (for Syria). The former remained low. Tracing the path of the deficit in Iraq, for example, shows that a balance was reached. Between 1932 and 1943, budgets alternatively presented a surplus or a deficit. The deficit was compensated for by the surplus, and treasury advances or temporary public debts were contracted on the domestic market. From 1928 onward, Iraq received new resources, namely the oil royalties which reached 18,000 pounds, that represented a fifth of public investments.[20] This situation revealed the low level of development of the state's capacities and of the financial market in both countries. In the 1930s (and until the 1950s), there were about two and a half million inhabitants. Expenditure reached 5 million pounds in Iraq, and 8.2 million French francs in Syria, in the mid-1930s (2.5 pounds/inhabitant in Iraq; 3.5 francs/inhabitant in Syria).[21] Those who made direct tax contributions were a minority. In 1950, in Iraq, only 24,000 citizens bore the burden of the majority of direct taxes.[22]

The budget maintained a fragile equilibrium. The local authorities, like most of the local borrowers, requested advances from foreign companies which paid royalties.[23] These advances could cover a small deficit, and created no incentive for a change in state revenues. However, a third factor affected this precarious balance from the outside: in the early 1930s, Syrian and Iraqi finances underwent the consequences of the economic crisis. Tariff revenues decreased as the global volume of exchanges plummeted. Prices dropped whereas the new state apparatus needed funds. The dual dynamic of growing expenditure and falling revenue created a major budgetary crisis first in Syria, then in Iraq. Parliamentary representatives tackled the issue by discussing the provision of new resources and fiscal reform. A major change took place. Indirect taxes increased, rather than land taxes, except in Iraq from 1936 to 1937.[24] This change put an end to the Ottoman legacy and to the free exchange agreement.

This fiscal revolution underlined the new dynamic between the elites. Large landowners constituted the great majority of parliamentary representatives. Since 1932, Iraq had become independent of British counsellors, and consequently, Iraqi representatives were free to decide the budget. In Syria, the new constitution of 1932 allowed a high degree of autonomy but constrained the budget to cover the expenditure of French civil servants. In the two countries, a new industrialist group emerged from the previous landowner elites. For example, in Syria, Lutfi Haffar launched the first water supply industry. The Iraqi and Syrian authorities elected in the 1930s faced a twofold challenge. They had to negotiate with the new fiscal law imposed by the Mandate powers and they had to reach an agreement with these elite groups. As most of the colonial powers reinforced their colonial pact and their currency block during the crisis, the new parliaments were able to make a fiscal turnaround which involved increasing tariffs in order to preserve local production and provide funds for the state, rather than implementing new land taxes. In Syria, the new National Bloc won the election in 1936 and tried to negotiate independently with France.[25] It refused to endanger its position by initiating discussions on land. In Iraq, the British countered nationalist ambitions by supporting the claims of the tribal chiefs who were the main landlords and the debate over land tax was frozen. In 1936, Sadr Biqdī instigated a coup and a new cabinet formed of young reformist politicians ruled the country for a few months. The new team briefly experimented with a land tax, but in the wake of World War II, the Iraqi cabinet halted the reform.[26] Between these two moments, several coups shook the regime and stopped the ordinary practices of the state. In this context, when the war broke out, both states shared common budgetary practices: an orthodox approach—keeping the balance between expenditure and revenue—and a low level of debt that could be reimbursed quickly.

From Crisis to the Development Approach

World War II aggravated the financial crisis. In 1941, the local authorities were side-lined by the French and the British and normal procedures ceased. New national governments were instituted in 1942 in Iraq, and in 1943 in Syria. In the first case, the British no longer ruled the country, and in the second, the 1932 constitution was re-established. These national governments had to tackle several challenges at the same time. Both countries experienced high levels of inflation: in Iraq, prices rose from 100 to 521 between 1939 and 1944.[27] This was the result of expenditure by the Allies who sent troops into both countries, but also the global growth of production to meet basic needs in the Middle East. Ordinary budgets remained low, as did their deficits. For example, in Iraq, deficits amounted to 790,000 Iraqi dinars, or 3.1 percent of global resources.[28] At the same time, both countries played an important part in the war market by providing supplies for the soldiers on the ground. The Iraqi and Syrian states owned quotas of frozen pounds, sums which covered British expenditure and could not be used directly. Therefore, they garnered resources but they could not use them. Moreover, the British and French reversed the balance by incurring debts for both countries. Finally, both countries witnessed strong Gross Domestic Product (GDP) growth due to the Allies' consumption, which led to an increase in bank deposits and assets. In Iraq, bank deposits rose from 100 in 1939 to 1050 in 1944.[29] This phenomenon created scarcity in state resources and the inflow of private capacities. However, relations between the authorities and the elites continued to take place firmly within the previously established framework.

In the aftermath of 1941, war operations ceased in the region, but the armies remained stationed on the ground. Both the British and the French launched certain initiatives to restore a new political order. In Iraq, after the invasion of 1941, the British tried to re-establish the legitimacy of the monarchy who had fled the country after a coup. At the same time, politicians who were in favor of the British had to negotiate with them to rebuild the tools of sovereignty. A new ministry led by Nuri al-Said was formed in 1942 and tackled the financial crisis. The Iraqi government borrowed 50,000 Iraqi dinars from the local market. Then, in 1943, the Bank of the Two Rivers issued a loan of 3 million dinars on the local market with a 2 percent tax-free revenue.[30] The authorities had two goals in what turned out to be a success: to draw on private surplus to correct inflation and to provide resources that would enable them to implement plans for new infrastructures. Nevertheless, it became obvious to the British and the Iraqi authorities, as they confessed, that it would be easier to solicit the British market, as it prevented public opinion from demanding political reform. Moreover, as the British consul pointed out, launching this kind of loan was the proper way to avoid new taxation, and to develop the country. Cabinets would avoid long parliamentary debates on how to expand taxes affecting the social and economic base of members of the Senate and the House of Representatives. Indeed, the budget voted in June 1941 presented a surplus: ordinary resources reached 10 million Iraqi dinars, and expenditure 8.6 million (in 1941). However this did not cover public works. An addendum in October underlined the budget deficit that required some external resources. In 1943, a new equation emerged in Iraq: debts could provide the resources that would help build the necessary infrastructures.

In Syria, the newly elected parliament and president of the Republic fought arduously with the Free French to resecure the national prerogative and, at the end of 1944, they finally gained control over the budget. However, it took several months to prepare the annual budget. Discussions in 1946 in the House of Representatives (*majlis al-niyābī*) highlighted key elements of the financial aspects of sovereignty and the debt legacy. Three aspects shed light on the new practices. First, deputies agreed to integrate debt from the ordinary budget for the Alawite territory. They denied this territory any financial autonomy. Second, they confessed that resources remained scarce and highly dependent on agricultural income. They discussed the possibility of dividing the financial year into two sessions, before and after the harvest. They ended up rejecting the idea, but they recognized the need for extraordinary expenditure in favor of major development projects. Third, they discussed taxes and tariffs in detail in order to develop state capacities without infringing privacy. Therefore, some representatives argued in favor of taxes on revenue as a tool for social justice, while others were against it. All these elements provided the background for debt discussions.

In 1946, the budget debate remained a key issue in the parliamentary session. Through these tools, representatives intended to sell out Mandate legacies. The resources reached 92.5 million Syrian lira with 30 million royalties (railways and pipeline revenues) and expenditure 113 million.[31] General debts accounted for 6.1 million Syrian lira and amounts left over from other budgets. As the minister of finance explained, the increase in debt was the result of different factors: the rise in civil servants' salaries, retirement, and the annexation of debt from the Druze and Alawite territories. The minister suggested in his proposal to cover 5.2 million Syrian lira of the previous debt. In parliament, the budgetary commission preferred to reimburse more, that is, a sum of 6.1 million, by exploiting different financial tools. This underscores why the budget committee was central. As Habīb al-Kahhāla pointed out in his memoirs,[32] parliamentary representatives ascribed a high value to the budget committee, membership of which was hotly contested. Within the committee, representatives negotiated the allocation of resources and campaigned to obtain credits for their own constituencies. Benefiting from the assembly was proof of their influence for their voters. At the same time, most of them refused any kind of taxes that might decrease their revenue. The commission also exploited the different financial tools. Part of the resources came from the *awqaf*, religious endowments controlled by the state. The state could offer loans via the *awqaf*, which could be reimbursed at different levels. It appeared that the great bulk of this public debt was managed by the state, which could borrow the amount on the private markets. However, even if the representatives wanted to reimburse and to alleviate the debt burden, they concluded that the resources would not offer a great range of opportunity: due to the increase in expenditure, the government could only requisition the waqf administrations, which normally had been devoted to religious affairs.

In both cases, the authorities inherited precarious situations in which inflation, links with European currencies, and budgetary orthodoxies left them with scarce resources. As exemplified by Iraq, local loans and then foreign loans could provide new opportunities in order to meet the challenges of independence.[33] In Syria, the conclusion was less clear. Representatives recognized the need for change but they did not articulate it with any new budgetary mechanism. They exploited traditional tools to collect a few more thousand Syrian lira to pay the interest. In both cases, the representatives looked to satisfy their own interests, their financial philosophy and the needs of the state. At the same time, they were under pressure from public opinion. The Syrian newspaper *Alif Bā'* thus called in 1946 for "a budget [that] would surprise."[34] Syria and Iraq sought to secure other resources in order to meet these demands.

While debt ratcheted up, Iraq and Syria were faced with the problem of finding financial backers. Syria belonged to the French franc zone and Iraq was pegged to the British pound. Even if they regained access to a certain amount of the frozen pounds, because they faced deficits on the British market, they were unable to decide on a global plan for their resources as each reimbursement was conditional on fresh negotiations. Each negotiation meant discussing financial issues but also defense, imperial policies, and so on. These talks took place within a tense context at a time when events in Palestine had a profound impact on public opinion.[35] It became difficult for any government to engage in discussions with the British without becoming embroiled in the struggle for Arab rights. But, through a set of initiatives, the British maintained their ascendancy over the Middle East: no other power could give the new countries assistance.[36] The first break in this asymmetric relationship came from international organizations.

At the end of World War II, the new authorities took part in building international organizations. Belonging to the International Monetary Fund (IMF) or the United Nations highlighted that they were part of the Allies and that they had contributed to winning the war. Membership of these institutions created after World War II was also celebrated in these countries as proof of having achieved independence. Debates in the Iraqi parliament illustrated the main bone of contention.[37] On the one hand, ministers claimed that membership of these institutions represented an important victory in the struggle to become a fully sovereign nation, as the Iraqis entered into discussions with the British on an equal footing. Moreover, it was thought that these institutions might provide Iraq and Syria with a loan, without the constraints of foreign powers. This fear of Western encroachment demonstrated the persistence of the state's collective memory of the late nineteenth century, when European powers dominated the late Ottoman Empire through their debts, as well as contemporary concerns regarding the asymmetric debate between a dominant power and the new authorities. Avoiding the same kind of evolution was deemed possible through membership of the IMF. On the other hand, some representatives argued that becoming a member of these institutions would lead the local currency to be controlled and that this would be equivalent to losing sovereignty. However, these new steps illustrate how sovereignty became the key point in the debate. Moreover, it shows how political factions struggled over the issue in order to promote certain policies under constraints. While most politicians avoided requesting parliament to create progressive taxation, and while needs increased and the deflationist effect on the debt aggravated the balance, a new international order was shaped in which each internal faction sought out several partners.

In this context, 1948 sent profound shockwaves through both countries. In 1948, Iraq experienced two major crises. First, in January, demonstrations broke out in the capital condemning the new treaty with Great Britain. Within a few days, the authorities lost control of the capital and protestors called for the end of the monarchy. On the final day (January 27), the crowd denounced the soaring price of bread. Finally, troops opened fire on the demonstrators, the treaty was canceled and a new cabinet was formed. A few months later, Iraq and Syria faced the Palestine war. Their politicians announced the victory of the Arab troops against Zionist forces. However, the Iraqi and Syrian armies could not win and, in December 1948, the governments recognized their defeat. This news deeply shocked Syria and Iraq. In Damascus mass demonstrations erupted, soon followed by other major cities, calling for an investigation into the defeat. The authorities came to the same conclusion: the lack of modern equipment and the lack of development were responsible for the country's backwardness, and therefore its defeat.[38] It was not a case of David against Goliath, as the Arabs were not able to get access to military supplies. Suddenly, national issues of development became the political priority of both governments. Legitimacy was directly connected to the capacities of the ministers to build up modern troops and to organize retaliation.

Both countries were rocked again in 1949. In Syria, three coups shook the political system.[39] In Iraq, emergency laws stopped all kinds of political activity in the public sphere. Parliaments were at a standstill for a few months before being re-opened. A new vocabulary emerged from this turmoil. The country had to get access to modern equipment, and social and economic conditions had to improve very quickly in order to counter Israeli progress. A new grammar of power was elaborated: efficiency and national cohesion became the key mottos for implementing change. Nevertheless, this did not bring the cabinet new resources. On the contrary, Iraq lost oil revenues, as it refused to use the Haifa refinery controlled by Israel. Syria freed itself from Lebanese intrusion in customs revenues as it brought an end to the "common interest" institutions. Therefore, on the one hand, the Syrian authorities were able to define national priorities, such as building a seaport to become independent from Beirut's infrastructure, but on the other hand, their revenues decreased as breaking the economic union disturbed the economic networks. Both countries faced a fiscal crisis at the beginning of the 1950s, as populations required their immediate needs to be met and the resources of the state remained limited or depleted. This was particularly apparent in the scarcity of liquid assets, a phenomenon duly mentioned which could be linked to excessive debt on the monetary circuit.[40]

Financing Development Through Foreign Assistance in the 1950s

In this context, several initiatives were undertaken by Iraqi and Syrian protagonists. At the beginning of the 1950s, governments faced a multi-faceted crisis. On the one hand, rural crisis, military demands and public works to equip the country created a budgetary burden. On the other hand, parliamentary debates blocked any initiative to expand taxation on the land. A common answer emerged from the debates. The crisis made it necessary to find foreign partners in order to sustain development projects and to bypass fiscal changes. Thereafter, the Iraqis and Syrians followed two different paths, which finally converged in the late 1950s. In Iraq, in late 1949, the post-crisis government quickly requested aid in order to develop the country. Nuri al-Said headed the cabinet which ended the financial crisis by reaching a deal with the British. He turned toward the British and the new international institutions when he wanted to create new infrastructures. A generational effect was at work here: Nuri al-Said entered politics at the beginning of the 1930s, he became an expert in negotiating with the British, and he handled Iraqi difficulties in matters of development, mostly in relation to agricultural and industrial issues. As the first British mission in 1937 had recommended, he tried to implement combined solutions in which building infrastructures would help to improve the quality of the land, thereby expanding the area suitable for cultivation, but would also allow for industrial use. Nuri al-Said also played a key role in exchanges with foreign powers. He belonged to the first mission, which asked for a loan in 1939, but was denied. He was the key figure in stabilizing the monarchy after the troubles of 1948, even if he had already started to search for new figures in order to ensure the stability of the regime.

To this end, he pursued talks with the British but also with a new institutional body, the International Bank for Reconstruction and Development (IBRD).[41] As the Iraqi government requested liquidity and as most of the resources were frozen due to the closure of the Haifa pipeline, Nuri al-Said and his minister of Finance, Tawfiq al-Suwaydī, first turned to the British market. Discussions began with Barings to issue 3 million pounds in loans.[42] At the same time, Nuri al-Said submitted a request to the IBRD. Initially, he asked for a sum of 6.5 million pounds toward the improvement of the railways. As the representatives of the IBRD mentioned to the British, the Iraqi request proved that the authorities did not know their own resources or their needs. After enquiring into the railway system, the IBRD concluded that it might constitute the right basis for development in Iraq. The British pushed the IBRD to deliver the loan on condition that the Haifa pipeline be re-opened. At the same time, the Iraqi government finally rejected the conditions offered by Barings, as it would prove its subordination to the British government. A new project emerged from the debates between the three partners (IBRD, the British and the Iraqi government) fueled by the Americans: the expansion of the IBRD loan to 12.5 million pounds. These new resources would be employed following the conclusion of a review from the Bank. Consequently, international loans would complete scarce resources, and allow for the construction and extension of infrastructures, mainly the Tharthar project, by implementing final expertise. A new dialogue had been created between international partners and local actors which allowed them to avoid the national arena of negotiations.

In January 1950, President Truman announced that Middle Eastern countries could benefit from new development aid. This quickly became known as the "Point IV Program" and it allowed funds to be granted subsequent to a survey of national resources.[43] The ultimate purpose of Truman's policy was to solve the Palestinian refugee problem by improving local economic conditions. It exported European patterns: the Marshall Plan helped to settle difficulties regarding population movements after the war. This nevertheless did not come up to Arab expectations. Two paths emerged from the negotiations for potential loans. In the Iraqi case, the government did not immediately refuse the help on offer.

Parliament debated for a while about how the US proposal could possibly fit with local needs. The process did not lead to a specific agreement but it gave the Iraqis some leverage in their negotiations with the British. When the latter canceled discussions about financial resources, the Iraqis turned to the Americans and requested talks with them about air bases, military supply and debt.

On the contrary, in Syria, any discussion about the Point IV Program radicalized the debate. Politicians associated the refugee problem with the Palestine issue and they refused to resettle Palestinians in Syria while Israel maintained its domination. As a result, it was thought that refugees should have the opportunity to go back to their homeland. Economic support was considered as a domestic problem and it had to be tackled in a proper way. From this point of view, as Western powers were responsible for colonization and backwardness, they had to help southern countries, but they could not tie their aid to regional or international problems. The entrance of the United States into the field of suppliers enlarged the potential scope for aid to the Middle East. Negotiations underscored how debts and loans were part of a broader dialogue on policy-building.

A new group came to power in Syria in 1950. Adīb al-Shīshaklī staged the third—and final—coup in December 1950. He refused to lead the government or to accept a ministry. A new cabinet was formed. Informally, however, it was Adīb al-Shīshaklī who ruled the country. His manner of dealing with debts and loans highlighted his ability to direct policy. When in February 1950, the Syrians were opposed to the Point IV Program, Shīshaklī then headed a delegation to Saudi Arabia. This move showed that the Arab East had split into two factions. Saudi Arabia and Egypt feared the Hashemite influence and tried to curb the predominantly Iraqi show of power. The "struggle for Syria" began.[44] From this perspective, Shīshaklī won over the Iraqi faction led by the People Party (*hizb al-shaab*). He immediately began to look for funds. His conduct remained non-institutionalized, as he acted without a clear mandate. Contrary to the Iraqis, he preferred to deal with regional rather than foreign states. This allowed him to escape any kind of foreign pressure. He managed to secure a loan within a few days: Saudi Arabia provided 6 million dollars. This amount allowed the new Syrian cabinet to experiment with new economic and social policies.

The new loan highlighted how several interests interplayed to build the budget. Important developments took place on two different levels. On the regional stage in the Middle East, Saudi Arabia used the loan to create a new partnership. It forced the Aramco oil company to increase royalties in order to fill the dollar gap. A chain of financial supply appeared to support the loans and debts: Syria contracted a loan, with no interest owed to Saudi Arabia, which helped a political faction to control Syrian institutions; Saudi Arabia proposed a loan by putting pressure on international actors such as the oil companies. On the local stage, discussions involving the Prime Minister, Khālid al-'Azm, pinpointed the main objective of this loan. While some deputies pointed out that the loan would compensate for the yearly remaining amounts of internal debts, the government refused to use the loan for this purpose. On the contrary, 'Azm declared that the loan would be entirely devoted to new infrastructures. The government received support from a wide range of representatives who ratified the new Saudi-Syrian agreement.

Shīshaklī's move also demonstrates how this powerful new politician acted on the Syrian stage. He did not first establish new institutions nor did he halt the everyday practices of the state. He endorsed the policy of the new government leader, Khālid al-'Azm, whose program mainly focused on internal reforms and new infrastructures. The new prime minister clearly stated that the Saudi loan would provide resources for infrastructure—such as the extension of the port of Lattakia—and developmental policies, rather than for the repayment of old debts.[45] A new logic emerged, to invest rather than to pay the debt. He promoted a technocratic approach to policy-making, which distanced him from the two main political groups. More broadly, there were several points on which Shīshaklī and 'Azm converged, notably economic development and a Syrian-centered focus.

Officers and bureaucrats had no revolutionary plans: they implemented a reformist approach. Consequently, Shīshaklī and 'Azm did not implement the transfer of property either in rural provinces or in industry. Admittedly, they looked to change the nature of state resources. However, in 1950, internal fighting between parliamentary groups and military factions prevented the cabinet from ensuring continuity. By accepting the Saudi loans, the new government was able to launch some projects without fear of disruption from the parliament.

Iraq and Syria took two different paths. Both found similar solutions which explained the further steps taken toward expanding public debt. Firstly, they were able to obtain emergency loans: in a matter of a few weeks, resources could be made available. Secondly, they managed to obtain loans that allowed the authorities to bypass internal debates, which involved general discussion on how to develop the country. Thirdly, they devoted resources to exceptional expenditures—particular projects, rather than ordinary budgetary practices. Fourthly, they permitted the cabinet to make contact with the "international community": while discussing a loan, the ministers could request military tools or technical assistance. These similarities and differences explained the next steps taken by each parliament.

At the beginning of the 1950s, debates revolved around the same issues in Syria and in Iraq. The state wanted to increase its resources, and most of the young politicians, or technocrats, insisted on the paramount importance of agricultural revenue and land. On the one hand, governments acting in the name of the state wanted to control rural areas, which could be achieved by taxing land. This approach meant conducting proper surveys of the land in order to clarify the different types of land. However, most of the new Middle Eastern states had not undertaken any surveys since the 1920s. Some land belonged to private landowners, some were not registered, some were part of the imperial lands left over from the Ottoman Empire, and formally fell within the jurisdiction of the state. This point became crucial in two ways. Firstly, securing state-held land could provide opportunities for implementing agrarian reform without the need to take control of private land. The state could supply its own lands. Secondly, identifying the type of land helped to determine an accurate tax rate. On the other hand, governments faced other institutional components, mostly representatives who prevented any new tax measures from being voted. Both cabinets stalled in their attempt to establish any real new land legislation. In Syria, this became part of a broader plan: the state needed audits and expertise to properly define its fiscal policies. Therefore, it was not possible to use this tool immediately. In Iraq, the first attempts at investigations in rural areas met with a brutal campaign of violence. It triggered a population exodus; people were afraid of the landlords. Finally, Nūrī al-Said was forced to concede that any agrarian reform would lead to civil war. As a consequence, cabinets were not able to subsidize further resources to concessions, royalties and loans.

In this context, in 1952 the Iraqi government invited the IBRD to undertake a broader investigation, as it was bringing a last round of negotiations with the Iraqi Petroleum Company (IPC) to a close.[46] The Iraqi government and the IPC reached an agreement at the beginning of 1952 and Nuri al-Said managed to have the parliament ratify it. He then negotiated with the court that the regent would dissolve parliament in order to secure a clear majority in favor of implementing the new budget. While

Nuri al-Said called for a new parliament, intended to include representatives who endorsed the new treaty and supported his leadership, several groups raised opposition to his project. Twin processes animated the negotiations: the court tried to sideline Nuri al-Said and to regain its ascendency over the institutions, while the opposition called for more liberal measures before agreeing to participate in the elections. Their disagreements led to overt and serious tensions. All the actors avoided solving the conflict: demonstrations duly followed. In this context, the IBRD mission sent its recommendations on how to develop the country. Social demands became a sensitive issue as crowds took to the streets and riots spread around the country.

The IBRD survey report highlighted how requesting aid from an international agency could bring about change in administrative tools. The Iraqi government requested that any British infringement be prevented. However, the British had to agree to any involvement from the IBRD.[47] The mission was nevertheless completed and sent to the Iraqi authorities, along with its principal observations. Many of them dealt with accounting for and developing the statistical apparatus. The report concluded that the acquisition of statistics required heavy investment as neither the authorities nor the members of the missions were able to collect useful data. It also proposed methods for calculating the national revenue and for anticipating the results of the main reforms. This survey was delivered along with the first loan. Its principal purpose was to help improve the administrative apparatus in order to provide the necessary funds for development projects. It was part of a more long-term trend which began in 1947, when the first census was completed. From this perspective, resorting to aid from the IBRD highlighted how loans—and debts—were a key element of broader negotiations. It showed that governments dealt with internal opposition on this issue; that the prime minister could negotiate with different powers; and that he could indicate with which alliance Iraq would align itself. Finally, getting a loan meant further administrative reforms to improve fiscal efficiency without engaging major social changes. However, when the IBRD concluded its report, the national budget had changed as royalties were to quickly increase thanks to the new agreement. It became obvious that oil revenues would cover future loans. The mechanism for the rentier state started to be put in place: because taxation was difficult to establish, the authorities looked for other sources of funding and they negotiated their international position in exchange for loans. This dynamic was reflected in the budget: an "extraordinary" budget grouped together all expenditure on infrastructure. In the mid-1950s, this became unnecessary as oil revenues grew and were soon high enough to cover exceptional expenditure. This evolution proves how rent and debts could be substituted in the Iraqi case.

In Syria, debates did not follow the same path. The institutional game changed in late 1951 when Shīshaklī staged a fourth coup and brought everyday procedures to a standstill. All political parties were forced to dissolve, General Salu then Colonel Shīshaklī headed the government, and no constitution was instituted before summer 1953. In this context, the cabinet maintained its previous course by attempting to generate greater national revenue and make universal improvements in living standards. The main target remained to challenge Israel, which required the acquisition of military equipment and an increase in the level of development. In order to provide supplies for his initiatives, Shīshaklī had to interact with foreign partners. He soon hosted the Secretary of State John Foster Dulles in Damascus and tried to convince him that providing weapons to the Arab world would help moderate governments to defend Western values. The Syrian leadership, Shīshaklī contended, was fully committed to the fight against communism through the instigation of reforms. In this context, the United States offered aid to Syria, but it was decided to channel it through the IBRD, so that Shīshaklī could not be accused of selling the country to the imperialist powers.

The mission was welcomed by a speech in the new parliament in February 1954. Although Shīshaklī was overthrown soon after its arrival, the mission continued to conduct its research. Its main conclusion pointed out that the scarce resources of the financial market were difficult to mobilize through public debt and that Syria had only agreed to borrowing from Saudi Arabia. It concluded that loans attached to further projects would improve conditions in Syria. The report nevertheless was sent to a new team. In late February 1954, Shīshaklī was overthrown and the parliamentary regime was re-established. Its members rejected old regime practices and agreements, and did not endorse the conclusion of the IBRD. They nevertheless faced the heavy burden of finding resources to improve the country. At the same time, removing Shīshaklī renewed the "struggle for Syria": each faction of the new parliament looked for allies to reinforce their internal position. Securing loans or supplies was proof of their ability to rule the country. More precisely, as the parliament was divided into equal groups—the major parties each held a fifth of the seats—the rulings of certain commissions became decisive. As the Baath Party conquered the commission of Foreign Affairs, it imposed a certain grammar of partnership. Neutrality meant refusing any alliance which forced Syria to endorse a Western position. It was synonymous with being aligned with certain regional powers. In 1955, while the Syrian government faced difficulties in terms of economic and military support, they turned toward the "neutral" groups of Arab powers to sign an agreement. At the end of the year, a tripartite agreement bringing together Egypt, Saudi Arabia and Syria offered a new way forward with the help of resources from Arab suppliers.

* * *

This long-term overview, from the beginning of the mandate period to the mid-1950s, shows how public debt was part of a broader debate. While Mandate authorities avoided expanding the capacities of the state, a change occurred in the late 1930s. Following the economic crisis, the tight balance between expenditure and resources could no longer be sustained. Moreover, during World War II, additional duties were required of the authorities. Becoming independent meant that the state had to take on new missions toward the population. Faced with the growth of expenditure due to necessities, the representatives had to find new tools. The paradox of the late 1940s and early 1950s in the Middle East was the junction of internal and external dynamics. Internally, the old elite classes refused to change the fiscal apparatus of the state while developing a discourse of the state's development mission. Externally, foreign actors such as international institutions provided funds that matched the demands of the countries. The Iraqi and Syrian authorities shifted their major resources from indirect taxes and tariffs to loans in order to face the social demands for infrastructures and military equipment. These dynamics paved the way for establishing the political mechanism of the rentier system—receiving an amount of wealth superior to needs.

Therefore, "representation without taxation" resulted from the functioning of the parliamentary systems. Several contextual elements forced the growth of expenditure such as the need for modern military equipment to match that of Israel, for public works to equip the country, and so on. As financial issues shook the governments, most of them moved away from the arena of the Assembly toward international institutions or regional partners. Requesting a loan seemed proof of being modern and fully equal on the international stage. Consequently, from local politicians' perspective, the IMF and IBRD could provide expertise and assistance without encroaching on sovereignty. On the contrary, discussing the land or revenue would jeopardize the economic base of representatives. Parliamentary dynamics paved the way for creating a credible debt on the external stage, a mechanism that avoided a certain accountability. When new military elites seized power in the 1960s, fiscal systems were already in place to allow the rentier system.

Notes

1. *Alif Bā'*, July 12, 1946.
2. Abd al-Razzaq al-Hasani, *Tārīkh al-wuzārāt al-'iraqiyya* [History of the Iraqi governments] (Saida: Matba'at al-'Irfan, 1965), t. 6.
3. Joel Migdal, *State in Society: Studying How States and Societies Transform and Constitute One Another* (Cambridge: Cambridge University Press, 2012).
4. Karl Wittfogel, *Oriental Despotism: A Comparative Study in Total Power* (New Haven: Yale University Press, 1957); Nazih Ayubi, *Over-Stating the Arab State: Politics and Society in the Middle East* (London: I.B. Tauris, 2009).
5. Odd Arne Westad, *The Global Cold War: Third World Interventions and the Making of Our Time* (Cambridge: Cambridge University Press, 2007); more generally on the Cold War in the Middle East, Rashid Khalidi, *Sowing Crisis: The Cold War and American Dominance in the Middle East* (New York: Beacon Press, 2009); Roby Barrett, *The Greater Middle East and the Cold War: US Foreign Policy under Eisenhower and Kennedy* (London, New York: I.B. Tauris, 2007); Salim Yaqub, *Containing Arab Nationalism: The Eisenhower Doctrine and the Middle East* (Chapel Hill: The University of North Carolina Press, 2004).
6. Henry Laurens, *Les crises d'Orient, 1949–1956* (Paris: Fayard, 2020).
7. Hazem Beblawi and Giacomo Luciani, eds., *The Rentier State* (London: Croom Helm, 1987); on the development of oil, Matthieu Auzanneau, *Or Noir: La grande histoire du pétrole* (Paris: La Découverte, 2015).
8. The second article of the Mandate over Syria and Lebanon recognized France as a ruler who would guide the local populations toward self-development without specifying the time-horizon, https://mjp.univ-perp.fr/constit/sy1922.htm (accessed December 19, 2019).
9. Philip Khoury, *Syria and the French Mandate: The Politics of Arab Nationalism, 1920–1945* (Princeton: Princeton University Press, 1987).
10. Ian Rutledge, *Enemy on the Euphrates: The British Occupation of Iraq and the Great Arab Revolt, 1914–1921* (London: Saqi Books, 2014).

11. The final statement was issued on April 18, 1925, and the settlement of the debts went with the moratorium in 1932.
12. *Reports of International Arbitral Awards*, April 18, 1925, vol. 1, 529–614. Several discussions followed to decide whether Iraq, Lebanon and Syria had to pay back in gold or in nominal currency. Negotiators finally agreed on nominal.
13. Ali Alawi, *Faysal I* (New Haven: Yale University Press, 2014).
14. Peter Sluglett, *Britain in Iraq: Contriving King and Country* (New York: Columbia University Press, 2007).
15. In 1921, the revenue was £3.9 million, £3.5 million in 1922, and £3.7 million in 1923. The expenditure was £4.2 million in 1921, £3.5 million in 1922, and £3.1 million in 1923, R. Jarman, ed., *Political Diaries of the Arab World: Iraq 1920–1965, Vol. 5* (Oxford: Archive Editions, 1992).
16. Geoff Burrows, Phillip Cobbin, "Financial Nation-Building in Iraq, 1920–1932," Department of Accounting & Business Information Systems, The University of Melbourne, Unpublished Paper (2010), https://pdfs.semanticscholar.org/ebb3/23c20edd09a571865181b707ff7950fbb533.pdf (accessed January 22, 2020).
17. In 1924, the amount was £173,000, £425,000 in 1925, £370,000 in 1926, £351,000 in 1927, £272,000 in 1928, £272,000 in 1929, £271,000 in 1930, see *Report of the Society of Nations, Iraq, 1930*.
18. Jean-David Mizrahi, *Genèse de l'Etat mandataire. Service de renseignements et bandes armées en Syrie et au Liban dans les années 1920* (Paris: Publications de la Sorbonne, 2003), 105–107.
19. Edmond Chidiac, "*Le bilan économique du mandat français en Syrie et au Liban (1920–1946)*" (Ph.D. diss., INALCO, 2003), 86–87.
20. al-Hasani, *Tarikh al-Wuzarat al-Iraqiya*, vol 1.
21. The expenditure was 8.2 million with the addition of the Druze and Alawite territories, and the revenues 8.1 million francs in 1936. Chidiac, *Bilan*, 176.
22. International Bank for Reconstruction and Development, Report on the Economy of Iraq, 25 February 1949.
23. Abd Allah Ismā'il, *Mufāwaḍāt al-'Irāq al-nafṭiyah, 1952–1968* [Oil Negotiations of Iraq, 1952–1968] (London: Dār al-Lām, 1989).
24. Mohammed Hadid, *Mudhakkirātī: al-ṣirā' min ajl al-dīmūqrāṭiyah fī al-'Irāq* [My Memoirs: The Fight in Favor of Democracy in Iraq] (Beirut: Dār al-Sāqī, 2006).
25. Khoury, *Syria*.
26. Muhammad Hadid, *Mudhakarrātī, al-sira'min ajl l-dimuqrati fi-l-'Iraq* (London: Saqi Books, 2006).
27. Joseph Sassoon, *Economic Policy in Iraq, 1932–1950* (London: Routledge, 1987), 117.

28. "Budget Irakien", Bagdad, July 21, 1945, box 456, Iraq 1944–1952.
29. Sassoon, *Economic Policy in Iraq*.
30. January 16, 1945, Baghdad, FO 371/45,321 (Kew); Daniel Silverfarb, *The Twilight of British Ascendancy in the Middle East: A Case Study of Iraq, 1941–1950* (New York: St. Martin's Press, 1994).
31. Majlis al-nuwwāb, *Mudhakkirat al-niyābiya* (Damascus, 1946).
32. Habib Kahhāla, *dhikkriyat al-na'ib* [Memoirs of the deputy] (Damascus: s.n, 1963), 17.
33. Majlis al-a'yân al-`irāqī (1946–1947), 4th session, January 28, 1946; Tawfīq al-Suwaydī, *Mudhakarrat* [Memoirs] (London: Dar al-hikma, 2006), 441–442.
34. *Alif Bā'*, July 12, 1946.
35. Michael Eppel, *The Palestine Conflict in the History of Modern Iraq: The Dynamics of Involvement, 1928–1948* (London: Frank Cass, 1994).
36. Roger Louis, *The British Empire in the Middle East 1945–1951. Arab Nationalism, the United States and Postwar Imperialism* (Oxford: Clarendon Press, 1984).
37. "Quota – IMF", August 21, 1946, file 10, S-0969-0002, United Nations (New York); Majlis al-A'yān al-`irāq (1945–1946), 2nd session, December 23, 1945.
38. Matthieu Rey, "How Did the Middle East Meet the West? The International United Nations Agencies' Surveys in the Fifties," *Middle Eastern Studies* 49, no. 3 (April 2013): 477–493.
39. Matthieu Rey, *Un temps de pluralisme au Moyen Orient, Le système parlementaire en Irak et en Syrie, de 1946 à 1963* (Paris: Ehess, 2013).
40. IBRD, *Economic Development of Iraq* (Baltimore: Johns Hopkins University Press, 1952).
41. Documents in FO 371/75153 and FO 371/75154 (Kew).
42. Note 9912; August 1949, FO 371/75153 (Kew).
43. Michael Heilperin, "Le Point IV du président Truman," *Politique Etrangère* 15, no. 2 (1950).
44. Patrick Seale, *The Struggle for Syria. A Study in Post-War Arab Politics, 1945–1958* (London: I.B. Tauris, 1987).
45. Notes in FO 371/82663; Matthieu Rey, "L'extension du port de Lattaquié (1950–1955), étude sur les premiers temps de la fabrique du développement en Syrie", in *Cahier de l'Ifpo* (2013): 59–82.
46. Rey, "How did the Middle East meet the West?"
47. At the same time, the IBRD tried to settle the contentious discussion between Great Britain and Iran.

PART IV

The Political Roads to Financial Markets and Global Debt Crisis (1970s–)

Few people would contest the idea that we now live in the age of a globalized financial capitalism, characterized by market deregulation, massive international flows of capital, and diminished political sovereignties. But how did we get there? Common narratives about financialization stress the critical role played by the "shock of the global" in the 1970s, with the rise of neoliberal ideas and the revolt of capital against welfare states as the usual suspects.

The four chapters gathered in Part IV tell another story: they argue that the turn to a *financialized debt regime* was fundamentally driven by political and social motives in the 1970s and 1980s, rather than produced by the invisible hand of the market, as if globalization had no political underpinnings. The decision to move from *regulated debts* to *marketized debts* originated in the late 1960s and 1970s, when many technocrats and political actors considered that the *dirigist debt regime*—which, together with steep progressive taxation, had been sustaining the funding of mixed economies since 1945—was generating too many inflationary political demands they could (or would) no longer cope with. Acting as if they were willing to "depoliticize" public debts and delegate their management to supposedly apolitical market actors, these reformers made a political choice that had far-reaching consequences, as shown in Chap. 15 by Anush Kapadia and Benjamin Lemoine in their comparative take on France and India. This complete change in public debt management led to a shift of power from state treasuries to central banks and international financial markets—as the Italian example studied by Alexander Nützenadel in

Chap. 16 illuminates—through a mix of half-improvised remedies to short-term crises and willful restraints put on state intervention in the economy. But politics did not disappear: instead, it was transferred to domestic and international institutions which were designed to be insulated from democratic accountability. Hence the growing feeling that financial markets can impose whatever they want on politically deprived communities, as was the case during the Greek crisis in the 2010s.

Nonetheless, states remained crucial actors, as their intervention and bailout plans demonstrated after the 2008 crisis. For most large advanced economies it has been a period of unprecedentedly easy borrowing. States still have the capacity to sustain high debts, but at a political cost that weakens their democratic institutions. The international relations of public debts also highlight this dimension: Jérôme Sgard shows in Chap. 17 that the debt settlement mechanism experimented by the International Monetary Fund during the Latin American debt crisis of the 1980s, for all its market-oriented reform packages, still relied on intergovernmental negotiations that had the power to exert control over the banking sector. Paradoxically, the triumphant "hyper-globalization," which followed suit in the next two decades, with greater capital account liberalization and bank deregulation, did not produce any international framework for the resolution of debt disputes, but rather a "reterritorialization" of its rules under the US legal system, as the conflict between Argentina and vulture funds illustrated in the 2000s.

The discrepancy between the financial networks of globalization and their political regime has never been so wide, which explains many of the political developments and crises that have occurred in the 2010s, especially in the Eurozone. In Chap. 18, Adam Tooze chronicles those shifts through a focus on the men who styled themselves "bond vigilantes," and their role in working this new financialized debt regime to its limits. In doing so, he highlights the close connection between the new forms of high public indebtedness, the growing economic inequalities, and the widespread dissatisfaction with democratic institutions that feed the dangerous political reactions that have swept across a large part of the world in recent years. But instead of lamenting the global "dominance of financial markets," what is needed is an account of how power relations between debtors and creditors are continuously reshaped in this new environment. As Tooze concludes, "the political economy of sovereign debt is a strategic game and it is political all the way down."

CHAPTER 15

From Debt *Dirigisme* to Debt Markets in France and India

Anush Kapadia and Benjamin Lemoine

Our contemporary wisdom on debt management is by now familiar. In 2014, the International Monetary Fund (IMF) published and circulated their Guidelines for Public Debt Management.[1] The script for international bureaucracies aimed at making market devices for managing debt the standard, legitimate, and unimpeded method by which the state should be financed. A state should hang out its shingle like any market agent and try and sell its bonds. Yet for much of the postwar period, the states of major economies from India to France used "non-market financing channels" to raise debt. These were legal mandates on banks and other financial institutions to either purchase government debt or, equivalently, deposit cash at the Treasury. Our present neoliberal common sense, illustrated by IMF instructions, sees this set of non-market techniques, which

A. Kapadia (✉)
Humanities and Social Sciences, Indian Institute of Technology, Bombay, India
e-mail: akapadia@iitb.ac.in

B. Lemoine
CNRS, IRISSO, Paris, France
e-mail: benjamin.lemoine@dauphine.psl.eu

were tightly embedded in political authority, as "distorting," unsound practices, uncompetitive and non-modern arrangements, in sum "pitfalls to avoid."

This now-standard narrative assumes that there is only one good way to achieve sound credit. This chapter challenges this idea by charting a paradigm shift in the techniques and politics governing sovereign debt that occurred in two seemingly incommensurable countries: France and India. We analyze how a system of sovereign debt management that was embedded in political authority and administrative rules and control, what we call *debt dirigisme*, was dismantled and why it has been forgotten and made unthinkable. Cutting across the developed-developing divide, market-based techniques of debt governance came to be extremely widespread between the 1960s and 1990s.

What accounts for similar techniques of debt management to crop up in such diverse locales? One answer is that France and India are less divergent than they might appear, at least at the level of statist techniques marked by an elite, technocratic *dirigisme*. A second is that both nations, albeit to differing degrees, exposed themselves to neoliberal globalization, both ideologically and institutionally. This chapter traces the establishment, crisis, and subsequent transformation of debt management techniques in France and India in order to provide two distinct entry points into a world historical shift.

In trying to assess the respective historical weight of ideological and institutional pressures being brought to bear on the French and Indian debt management systems, it is important to recall the fact that administered, non-market techniques for managing debt actually worked well, durably supplying liquidity to the state so that it could pursue social goals. Beneath the now-hegemonic rhetoric, there is a rich catalogue of historical examples where states did not draw their financial means from a market governed by the appetites and wishes of the (international and/or domestic) financial class but instead relied on regulations that were politically, administratively, and legally established to tap domestic resources.

There is nothing "natural" or obvious about resorting to the capital markets in order to finance the state; nor is it inevitable to expose the state's credit by allowing rating agencies and private investors to monitor public policies. On the contrary, between the beginning of postwar reconstruction and the current period, governments were involved in a social, political, and institutional endeavor designed to undermine and deconstruct the power of banking and financial institutions: their purpose was to discipline the financial industry in order to make it the instrument of collective projects, broad public services, and social progress. The financialization of sovereign debt management, and more broadly of the state apparatus and modes of management, that developed worldwide actually served to narrow the institutional space for these social goals.[2] We show how in both France and India, a critical conjunction of cyclical institutional weakness, vulnerability on the international front, and ideological robustness created the conditions for a structural transformation in debt management techniques.

In countries like Germany, Italy, and France, the public debt was said to be "non-marketable" at the end of the Second World War; the proportion of debt collected and managed through administrative and political regulations was considerably larger than its "marketable" or commercial counterpart, including bonds that were issued, sold, and distributed in conformity with market procedures.[3] In the United Kingdom, during that same period, the public debt was evenly divided into negotiable and non-negotiable portions.[4] By 1993, however, the commercial share of the debt had risen to 82 percent in the United Kingdom while in Germany, it grew from 8 to 81 percent between 1953 and 1993. Altogether, the so-called Golden Age of Western capitalism—from 1945 to the mid-1970s—was basically underwritten by the non-market financing of the state. In the countries where the marketable debt had been hitherto dominant, its proportion diminished notably during those years.

Commonalities across such diverse constituencies as France and India are, in the last instance, a result of both nations being component parts of a global, capitalist division of labor. It is easy to forget that France started out the postwar period as a "peripheral" economy to the American "core" before graduating to a core nation itself.[5] Both France and India have been subjected to bouts of emulative state formation by technocratic elites in alliance with party-political actors.[6] *Dirigiste* industrial policy was followed by the neoliberal planning and designing of a market economy in both nations. The different degrees of success of market planning in the two nations ultimately come down to the balance of power within nations and between these nations and global finance. Yet, even today, France's "state-directed" variety of capitalism might have more in common with Asian developmental states than European or Anglo-American varieties of capitalism.[7]

Local barricades only yield to global pressures under very specific conjunctures, and they yield in very diverse ways through active political mobilization inside the administrative apparatus. Local players use global discourses in their internecine disputes, otherwise global discourse fails to gain traction locally. On the ideological front, the period under discussion saw the rise of a narrative, issued by technocratic actors, that marked an opposition between an "ancient regime" of regulated debts and the "modern market" for sovereign debt and its "sound" management. This distinction commenced with the stabilization of "models" and standards for economic development. The end result was to frame a set of techniques as coterminous with "modernity" itself. This chapter explains how shifts and displacements regarding the *sense of normality* for public debt techniques occurred.

The application of a particular technology within historical configurations not only generates path dependency and lock-in features in policy making, but also "political" properties[8]: a certain political representation (administrative authority and political legitimacy versus market transparency, economic performance, "modernity"); a particular target for economic policies (inflation versus economic growth and reconstruction); and a specific ordering of the state's commitments and priorities (financial debt repayment versus social spending).

How did institutional arrangements that were legitimate during the era also known in the West as the "Glorious Thirty"—an era of productivity, growth, and financial "repression"—become heretical in both France and India?[9] Historicizing the present moment of hegemony of the market discourse (and practice) shows how it is actually the result of intra-elite, political fighting and competing factions *within* the state in democratic contexts. In this story, "operational" economic ideas (i.e. that directly affect reality) are mainly produced by the technocratic actors who benefit from concrete powers, capacities of action and hierarchical legitimacy.[10] In practice, however, the question does not arise in terms of a scholastic economic division; for instance, the actors do not care whether they are qualified, in these transformations, as "Liberals," "Keynesians," or "Monetarists." However, we observe a tangle of "technico-ideal" devices, where the instruments and expertise mobilized are both technical in nature and convey different conceptions of what the state and the economy should be: a greater or lesser sensitivity to (or condemnation of) *dirigisme*, different beliefs in the efficiency and legitimacy of markets in ordering or governing behaviors (including that of the administration itself). These arrangements lead to diverse relations with the state and degrees of intrusion of politics in monetary and economic affairs.

In nations that successfully climbed out of post-colonial poverty, the development state, capital controls and debt *dirigisme* all formed an institutional complex that husbanded resources to a state that in turn used a non-market mode of firm control, dubbed a "reciprocal control mechanism" by Alice Amsden, in order to subsidize growth while ensuring discipline and minimizing capture.[11] The development state was the global south's form of "embedded liberalism," and where it worked, it worked very well. It might have failed to produce East Asian levels of growth in India, but where East Asian autocracy drove an austere productive machine, India's most successful product was its vibrant democracy itself. None of these successes would have been conceivable without debt *dirigisme*.

How then did this house come tumbling down? The main contrast between our two cases is that while France went neoliberal in its debt structures, Indian debt *dirigisme* lives on in substance if not in form. Why did actors in constituencies as far apart as France and India (try to) pick apart this machine while using sophisticated arguments to legitimate the paradigm shift? Why did they succeed in some places and fail in others?

By breaking with a clear-cut divide between developed and developing states—in France, the reconstruction phase of an old European nation-state, and in India, a new nation-state born out of the crisis of the British Empire—this comparison offers a general understanding of the career of public debt but also of the economic logic behind the shift from regulated debts to marketized debts that occurred between the 1960s and 1980s.

First, we outline how debt was generated and institutionally fixed in India and France during the heyday of their respective *dirigiste* formations. Then, we explore how particular crises were opportunistically used to make the existing common sense look shopworn: internal wear and tear, external pressure, and an altered balance of power in intra-elite politics started to take a toll at particular moments in the life cycles of these institutions. Given the global nature of capitalism, paradigm shifts in debt management tend to occur when the international and domestic scenes align in a particular way; such conjunctures occurred in both our cases, as we discuss.

The Heyday of Debt *Dirigisme*

To use Peter Hall and David Soskice's term, the French "variety of capitalism" falls much closer on the spectrum to Germany's "coordinated market economy" than to the Anglo-sphere's "liberal market economy."[12] Vivien Schmidt goes further and views the French economy as more than simply "coordinated," and rather as a "state-influenced market economy" in which an elite-led state intervenes where and how it sees fit, sometimes in the mode of outright nationalization, sometimes through industrial policy, and at other times through a more coordinated-market type consolidation of wage bargains.[13] Schmidt notes that the developmental states of East Asia could also be classified in this manner.

The story of India's *dirigisme* is rather less felicitous. As many observers have noted, unlike its East Asian and European counterparts, Indian industrial policy lacked a critical outward orientation. Exports not only provided lucrative markets for peripheral nations, but also, more importantly, success in the highly competitive global market formed an objective benchmark for performance that enabled the state to allocate subsidies in a meritorious, productivity-enhancing fashion, visibly rewarding success in a way that the invisible hand of the global market would not. As a *dirigiste* economy, India had a highly protected home market before "liberalization" in 1991, but the firms it protected were not subject to export-based performance measures as they were in the case of successful developmental states. Industrial policy and the subsidy regime were therefore captured by unproductive but politically well-entrenched firms and substantial agrarian landlords, and India's growth potential remained unfulfilled.

If India had success, it was in securing democracy itself. Indeed, one can read the choices of debt management techniques directly off the democratic political settlement: market-based techniques would simply give market actors degrees of operational freedom in the debt market and quasi-sovereign power over fiscal priorities that would be inconsistent with a poor, populist democracy. Here India's development state forms a structural parallel with the *dirigisme* of the postwar period worldwide, and control naturally extended to the critical function of government debt.

The Indian and French cases of *dirigisme* came to be drawn into the neoliberal orbit for rather distinct reasons at distinct time intervals. Common to both constituencies was a set of elite technocrats who formed the conduits for an emulative state formation but also used these ideas in the service of their own power plays. Given the centrality of government debt in all state formations, technical struggles between elites over market design almost always encode deeper struggles over the very nature of the state and which constituency it served.

Techniques of *Dirigiste* Debt

What then did *dirigisme* in debt structures actually look like in institutional terms in France and India? A combination of capital controls on the external front and quantitative controls over the banking system on the internal front meant that the state had captive sources of domestic borrowing that were not subject to market discipline from within or without. This did not mean that there was no discipline on state borrowing per se, just that market discipline through the sale/purchase of government debt and the concomitant movement of interest rates was not the mechanism by which state borrowing was disciplined. Contrary to neoliberal common sense, the function of "discipline" can be performed by a variety of institutional forms and political settlements.

Just so, intra- and inter-institutional equilibria between the Treasury, the central bank, and nationalized commercial banks served to prevent borrowing excesses spilling over into inflation and/or balance of payments crises. The main goal of such institutions was, at this time, to channel, control, and direct money distribution in the whole economy, through the supervision of bank activities and/or direct or indirect nationalization.[14] Capital controls during the Bretton Woods era enabled this form of institutional discipline by limiting the presence of foreign capital and therefore the threat of a "sudden stop" of flows to the state.[15] While technocrats staffed these commanding heights of liquidity, their field of operation was itself contoured by broader socio-political contracts that demanded the delivery of economic growth and/or the containment of inflation.

In the aftermath of the Second World War and right up until the 1960s, the French state had several techniques at its disposal that made borrowing outside its own public circuits merely optional. The first five-year plan for "modernization and equipment" (from 1945 to 1950) sought to "ensure a rapid rise in the population's quality of life, and particularly with respect to food provision." Projected in the program were (1) the reinstatement of basic industries that had been damaged or destroyed during the war (coal, electricity, steel, cement, agricultural engineering, and transportation); (2) the modernization of agriculture; (3) assistance to the construction industry (buildings and public works); (4) the development of export industries; and (5) the transformation of living conditions (particularly housing). It is noteworthy how priorities were defined at the time, including by Charles de Gaulle; what counted as absolute necessity had nothing to do with today's austerity and budgetary discipline. "As far as the economy is concerned," and in order to "use common resources for the benefit of all," de Gaulle declared, "the pursuit of particular interests must always give way to regard for the general interest."[16] Here was a particular, Gaullist social contract at work, a contract that expressed itself in the formation and operation of debt structures.

After the war, there were no reserves to pay for the first plan, and the structures capable of creating, sustaining, and collecting the necessary funds needed to be reinvented. In 1945, the French Ministry of the National Economy was given the task of supervising the financing of public investments. Economic planning and a tight control of the banking system and financial markets, as well as a public and centralized system of collection and reallocation of savings in the national economy, embodied this deployment of state power. The Treasury established mechanisms that procured easy, regular, and secure resources for the state in order to provide "available liquidity in all circumstances."[17]

As for covering public deficits, the public authorities did not have to deal with interest rates established by financial markets; rates may have been low and profitable, as is currently the case, but nonetheless subject to inherent and often irrational volatility. The organization of cash flow at the time made the state the investor and the banker of the national economy: this was known as the "Treasury circuit."[18] This notion reveals how administrative daily practices, rules and mechanisms, implemented for down-to-earth reasons, could be transformed by technocrats themselves into a theoretical systematization of economic reality. It included a variety of more or less constraining mechanisms and compelled a number of financial institutions to deposit resources they had themselves collected in the economy at the Treasury.

The French Treasury functioned as the main banker in the economy, collecting deposits that allowed for a large proportion of public deficits to be covered almost automatically and outside of any market procedure. It received the funds deposited—mandatorily—by its correspondents and settled their expenses for them according to their orders, just like a commercial banker. At the same time, these deposits represented "spontaneous resources" (in the administrative jargon of the time) for the Treasury, which passively centralized these flows, there again, like a present-day large commercial bank.

This mode of financing is entirely different from the way we currently think about debt. When it did go into debt, the Treasury seldom appealed to creditors outside its own purview but instead collected and mobilized the resources of its own network of savers—the "Treasury's correspondents," composed of deposit accounts of households, civil servants or other citizens who use the French Treasury as a bank (the *guichets du Trésor*), but also public banks and institutions that had to deposit a certain percentage of their cash flows on the Treasury account at the central bank. Far from making the state dependent on external lenders, the "Treasury circuit" was a structure that made for the deployment of a truly public financial capability.

Within the circuit, interest rates were determined by the state and thus not subjected to the law of supply and demand. Money circulated within a public network of individuals or institutions that acted as depositors and short-term lenders. The state, via the Treasury, was a privileged financial actor since the resources automatically came under its purview. By 1955, this system had made the Treasury the largest collector of funds (with the exception of the Banque de France) in the French economy: "It alone collects more capital (695 billion francs) than the banking sector (617 billion) and allocates more funds (783 billion) than the entirety of the public and private institutions involved in granting credits (715 billion)."[19]

This public "earmarking"[20] of money was tethered to the nationalization of the banking and credit industry, two-thirds of which—including the Banque de France, nationalized in 1945, and four major commercial banks—was controlled at the time by the public and quasi-public sectors. Thanks to this system, the issuing of medium- and long-term bonds, which exposes the state's credit to the judgment of the markets, was no more than an optional instrument—though one that provided a complementary lever to which the French state did resort.

India had a very similar set of institutions that governed the accumulation and distribution of debt. The normative social contract was of course one of a new state promising development to a vast and poverty-stricken nation, but the operative social contract, more implicit, was a peace pact between rival factions of a dominant coalition, none of whom could dominate the others. "Democracy" in the Indian context might best be seen as a *modus vivendi* between these competing factions, more a neutral institutional dispute resolution mechanism rather than a deep commitment to inclusion or social transformation. This divided nature of dominant class power in India—a staple of the literature on India's historical political economy—generated a dynamic that gave rise to significant fiscal deficits.[21] The literature outlines the main members of these dominant classes: big business, rich agri-capitalists, and the administrative technocracy, all competing for their share of state patronage.[22] Yet, unremitting poverty and a post-colonial elite's natural obsession with sovereignty set structural limits on how this deficit could be financed.

As a poor, agrarian nation, its polity was also extremely sensitive to inflation. The demands of the political society, from both elite and subaltern constituencies, interacted with these constraints to generate an idiosyncratic institutional complex: the banking system was configured to plough substantial household savings into government paper to finance the debt. This institutional complex might be called India's fiscal-monetary machine, a structure completely analogous to France's "Treasury circuit" outlined above. Whereas in France, the Treasury itself took in deposits as liabilities and made loans or investments as assets, in India the system worked less directly. The Indian state would borrow for investment by floating bonds that were compulsorily purchased by nationalized banks and insurance companies who in turn mobilized household savings.

This machine/circuit was assembled in two main phases, the main push coming in 1969 with the nationalization of the fourteen largest commercial banks, and the second with the nationalization of six more banks in 1980. These dates mark the bookends of the Indira Gandhi regime, an authoritarian populism that required access to huge amounts of liquidity in order to keep it running. By the time the 1980s rolled around, the machine was ramshackled from overuse and foreign debt had to be resorted to in increasing amounts. Still, the machine limped on through the decade only to give way in 1991 as a global crisis of liquidity struck the world economy. Large and enduring fiscal deficits are implied by the structure of power in India: the wariness of taxing certain parts of the dominant coalition (well-connected firms, powerful rural landlords) and the requirement to subsidize others interacted with the politically magnified inefficiencies of state-run enterprises to atrophy the revenue stream of the state, while expenditures could only increase with the fractalization of politics.[23] How were these structural deficits (that one can find in France for other reasons) to be funded while avoiding inflation, maintaining sovereignty, and remaining "democratic"? India's banking system provided the institutional fix to this foundational problem.

Much like in France, the most significant regulatory feature of Indian banking was what came to be known as the "preemption" of the bank's resources by the government by means of statutory requirements. By 1991, on the eve of the crisis-fueled liberalization of the economy, commercial banks owned 59 percent of all state and central government securities combined. The Reserve Bank of India (RBI) held 20 percent and the nationalized Life Insurance Corporation 12 percent. Together therefore, these three entities held a staggering 91 percent of all outstanding government debt on the eve of reforms. The government bond "market" was truly captive. This holding had been built up over the years thanks to something called the Statutory Liquidity Ratio (SLR), namely the quantum of a bank's loan assets that must be held, by law, in government paper, calculated as a ratio of its deposit liabilities. The SLR dictates the minimum amount a bank must lend to the government itself for putatively regulatory reasons. In addition, the banks are subject to a Cash Reserve Ratio (CRR), namely the amount of cash (which earns no interest) they must deposit at the RBI.

The history of these ratios is therefore a story of the degree of fiscal imbrication in the monetary system. By the end of the 1980s, the SLR had hit its all-time high of 38.5 percent; the CRR would hit 15 percent excluding that on incremental deposits. By the time the fiscal expansion of the 1980s had done its work, in other words, over 53 percent of the entire resources of the whole banking system was being mandatorily shoveled into government debt. Banks routinely had debt holdings above the statutory limit.

As in postwar France, the Indian banking system acted as a great big intermediary between the public—who deposited their savings in the banks—and the government—to whom the banks lent via their compulsory purchases of government securities. Household balance sheets had therefore given over their leverage capacity to the government and thereby enhanced the latter's ability to achieve comparatively high yet stable debt ratios. India routinely saved upwards of 30 percent of GDP, so the savings base that the fiscal-monetary machine was built on is and remains substantial.

The Political Justification for Captive Resources

These debt machines in both France and India worked in one critical sense: they served to insulate the fisc from private capital, to govern money circulation in the economy, and thereby generate space for *dirigiste* policies. These debt machines were therefore key pillars of "embedded liberalism" in their respective constituencies.

In France, the "Treasury circuit" represented a particular vision of democracy. The technocrats from the Ministry of Finance embodied the political legitimacy of the state, which allowed them to intervene in the economy and to manage financial and monetary problems in a position of supremacy over private actors and even public opinion. The circuit acted as an efficient protection against the return of the "money wall" (*le mur d'argent*)—the obstacles previously raised by financial capitalists in order to undermine a government's attempt to engage in non-orthodox social, fiscal, and monetary policies, or, more generally, to take measures that went against their class interests.[24] Throughout the thirty years following the end of the Second World War, the average debt to GDP ratio was stable: around 15 to 20 percent as opposed to almost 100 percent today. The circuit also enabled French authorities to spare themselves the political liability of turning too systematically to the Banque de France for an advance.[25]

At the time, a government considering such an option needed to get parliamentary approval and was usually faced with a bit of popular uproar and a heated public debate. Regular parliament checks on state resources at the Banque de France (with a legal ceiling), or explicit appeals by the state to public and national savings (through a policy of Grand Loans, known as *politique des grands emprunts*) was a politically risky mode of financing, because it implied public visibility and general discussion, compared to automatic devices of debt *dirigisme* and bank supervision. As early as 1948, the state also established a system of liquidity oversight according to which banks were obliged to acquire and keep a set amount of Treasury bills. A legal provision—an equivalent of Indian SLR—known as the "Treasury bills threshold" (*bons planchers du Trésor*) required banks to purchase and hold short- and medium-term Treasury bonds in their portfolios, allowing administrative decision-making to determine rates and prices for debt and Treasuries. Such a requirement, understood as a "forced loan," was a way of making sure that the banks did not get rid of the state securities, but was also a way of controlling their activity. It worked somewhat as a system of mandatory reserves—but one in which the banks' liquid assets, instead of being deposited in the Central Bank, were systematically invested in Treasury bills. Rather than a permanent opportunity for monetary laissez-faire, these obligatory Treasury bill provisions were a lever for monetary action that could work both ways: having to keep a certain amount of state securities in their coffers, banks were restrained in their ability to over-lend to companies or households in times of inflation—while still keeping the state afloat.

Though the "Treasury circuit" model is often associated with the danger of runaway inflation, it must be recalled that in its heyday, namely the 1950s and 1960s, inflation was contained below a 6 percent average.[26] Above all, far from being limited to the management of the cash flow, the tools that were then allotted to the Treasury enabled the state to play an important role as a regulator for the *amounts* of currency and credit in circulation and a driver of economic growth. This was institutional discipline in operation.

The financing techniques of the "golden age" in France established a particular political relation between public authorities and financial institutions. In the name of general interest,[27] this technique introduced a political and administrative coordination of monetary and financial functions. For François Bloch-Lainé (one of the most famous senior civil servants in postwar France), this specificity had to do with state domination and control over the banks and short-term bills market mechanisms. He compared the French Treasury of the time with the British Treasury that "suffers the market rate instead of creating it."[28] Thanks to regulated debt, "the French Treasury remains master of the maneuver in terms of short-term rates. It is the Treasury that makes […] the law of the market by setting its own rates."[29] By making it mandatory for banks to acquire its bills, the Treasury imposed an earmarking of their money supply. The continuous issuing of securities ensured that the needs of the state were covered at all times and dispelled the threat that the markets would price its bonds unreasonably. It thus turned the state into an uncommon borrower, endowed with the power to make the rules regarding its own debt and to impose its authority on the banking and financial world. Money flows were produced, directed, and controlled by the public authorities, which devoted them to dedicated economic objectives that fulfilled the postwar Gaullist social contract: reconstruction and full employment of the means of production.

Likewise, India's fiscal-monetary machine acted as a captive source of savings from which the state could borrow, while the banking system made sure that the "preemption" of resources by the state would remain within the bounds of politically critical inflation. By capping savings rates in banks and thereby implicitly taxing savers, the system ensured that negative real interest rates were passed on to a debt-hungry state. There are no domestic or foreign debt-holders demanding fiscal rectitude from the Indian state, no bond market vigilantes as in the prototypical "third world debtor" nations such as Greece or Argentina, because the Indian state itself owned (and still owns) its major creditor, namely the nationalized banking system. There was, in the 1970s and early 1980s, plenty of room on the margin before this regime took on unstable proportions, and successive political establishments milked this margin. By serving as a critical means by which an agrarian economy was monetized, the banking system served to financialize rural savings and render them mobile in the service of running the dominant coalition.

Without this domestic source of captive finance, the dominant coalition would arguably have succumbed to crisis long before it did. Although India did have its own foreign debt crisis in the early 1990s, there was never a default on its sovereign obligations. The timing of this crisis is noteworthy: most other developing nations succumbed to international debt much sooner, pitching in to crisis in the 1970s. East Asian economies also felt the whiplash of international debt inflows and outflows in the late 1990s. India's fiscal-monetary machine served as a bulwark against foreign capital flows, often the scourge of developing economies, for most of its independent existence. Only once did this insulation give way, namely at the watershed moment of the 1990s, leading to a "liberalization" of a kind.

One could of course make the counterfactual argument that a harder budget constraint on the Indian state might have led to more productive outcomes: the very inefficiency of the state is enabled by the captive nature of its borrowing. This is no doubt true, but it misses the broader point about the underlying social contract performing some kind of last resort discipline, especially with respect to inflation. Indian political parties had to get reelected, and inflation beyond a certain point would have killed them at the polls. This political discipline might well have been too little too late, but the experience of other developing nations indicates that market discipline might well be too harsh for the political equilibrium to bear.

This section has established how institutions and techniques of state-managed debt were critical to the successes, in either political or economic terms, of *dirigiste* regimes in France and India. Savings were forced into the state's debt instruments which were then held in the banking system or by the Treasury itself. This mobilization enabled an industrial policy in France that was critical in helping a war-torn economy to rejoin the ranks of the global core economies. Moreover, this planned economic growth was achieved while containing inflation, contrary to monetarist common sense. In India, success in economic terms was not unsubstantial given the colonial record, but was more directly visible in political terms, creating the means to keep a heated, divided polity on its democratic rails even while containing inflation and keeping international capital at bay. As with any complex institutional mechanism, there was nothing inevitable about the destiny of these devices, their durability or their deletion. In the final instance, these institutions rested on a political equilibrium. If the regular, periodic need for institutional fixes coincided with a fraught political conjuncture, these institutions could be transformed. It is to an examination of these critical conjunctures that we now turn.

THE DESTABILIZATION OF DEBT *DIRIGISME*

This section examines how cyclical institutional crises in both India and France were successfully framed by an emerging neoliberal ideology and as such, requiring major institutional surgery rather than temporary patchwork. One of the key asymmetries that drove the transformation is that administrative controls did not themselves have an ideological axe to grind: they were more or less pragmatic responses to requirements for liquidity from within an overall *dirigiste* paradigm. The same is not true for market-based techniques: we only have to think of the emblematic role played by auctions in the neoliberal paradigm.

Thus in France, the economic framing of administrative tools and decisions was only implicitly justified by theory. Bloch-Lainé talks about a "rudimentary Keynesianism" of his services: "With very imperfect observation and intervention instruments, we have constantly applied ourselves to the 'good use of money printing.' Our dominant conviction (which did not exclude sadness due to loose morals) was that without sustained public investment, almost at all costs, take-off was impossible."[30] Technocrats of the time used an almost religious vocabulary to describe the behavior and beliefs of their opponents who at the outset wanted to end the use of the instruments of debt *dirigisme* and return to the natural order and legitimacy of the laws of the market in credit distribution:

> Some even piously claimed to adhere to a religion which we have, indeed, offended by objectively reprehensible sins, such as inflation. But, under the mask of an irreproachable monetary theology, they expressed displeasure, rather than exhaled virtues. They said 'growth based on a franc which is at bottom factitious, one does not progress at this price, one necessarily regresses.'[31]

But the opportunity, necessity, precise conditions, timing, and implementation of these supposedly "back to normal" market pre-war rules were not predefined or given. This framing of the postwar institutional structure as an aberration from the norm is of course a standard rhetorical move in the attempt to (re)establish hegemony. Never mind that the entire war enterprise and thirty years of successful economic growth—basically, an entire generation—were governed by these institutions. Questioning the legitimacy of debt *dirigisme* becomes a potent discursive weapon in the hands of market reformers when a moment of vulnerability in the system emerges. "Normal" crises can then be framed as systemic.

As the French case shows, destabilization can come from within the administrative apparatus and can modify, piece by piece, the whole system. Reformers can trigger crisis within a system by criticizing it, mobilizing the political class and public debate in order to accept moves and changes. The dismantling of "above the market" mechanisms began at the end of the 1960s with the precise goal of removing the state from its pedestal. The state-as-banker was undone in the name of competition and for the sake of "freeing" a sizeable portion of the financial sector. Broader ideological shifts combined with changes in technique. Liberal reformers and policy experts undertook the commodification of public debt at the Ministry of Finance for both ideological and pragmatic reasons: to prevent inflation, which became a national priority for policy makers, and to demonstrate the state's ability to act and overcome this risk.

The prioritization of struggling against inflation rather than full employment already signals a rupture in the postwar social contract between labor and capital.[32] Inflation ceased to be seen as an inevitable outcome, one that was tacitly accepted by the administration as a necessary consequence of its legitimate policies. Instead, and even if its level at this time seem contained and reasonable, inflation started to be viewed as a matter of urgency which governments needed to resolve. The Treasury's liberal reformers, and ideologist "counselors of the prince" such as Jacques Rueff, identified state-administered Treasury instruments as unsound money that led to monetary and budgetary chaos, and the cause of inflation that could be easily overcome. The shift to market financing mechanisms could, according to such officials, free the government to borrow without being concerned about inflation.[33] Of course, inflation in the late 1960s also signaled a slowing down of the postwar economic machine in many developed nations as productivity faltered even while wage demands were not trimmed.[34] Foregrounding inflation enlisted the technocrats, whether knowingly or not, in a battle to bring wage demands in line with waning productivity: economic growth would have to be curtailed to fight inflation, and thereby wage demands would have to be moderated.

Auctions became the reformer's technique of choice. Auctions of government debt instruments, argued Jean-Yves Haberer and other French reformers, allowed what they considered as true market democracy and transparency to emerge against the deprecated "excessive" bureaucratic powers and *dirigisme* of the legal requirement to hold debt. Market devices would reconstruct the interest rate level as a constraint on government borrowing instead of the state decision that prevailed under the threshold system. The gradual dismantling of the circuit was therefore not only motivated by its internal dysfunctions; it was also part of a project to limit the role of the state in monetary and budgetary affairs.

This discipline imposed on the state would prevail only after the gradual withdrawal from certain practices, disparagingly called "interventionist" at the time. The measures of the 1960s–1970s, which "consisted in putting an end to the prerogatives that the Treasury granted itself," were designed, in Haberer's words, to "introduce a *dose* of liberalism" and to return to a strong currency. But further, as the work of Éric Monnet shows, the postwar paradigm of quantitative and "qualitative" controls over money and debt was a way of imposing counter-cyclical discipline on the French monetary system without any recourse to market-based price controls, namely interest rates and discount rates. Thus, even if inflation was a concern—and whether it was an objective concern is itself a political question—the question of the choice of technique to control inflation remained.

In the Indian case, there was evidence that the system lurched into a full-blown balance of payments crisis. At the deepest level, the crisis was the result of the failure of the state's soft budget constraint to contain demands for unproductive subsidies emerging from the dominant coalition, leading to an unsustainable bloat in the fiscal deficit. As the fiscal-monetary machine became saturated with government debt, direct monetization of the deficit was increasingly being resorted to by the RBI by the mid-1980s, leading to a pushback from the technocrats at the central bank. This meant that rather than compel commercial banks to buy its debt, the government went directly to the central bank and had it credit the government's account with the central bank with more funds against the issuance of more debt. This is one way of "printing money" in a state-credit money system, with all the inflationary risks attendant to that term.

In short, central bankers were being made responsible for fueling inflation. The technical means by which these technocrats sought to push back was again the marketization of government debt. Yet, this came too late to stop the leveraging up of the nation on short-term foreign debt from highly liquid global markets, itself a direct result of the saturation of the fiscal-monetary machine.

The Indian crisis was in substantial measure born out of a political abuse of the machine erected to institutionally paper over the country's divided polity. The political system was leveraging up its banks to saturation point. SLR (the ratio of bank deposits that had to be invested in government paper) increased 8 percent over the 1970s and just 4.5 percent over the 1980s, a period when the government debt ballooned. Even though the need for resource preemption increased with the huge increases in the fiscal deficits, the rate of preemption declined, a clear indication that the system was saturated. The politics of the system began to push against its limits. Growth of this form of preemption is predicated on the healthy growth of the banks, yet the very fact of preemption acted as a tax on that growth in the Indian context.

As the fiscal-monetary machine overheated with ever-increasing resource preemption, the debt-carrying capacity of the banking system reached saturation point. With the loan book itself politicized, non-performing assets started to rise as well as the 1980s progressed. With fiscal pressure unabating, the system found a solution by going one level higher up in the hierarchy, to the central bank itself. It was at this point that reform-minded technocrats across the government started to push back.

This also happened to be the point at which the *dirigiste*, Keynesian common sense of the postwar period began to fade globally. With the disrepair of the growth machine in the developed West, the strident counter-hegemony of monetarism began to take hold. In order to contain the increasing menace of inflation, this ideology held that central bankers ought to be statutorily independent from the fisc and focus narrowly on targeting the money supply in order to contain inflation. Because the fisc's money creation was often considered as the main (but not the only) source of inflation, containing inflation was tantamount to containing the fisc. Far from being merely a technocratic operation, monetarism aimed to change the political settlement itself, as its progenitors were well aware, albeit it by technocratic and therefore less publicly visible means. Indian central bankers started to use monetarism to hold back the fisc as the fiscal-monetary machine overheated and the balance sheet of the central bank itself was being encroached upon, leading to a dangerous increase in inflation. With the formation of the Committee to Review the Working of the Monetary System, which gave its report in 1985, Indian central bankers were giving notice that they had been pushed far enough.[35]

Monetarism was the discursive means by which the system was seeking to self-correct. This meant creating a market for government paper in which the RBI could intervene to control the money supply rather than having the state fund itself from banks and the central bank itself. Market discipline was meant to harden the state's budget constraint. The balance of the Committee's membership was framed to push this line. The Committee concluded that "it would be desirable, in the Indian context, to assign to the monetary authority a major role in promoting price stability, and also to accord price stability a dominant position in the spectrum of objectives pursued by the monetary authority."[36] In order to pursue this objective, the RBI should adopt "monetary targeting with feedback," a convoluted formulation that undid the strictures of conventional monetary targeting because any rigid policy rule that targeted money growth would constitute more discipline on the fisc than the political settlement could bear; "feedback" conceded this point. In the case of France, monetarism was introduced more covertly.

Populist politicians in India who live through the distribution of often unproductive patronage, jealously guard their fiscal autonomy. Unlike the reciprocal control mechanism of a well-functioning development state, in India, subsidies are not being exchanged for measurable performance: they are tokens of patronage that maintain a dividend distribution of power. As they are driven by electoral discipline that is also the source of their patronage powers, the one thing that disciplines populists is inflation. Populists are therefore disciplined by democracy, but there is plenty of space before inflation kicks in to run a patronage game. Once inflation above 10 percent kicks in, all populists are similarly constrained, and therefore trim their sails correspondingly.

Cultivated Exposure to International Finance

If debt *dirigisme* is defined by an institutional insulation of state borrowing from foreign capital and private investment, then its demise is signaled by the penetration of these defenses by global markets. After all, liquidity can be sourced from various locales, but the attendant politics of that liquidity will substantially differ depending on the source. The French and Indian cases show how domestic disputes over debt management coincided with a major climate change in the global financial weather system. Jacques Rueff, one of the main French critics of what he called the "unsound" international inflationist regime of Bretton Woods, was simultaneously calling for auctions of state debt to finance the national state.

This argument had some resonance during the 1960s because de Gaulle became sensitive to complaints against the hegemony of the dollar.[37] As the argument to maintain the international standing of the franc was strengthened within the administration, alternative explanations were ruled out. Indeed, another thesis was available but was losing strength: it consisted in accusing the lack of monetary cooperation and economic diplomacy between states.[38] It was not "the economic policy of France" per se that was the problem, but rather "the failure of an attempt to organize international relations within Europe in the face of erratic capital movements."[39] In the 1980s, even within the socialist camp, this problematization was marginalized. Once again, national and international reforms, criticisms, and strategic moves were interacting in a reciprocal and reinforcing manner.[40]

The critical functional predicate for the effectiveness of quantitative, administrative controls over a credit system is capital controls: financial autarky is a corollary of functional financial control of the debt-*dirigiste* type. Debt *dirigisme* is after all a species of *dirigisme* more generally; it can only work if the state can administratively inflate and deflate the economy without the opposition that comes from deep and liquid money markets. Another way of saying this is that workable administrative controls require a state to be able to vary its exchange rate and its interest rate independently of each other in a cooperative and diplomatic way—as Bretton Woods institutions originally allowed. As the so-called trilemma of open economy macroeconomics—wherein a government can choose only two out of three levers to control: capital flows, interest rates, or exchange rates—came to be configured to open the capital account de facto in the late 1950s, governments gradually lost operational freedom over money as another player of substantial size could now move money in and out of sovereign economic space, namely global capital markets. By 1959, most European nations had returned to full convertibility on the trade account even while the capital accounts of many would remain controlled well into the 1980s. Thus capital flows could be disguised as trade flows through techniques such as over/under invoicing of imports/exports. This started to let the air out of the apparatus of administrative control.

With the capital account now increasingly open *de facto*, debt *dirigisme* became increasingly difficult as international constraints rapidly became more binding. Once the link between domestic and international liquidity was reestablished in practice, international capital could now express its views in a meaningful way on the currency markets. The threat of this daily referendum[41] on monetary and fiscal policies pushed nations to extreme positions as regards the management of their currencies. Nations either gave up controlling currencies altogether and let the market decide in a way that made the price of currencies flexible, or they sought to fix their currencies permanently to other currencies, mainly those of trade partners, in order to minimize the deleterious effects of currency volatility on vital trade relations. Europe obviously went the latter path, permanently handing over monetary sovereignty to an autonomous body and thereby limiting the scope of any future debt *dirigisme* forever.

This transition did not occur overnight, with many intermediate steps that entailed careful management of the currency and debt markets before a complete handover to the market could be carried out; most OECD nation currencies were still managed by respective central banks in the 1970s and 1980s. But a section of the French establishment, keen Europeans, sought to peg the franc to the mark and create a pan-European system to discipline nation-states and their money.[42] A classic, Polanyian double movement was coming into focus. Liberals sought to construct a global market, facilitate the untrammeled movement of capital, and curtail the state, while the social contract pushed the fisc to expand in ways that were becoming increasingly constrained. The incoming socialist government of François Mitterrand soon discovered these constraints in 1981 as its expansionist policies led to an attack on the franc and a curtailment of expansion.

Re-constructing Capital Markets with Sovereign Debt

While the early 1980s were a neoliberal watershed in many constituencies, it was often the case that left-wing governments were the agents of neoliberal reforms, such was the extent of international financial pressure coupled with a new technocratic consensus. This was the case in France, where 1981 saw the emergence of an avowedly socialist government under François Mitterrand. As with Bill Clinton a decade later in the United

States, Mitterrand entered office with plans that would expand the fisc, only to find that the constraints of a reemerging finance were very binding. But it fell to the socialists to find a narrative to legitimate bringing market techniques into a world of debt *dirigisme*. The 1980s were an important moment for bond market naturalization in France, because it won political legitimacy, by being approved by the socialist experience of François Mitterrand. Pierre Bérégovoy, one of the most famous socialist ministers of Finance, known for his working-class origins, justified these reforms "in the name of the ordinary man" and as a protection of small savings: the continuation of disinflation was the guarantee meant to sell market techniques to the socialist voter. The mechanisms of competition would reduce the cost of credit and interest rates and favor the average Frenchman rather than the speculator.[43] According to Jean-Charles Naouri, his main cabinet advisor:

> In Bérégovoy's cabinet, we knew what had to be done. This had been evident for a decade at least. The first thing was to be sure that Bérégovoy was with us in that 'coup'. We had many compelling arguments with which to defend [the reforms]. But Bérégovoy was obsessed with only one question: will it make credit less expensive for the French?[44]

In the name of small savings and the lower middle-class (a political justification one can observe in many other historical situations),[45] the socialist minister broke the barriers of financial regulation and paved the way for a large French capital market open to global capital. Left-wing leaders who implemented the reforms during these years were by no means new converts to financial orthodoxy and deregulation: they were the "usual suspects," namely the liberal wing of the socialist party.[46] Thus, Jacques Delors, whose Christian and social democrat leanings by no means tended to "Jacobinism" or "state *dirigisme*," was quite prepared to break with any form of administered economy. The 1980s can be understood as an ideological and technical U-turn for socialism, that is to say, an acceptance of market exclusivity in state financing techniques, and the refusal of plurality and pragmatism regarding market techniques or regulated debt. Jean-Yves Haberer, who meanwhile had become the Treasury manager, explicitly refused, in the early years of the Mitterrand presidency, to examine *dirigiste* solutions aimed at financing the state (i.e. the "Treasury bills threshold") stigmatized as residues of an "archaic past." This refusal might have been couched in technical terms, but it encoded a political, indeed ideological, preference. With the reopening of global markets and the binding of the external liquidity constraint, the liberal wing of the socialists was emboldened. And with purportedly left-wing parties now legitimizing the new market techniques in the name of the common citizen, the way was open for the full-fledged dismantling of debt *dirigisme* in France.

Market techniques, initially a political and technocratic project in managing the economy and monetary affairs, became fully depoliticized. By the end of the 1980s, politics had become inoffensive for financial actors, as proclaimed by a bank presentation performed during a road show of the French Treasury: "Regardless of who wins presidential election in May 1988, the French Bond Market will not suffer."[47] It was quite a performance: socialism in France turned to the capital markets as a solution for economic diseases, whether inflation or "lax" fiscal and monetary policies. Market devices—and the related deregulation of capital markets—were also understood as a way to promote healthy growth, based on real savings and "sound" money, but also to organize the access to cheap credit for the middle class, considered as the socialist party's new core electorate.[48] Describing the politics of this transformation brings out the changing nature of state agency, which behaved "as if" it was a regular borrower,[49] an issuer among many others and "a *homo economicus* preoccupied with calculating its own financial benefit."[50]

In the Indian case, as the domestic debt engine overheated with deficits rising from political demands, marginal liquidity was sought at ever-higher levels of the credit system. Demands moved from the banking system to the central bank's balance sheet. When the technocrats at the central bank pushed back, the system sought liquidity even higher up in the hierarchy of money, namely the international money markets. These markets were of course much less forgiving as creditors than the captive fiscal monetary machine to which the Indian settlement was accustomed. Through the 1980s as a more neoliberal regime was becoming embedded in the ruling Congress Party, borrowing on the sovereign account was increasingly done at short durations and in foreign exchange. A substantial IMF loan, the Fund's largest up to that date, in 1980 provided a good housekeeping seal of approval for foreign creditors flush with funds from the latest oil shock. External debt to GDP went to 30 percent by the end of the decade, with short-term debt steepling to almost four times as much as foreign exchange reserves.

Skating on thin ice, the shocks of the early 1990s were enough to plunge India into its worst-ever balance of payments crisis since independence, providing Indian neoliberals with a historical opening and ushering in India's own "liberalization" moment. Government debt is about getting liquidity in real time to the state. As the biggest economic entity in the land (even liberal states are upwards of a full third of their economies), the state's liquidity operations will affect the entire liquidity conditions of any economy. To ensure the state's capacity to undertake liquidity actions with minimal opposition was the stated aim of debt *dirigisme*. The stated aim of neoliberalism was to counterbalance the state in this regard. Its preferred method was a market for liquidity that was global so that the entire heft of global finance could be brought to bear in disciplining state finances.

Thus whether through inflation in France or foreign debt in India, the international sphere was brought into contact with state finance and debt *dirigisme* was substantially dismantled. The developing Indian nation held on to its nationalized banks even after liberalization and continued to "repress" finance to a substantial degree, keeping foreign investors largely out of the domestic government bond market. Debt *dirigisme* was too critical a prop for India's political balance to give up; it returned to the insulation of its domestic fiscal-monetary machine as soon as the machine was repaired. By then, the fisc had been shrunk to some extent and the script flipped in favor of a dominant neoliberal narrative. But the institutional ensemble of the fiscal-monetary machine trundled on albeit in truncated form, producing India's democracy rather than robust capitalism. India's debt management system was and remains subservient to the reproduction of its clientelist politics with democratic features. With the rise of neoliberalism in the early 1990s, the Indian debt management system has been given a thin veneer of market structures with the RBI now limited in what it can do directly, but the ownership of public debt remains largely in the hands of nationalized banks and insurance companies. The ideology of "fiscal responsibility," read as keeping the ratings agencies happy, contains the debt. Thus, unlike in France, India's "Treasury circuit" remains substantially intact even as it is continually criticized as premodern.

* * *

We have outlined the career of debt management institutions and ideologies at similar conjunctures in two state-dominated economies: India and France. The domain of debt management is an elite-dominated space where a small, tightly networked set of people make micro-technical choices with macro-political implications. What we document here, therefore, is a shift in planning techniques from *dirigiste* to neoliberal. Whereas in the first paradigm, the pretensions to planning sit on the surface, in the second they hide behind discourses of market liberalism.

Yet markets themselves are highly engineered spaces, a point made two generations ago by Karl Polanyi. Neoliberalism distinguishes itself from classical liberalism (Polanyi's concern) by the explicit use of planning methods that seek to actively design markets and thereby achieve liberal ends.[51] Classical liberalism advocated a night watchman state that let the market get on with it; that ideology died in the epic trauma of what Churchill called the Second Thirty Years War in which the Great Depression marked half time. No more could "the market" be left to itself, at least at the operational level. Whatever rhetorical devices were used outwardly, market structures would have to be consciously constructed, planned, organized, and systematically reinforced by a committed, technocratic elite using state power.

This process of neoliberal capture is essentially contradictory because the self-presentation of neoliberalism continues to be that of classical liberalism, namely an advocacy of rolling back the state.[52] Nowhere is this contradiction more apparent than in the battle over the design and construction of government bond markets. Monetary systems are inherently hierarchical, but there is always a political struggle to determine the contours of this hierarchy.[53] The state's bond is the benchmark bond, the safest asset, the price of which sets the terms of borrowing in the entire economy. And the price of state bonds can be set either administratively or through a government bond market.

The government debt market is therefore the taproot of the fisc, but it is only one choice along a continuum of planning and control techniques. Recall that even today, the benchmark price of money, the interest rate, is a fixed price set administratively by a central bank. Far from being a market price, the markets take their cue from this administered price. In the monetary space with its natural hierarchy, the distance between *dirigiste* and neoliberal planning techniques can be short indeed. This concentration of monetary power makes debt management techniques, administered or market-based, a key battlefield in the struggle to control the economy as a whole. This is why the formatting of the debt management function is a subset of broader economic planning operations whether of the *dirigiste* or neoliberal variety.

This chapter has outlined two formatting struggles over the institutions of government debt in two constituencies defined by the guiding hand of the state in economic life. Like the French establishment, India has cultivated an elite stratum of technocrats. Being *dirigiste* operations, both political economies evolved in similar ways under neoliberalism. As the *dirigiste* grip on the French economy began to slip in the 1970s and especially the 1980s, the degree of discipline and orientation the French state could impose on large, well-connected firms began to ebb. Even if France didn't evolve into a full-fledged liberal market economy of the Anglo-American type, financial markets pressured French currency, public finance, and social spending.

India's failure to develop in the first instance can, in large measure, be written up to its inability to drive its corporate oligarchs into a more productive direction. "Liberalization" merely accentuated the freedom of Indian oligarchs and indeed added substantially to their number. Thus a corporate, oligarchical elite emerged as increasingly autonomous from both the state and the market in the post-*dirigiste* period in India. In retrospect, part of the ultimate failure of the debt *dirigisme* regime was not that "unnatural" restraints on capitalism were bound to fail, but that such an invocation of capitalist teleology failed to find its equivalent in the nationalist alternative that was put in place. There was no counter-hegemonic narrative that the welfare state and administered capitalism could be said to express. When the latter was criticized and thrown into crisis, therefore, it was a relatively easy discursive task to cast these failures as inevitable and trot out the argument from freedom: French neoliberal planners in particular adopted this rhetorical strategy but so did India's.

In the case of the developing world, this discursive imbalance was amplified by being overlaid with another potent ideological asymmetry, that of the Occident and the Orient. This combined with the peripheral nature of India's economy to give its elites less room to maneuver, but the common contours with the French system are apparent. India is a good test case for the operation of capitalist discursive power given the relative political weakness of market-based reformers in this poor democracy. Even today, a full quarter century after the signal crisis of 1991, the market-based paradigm reigns supreme at the level of technical discourse, even as it is honored largely in the breach. This shortfall is written up merely as contextual and conjunctural: best practice tells us where we have to go, we just need to account for some local infelicities in order to get there. The internalization of an orientalist, end-of-history ideology is hegemonic at the level of the dominant legitimating discourse. In both France and India, the argument from nation and state tends either in the direction of rightwing populism or moth-eaten, ameliorist left-wing welfarism. Neither has as yet managed to breach the hegemonic dominance of market-constructing neoliberalism. But the game is still in play, and new counter-hegemonic players may yet emerge from the nation.

NOTES

1. "Revised Guidelines for Public Debt Management," prepared by the Staffs of the International Monetary Fund and the World Bank, March 2014, Washington, International Monetary Fund. See also the common framework edited by the staff of the IMF and the World Bank in 2001 and prepared by a working group and task force that included government members, Treasury, and Central bank representatives of many economies of the world.
2. Christine Trampusch, "The Financialization of Sovereign Debt: An Institutional Analysis of the Reforms in German Public Debt Management," *German Politics* 24, no. 2 (2015): 119–136; Andrea Lagna, "Derivatives and the Financialization of the Italian State," *New Political Economy* 21, no. 2 (2016): 167–186; Florian Fastenrath, Michael Schwan, and Christine Trampusch, "Where States and Markets Meet: The Financialization of Sovereign Debt Management," *New Political Economy* 22, no.°3 (2017): 273–293.
3. In Canada, from 1946 to 1976, public debt went down from 85 to 37 percent; in the Netherlands from 99 to 61 percent, and in Spain from 100 percent in 1945 to 22 percent in 1978. In France, even throughout the 1970s, three quarters of the techniques of state financing still pertained to the "non-negotiable," or in other words administered, share of the debt. From 1987 onward, however, the proportion was reversed and the "negotiable" instruments, subjected to the law of the financial markets, became predominant. Cf. S. M. Ali Abbas et al., "Sovereign Debt Composition in Advanced Economies: A Historical Perspective," *International Monetary Fund*, Fiscal Affairs Department, September 2014.
4. Abbas et al., "Sovereign debt composition."
5. See the influential paper by Michael P. Dooley, David Folkerts-Landau, and Peter Garber, "An Essay on the Revised Bretton Woods System," National Bureau of Economic Research, Working Paper 9971 (2003).
6. See Benedict Anderson, *Imagined Communities: Reflections on the Origin and Spread of Nationalism* (London: Verso, 1991) and Partha Chatterjee, *The Nation and its Fragments: Colonial and Postcolonial Histories*

(Princeton: Princeton University Press, 1993) for arguments concerning the emulative modularity of nation-state forms.
7. Vivien Schmidt, "Varieties of Capitalism: A Distinctly French Model?" in *The Oxford Handbook of French Politics* (Oxford: Oxford University Press, 2016), 11–10. See also Bruno Amable, *The Diversity of Modern Capitalism* (Oxford: Oxford University Press, 2003).
8. Science studies scholars observe how technologies and sciences problematize political decision-making and democracy. Langdon Winner, *The Whale and the Reactor: A Search for Limits in an Age of High Technology* (Chicago: University of Chicago Press, 1986); Brice Laurent, *Democratic Experiments. Problematizing Nanotechnology and Democracy in Europe and the United States* (Cambridge, Mass.: MIT Press, 2017). This paper extends this scope by considering how public administration devices (such as fiscal tools) perform a trade-off between social categories, transform, and then stabilize a particular political order.
9. Rawi Abdelal, "Writing the Rules of Global Finance: France, Europe, and Capital Liberalization," *Review of International Political Economy* 13, no.°1 (February 2006): 1–27; Eric Helleiner, *States and the Reemergence of Global Finance* (Ithaca: Cornell University Press, 1994); Barry Eichengreen, *Globalizing Capital: A History of the International Monetary System* (Princeton: Princeton University Press, 1996).
10. Cf. the chapters by Alexander Nützenadel and Jérôme Sgard in this volume.
11. Alice Amsden, *Asia's Next Giant: South Korea and Late Industrialization* (Oxford: Oxford University Press, 1992).
12. Peter A. Hall and David Soskice, *Varieties of Capitalism: The Institutional Foundations of Comparative Advantage* (Oxford: Oxford University Press, 2001).
13. Schmidt, "Varieties of Capitalism."
14. Éric Monnet, *Controlling Credit: Central Banking and the Planned Economy in Postwar France, 1948–1973* (Cambridge: Cambridge University Press, 2018).
15. Helleiner, *States and the Reemergence of Global Finance*.
16. Speech by the Général de Gaulle, 12 September 1944, at the Palais de Chaillot, quoted by Claire Andrieu, *Le programme commun de la Résistance, des idées dans la guerre* (Paris: Les éditions de l'Érudit, 1984), 114.
17. Laure Quennouëlle-Corre, *La Direction du Trésor, 1947–1967: l'état-banquier et la croissance* (Paris: Institut de la gestion publique et du développement économique, 2000), 244; Jean-Pierre Patat and Michel Lutfallah, *Histoire monétaire de la France au XXe siècle* (Paris: Economica, 1986), 121.
18. For another presentation of the "circuitist view," see Éric Monnet and Blaise Truong-Loï's chapter in this volume (Chap. 19).

19. See the chapter by Eric Monnet and Blaise Truong-Loï in this volume.
20. Viviana Zelizer, *The Social Meaning of Money. Pin Money, Paychecks, Poor Relief and Other Currencies* (New York: Basic Books, 1994); Vincent Gayon and Benjamin Lemoine, "Argent public," *Genèses* 80, 2010; Nathalie Daley, "La banque de détail en France: de l'intermédiation aux services" (CERNA, Mines Paris Tech, 2001).
21. See among others, Pranab Bardhan, *The Political Economy of Underdevelopment in India* (New Delhi: Oxford University Press, 1984); Michal Kalecki, *Essays on the Economic Growth of the Socialist and the Mixed Economy* (London: Unwin, 1972); Kakkadan Nandanath Raj, "The Politics and Economics of Intermediate Regimes," *Economic & Political Weekly*, 7 July 1973; Partha Chatterjee, "Democracy and Economic Transformation in India," *Economic & Political Weekly*, 19 April 2008; Matthew McCartney and Barbara Harriss-White, "The Intermediate Regime and Intermediate Classes Revisited: A Critical Political Economy of Indian Economic Development From 1980 to Hindutva," *Working Paper Series of Queen Elizabeth House*, Oxford, 2000; Vamsi Vakulabharanam, "Does Class Matter? Class Structure and Worsening Inequality in India," *Economic & Political Weekly*, July 17, 2010.
22. See Pranab Bardhan, *The Political Economy of Development in India* (Oxford: Basil Blackwell, 1984) in particular.
23. See Sanjay Reddy, "A Rising Tide of Demands: India's Public Institutions and the Democratic Revolution," in *Public Institutions in India: Performance and Design*, eds. Devesh Kapur and Pratap Bhanu Mehta (New Delhi: Oxford University Press, 2007).
24. In France, the expression became famous after the traumatic Treasury crisis faced by the so-called Lefts Cartel government in 1924. Edouard Herriot, then head of the government, coined it to characterize the hostility of the banking and financial milieus to his reformist agenda and their attempts to dissuade him by undermining the French economy. Jean-Noël Jeanneney, *Leçons d'histoire pour une gauche au pouvoir. La faillite du cartel (1924–1926)* (Paris: Seuil, 1977, ²2003).
25. See Stefanie Middendorf's chapter on Germany in this volume.
26. Inflation was indeed stable during that period, except for a non-negligible hike of 15.8 percent in 1958. However, it returned to double figures starting in 1974. Thomas Piketty, *Les hauts revenus en France au XXème siècle. Inégalités et redistribution (1901–1998)* (Paris: Grasset, 2001), 689–90.
27. September 12, 1944, speech by Charles de Gaulle at the Palais de Chaillot, cited by Andrieu, *Le Programme commun de la Résistance*, 114.
28. François Bloch-Lainé, *Profession fonctionnaire* (Paris: Seuil, 1976), 70.
29. Bloch-Lainé, *Profession fonctionnaire.*

30. François Bloch-Lainé and Jean Bouvier, *La France restaurée. Dialogue sur les choix d'une modernisation* (Paris: Fayard, 1986).
31. Bloch-Lainé and Bouvier, *La France restaurée*, 106.
32. Wolfgang Streeck, *Buying Time. The Delayed Crisis of Democratic Capitalism* (London: Verso, 2014).
33. Monnet, *Controlling Credit*.
34. Robert Brenner, *The Boom and the Bubble: The US in the World Economy* (London: Verso, 2002).
35. *Report of the Committee to Review the Working of the Monetary System* (Bombay: Reserve Bank of India, 1985).
36. *Report of the Committee to Review*, 146.
37. Christopher Chivvis, "Charles de Gaulle, Jacques Rueff and French International Monetary Policy Under Bretton Woods," *Journal of Contemporary History* 41, no.° 4 (October 2006): 701–720.
38. The "failed cooperation of the 1970s" that Eric Helleiner emphasizes, *States and the Reemergence of Global Finance*.
39. Alain Boublil, an adviser to François Mitterrand, who often defended heterodox positions between 1981 and 1983. Memo by Alain Boublil, 5 April 1982, Elysée Archives. Quoted by Anthony Burlaud, "Les Socialistes et la rigueur" (Master's diss., University Paris I, 2011), 85.
40. Rawi Abdelal, Mark Blyth, and Craig Parsons, eds., *Constructing the International Economy* (Ithaca: Cornell University Press, 2010).
41. Wolfgang Streeck explains and extends this mechanism to government debt auctions in *Buying Time*; Benjamin Lemoine, "Democracy and the Political Representation of Investors. On French Sovereign Debt Transactions and Elections," in *The Making of Finance. Perspectives from the Social Sciences*, eds. Isabelle Chambost, Marc Lenglet, and Yamina Tadjeddine (London: Routledge, 2018).
42. David R. Cameron, "From Barre to Balladur: Economic Policy in the Era of the EMS," in *Remaking the Hexagon: The New France in the New Europe*, ed. Gregory Flynn (Boulder: Westview Press, 1995), 124–128. On the same period, see David R. Cameron, "Exchange Rate Politics in France, 1981–1983: The Regime-Defining Choices of the Mitterrand Presidency," in *The Mitterrand Era. Policy Alternatives and Political Mobilization in France*, ed. Anthony Daley (New York: New York University Press, 1996), 56–82. Giscard and Schmidt and their initiative on the EMS, cf. Eichengreen, *Globalizing Capital*.
43. Paul Lagneau-Ymonet and Angelo Riva show the correlation between liberalization and the defence of "popular capitalism": "La privatisation paradoxale d'un étrange bien public: la bourse de Paris dans les années 1980," *Genèses* 3, no.° 80 (2010): 49–69.

44. Interview by Rawi Abdelal, *Capital Rules. The Construction of Global Finance* (Cambridge, Mass.: Harvard University Press, 2009), 61.
45. This language is mobilized across history and sometimes for completely different ends. See, for instance, Nicolas Delalande's chapter on the First World War in this volume.
46. Marcos Ancelovici, "The Unusual Suspects: The French Left and the Construction of Global Finance," *French Politics* 7, no. 1 (April 2009): 42–55.
47. Archives of the Centre des Archives Économiques et Financières (CAEF), French Ministry of Finance, consulted by Benjamin Lemoine.
48. Benjamin Lemoine, *L'ordre de la dette. Les infortunes de l'État et la prospérité du marché* (Paris: La Découverte, 2016); Mathieu Fulla, *Les socialistes français et l'économie (1944–1981). Une histoire économique du politique* (Paris: Les Presses de Sciences Po, 2016), 470.
49. Jérémy Morales, Yves Gendron, and Henri Guénin-Paracini, "State Privatization and the Unrelenting Expansion of Neoliberalism: The Case of the Greek Financial Crisis," *Critical Perspectives on Accounting* 25, no.°6 (2014): 423–445.
50. Roi Livne and Yuval Yonay, "Performing Neoliberal Governmentality: An Ethnography of Financialized Sovereign Debt Management Practices," *Socio-economic Review* 14, no.°2 (April 2016): 339–362.
51. Philip Mirowski and Dieter Plehwe, eds., *The Road from Mont Pèlerin: The Making of the Neoliberal Thought Collective* (Cambridge, Mass.: Harvard University Press, 2009).
52. Mirowski and Plehwe, *The Road from Mont Pèlerin*, 38–44.
53. Perry Mehrling, "The Inherent Hierarchy of Money," in *Social Fairness and Economics: Economic Essays in the Spirit of Duncan Foley*, eds. Lance Taylor, Armon Rezai, and Thomas Michl (New York: Routledge, 2013); Anush Kapadia, "Europe and the logic of hierarchy," *Journal of Comparative Economics* 41 (2013): 436–446.

CHAPTER 16

The Political Economy of Debt Crisis: State, Banks and the Financialization of Public Debt in Italy since the 1970s

Alexander Nützenadel

In January 1976, the governor of the Italian Central Bank Paolo Baffi received an alarming note from the director of the research division Tommaso Padoa-Schioppa. "The complete depletion of all foreign reserves and credit has brought Italy to a dramatic national crisis, similar to the landing of American troops in Sicily in 1943 ... In this situation, economists cannot claim that the origins of the crisis are non-economic, and that suggesting political measures would mean exceeding their competence. Instead, economists have to assume responsibility and propose solutions based on economic and not political considerations." Important actions, according to Padoa-Schioppa, consisted in a mobilization of private savings, a more efficient tax system, and the privatization of public economic activities (especially state participation and planning in industry and banking) in order to create a more competitive economy.[1]

A. Nützenadel (✉)
Department of History, Humboldt University, Berlin, Germany
e-mail: nuetzenadel@geschichte.hu-berlin.de

© The Author(s) 2020
N. Barreyre, N. Delalande (eds.), *A World of Public Debts*, Palgrave Studies in the History of Finance,
https://doi.org/10.1007/978-3-030-48794-2_16

This letter documents that the growing public debt of the 1970s was perceived as a deep crisis not only of public finance but also of the entire political system. Beside the financial and economic problems that Italy—like most other European countries—had to face as a consequence of the oil crisis and the breakdown of the international monetary order of Bretton Woods, massive tensions threatened the fragile political consensus that had emerged in Italy during the postwar reconstruction. A wave of strikes and social conflicts since 1969 challenged the "historical compromise" between the Communist and the Christian Democratic Party. The rise of extra-parliamentary forces and terrorist attacks from right- and left-wing groups undermined the authority of democratic institutions. In this situation, technocratic government became an attractive option to resolve the economic, social and political crisis.

Tommaso Padoa-Schioppa was a key figure in this new generation of technocratic economists and financial experts who gained tremendous influence on debt management, fiscal consolidation and monetary policy. Trained at the University of Bocconi and the MIT in Boston, after a brief experience in private management, Padoa-Schioppa made a career within the Banca d'Italia. At the same time, he served as an influential advisor of numerous economic bodies and institutions including the Washington-based Group of Thirty. From 1993–97, he was president of the Basel Committee on Banking Supervision, and in 2006 he was appointed as Minister of the Economy and Finance in the government of Romano Prodi, serving in that post until May 2008. Like many other economist-technocrats of his generation—including Romano Prodi, Beniamino Andreatta, Mario Monti or Mario Draghi—Padoa-Schioppa aimed at a radical reform of political and economic institutions. While the state became increasingly weak during the political crisis of the 1970s with repeated government reshuffles, massive social conflict and rising problems of terrorism, the central bank apparently constituted a haven of stability.

The argument of this chapter is that the debt crisis opened new and unexpected room for maneuver in Italy, which radically changed the financial and economic system during the 1970s and 1980s. The term "crisis," in this sense, takes on a different meaning from the one it is usually given by economists. Hansjörg Siegenthaler redefined the concept of crisis by relating economic crisis to institutional change and social learning.[2] Siegenthaler describes modern economic development as a series of periods marked by structural stability and crises. In periods of structural stability, economic fluctuations may occur, but social norms and regulatory systems remain unchanged, whereas crises are characterized by a fundamental loss of trust in the existing order. Accordingly, crises are moments of "fundamental learning" during which new cognitive and institutional regulatory systems are developed.

Recent studies in economic and political sciences have stressed the common patterns of debt growth in Southern Europe in the past decades.[3] Instead, I will argue that the Italian experience is somewhat different. While Greece, Spain and Portugal traditionally had high private external debt, in Italy a large share of public debt was financed internally. As I will show, private household savings contributed massively to covering public deficits. This, however, was only possible by restructuring financial and monetary policy and the marketization of debt which occurred during the 1970s and 1980s. The Italian case provides evidence that financialization was not necessarily driven by the logic of deregulated markets alone. Here, it was rather the specific interplay of governments, central banks and private investors that shaped financial innovations since the 1970s. This also makes clear why technocrats and central bankers played such an important role in the transformation of financial markets. While often pursuing a national political agenda, they usually had excellent international connections through activities in institutions such as the World Bank, the International Monetary Fund (IMF) or the Organization for Economic Cooperation and Development (OECD).

The End of Economic Growth and the Debt Crisis of the 1970s

In a long-term perspective, the Italian debt crisis of the 1970s was not unprecedented.[4] Already in the nineteenth century, the debt to Gross Domestic Product (GDP) rate rapidly increased due to the enormous costs of nation-building such as infrastructures, public administration and military structures.[5] Economic backwardness, and the topography demanded high investments that could not be financed by the weak domestic capital market. After the turn of the century, the debt ratio continuously declined as a result of fiscal consolidation and high economic growth, only to rise rapidly again during World War I. As with most European countries, the war created enormous financial costs which created a huge burden for postwar governments and economic consolidation. The inter-war period was initially characterized by an attempt to bring public expenditure under control and absorb the burden of debt from the war, but these efforts were spoiled by the Great Depression and World War II.[6]

After 1945, Italy—along with many other European countries—experienced massive debt relief for the public sector driven by inflation and currency reforms.[7] The national debt ratio fell to roughly 30 percent and remained at this level for over two decades.[8] In the newly established republic, the liberal Finance Minister Luigi Einaudi and his central bank president Donato Menichella pursued conservative budgetary and monetary policies that gave priority to a balanced budget and low inflation rates. This was in keeping with the guidelines established by Italian economic policy in the reconstruction phase. By the same token, monetary policy primarily aimed for a stable currency, as reflected in the Italian Constitution of 1948, which protected people's savings (Art. 47).[9] Moreover, Italy pursued a policy of free trade in Europe, particularly after the establishment of the European Economic Community (EEC) in 1957.[10] Along with the other European countries and in compliance with the principles of Bretton Woods, Italy liberalized its foreign exchange and capital movements in the late 1950s. After the lira was made freely convertible, however, the central bank had to intervene on numerous occasions to stabilize the exchange rate. The Banca d'Italia, which had received extensive authority during the course of the reform of 1936, played a key role during the postwar decades that went far beyond the traditional functions of a central bank. It administered, for example, the financial payments under the Marshall Plan and loans from the World Bank. The Banca d'Italia cooperated closely with the central government and was, in contrast to Germany or the United States, not fully independent. For example, interest rates ceilings, liquidity requirements and minimum reserves for commercial banks were determined by the Interministerial Committee for Credit and Savings (Comitato Interministeriale per il Credito e il Risparmio), which was chaired by the minister of the treasury.[11]

In general, the economic system in Italy exhibited strong similarities with the French *planification économique*.[12] The Italian government intervened not only on the macroeconomic level by means of fiscal and monetary policy, but owned—or at least controlled—considerable segments of heavy industry and the banking system. A key actor was the Istituto per la Ricostruzione Industriale (IRI), a public holding founded in 1933 in the context of the Great Depression. Even though the IRI was a creation of the fascist regime, it survived the political and economic transformations after 1945. This continuity stood in contrast with the more liberal economic rhetoric of postwar governments and led to a specific mix of laisser-faire (especially in foreign trade) and state dirigisme. As in France, industrial policy and investment planning played a key role in the long-term strategy to modernize the Italian economy.[13] Extensive investments were made to create a modern infrastructure and to industrialize southern Italy. However, during the high growth of the 1950s and 1960s, the country managed to keep public debt low, and even to reduce the debt GDP ratio during the 1950s. This was one of the positive side-effects of the *miracolo economico*, which finally transformed Italy into a modern industrial nation. Growth, however, also constituted an engine of political and social cohesion. In average, Italian real GDP increased at a rate of 5 percent between 1950 and 1973, exceeding most other OECD countries.[14] Moreover, the moderate inflation rates of the postwar period helped to reduce public debt consistently.

A radical change occurred in the early 1970s, when the debt to GDP ratio increased considerably.[15] As in most other industrialized countries, this increase was caused by a coincidence of different factors. Due to the oil price shock of 1973–74, growth rates declined sharply, followed by lower incomes and tax revenues. At the same time, public expenditure continued to grow, mainly due to the rising cost of welfare (especially pensions and health) and public administration, while investments by and large stagnated, with potentially negative effects on the infrastructure of the country.[16] Moreover, due to rising deficits and interest rates, the cost of debt service and amortization increased significantly. Although the average interest rates for government bonds remained under 5 percent until the mid-1960s, they rose steadily in the following years. During the second half of the 1970s, between 10 and 12 percent interest rates had to be paid for long-term bonds, while short-term bonds earned between 15 and 20 percent. The interest costs on government bonds during this period corresponded to roughly 10 percent of the country's gross domestic product.[17] Italy's debt ratio quadrupled within two decades to roughly 120 percent. During the 1990s and after the introduction of the Euro, the Italian government was able to consolidate public debt on a more sustainable level, while the GDP debt ratio surged again with the outbreak of the global financial crisis in 2007.

In order to explain this development—which in Italy was much more dramatic than in other industrialized countries—the specific historical circumstances and institutional changes have to be considered, which are not reflected by macroeconomic indicators. In particular, I will look at the strategies and patterns of debt management employed by the treasury, the central bank and other relevant institutions. Three aspects in particular are analyzed: first, the liberalization of the market for sovereign bonds; second, the close institutional connection between monetary policy and debt management by the Banca d'Italia; and third, the specific investment behavior of private households in Italy.

The Reorganization of Sovereign Bond Markets

Until World War II, state debt was financed primarily with conventional fixed interest government bonds with maturities of 10 to 15 years, while short-term deficits were covered by loans of the central bank. After 1945, as in many other countries, the Italian state took advantage of other sources:[18] first, short-term treasury bonds with a maturity of less than one year (*buoni ordinari del Tesoro*, BOT) were introduced in order to create a more flexible form of debt regulation; second, a growing proportion of the government budget was covered by loans from public banks (including the banks of the postal service) and directly through central bank credits. While relatively small budget deficits and low interest rates made it easy to finance debt via the money and credit markets during the postwar years, starting in the early 1970s this proved to become more difficult, as the gap between government revenues and expenditures continued to increase.

More importantly, soaring inflation rates of 15–20 percent made debt management extremely difficult since fixed interest long-term bonds were no longer marketable, causing a shift toward short-term treasury bills. While short-term bonds made up one-fifth of securities in the 1960s, their share increased to nearly 50 percent by the mid-1970s.[19] This forced the state to issue new bonds and to restructure budgets continuously.[20] Starting in 1975, with support from the Banca d'Italia, the Ministero del Tesoro released large numbers of new bonds.[21] For the most part, these were bonds with a maturity of between one and three years and variable, inflation-adjusted interest rates. Furthermore, non-interest-bearing zero-coupon bonds were introduced, whose yields consisted of the difference between the face value and the purchase value. As a result of this restructuring, the maturity periods of sovereign bonds were significantly reduced, going from nearly ten years in the early 1970s to a little over one year by the late 1970s.[22]

The decisive innovation was that, starting in 1975, sovereign bonds were no longer issued by the Italian Ministry of the Treasury, but by auctions on the financial market. Auctions had already been introduced for a small proportion of treasury bills in 1962, but without establishing a full money market. Given that only a small percentage of the bonds were sold in auctions and rigid legal regulations were enforced, there was no real secondary market for government bonds prior to the mid-1970s.[23]

In 1975, Giudo Carli, who had been governor of the Banca d'Italia since 1960, was replaced by Paolo Baffi. Carli was considered a moderate Keynesian who believed in the power of macroeconomic fine-tuning and growth policies. Also, Carli had initiated a process of internal professionalization, including the establishment of econometric forecasting and risk surveying. Even though Carli had criticized uncontrolled budget expansion, he supported the policies of industrial growth and modernization pursued during the 1960s. Moreover, the cooperation between the Treasury and the Central Bank had worked fairly well. Instead, Paolo Baffi—who himself had started his career in the Banca d'Italia in 1936— paid more attention to the political autonomy of the Banca d'Italia and was rather skeptical toward industrial planning. Moreover, under his direction, monetary and credit policy underwent massive changes after 1975. Baffi aimed at the creation of an efficient money market in order to prevent the Central Bank from being involved in financing state deficits directly. Baffi therefore pushed forward a reform of the auction process. According to the new legislation passed in 1976, all treasury bills were emitted by market auctions. Bidding was no longer limited to financial institutions, but was also extended to insurance companies and welfare institutions. Also, the Banca d'Italia was officially authorized to make bids. Even more important was the creation of a secondary market: Italian sovereign bonds could now be traded on the stock exchange. This reform was expected to enlarge the market for treasury bonds—which had often proved difficult to place in the past—resulting in higher yields.[24] Indeed, since the early 1970s most government bonds had been sold significantly below their nominal value in a desperate effort to find purchasers. The sales value was at times 10 to 15 percent below par, which resulted in a significant loss for government funds.

An additional measure designed to improve the placement of government bonds was enabling the Banca d'Italia to purchase unsold bonds at a minimum price. While this aimed at stabilizing the market for government bills, it also had the effect that the Central Bank acquired an increasing share of sovereign bonds.[25] Furthermore, since commercial banks used their government bonds for refinancing, this led to an increase in the amount of money in circulation, which fanned inflation even further.

The majority of government bonds were not directly purchased by private investors, but by banks and institutional investors (primarily insurance companies), which were required to maintain a minimum amount of "safe" securities in their portfolios. The banks either sold these securities to private investors or retained them to safeguard new financial transactions. This secondary market driven by sovereign bonds played a key role in the expansion of the Italian financial sector and ultimately gave a significant boost to the country's banking business. In fact, already in 1973 bonds worth 8000 billion lira were sold to the Italian bond market, whereas the value of shares traded on the stock exchange only amounted to 2000 billion lira.[26] While the stock market stagnated in the 1970s due to the difficulties of the Italian economy, trading in government bonds boomed and triggered an unprecedented growth in the financial sector in Italy. Between 1975 and 1980 alone, the volume of this sector tripled in value. Moreover, state-owned companies began to issue bonds at a large scale and thus substantially contributed to the process of financialization. For instance, the state railway (Ferrovie di Stato) had been issuing guaranteed bonds since 1967 which by 1972 already made up 5 percent of marketable public debt. Other important emitters of public bonds included the post banks and the Credit Consortium for Public Works (Consorzio di Credito per le Opere Pubbliche).[27] While the deregulation of the stock market and the privatization of the banking sector were implemented only under the Minister of the Treasury Giuliano Amato in 1990, the financialization of sovereign bonds was caused by the economic turmoil of the 1970s and the urgent need to generate new income sources for the public sector. This time lag between the forceful marketization of state bonds and the liberalization of financial markets in general shows that the overall process of "neo-liberal" reform was much more complex and fragmented. And it was closely intertwined with the specific institutional responses to the crises.

The Banca d'Italia: Monetary Policy and Debt Management

During the course of the debt crisis of the 1970s, the Banca d'Italia emerged as one of the most professional, largest and most powerful central banks in Europe.[28] The end of the Bretton Woods system and the abolition of fixed exchange rates meant that central banks no longer had to intervene in the currency market to stabilize the exchange rate. This created new room for maneuver for monetary policy and allowed the Banca d'Italia to use interest rates and open market operations for macroeconomic policy. Until then, monetary control had been exerted with a minimal reserve policy, which had always been a relatively weak instrument. By effectively controlling interest rates and open market transactions on the money and credit market, the Banca d'Italia had become a powerful actor in both monetary and fiscal policy. Moreover the bank assumed an important role in the international financial relations of Italy. Italian central bankers were internationally well connected and often had earned academic degrees in prestigious universities in North America or the United Kingdom. While Guido Carli had been director of the IMF before his career in the Banca d'Italia, Baffi had pursued economic research on the Bank of England in London. International agencies such as the World Bank, the IMF, or the Basel Committee played an important role for both academic and political exchange. During the currency crises of 1974 and 1976, the Banca d'Italia was a central institution in the negotiations with foreign creditors.[29] This was partly due to the deep crisis of political parties and the continuous reorganization of the cabinet and ministries. Against this background, the central bank gained a leading role in economic policy and international negotiations. The fact that Italy was accepted as a full member of the European Monetary System in 1979 with favorable conditions (primarily greater exchange rate band widths), despite the country's massive currency problems, was an accomplishment attributable to the Banca d'Italia, which in turn gained in reputation thanks to its successful crisis management.

Moreover, the power of the Banca d'Italia grew to the extent that the government was no longer capable of financing its expenditure via conventional bonds and hence relied on the support of the central bank, which was increasingly used as a source of short-term loans. Senior management at the Banca d'Italia viewed this development with ambivalence, however, since this new role entailed considerable risks. Already by the late

1960s, central bank officials noted with concern that the Ministry of the Treasury could no longer find buyers for its bonds and frequently had to draw upon the reserves of the Banca d'Italia.[30] The debts owed by the Italian state to the central bank soared between 1968 and 1970 from 3018 billion to 6877 billion lira. By 1970, more than 30 percent of public debt was financed with loans from the central bank.[31] This amount continued to rise over the following years.[32] In September 1971, the director of the central bank Carli warned the government that "in this situation we have to refuse to finance the deficit of the Treasury by direct credits." Instead, he argued, the bank would support the government actively to "amplify the issue of short- and long-term government bonds on the market, accepting the effects on interest rates. This could lead to a restriction of credit supply from which the productive sector could suffer."[33] Yet, with the eruption of the oil price crisis of 1973–74 and mounting inflation rates, trade in government bonds suddenly collapsed, forcing the Banca d'Italia to purchase nearly all newly issued treasury bonds.[34] The central bank went from owning nearly 15 percent of all government bonds in 1968 to possessing nearly 40 percent in 1976.[35]

The Banca d'Italia was not merely passively involved in state debt management, however, but rather assumed growing responsibilities. Since 1975, it cooperated with the Ministry of the Treasury to restructure the government bond market. For the bank, this had unintended and ambiguous effects. The fact that the Banca d'Italia acquired a large share of securities caused a conflict of interest between monetary policy and debt management. For instance, the central bank had to ensure that the returns on government bonds remained lucrative despite high inflation.[36] Already back in 1973, the bank had warned of the baleful consequences of "political embroilment in interest rate policies."[37]

This conflict of interest was recognized by many experts and already viewed at the time as an obstacle for the integration of Italy into the European Monetary System (EMS). The center-left government under Prime Minister Arlando Forlani therefore campaigned for a "divorce" between the Banca d'Italia and the Ministry of the Treasury, which was carried out in July 1981. The economist and Treasury Minister Beniamino Andreatta and Carlo Azeglio Ciampi, who had been appointed governor of the Italian Central Bank in 1979, were the driving force behind this initiative. Both belonged to the group of "technocrat" economists who favored fully integrating the Italian economy in the European Community. In view of the country's high rate of inflation, they urged sweeping reforms of monetary policy—measures which, following Italy's accession to the EMS, were also called for by the other European member states.

The reform of 1981 had far-reaching consequences for the organization of the bond market. Henceforth, the Ministry of the Treasury established the guidelines for the structure of the bond portfolio along with the market conditions (returns, maturities, etc.). Sales of government bonds were now controlled by a private banking consortium that had to offer them at market prices. Furthermore, the Banca d'Italia was no longer required to purchase bonds, which triggered a rapid decline in the number of treasury bills owned by the central bank.[38] A consequence of this measure was that government bonds now had to be sold at market prices. This significantly increased interest payments and tended to make it more difficult for the Treasury to manage the burden of debt.[39] It made financial repression more difficult. A further growth of public debt was an unintended effect of the central bank independence.

Despite this radical reform, the separation between central bank and government was not as strict and legally formalized as in Germany. In fact, the Banca d'Italia continued to adjust monetary policy (in particular open market operations) to keep public debt sustainable. Although the central bank was no longer obliged to buy a certain number of bonds, it intervened on a regular basis with purchases to stabilize the sovereign bond market. Furthermore, the Banca d'Italia supported the government to overcome short-term deficits by making loans available to the Italian state at a symbolic interest rate of 1 percent.[40]

FAMILY AND THE STATE: MOBILIZING PRIVATE HOUSEHOLD SAVINGS

The massive credit problems of the 1970s cannot detract from the fact that Italy has ultimately provided an example of effective debt policy and has largely been able to avoid severe sovereign debt crises right up to the present.[41] Despite considerable liquidity problems, the country has been spared severe turmoil on financial markets, the monetary system has remained viable and major bank failures have been avoided. Moreover, in spite of a growing balance of payments deficit, the Italian state managed to finance the vast majority of its public debt from domestic sources, although this was only possible with massive interventions on the monetary and currency markets. Starting in 1974, foreign exchange transactions were regulated by the state and a mandatory deposit of 50 percent on trade transactions was introduced. In 1976, these deposits had to be made in the form of sovereign bonds that were issued specifically for this purpose, which de facto amounted to a forced state loan.[42] These loans not only placed a significant burden on Italian exports but also contradicted the free trade principles of the European Community that Italy had committed to since its foundation.

An examination of the structure of public debt reveals a clear shift in the 1970s (Table 16.1). While interim loans from banks and deposits at the post banks and state banks waned in importance, government bonds became a key source of debt funding. Thanks to the introduction of new, attractive treasury bills and a flexible market-based process of placement, government bonds became more appealing—and not just for the traditional investors such as banks and professional financial investors, but also for private households. In cooperation with the central bank, this allowed the Italian state to gradually consolidate government debt. Although the government deficit was largely financed with short-term money market papers until 1975, certificates with longer maturities gradually gained in importance. This had less impact on long-term bonds with a maturity of between six and ten years—which remained unpopular among buyers due to high inflation—than it did on medium-term bonds with a maturity between one and two years.[43] Short-term treasury bills still served to finance the government deficit, but on average their maturities slightly increased again.[44]

Foreign loans played practically no role in the public debt portfolio. Although Italy received large loans from the IMF during the 1970s in

Table 16.1 Distribution of public debt in Italy (1970–92)

	1970–74	1975–79	1980–84	1985–89	1990–92
Credits of the Banca d'Italia	43.60%	16.49%	14.17%	9.13%	12.62%
Credits of the post bank	14.06%	16.21%	5.47%	9.9%	7.45%
Private bank credits	20.08%	3.30%	5.97%	2.48%	8.15%
Foreign credits	0.45%	0.95%	2.63%	3.73%	4.31%
Government bonds	20.45%	62.44%	71.53%	74.68%	67.34%
Other	1.36%	0.61%	0.23%	0.08%	0.13%
Total	100.00%	100.00%	100.00%	100.00%	100.00%

Source: Giandomenico Scarpelli, *La Gestione del Debito Pubblico in Italia* (Roma: Bancaria Editrice, 2001), 26

order to overcome its massive currency problems, foreign loans actually became less important for the public sector. Foreign debt went from over 10 percent of total government debt in the mid-1960s to under 3 percent during the course of the 1970s, and never rose above 6 to 7 percent until the introduction of the Euro.[45] This was only possible because Italy—similar to Japan—had an extremely high savings rate.[46] While the government deficit rose at an above-average rate, private indebtedness remained extremely low compared to other countries. Moreover, the vast majority of private debt was not tied to private households, but rather to businesses and banks that increasingly relied on interbank loans.[47]

The traditionally high savings rate can be attributed to a low propensity to consume, but is primarily due to a family-oriented model of long-term capital accumulation used by Italian households to compensate for the lack of income security. Despite high inflation and negative real interest rates, the tendency to save money increased even further among private households during the 1970s (Fig. 16.1). This was probably a consequence of the economic crisis, which spurred households to consume less and save more in anticipation of future losses of income.[48] Already by the year 1970, the savings rate among private households was 14.8 percent and thus far above the level of all other industrialized nations. While there

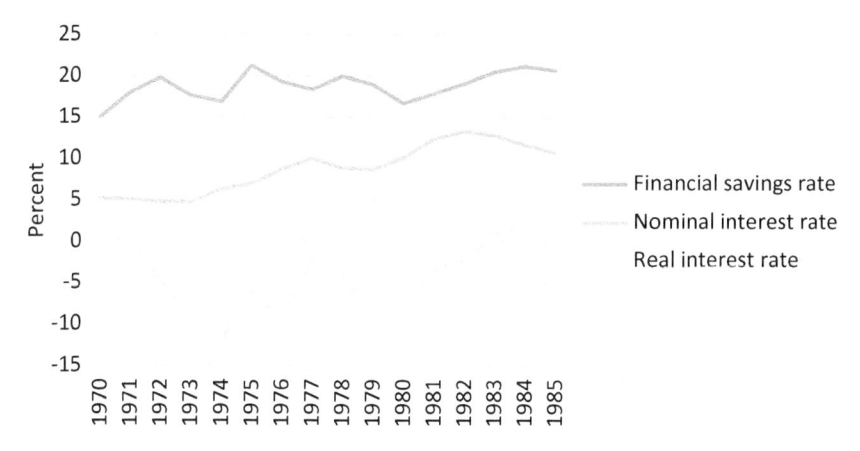

Fig. 16.1 Savings and interest rates (1970–85). (Source: Ministero del Tesoro, *Ricchezza finanziaria, debito public e politica monetaria nella prospettiva international*, Rapporto della Commissione di studio nominate dal Ministero del Tesoro (Roma: 1987), 157)

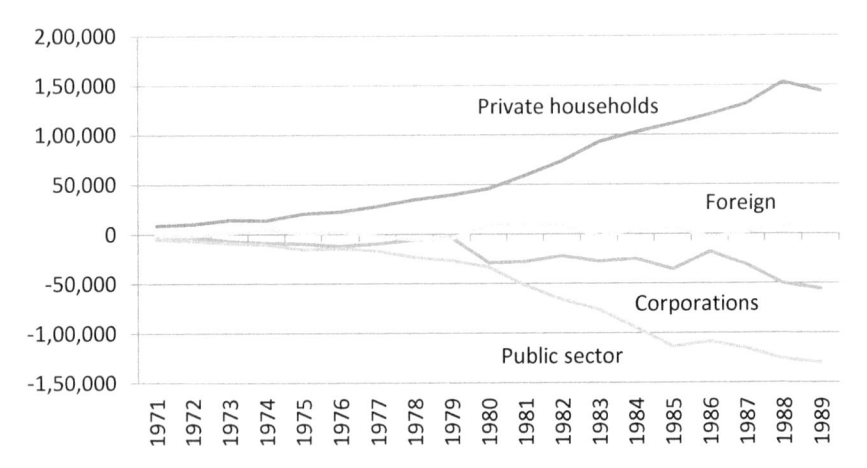

Fig. 16.2 Balance of financial assets/liabilities (1971–89). (Source: Mario Baldassari and Maria Gabriella Briotti, "Bilancio pubblico ed economia italiana negli anni '70 e '80: dalle radici del debito alla manovra di risanamento, una 'ristrutturazione' da fare," *Rivista di Politica Economica* LXXX (1990), 371–438, 405)

was a reduction in the tendency to save in many countries, such as Germany and the United States, during the 1970s Italians saved an ever-growing share of their income: In 1974 the savings rate was 16.3 percent, and in 1978 it was 18.7 percent.[49] As can be seen in Fig. 16.2, the financial surpluses of private households have continuously increased since the early 1970s. They not only contributed to financing the deficits of the public sector, but also of the highly indebted private companies, which were able to take out loans on the domestic capital market. The mobilization of private household savings for the state and private corporations is a crucial element in explaining Italy's relative stability. It meant, however, a substantial loss of private wealth, especially of small savers who had few investment alternatives.

The restructuring of private household investment was partly based on the improvement of nominal interest rates. In general, private households continued to acquire real estate and place funds in savings accounts (where banks and above all the post banks played a major role) and insurance policies. However, a significant reallocation of funds can be observed in their asset portfolios during the second half of the 1970s. Volatile market prices and low returns caused the demand for company shares to plummet, and the same was true for savings accounts due to high inflation and negative

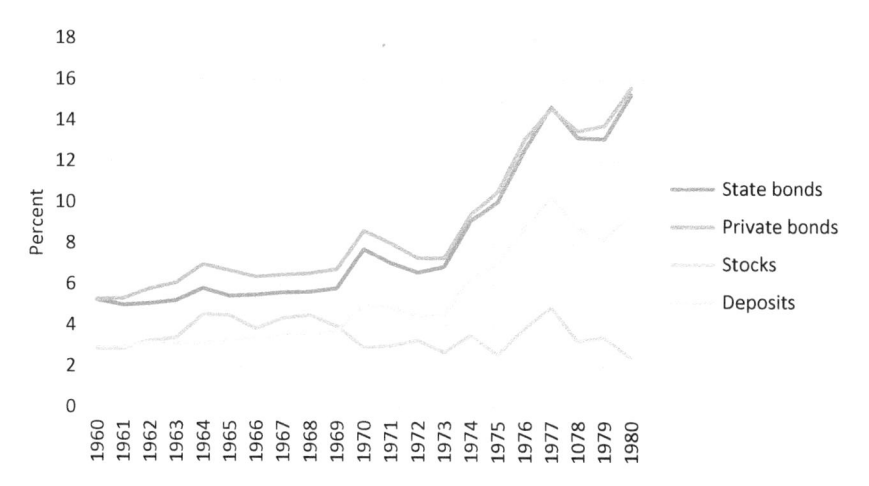

Fig. 16.3 Rate of return: state bonds, private bonds, stocks and deposits (1960–80). (Source: Ministero del Tesoro, "La difesa del risparmio finanziario dall'inflazione," in *Rapporto della Commissione di studio nominate dal Ministero del Tesoro* (Roma: 1991), 42)

real interest rates. By contrast, government bonds became more and more attractive, as the returns were significantly greater than other financial investments, not least because the Italian state encouraged investors with tax incentives (Fig. 16.3). This restructuring of private asset portfolios is statistically well documented.[50] In 1980 private households owned 19 percent of all government bonds; by the mid-1980s, their share had grown to approx. 30 percent.[51] Government treasury bills, which had earlier been primarily acquired by institutional investors, thus became one of the most popular private financial investments. Even without any reliable data on the distribution among income groups, it is clear that a growing number of small investors and middle income families were purchasing government bonds, which were viewed as high-yielding and safe forms of investment.[52]

The acquisition of government bonds thus turned out to be highly lucrative for many Italian investors and households. This may explain why the massive increase in public deficits did not spark any major political turmoil, but instead enjoyed a relatively high degree of social acceptance.[53] Not only members of the political parties but also trade unions saw the increase in public deficits as a more or less necessary evil associated with the crisis, especially since high inflation rates facilitated to eradicate at least some of the debt. The labor organizations had largely come to terms with the difficult economic conditions and their impact on financial policy, and had made the best of the situation with lavish wage agreements and an automatic cost-of-living adjustment to account for inflation (*scala mobile*), which was initially introduced for Italian industry in 1975 and in subsequent years also applied to other sectors, including public service workers. An additional incentive to accept the debt situation was that the increase in government expenditure was primarily used to bankroll the state social system, particularly the generous pension benefits that were the envy of many other countries.[54]

* * *

After the financial crisis of 2008, the Euro Zone was confronted with massive fiscal and monetary imbalances. Especially Spain, Greece, Italy and Portugal had to face enormous public deficits. However, a comparative historical analysis shows that there is no common pattern of debt evolution in Southern Europe. While Spain and Greece traditionally relied on foreign sources to cover public (and private) debts, the Italian state was able to mobilize domestic savings for public deficits. This model emerged already during the 1970s when a mixture of high inflation, rising welfare spending and foreign account deficits forced the Italian government to develop new strategies of debt management. The Banca d'Italia and the Ministry of Treasury successfully reorganized the bond market and introduced a series of financial innovations such as auctions and index-linked bonds which became highly attractive for both institutional and private investors—including many households—which, often for the first time, came in touch with financial markets. The securitization of sovereign debt was therefore the main driver of financialization, while global capital mobility and the deregulation of the private banking and the stock market were far less important. The state in desperate search for domestic sources of income thus generated and dynamized financial markets. From this perspective, it was by no means accidental that banks and large industrial corporations remained under public control until the early 1990s. The state had little interest to compete with private companies and banks on the financial market. This attitude was similar to the French model of "debt commodification" that turned the state into a regular borrower during the 1970s.[55]

Even if external shocks sparked the Italian debts crisis, an explanation of Italy's debt growth must take political and institutional factors into account. Against the background of a highly instable electoral system and rising internal conflicts, a social consensus had to be continuously negotiated between political parties, economic interest groups and trade unions. In this situation, it would have been extremely difficult to reach fiscal adjustment through higher tax revenues. With the securitization of sovereign debt, the state was able to gain time and to consolidate structural budget deficits.[56] In view of the massive currency problems and economic shocks of the 1970s, the "Italian solution" of the debt problem was highly efficient. In terms of sustainability, the marketization of public debts created long-term burdens which persist until today.

Notes

1. Archivo storico della Banca d'Italia (ASBI), Carte Baffi, Monte Oppio, b. 24, fasc. 1: Guido Carli to Minister of Treasury Ugo La Malfa, 8/8/1973: Tommaso Padoa-Schioppa to Paolo Baffi, 23/1/1976.
2. Hansjörg Siegenthaler, *Regelvertrauen, Prosperität und Krisen: Die Ungleichmäßigkeit wirtschaftlicher und sozialer Entwicklung als Ergebnis individuellen Handelns und Lernens* (Tübingen: Mohr Siebeck, 1993).
3. See, for example, Stefano Battilossi, "Structural Fiscal Imbalances, Financial Repression and Sovereign Debt Sustainability in Southern Europe, 1970s–1990s," in *The Political Economy of Public Finance. Taxation, State Spending and Debt since the 1970s*, eds. Marc Buggeln, Martin Daunton and Alexander Nützenadel (Cambridge: Cambridge University Press, 2017), 262–98.
4. See Roberto Artoni and Sara Biancini, "Il debito pubblico dall'Unità ad oggi," in *Storia Economica d'Italia*, eds. Pierluigi Ciocca and Gianni Toniolo (Rome/Bari: Laterza: 2004), 269–380; Franco Spinelli, "Dimensione, composizione, quotazioni e costo del debito pubblico interno dal 1861 al 1985. Con una appendice sul debito estero," in Idem, *Per la storia monetaria dell'Italia* (Turin: Giappichelli, 1989), 301–55; Francesco Rèpaci, *La finanza pubblica nel secolo 1861–1960* (Bologna: Il Mulino, 1962); see also Alexander Nützenadel, "Im Schatten des Staates. Öffentliche Schulden, Kreditmarkt und private Vermögensbildung in Italien nach 1945," *Geschichte und Gesellschaft* 41 (2015): 447–464.
5. See Ragioneria Generale dello Stato, *Il bilancio del Regno d'Italia dal 1862 al 1912–13* (Rome: Tipografia dell'Unione, 1914); Giuseppe della Torre, "Collocamento del debito pubblico e sistema creditizio in Italia (1861–1914)," in *Storia d'Italia, Annali 23: La banca*, eds. Alberto Cova et al. (Torino: Einaudi, 2008), 401–20.

6. Giancarlo Salvemini and Vera Zamagni, "Finanza pubblica e indebitamento tra le due Guerre Mondiali: Il finanziamento del settore statale," in *Ricerche per la Storia della Banca d'Italia. Problemi di finanza pubblica tra le due guerre, 1919–1939*, eds. Sergio Cardarelli et al., vol. 2 (Rome/Bari: Laterza, 1993), 139–234.
7. Paolo Baffi, "La lira nell'ultimo quarto di secolo," in *L'economia italiana dal 1861 al 1961* (Milan: Giuffré, 1961), 453–86.
8. See Carmen Reinhart and Kenneth S. Rogoff, *This Time is Different: Eight Centuries of Financial Folly* (Cambridge, Mass.: Harvard University Press, 2009), database: http://www.reinhartandrogoff.com/data/browse-by-country/countries/italy/
9. Gianni Toniolo, "La politica monetaria degli anni '50 (1947–1960)," in *Sviluppo e crisi dell'economia italiana*, ed. Giampiero Franco (Milan: Etas Libri, 1979), 48–71.
10. Rolf Petri, *Storia economica d'Italia. Dal fascismo al miracolo economico (1918–1963)* (Bologna: Il Mulino, 2002), 197–203.
11. The Committee was established in 1947 as a supervisory body for the banking system and monetary policy in general. The Minister of the Treasury was also the head of two other important bodies of monetary policy, the Permanent Commission of Supervision of Note Circulation and the Commission of the Bank of Issue. Moreover, a high official of the Ministry was present at all meetings of the Board of Directors of the Central Bank; see Fulvio Fenucci, *Il concorso del Comitato interministeriale per il Credito e il Risparmio alla determinazione dell'indirizzo economico* (Naples: Liguori, 1984).
12. Eric Monnet, *Controlling Credit. Central banking and the planned economy in postwar France (1948–1973)* (Cambridge: Cambridge University Press, 2018).
13. Christian Grabas, "Planning the Economic Miracle? Industrial Policy in Italy between Boom and Crisis," in *Industrial Policy in Europe after 1945. Wealth, Power and Economic Development in the Cold War*, eds. Christian Grabas and Alexander Nützenadel (Basingstoke: Palgrave Macmillan), 2014, 182–214.
14. Ignazio Musu, *Il debito pubblico* (Bologna: Il Mulino, 1998), 80–85.
15. Piero Giarda, "La crescita della spesa pubblica negli anni '70," *Rivista Milanese di Economia* 5 (1983): 139–60; Giancarlo Morcaldo and Giancarlo Salvemini, "Il debito pubblico. Analisi dell'evoluzione nel periodo 1960–83 e prospettive," *Rivista di Politica Economica* LXXIV (1984): 1407–45.
16. Figures in Ministero del Tesoro, *Relazione*, p. 65; see also ASBI, Direttorio, n. 65, fasc. 1: Guido Carli to Minister of Treasury Emilio Colombo, 13/1/1970, 2; see also: Maurizio Ferrera, *Il welfare state in Italia. Sviluppo e crisi in prospettiva comparata* (Bologna: Il Mulino, 1984).

17. Spinelli, *Dimensione*, 334, 343.
18. See Chap. 15 in this volume.
19. Spinelli, *Dimensione*, 323.
20. Already in 1973, treasury bonds issued with an interest rate of 7 percent were not sold on the market anymore; see ASBI, Direttorio, n. 67, fasc. 3: Guido Carli to Minister of Treasury Ugo La Malfa, 24/7/1973 and 8/8/1973.
21. Ministero del Tesoro, *Relazione del Direttore Generale alla Commissione Parlamentare di Vigilanza. Il Debito Pubblico in Italia 1861–1987*, vol. 1 (Rome: Istituto poligrafico e Zecca dello Stato, 1988), 78.
22. Morcaldo and Salvemini, "Il debito pubblico," 1418.
23. ASBI, Carte Baffi, Monte Oppio, n. 80, fasc. 4: Tommaso Padoa-Schioppa, *Tecniche di Emissione dei Buoni Ordinari del Tesoro*, 1975.
24. This manifested itself already one year after the introduction of the new auction process; see Banca d'Italia, *Relazione annuale 1975* (Rome: Centro di Stampa, 1976), 230–1.
25. Following a temporary reprieve in 1974/75 in the wake of the introduction of the auction process, in 1976 the central bank again had to acquire sovereign bonds to the tune of 9280 billion lira (compared to 5410 billion lira in 1975); see Banca d'Italia, *Relazione annuale 1976*, 214.
26. Francesco Balletta, "Debito pubblico ed efficienza del mercato finanziario in Italia nella seconda metà del Novecento," in *Debito pubblico e mercati finanziari in Italia: secoli 13.-20*, eds. Guiseppe de Luca and Angelo Moioli (Milano: Franco Angeli, 2007), 642.
27. Ministero del Tesoro, *Relazione*, 68.
28. See Marcello De Cecco, "Banca d'Italia e conquista politica del sistema del credito. Tecnocrazia e politica nel governo della moneta tra gli anni '50 e '70," in Idem, *Il governo democratico dell'economia* (Bari: De Donato, 1976); Alberto Predieri, *Il potere della banca centrale: Isola o modello?* (Citta di Castello: Passigli 1996).
29. Salvatore Rossi, *La Politica Economica italiana 1968–1998* (Rome/Bari: Laterza), 46.
30. ASBI, Carte Baffi, Monte Oppio, n. 115, fasc. 5: Rapporto Servizio Studi, 14/7/1969.
31. Banca d'Italia, *Relazione 1970*, 195.
32. Banca d'Italia, *Relazione 1975*, 231.
33. ASBI, Direttorio, n. 66, fasc. 1: Guido Carli to Minister of Treasury Emilio Colombo, 19/9/1971.
34. Banca d'Italia, *Relazione 1973*, 240.
35. Giandomenico Scarpelli, *La Gestione del Debito Pubblico in Italia: obiettivi e tecniche di emissione dei titoli di Stato dagli anni settanta ai giorni dell'euro* (Rome: EDI Bank-Bancaria editrice, 2001), 27.

36. ASBI, Banca d'Italia, Direttorio – Carli, Pratiche, n. 67.0, fasc. 3: Guido Carli to Minister of Treasury Ugo La Malfa, 8/8/1973; see also Francesco Balletta, "Debito pubblico," 640–1.
37. Banca d'Italia, *Relazione 1973*, 241.
38. By the early 1980s, the bank's share had dropped to below 20 percent of the bonds in circulation; see Balletta, "Debito pubblico," 656 and 658.
39. Spinelli, *Dimensione*, 332–3.
40. Ibid.
41. See Antonio Confalonieri and Ettore Gatti, *La Politica del Debito Pubblico in Italia*, vol. 2 (Bari/Rome: Laterza 1986); Giancarlo Morcaldo, *La Finanza Pubblica in Italia* (Bologna: Il Mulino, 1993).
42. Ministero del Tesoro, *Relazione*, 71.
43. Banca d'Italia, *Relazione 1978*, 193.
44. See Morcaldo and Salvemini, "Il debito pubblico," 1408–55.
45. Spinelli, *Dimensione*, 350; nevertheless, state companies such as Enel increasingly relied on foreign loans from the early 1970s; see Ministero del Tesoro, *Relazione*, 68; ASBI, Direttorio, n. 65, fasc. 1: Guido Carli to Minister of Treasury Emilio Colombo, 13/1/1970, 2.
46. W. Elliot Brownlee and Eisaku Ide, "Fiscal Policy in Japan and the United States since 1973: Economic Crises, Taxation and Weak Tax Consent," in *Political Economy of Public Finance*, 57–82.
47. For a general comparative account see Sheldon Garon, *Beyond Our Means: Why America Spends While the World Saves* (Princeton: Princeton University Press, 2012).
48. Ministero del Tesoro, *Relazione*, 61.
49. Mario Baldassarri and M. Gabriella Briotti, "Bilancio pubblico ed. economia italiana negli anni '70 e '80: dalle radici del debito alla manovra di risanamento, una 'ristrutturazione' da fare", *Rivista di Politica Economica* LXXX (1990): 421–38. It was thus significantly higher than in Japan or West Germany, which had savings rates at the time of 11 percent; see ibid.
50. Ibid., 423.
51. Ministero del Tesoro, *Relazione*, 85.
52. Scarpelli, *Gestione del Debito*, 29; Salvatore L. Francesca, "Sistema bancario e mercato obbligazionario in Italia nella seconda metà del Novecento," in *Debito pubblico e mercati finanziari in Italia (secoli XIII–XX)*, eds. Giuseppe De Luca and Angelo Moioli (Milan: Franco Angeli 2007), 704.
53. Also see Filippo Cavazzuti, *Debito pubblico, ricchezza privata* (Bologna: Il Mulino, 1986).
54. Michele Salvati, "Gli anni ottanta e il debito pubblico," in *Pensare la contemporaneità. Studi di storia per Mariuccia Salvati*, eds. Paolo Capuzzo et al. (Rome: Viella, 2011), 257–72.

55. Benjamin Lemoine, "The Politics of Public Debt Financialization: (Re)Inventing the Market for French Sovereign Bonds and Shaping the Public Debt Problem (1966–2012)," in *Political Economy of Public Finance*, 240–261; see also Chap. 15 in this volume.
56. Wolfgang Streeck, *Buying Time: The Delayed Crisis of Democratic Capitalism* (London and New York: Verso Books, 2017).

CHAPTER 17

From a Multilateral Broker to the National Judge: The Law and Governance of Sovereign Debt Restructuring, 1980–2015

Jérôme Sgard

Sovereign debts are no ordinary contracts. Although they are typically written and talked about in the language of private contracts, even a cursory look at how they work reveals how specific they are. Let us take the issue by its roots. Beyond the naturalized image of "a meeting of minds", based on "the will of the parties", the question almost always arises of why contracts in general hold and why they can indeed be construed as "a law unto the parties", as the French Civil Code aptly says.[1] This phrase implies that once commitments between private parties have been exchanged and expectations shared regarding their respective course of action, these commitments should be as binding on the parties as the law per se. Hence, the enforcement of contracts should benefit from the same ultimate guarantees as those typically provided by the sovereign in a classic liberal framework. When confusion and discord arise, private contracts may eventually

J. Sgard (✉)
Sciences Po, CERI, Paris, France
e-mail: jerome.sgard@sciencespo.fr

© The Author(s) 2020
N. Barreyre, N. Delalande (eds.), *A World of Public Debts*, Palgrave Studies in the History of Finance,
https://doi.org/10.1007/978-3-030-48794-2_17

be interpreted by a court of law and extra enforcement guarantees offered against cheating, opportunism and evasion, which are the natural outcomes of free-wheeling bargains. This is the job of civil justice and the executive.[2]

In the case of sovereign debt this framework does not work, of course. The sovereign borrower cannot be declared bankrupt and liquidated, its political regime changed and its land assets seized. There is no superior, uncontested authority that can neatly exclude the defaulting borrower from market transactions and restructure its economy.[3] Similarly, there is no way a judge can suspend contractual relationships between investors and sovereign borrowers and impose that they all move to a single, collective discussion forum, which he supervises and where their majority decisions will be confirmed and enforced. Such a framework has never existed in the case of sovereign debt. No multilateral judge has ever received the legal right to suspend the execution of contracts signed under US, English or Luxemburg law and to summon creditors to his office.

Significantly, whereas the key features of bankruptcy laws for private businesses were established by the end of the Middle Ages, the history of sovereign debt restructurings presents the exact opposite image: rules keep changing over time and they rarely come with the high degree of predictability that is generally observed with private firms at the domestic level. They have always remained more fluid and contested, so that they have also been regularly subjected to power relationships that play out openly. Strong states and weak states, rich nations and poor ones, multilateral coordination or not, a bond-based or loan-based debt market, the presence or not of an uncontested hegemon—all these variables weigh heavily on how sovereign debt contracts are framed and restructured, hence on how we conceive them as a social and legal artifact.

This chapter tells the story of how the sovereign debt market shifted radically, between the 1980s and the 2000s, from a model where debt settlements were brokered by the IMF, hence in a framework marked by strong multilateral rules and the direct oversight of key industrialized countries, to a model where restructurings are adjudicated by national courts. In practice this means the New York South District Court which has jurisdiction over Wall Street. This structural shift is of course a substory in the broader movement from the post-war domestic and international settlements to the Second Global Era. It is part and parcel, it will be argued, of the emergence of global capital markets, on the back of capital movement liberalization (on the external front), and financial deregulation (on the domestic front). Market regulations thus became much more dominated by private actors: international lawyers, investment bankers, hedge fund managers, and so on. And as the actors and the forum changed, the legal and judicial practices were structured much more strongly by a language of private law and private contracting. Whereas everybody agrees that a private and a state debtor are entirely different animals, sovereign debt restructurings are framed today, as much as possible, as if they were essentially similar to a private bankruptcy. The agents in charge of these operations seem to assume that what similarity there is between them is enough to justify the convergence in legal strategies.

Two neglected yet defining features of this experience are singled out and analyzed in this chapter. First, the rules that were adopted in 1982 by the International Monetary Fund (IMF) and its patrons were clearly anchored in the "old world" of post-war economic policy-making, where states kept a strong capacity to act discretionally, to suspend or redraw rules when needed and, not least, to interfere directly in private property rights and contracts. In this sense, the success of this historically unique multilateral approach to sovereign debt restructurings hinged critically on this very specific and already declining political economic regime. Moreover, the crisis itself became a major factor in making these interventionist methods obsolete or illegitimate. This is one of the most paradoxical dimensions of this episode.

Second, the ensuing secular evolution had far-reaching consequences regarding what used to be called the "international financial architecture". Rather than triggering a move toward stronger global rules and procedures, the emergence of a large, integrated sovereign debt market has led paradoxically to a re-nationalization of the overall dispute resolution mechanism and a serious weakening of multilateral principles. This should not come as a complete surprise to the historically minded: in this volume, Adam Tooze underlines how today's capital markets and their crisis are shaped by the interaction between markets and policy makers. Closer to the point, the experience of the pre-1914 era shows that, as a rule, sovereign debts tend to be restructured in the financial places where they were initially issued (Part II in this volume). And contrary to what a standard critique of the IMF might have implied, this has not delivered a relative depoliticization of the debt regime, but a fragmentation that rather increases the room for uneven treatments and strong-arm politics: rules of "comparative treatment" between countries, or the strong link that was once observed between debt restructuring and macroeconomic stabilization, are now considerably shallower.

From a long-term perspective, this remarkable movement marks a major reversal in the trend toward multilateralism that was initiated by the League of Nations during the 1920s and which culminated during the post-1945 decades, say between the Bretton Woods Conference (1944) and the developing countries debt crisis of the 1980s. At the same time, this evolution does not mark either a clear-cut return to pre-1914 rules, when private actors and disintermediated finance also dominated the sovereign debt market. The current trend toward legalization and judicialization is largely novel and suggests that the Second Global Era (since 1990) does not rest on the same legal underpinnings as the First Global Era (1870–1914). Something entirely new is at stake that reflects a new relationship between sovereignty and private rights, hence between state power and private wealth.

Sovereign Debt Renegotiation from a Historical Perspective

During the first era of financial globalization, before 1914, no formal contingent rule or multilateral agent mediated between the defaulting sovereign and the private (bond) investors. Bilateral negotiations exclusively aimed at reinstating the contractual rights of creditors who, in principle, could not count on the active support of their governments. Though there are still discussions on the extent of their actual intervention, the rule is that they would enter the fray only when the debtor country was acting in obvious bad faith or refused to negotiate. In the absence of multilateral financial institutions, information gathering and economic monitoring was undertaken by private bondholders' associations and by the largest international banks (Rothschild, Baring, Crédit Lyonnais, etc.).[4] Representatives of these associations, in particular, regularly took control of part of the fiscal administration of debtor countries so as to control their financial position directly: Turkey, Greece and Tunisia are the best-known examples of such direct infringement of state sovereignty, which extended much deeper than anything the IMF would do.[5]

The early years of the twentieth century then witnessed a gradual move toward a more structured framework for debt renegotiations with explicit mediations in place. First were the US Money Doctors, that is, professors of economics in a major East Coast university, fully armed with their modern, scientific, neutral knowledge. Their role—not entirely different from that of the later IMF—was to produce a comprehensive account of the country's economic and financial position, and of its capacity to resume debt service; they would then recommend a stabilization policy and give their own seal of approval to the government's commitments. In turn this would open access to a financial agreement, typically with a new bond issue, launched by US banks in Wall Street. Official reserves would most probably be invested in New York and a trade agreement with the United States could well be forthcoming.[6] This was the time of Rooseveltian imperialism and the main countries concerned were either Central or South American. The most well-known money doctor, Edwin Kemmerer, intervened along these lines in Guatemala, Colombia, Chile and Peru.[7]

Of course the Money Doctors did not always prove immune to corruption, they could also be plain wrong, and they were ill-equipped to address the problems of enforcement and moral hazard which rapidly came to the fore. Still, the long-term trend was in the direction of a reinforcement and institutionalization of this third-party mediation based on expertise and the pretense of scientific neutrality. Since then, and with very few exceptions, private investors have never attempted to reintegrate these two key functions—economic expertise and third-party mediation. Drawing on Alec Stone-Sweet's argument, a "dyadic" conflict resolution framework was substituted by a "triadic" one, which he interprets as a first, qualitative step toward institutionalized governance.[8]

In the 1920s, the interventions of the League of Nations in Austria, Hungary and Romania were a further breakthrough in this direction: the third-party mediator was no longer a private person, working exclusively for American banks and investors, but a multilateral body, however weak, contested and economically conservative. The first ever multilateral stabilization program was thus negotiated with the Austrian government in 1922 and then closely monitored by a High Representative of the League in Vienna: he had direct access to economic information but also to policy makers, which he could thus supervise from close up, in a way quite similar to what IMF missions would later do. In the meantime the League became the channel through which some of its key members offered their guarantees on a sovereign bond issued by the Austrian government. This was not a multilateral loan, but neither was it pure private lending nor a blatantly clientelistic bail-out.[9] As was later written by Jean Monnet, who worked in the economic and financial section of the League: "Not only did Austria not lose anything in terms of independence as it relied upon foreign aid; it actually reinforced its independence, thanks to international guarantees and internal reforms".[10] Still today, any IMF intervention in a crisis-stricken country can be justified in the same way.[11]

Between 1944 and 1980, the "first IMF" did not deal much with sovereign debt: capital markets had entirely collapsed in 1932–1933, reopening them was clearly not a priority at Bretton Woods, and most domestic economies operated under a regime of heavily regulated finance (as shown by Kapadia & Lemoine and Nützenadel in this volume). Capital markets re-opened only during the 1960s as regards the developed countries, and a decade later for the developing ones. The 1950s were nevertheless the period when the key concept of IMF bilateral conditionality was gradually developed by way of experience and precedents. The very notion that the IMF could indeed lend against policy commitments (adjustment measures) started to emerge only in 1952 when the framework of the Stand By Agreement was invented. But it was only in 1956–1958 that conditional lending became formalized with the introduction of quantitative performance targets stipulating that if these policy objectives were missed, the loan would be automatically suspended and new discussions would have to take place with the Fund's staff. However, this practice was developed in a highly experimental way and became formalized as broad guidelines only in 1979. The IMF know-how on conditionality monitoring and conditionality enforcement remains till today a highly specific asset, which the World Bank, the Organization for Economic Cooperation and Development (OECD), the Central banks, not to speak of the European Commission, do not have.

Most significantly however, conditional lending, which is a form of sovereign borrowing, was explicitly conceived as a non-contractual transaction. A lot of confusion often arises here from the common perspective that envisages IMF conditionality as a substitute for the many private law techniques whereby, at the domestic level, investors' rights are protected against opportunistic debtors (collateral, monitoring clauses, bankruptcy, foreclosures, etc.). Against this banal conception, Joseph Gold, who was the major figure in the formation of the Fund's legal doctrine, always insisted that conditionality should not be interpreted in this contractual language. He stressed in particular the fact that policy commitments are too broad and imprecise for this and that the Fund's discretion when deciding to keep lending should not to be constrained ex ante by commitments that would be framed as "a law unto the party". This should not necessarily be seen as a signal that restructurings are essentially political, that is, shaped by power relationships, policy-based consensus and hegemonic leadership. These factors certainly have a bearing on which rules weigh significantly on outcomes, though within a multilateral arena. Critically, the practice of IMF conditional lending fully recognizes the sovereign character of the borrower: even though its leeway is diminished by the financial crisis and by the intervention of the Fund, it strategizes, breaks rules and reneges on commitments just like any Westphalian animal, and not like a private business.[12]

IMF lawyers have thus kept stressing that an agreement with the Fund is made in fact of two parallel, unilateral transactions: a loan and a set of policy commitments. First, the Letter of Intent, which summarizes the sovereign's commitments, is signed only by the country's authorities. Provided its Executive Board agrees with it, the Fund then separately announces that financial resources are made available to the country. No single document, signed by the two parties, ever sums up the respective rights and obligations. Following the same logic, the policy targets and criteria are considered only as indicators within the broader process of economic policy monitoring, which is the core of the strategic interaction between the Fund and the sovereign, that is, the actual basis on which a stand-by agreement will be suspended or continued, a new Letter negotiated, targets adjusted, waivers obtained, and so forth. This framework of interaction works therefore on the assumption that successive commitments by the two parties will be open to cheating, renegotiation, arm-twisting and so forth. It is thus entirely built on the full recognition that the member-state that negotiates with the Fund is a sovereign and is expected to behave accordingly, that is, in a "realistic", opportunistic way. Rather than being assessed on the basis of a series of detailed commitments, written into the Letter, this expected outcome is in fact much broader: the country should be able to return to the market and restore its capacity to conduct its foreign payments on its own, without excessive stress or breakdown. At that point of course, the painful relationship with the Fund will be thankfully over.

One immediate implication of this realistic, Westphalian relation is that all countries are not equal with respect to an in-coming IMF mission: geopolitical leverage and local economic expertise will bear heavily. But the fast-track conclusion that Fund practice is intrinsically political may also lead to serious misunderstanding of what its rules are about and why their relative decline is so significant. Multilateral rules demanded that the game between a crisis country and the Fund unfold within rather sophisticated rules that have been indeed developed over the decades and which are still today a key element of the Fund's toolbox. These rules structure the game and bear on its outcomes.

"Comparability of treatment", for instance, is a principle that may easily be discarded as full daylight hypocrisy, yet it is also an argument, or a tactical resource, that the parties may actually mobilize in their dealings—including at the IMF board when a large shareholder (say France) defends a bit too heavily a given ally (say Côte d'Ivoire). The Fund itself knows very well that its legitimacy and efficiency require that it should not be seen blatantly ignoring the core rules of multilateral action and playing overtly to the interests of this or that party. The gap between acting as the faithful agent of dominant powers and preserving a modicum of multilateral principles and institutional consistency is what makes the Fund interesting and what justifies its existence. It also helps understand the unique, multilateral character of the restructuring regime of the 1980s and, by contrast, the radical evolutions seen since the early 2000s.

CLASSIC MULTILATERALISM AND CONDITIONALITY: THE DEBT CRISIS OF THE 1980S

The experience of non-contractual, conditional lending that had been capitalized over hundreds of IMF economic programs since the 1950s proved remarkably flexible when sovereign debt issues landed on the Fund's broad desk. After the Mexican quasi-default of August 1982, the mechanics of IMF conditional lending was immediately mobilized as the core of the new restructuring framework. This allowed the IMF to take up immediately the central role in the overall crisis management, exactly at the place where the Money Doctors and the League of Nations had been standing in the past. That is, it acted altogether as a (nominally) independent neutral economic policy expert, a third-party broker, a crisis lender, and a provider of enforcement guarantees. The defining innovations *vis-à-vis* the experience of the 1920s were the monopoly of the Fund over these operations, its capacity to lend, the sheer number of countries in which it intervened and the amount of debts it restructured.

Of course, the 1980s debt crisis took an extremely long time to solve—almost seven years. This reflects primarily the assumption by developed countries that the whole issue, in all countries, was not one of insolvency, a diagnostic that would have called for immediate write-offs. For years, it was assumed that it was only a liquidity crisis that only required some rescheduling of debt service and macroeconomic adjustment. Despite all the tensions and undue costs that this caused, the IMF-centered procedure for restructuring resisted all opt-out strategies. This was clearly not a foregone conclusion. In 1982 and till the end of the decade, dissenting voices, primarily from commercial banks, asked more or less explicitly to be bailed out by Western governments, hence at the expense of Western taxpayers. The IMF was thus instrumental in imposing on banks an active contribution to solving the problem and "sharing the burden". During all those years, the smaller or regional banks in particular were exposed to very strong pressures.[13] If a bank with a marginal interest in foreign operations refused for instance to contribute to a "new money loan" designed to help out crisis countries, it would probably receive telephone calls from its largest competitors threatening retaliations, for instance in access to capital markets. And if these threats failed, the public regulator and the central bank would probably be the next to call—in the United States and in Europe. The Fed was at this point a powerful enforcer, during the whole decade.

This met, up to a point, the pressure that was exercised at the same time on the debtor countries that had little alternative to actually accepting IMF intervention and macroeconomic stabilization. Geopolitical leverage was clearly applied at this point, most clearly in Latin America, in spite of the difficulties encountered by new democratic governments, such as Argentina and Brazil. Debt write-offs were never envisaged as some kind of one-off support given to these new regimes. At the same time, the attempts by the same Latin American governments to coordinate on debt matter never took off, whatever the anxiety manifested by some, in Washington.[14]

Let's look into more detail at how these debt restructurings were handled during those years.[15] The old two-way relationship on which conditionality had been developed since the 1950s was opened up in practice to creditor banks. Informal representative groups of six to ten commercial banks (the so-called London Clubs), which negotiated with the debtor country, were drawn during all those years from the same group of 20–25 major international banks, which therefore sat on several such committees.[16] These banks were thus de facto co-opted within this forum that had been developed since the 1950s by sovereigns and for sovereigns, within a multilateral agency, the IMF, that was de facto controlled by the dominant, Western countries.[17] Decision-making rested on a remarkable three-way, mutual right of veto. First, the Fund's agreement upon a macroeconomic program was a pre-condition for the conclusion of any financial accord with the private investors and, hence, for a return to the primary capital markets.[18] Put differently, the IMF acted as a powerful third-party and a gate-keeper. But in turn this large power was balanced by the second step requirement that banks agree upon a debt restructuring agreement before the IMF could actually disburse its loan. In other words, if the banks believed that the Fund was too soft on a country, because of its "preferred pupil" status for instance, they could reject the whole plan.[19] And of course, the country's government had to sign both accords.

Here is a paradox. On the one hand, the Fund was at the core of the game, not least as an enforcer. If indeed, post-restructuring, the sovereign were again to follow "bad policies" and to default, the financial concessions by the investors would have been of no effect; that is, the equity criteria in the initial agreement would have been violated ex post. A key contribution of the Fund was thus to give credibility to this settlement, hence to give to the three-way bargain a sufficiently long time horizon. Still, on the other hand, one may wonder what the Founding Fathers of the IMF, at Bretton Woods, would have thought of the IMF now accepting that its decision to lend to a member-country could be de facto vetoed by an informal group of private bankers with no formal mandate.

Part of the answer, probably, is in a pattern of thorough deformalization. Just like conditional lending at its beginning, the new practice with banks presented a remarkably limited legal and judicial character: the whole approach was essentially developed and justified in terms of expediency and a pragmatic, problem-solving approach. Critically, this required that all external legal and contractual bonds were de facto suspended.[20] The terms of the initial debt contracts, in particular, had very limited influence on the restructuring process. *Ditto* with international private law, with precedents, and of course any customary practice that could have been imported from private sector restructurings. Not least, bank regulations also had to be adjusted or suspended, when needed: if Western commercial banks had had to classify as "non-performing" all sovereign loans that were not serviced or that were being restructured, many among them, in 1982–1983, would have posted large losses. In turn their own solvency might have come into question, and with it the stability of the whole Western financial system. In other words, the risk of an international systemic crisis was immediate, in fall 1982. But contrary to what happened with the sub-prime loans after 2007, national governments then decided to suspend the key regulations and follow a policy of forbearance, so that no losses would have to be posted on restructured sovereign loans to developing countries.[21]

What this tells, from a broader perspective, is that the debt strategy of the 1980s was not just predicated on the pre-eminent position of the Fund and its capacity to leverage its key resources—expertise, crisis lending, conditionality enforcement, and so on. At the core of this experience is primarily a remarkable convergence of the two dimensions of the Western post-war settlement: first, the strong hand of the Western-controlled IMF and the G7 countries themselves vis-à-vis developing countries; and second, the capacity of the same Western governments to interfere directly in their own domestic banking system, to rewrite rules when needed and to force the bankers' hands if they resisted. Governments de facto intervened in private contracts and property rights, without being subjected to strong legal or constitutional constraints or to rules of due process. The "Keynesian compact" at the domestic level thus worked in sync with the multilateral "Bretton-Woods compact". And at the core of all this, we find the smart, discrete and highly flexible strategy of non-contractual conditional lending.

THE BREAKTHROUGH TO GLOBAL CAPITAL MARKETS

The parallel demise of these two "compacts" was a full part of how the debt crisis was eventually resolved. The 1980s, as is well known, were the years of financial deregulation and capital account liberalization: first in the United Kingdom and the United States at the turn of the decade, then in Continental Europe. Short-term capital movements were essentially free among OECD countries by 1989. This of course entirely redesigned the rules of the game and the political economy of the relationship between large private banks and governments. On the one hand, deregulation came over time with more supervision, for instance regarding the treatment of non-performing loans or capital adequacy norms. On the other hand, discretionary pressures by governments clearly became more difficult. They were not only becoming illegitimate, including within national bureaucracies; they also became more difficult to exercise, as banks were gaining more room to shift their activities across countries and resist pressure from local governments or politicians.

The debt crisis of the 1980s, especially in Latin America, was a major chapter in this broad secular transition. Within these economies, the conjunction of the foreign debt crisis and episodes of high inflation, if not hyperinflation, signaled in a most brutal way the failure of the growth cycle of the 1970s and the collapse of the "developmentalist", or state-led economic model, typically associated with import-substitution. This broad paradigm had gradually emerged in Latin America from the turn of the twentieth century onward, before gaining predominance during the 1930s and coalescing during the post-war decades.[22] It thus extends broadly over the five or six central decades of the century, with many more or less distant parallels being observed across the world, such as the Soviet-type economic model in post-colonial countries, authoritarian modernization, and of course the New Deal and its influence on the early years of the World Bank.[23] In a similar manner, broad ideological shifts at the international level also played a role in delegitimizing the import-substitution paradigm in international arenas, including at the World Bank and the Fund. But the declining effectiveness of this model, especially in Latin America, where it had remained largely intact, and the loss of domestic legitimacy also bore heavily. The shift in economic policies during the 1980s would have not been as large, and sudden, and enduring if it had been defended only by foreign or multilateral interests, plus a few domestic allies—say, the proverbial *comprador bourgeoisie* and a gang of radical economists.

The broad narrative on the end of classic import-substitution crosses the story of the debt crisis exactly in 1985. The strategy regarding the debt crisis that had been adopted in 1982 rested mostly on debt restructurings and "macroeconomic adjustment" (i.e. budget, money and the foreign exchange). Progress was made on this later count but countries did not regain access to capital markets, primarily because their debt levels remained extremely high so that their overall position was seen as utterly fragile. Brutal hyperinflations during those years attest to this. The short-lived "Baker Plan", launched in 1985, rapidly failed for the same reason but left an enduring legacy: macroeconomic adjustment was now complemented by "structural adjustment", that is, trade liberalization, labor market reforms, privatization, and so on. In other words, this was the time when the "Washington Consensus" was actually formed, before it received its name.[24]

By 1987, however, a growing consensus was emerging that large debt write-offs were called for if these countries were to grow again and, in a number of cases, to consolidate their new democratic institutions. Whereas, initially, the transition from military rule in countries like Argentina and Brazil was not seen as a key variable in the debt strategy, this gradually changed as low growth, hyperinflation and the continuing debt problem started to weaken the first democratic governments, critically the Alfonsin government in Argentina. The perspective of seeing these countries moving back to a military regime or being taken over by the radical left was indeed in the background, in the late 1980s. But even then, it was only with the Bush presidency, from early 1989 on, that the principle of debt write-offs was at last accepted. Before that, the US Treasury, in particular Treasury Secretary Jim Baker, had imposed a full veto on any official discussion over such a move, at the Fund or for instance at the G7.

The result was the so-called Brady Plan (1989) which led to 25 to 40 percent cuts on debt in gross terms, depending on the situation of each country. But all past loans that had often been restructured two or three times since the beginning of the decade were also exchanged against dollar-denominated, tradable bonds—the so-called Brady Bonds. The write-offs, the debt exchanges and the turn to structural adjustment opened the way to massive changes in the economic and financial landscape. First the fiscal position of the countries was stabilized, hyperinflations were gradually brought under control, growth resumed and, in some cases, rapid economic catch-up followed. Then, countries that had been in default for years soon regained easy access to the capital markets, though primarily by way of bond issuance. And rather than being dominated by the largest international banks, markets were now peopled as well by investment funds of different varieties, insurance companies, multinational enterprises and, quite soon, by personal investors acting via the Internet. The 1989 breakthrough on developing country debt was thus directly instrumental in the birth of both the "Emerging economies" (structural adjustment and growth recovery) and the "Emerging markets" (debt write-offs and participation in capital markets). This is where the story of the debt crisis since 1982 merges with the broader narrative of the emergence of the Second Global Era, during the 1990s.

What had not been foreseen in 1989 was the speed with which financial globalization would follow. Significantly, in John Williamson's celebrated 1990 essay on the "Washington Consensus", capital account liberalization, which strictly conditions participation in international capital markets, is not mentioned. In fact, capital account liberalization was typically decided by countries' governments themselves and followed the success of the Brady Plan. It became a policy must only after 1992. This was the time when private bankers, institutional investors, policy wonks, well-meaning economists and Fund officials repeated every morning that once foreign trade had been liberalized, there was no reason not to do the same with capital flows. The law of comparative advantages applied in a similar manner to both, they kept repeating. What the actual policy consensus of those years missed entirely was the new risks of crisis to which the "emerging economies" were now exposed. For instance, the list of seminars held at the Research Department of the IMF between 1990 and 1994 does not signal any anticipation that free capital movement and bank deregulation may soon cause new crises, whose dynamics would be entirely different from those of the previous decade.

A "Bankruptcy Court for Sovereigns"? A Failed Project

The radical innovations at the turn of the 1990s had not only a direct, massive effect on how the sovereign debt market operated. Its much broader and diversified basis of investors also implied that, in the event of default, renegotiation would be considerably harder to obtain than in the bank-based regime. In time of crisis, investors may just sell out their bonds, causing their price to fall further and the payment crisis to extend. Various classes of investors also respond to very different investment objectives, time horizons, regulatory and contractual constraints, so that confronted with market stress they may react in wholly divergent ways. In other words, exit, leading potentially to a disorderly massive sell-out, is an easy option, whereas voice and renegotiation have become much more complex and costly than they used to be. Lastly, the time-frame of this strategic interaction is dramatically shortened, while the systemic risk in the capital markets can exercise extremely brutal pressure on policy makers and their bureaucracies. This was demonstrated most spectacularly at the time of the crisis in Mexico (1994–1995) and Asia (1997–1998) when a number of central banks essentially lost control over their monetary and financial system.

However, during the 1990s, and with the only exception of Russia (1998), sovereign insolvency was not a burning issue: the main fragilities of the emerging countries were in their banking sector (Asia) or on the liquidity side of their public debt strategy (Mexico, 1994). Barry

Eichengreen and Richard Portes rang the bell early on, and so did Jeffrey Sachs: if, and when, sovereign defaults make their comeback, the global policy toolbox would be found wanting.[25] But one of the main official contributions to the international policy debates during those years, the Rey Report (1996), clearly opposed any radical innovation regarding sovereign debt workouts. Another landmark contribution, the Meltzer Report (2000), submitted to the US Congress, clearly opposed any official intervention in sovereign debt restructuring and criticized retrospectively the practice of the 1980s.[26]

One had to wait until the Argentine debt default of 2001 for the first confirmation that the sovereign debt problem was serious, even though a full account was not obtained before 2015: this largest default ever took indeed fifteen years to be settled.

The Argentine default was the context in which the project of a "bankruptcy court for sovereign borrowers" (or Sovereign Debt Restructuring Mechanism, SDRM) emerged, in 2002 and triggered an intense policy debate, at the IMF, in national governments and in the academia.[27] While the whole episode is often remembered as a freewheeling, global seminar of no practical consequence, it shaped strongly, though by default, the subsequent debates on sovereign debt. It also underlines with hindsight the spectacular break with past practices that would soon appear. The initial attraction of the Fund's proposal derived from the perceived risk that, in times of sovereign debt crisis, de-coordination among creditors would soon be followed by a free-for-all, that is, a panic. This, it was assumed, called for an institution with the legal power to halt such dynamics, hence to suspend the contractual rights of investors to sell out and exit. A good part of the publicity gained by the Fund's proposal came from its being openly inspired by Chapter 11 of the US bankruptcy code that allows the managers of distressed enterprises to suspend litigation by creditors, so as to negotiate a restructuring plan under the protection, and the supervision, of courts.[28] At the same time, the management may suspend debt service for a non-negligible period of time (several years in the worst cases), but it can also have access to fresh money so that the firm keeps operating (like a country under debt restructuring). Lastly, under the US Chapter 11, the management (read the government) remains a key player in the discussion.

From this US experience derived the proposal to create within the Fund an independent, quasi-judicial body which could apply a similar procedure to sovereign debtors and their creditors. The proposal called for an ad hoc "Forum" to administer debt renegotiation and then legally sanction the restructuring agreement. Provided a qualified majority (75 percent of holders) accepted it, minority investors would not be able to hold-out and resist the majority decision. In particular they would lose the capacity to sue the sovereign or the majority creditors after a write-off, for instance in a US court.[29] The condition for this breakthrough, however, was that jurisdiction over the sovereign debt contracts would be lost by national courts, to the benefit of this new, to-be-invented, supranational court. Compared with the experience of the 1980s, debt restructuring would thus be based less on brokering and more on a judicial model of dispute-resolution, although this quasi-judicial forum would de facto have a supra-national character.

Oddly enough, the Fund wholly under-estimated at the time the extent to which this logic of judicialization required a profound redefinition of its own operating rules. In fact, the Fund's thinking actually evolved over time, as if it discovered only progressively the internal consistency of its initial proposal as well as the problems of institutional design that it raised. Take just as an example the question of the forum where proceedings would take place. Initially the renegotiation process was to take place within the Fund's existing structure, with few institutional guarantees as regards judicial independence. Apparently, this would be in a classic set-up, very similar to the one applauded by Jean Monnet in 1922, where efficiency and legitimacy would flow from the old pretense of multilateralism being disinterested, neutral and apolitical. But this position was gradually abandoned and a so-called "Debt Resolution Forum" was soon envisaged that would have been endowed with a de facto independent, judicial constitution and with a capacity to interpret its own legal rules.[30] Later an appellate body was even added, which would have further formalized the Forum's capacity to develop a (non-binding) case-based jurisprudence.[31] Finally a complex procedure was proposed to guarantee the independence of the three "bankruptcy judges" put in charge of each specific case. At that point, the IMF would be only a benevolent and discrete host, providing the premises and perhaps a secretariat.

What had started as a cooperative and rather loose negotiation framework in which the parties would have sorted out all the problems caused by a default, ended up as an almost paradigmatic model for a civil or commercial court. In particular, while renegotiations were initially to be closely linked to economic crisis management—as they were in the 1980s—the end result codified how these two concerns should be carefully separated one from the other. As all practical responsibilities concerning the unfolding of negotiations were left squarely in the hands of the parties, any de facto link to policy conditionality was excluded by construction. In order for the judicial, process-based character of this forum to be acceptable, the restructuring process had to be wholly out of reach from any policy maker. Remarkably, in the final version of the IMF proposal, the term "conditionality" is mentioned only once in 75 pages. Consequently, the formal link with conditionality enforcement by the IMF, hence with the guarantees of execution attached to a debt agreement, was also broken. In this sense, the end of the multilateral approach to sovereign debt restructuring was not just about actors and the forum. It was very much about the dynamics of bargaining and enforcement, and about the absence, or weakness, of the guarantees of consistency and relative fairness that the Fund used to provide.

Still, all these blueprints and seminars, at the IMF and beyond, were not enough: the whole attempt entirely failed, of course, not least because the whole private financial sector, especially in the United States, was entirely set against this proposal, from Day One.[32] Beyond interests and ideological preferences lay, however, a more potent proposition: since 1990, property rights and contracts, including contracts with sovereign debtors, had been thoroughly redefined and hardened by relying directly on the language of the classic theory of contracts where their integrity and their full enforcement by sovereign courts are seen as a basis of efficient markets and a stable social order.

The failure of the SDRM proposal just told us that this core legal, political, and ideological construction could not be easily amended or redrawn. In such a world, one cannot bring private contracts under a new supranational jurisdiction as a matter of policy expediency—whatever the intrinsic merits of the proposal.[33] As the 1804 Civil Code implicitly stated, contracts have no existence, or at least they have a very different existence if they do not come with a jurisdiction, or if they are suddenly given an entirely new supra-national jurisdiction, with its own, different substantive and procedural rules. And once hundreds of billions of dollars have been invested by thousands of investors in a new species of "quasi-private" sovereign debt contracts, with their legal construction and attached political guarantees, any attempt to redraw those rights and transfer them under a new supra-national authority is doomed to mobilize massive vested interests. Investors do not only invest in token bonds, they also adhere to the institutions that back them up. In fact, what the Fund and its patrons were eventually told is that anything short of full-fledged *national* courts, with all their constitutional and judicial guarantees, would be rejected. The IMF, with its highly specific governance, its taste for ad hoc rules and its poor record regarding external legalities could just not be seen hanging around.

Back to Contracts and National Courts

Since 2003, this core point of liberal constitutionalism has never been seriously contested: the forum where disputes are resolved and debt contracts interpreted is the national courts, primarily the courts that have jurisdiction over bond issues—such as the New York South District Court, to start with. The core question since then has been how to solve, within this new landscape, the hard problems of collective action that arise from debt defaults and which, for centuries, have been addressed most efficiently by private bankruptcy procedures. Here is the irony: while sovereign debt restructuring is now conducted in the language of private contracting and before national courts, the bankruptcy paradigm was entirely left aside, at the moment when the IMF proposal for a bankruptcy court was dropped.

In the aftermath of the 2003 withdrawal of the Fund's proposal, the key concept at the center of the policy debate was Collective Action Clauses (CAC), which came to be seen as a partial, contract-based alternative to a statutory approach, based indirectly on the experience of private bankruptcies. CACs, in practice, are written in the original debt contracts so as to define on an *ex ante* basis how a possible default would be dealt with by the holders of each given bond.[34] Within this limited framework, CACs thus address the basic collective action problems of coordination between investors, plus issues of circulation of information, representation and qualified majority decision-making. Yet, investors remain "encapsulated" in the closed structure of their original debt contracts. How should holders of different bonds be coordinated? How can they transfer the right to renegotiate the contract to a joint representative? What should be done with the bonds which do not include CACs? Today, the CAC approach is most often seen as, at best, a step toward a safe and predictable regime for debt restructuring. Certainly not as a silver bullet. For some, in fact, CACs are rather a false answer offered by smart private lawyers to politicians after the proposal for a supra-national court had been withdrawn.

Then came the long saga of the Pari Passu clause, at the core of the long saga of the Argentine debt restructuring. The underlying story is well known.[35] A now famous investment fund, Elliott Associates, had bought a substantial amount of Argentine debt shortly after the 2001 default, held it for years, and successfully blocked all attempts at enforcing a large write-off, even when more than 90 percent of bondholders had accepted it. The "reinvention" of the Pari Passu clause was at the heart of its strategy. After it had been a silent clause in many sovereign debt contracts, and its exact legal implications had been lost for a long time, a Brussels court (2000), followed by the NY South District Court endorsed an interpretation that directly reinforced the interests of minority bondholders against the will of a majority.[36] The NY Appellate Court then confirmed the decision and the US Supreme Court decided it had no base for taking on the said case. Lastly, the same NY Court offered legal instruments to minority bondholders, allowing them to seize foreign payments made (in that case) by the Argentine governments, provided they transited through a US-registered bank or through a dollar clearing house. This series of landmark decisions rested entirely on a logic of absolute defense of the individual rights of contractants, but the overall outcome was also to entirely push aside the classic paradigm of private bankruptcies, which is actually founded on the principle of a qualified majority vote. Eventually, in 2015, the incoming government of President Macri sued for peace, launched a mega-bond issue in New York and paid back Elliott Associates the debt it owned, at face value.

This evolution clearly plays into the hands of the new class of specialized hedge-funds, exemplified by Elliott Associates, that now make profits by buying the debt of distressed countries at a low price, before obtaining full, face-value service, hence by rejecting any constructive settlement that would include financial concessions by investors. How far this precedent and the success of this disruptive strategy will weigh on future restructuring is still open for question. A later decision by the same New York Court suggested that the Argentine case might remain an outlier and that a more constructive regime might emerge in the future.[37] But this remains at this point one possible scenario among many others.

* * *

With hindsight, there is little doubt that a strong link ties together the three events we have analyzed in this chapter: the conditions under which the debt crisis of the 1980s was managed and eventually resolved, the failure of the IMF to establish a supra-national debt court in 2001–2003, and the present regime where national jurisdictions have taken over and the IMF has receded into the background. Of course, the present rules are part of the broader patterns that we typically associate with the emergence of a globally integrated economy and widespread liberalization. At the same time, the story of how the sovereign debt market evolved was not foretold and it would be certainly unwise to frame it, ultimately, as just a variation, or a long comment, on a broader generic narrative.

The IMF-centered approach to debt restructuring that was adopted during the 1980s was rooted in the post-1945 "Keynesian compact", both at the domestic level (economic *dirigisme*, hands-on banking regulations, etc.) and at the multilateral one (close, ad hoc coordination between the Fund and national regulators). The curiosity here is that this rather archaic strategy was adopted at the exact time when the Keynesian policy compact was being dismantled, first in the United States and in Great Britain, then in Continental Europe and Japan, as shown in previous chapters. This chronological misalignment was however resolved with the 1989 Brady Plan which finally brought the debt crisis to an end while being entirely founded on the new, free-market consensus. Indeed, the US Treasury, its G7 counterparts and the private financial sector easily agreed on an exit strategy that would make a re-run of the 1980s' debt strategy de facto impossible. Never again should this heavy-handed strategy be used with banks.

From this perspective, and with hindsight, the proposal of a "Bankruptcy court for sovereigns" can be interpreted as a late attempt at re-inventing a strong, multilateral, government-led mechanism for sovereign debt restructuring, though within a world of dis-intermediated finance. In the wake of the Asian, Russian and Argentinean crises, Western governments and financial technocrats had come to doubt seriously that the private sector could be entirely trusted in identifying and adopting new norms and rules for debt restructuring. So they considered taking sovereign debt crisis back into their hands by building an ad hoc forum, well inside their common house—the IMF. This was not a benign or inconsequential proposal: this "neo-Keynesian project" called indeed for the property rights of sovereign debt investors to be thoroughly intervened in. And rather than being interpreted and restructured by a well-established national sovereign court, as in classic liberal constitutionalism, these contracts would be put into the hands of a new, untested supra-national jurisdiction.

After 2003 the entire failure of this project made it clear that the new understanding of "what a sovereign debt contract is" had to be taken to its ultimate consequences. This bizarre legal artifact, whose shape has proved so unstable over time, had now been reframed as a near equivalent of a classic private contract, backed up by a sovereign authority, even though a sovereign state also stands on the debtor side of the said contract. This new set-up could not contrast more with the experience of the 1980s, when restructurings were in the hands of the IMF, a cooperative of sovereigns, with its highly specific practice of "non-contractual conditionality" and its veto-based rules for decision-making.

Today, the new debt framework clearly lacks a predictable, rule-based framework for debt restructuring. The coordination of creditors, a qualified majority rule among them, and credible guarantees of execution remain the three strategic challenges on which any future restructuring regime will have to be founded. Whether or not the extremely dysfunctional process that was followed in the Argentine case will remain in the future an outlier is still an open question. At least, this experience demonstrated the many adverse effects that flawed rules can have on restructuring, more generally on the sovereign debt market as such. Still, the current trade war between the United States and China and the considerable pressures on the post-1945 multilateral architecture also underline the new, broader underlying risks of dislocation that may affect the stability of this global market. Until now the aim of a unified regime for debt restructuring, hence of a broadly integrated, law-based debt market has remained a shared objective across the world. Any bifurcation toward, say, a US-led and the China-led debt markets would clearly cause unknown financial and political tensions, not least at the IMF. The case of Venezuela as of a number of over-indebted African countries might offer early signals of things to come.

Notes

1. "*Les conventions légalement formées tiennent lieu de loi à ceux qui les ont faites*" (Art. 1134).
2. This chapter is based on my forthcoming book: *Debt, Sovereignty and the IMF. An Oral History of the 1980s Debt Crisis*, to be published in 2020 by E. Elgar, Cheltenham (UK).
3. Jonathan Eaton and Mark Gersovitz, "Debt with Potential Repudiation: Theoretical and Empirical Analysis," *Review of Economic Studies* 48, no. 2 (April 1981): 289–309; Jeffrey Sachs, *Theoretical Issues in International Borrowing*, Princeton Series in International Finance, 54 (Princeton:

International Finance Section, Dept. of Economics, Princeton University, 1984); Barry Eichengreen, "Restructuring Sovereign Debt," *Journal of Economic Perspectives* 17, no. 4 (2003): 75–98; Odette Lieneau, *Rethinking Sovereign Debt. Politics, Reputation, and Legitimacy in Modern Finance* (Cambridge, Mass.: Harvard University Press, 2014).

4. Charles Lipson, *Standing Guard, Protecting Foreign Capital in the Nineteenth and Twentieth Centuries* (Berkeley: University of California Press, 1985); Paulo Mauro and Yafeh Yishay, *The Corporation of Foreign Bondholders* (Working Paper, International Monetary Fund WP/03/107, Washington, DC, 2003); Michael Waibel, *Sovereign Defaults before International Courts and Tribunals* (Cambridge: Cambridge University Press, 2011); Marc Flandreau, "Sovereign States, Bondholders Committees and the London Stock Exchange in the Nineteenth Century (1827–68): New Facts and Old Fictions," *Oxford Review of Economic Policy* 29, no. 4 (2013): 668–96.

5. See Part II in this volume, especially the chapters by Malak Labib and Ali Coşkun Tunçer.

6. Marc Flandreau, ed., *Money Doctors: The Experience of International Financial Advising 1850–2000* (London: Routledge, 2003); Barry Eichengreen and Peter H. Lindert, *The International Debt Crisis in Historical Perspective* (Cambridge, Mass.: MIT Press, 1989); Elisabeth S. Rosenberg, *Financial Missionaries to the World, The Politics and Culture of Dollar Diplomacy—1900–1930* (Cambridge, Mass.: Harvard University Press, 1999).

7. Edwin Kemmerer, "Economic Advisory Work for Governments," *American Economic Review* 17, no. 1 (March 1927): 1–12; Albert O. Hirschman, *Journeys Towards Progress* (New York: The Twentieth Century Fund, 1963), 162–191; Flandreau, *Money Doctors*.

8. Alec Stone-Sweet, "Judicialization and the Construction of Governance," *Comparative Political Studies* 32, no. 2 (April 1999).

9. Louis W. Pauly, *The League of Nations and the Foreshadowing of the International Monetary Fund*, Essays in International Finance 201 (Princeton: International Finance Section, 1996); Eichengreen and Lindert, *International Debt Crisis*; Juan Flores and Yann Decorzant, "Going Multilateral? Financial Markets' Access and the League of Nations Loans, 1923–28," *The Economic History Review* 69, no. 2 (May 2016): 653–678; Nathan Marcus, *Austrian Reconstruction and the Collapse of Global Finance, 1921–1931* (Cambridge, Mass.: Harvard University Press, 2018).

10. See Jean Monnet, *Mémoires* (Paris: Fayard, 1976), 129–130 (paperback edition).

11. The main components of a multilateral approach were indeed present in the 1920s. See Michael N. Barnett and Martha Finmore, "The Politics, Power, and Pathologies of International Organizations," *International Organization* 53, no. 4 (1999): 699–732; John G. Ruggie, "Multilateralism: The Anatomy of an Institution," *International Organization* 46, no. 3 (1992): 561–598; Robert O. Keohane, "Reciprocity in International Relations," *International Relations* 40, no. 1 (1986): 1–27.

12. Joseph Gold, "The Law and Practice of the International Monetary Fund with Respect to 'Stand-By Arrangements,'" *The International and Comparative Law Quarterly* 12, no. 1 (1963): 1–30; Joseph Gold, *Conditionality*, IMF Pamphlet Series 31 (Washington: International Monetary Fund, 1979).

13. See, for example, Charles Lipson, "Bankers' Dilemma: Private Cooperation in Rescheduling Sovereign Debts," in *Cooperation under Anarchy*, ed. Kenneth. A. Oye (Princeton: Princeton University Press, 1986).

14. Jacek Kugler, "The Politics of Foreign Debt in Latin America, a Study of the Debtors' Cartel," *International Interactions* 13, no. 2 (1987): 115–44; Riordan Roett, "Latin America's Response to the Debt Crisis," *Third World Quarterly* 7, no. 2 (1985): 227–41.

15. Jérôme Sgard, "How the IMF Did It: Sovereign Debt Restructuring, 1970–1989," *Capital Market Law Journal* 11, no. 1 (2016): 103–125.

16. These clubs did not have any legal or institutional existence and they were not coordinated: there was a London Club for Mexico, another for Argentina, a third one for Côte d'Ivoire and so on. A lead bank would just do the paper work and interact (also informally) with the IMF and national authorities. Stanley F. Farrar, "Rights and Duties of Managing and Agent Banks in Syndicated Loans to Government Borrowers," *University of Illinois Law Review* 1 (1982): 229–249; Alfred Mudge, "Sovereign Debt Restructure: A Perspective of Counsel to Agent Banks, Bank Advisory Groups and Servicing Banks," *Columbia Journal of Transnational Law* 23 (1984): 59–74. On the other hand, the Paris Club dealt with debts extended by public entities, such as development aid or export insurance. Being hosted by the French Ministry of Finance, it has kept extensive archives. During the 1980s, the Paris Club rather ran a side show, primarily because, in its meetings, the key voices on the creditor side were in fact the G7 countries, which also dominated the discussions at the IMF, in Washington. So there was no significant problem of coordination and negotiation between the two.

17. The intense power struggle between the banks and the policy makers on a strategy to address the Mexican default is vividly analyzed by Joseph Kraft in his book *The Mexican Rescue* (New York: Group of Thirty, 1984). On the enforcement of the collective action rules on potentially diverging

actors, see also Sebastian Alvarez, "The Mexican Debt Crisis Redux: International Interbank Markets and Financial Crisis, 1977–1982," *Financial History Review* 22, no. 1 (April 2015): 79–105.
18. Most countries also had bilateral official debt with national governments, which was coordinated within the Paris Club, and multilateral debt which was excluded from any formal renegotiation.
19. For broad narratives of the debt crisis, see John Boughton, *Silent Revolution, the International Monetary Fund 1979–1989* (Washington: International Monetary Fund, 2001); William R. Cline, *International Debt Reexamined* (Washington, DC: Institute for International Economics, 1995); Michael Dooley, *A Retrospective on the Debt Crisis* (NBER Working Paper 4963, 1994); Benjamin Cohen, *In whose interest? International Banking and American Foreign Policy* (New Haven: Council of Foreign Relations/Yale University Press, 1986).
20. Sgard, "How the IMF Did It."
21. In the case of the United States, the whole problem was solved in one sentence by Paul Volcker, then Governor of the Federal Reserve: "In such cases, where new loans facilitate the adjustment process and enable a country to strengthen its economy and service its international debt in an orderly manner, new credits should not be subject to supervisory criticism" (quoted in Kraft, *Mexican Rescue*, 49).
22. Joseph L. Love, "Raul Prebisch and the Origins of the Doctrine of Unequal Exchange," *Latin American Research Review* 15, no. 3 (1980): 45–72.
23. Eric Helleiner, *Forgotten Foundations of Bretton Woods. International Development and the Making of the Postwar Order* (Ithaca: Cornell University Press, 2014); Kiran Klaus Patel, *The New Deal, A Global History* (Princeton: Princeton University Press, 2016).
24. John Williamson, "What Washington Means by Policy Reforms," in *Latin American Adjustment: How Much Has Happened?* (Washington: Institute for International Economics, 1990), 7–20; John Williamson, "A Short History of the Washington Consensus," (paper presented at the *Forum Barcelona*, "From the Washington Consensus towards a new Global Governance," Barcelona Center for International Affairs, Barcelona, 2004), 14 pages.
25. Barry Eichengreen and Richard Portes, eds., *Crisis? What Crisis? Orderly Workouts for Sovereign Debtors* (London: Center for Economic Policy Research, 1995); Jeffrey D. Sachs, "Do We Need an International Lender of Last Resort?" (Frank D. Graham Lecture, Princeton University, Princeton, 1995).
26. Group of Ten, *Report* (Basel: Bank for International Settlements, 1996 [Rey Report]); International Financial Institution Advisory Committee,

Report (Washington, DC: US Congress, Joint Economic Committee, 2000 [Meltzer Report]).
27. This project was known officially as the "Sovereign Debt Restructuring Mechanism" (SDRM) as well as by the name of the IMF official who led the institution's work on it—Anne Krueger. Anne Krueger, "International Financial Architecture for 2002: A new Approach to Sovereign Debt Restructuring," (Washington: National Economists Club/ American Enterprise Institute, November 26, 2002), 7 pages; International Monetary Fund, "A New Approach to Sovereign Debt Restructuring: Preliminary Considerations" (Washington: International Monetary Fund, November 30, 2001), 18 pages; International Monetary Fund, "The Design of the Sovereign Debt Restructuring Mechanism – Further Considerations" (Washington: International Monetary Fund, November 27, 2002), 76 pages.
28. On private bankruptcies, see Thomas H. Jackson, *The Logic and Limits of Bankruptcy Law* (Cambridge, Mass.: Harvard University Press, 1986). On US Chapter 11, see Douglas G. Baird, *Elements of Bankruptcy* (New York: Foundation Press, 2001). On a comparison between US Chapter 11 and the SDRM proposal, read Patrick Bolton, "Towards a Statutory Approach to Sovereign Debt Restructuring, Lessons from Corporate Bankruptcy Practice around the World," *IMF Staff Papers* 50, Special Issue (2003): 41–71; Nouriel Roubini, "Do we Need a New Bankruptcy Regime?" *Brookings Papers on Economic Activity* 2002, no. 1 (2002): 229–255.
29. Compared to the 1980s regime, this would have also reflected a shift to a fully-fledged compulsory conflict settlement mechanism.
30. International Monetary Fund, "Sovereign Debt Restructuring Mechanism—Further Considerations" (Washington: International Monetary Fund, August 14, 2002), 33 pages; International Monetary Fund, "A New Approach."
31. International Monetary Fund, "Sovereign Debt Restructuring Mechanism"; International Monetary Fund, "A New Approach."
32. Anne Krueger, "Sovereign Debt Restructuring: Messy or Messier?" *The American Economic Review* 93, no. 2, Papers and Proceedings (2003): 70–74.
33. A high-level working group organized by the Brookings Institution underlined in 2013 that the bankruptcy paradigm remained the first best option, though it also recognized that the perspective of an evolution in this direction seemed very narrow. Lee C. Buchheit et al., *Revisiting Sovereign Bankruptcy* (Washington: The Brookings Institution, 2013).
34. On CACs, see Eichengreen and Portes, *Crisis?*; Liz Dixon and David Wall, "Collective Action Problems and Collective Action Clause," *Financial Stability Review,* Bank of England (June 2000):142–151; Mark

C. Weidemaier and Mitu Gulati, "A People's History of Collective Action Clauses," *Virginia Journal of International Law* 54, no. 1 (2013): 51–95. CACs have traditionally been included in London bonds, contrary to New York ones. This is why the discussion centered on New York law and legal practices. More generally, CACs reflect a logic whereby national jurisdictions and legal frameworks compete one against the other. The point is that competition has already delivered its result, under the form of a de facto duopoly between the two large financial centers: markets are vertically or geographically integrated with legal institutions.

35. Mark Weidemaier, "Sovereign debt after *NML v Argentina*," *Capital Markets Law Journal* 8, no. 2 (2013): 123–31; Lee C. Buchheit and Mitu Gulati, "Restructuring Sovereign Debt After *NML v. Argentina*," *Capital Markets Law Journal* 12, no. 2 (2017): 224–238. The main argument against any public intervention in sovereign debt restructurings claims that controlling these "realist" debtors is always highly difficult; helping them out when they are in difficulties is thus doomed to create a moral hazard, hence even greater difficulties in enforcing sovereign debt contracts. Protecting the market thus requires that the costs of defaulting for borrowing states be maximal, so that their own self-interest is indeed to protect their reputation, or track-record. See Anna Schwartz, "Do Sovereign Debtors Need a Bankruptcy Law?" *Cato Journal* 23, no. 1 (2003): 87–100.

36. Mark Weidemaier, Robert Scott and Mitu Gulati, "Origin Myths, Contracts, and the Hunt for Pari Passu," *Law & Social Inquiry* 38, no. 1 (2012): 72–105.

37. Lee C. Buccheit and Andrés de la Cruz, "The Pari Passu Fallacy – *Requiescat in Pace*," *International Financial Law Review* (February 2018): 32–33.

CHAPTER 18

Of Bond Vigilantes, Central Bankers and the Crisis of 2008

Adam Tooze

The political economy of the late twentieth century was marked by a striking juxtaposition. From the mid-1970s an unprecedented peacetime surge in public debt coincided with the liberalization of international capital transactions. In 1970 the debt to GDP ratio of a sample of major OECD countries stood at 40 percent. By the mid-1990s, as an unweighted average, this had doubled to 80 percent. Over the same period the capital account restrictions of Bretton Woods were dropped. Capital moved with a freedom last seen in the 1920s, and it moved through financial markets and bank balance sheets at greater speed and in greater volume than ever before. The combination was explosive. From the 1970s, spooked by large deficits and accelerating inflation, capital markets became jumpy. The history of public finances was punctuated by a succession of crises. In 1976 heavy selling in forex and gilt-edged markets forced both Italy and Britain to borrow from the International Monetary Fund (IMF). The Latin American debt crisis erupted in Mexico in August 1982. In 1983, in

A. Tooze (✉)
Department of History, Columbia University, New York, NY, USA
e-mail: adam.tooze@columbia.edu

© The Author(s) 2020
N. Barreyre, N. Delalande (eds.), *A World of Public Debts*, Palgrave Studies in the History of Finance,
https://doi.org/10.1007/978-3-030-48794-2_18

France the socialist government of François Mitterrand surrendered to the force of the market. Not by coincidence 1983 was also the year in which the phrase "bond vigilantes" was coined by the American brokerage house economist Edward Yardeni.

"Bond investors are the economy's bond vigilantes," Yardeni declared. "So if the fiscal and monetary authorities won't regulate the economy, the bond investors will. The economy will be run by vigilantes in the credit markets."[1] As Yardeni later spelled out: "By vigilantes, I mean investors who watch over policies to determine whether they are good or bad for bond investors [...] If the government enacts policies that seem likely to reignite inflation," Yardeni elaborated, "the vigilantes can step in to restore law and order to the markets and the economy."[2]

In fact, as Yardeni coined his phrase, the authorities in all the major advanced economies were reasserting control. They did so, not by limiting capital movement, but by following the lead taken by the US Fed with its interest rate hike of October 1979.[3] What became known as the "Volcker shock" stopped inflation. Much of the disinflationary work was done by high unemployment. It was this spectacular squeeze that set the stage for the "great moderation" of the 1990s. Inflation calmed, but in a world of unrestrained capital mobility, the vigilantes could strike anyone, anywhere, at any time. In 1992 Britain and Italy again felt the pressure of currency and bond markets. As Bill Clinton took office in early 1993, the first Democrat to do so in twelve years, there was anxiety on Wall Street that he would overturn the anti-inflation consensus of the 1980s. For Yardeni this was the real "heyday" of the bond vigilantes. The assessment of the *LA Times* was blunt: "Power will not be held only by the Treasury, the Federal Reserve and Congress. Thousands of bond owners and portfolio managers around the world also will have a collective influence—some economists even say veto power—over the Clinton Administration's policy choices."[4] When newspapers reported that Clinton might be considering a significant fiscal stimulus, rates shot up. Bond markets calmed only when Clinton and his team disavowed any such plan. As Yardeni approvingly remarked: "What is striking is that just a modest uptick in yields got the prompt attention of Clinton and his policy-makers."[5] Indeed, they did not just get the attention of the Clinton administration. As Bob Woodward chronicled in his highly influential inside report, *The Agenda*, they changed the direction of the presidency.[6] The Clinton administration implemented a regime of budget balance and "welfare reform" that more than satisfied the markets. Having climbed from 5.2 percent to just over 8.0 percent between 1993 and 1994, by 1998 ten-year Treasury yields eased back to 4 percent. It was against this backdrop that political advisor James Carville, the architect of Clinton's electoral win, commented in February 1993:[7] "I used to think that if there was reincarnation, I wanted to come back as the president or the pope or as a .400 baseball hitter. But now I would like to come back as the bond market. You can intimidate everybody."[8]

After the Europeans and the United States in the early 1990s, the Asian economies, Russia and then Latin America were next. Between 1997 and 2001 they were convulsed by a series of "twin crises"—capital market and foreign exchange runs—that stretched from Thailand to Argentina. As the new century began, the idea that liberalized capital markets exercised veto power became common sense. In academic economics it was formalized in the notion of the trilemma. A country might wish to have a stable currency, enjoy the benefits of capital mobility and the autonomy to conduct its own economic policy. But all three of these goals were unattainable. The best that any state could do was to choose two. If it acceded to the advice of the OECD and the IMF to liberalize capital, a country was left with a choice between stabilizing its exchange rate and conducting an autonomous economic policy. It could not have both.[9] If that sounded tough, many were convinced that the trade-off was, in reality, even more severe. Given that a dramatic slide in currency values in an emerging market was likely to unleash an avalanche of outflows, for most states, exchange rate flexibility was not an option. So what governments faced was not in fact a trilemma but a stark choice.[10] One could choose to put on the golden handcuffs of global financial integration, and abandon any pretense to national sovereignty in economic policy, or one could impose exchange and capital controls and retain a degree of economic policy autonomy. In practice there were no takers for the latter option, market liberalization and fiscal consolidation became the norm.

In April 2000, Rolf Breuer, the head of the Deutsche Bank, told *Die Zeit*, economic and social policy would "more than ever [have to be] formulated with an eye to the financial markets: if you like, they have taken on an important watchdog role alongside the media, almost as a kind of 'fifth estate.' " In Breuer's view, it would "perhaps not be such a bad thing if politics in the twenty-first century was taken in tow by the financial markets". For, in the end, "Politicians (…) themselves contributed to the restrictions on action (…) that have been causing them such pain. Governments and parliaments made excessive use of the instrument of public debt. This entails—as with other debtors—a certain accountability to creditors. (...) If governments and parliaments are forced today to pay greater heed to the needs and preferences of international financial markets, this (...) is attributable to the mistakes of the past."[11] In 2007 former Fed chair Alan Greenspan summed up the wisdom of the new era of globalization. In an interview with the Zürich daily *Tages-Anzeiger* on 19 September, he opined that in the upcoming US presidential election it mattered little which candidate he supported, since "(we) are fortunate that, thanks to globalization, policy decisions in the US have been largely replaced by global market forces. National security aside, it hardly makes any difference who will be the next president. The world is governed by market forces."[12]

That was in 2007, before the financial crisis hit. The question is how this narrative stands up in the wake of a decade of financial turmoil and policy innovation. Is the image of sovereign debt politics shaped between the 1970s and the early 2000s still plausible?

The Power of Bond Markets

On the face of it, it seems that the crisis must have tightened the grip of financial markets on politics. Prior to the COVID shock of 2020, the increase in public debt after 2007 was the most dramatic ever seen in peacetime, dwarfing the debt shock of the 1970s and 1980s. In the US alone, the increase in Treasury liabilities between 2008 and 2015 came to $9 trillion. According to the logic espoused by the likes of Breuer, it is hard to see how this could not have increased the leverage of bond markets.

In May 2009, as the scale of the fiscal shock became clear, Bloomberg and the *Wall Street Journal* reported that markets were up in arms. Yardeni was once more to the fore warning that "Ten trillion dollars over the next 10 years is just an indication that Washington is really out of control."[13] On 29 May 2009 the *Wall Street Journal* announced that in light of "Washington's astonishing bet on fiscal and monetary reflation," the bond vigilantes were swinging back into the saddle. "It's not going too far to say we are watching a showdown between Fed Chairman Ben Bernanke and bond investors, otherwise known as the financial markets." "When in doubt", the *Journal* advised its readers, "bet on the markets."[14] It was a message that had particular resonance inside an Obama administration staffed by veterans of the Clinton years and haunted by memories of the 1990s. In May 2009 Obama commissioned his budget director Peter Orszag to prepare contingency plans for a bond market sell off.[15] Orszag was a protégé of Clinton-era Treasury Secretary Robert Rubin. In the locust years of the Bush presidency, Orszag, working with Rubin, had anticipated Obama's request by crafting an agenda of budget consolidation for the next Democratic presidency.[16]

In early 2010, the appearance of "Growth in a Time of Debt", a highly influential paper by Professors Carmen M. Reinhart and Kenneth S. Rogoff, added intellectual weight to fear of the bond market.[17] The two former IMF economists claimed to have identified a critical threshold. When debt reached 90 percent of GDP, growth declined sharply, leading to a vicious spiral of rising debt burdens and slowing growth. Since markets could anticipate this outcome, debt levels above 90 percent of GDP risked a sudden loss of market confidence. "I certainly wouldn't call this my baseline scenario for the US", Reinhart warned in one interview— "but the message is: think the unthinkable."[18] On Fox TV, historian Niall Ferguson invoked the collapse of the Soviet Russia to make the same point. A world power could be brought down by financial excess with catastrophic speed.[19] In light of the intensifying Eurozone crisis, Ferguson's message to American audiences was stark: "The PIIGS R US". The PIIGS here refers to Portugal, Ireland, Italy, Greece and Spain, the main casualties of bond market pressure in the Eurozone.

As the Greek debt crisis went critical in the spring of 2010, fear of debt spread around the world. By May 2010, as Alan Blinder put it, the vigilantes were "riled up" and had formed "an electronic mob" circling the globe "faster than Hermes".[20] The sovereign bond spreads not only for Greece, but Ireland, Portugal, Italy and Spain were all moving upward. And the tension spilled beyond the Eurozone. The hotly disputed and inconclusive UK election of 6 May 2010 came in the most acute early phase of the Eurozone crisis. As British voters cast their ballots, rioting convulsed Athens and the "flash crash" disrupted US financial markets. Not surprisingly, in the aftermath nerves were on edge. Getting Britain's deficit under control was the central preoccupation of the ensuing coalition negotiations between the Tories and the Liberal Democrats.[21] For the Tories and their advisors, it was clear that the budget talks would be "regarded by the financial markets as a test" of their government's credibility. Market pressure would become the main justification for Britain's severe austerity course. Even more drastic was the experience of the Eurozone crisis cases, all of which underwent budget tightening enforced by the threat of rising bond yields. "Spreads" became the stuff of daily conversation across Southern Europe. In the Greek case, debt restructuring would become a brutal trial of strength. Negotiations stretched for nine months and resulted in 2012 in a debt restructuring that only partially disencumbered the Greek state.[22]

What were the forces, who were the decision-makers moving the bond markets? In the wake of the crisis, this was no longer a question only for market insiders. Campaigning organizations such as the Trade Union Advisory Committee to the OECD and the International Trade Union Confederation began compiling statistics on global asset managers. The sheer size of the capital accumulated by these firms gives an impression of formidable power. The largest of them manage portfolios comparable to the sovereign debt of large European countries. BlackRock in 2010 already boasted a portfolio of $3.5 trillion.[23]

The giant bond funds bring to mind not so much the vigilantes of the Wild West as the capitalist empire-builders who displaced them. Truer to the vigilante imagery were the hedge funds. These are far smaller than the asset managers. Only a few of the very largest hedge funds had more than $30 billion under management. But they were also more aggressive and willing to take risks on massively discounted sovereign bonds. A handful of so-called "vulture funds" snapping up a few billion dollars' worth of devalued debt could exercise huge leverage in complex debt negotiations.

Whether large or small, the spokesmen and -women of the bond market were not shy about announcing their power. They liked their role as market enforcers. In the spring of 2011, "bond king" Bill Gross of PIMCO, which had more than $1 trillion under management, gave an interview in which he threatened a market rebellion against government deficit. In language reminiscent of the Tea Party, Gross told *Atlantic* magazine: "Sale of Treasury bonds is the easiest way of staging a mini-revolution."[24] As *Wall Street Journal* blogger Neal Lipschutz opined on 23 November 2011: "There is a significant disconnect between the every person has a vote doctrine of representative government and the blunt collective power of money and markets. Most of the time this disconnect is hidden and doesn't really matter. In times of crisis, as we have seen in Europe, it can become the only thing that matters, overshadowing coalition governments, parliamentary squabbles, constitutional prohibitions and all the rest."[25] As Kathleen Gaffney who co-managed $80 billion in bonds for the Loomis Sayles group, owned by Natixis, put it to the *Financial Times*, the governments of Greece and Portugal would "pay the price for not being harder on the populace".[26]

Talk of "bond kings", "mini-revolutions" and the need to squeeze the "populace" unsurprisingly drew the attention of a new breed of left-wing thinkers interested in political economy.[27] Slavo Žižek, *enfant terrible* of the radical scene asked rhetorically, "What, then, is the higher force whose authority can suspend the decisions of the democratically elected representatives of the people? As far back as 1998, the answer was provided by Hans Tietmeyer, the then governor of the Deutsche Bundesbank, who praised national governments for preferring 'the permanent plebiscite of global markets' to the 'plebiscite of the ballot box'."[28] At a conference hosted by the Soros-funded platform for alternative economic thought, INET, German literary theorist and social critic Joseph Vogl remarked: "The markets themselves have become a sort of creditor-god, whose final authority decides the fate of currencies, social systems, public infrastructures, private savings, etc."[29]

The most systematic and influential analysis of public debt from the left was that offered by economic sociologist Wolfgang Streeck. According to Streeck, indebted capitalist democracies, what he calls "debt states", face a systematic double bind. They are answerable not just to their citizens, but to a new constituency, the owners of government bonds. Unlike citizens, credit markets are internationally organized. Their claims are enforceable in law. Bondholders can exit whenever they like. The interest rates set by bond auctions "are the 'public opinion' of the *Marktvolk* (i.e. 'market citizenry')". They are more precise and more pressing than the vague soundings of public opinion. Whereas the debt state "can expect a duty of loyalty from its citizens, it must in relation to its *Marktvolk* take care to gain and preserve its confidence, by conscientiously servicing the debt it owes them and making it appear credible that it can and will do so in the future as well."[30]

Of course, this left critique of capital markets has a long and distinguished pedigree. The idea of bond markets acting as a countervailing force against left-wing governments stretches back at least as far as the early twentieth century when social democratic parties first took the gamble of trying to govern capitalist states. In 1924 the government of the *Cartel des Gauches* in the French Third Republic was hobbled by what they dubbed the "*mur d'argent*" (wall of money).[31] In 1931 the British left denounced the "bankers ramp" that split the second Labour government of Ramsay MacDonald.[32] In 1943 Polish economist Michael Kalecki theorized that any progressive administration seeking to adopt a Keynesian approach to full employment would face a capital strike.[33] In 1944 Karl

Polanyi, in *The Great Transformation*, pointed out that financial markets are governed "by panic".[34] Under Bretton Woods, after 1945, the restriction of capital mobility was designed precisely to limit the danger of capital flight. And those fears were amply reconfirmed once capital mobility returned. In the early 1980s the hobbling of Mitterrand's government by capital market panics reawakened memories of the *mur d'argent* of the 1920s.[35] Thirty years later, in the eurozone crisis, the breaking of PASOK in Greece and the Spanish social democratic administration followed a familiar script and the enormous pressure directed against the left-wing governments of Greece and Portugal in 2015 made the rule of capital seem more absolute than ever.[36] It was not for nothing that Streeck in 2012 positioned his Adorno Lectures, published as *Buying Time*, as a self-conscious revival of earlier generations of crisis theory.

The convergence between the cheerleaders of the bond vigilantes on the one hand and the left critics of financial capitalism is striking and by no means accidental. Both have a stake, though from opposite vantage points, in highlighting capital's watchdog role. What both downplay is the fact that the pressure of bond markets on sovereign borrowers was far from uniform. Capital markets are hierarchically differentiated and power relations between debtors and creditors are more complex than the simple model of creditor dominance would suggest. Investors have to put their money somewhere and they have a deep interest in security. A fund manager with hundreds of billions of dollar to invest faces a serious problem of finding the right balance of risk and return. As Streeck himself grudgingly acknowledges, dependence runs both ways. Investors need government debt issuance to provide them with "safe assets".[37] Furthermore, if they so choose, governments do have the option of exercising sovereign power over capital markets. They can engage in what is commonly termed "financial repression"—requiring funds to be allocated to low-risk assets and capping interest rates. Furthermore, there is, as Streeck recognizes, a more elemental risk in lending to sovereigns. "They may also at their discretion one-sidedly 'restructure' government debt, since as 'sovereign' debtors they are not subject to any legal bankruptcy procedure. [....] That is a constant nightmare for lenders."[38] Indeed, it is with that problem of "original sin" that mainstream economic accounts of public debt markets begin.[39] Governments as sovereign borrowers have a credibility issue. How does a sovereign borrower persuade private lenders that it will respect their property rights? As Jerome Sgard's chapter in this volume shows, this is the question that was actively contested in the courts over Argentina's default of 2001.

Though it is tempting to paint a picture of market dominance over democratic government, as Streeck recognizes the interaction is better described as a never-ending "strategic game".[40] And the crucial question is, at any given moment, what defines the terms of the game? To offer a more specific answer, we need to marry general sociological observations to a systematic international political economy. The pressure the capital markets exercise depends on the position of a state in the global financial hierarchy (international relations), the political forces that can be mobilized by both sides and the kinds of legal strategies analyzed by Sgard (political economy), the dynamics of financial balance sheets (microfinance), and the general balance between borrowers and lenders in global capital markets (macroeconomics).

The Strategic Game Since 2008

If we focus on the financial crises that began in 2008, we observe a starkly differentiated experience. The victims of the Eurozone crisis such as Greece, Portugal and Ireland found themselves in extreme difficulties. But this was because they were small borrowers and they had surrendered control of their currency to the Eurozone system. They could not devalue. And even if they had been willing to take the risk of leaving the Eurozone, the scale of their debts in euro made the risk of a disruptive avalanche too great. That same constraint applied even to those EU members who were not members of the Eurozone. For Latvia, in 2009, for instance, a devaluation as recommended by the IMF would have been tantamount to a comprehensive default on its euro-denominated debts. Despite the political pain it caused, Latvia's government stayed the course of austerity. This held Latvia on course for Eurozone membership and launched the remarkable European political career of Valdis Dombrovskis, who rose to occupy a key position in Urusula von der Leyen's Commission of 2019.

Greece, Portugal, Ireland and Latvia provide graphic illustrations of the power of creditors. But add them all up and they account for an insignificant slice of global bond markets. The largest sovereign borrower, the United States, has played the strategic game with its creditors on entirely different terms.

As Paul Krugman insists, as far as the United States is concerned, those who sought to revive the memory of the 1990s bond vigilantes to greet the Obama administration in 2009 were indulging in fear-mongering. Not only were the size and the number of the vigilantes exaggerated, but "even if for some reason the vigilantes did attack, it's very hard to see how they could cause a recession in a country that retains its own currency and doesn't have large amounts of debt denominated in foreign currency. (…) A loss of confidence would lead not to a contractionary rise in interest rates but to an *expansionary* fall in the dollar."[41] According to Rudiger Dornbusch's seminal macro model of "exchange rate overshooting", so long as the central bank held its nerve and was willing to hold short-term interest rates down, the effect of a speculative attack would be to depreciate the currency to the point at which the expected future appreciation provided investors with the rate of return that they needed. In the meantime, a lower exchange rate would add to export competitiveness. The vigilantes would be doing their supposed victims a favor.

Such qualifications are a salutary corrective to monolithic views of creditor power. But they do not go far enough in addressing the remarkable events we have witnessed since 2008. While on the periphery of the Eurozone, Greece, Ireland, Portugal and Spain enacted a stylized rerun of the clashes of the 1980s, by 2014 global investors were paying Germany to take their money. Contrary to the bond vigilante story line, the crisis led investors to see the bonds of countries like the United States, Germany and the United Kingdom as safe havens. The cost of borrowing held steady or fell even as the volume of sovereign debt issued increased spectacularly.[42] Rather than facing a vicious spiral of waning confidence, rising borrowing costs, insolvency and crisis, the period after 2008 saw treasuries and central banks open up a virtuous circle in which lower rates made larger debts more affordable. As a result, even as America's debt surged, its costs of debt service fell from $451 billion in 2008 to $383 billion in 2009. And investors were not put off. Even with lower yields and surging volumes of debt issued, the bid-to-cover ratio, which measures the ratio of bids to the quantity of Treasury bonds offered, rose from 2.41 in 2004–2008 to 2.63 in 2009 and 3.21 in 2010.[43]

The point of these remarks, of course, is not to erase the extreme victimization of borrowers like Greece. The point, rather, is to throw into stark relief the ideological work done by slogans such as "The PIIGS R US". Among the larger borrowers outside the Eurozone, it took blatant scaremongering to maintain the pressure for austerity and to keep borrowing in check even as the terms of borrowing eased. Furthermore, by asking why experience in credit markets was so polarized we are driven to reexamine two assumptions presumed by the familiar narrative of bond market power, but too rarely spelled out. The first concerns the attitude of the central bank, the agency that mediates between the state and bond market. The second concerns the underlying condition of the global economy.

Central Banks Come into Play

Relations between elected governments and capital markets are triangulated by a third pole, the officials, technicians and economists who craft financial and monetary policy in Treasuries and above all in central banks. The most immediate explanation for the extraordinarily easy conditions enjoyed by the largest sovereign borrowers since the onset of the 2008 financial crisis is the action of their central banks. The central banks made themselves into purchasers of government debt on a scale unprecedented in peacetime. The Fed led the way with three consecutive quantitative easing programs, in 2009, 2010 and 2012. The Bank of England was a major buyer of gilts in 2009. The Bank of Japan adopted QE on a huge scale in 2013, as did the European Central Bank (ECB) in 2015. By 2017, according to IMF data, G4 official purchases had absorbed two-thirds of the $15 trillion in new sovereign debt issued since 2010.[44] Not surprisingly, this scale of official purchases helped to keep bond prices up and yields down.

This contrasted sharply with the conduct of central banks during the era of the "Volcker shock" and its aftermath. During the long war against inflation from the 1970s to the 1990s, central bankers took the lead in driving up rates. It was this historical experience that became the unspoken assumption of theories of bond market dominance. The central bank was assumed to be passive or even to be taking the side of the bond vigilantes against high-spending governments. To that extent, theories of capital market dominance were really describing a struggle within the apparatus of the state. The vast economic policy literature on central bank "independence" is testament to this point.[45] In the central banking tradition exemplified by the Bundesbank and personified by Paul Volcker, "independence" means the ability and willingness of central bankers to defy the wishes of elected governments. It does not mean that central banks are "independent" with respect to the interests or ideas of "the markets". Though they pursue their careers in ministries and central banks, financial officials commonly maintain close relations with the markets and often pass through revolving doors into and out of positions in the private sector.

The cohort of central bankers who faced the crisis of 2008 were the self-conscious inheritors of the Volcker tradition. Notably in Europe they played the role of watchdogs over fiscal policy. Mervyn King of the Bank of England had no compunction in the spring of 2009 in going on record in Treasury Select Committee to assert: "I do not think we can afford to wait until the Parliament after next before taking action to demonstrate credibly that the United Kingdom is going to reduce its deficit and that fiscal policy will be credible."[46] It was no slip of the tongue. King repeated the message a year later. On 12 May 2010, he told the incoming Tory-Liberal coalition government: "The most important thing now is for the new government to deal with the challenge of the fiscal deficit. It is the single most pressing problem facing the United Kingdom; it will take a full parliament to deal with (…) I think we've seen in the last two weeks, particularly, but in the case of Greece, over the last three months, that it doesn't make sense to run the risk of an adverse market reaction."[47] King was acting the role of the "independent" enforcer demanding that Britain's elected politicians deliver a credible commitment to austerity. But he was playing a delicate game. The central banker needed to vigorously assert his independence in part also because the Bank of England was itself engaged in a highly unconventional role. Since 2008, it had been propping up the bond market on a massive scale. It was to make this task manageable that King was asking for fiscal consolidation.

In the Eurozone, given the unsettled state of its constitution and the high debt levels in Greece, Italy, Ireland and Portugal, the rules of the "strategic game" were even rougher. The rhythm of the crisis was set by the cat and mouse game between the ECB, Germany and the lesser players of the Eurozone. The three periods in which tension within the Eurozone built to unbearable levels—November 2009–May 2010, March–August 2011, May–August 2012—were phases in which the ECB ostentatiously refused to support the public bond market of the common currency zone. Jean-Claude Trichet of the ECB made no secret of the fact that he used these tactics to force the slow-moving Eurozone governments to consolidate their budgets.[48] And when that was not enough Europe's central bankers went further. In Greece, Ireland and Portugal, the ECB joined the troika overseeing the "program countries". Nor did the ECB confine itself to disciplining the "program countries". In August 2011, Trichet fired off extraordinary missives to the prime ministers of Spain and Italy demanding fiscal retrenchment and institutional "reforms". The letter to Berlusconi was cosigned by Mario Draghi as president of the Bank of Italy and Trichet's successor at the ECB. The ECB's threat was that unless the governments acted as the central bank demanded, it would withdraw support both for sovereign and bank debt, allowing the sovereign-bank doom loop to take full effect. Seen from this angle, to talk in terms of "bond market vigilantes" imposing the rules is euphemistic.[49] The role of bond markets in relation to the ECB and the dominant German government was less of a freewheeling vigilante, than of state-sanctioned para-militaries delivering a punishment beating while the police looked on.[50]

The question, as with para-militarism, was whether the extra-judicial threat once unleashed could be contained or whether "austerity by fear" would take on a life of its own. By the summer of 2011, it was increasingly apparent that the strategy of tension had produced something akin to hysteria in Eurozone sovereign bond markets. Far from helping to "restore law and order", the markets were in the grip of a panic. Furthermore, the uncertainty that surrounded Italy, at the time the fourth largest sovereign debtor after the United States, Japan and Germany, created an existential risk for the Eurozone. The state of panic in the market could be judged by the fact that CDS quotations implied that Italy's probability of default was greater than that of Egypt in the midst of the Arab Spring.[51] Three years earlier the same Italian bonds had traded on terms practically identical to Bunds.

This lurching adjustment of market judgment inverted the terms in which the bond vigilante argument was usually cast. Rather than short-sighted governments being disciplined by the "logic of the market", it was the markets whose rationality was in question. Of course, intelligent advocates of markets do not claim that market actors are individually correct in their forecasts or necessarily rational in their individual behavior. The claim is that markets are collectively rational and optimizing. This, however, depends on the operation of checks and balances. So long as the bets by market actors offset each other, speculation will be self-stabilizing. But in a collective panic, even well-judged contrarian bids will be swamped by the general market movement.[52] The vigilantes themselves, on whose sound judgment the corrective mechanism supposedly depends, risk becoming victims of the financial stampede.[53] In the fall of 2011, it became difficult for cool-headed investors to place bets on the survival of the Eurozone, not because they were wrong, but because the rest of the market believed they must be wrong.

A case in point was MF Global, the main victim of the huge surge in uncertainty in the fall of 2011.[54] MF Global was a large derivatives broker, headed by a former CEO of Goldman Sachs. It went bankrupt because it had placed a major play not on the collapse but on the survival of the Eurozone. The problem was not that MF Global suffered a default on its portfolio of 6.3 billion dollars' worth of Eurozone bonds. In fact, it stood to make a handsome profit. The problem was that market anxiety about that long bet cut off MF Global's funding. In desperation its managers then cooked the books. Significantly, as MF Global's portfolio was liquidated in December 2011 George Soros was on hand to buy up a large slice.[55] The difference between MF Global and Soros was that Soros was operating as a private investor betting his own money.[56] He could thus afford to ignore short-term market sentiment. Most fund managers don't enjoy that luxury. They too are subject to the diktat of market sentiment.

It was the judgment on the part of the new management team that took charge of the ECB in December 2011 that markets were dysfunctional and the risks posed by a panic in the market for Italian and Spanish sovereign debt that caused the ECB to abandon Trichet's tactics and to commit finally to market stabilization.[57] It was no longer strictly financial issues that were at stake. The message that Draghi delivered in London in July 2012 was that European politicians were changing the game.[58] Europe was in the process of building a new state structure. If bond markets did not understand this, the ECB would do whatever it took to convince them.

In his famous speech, Draghi implicitly articulated four essential facts about the strategic game of sovereign bond markets. First, modern financial capital has been politically and legally framed since its inception. Since the 1600s financial markets have been imbricated with the state and its currency. It is a constantly evolving relationship and the Eurozone in the crisis that began in 2010 was adding a new chapter to that history. Second, in moments of stress what mattered were not just structures and institutions but governmental action—the ECB would *do* what was necessary. Third, its action was generative. The state had the capacity to change the rules of the strategic game. It is not only market actors that innovate. As Draghi said, the ECB would do "*whatever* it takes". And, fourth, in a fiat money regime, state actors have vast resources at their disposal. Hence the significance of Draghi's emphatic follow-up: "Believe me! ... It will be enough."

Draghi is a devout European. And he clearly intended to make a statement about the progress of European state-building. But what global markets heard was a simpler message. Draghi was promising that the ECB would henceforth act like a regular central bank when faced with a financial crisis. What that meant was that the ECB would abandon its fixation on "independence" and the hands-off strategic game with the politicians that this implied. Instead, it would act as a proactive stabilizer both of private and public asset markets.

Under Bernanke as Fed chair, in the face of the financial crisis, the relationship between the Fed and the US government since 2008 had been not one of "independence" but of cooperation and complementarity. There was, on the part of the Fed, none of the monetary rigor of the Volcker era, nor Greenspan's prevarication in relation to the Clinton administration, which had opened the door to the bond vigilantes in the early 1990s. Faced with the crisis of 2008 Bernanke had thrown the full weight of the Fed behind the efforts of the US Treasury to stabilize the US economy. He had provided liquidity to banks from around the world on a massive scale, while through the asset purchases of QE1 and QE2 he had pushed down the interest rates on US sovereign bonds. In September 2012, when Bernanke launched what became known as QE3 he went a step further. He committed to buying bonds and holding down interest rates until America's "real" economy recovered. He thus inverted the priorities inherited from 1979. Whereas after the Volcker shock, interest rates were sent sky high and the hammer of unemployment was used to bring down inflation, now bond markets would be wrenched out of shape by Fed bond purchases until unemployment fell below 6 percent. Bernanke took this step not only because the US economic recovery was painfully slow, but also because following the Republican midterm victory in November 2010, the relationship between the executive branch and Congress had become so dysfunctional that there was little hope of any fiscal stimulus being forthcoming. Here too the central bank's role in relation to the bond market was conditioned by tensions internal to the state. The partisan hostility between the Fed and the Republicans that burst into the open in Donald Trump's first term originated in Bernanke's refusal to participate in the Republican fiscal blackmail of the Obama administration.

The Demand for Safe Assets

Not only did the major central banks engage in proactive intervention in the 2008 crisis, their actions had the effect that they did because they acted in concert with broader financial forces. The jumpiness of investors in "peripheral" Eurozone sovereign debt markets was not typical of their behavior toward sovereign debt in general. In general, from the early 2000s onward the balance in sovereign bond markets favored the issuers of debt not the investors. Before 2008, it is worth remembering, even the PIIGS could borrow on terms almost as good as Germany and following the stabilization of the Euro spreads once again converged despite a distinct relaxation of austerity. In the early 2000s, far from facing difficulty in funding the deficits of the Bush years, the US found huge demand for Treasuries among sovereign wealth managers in emerging markets and the petrostate. Their huge current account surpluses needed to be placed abroad in low-risk assets. US Treasuries offered by far the largest and most liquid market for foreign investors.[59] The global demand for US Treasuries was so great in the early 2000s that it led Bernanke to complain of a "savings glut" that frustrated the Fed's efforts to raise long-term rates.[60] Unsurprisingly, the huge build up of foreign holding of US sovereign debt led many observers to predict the ultimate bond vigilante attack: a China-led bond market sell off. Indeed, this was the consensus view of the likely crisis ahead. But that was not what transpired in 2007–2008. What collapsed was not demand for Treasuries but for private label asset-backed securities (ABS).

The two are interrelated. In the early 2000s it was the roaring demand for sovereign debt that created a market opportunity for financial engineers.[61] Through securitization they turned private debts, like mortgages, into highly rated asset-backed securities that ratings agencies were willing to classify as close substitutes for government bonds. When the real estate bubble burst, it was the market for mortgage-backed securities that collapsed not the sovereign debt market. Since trillions of dollars of privately generated securities could no longer be classed as safe assets, government securities offered the only possible alternative.[62] If China at that moment had decided to unload its huge holdings of US Treasuries, as Moscow apparently urged it to do, that would certainly have sent an unfriendly signal to Washington. But as a means of exerting pressure on the United States it would have been ineffective. As investors fled from privately issued mortgage-backed securities there was huge demand for US

Treasuries. Amid the turmoil of the Lehman crisis, the dollar rose. China continued to increase its holding of US government debt all the way up to the US government budget crisis of 2011.

Once the panic of 2008 had worn off, the desire of the private sector to deleverage, added to the demand for sovereign debt. As households, corporations and banks all tightened their belts, this added to the demand for safe government-issued securities. As a result, the $9 trillion in new debt issued by the US government between 2008 and 2015 were absorbed at lower interest rates than the US had paid between 2001 and 2007 when issuance came to "only" $2 trillion.

If the acute crisis of 2008 drove investors into Treasuries, one might have expected the recovery to induce a reverse shift. Interest rates would gradually rise, restoring more normal conditions in capital markets. But that is not what happened. Real rates continued to decline, so much so that in 2013 economists began debating what Larry Summers would dub "secular stagnation".[63] Growth in GDP and productivity were both slow and long-run real interest rates were falling as well. Thus mainstream policy analysts found themselves in surprising agreement with Marxisant political economy in diagnosing a declining vitality of Western capitalism.[64] But this has an ironic consequence, which escapes Streeck. If the "ultimate cause" of the public debt build up is "a secular decline in economic growth", which governments seek to compensate for with new spending, then that same deterioration in private sector growth prospects also makes it unprecedentedly cheap for governments to borrow.[65] The lack of profitable private investment crowds lenders into unexciting but safe public debt.

The surprising upshot was that in an era in which public debt increased more rapidly than ever before, the bond markets lost their bite. In September 2012, Yardeni, the original champion of the bond vigilantes, commented despairingly that the Fed's quantitative easing had made it "next to impossible for vigilantes to ply their trade".[66] "The bond vigilantes operate in a free market. When you allow them to make judgment calls on what they really want to pay for a bond and what policies are doing and whether those policies suggest that yields should be higher or lower, then the bond vigilantes can do their job. But … [h]ow can there be a market when this massive government entity is intervening to peg interest rates at zero?"[67] At PIMCO, there was a similar atmosphere of defeatism. As Bill Gross explained, the mechanics were those of a merry-go-round. "At 8 a.m., the Fed calls up and asks our Treasuries desk for offers to buy, and one hour later, the Fed's asking for bids to sell them."[68]

From Strategic Game to Reflexive Psychodrama

But are the central bankers really the rulers of the market? Can they dictate terms? The first test of the question came in 2013 when the Fed decided to test the possibility of ending QE3. Ben Bernanke first raised the possibility of "tapering" in May. Then, at 2.15 pm on 19 June 2013, the Fed chair confirmed that bond purchasing might be scaled back from $85 billion to $65 billion at the upcoming September 2013 Federal Open Market Committee (FOMC) meeting, conditional on positive economic news. He also suggested that the bond-buying program could wrap up by mid-2014. The response in the markets was instantaneous and violent. In a matter of seconds, yields surged from 2.17 to 2.3 percent. Two days later they had risen to 2.55 percent and would peak at 2.66 percent. These were small changes in absolute terms, but amounted to an increase in borrowing costs of almost 25 percent and inflicted a correspondingly serious capital loss on everyone holding bonds. In the periphery of the world economy the effect was even more dramatic. Emerging market borrowers suffered a savage shock.

If Bernanke had meant to suggest the need for a tightening of monetary policy, his words alone had produced that effect. To Richard Fisher, chair of the Dallas Fed and himself a former hedge fund manager, it was reminiscent of one of the great moments of market vigilantism—the 1992 attack on the Bank of England led by George Soros. The markets were testing the Fed's resolve. But this was the logic of the bond vigilantes in reverse. The Fed was not backsliding on inflation, it was talking tough. The question was whether it had the nerve to carry through. As Fisher put it to the *Financial Times*: "Markets tend to test things." "We haven't forgotten what happened to the Bank of England. I don't think anyone can break the Fed (…) but I do believe that big money does organize itself somewhat like feral hogs. If they detect a weakness or a bad scent, they'll go after it."[69] For Fisher it "made sense", for the Fed "to socialize the idea that quantitative easing is not a one-way street". But given the likely impact on the fragile recovery of a rapid surge in interest rates he did not expect Bernanke to go from "Wild Turkey to 'cold turkey' overnight". Nevertheless, when the FOMC decided on 18 September 2013, that it "would await more evidence that progress will be sustained before adjusting the pace of its purchases", it came as a shock. The Fed had pulled back. Were the doves on the Fed Board too weak-kneed to impose an interest rate shock? Was monetary policy now dominated by the desire to hold down rates? Was it time for the bond vigilantes to ride again? Or was the US economy simply not ready for a tightening? Perhaps it was the Fed testing the markets, not the other way around. Did Bernanke want to demonstrate that neither quantitative easing nor tapering were a one-way bet?[70]

The strategic game between the Treasury, the Fed and the bond markets was dizzyingly reflexive. The result was not a simple power dynamic running in either direction, but a relationship that had about it the air of psychodrama. In October 2014, as the Fed finally steeled itself to end Quantitative Easing (QE), the *Financial Times* was moved to invoke the box office hit, "Gone Girl":

> 'I will practice believing that central banks love me,' is a phrase that may as well have been recited by investors who have tried, for lack of a better alternative, to believe the Fed was their best friend for the past five years. They have been herded into similar positions thanks to years of easy money.
>
> 'What are you thinking? What are you feeling? What have we done to each other? What will we do?'—a refrain equally applicable to a concerned policy maker as a nervous husband. The Fed must be eyeing this latest market sell-off very warily.
>
> The whole thing reeks of a marriage built on shaky foundations. Mutual distrust that can lead to a highly combustible situation as investors reassess their historical relationship with unconventional monetary policy at any given time—with deeply unpredictable results.[71]

In the event, with the unemployment numbers at satisfactory levels, Janet Yellen, Bernanke's chosen successor, wound up QE on 29 October 2014 without incident. The recovery in the United States was anemic, but it was at least firmly established. The same could not be said for the Eurozone. On 22 January 2015, to counter acute fears of deflation, the Governing Council of the ECB decided that it would begin buying bonds at the rate of 60 billion euro per month.

This had a dramatic impact. It was one thing to operate QE in a situation in which governments were issuing large quantities of new debt. Those had been the conditions under which QE was first introduced in the United States and the United Kingdom in 2009 and 2010. By 2015 in the Eurozone the balance was tilted the other way. That year the Eurozone countries were expected to issue only 162 billion euros in new debt. With Draghi's purchases set to run to 427 billion euro, the net supply of bonds for the Eurozone financial markets in 2015 was expected to be negative by 265 billion euro. With Germany issuing barely any new debt, the supply of Bunds was squeezed particularly severely.

The ECB was not just propping up the market, it was draining it of euro-denominated bonds. In 2017 the IMF published a projection that revealed in stark terms both the reshaping of global public debt markets in the wake of the crisis and their likely future development. It is a picture very different from that which shaped the political economy of sovereign borrowing in the 1970s, 1980s and early 1990s.

Between 2010 and 2012, of the roughly $9 trillion issued by the governments of the advanced economies half had been absorbed by central banks. Of the remainder which was placed with private investors, roughly half was issued by the United States. By 2017 the balance had dramatically shifted. Of the $15 trillion in sovereign debt issued since 2010, two-thirds had been absorbed by official purchases, including the entire new issuance of Eurozone and Japanese debt. Virtually all the bonds left for private investors were issued by the United States with a small fraction coming from the United Kingdom. Over the next five years the IMF predicted that fiscal restraint in Europe and continuing bond purchases by the Bank of Japan and the ECB would tilt the balance further. In effect the United States would be the only supplier of highly rated advanced country sovereign debt to world markets. The stance adopted by the ECB and Japan might shift the balance somewhat. But as far as the gigantic global asset managers are concerned, the balance of force between borrowers and lenders took on a stark simplicity. The US sovereign debt market watched over by the Treasury and the Fed was the only "strategic game" in town.

* * *

The world described both by boosters and critics of globalization was flat. All sovereign borrowers, even the United States, were subject to the same capital market pressure. If that was ever a reasonable description it described at most an episode. The period in which the United States was subject to recurring and serious bouts of bond market pressure extended from the breakup of Bretton Woods in the early 1970s to the mid-1990s. It did not last. The world of sovereign debt revealed by the crisis of 2008 has been anything but flat. There have been victims of bond market pressure, notably among the weaker "periphery" of the Eurozone and troubled emerging markets such as Argentina and Ukraine. But for most large advanced economies it has been a period of unprecedentedly easy borrowing. Despite the giant turmoil in financial markets no member of the G7 found itself shut out of bond markets or faced a prolonged period of elevated yield sufficient to put its financial sustainability in question. When Italy did seem on the brink in 2011–2012, this triggered a dramatic institutional and policy shift on the part of the ECB. Of course, this came at a price. Conservative political forces insisted on austerity and insisted that this was necessary to preempt bond market pressure. And at times they were successful in their campaign. But after 2016 both the United Kingdom and the United States demonstrated the extraordinary degrees of freedom that bond markets will grant even to avowedly populist governments. Japan, meanwhile, continues to demonstrate the basic insight of functional finance that there is unlikely to be a firm upper limit to public debt, if you "owe it to yourself". And the COVID crisis of 2020 would drive home the remarkable latitude enjoyed by sovereign borrowers.

The political economy of sovereign debt is a strategic game and it is political all the way down. That applies to the political discourse of debt as well. For obvious reasons the householder analogy has long been beloved of conservatives. In 2010, the discourse of "critical thresholds" and "slippery slopes" was powerful in energizing the campaign for austerity. But the same applies to denunciations of "debt slavery" and clichés about the "dominance of financial markets". Such rhetoric, both in its left and right variants, can be understood as the expression of a populist moment. Those of us interested in holding open other political options must do the work of developing a realistic account of the variable and complex geometry of the strategic game between debtors and creditors. These are the contemporary stakes in the study of the history of public debt. They are made even more urgent by the dramatic fiscal legacy of the COVID crisis.

Notes

1. Ed Yardeni, "A Brief History of Ed Yardeni's 'Bond Vigilante' Model," Business Insider, Dr. Ed's blog, November 13, 2013, accessed January 25, 2020, http://www.businessinsider.com/bonds-and-nominal-gdp-2013-11

2. Victor F. Zonana, "Bond Market Packs a Punch Clinton Is Already Feeling," *LA Times*, November 21, 1992, accessed January 25, 2020, http://articles.latimes.com/1992-11-21/news/mn-734_1_bond-market
3. Eric Helleiner, *States and the Reemergence of Global Finance. From Bretton Woods to the 1990s* (Ithaca: Cornell University Press, 1996).
4. Zonana, "Bond Market."
5. Zonana, "Bond Market."
6. Bob Woodward, *The Agenda: Inside the Clinton White House* (New York: Simon and Schuster, 2007).
7. Megan Mcardle, "The Vigilante," *The Atlantic*, June 2011 accessed January 25, 2020, http://www.theatlantic.com/magazine/archive/2011/06/the-vigilante/308503/
8. John Greenwald, "Greenspan's Rates of Wrath," *Time* 28 November 1994, accessed January 25, 2020, http://content.time.com/time/magazine/article/0,9171,981879,00.html.
9. Barry J. Eichengreen, *Globalizing Capital: A History of the International Monetary System* (Princeton: Princeton University Press, 1998).
10. Hélène Rey, "Dilemma not Trilemma: The Global Financial Cycle and Monetary Policy Independence," No. w21162. National Bureau of Economic Research, 2015.
11. Rolf E. Breuer, "Die fünfte Gewalt," *Die Zeit*, April 27, 2000, accessed January 25, 2000, http://www.zeit.de/2000/18/200018.5._gewalt_.xml
12. "Greenspan: Interview," *Zürcher Tages-Anzeiger*, September 19, 2007.
13. "Return of the Bond Market Vigilantes," *Wall Street Journal*, May 29, 2008, last accessed January 25, 2020, http://blogs.wsj.com/marketbeat/2008/05/29/return-of-the-bond-market-vigilantes/
14. "The Bond Vigilantes," *Wall Street Journal*, May 29, 2009, last accessed January 25, 2020, http://www.wsj.com/articles/SB124347148949660783
15. Ron Suskind, *Confidence Men: Wall Street, Washington and the Education of a President* (New York: HarperCollins, 2011).
16. Robert E. Rubin, Peter R. Orszag, and Allen Sinai, "Sustained Budget Deficits: The Risk of Financial and Fiscal Disarray," in *AEA-NAEFA Joint Session, Allied Social Science Associations Annual Meetings*, 2004.
17. Carmen M. Reinhart and Kenneth S. Rogoff, "Growth in a Time of Debt," *American Economic Review* 100, no. 2 (2010): 573–78.
18. Mcardle, "The Vigilante."
19. Gregory White, "Here's Niall Ferguson's Complete and Definitive Guide to the Sovereign Debt Crisis," May 19, 2010, last accessed January 25, 2020, http://www.businessinsider.com/niall-ferguson-sovereign-debt-2010-5

20. Alan S. Blinder, "Return of the Bond Market Vigilantes," *Wall Street Journal*, May 20, 2010, last accessed January 25, 2020, http://www.wsj.com/articles/SB10001424052748703315404575250341585092722
21. Patrick Wintour, "Mervyn King Shaped Tough Deficit Policy – but was it Political Bias?," *The Guardian*, November 30, 2010, last accessed January 25, 2020, https://www.theguardian.com/business/2010/nov/30/mervyn-king-deficit-policy-neutrality
22. Jeromin Zettelmeyer, Christoph Trebesch, and Mitu Gulati, "The Greek Debt Restructuring: An Autopsy," *Economic Policy* 28, no. 75 (2013): 513–563.
23. Pieer Habbard, "The Return of the Bond Vigilantes," Trade Union Advisory Committee of OECD, Working Paper, March (2012).
24. Mcardle, "The Vigilante."
25. Neal Lipschutz, "Bond Vigilantes Make Their Votes Known in Europe," *Wall Street Journal, Real time economics blog*, November 23, 2011, last accessed January 25, 2020, http://blogs.wsj.com/economics/2011/11/23/bond-vigilantes-make-their-votes-known-in-europe/
26. Sophia Grene, "Bond Manager Bets on Greek Debt," *Financial Times*, December 3, 2011, last accessed January 25, 2020, https://next.ft.com/content/4c0670f6-1c29-11e1-9631-00144feabdc0
27. See for instance: Ole Bjerg, *Making Money: The Philosophy of Crisis Capitalism* (London: Verso Trade, 2014); David Graeber, *Debt: The First 5000 Years* (New York: Melville House, 2011); Maurizio Lazzarato, *The Making of the Indebted Man* (New York: Semiotext(e), 2012).
28. Slavoj Žižek, "How Capital Captured Politics," *The Guardian*, July 13, 2014, last accessed January 25, 2020, http://www.theguardian.com/commentisfree/2014/jul/13/capital-politics-wikileaks-democracy-market-freedom
29. Joseph Vogl, "Sovereignty Effects," INET Conference Berlin, April 12, 2012, last accessed January 25, 2020, https://ineteconomics.org/uploads/papers/Vogl-Paper.pdf
30. Wolfgang Streeck, *Buying Time: The Delayed Crisis of Democratic Capitalism* (London: Verso Books, 2014).
31. Hubert Bonin, "Les banques françaises devant l'opinion (des années 1840 aux années 1950)," 2011, Post-Print hal-00800238, HAL.
32. For the current state of play on 1931 see Robert Boyce, *The Great Interwar Crisis and the Collapse of Globalization* (London: Palgrave Macmillan, 2009), 298–344.
33. Michael Kalecki, "Political Aspects of Full Employment 1," *The Political Quarterly* 14, no. 4 (1943): 322–330.
34. Karl Polanyi, *The Great Transformation* (Boston: Beacon Press, 1957), 229.

35. Bonin, "Les banques françaises" and Vincent Duchaussoy, "Les socialistes, la Banque de France et le 'mur d'argent' (1981–1984)," *Vingtième Siècle. Revue d'histoire* 2 (2011): 111–122.
36. Adam Przeworski and Michael Wallerstein, "Structural Dependence of the State on Capital," *American Political Science Review* 82, no. 1 (1988): 11–29.
37. Gary B. Gorton and Guillermo Ordonez, "The Supply and Demand for Safe Assets," No. w18732, National Bureau of Economic Research, 2013 and Streeck, *Buying Time*, 132.
38. Streeck, *Buying Time*, 132.
39. Douglass C. North and Barry R. Weingast, "Constitutions and Commitment: The Evolution of Institutions Governing Public Choice in Seventeenth-century England," *The Journal of Economic History* 49, no. 4 (1989): 803–832; Barry Eichengreen and Ricardo Hausmann, "Exchange Rates and Financial Fragility," No. w7418, National Bureau of Economic Research, 1999; Michael D. Bordo, "Growing up to Financial Stability," No. w12993, National Bureau of Economic Research, 2007.
40. Wolfgang Streeck, "The Politics of Public Debt: Neoliberalism, Capitalist Development and the Restructuring of the State," *German Economic Review* 15, no. 1 (2014): 143–165.
41. Paul Krugman, "Bond Vigilantes and the Power of Three," *New York Times, The conscience of a liberal Blog*, December 24, 2012, last accessed January 25, 2020, https://krugman.blogs.nytimes.com/2012/12/24/bond-vigilantes-and-the-power-of-three/
42. Daniel Kruger, "Where have all the Bond Vigilantes Gone?," *Bloomberg Businessweek*, April 29, 2010, last accessed January 25, 2020, http://www.bloomberg.com/news/articles/2010-04-29/where-have-all-the-bond-vigilantes-gone
43. Scott Carmack, "The U.S. Treasury Auction – Who Is Showing Up?," Seeking Alpha, January 26, 2016, last accessed January 25, 2020, https://seekingalpha.com/article/3835426-u-s-treasury-auction-showing
44. IMF, *Global Financial Stability Report* October 2017, last accessed January 25, 2020, http://www.imf.org/en/Publications/GFSR/Issues/2017/09/27/global-financial-stability-report-october-2017
45. Carl E. Walsh, "Central Bank Independence," in *Monetary Economics*, eds. Steven N. Durlauf and Lawrence Blume (London: Palgrave Macmillan, 2010), 21–26.
46. Neil Irwin, *The Alchemists: Three Central Bankers and a World on Fire* (London: Penguin, 2013), 237–238. See also Wintour, "Mervyn King."
47. Irwin, *Alchemists*, 246.
48. Carlo Bastasin, *Saving Europe: Anatomy of a Dream* (Washington: Brookings Institution Press, 2015).

49. David M. Woodruff, "Governing by Panic: The Politics of the Eurozone Crisis," *Politics & Society* 44, no.1 (2016): 81–116.
50. Bastasin, *Saving Europe*.
51. Bastasin, *Saving Europe*, 313.
52. Steve Johnson, "Bond Fund Managers Brave 'the Ring of Fire'," *Financial Times*, February 7, 2010, last accessed January 25, 2020, https://next.ft.com/content/c725a322-1287-11df-a611-00144feab49a#axzz1gawCMzGp
53. John Beirne and Marcel Fratzscher, "The Pricing of Sovereign Risk and Contagion during the European Sovereign Debt Crisis," *Journal of International Money and Finance* 34 (2013): 60–82.
54. "Eurozone Crisis Claims MF Global," *Financial Times*, October 31, 2011, last accessed January 25, 2020, https://www.ft.com/content/138241f6-03dd-11e1-98bc-00144feabdc0
55. Gregory Zuckerman and Dana Cimilluca, "Corzine's Loss May Be Soros's Gain," *Wall Street Journal*, December 9, 2011, last accessed January 25, 2020, http://www.wsj.com/articles/SB10001424052970204319004577086652040716704
56. Antonia Oprita, "Soros Bought $2 Billion Ex-MF Global Europe Debt: Report," CNBC, December 9, 2011, last accessed January 25, 2020, https://www.cnbc.com/id/45610428
57. Harm Schepel, "The Bank, the Bond, and the Bail-out: On the Legal Construction of Market Discipline in the Eurozone," *Journal of Law and Society* 44, no.1 (2017): 79–98.
58. "Verbatim of the Remarks made by Mario Draghi," ECB, July 26, 2012, last accessed January 25, 2020 https://www.ecb.europa.eu/press/key/date/2012/html/sp120726.en.html
59. Gary Gorton, "The History and Economics of Safe Assets," *Annual Review of Economics* 9 (2017): 547–586.
60. Ben S. Bernanke, "The Global Saving Glut and the US Current Account Deficit," Sandridge Lecture, Virginia Association of Economists, Richmond, Virginia March 10, 2005, https://www.federalreserve.gov/boarddocs/speeches/2005/200503102/
61. Ben S. Bernanke, "International Capital Flows and the Returns to Safe Assets in the United States 2003–2007," *Financial Stability Review* 15 (2011): 13–26 and Richard J. Caballero, "The 'Other' Imbalance and the Financial Crisis," No. w15636, National Bureau of Economic Research, 2010.
62. Richard J. Caballero, Emmanuel Farhi, and Pierre-Olivier Gourinchas, "The Safe Assets Shortage Conundrum," *Journal of Economic Perspectives* 31 (Summer 2017): 29–46.

63. Lawrence H. Summers, "US Economic Prospects: Secular Stagnation, Hysteresis, and the Zero Lower Bound," *Business Economics* 49, no. 2 (2014): 65–73.
64. Fred Magdoff and John Bellamy Foster, "Stagnation and Financialization: The Nature of the Contradiction," *Monthly Review* 66, no. 1 (2014): 1.
65. Streeck, "Politics of Public Debt."
66. Ed Yardeni, "Bond Vigilantes Get to Work in the Eurozone," https://www.youtube.com/watch?v=_DQHLqhM2uA
67. Yardeni, "Bond Vigilantes."
68. Mcardle, "The Vigilante."
69. "Fed Fights back against 'Feral Hogs'," *Financial Times* June 24, 2013, last accessed January 25, 2020, https://next.ft.com/content/9d8fa63e-dce6-11e2-b52b-00144feab7de
70. Anatole Kaletsky, "The Markets and Bernanke's 'Taper Tantrums'," Reuters, September 19, 2013, last accessed January 25, 2020, http://blogs.reuters.com/anatole-kaletsky/2013/09/19/the-markets-and-bernankes-taper-tantrums/
71. Tracy Alloway, "A Marriage of Convenience Comes to an End," *Financial Times* October 17, 2014, last accessed January 25, 2020, https://next.ft.com/content/524a2226-55c1-11e4-93b3-00144feab7de

Conclusion: On the Historical Uses of Numbers and Words

CHAPTER 19

The History and Politics of Public Debt Accounting

Éric Monnet and Blaise Truong-Loï

At first sight,[1] the debates on public debt that emerged from the 2007–2008 global financial crisis and the 2010–2012 European debt crisis focused mainly on drawing economic policy conclusions from the level of debt relative to Gross Domestic Product (GDP), without raising many questions about the definition and accounting of public debt.[2] Economic and moral arguments, embedded in different political repertoires,[3] were called upon to discuss what is "too much debt". This debate around numbers mostly took the quantity of debt as given. In several cases, however, accounting issues have been in the forefront. A striking example—although unnoticed outside

---

The original version of this chapter was revised. Correction to this chapter can be found at DOI https://doi.org/10.1007/978-3-030-48794-2_21

É. Monnet (✉)
EHESS, Paris, France

Paris School of Economics, Paris, France
e-mail: eric.monnet@ehess.fr

B. Truong-Loï
Sciences Po, Paris, France
e-mail: blaise.truongloi@sciencespo.fr

© The Author(s) 2020, corrected publication 2020
N. Barreyre, N. Delalande (eds.), *A World of Public Debts*, Palgrave Studies in the History of Finance,
https://doi.org/10.1007/978-3-030-48794-2_19

circles of specialists—was the publication in 2011 of the first official global methodological guide on public sector debt statistics by nine international organizations.[4] Statistical issues also attracted some attention in the public and academic debates. Greek creative public accounting (helped by the advisers of the US bank Goldman Sachs) in the decade preceding the debt crisis was a reminder that some legal financial arrangements can quite easily be used to circumvent such rigid and comprehensive accounting rules as those of Eurostat, the European Commission Directorate-General in charge of collecting and publishing the official statistics of the European Union (EU) members.[5] For some observers, the Greek scandal simply reflected the inability of the current Eurostat definition of public debt to incorporate derivative liabilities, and, thus, to account for changes in financial instruments that affect the nature and politics of public debt.[6] The ability of standard definitions of public debt to account for major public policy challenges was further called into question by the fact that the implicit guarantees provided by governments to domestic banks were not accounted as public debt.[7] In the same vein, accounting issues struck back about the focus of official statistics on gross debt only. Accountants do not subtract the financial assets of the state from the liabilities. The link between public debt and public wealth is indirect, at best.[8] Although public assets are usually not considered in comparisons of public debt across countries, they play a key role in the assessment of the size of public debt and, of course, during debt settlements. For instance, the Greek government was forced by creditors to sell state assets to repay the national debt.

The gross/net distinction and the incorporation of derivative liabilities in the scope of public debt are not the only issues that spur conflicts between public debt statistics and financial theory. Reacting to recent debates on public debt, some economists emphasized that standard statistics are based on definitions at odds with economic reasoning. Most prominently, national accountants calculate the stock of nominal debt as it is issued (i.e. at the repayment value of the principal) rather than as the sum of government's outstanding promises to pay coupons.[9] In the words of Alessandro Missale: "Indeed, theory and policy speak different languages: while the former focuses on the market value of the debt and rates of return, policy makers are concerned with national accounting figures; the book value of the debt and the interest payments."[10]

During the European sovereign debt crisis, some hardly noticed details in public debt statistics also made it clear that the definition of public debt relies on a definition of the sovereign state and thus implicitly defines the boundaries of the relevant sovereign. Eurostat states that "Government loans (IGL) to other EU governments have been deducted from euro area and EU debt."[11] Put differently, loans to Greece granted by other EU governments do not increase the official total amount of EU's public debt.[12] In this case, they even pushed it down since the Greek government used them to reimburse its previous existing debt. As in the Maastricht definition, public debt is consolidated between the different elements of a sovereign state.[13] These accounting options reveal that, at least in the statistics, the European Union is not merely a sum of member states.

This set of recent examples shows that the definition of public debt reflects both geographical and economic boundaries of the state, different financial reasoning or financial practices, as well as different political uses of statistics. Neither attempts by international financial institutions to standardize concepts and definitions of public debt—which are rather recent in historical perspective—nor recent noted publications of long-term historical series of public debt should lead one to believe that alternative quantitative perspectives and definitions of public debt are illegitimate or misguided, and that a gold standard has been reached regarding the calculation of public debt figures.[14] On the contrary, understanding how public debt statistics were constructed and used and why such methods have changed over time is key to fully appreciating the politics of public debt. Uses of international statistics on public debt—including historical series reconstructed by academic and international policy institutions—are a typical example of a globalized discourse of technical expertise which shapes policy options and the view of macroeconomic realities. Statistics of public debt, standardized and compared, participate in the construction of a global objectivity, by numerous actors and institutions. They determine how we see the world.[15] A historical perspective sheds light on how such discourses have changed over time, while also highlighting persistent issues.[16] It is also important to acknowledge and understand why the standardization of international statistics on public debt occurred much later than for other major macroeconomic statistics, such as prices, production, national income and trade. The "delayed" international standardization of public debt statistics reflects as much accounting difficulties as shifting political interests.

This chapter does not intend to provide new computations of historical series of public debt—although in some cases we will highlight how series differ.[17] Instead, our goal is to review different methods of public debt accounting and narrate their historical evolution. Our contention is that in many cases, available long-term public debt series published by contemporaneous national or international institutions (and compiled recently by economists) are too limited to understand the political economy of public debt. A posteriori reconstructions and compilations of macroeconomic long-run series often miss the politics that lie behind the numbers. What is the interplay between the evolution of accounting practices and concepts and their functioning within the state and among contemporary economists? How have international comparisons of public debt statistics participated in the construction of a global discourse on debt sustainability and good economic policies? What was measured and why? What preconceptions lie behind statistical constructs? With such questions in mind, this chapter proposes a short and inevitably partial journey into the history of the accounting practices of public debt. It also tries to offer a general perspective on how figures and politics entangle all along the four parts of this collective book.

Historical Series of Public Debt and Methodological Issues

Pre-1914 External Debt and Financial Accounting

Despite well-known difficulties, there have been several recent attempts by economists or economic historians to build long-term public debt series for as many countries as possible. A first wave of comparative studies emerged in the 1980s after the Latin American debt crises. Prominent examples are articles by Barry Eichengreen, Richard Portes, Peter Lindert and Peter Morton.[18] Following these studies, and as part of the widespread interest in the first age of globalization (1880–1914) that developed in the 1990s, other authors attempted to compute public (and mostly external) debt figures for the pre-1914 period.[19] The most complete work was the one of Marc Flandreau and Frédéric Zumer, which has since served as a basis for most subsequent work.[20] Fifteen years later, the recent financial and debt crises gave birth to a more ambitious literature culminating in the historical databases produced by Carmen Reinhart and Kenneth Rogoff as well as by economists of the International Monetary Fund (IMF) which cover dozens of countries since the late nineteenth century.[21]

In a nutshell, three main kinds of sources are used in these comparative works. For the period before 1914, private sources prevail. Flandreau and

Zumer mostly relied on statistics produced by the Credit Lyonnais—the biggest French bank of the time, which hosted an international research department.[22] They compared them to other contemporary sources such as *The Economist* and, most importantly, the *Statesman's Year Book* which published and commented on public debt statistics on an annual basis, among other things. The database constructed by Flandreau and Zumer is the main source of Reinhart and Rogoff and the International Monetary Fund's datasets for the pre-1914 period. Lindert and Morton also used private sources: the annual reports of the British Corporation of Foreign Bondholders (CFB) before 1930 and Moody's annual reports in the 1930s. For the interwar period, the standard source is the League of Nations which undertook a far-ranging collection of international statistics, including public debt. Since World War II, the United Nations (UN) and the IMF serve as references. United Nations yearbooks are especially used for the period until the 1970s. It was only after its involvement in the Latin American public debt crises in the 1980s that the IMF implemented a consistent policy of publishing and comparing continuous series of public debt, although some figures on public debt appeared in the *International Financial Statistics* volume as early as 1947. In some few cases (the United Kingdom and the United States), comparative studies have relied on national sources instead of UN or IMF statistics.

All the studies quoted above have a common characteristic: rather than using national official sources, they are based on earlier attempts by private or public institutions to standardize and compile public debt statistics. The persistent reluctance to rely on published national sources reflects scholars' widely held belief that, for a long time, statistics of public debt produced by governments were not comparable. Besides deliberate misreporting and falsifications, the accounting choices and definitions of state entities varied too much across countries to allow straightforward comparisons. Flandreau and Zumer stressed in the following way how these difficulties affect the work of economic historians: "Data on [...] public debts may seem, superficially, relatively easy to gather, which should permit researchers to place much of the data-collection burden upon research assistants. This strategy would be very inappropriate. The task requires that senior researchers get personally involved."[23]

Difficulties in international comparability of public debt have been stressed by all comparative attempts to standardize figures, in the past and today alike. This issue went much beyond debates of accountants and economists. Public debt statistics were often constructed to legitimate international financial control.[24] Given the huge amount of work involved in collecting official statistics and making them comparable, historians have no choice but to rely on such earlier attempts. What is important is to understand the choices that were made—or not made—by past comparative economists. For example, the Crédit Lyonnais—the source of Flandreau and Zumer's work—adopted a very financial perspective and focused on comparing debt service to government revenues (excluding debt or net income from public companies). What may look like a bias or limitations in the production of statistics is the price to be paid for an exceptionally rigorous work of standardization of international statistics. By contrast, other private sources did not produce continuous series with a unique definition. In such a case, as noted by Lindert and Morton about the Corporation of Foreign Bondholders: "The mass of data available from the sources mentioned above was assembled for the benefit of contemporary investors, not subsequent scholars. Definitions and categories shift over time and make it necessary to apply some criteria in deciding what to include and what to leave out."[25] An illustration of these issues is the figures published by the *Statesman's Yearbook* on Chinese public finances in the late nineteenth century. The Qing dynasty's foreign debt arose almost entirely out of the 1894–1895 defeat against Japan, which resulted in a £33 million indemnity.[26] To meet the cost of reimbursement, the Chinese government borrowed £48 million on European markets in 1895, 1896 and 1898. The *Statesman's Yearbook* then faced immense difficulties deciding where public debt was: in the indemnity? in the loans? in both? Decisions varied from year to year of publication. On the one hand, adding the indemnity to the loans was redundant. It would count the same amount twice. This probably explains why the authors of the 1897 issue of the *Statesman's Yearbook* only considered the borrowing from Europe as external debt. On the other hand, the aggregated sum raised by the Chinese government for these three years clearly exceeded the amount of the indemnity. Furthermore, whereas the indemnity was to be paid back in seven years, the 1895, 1896 and 1898 European loans had a thirty-six-year maturity. Part of it must have been spent for another purpose than paying back Japan. Consequently, it made sense to include both the loans and the indemnity, as the authors of the 1896 *Statesman's Yearbook* did.[27] Neither of these two perspectives is wrong if properly justified but switching from one to the other is highly problematic for those looking for time-consistent data on the Chinese debt.

The League of Nations and the Interwar Duplication of Public Debt

In the interwar period, the League of Nations published figures produced by governments without standardizing them *ex post*. However, the League sent a questionnaire to each country to present final statistics in harmonized categories. A general rule was applied: only central government debt had to be considered; debts of local governments were excluded. Despite this attempt to harmonize statistics *ex ante*, the retrospective volume of the statistics of the League of Nations, published by the United Nations in 1948, still shows very different accounting practices across countries, which often changed over time.[28] This was prominently the case for war reparations or sinking funds liabilities.[29] As acknowledged in a long introductory note, the continuity in the published series is most of the time an artifact and hides changing definitions over time.

The League of Nations' efforts to standardize economic statistics across countries led to major successes. Breakthroughs were mostly made in the field of statistics on production and trade.[30] By contrast, little progress was made on public debt statistics, despite the publication of several "Memorand[a] on public finance". Memoranda on public finance focused on describing governments' budgets and the League of Nations did not go beyond identifying the different technical procedures followed by national governments to compute published public debt statistics. It was not until 1938 that decisions were made to draw up a new questionnaire on public debt that would record all public liabilities, and especially claims and liabilities between several public institutions. The method was new in that it viewed public debt in the context of the total balance sheet of a country. It was especially motivated by the fact that, in the 1930s, financial linkages between state institutions (within a given country) had strongly increased.[31] The role of international financial markets in the financing of government had decreased and domestic financial arrangements became predominant, as it clearly appears in Part III of this volume. As a result, the balance between marketable and non-marketable debt, as well as between internal and external debt shifted greatly. This was not only the case in the USSR,[32] Fascist Italy and Nazi Germany.[33] In France, for example, a sinking fund (Caisse Autonome d'Amortissement) and a public credit institution (Crédit National), set up in the 1920s to finance reconstruction and settle war debt, created financial linkages between different bodies of the state. These connections were not completely new, as they already existed before 1914, particularly between states and railway companies. Yet, they burgeoned during World War I and the interwar period, changing the nature of public debt and the interpretation of statistics. In his comparative work on English, German, French and US public debt from 1914 to 1944, the French economist Henry Laufenburger called such a change the "dedoubling (*duplication*) of public credit". He described it in the following way: "Not only does the state multiply the number of bodies and institutes which issue bonds and commit to repay debt, but the massive debt of the state increasingly relies directly on commercial and saving banks which both collect deposits."[34] For the same reasons, League of Nations economists realized that a full assessment of public debt required looking beyond the gross liabilities of the central government.[35] The (failed) attempt of the League of Nations to compute public debt statistics based on estimations of public sector total liabilities rather than on figures of marketable debt issuance or budget expenditures was a sign of the times. It bears witness to the questions contemporary economists were asking about the financial boundaries of the state. Besides the writings of Laufenburger quoted above, it is worth mentioning the book of the British economist Henry Campion. Published in 1939, it was a seminal attempt to estimate public wealth and, thus, to account for the total assets and liabilities of the state, rather than looking merely at external and marketable debt.[36]

From Bretton Woods Neglect of Public Debt to Recent International Benchmarking

After World War II, the accounting of public debt was not the main priority for the statistical offices of international organizations. In the "Articles of Agreement of the International Monetary Fund" signed at the Bretton Woods Conference, members of the future IMF committed to provide statistical information to the Fund.[37] A long list of relevant macroeconomic statistics featured in the agreement (trade in goods and services, international investment position, foreign exchange reserves, prices, national income, etc.) but the list did not include statistics on public debt. The Articles of Agreement of the International Bank for Reconstruction and Development (IBRD, the future World Bank) do not include a commitment to furnish statistical information in exchange for a loan. In its first years of operations, the IMF mainly focused on standardizing balance of payments statistics (the first edition of the *Balance of Payments Manual* was published in 1948) and foreign reserves data. The IMF then started to produce numerous studies on the "adequate level" of foreign reserves.[38] Such a benchmarking procedure was not attempted on public debt comparisons. Although defaults on public debt had been a major economic event of the 1930s, the political lessons learnt from the interwar period by postwar reformists focused on demand management, financial and payments imbalances rather than on the danger of public debt. The new world emerging from the ashes of the Great Depression and World War II did not want to let the states depend on financial markets, nor the "burden" of public debt to impede the development of welfare states and new growth strategies.[39] The Bretton Woods—or, let's say, Keynesian—moment, which created a major push for the development of macroeconomic statistics, hence left aside the accounting of public debt. This was true both at the international and at the national level. In the United Kingdom, the 1944 White Paper on Employment Policy, which laid out the principles of postwar economic policy and led to an unprecedented program of construction of macroeconomic series and figures,[40] urged for the creation of statistics on unemployment, national income, production, prices, money, credit, payments, foreign capital movements and balance of payments, but no distinct series on public debt.

In the late 1940s and 1950s, when international organizations dealt with government debts, they did not try to implement a global and standardized statistical apparatus. Documents produced by the World Bank about the countries that were granted a loan during that period are models. They merely documented the history of default on external public debt and repayments for each country.[41] In the 1960s, after several "developing" countries experienced great difficulties in servicing their external debt and had to reschedule their loan repayments, extensive research was undertaken in academia and international institutions, but its focus was again on debt service and on external debt only. Approaches and issues were similar during the Latin American debt crisis of the 1980s.[42] The issue of global standards of public debt accounting hence remained unexplored for long. Therefore, while the first international guide to the System of National Accounts (SNA) was published in 1953 by the UN (with major revisions in 1968, 1993 and 2008), an equivalent guide for public debt accounting was only published in 2011. The first global guide on public sector debt statistics was prepared and published under the joint responsibility of nine organizations: the IMF, the Organization for Economic Cooperation and Development (OECD), Eurostat, the UN, the Bank for International Settlements (BIS), the European Central Bank, the Commonwealth, the World Bank and the Club de Paris. Note that, like the SNA, this is a guide that provides recommendations and no compulsory rules. Contrary to the SNA, whose primary targeted readership is national institutions, this guide is mainly intended to help statisticians who are compiling national sources. The only precedent to this guide had a much narrower focus and had been published in 1988, motivated by the Latin American debt crisis. Originally called *External Debt: Definition, Statistical Coverage and Methodology*, it was revised in 2003 under the name *External Debt Statistics: Guide for Compilers and Users*, so as to be consistent with the 1993 SNA and to cope with recent developments in international capital markets. The only previous attempt to standardize statistics of public debt across countries—in a compulsory way—came from the Maastricht Treaty and was applied to the members of the European Union. It gave birth to a peculiar definition of public debt, named "debt in the sense of Maastricht".[43] In that definition, the "public sphere" encompasses four elements: the central state, central government bodies,[44] local administrations and social security funds. "Debt in the sense of Maastricht" is a gross, consolidated and nominal debt (it is evaluated at the repayment value of the principal).

The Maastricht debt definition, along with the 2008 and 2011 *Guide of Public sector debt statistics*, illustrates a quite recent wave of attempts to find a common definition of public debt at an international level. It has converged toward a standard definition of debt that can be summed up in three main elements. First, it is a gross debt: government assets are not subtracted from the total amount of debt. Second, it is the "general government" debt: it includes the debt of the central government and the main bodies of the state (regional states, municipalities, etc.) but not the total debts of state-owned corporations. Third, it excludes contingent liabilities, guarantees and financial derivatives.

Such a recent convergence is remarkable in historical perspective and arguably seen as a great achievement for the production of international statistics. However, even proponents of the new standard stress that this common definition is somewhat arbitrary and could have significant limitations, depending on the purpose of the analysis. A 2012 study written by staff economists of the IMF, whose primary goal was nonetheless to apply the standard nomenclature of the *Public-Sector Debt Statistics Guide* to improve data comparability, clearly emphasizes the issues at stake:

While key macroeconomic indicators such as Gross Domestic Product (GDP) or Consumer Price Index (CPI) are based on internationally accepted methodologies, indicators related to the debt of the public sector often do not follow international standards and can have several different definitions. [...] The absence of the standard nomenclature can lead to major misunderstandings in the fiscal policy debate. [...] The authors suggest that gross debt of the general government should be globally adopted as the headline indicator supplemented by other measures of government debt for risk-based assessments of the fiscal position. Broader measures, including net debt and detailed information on contingent liabilities and derivatives, could be considered.[45]

WHY DO STATISTICS DIFFER? CONSEQUENCES FOR ECONOMIC HISTORY

The IMF 2012 study quoted above is only one example among many recent papers that have stressed how the estimations of public indebtedness may vary to a large extent and why a new standard definition of public debt should not prevent economists from studying and using alternative definitions. This scholarship, that complements the numerous official attempts to come up with a common nomenclature, furnishes insights that have received surprisingly little attention in the economic history literature that has devoted considerable effort to collecting long-term data on public debt.[46] This is not to argue that comparisons of public debt across countries should be avoided, but to raise questions on accounting methods and to emphasize the need to develop alternative indicators to assess the historical financial and political issues around public debt. As OECD economists recently warned: "There is no single 'best' indicator for analyzing general government debt."[47] According to them, it is crucial to realize that accounting differences as well as variations in the perimeter of public debt exist because each country has a different state organization. We believe that such insights and conclusions are even more valid for the economic history literature.

What is especially striking for historians is how these recent warnings and discussions are reminiscent of the writings of previous economists, decades or a century ago. Despite efforts in constructing a common accounting framework and despite the evolution of debt instruments over time, the same conceptual issues stand out. In his far-ranging comparative book *Les dettes publiques européennes* (*The Public Debts of Europe*), written in 1887, the French economist and journalist Alfred Neymarck did not provide a full notice nor an introduction to accounting issues. Yet, he emphasized that, for many countries, the definitions of public debt and accounting practices were problematic.[48] The case of the railways is a good example. While most of the time, the debt of state-owned railway companies was included in the public debt, Neymarck claimed that it should not be, since the activity of the railway companies was not a burden on the budget of the state and was not important to understand the tax pressure on citizens.[49] However, he acknowledged that this issue was sometimes more complicated, for example, when the Danish government issued public bonds to buy stocks of railway companies in 1880.[50] It was even more complicated to identify the guarantees of the bonds issued by public companies and to assess whether they would finally be a burden on taxpayers. In the case of Serbia, Neymarck provided a thorough discussion of the issue: "The funds borrowed by the railway companies are guaranteed by their revenues from the railways […] but, in second line, the guarantees are the revenues of the customs, then of general taxes, and then of any resource of the Serbian government."[51] Public debt accounting already faced issues of state boundaries and contingent liabilities.

Accounting difficulties created by the variety and nature of financial instruments are not new either. Neymarck rightly noted that computing the level of French public debt by adding the nominal capital of perpetual bonds (*rente*), which is never repaid, and the capital of debt repayable by annuities was not meaningful from an economic point of view.[52] Moreover, in some cases—and not always in a consistent way—Neymarck referred to the concept of net debt. For example, he stated that the current debt of the French state should be assessed in the light of the future revenue and assets of the railway companies which had been purchased by the French government in 1881.[53] Four years earlier, in his *Traité de la science des finances*, Paul Leroy-Beaulieu had already voiced this general warning: when analyzing a state's debt burden, "one must subtract from state liabilities all the assets which generate public revenues. If not, it is absolutely impossible to assess properly how indebted this state is."[54] In the 1900s, when the economists of the Crédit Lyonnais tried to depict Chinese public finances in a big table, they did include a "public asset revenues" column and an "asset value" column to assess in two final columns a "net debt service" and a "net outstanding debt". Yet, as they lacked data, the first two columns remained empty whereas the last two ones were just a copy of the columns (gross) "debt service" and (gross) "outstanding debt."[55] The result they obtained was thus explicitly unsatisfactory. Empty columns were a clear message: gross figures were only used for want of anything better. It is then striking that nowadays, the preference for "gross" numbers is hardly ever discussed and taken as given whereas it often resulted in the past from a lack of data on the value of public assets.

What public debt should be compared to (population? trade? government's assets? national revenue?) was also a key—but unsolved—issue in pre-1914 writings on public debt statistics. Around 1900, most economists agreed that, for a financial risk assessment, it was meaningful to compare debt service to government revenue. There was no consensus, however, on the denominator of a public debt ratio, because estimates of national income were not widespread and usually very rough at that time.[56] It was probably not needed for investors, but economists whose goal was to assess the actual and potential burden of debt on the nation (because they viewed debt as a source of future taxes) had to choose a way to compare nominal levels of public debt. For example, Neymarck ranked countries by the growth rates of their debt from 1870 to 1885. Alternatively, following previous publications by the Société de Statistique, he also mentioned levels of public debt per inhabitant.[57] As for Leroy-Beaulieu, he focused on the debt interests/government overall budget ratio and mentioned, without any justification, two important thresholds: 35 percent and 45 percent (respectively the vigilance threshold and the alarming threshold).[58]

In the interwar period, to our knowledge, the League of Nations did not discuss the issue of the denominator in its publication on public debt statistics. The only other economic variable which was published in the columns next to the public debt statistics was a price index. Given the high inflation rates during and after World War I, it was essential to compare the nominal growth rate of public debt to the evolution of prices. A notable exception was the 1938–1939 World Survey of the League of Nations which, for the first time, featured a brief comparison of public debt to national income for a limited number of countries. The issue was prepared by James Meade, the Keynesian economist who would later become one of the fathers of national accounts. However, only modest conclusions were reached from this comparison besides stating that the United Kingdom and France had more debt relative to their national income than Sweden because of the "long avoidance of war" in the latter country. And the usual caveats applied: "It is not possible to use this table for strict international comparisons, because both the figures of national income and those of public debt are not properly comparable." This publication also contained few words on the ratio of public debt to population: "Whereas in the nineteenth century, the burden of state debt per head of the population was reduced by a rapid growth of the population, the opposite development is to be expected in a declining population unless the burden of debts is rapidly reduced by, for instance, repayment or a rise in prices."[59] While the League of Nations left aside the discussion on which variables should be compared to public debt, it confronted directly and openly the issue of accounting and statistical definition of public debt and revenues. Yet, they did not find a common method to deal with these issues, as we have discussed previously. In the *Memorand[a] on Public Finance*, cautionary notes reminded the reader that comparability of public budgets and debts was almost an impossible task and that an "extreme prudence" was necessary to compare the figures of one country to those of another one. The 1948 retrospective volume on public debt contained a longer methodological introduction that explained the main sources of variations in definitions and accounting practices across countries: "The main object of this note is to indicate, in broad lines, the differences in *national concepts of public debts* in various countries. These differences are chiefly the result of diversity in type of state organization, in government functions, and in budgetary and accounting methods."[60] This document hence sums up the different elements to bear in mind when producing or reading statistics on public debts:

- The *type of state organization*.
- The *extent of economic activities* in which the various governments are engaged.
- The *budgetary methods and accounting practices*.[61]
- Public debt can be shown on a *"net" or "gross" basis*, and the meaning of these terms is not the same everywhere.[62]
- *Methods of conversion of foreign debt* (parity rates or market rates of exchange at the time of the issue of debt, etc.).

Such a list is strikingly similar to the one in a recent BIS paper which introduces a new international public debt database and notes that "the main discrepancies in the reporting of government debt figures relate to the following dimensions":[63]

- *Sector coverage* (e.g. public enterprises, subnational authorities such as states or regions, social security funds).
- *Instrument coverage.*
- *Consolidation.*
- *Netting.*
- *Valuation method.*

If public debt accounting tends to be more and more unified and coherent, very different measures still exist. They do not imply the same perspective and do not raise the same political questions on public debts. The next section therefore tries to make these underlying issues more explicit, and discusses how different perspectives prevailed at different times.

What Lies Behind Public Debt Statistics? Some "Ideal-Types"

The issue of public debt accounting is not only a challenge for statisticians and economists. Excluding components from the scope of public debt, shifting from one sustainability ratio to another, or reasoning with gross figures rather than with net, raise first and foremost very political questions. We aim to understand them through a typology of perspectives on public debt accounting and hereby distinguish three ideal-types that correspond to different ways of defining public debt and performing comparisons: a *financial* view which emphasizes external and marketable debt and focuses mostly on debt services and the history of repayment to evaluate the risk of public debt; a *circuitist* view which emphasizes the interlinkages between the several bodies of the state, as well as their role as financial intermediaries, and thinks mostly in terms of domestic assets and liabilities to evaluate the role of the state (the "public") in the economy; a *benchmarking* perspective whose primary aim is to provide international harmonized definitions and public debt ratios—as arbitrary as they may be—for explicit political guidance and salience. Each of them tends to focus on a specific question of what is at stake in the political economy of public debts. Finally, as we will discuss at the end of the section, each of these perspectives had its historical moment, broadly corresponding to the last three parts of this collective book.

The Financial View

The first perspective is a *financial view* (or *market-based view*) of public debt. This view is mainly that of investors. The perimeter of public debt is assumed to be quite narrow in this perspective because investors are interested in marketable debt (i.e. debt issued on financial markets, that can be traded easily) and in the debtor with whom they contract. Public debt is viewed as a potential substitute to private debt, without any difference in nature. Hence, debts of state-owned companies or local governments are viewed as separate entities from the central government and then usually excluded from general statistics on public debt. By contrast, foreign/external debt deserves a special attention in such a perspective. Financiers mainly assess debt sustainability by comparing debt service to government revenues.

Such a view is epitomized by the various financial analysts or institutions that were constructing and publishing their own figures of public debt in the late nineteenth century (the "First Age of Globalization", studied in the second part of this volume) and has remained prevalent over time. The big table on Chinese public finances mentioned above is a good illustration of that perspective. It was made by the Credit Lyonnais employees to compare the evolution of public revenues and debt service. For the years ranging from 1890 to 1902, the economists of the Service des Études financières (the "Financial Studies Department") reported the amounts associated to the state's different sources of revenues (maritime customs, local customs, taxes and others) and debt service. In doing so, they tried to evaluate the solvency of China, whose many bonds had been issued in Paris by a consortium of Western banks including Le Crédit Lyonnais.[64]

In this perspective, the government is expected to publish as many details as possible on marketable debt (volume and date of issue, amortization, debt service, etc.) so that risk on its debt can be calculated easily.[65] Otherwise, reluctant states may face sanctions imposed on international capital markets by those Adam Tooze refers to as "bond vigilantes" (Chap. 18).[66]

The Circuitist View

The second perspective is that of a *circuit economy* and it was developed in the interwar and postwar period (see the third part of this volume). Following this view, public debt is equivalent to the total liabilities of the state, and thus needs to be assessed with regard to the assets. The size of public debt reveals the importance of the state as a financial intermediary in the economy, that is, to what extent domestic savings are intermediated (directly or indirectly) by the state to finance investment. Consequently, outstanding debt matters much more than debt service and the external debt is likely to be neglected, except when debt is consolidated on an international or regional scale. On the contrary, debts of all state entities are included, although their frontiers may be blurred. Non-marketable debt is included and deserves a special analysis since it reveals the state capacity to escape the constraints of financial markets and oblige domestic institutions to own debt, for example, as regulatory capital or forced savings. The circuitist view is hence adopted when paying attention to the structure of public debt ownership,[67] when the role of the state in the financing of the economy is high or when a significant share of public debt is not marketable. In this perspective, different estimates may be used by economists or governments to assess the size of public debt, depending on the relevant perimeter of the state.[68] Alternative measures of state indebtedness are also used, such as "credit to the government", which is the counterpart of the money supply. Hence, in a circuitist perspective, public debt is not measured to evaluate its risk but to estimate the state's role in money creation, financial intermediation, or capital accumulation.

Such a perspective is naturally consistent with mercantilist views of public debt ("The debts of a state are debts from the right hand to the left hand," as famously stated by Jean-François Melon and criticized by Adam Smith)[69] and other circuitist perspectives that were prevalent in most countries from the 1930s to the 1970s and viewed public intervention as a necessary feature of wealth accumulation. It supports justifications for forced savings, backed by Keynesian macroeconomic arguments on aggregate demand and market failures, especially in war or planned economies.[70] However, the statistics produced in this perspective can also be used by critics of state interventions. This was, for example, the case when public debt was viewed as an inflationary burden in the 1970s,[71] or by critics of state-owned firms, or of social security systems, that considered the state's share in total national wealth should be minimal, whatever the interest paid on public debt.[72]

A good illustration of the consequences of the circuitist perspectives for the politics and accounting of public debt is seen in the financial relationship between the government and the central bank in postwar France.[73] From the mid-1950s to 1973, half of the financing of the *Banque de*

France—the French central bank—to the government was hidden. It did not appear as such in the balance sheet of the central bank and was not counted as "official" public debt. Yet, the Treasury and the central bank considered this unofficial debt as a normal circuit of government financing and kept track of the relevant figures. Such hidden financing relied on complex mechanisms and interconnections between several state-owned financial institutions: the central bank was lending to the Caisse des Dépôts—a developmental bank—which deposits these funds with the Treasury. These financial schemes reflect the general trend toward cross liabilities between several bodies of the state, in a context where policies aimed at decreasing the war debts of European states and increasing government intervention in the financial system. They reveal the nature of a state whose boundaries seem undefined but they should not be interpreted as a mere sign of free financing to the state, as, by other means, the central bank was able to cut credit to the government and the private economy in case of inflationary pressures. A 1973 law that abolished such a practice was officially justified as a way to provide more transparency on the financing of the government. The 1973 reform should also be understood in the context of the "rationalization of public policies" that started in the late 1960s in France:[74] reforms took place following the objectives of simplification and rationalization of state procedures, looking for more accountability and transparency (typical features of the financial perspective). Initial attempts to liberalize financial markets and decrease the role of state occurred at the same time. Changes in statistics reflected changes in the nature of the state and in the accountability of monetary and fiscal policy.

The Benchmarking View

The third perspective is the *benchmarking view*. Here, the main objective is to standardize and compare statistics of public debt across countries in order to derive policy implications. Consequently, the economic logic behind the definition of public debt is less clear, even if numbers enter into the formulation of policy rules. International institutions—from the League of Nations to the IMF—have obviously played a major role in diffusing the benchmarking view, as they supervised many quantitative and comparative studies and implemented public debt accounting standards. Yet, advocates of the benchmarking perspective are also more prone to acknowledge that statistics are somewhat arbitrary: if choices need to be made for international comparability, it is obvious that alternative definitions could be used. Harmonization aims first and foremost to produce long-term and international series to identify regular patterns and minimize biases due to different accounting systems. This is quite different from the financial perspective which relies on the idea that the information could be complete if governments were totally transparent on their debt management—an argument that became the dominant narrative in the 1980s. In the benchmarking perspective, there is no belief in that possibility: aggregated data demand sacrifices in terms of accuracy. Yet, the political impact of such statistics is key and justifies their production.

Besides financial considerations, the objective of Neymarck's *Les dettes publiques européennes* was, for example, to discuss the danger of rising public (war) debts in continental Europe while American and English debts were decreasing. In this perspective, comparing public indebtedness led to a very clear policy message regarding the economic and social burden of wars. Neymarck acknowledged key differences in the accounting of public debt across countries—which prevent robust financial comparisons—but however undertook an international analysis to highlight the consequences of relative patterns of public debt for public policy. In 1871, compiling figures on the *National Debts of the World* had also led Robert Dudley-Baxter, from the Royal Society of Statistics, to make clear distinctions between the countries of the globe. According to him, marketable debt was a characteristic of "civilized" countries, but over-indebtedness was a common feature among countries eager to look more developed than they were. Following this reasoning, he identified three groups based on racial characteristics. First, the "Germanic peoples" (England, the United States, Belgium, Holland, Germany, etc.) who take care to repay their loans since they are "industrious and thrifty".[75] Second, the "Latin peoples" (France, Italy, Spain, Portugal and Latin American countries), "sober and careful" but who suffer from "expensive governments".[76] The third group is composed of "peoples without many racial affinities but who share geographical situation and political conditions": military, absolute and irresponsible governments (Russia, Turkey, Greece, Egypt, Morocco, etc.). These countries are to take out loans and be unable to repay them,[77] which eventually legitimates the creation of international financial controls by Western powers, studied in the second part of this book.[78] For Dudley-Baxter, figures of public debt were thus tools for a racial and comparative reasoning which endowed peoples with moral virtues according to their creditworthiness. In his *Traité de la science des finances,* Leroy-Beaulieu nevertheless leveled criticism at this approach and provided alternative figures on public indebtedness, stressing that most indebted countries (both in absolute and relative terms) belonged to Dudley-Baxter's first category, the allegedly "Germanic countries."[79] Nationalist considerations are thus never far when comparing public indebtedness. During World War I, it was a frequently monitored indicator to assess belligerents' strength or weakness.[80]

The recent work by the economists Reinhart and Rogoff has renewed the long tradition of a comparative perspective on public debt, building on the more recent expansion of benchmarking practices by international organizations. Benchmarking practices and reasonings are also widespread today in the political role attributed by governments to rating agencies.[81] Contrary to the nationalist narratives of the late nineteenth century, today's benchmarking practices by international organizations tend to neglect domestic peculiarities and to make all states commensurable and similar to private debtors.[82]

Historical Interactions of the Three Perspectives

Our three perspectives are ideal-types and certainly coexist, but each of them had its historical moment of domination. The financial view developed in the first age of globalization, when Europe was the "world's banker"[83] (Part II of this volume). The circuitist view accompanied the rise of macroeconomic accounting and heavy state intervention in the financial sector, when non-marketable debt represented a large share of public debt, and when the transparency of financial arrangements was not a key signal of good behavior (Part III). The benchmarking view has gained prominence since the 1980s, when marketable debt regained importance and international organizations started to standardize public debt accounting to prevent sovereign defaults (part IV). These three perspectives may not capture properly the period covered by the first part of this book (1770s–1860s), when statistics on public finances mainly focused on spending or revenues and financial globalization was in its early stage. We suggest, however, that the eighteenth century saw the emergence of the financial perspective (rise of marketable public debts in London, Paris and Amsterdam) while a form of circuitist perspective was still dominant, in line with mercantilist principles and the politics of empire.[84]

Like any ideal-type, our three perspectives are often confounded in a single work or publication. For example, the books by Reinhart and Rogoff or the current IMF debt sustainability framework[85] interconnect the financial and benchmarking views, mixing financial reasoning on debt sustainability and long-term series from which they infer strong policy conclusions on the good behavior of public finance. Moreover, in the late nineteenth century as today, benchmarking practices have played a key role in assessing financial risk, especially when information on public debt and domestic policies was limited or imperfect. The statistics published by the League of Nations in the interwar years were the first attempt to provide an official standardization of public debt categories but they also assisted the League in its role of a rating agency, aimed at influencing financial decisions.[86] Immediately after World War II, it is also that combination of financial and benchmarking perspectives that prevailed when international organizations paid attention to statistics of public debts. The main question of a 1957 study published by the World Bank comparing the level of public external debt across countries was whether post-1945 accumulation of external debt had handicapped economic growth and whether the debt service of external debt was sustainable. The approach followed by the World Bank was very much that of a financial lender. A 1949 report on "Turkey's external public debt history" is exemplary. It contains tabs offering information on interest and amortization payments on the external debt. However, unlike the Crédit Lyonnais' employees, World Bank economists did not try to compare these sums to state revenues. Instead, they related them to projected dollar and exchange receipts and imports (in percentage).[87]

The current international SNA, which provides a definition of government liabilities, articulates the circuitist view with the benchmarking perspective. National accounting may, at first sight, look like a mere example of the circuitist perspective but the need to standardize accounts internationally has led accounting practices to bypass national specificities about the definition of the public sector. As we explained in previous sections, the development of the SNA—and the benchmarking practices associated with it—has pushed to replace the term of "public debt" by "general government debt", and thus to avoid defining the "public" sector which is at the core of the circuitist logic. Such an evolution is in fact not specific to public debt. It reflects a more general process in the history of national accounting, from a strong macroeconomic circuitist and national view to a paradigm of international comparability.[88]

Finally, note that the term "debt burden"—that appeared regularly in the writings of economists and financiers in the nineteenth century and has continued to be widely used throughout the twentieth century—is not especially associated with one perspective. It is found in various types of argument and is itself subject to various interpretations. In the financial perspective, the burden is what will increase the probability of default. In the benchmarking perspective, the debt burden is what prevents the state or the nation from acting. It is then mostly associated with a tax burden weighing on the economy.[89]

More importantly, governments themselves may play with the three perspectives described above because they have to respond to different demands (from domestic and international creditors or observers as well as from their taxpayers and citizens) and because public debt statistics are published on different supports and articulated with various types of official publications: central government budget, wealth accounts, money and financial statistics, retrospective national accounts and so on. This ambiguity and the multifaceted definition of public debt partly explain why economists and historians have emphasized the many difficulties in comparing public debt statistics across time and countries.

* * *

Long-term series of public debt show, in most countries, a striking decrease in the public debt-to-GDP ratio in the three or four decades after World War II. It may seem paradoxical that this decrease corresponds to the times when the state intervention in the economy was much higher than before or since. Conversely, the subsequent increase in public debt ratios at the turn of the 1970–1980s paralleled a decrease in state intervention. Wolfgang Streeck has described such a phenomenon as the transition from a fiscal state to a debtor state.[90] From such figures, one may conclude that the debt-to-GDP ratio is a very bad indicator of the state's role in the economy and of its liability, since the numbers are limited to general (or even central) government debt and do not include key liabilities of the welfare state such as pensions, or guarantees offered to failing banks. Not only are such ratios poorly informative about the relative size and indebtedness of the private and public sectors, but they are also silent on the risk associated with the debt, since they neglect the nature of the debt instruments and the identity of debt holders.[91] Can we compare a world where the public debt is mainly held (sometimes through various mechanisms of forced savings) by domestic banks and other financial institutions which are mainly state-owned to a world where the debt is massively issued and traded on international markets? Is it meaningful to compare the debts of nineteenth-century economies, caused by war expenditures and the expansion of railway companies, to the debts of modern welfare states excluding contingent liabilities? Opening the black box of public debt statistics and understanding their historical use by contemporaries (both of official and alternative estimates) is an essential step toward a better understanding of the politics of debt. This chapter has shown that there is no single indicator for estimating and analyzing central government, general government and public debts, and that, over the course of history, economists and accountants have used different definitions depending on their interest and perspective. Defining public liabilities goes beyond standardizing accounting practices; it implies choices and results from constraints, both strongly shaped by the historical context.

NOTES

1. This chapter has greatly benefited from the comments and lively discussions with the members of the collective *A World of Public Debts: A Political History*. We especially thank Nicolas Barreyre, Nicolas Delalande, Noam Maggor and Stephen Sawyer for detailed feedback on a previous draft. We also thank Thomas Piketty and Angelo Riva for important suggestions and help with references. We owe a special debt to Adam Tooze for pushing us to write this paper and discussing these ideas on several occasions.
2. See Mark Blyth, *Austerity: The History of a Dangerous Idea* (New York: Oxford University Press, 2013), for a critical review of the debates. Philip R. Lane "The European Sovereign Debt Crisis," *The Journal of Economic Perspectives* 26, no. 3 (2012): 49–67 provides a quantitative account of the debt crisis. On the US debate on debt limit, see D. Andrew Austin, *Debt Limit: History and Recent Increases* (Washington DC: Congressional Research Service Report, 2015).
3. In this volume, see Chap. 20 by Nicolas Barreyre and Nicolas Delalande.
4. International Monetary Fund, *Public Sector Debt Statistics: Guide for Compilers and Users*, 2nd edition (Washington DC: IMF publications, 2013).
5. Beat Balzli, "How Goldman Sachs Helped Greece to Mask its True Debt," *Spiegel Online*, February 08, 2010 http://www.spiegel.de/international/europe/greek-debt-crisis-how-goldman-sachs-helped-greece-to-mask-its-true-debt a 676634.html
6. Agnes Tardos, "The Story Told by Debt Indicators and the Hidden Truth," *IFC Bulletins chapters* 36 (2013): 351–365.

7. Such "contingent" liabilities are off balance sheet in the standard definition of public debt (which, in the European Union, is called "debt in the sense of Maastricht"). Angelo Baglioni and Umberto Cherubini, "Bank Bailout Guarantees and Public Debt," *VoxEu*, December 1, 2010, http://voxeu.org/article/bank-bailout-guarantees-and-public-debt; "Marking-to-Market Government Guarantees to Financial Systems: Theory and Evidence for Europe," *Journal of International Money and Finance* 32 (2013): 990–1007.
8. Thomas Piketty, *Capital in the Twenty-First Century* (Cambridge, Mass.: Harvard University Press, 2014), Chap. 4.
9. George J. Hall and Thomas J. Sargent, "A History of U.S. Debt Limits," NBER Working Paper, no. w21799 (December 2015). According to Missale, this accounting mistake prevents government from using public debt as an insurance against macroeconomic shocks to the government budget. Alessandro Missale, "Sovereign Debt Management and Fiscal Vulnerabilities," BIS Papers, chapter 65 (2012): 157–176. A more critical perspective is given by Yuri Biondi: "This driving reference to and preference for a market-based view on public finances" reflects a new "business-style accounting" which "is one of the pillars of 'new public management'". For Biondi, assuming an equivalence between public and private accounting is not desirable: it neglects specificities of public finances, and is not sustainable in the long run. Yuri Biondi, "Public Debt Accounting and Management in UK: Refunding or Refinancing? Or the Strange Case of Doctor Jekyll and Mr. Hyde in the Aftermath of the Global Financial Crisis," *Accounting Forum* 40, no. 2 (2016): 89–105; Id., "Accounting Representations of Public Debt and Deficits in European Central Government Accounts: An Exploration of Anomalies and Contradictions," *Accounting Forum* 40, no. 3 (2016): 205–219.
10. Missale, "Sovereign Debt Management", 159.
11. Eurostat, "Third quarter of 2016 compared with second quarter of 2016, government debt fell to 90.1 percent of GDP in euro area", *Newsrelease. Euroindicators*, 15/2017 (January 23, 2017): 3. http://ec.europa.eu/eurostat/documents/2995521/7826125/2-23012017-AP-EN.pdf
12. In 2016, intergovernmental loans were equal to 2.2 percent of the Euro Area GDP.
13. Consolidation makes it possible to produce a unique set of accounts to represent the financial situation of different entities which can be considered relevantly as a whole. Here, the issue at stake is: can member-states of the European Union be considered as parts of a sovereign entity?
14. Yuri Biondi even advocates abandoning the balance-sheet accounting approach and suggests implementing new standards to get better account-

ing representations of public finances. See Biondi, "Accounting Representations of Public Debt".
15. Some recent studies have highlighted the role of economic statistics in shaping globalization. Daniel Speich studied how the production of global figures on economic inequality has nurtured for seventy years a "conceptual world economic order of nations" which is today widespread and taken for granted. Daniel Speich, "The Use of Global Abstractions: National Income Accounting in the Period of Imperial Decline," *Journal of Global History* 6, no. 1 (2011): 7–28. Quinn Slobodian showed that, as early as the late nineteenth century, some German and Austrian economists mobilized statistics "to make visible what they called the 'world economic organism'": Quinn Slobodian, "How to See the World Economy: Statistics, Maps, and Schumpeter's Camera in the First Age of Globalization," *Journal of Global History* 10, no. 2 (2015): 307–332.
16. As pointed out by Thomas Piketty about GDP statistics, "One conclusion stands out in this brief history of national accounting: national accounts are a social construct in perpetual evolution. They always reflect the preoccupations of the era when they were conceived. We should be careful not to make a fetish of the published figures." Thomas Piketty, *Capital*: 58.
17. For a recent presentation and discussion of widely used public debt statistics, see Ali S. Abbas, Alex Pienkowski and Kenneth Rogoff, eds., *Sovereign Debt: A Guide for Economists and Practitioners* (Oxford: Oxford University Press, 2019). As for the evolution of debt-to-GDP ratios over two centuries in major economies, there is no clear evidence that alternative sources would lead to very different long-term patterns from the one that has been emphasized in recent publications. The amount of public debt arguably increases when a country is at war.
18. Barry Eichengreen and Richard Portes, "Debt and Default in the 1930s: Causes and Consequences," *European Economic Review* 30 (June 1986): 599–640. See also: Rudiger Dornbusch and Mario Draghi, *Public Debt Management: Theory and History* (Cambridge: Cambridge University Press, 1990); Peter Lindert and Peter Morton, "How Sovereign Debt Has Worked," in *Developing Country Debt and Economic Performance, Vol. 1: The International Financial System*, ed. Jeffrey D. Sachs (Chicago: Chicago University Press, 1989): 39–106.
19. Michael D. Bordo and Lars Jonung, "Monetary Regimes, Inflation, and Monetary Reform: An Essay in Honor of Axel Leijonhufvud," in *Inflation, Institutions, and Information: Essays in Honor of Axel Leijonhufvud*, eds. Daniel Vaz and Kumaraswamy Velupillai (London: Palgrave Macmillan, 1996): 157–244; Maurice Obstfeld and Alan Taylor, "Sovereign Risk, Credibility and the Gold Standard: 1870–1913 versus 1925–3," *The Economic Journal* 113, no. 487 (April 2003): 241–275.

20. Marc Flandreau and Frédéric Zumer, *The Making of Global Finance. 1880–1913* (Paris: OCDE Development Centre Studies, 2004). The compilation of statistics by Mitchell also contained statistics on public debt but most series were discontinuous, and no effort was made to make them comparable. Mitchell relied on official government sources: Brian R. Mitchell, *International Historical Statistics: Europe 1750–1988* (New York: Stockton Press, 1983); *International Historical Statistics: The Americas, 1750–1988* (London: Macmillan, 1983).
21. Carmen M. Reinhart and Kenneth S. Rogoff, *This Time is Different: Eight Centuries of Financial Folly*, (Princeton: Princeton University Press, 2009); S. M. Ali Abbas, Nazim Belhocine, Asmaa El-Ganainy and Mark Horton, "Historical Patterns and Dynamics of Public Debt–Evidence from a New Database," *IMF Economic Review* 59, no. 4 (November 2011): 717–742; S. M. Ali Abbas, Laura Blattner, Mark De Broeck, et al. "Sovereign Debt Composition in Advanced Economies: A Historical Perspective," IMF Working Paper, WP/14/62 (September 2014).
22. Marc Flandreau, "Le service des études financières sous Henri Germain (1871–1905): une macro-économie d'acteurs," in *Le Crédit Lyonnais (1863–1986). Études historiques*, eds. Bernard Desjardins et al. (Geneva: Droz, 2003): 271–301.
23. Flandreau and Zumer, *The Making of Global Finance*, 98.
24. In this volume, see Chap. 6 by Ali Coşkun Tunçer and Chap. 7 by Malak Labib.
25. Neymarck collected figures directly from governments and presented them without statistical processing, but he stressed several times in his study the imperfection of official statistics and different accounting practices across countries (see below). Lindert and Morton, "How Sovereign Debt Has Worked," 80.
26. See in this volume Chap. 9 by Dong Yan.
27. In 1896, the authors of the *Statesman's Yearbook* asserted that the Chinese debt had increased from £13 million to £53 million within the previous two years. To get this increase, they must have added the Japanese indemnity, the 1895 loan and the 1896 loan. Then, they subtracted the first two instalments of the indemnity and the part of the pre-war debt that was paid back. In 1897, the authors mentioned a £15 million decrease. Since, within a year, the Chinese government only paid back a new instalment of the indemnity and the first instalments of the 1895 and 1896 loans, there can be only one explanation for this decrease: the remains of the 1895 indemnity had been removed from the outstanding amount.
28. United Nations, *Public Debt 1914–1946* (Lake Success: New York, 1948).
29. The debate on how to account for war reparations and subsequent debt accords is not settled and still gives rise to historical debates. See, for

example, the new series of Italian foreign debt, that significantly differs from earlier ones: Marianna Astore and Michele Fratianni, "'We can't Pay': How Italy Dealt with War Debts after World War I," *Financial History Review* 26 no.2 (2019): 197–222.
30. See especially the 1928 Geneva international conference relating to economic statistics.
31. See in this volume Chap. 12 on interwar Germany, by Stefanie Middendorf.
32. In this volume, see Chap. 13 by Kristy Ironside and Étienne Forestier-Peyrat. After the repudiation of the Tsarist debts, the Soviet state resorted to lottery loans which aimed to attract a significant part of domestic savings.
33. In this volume, Chap. 12 by Stefanie Middendorf precisely shows that the traditional narrative, which focuses on the caesura of 1933, fails to explain how the structuration of the German public debt and its governance evolved in the Interwar period. Such an evolution was much more influenced by changes in the practice of power than by changes in the ideology of political regimes. On the computation of Italian domestic debt in the 1930s and the accounting issues related to state institutions financing the reconstruction (especially the Consorzio Sovvenzioni su Valori Industriali), see Vera Zamagni, "Italy: How to Lose the War and Win the Peace," in *The Economics of World War II: Six Great Powers In International Comparison*, ed. Mark Harrison (Cambridge: Cambridge University Press 2000): 177–223.
34. Henry Laufenburger, *Crédit public et finances de guerre, 1914–1944* (Paris: Librairie de Médicis, 1944): 9.
35. Denys P. Myers and Perry A. Wicks, "International Comparability of Public Debts," *The American Economic Review* 28, no. 4 (December 1938): 711–715.
36. Harry Campion, *Public and Private Property in Great Britain* (Oxford: Oxford University Press, 1939). Thomas Piketty considers this book as the very first attempt to calculate public assets. See Piketty, *Capital in the Twenty-First Century*, 591.
37. Keith J. Horsefield, *The International Monetary Fund, 1945–1965, Volume III: Documents* (Washington: International Monetary Fund, 1969).
38. Eric Monnet and Damien Puy, "Do Old Habits Die Hard? Central Banks and the Bretton Woods Gold Puzzle," IMF Working Paper, WP/19/161 (July 2019).
39. Eric Helleiner, *States and the Reemergence of Global Finance: From Bretton Woods to the 1990s* (Ithaca: Cornell University Press, 1996).
40. Harry Campion, "Recent Developments in Economic Statistics," *Journal of the Royal Statistical Society (Series A)* 121, no. 1 (1958): 2. See also Alan

Booth, "The 'Keynesian Revolution' in Economic Policy-Making," *The Economic History Review* 36, no. 1 (February 1983): 103–123.
41. See for example: World Bank, *Honduras' External Debt History* (Washington, DC: World Bank, 1948) http://documents.worldbank.org/curated/en/308151468274216187/Honduras-external-debt-history and World Bank, *Finland's External Public Debt History* (Washington: World Bank, 1948) http://documents.worldbank.org/curated/en/847541468256737689/Finlands-external-public-debt-history
42. Pieter Lieftinck, "External Debt and Debt-Bearing Capacity of Developing Countries," *Princeton Essays in International Finance* 51 (1966). See also: Charles R. Frank and William R. Cline, "Measurement of Debt Servicing Capacity: An Application of Discriminant Analysis," *Journal of International Economics* 1, no. 3 (August 1971): 327–344.
43. The Government Finance Statistics Manual first edition was published by the IMF in 1986.
44. A central government body is an institution whose mission, given by the central State, applies to a national scale. In national accounts, central government bodies are grouped together in several functions: general services, defence, public order and security, economic affairs, environmental protection, etc.
45. Robert Dippelsman, Claudia Dziobek and Carlos A. Gutiérrez-Mangas, "What Lies Beneath: The Statistical Definition of Public Sector Debt," *IMF Staff Discussion Notes*, SDN/12/09 (July 2012).
46. A recent exception is Andrea Papadia, *Sovereign Defaults during the Great Depression: The Role of Fiscal Fragility*, LSE Economic History Working Papers, no. 255 (2017). The author attempts to account for the debt of local governments and to reconstruct such series. Besides statistics of the League of Nations, he makes use of the international figures published yearly in the *Statistisches Jahrbuch für das Deutsche Reich*. He does not question, however, why accounting methods differed across countries.
47. Debra Bloch and Falilou Fall, "Government Debt Indicators: Understanding the Data," *Journal of International Commerce, Economics and Policy* 7, no. 1 (2016).
48. Ten years before, Paul Leroy-Beaulieu's *Traité de la science des finances* (Paris: Guillaumin et Cie, 1878) had quickly become the reference work on public finances in France. Sixteen of its forty-two chapters were devoted to "public credit". Among them one focused on "the different methods to evaluate the weight of a public debt".
49. Alfred Neymarck, *Les Dettes publiques européennes* (Paris: Guillaumin et Cie, 1887): 5.
50. Neymarck, *Dettes publiques*, 37.

51. Neymarck, *Dettes publiques*, 64. For more details on Neymarck, see in this volume Chap. 4 by David Todd and Alexia Yates.
52. Neymarck, *Dettes publiques*, 76.
53. Neymarck, *Dettes publiques*, 85.
54. Leroy-Beaulieu, *Traité*, 7th edition (Paris: Guillaumin et Cie, 1906): 656.
55. Crédit Lyonnais Archives, DEEF 73449.
56. See Adam Tooze, *Statistics and the German State, 1900–1945, The Making of Modern Economic Knowledge* (Cambridge: Cambridge University Press, 2001): 8.
57. Neymarck, *Dettes publiques*, 86–87.
58. Leroy-Beaulieu, *Traité*, 662.
59. *World Economic Survey, 1938/1939*, 8th year, League of Nations: 71.
60. United Nations, *Public Debt*, 7.
61. For example, amounts due to trust funds, deposits administered by the government, or even special advances of central banks may be excluded. War debts from 1914–1918 also received a different treatment across countries. Only some nations included them (Australia, Italy, France, Portugal and the United Kingdom) and the date of their exclusion varied. "As the amounts involved are often considerable, their inclusion or exclusion results in great differences in the foreign debt figure," cf. United Nations, *Public Debt*, 9.
62. In South Africa, "net debt" represented the "gross debt" after deduction of sinking funds, whereas, in Argentina, all bonds held by the government were deducted.
63. Christian Dembiermont, Michela Scatigna, Robert Szemere and Bruno Tissot, "A New Database on General Government Debt," *BIS Quarterly Review* (September 2015).
64. For more details on how foreign loans impacted Chinese economic and statistical knowledge, see in this volume Chap. 9 by Dong Yan.
65. Accordingly, the 1899 issue of the *Statesman's Yearbook* complained that "no general statement of the revenue and expenditures of China was made public." See *Statesman's Yearbook. Statistical and Historical Annual of the States of the World for the Year 1899* (London: Palgrave Macmillan, 1899): 460.
66. See in this volume Chap. 18 by Adam Tooze.
67. For an illustration focusing on the American case, see Sandy B. Hager, "Appendix: Accounting for the Public Debt," in Id., *Public Debt, Inequality, and Power: The Making of a Modern Debt State* (Oakland, CA: University of California Press, 2016): 105–122.
68. See Tooze, *Statistics and the German State*, 135, on how, in interwar Germany, annual surveys on government indebtedness took place in the

framework of the general circuitist perspective (especially on the circuit of payments) developed by macroeconomic statisticians.
69. Adam Smith, *An Inquiry Into the Nature and Causes of the Wealth of Nations* (London: J.M. Dent & Sons, 1910): 409
70. John Maynard Keynes, *How to Pay for the War: A Radical Plan for the Chancellor of the Exchequer* (London: Harcourt, Brace & Co, 1940).
71. See, about the United Kingdom: Nicoletta Batini and Edward Nelson, "The UK's Rocky Road to Stability," Federal Reserve Bank of St. Louis Working Paper, 2005-020A (2005).
72. On the evolution of these conceptions, see Chap. 15 of this volume by Anush Kapadia and Benjamin Lemoine.
73. This example is taken from Éric Monnet, *Controlling Credit: Monetary Policy and the Planned Economy in France, 1945–1973* (Cambridge: Cambridge University Press, 2018), Chap.5.
74. Philippe Bezès, *Réinventer l'Etat. Les réformes de l'administration française (1962–2008)* (Paris, Presses universitaires de France, 2009).
75. Robert Dudley-Baxter, *National Debts*, 2nd edition (London: Robert John Bush, 1871): 7–47.
76. Dudley-Baxter, *National Debts*, 48–63.
77. Dudley-Baxter, *National Debts*, 64–72.
78. In this volume, see Chap. 6 by Ali Coşkun Tunçer and Chap. 7 by Malak Labib.
79. Leroy-Beaulieu, *Traité*, 642–650
80. See Chap. 11 of this volume, by Nicolas Delalande.
81. See Chap. 18 of this volume, by Adam Tooze.
82. See Chap. 17 of this volume, by Jerome Sgard.
83. Herbert Feis, *Europe: The World's Banker, 1870–1914*, 2nd edition (New York: A. M. Kelley, 1964).
84. See Chap. 1 of this volume, by Regina Grafe.
85. International Monetary Fund, "Joint World Bank-IMF Debt Sustainability Framework for Low-Income Countries," *IMF Factsheet* (March 19, 2019): https://www.imf.org/external/np/exr/facts/jdsf.htm
86. Michel Fior, *Institution globale et marchés financiers. La Société des Nations face à la reconstruction de l'Europe, 1918–1931* (Bern: Peter Lang, 2008): 282.
87. International Bank for Reconstruction and Development, *Turkey's External Public Debt History*, Economic department report no. E39/49 (1949): http://documents.worldbank.org/curated/en/259561468337852342/Turkeys-external-public-debt-history
88. Adam Tooze, "Imagining National Economies: National and International Economic Statistics, 1900–1950," in *Imagining Nations*, ed. Geoffrey Cubitt (Manchester: Manchester University Press, 1998): 212–229;

Matthias Schmelzer, *The Hegemony of Growth: The OECD and the Making of the Economic Growth Paradigm* (Cambridge: Cambridge University Press, 2016); Fior, *Institution globale et marchés financiers.*

89. See the numerous uses of the term "debt burden," associated with "tax burden" in Dornbusch and Draghi, *Public Debt Management.* Finally, the influential paper by C. Reinhart and R. Rogoff is a prominent example where the "debt burden" is associated with lower economic growth. Carmen M. Reinhart and Kenneth S. Rogoff, "Growth in a Time of Debt," *American Economic Review*, 100, no. 2 (May 2010): 573–78. In this paper, it is not clear however whether high debt is a burden on economic growth because of a tax burden or because of its effect on the probability of crisis.
90. Wolfgang Streeck, *Buying Time: The Delayed Crisis of Democratic Capitalism* (London: Verso Books, 2014).
91. This chapter does not deal much with the identity of debtholders. International statistical standardization has failed to provide a unified framework to tackle this key issue, even though some attempts have been made to understand how sovereign debt composition has influenced the probability of default or choices regarding taxation since the 1950s. See Abbas, Blattner, De Broeck, et al., "Sovereign Debt Composition."

Open Access This chapter is licensed under the terms of the Creative Commons Attribution 4.0 International License (http://creativecommons.org/licenses/by/4.0/), which permits use, sharing, adaptation, distribution and reproduction in any medium or format, as long as you give appropriate credit to the original author(s) and the source, provide a link to the Creative Commons licence and indicate if changes were made.

The images or other third party material in this chapter are included in the chapter's Creative Commons licence, unless indicated otherwise in a credit line to the material. If material is not included in the chapter's Creative Commons licence and your intended use is not permitted by statutory regulation or exceeds the permitted use, you will need to obtain permission directly from the copyright holder.

CHAPTER 20

The Words of Public Debts: A Political Repertoire

Nicolas Barreyre and Nicolas Delalande

Historical *exempla* abound when public debt is in crisis. After the issue of the Greek debt became front-page news in 2011, for instance, the troubled past of the Greek state, and especially its default in the 1890s, were immediately conjured up as a lesson to the present. As the crisis deepened, however, historical counter-arguments also appeared: did not Germany, now so inflexible on debt payments, benefit from a generous debt write-off in 1953? This turn to history, however, dredged up more moral tropes and historical clichés than serious analyses. They were, in fact, easy shortcuts through a complex political and economic situation, boiling it down to sharp, contrasting positions. This is not an attempt to dismiss them, however: indeed, they had power. And this power is precisely what needs analyzing.[1]

N. Barreyre
Mondes Américains/CENA, EHESS, Paris, France
e-mail: nicolas.barreyre@ehess.fr

N. Delalande (✉)
Centre d'Histoire, Sciences Po, Paris, France
e-mail: nicolas.delalande@sciencespo.fr

© The Author(s) 2020
N. Barreyre, N. Delalande (eds.), *A World of Public Debts*, Palgrave Studies in the History of Finance,
https://doi.org/10.1007/978-3-030-48794-2_20

Reading through the historical cases explored in the present volume, one cannot but be struck by how many of today's political arguments used on public debt are echoes of past debates—sometimes, it seems, word for word. Many appeared as far back as the eighteenth century, and have long become tropes, circulating from place to place and from one period to the next, where they could be mobilized, reshaped, and retold in the same words but with different meanings attached. Politics has to be conveyed through discourse, and arguments on public debt emerged from specific contexts to weigh on specific policies, and more largely on the balance of power. Yet once they existed, those tropes did not simply disappear. Depending on context, some gained currency while others were demonetized. New ones emerged out of novel situations, but they always coexisted with older, persistent tropes. Individual arguments, while being drawn from the same political toolbox, would take new meanings by being bundled in new combinations.

To understand the political debates of today, we must therefore make sense of those tropes, where they came from, and what make them potent in the current situation of public debt crises. But we also must replace them in the full spectrum of their historical diversity, to illuminate which arguments have become invisible in today's debates. Recovering this discourse could also help build viable political alternatives to what seem to many as the impasses of our present day.

This chapter aims to make sense of the political *repertoire* that was built over time since the eighteenth century, when the idea of public debt took shape. It is not a comprehensive survey, but an attempt to pull together the different strands of arguments used across the period to politicize (or depoliticize) public debt. We recognize—and this is a crucial point—that those arguments were always used in, and adapted to, specific contexts, and that economic and political developments over three centuries also changed their respective impact and relevance. Yet putting them together allows us to see where the continuities, similarities and path dependencies lie, and explore the full range of the political implications of the sometimes technical and narrow discussions about public debt.

By repertoire, we mean the arguments about public debt that, once argued, entered the political culture and thus became readily available to political actors. As this volume suggests, the globalization of public debt in the nineteenth century also globalized a host of discourse justifying it.[2] In this repertoire, we identified four main registers of arguments, being as many interlinked but separate strands of political discourse on public debt operating at somewhat different levels, but all aiming to make sense of public debt and its *legitimacy*. Those four registers are morality, justice, power, and expertise.

The Moral Economies of Public Debts

We tend today to see public debt as a technical and economic matter, shaped by management imperatives, interest rates, and financial data. Yet at the same time, moral judgments always appear beneath the surface. Nietzsche could famously argue that Western morals were the result of converting material "debts" (*Schulden*) into "guilt" (*Schuld*).[3] The recent debt crisis in Greece provided obvious examples of such moral indictments: the Greeks were said to be "lazy" people, compared to thrifty and hardworking Germans. Those national prejudices and cultural stereotypes are also moral judgments, however ill-founded they might be. They point toward the dual nature of credit, which has historically been conceived as a *moral and social relationship* even before it became an *economic indicator*.

Debt, Credit, Honor

In the early modern period, the word "credit" would designate at the same time the moral and social value of a person (the reputation they enjoyed and the prestige attached to their name), and their capacity to borrow money and inspire trust. In Antoine Furetière's dictionary, published in 1690, the economic definition of credit came only third. The first meaning of the word referred to "belief, esteem that one acquires in public by one's virtue, probity, good faith and merit," and then to "the power, the authority, the wealth that one acquires by means of that reputation." Social respectability and financial trustworthiness were closely intertwined.[4]

States too had a moral record to honor. The language of honor, closely associated with the first conceptions of sovereignty, was central in the debates on public debt in the eighteenth and nineteenth centuries, more than in the recent period, when economic concepts and notions have become more dominant. The term "reputation," used in economic history and international finance as if it were neutral and objective, is clearly related to this traditional moral understanding.[5] Debts raise questions of honor; they involve judgements on the integrity of persons, states, and organizations. In the eighteenth century, most authors associated personal reputation with financial credit: a debt involved the debtor's word to repay. The moral imperative embedded in the debt relation was to honor one's word to do what one committed oneself to do. If, in the past three centuries, the word "credit" has gradually lost its plural meanings, it still carries its moral charge, connected with worldviews of morality, work ethics, and thrift.

This explains why countries with a record of debt failures and defaults could be met with virulent discourses of moral degeneracy. In the second half of the nineteenth century, Mediterranean countries were often described by West European diplomats or bankers as indolent, lavish, unable to discipline their subjects, desires, and finances. A corporal or carnal view of state finances was part and parcel of this development of "financial orientalism." Evelyn Baring, the consul-general of Egypt in the early years of the British protectorate, would complain about Egyptians' corrupted morals and uncivilized practices. "In no country has corruption—the cancer which eats away the heart of most Eastern governments—been more universal than it was in Egypt during the reign of Ismail Pasha," he opined. Egypt had suffered "from the ignorance, dishonesty, waste, and extravagance of the East, such as have brought her suzerain to the verge of ruin."[6]

Diplomatic visions of the Ottoman Empire also played on deeply entrenched cultural stereotypes, obsessed with the absolute power of the Sultan and the pernicious role of religious fanaticism. A French diplomat in Constantinople in 1876 regretted that "ministers, bankers, financiers, nobody is thinking here about the public interest. The patriotic idea does not exist. Only religious fanaticism is able to shake these people and take them out of their apathy."[7] Greece's position, in the late nineteenth century and today, has been that of a "split" country, between the East and the West. The language used by the International Financial Commission set up in 1898 incorporated elements that sound familiar when listening to the more recent European discourses on the Greek debt crisis: "The future of Greece now depends on her wisdom. If she applies herself to work, quiet and peace, in order to improve …, its financial situation will quickly recover … by brave and patient efforts."[8]

Thus, the morality of debt as a personal relationship, when applied to a country (confused with a people), carries more than the simple obligation to repay debts. It implies a whole political economy of the *correct* way to do it. At the time when Western countries were getting rid of debtor's prison, thus attenuating the moral infringement that incapacity to pay one's debt meant for society, they used the same arguments to justify the use of force to impose repayment of debts, and economic tutelage, on whole countries.[9]

But morality and honor were not so unequivocal as creditors (be they governments or interest groups) would have it. By the end of the nineteenth century, counter-arguments emerged in specific contexts, justifying repudiating a debt while impugning the morality of creditors. In post-1860s Mexico, for instance, repaying French bonds was rejected out of hand: it had been contracted by a regime that had been military imposed by France itself.[10] British bonds, were a different matter. Defended by many as "just claims," they were loudly denounced by nationalists, who saw them as another capitulation of the country's independence. Exchanging national pride for British capital would simply taint Mexico's reputation and jeopardize its dignity. In parliament in 1884, the debate was as much on finance as on morality and respectability. Rejecting payment of the British debt was, for many, a duty to "save our *patria* from the abyss and from dishonor." And the fight was not merely rhetorical: duels and street demonstrations accompanied this intense polemic on the *deuda inglesa*.[11]

Thus, the moral relationship created by a public debt could find itself at the heart of political contestation, all the more as the "collective" part of the "public" could mean many different things. But it could also call into question the very honor and moral claims of creditors. This became clear at the beginning of the twentieth century, when some public debts came to be construed as unjust or unsustainable burdens placed upon nations. The language of "odious debt" that emerged then, beyond its sophisticated legal details, carried views about moral and immoral debts. Democratic legitimacy and moral integrity could place limits on the notion of an everlasting debt, irrespective of changes of regimes and institutions. At the outset, the doctrine of the "odious debt" was much more an attempt at providing state repudiations with legal and political underpinnings rather than a purely moral assumption.[12] By the end of the twentieth century, however, movements for debt relief had endorsed it as a humanitarian discourse, calling on religious ideas of redemption. The Catholic Church called for an "ethical" treatment of the foreign debt crisis in 1986, in anticipation of the Jubilee. The international mobilization that took place in the 1990s relied on a mix of humanitarian feelings and mass media mobilization, with rock-stars like Bono touring the planet.[13]

These calls revived the idea of a "moral economy" of debt, where the unfair aspect of a debt could alter the moral value of the creditor powers.

This is precisely the kind of language anthropologist David Graeber mobilized in his recent bestselling *Debt: The First 5000 Years*, insisting on the primordial aspect of debt and the necessity to unveil its moral and violent foundations. In Greece as well, humanitarian arguments have been used to criticize the ruthlessness of the European "Troika." The conflict between economic austerity and its moral impact is nowhere more blatant than when foreign experts are confronted with images of starving children or impoverished old people. They echoed 1884 Mexico, when deputies warned against repaying the *deuda inglesa* while "the widows and the pensioners are dying of misery; there are public employees who commit suicide because they do not receive their salaries and lack the courage to see the horrible spectacle of their children's hunger."[14] This may explain why, in the past, financial conditionality and humanitarian interventions have been sometimes enacted simultaneously (for instance, after the two world wars), in order to convince people that economic calculations and empathy could work hand in hand.[15]

These moral counter-discourses have not neutralized the old argument about personal morality of honoring one's debts, however, either in its older form of trustworthiness or its newer form about market responsibility—that is, toward a system that would otherwise collapse, making repayment of public debt not a moral duty to the creditors in particular, but the collectivity as a whole.[16] They make it necessary, however, to morally defend claims in case of dispute: no longer can the moral polarity of default assumed.

The Ends of Debt

There is a second moral thread running through the political discourses on public debt. This one deals more with the finality of public debt than its payment. In the eighteenth century, large public debts became intimately linked to waging wars ever grander in scale and more imperialist in tenor. This led to a discourse hostile to public debt as a threat to peace itself. Adam Smith wrily pointed out that, without debt funding, "wars would in general be more speedily concluded, and less wantonly undertaken." James Madison was similarly convinced that "armies, and debts, and taxes, are the known instruments for bringing the many under the domination of the few."[17] As far as public debt was mostly contracted to wage wars, it became tarred by the same moral condemnations as warmongering itself.

In the nineteenth century, as nationalisms rose, however, this association between war and debt could be reversed, when the invention of public subscriptions led to associate patriotism and the love of the nation to the financial effort to pay for its wars. There is a rhetorical, and propagandic, thread here that can be followed from the Crimean War to the US Civil War to the French war indemnity in 1871, that culminated in the twentieth century with the two world wars.[18] The propaganda machines in all belligerent countries during those wars to dive deep into the savings of citizens powerfully equated public loans with patriotic fervor, to help fight the enemy and protect the nation. Moral suasion, sometimes outright pressure, was used on a wide scale to induce savers to invest in the national debt. Interestingly, those moral arguments were put forward both in democratic and authoritarian regimes.[19] While insisting on the supposed link between debt and freedom, all states aimed to turn debt-holding into a moral and political obligation. The propaganda in the United States and in Europe, including the Soviet Union, all pointed to the moral responsibility of each citizen in the war effort.[20]

In many ways, it was against this strong association between public debt and war that another discourse took shape in the nineteenth century, finding positive connotations to public debt, which could be presented as a marker of civilization, growth, and prosperity. In 1874, London-based *Fenn's Compendium* (the international reference for investors interested in public and quasi-public bonds) described the increasing public debt of the world not as a threat but as an opportunity, almost a blessing: "Judging from the past, there is nothing in this accumulation of debt which should give us cause of apprehension for the future. ... instead of being applied exclusively to war, and to the pressing exigencies of needy states, it is largely employed in the construction of railways, steamships, telegraphs, improvements of all kinds, at home, in our colonies, and in foreign lands, ... which promises well for the borrowers as for the lenders."[21] Rising debts, far from ushering chaos or breeding war, were the means through which modernity would improve mankind and living conditions. By the end of the nineteenth century, such positive pronouncements were widespread among economists and investors, but also in many polities looking to modernize their infrastructure and foster economic growth.[22]

Nowadays it seems hard to find any positive moral discourses on public debt, most often stigmatized as an excuse to irresponsibly let deficits run away. Yet amid negative interest rates and austerity measures playing havoc with liberal democratic regimes, new voices seem to emerge to plead for new borrowing that could actually rebuild better perspectives for the economic future of many countries. What is unsure at this stage is if such echoes of positive views of large-scale public borrowing for the welfare of society will change the political debate.[23]

Narratives of Justice and Inequality

The creditor-debtor relation gave rise to a second set of discourses and arguments that go beyond the realm of ethics, values, and respectability. It raised questions of justice, inequality, and redistribution. These issues are also moral ones, but they do not point to the personal morality of the creditor or the debtor, but rather the collective morality of the consequences of public debt. They are closely related to the distribution of economic resources and social justice. But public debt adds a very peculiar flavor to this well-known debate on "who gets what": they not only open questions of justice between social groups or classes, but also between the dead, the living, and "future generations." The articulation between economic justice and the relation to time might be one of the most striking features of the repertoire of political discourse on public debt as it emerged in the eighteenth century.

The Politics of the Past: Debts and Intertemporal Justice

Public debt might be the most salient political issue engaging political actors with the issue of time. As most debts were long-term (some even perpetual), the legitimacy and expediency of such an instrument necessarily engaged with the past and the future. Personal debts were part of the inheritance, and passed along in that fashion. But if the prince's debt was actually the nation's debt, did that still hold? Public debt thus became part of a larger discussion in the eighteenth century about the legitimacy of binding future generations.

The classical argument was maybe most forcefully put by Edmund Burke, in his rejoinder to the French Revolution: society is but "a partnership not only between those who are living, but between those who are living, those who are dead, and those who are to be born." But a new strand of thought had been chafing at this view for some time. Adam Smith found it "the most absurd of all suppositions, … that every successive generation has not an equal right to the earth, and to all that it possesses; but that the property of the present generation should be restrained and regulated according to the fancy of those who had died perhaps five hundred years ago." This contravened against what was then formulated as "the rights of men in society," which as Thomas Paine put it "are neither devisable, nor annihilable." And as "man has no property in man, neither has any generation a property in the generations that are to follow." The principle even appeared in the French revolutionary constitution of 1793: "A generation cannot bind future generations to its own laws," thus establishing the right to change legislation.[24]

This rising political view became particularly salient when discussing public debt. Would it not "be reasonable to fix some time, beyond which it should not be deemed right to bind posterity?" Joseph Priestley asked in response to Edmund Burke's pronouncements. "If our ancestors make a foolish *law*, we scruple not to repeal it; but if they make foolish *wars*, and incur foolish *debts*, we have, at present, no remedy whatever." This is precisely what Thomas Jefferson and James Madison wanted to prevent in the debates that so opposed them to Alexander Hamilton and the Federalists that it became the foundation of the first parties in the young United States. To a Hamilton eager to establish the credit of the new government by assuming the revolutionary debts and funding them, (debt-ridden) Jefferson would reply that "The principle of spending money to be paid by posterity under the name of funding is but swindling futurity on a large scale." For him, "the earth belongs in usufruct to the living; … the dead have neither powers nor rights over it." As Madison added, "each generation should be made to bear the burden of its own wars, instead of carrying them on, at the expence of other generations."[25]

It is striking that most of them were not talking about canceling past debt but devising the ways to prevent further borrowing. When later wars would be wars that endangered the nation itself, that vision of future generations would change too. After the US Civil War, for instance, many, like abolitionist senator Charles Sumner, found that "the generation that suppressed the rebellion" could not be expected "the added glory of removing this great burden" of debt: "the task was too extensive, and … it justly belonged to another generation."[26] This debate between loans and taxes, and the legitimacy of shifting war costs to future generations who would benefit from the human sacrifice of present generations, became a global one during the two world wars. There was a general consensus that the present costs of total war could not be met by taxes and that loans were required ("If this is a war to make democracy safe, this is certainly just that the coming decades which will enjoy the benefits of security should bear some part of the cost of preserving it," admitted Columbia economist Edwin Seligman), but several economists warned that future generations should not be overburdened with excessive indebtedness, lest the human costs of war should be worsened by economic devastation and hyperinflation.[27]

Of course, the same relationship of public debt to the political meaning of time could, and would, easily apply to past debts. It is significant that the French Revolution did not cancel past debts until very late—the first act of the national assembly was actually to confirm them.[28] Later revolutions, however, would view the public debts they inherited as part of the regime they overthrew. The repudiation of the Russian debt after 1917 might be the most famous example, but the question regularly came up in the twentieth century. The demise of Austro-Hungary and the Ottoman Empire after the First World War, for instance, opened debates about the territorial repartition of the debt, and the political legitimacy of such a debt for the newly established states of the region.[29]

But debts are more than financial obligations. They carry with them past memories and conflicts. Diplomatic disputes about debt repayments can last over several decades, as in the cases of the Haitian debt to France in the nineteenth century, the Russian bonds in the twentieth century, or the recent debates about German reparations and Greece's occupation during the Second World War. Public bonds, connecting different generations and contexts, can sustain and revive past grievances. The story of the Haitian debt offers a striking case. The Haitian Republic won its independence in 1804, but France recognized it only 21 years later, at the price of a steep indemnity, on the ground that former slave owners had to be compensated for their property loss. And for this, the Haitian state was forced to issue a loan in France. The country soon proved unable to pay its arrears, which opened a diplomatic dispute that lasted into the 1870s. In the complex and long story between France and its former colony, this issue of the 1825 indemnity and the debt it created has been a permanent subject of tension and resentment. In 2003, Haitian president Jean-Bertrand Aristide charged France for its past behavior and asked for the indemnity to be paid back, before being overthrown by a coup. Demands for reparations, which were again heard in 2010, show that financial debts are still the concrete vectors of larger representations.[30] As debts can last decades, the moral meaning attached to the reason they were contracted for is liable to change. And, with it, the very legitimacy of debt itself.[31]

Social Justice and Redistribution

The Haitian example shows debt is related both to time and to redistribution. Economically, public debts were conduits of financial transfers from taxpayers to bondholders. They were designed on the presumption that the bondholders needed to get back their capital with interest—that, indeed, it was their inducement for lending their money to begin with. (Of course, this assumption is crumbling in the era of negative interest rates, but this is too new a development to observe yet how it plays out historically.) Sometimes bondholders could get much more, if bonds were sold at a discount. Sometimes they got less, when inflation canceled the net gains. This redistributive effect did not always spark political debate, but when it did, it conveyed a competing sense of the legitimacy of such redistribution, and often also of the fairness of the amount of remuneration.

The political framing of such considerations mattered, as it defined the groups pitted against each other, and the legitimacy they might command in the political system. Especially when contracted in time of war, public debt could create competing images of sacrifice and profiteering that would either bolster or undermine the political legitimacy of creditors. In the nineteenth century emerged the image of the bondholder as the rich financier who did not fight the war, but insisted on profiting from it. In Europe, many radicals or socialists held the public debt as the enemy of the working class. Rich bondholders epitomized the power of elites, especially at a time when only a tiny portion of the population would have the right to vote and decide over budget issues.[32] Discourses about the value of thrift, advocated for by the liberal bourgeoisie, prompted fierce opposition. Members of the First International, convinced that public debts and permanent armies fueled nationalistic tensions and benefited only those who could invest in them, called for their abolition. Did not the Rothschilds make their immense fortune at incredible speed by lending to governments?[33] Later in the century, attacks against the *rentiers* and the *financiers* would also be tainted with antisemitism on the far left and right of the political spectrum.[34]

Against this discourse, a class-based counter-reading was sometimes offered. It was especially true when national wars started to be financed through public subscriptions. In the United States during the Civil War, holders of wartime public bonds were systematically presented as "the widow and the orphan," sometimes supplemented with the veteran. Public debt was sold to Americans as a form of popular savings, even linking it to the very survival of the families left behind by soldiers who died in the field. This was powerful rhetoric by those who wanted to defend public debt against cancellation or debasement (through monetary inflationary policies for instance)—whether this accurately reflected reality or not. Debates saw impassioned flights of oratory in defense of those widows and orphans, but also "the thrifty mechanic, farmer, retail dealer, washerwoman ... and so on" who sacrificed their savings to help prosecute the war.[35] In other political contexts, this trope would take different shapes, but its core of defending a public debt by legitimizing the recipients as the patriotic and deserving would prove irresistible in many places.

This wartime strategy was sometimes transferred to peacetime views of public debt. In late nineteenth-century France, the *rentier* became hailed as the paragon of republican stability, embodying the citizen literally investing in sovereign government. In the United States, the federal debt was defended during and after the Civil War as "a National Savings Bank for the earnings of laboring men and women." This line of argument did not win out, but was resurrected in another form during the First World War, that of the citizen-investor, whose financial judgement followed political profession.[36] Inflation and world wars mostly made such arguments irrelevant, however. Yet it is striking to see them resurrected in recent years by the massive transformation of old-age retirement welfare systems into market-investing pension funds. Suddenly, German pensioners had to be protected from any default of the Greek debt. Or Italian savers from manipulation by politicians, with central bankers at the rescue.[37]

These class-based readings, in their variations, were transferred to national readings of public debts when they were held internationally rather than domestically, especially in the twentieth century. Again, this resulted in the political framing of the debt reality, with variations depending on context, but it was a recurring trope, also involving a battle of legitimacy of the primary holders of the public debt, who had most to gain from interest payments and most to lose from cancellation or restructuration. In recent years, the perceived illegitimacy of claims by international debt-holders rested powerfully in the political images that channeled the anger of populations that were bearing the brunt of the economic situation. In Argentina, in the 2000s, the hedge funds that refused the restructuration of the debt and launched a legal assault against the country were soon called "vulture funds," wanting to make huge money out of the despair of the country where they had never invested in the first place—echoing debates in the 1790s United States where speculators had cheaply bought bonds from misinformed veterans and demanded payment in full from the brand new American government. If creditor's claims are unreasonable politically, then they become delegitimized and action against them becomes possible. Here it is a national framework that shapes the view of redistribution, of winners and losers, and of the fairness of the relationship.

Whether class-based or nation-based, however, this issue of redistribution through debt, especially as ever-harsher austerity policies are enacted across the world, has now moved again at the core of the scholarly debates on the current stage of capitalism, with sociologist Wolfgang Streeck now functionally distinguishing between two stakeholders of public policies: the *Staatsvolk* and the *Marktvolk*, with the latter viewed as systematically being catered to.[38]

Power and Sovereignty

Is public debt just another kind of debt, or is it something specific, something special precisely because it is public, and engages the sovereign, or if not at least the body politic? From the public nature of public debt emerged arguments either claiming the deeply political nature of this financial instrument, or on the other hand denying that any kind of special privilege, or treatment, should be applied to public debt compared to others. There would be fluctuations and cycles, of course, in the history of this particular register. Public debt is fundamentally linked to political power; and whether it should be tamed or unbound would time and again be at the heart of the debates each time public debt would be contested.

The Empire of Debt

Public debt is tightly connected to the issue of state sovereignty,[39] insofar as it was increasingly considered in the nineteenth century as a test for state claims to international recognition and belonging to the community of civilized nations. The inability to cope with public debt through taxes and state-building was a domestic problem for new states, but it was also directly connected to the issue of external interventions. European powers repeatedly used the issue to send military expeditions. The French expedition in Mexico in 1862 started as a joint effort with Britain and Spain to recoup debts. The "dollar diplomacy" inaugurated by the United States in the early twentieth century was partly triggered by a similar intervention threatened by the European powers in Venezuela. Tunisia, Egypt, the Ottoman Empire, Greece, China: all were imposed a form of Western-controlled institution to directly manage (part of) their fiscal system and directly pay their international creditors, effectively putting them under imperial tutelage.[40]

These interventions needed political legitimacy, however. Throughout the nineteenth century, Britain like France refused to let their justice system meddle with foreign public debts, stonewalling creditors' lawsuits in the name of the sovereignty of foreign states. Sending troops into another country was undeniably an act of aggression that could provoke either public opinion or rival powers. Responsible management of public debt, however, was during the same period constructed as the sign of a mature, civilized nation-state. The flip-side of such a discourse was that nation-states who could not manage their finances responsibly toward their international creditors needed to be disciplined. On the one hand, "delinquent" states would be characterized as uncivilized, or in a state of infancy—this was clear in the case of Latin American countries, for instance.[41] On the other, foreign intervention was couched in terms of universal rules, and gave rise to a framework of international law.

Law, in effect, is a discourse imbued with particular performative power. The many ad hoc solutions imposed on non-European powers who threatened default on their international debts in the late nineteenth century would become international law by the beginning of the twentieth, and soon integrated in international organizations.[42] In the 1920s, the League of Nations directly supervised what its experts perceived as a return to financial normalcy, notably in Central Europe in the first part of the decade. They were instrumental in organizing nine loans for fledgling European countries, giving birth to a few *causes célèbres* such as loans to Austria, Greece, and Bulgaria.[43] Economic and political strings attached to the loans were already the topic of much debate, as well as when the Portuguese government and its republican opposition in exile fought over a possible loan in 1927.[44]

The role of international institutions and foreign bondholders however was repeatedly met with growing anti-imperialist discourses and protests. Nothing exposed more the raw power play at the heart of public debt than the movements opposing the Western powers' interventions to defend privately held sovereign debt, starting with Arab nationalist movements in the 1880s, on to the Young Turks, Iranian constitutionalists and Chinese nationalists in the early twentieth century, who all saw the mechanisms of public debt as the main channel for foreign capital and interventionism. This overall hostility was not exclusive of some measure of interest in—or even admiration for—the foreign-controlled administrations of public debt as models of modernity and efficiency to be emulated. Moreover, local elites often grew involved in ambiguous schemes, using foreign capital while at the same time stoking nationalist feelings. That was the case in the Ottoman Empire, where Pan-Islamism could go hand in hand with massive import of foreign capital.[45]

Criticism of the imperialist and neo-colonialist overtones of debt relationships became a cornerstone of resistance movements in Asia, Latin America, and Africa in the second half of the twentieth century. The debt crisis of the 1980s gave considerable momentum to this discourse among African and Latin American leaders. Throughout the decade Fidel Castro regained great popularity on the continent when he railed against the "unpayable debt" of Latin American countries. The congress he organized in August 1985 in Havana was widely welcomed as a milestone in the fight against financial oppression.[46] The strongest attack on the debt order was made in July 1987 when Thomas Sankara, then president of Burkina Faso, called for a general cancellation of African debts: "We think that debt has to be seen from the standpoint of its origins. Debt's origins come from colonialism's origins. Those who lend us money are those who had colonized us before." He simply rejected the moral standards that sustained the debt order: "The rich and the poor don't share the same morals."[47]

This is partly to neutralize the potency of such discourse that the debt order has been moved steadily away from the arena of international institutions like the IMF toward a legal framework of the market, in ways similar to the turn from a dirigiste debt regime to a financialized one within countries.[48] Postcolonial international relations, however, put in a stark light the very old issue of properly defining the relation of sovereign debt to the world private economic transactions (the "market").

The Autonomy of the State Versus the Logic of the Market

The "public" in "public debt" may refer to several meanings. One relates to public affairs as opposed to private business, implying a reflection about the autonomy of the state and its capacity to control private funds for collective purposes. Another, closely related to democratic accountability of state institutions, talks of the "public" in terms of both committing the sovereign and legitimating its actions. Both debates are linked, although in non-simple ways.

Are public debts different from private debts? What kind of relations do they entertain? This is a classical debate in political economy, whose first steps can be traced back to the eighteenth century, when many authors started arguing about the usefulness of public indebtedness, and its peculiarity, while others would insist that "the economy of a state is precisely only that of a large family," as Voltaire put it.[49] There were two strands to this debate. One was political, and related to the relative strength of creditor and debtor to enforce the loan agreement. Sovereign debts were said to be different from other debts, because no enforcement could be imposed on a state, which had the power to repudiate its debts, imprison its creditors, and wipe off its pledges. That is why David Hume feared that heavy debts would lead to state tyranny; by repudiating their debts, states could ruin their creditors and arbitrarily expropriate private property. The examples coming from absolute monarchies such as Spain or France were taken as a warning.[50]

However, the eighteenth century was also the period when it became commonplace to assume that a state's power and reputation were linked to its ability to repay its debt and honor its commitments. The strength of the state was no longer conceived as deriving from its ability to punish creditors, but rather as its capacity to stick to its promises and build trust relationships with private investors. This conception became an international criterion over the nineteenth century.[51] Two types of states were thus identified: those complying with their duties, and those unable to honor their commitments. By the turn of the twentieth century, experts routinely distinguished between good, modern, and faithful states, on the one hand, and weak, fragile, and untrustworthy states, on the other. Those discourses did not go unchallenged, but were dominant before the First World War. They underpinned the sometimes-hysterical defense of public credit: "Public credit should be 'like Caesar's wife, above suspicion.'"[52]

The Bolshevik repudiation in 1918, then the 1931 general moratorium on debts, put an end to this clear divide and ushered a period during which it was conceivable to erase debts and impoverish bondholders for the sake of economic or political stability. In the age of total wars, interrupting the normal course of repayment would be acceptable, inasmuch as it served geopolitical aims and struggles. The fate of German foreign debts after 1945 is a good example of this, as Western powers agreed to a historical debt cancellation to avoid the repetition of interwar political failures and conflicts. The preamble of the 1953 London Treaty stated that it was necessary to "remove obstacles to normal economic relations between the Federal Republic of Germany and other countries and thereby to make a contribution to the development of a prosperous community of nations."[53] In this case, after the Second World War's millions of deaths and casualties, and at the onset of the Cold War, writing off past debts made sense to prepare for a brighter future: the lessons taken from the recent past had led to a dramatic shift in international financial policies, where debtor states could be absolved for the sake of growth and stability.[54]

This geopolitical transformation took place precisely at the moment when the Keynesian theory was asserting a clear distinction between public economics and the state, on the one hand, and microeconomics and household behavior on the other. This is the second strand of debates hashing out the distinction between public and private debt. The idea that the logic of the state was qualitatively different from that of private actors was reminiscent of earlier debates going back to the eighteenth century. Then, some started arguing that, while "the interest of a private debtor is simple and uncompounded; that of a state is so complex, that the debts they owe, *when due to citizens*, are, on the whole, rather advantageous than burdensome: they produce a new branch of circulation among individuals, but take nothing from the general patrimony." Here mercantilist thinking ("It is a contradiction to suppose that a nation can become bankrupt to itself") opposed the liberal views of an Adam Smith, a David Hume, or an Antoine Destutt de Tracy.[55]

The debate between economists had shifted by the twentieth century, but its deep political nature is still very much in evidence. Keynes's idea that debts and deficits could be useful when used for counter-cycle purposes, was ominous to anti-Keynesians. James Buchanan and other public choice economists condemned this way of thinking, which they considered to be a dangerous fallacy. In his 1958 *Public Principles of Public Debt*, Buchanan launched a first attack toward what he branded the "new orthodoxy," arguing that he had come "to realize that the analogy between the public economy and the private economy is applicable to most of the problems of the public debt."[56] This intellectual offensive led to what is sometimes called the "neoliberal turn." Shifting intellectual positions on the nature of the state and its role in the economy contributed to a turn in financial policy in the 1970s and 1980s, when states moved again to the financial markets to raise money.[57] In one generation, the "orthodoxy" flipped from the theory of productive deficit to that of expansionary austerity, as famously expounded by economists Alberto Alesina and Silvia Ardagna in the late 1990s: "The next decade has to witness a strong reversal of the growth of government into a shrinking of government."[58]

Languages of Expertise and the (De)Politicization of Debts

Such discourse was a direct challenge to the very legitimacy of democratic accountability of public debt. In that sense, it is inscribed in a long tradition of denying that public debt should be the object of political contention. As we saw, in the nineteenth century, the moral discourse of obligation and honor was most likely to be the vehicle of such a view. By the end of the century, however, another discourse had emerged, one that is very present today: it asserts that public debt is a matter of technical management better left to experts and out of the hands of fickle, populist politicians. They are directly connected to a general attempt at depoliticization spreading to the entire economic sphere, which should be preserved from "irrational" democratic intervention.

The Discourse of Neutral Expertise

What has sometimes been called a "new constitutionalism" by critical thinkers does indeed rely upon the establishment of ideological and constitutional barriers to political action on public debt.[59] Recent German initiatives to set up constitutional constraints to public indebtedness through the so-called "debt brake" and measures adopted in the framework of the European Union to limit the margin of national governments have given birth to critical discourse about the "authoritarian constitutionalism" inherent to the new regime of public debt.[60] This way to constrain public action thus relies ideologically upon the idea of an efficient market, but uses the very attributes of state sovereignty to stripe political actors of key competences.

Beyond constitutional mechanisms and theoretical justifications, this depoliticization also draws upon configurations that allocate power and accountability across different categories. Public debt management has been through time shared among a great variety of actors. Elected officials and even public servants active in state institutions seem to have lost ground vis-à-vis other actors, notably central bankers in recent years. The emancipation of central banks from state tutelage completed through the 1990s in many countries was frequently justified by the necessity to carve out a distinct field of action for their technical know-how and expertise.

These institutional arrangements give powerful force to the political claim that public debt, once contracted, is beyond the realm of politics and a matter of technical management. Yet the stance itself goes back to, at least, the end of the nineteenth century, when some economists started seeing the economy as subject to universal, impersonal laws that simply need to be uncovered and then applied. Coupled with professionalization, it fed the rise of the expert, who took pains to present himself as "neutral" and "objective." This was often a very conscious stance, especially in case of international credit relations. The Americans who became international financial advisors in the first decades of the twentieth century, and conducted missions of reorganization of public finances in many Latin American countries, but also post-1918 European countries like Germany or Poland, all endeavored to present themselves as professional experts acting objectively, free of political interests—a stance belied by their previous careers as colonial administrators, or the fact that their work was mostly imposed as part of bank loan contracts, or even US intervention.[61] This thread of expertise runs throughout the twentieth century, although the actual policies implemented could vary significantly.

A wide array of metaphors has been used to construct this professional expertise and, by contrast, the inability of the layperson to properly understand, much less influence, decisions about public debt. Indebtedness has thus been compared to a drug addiction,[62] an illness requiring "doctors" to provide with cures and medicines. The concept was popularized in the 1920s as Edwin Kemmerer, then a leading economic expert, was widely known abroad as a "famed money doctor." Arthur Millspaugh, financial advisor to Persia in the 1920s, was greeted by a Persian newspaper in the following manner: "You are a physician called to the bedside of a very sick person. If you succeed, the patient will live. If you fail, the patient will die."[63] Those were self-serving metaphors, of course: those of the professionals armed with arcane knowledge who need to be trusted in what only they can do—manage public finance.

Opacity and Visibility

The tension between specialized understanding of the topic and the demands for transparency and public accountability has a long history. Already in the early eighteenth century, Daniel Defoe pointed to the immaterial nature of "public credit," which was essential for the nation's economy but could hardly be felt or touched upon:

> I am to speak of what all people are busie, about, but not one in Forty understands: every man has a concern in it, few know what it is, nor is it easy to define or describe it … *Like the Soul* in the Body, it acts all substance, yet is it self immaterial; it gives motion, yet it self cannot be said to exist; it creates *forms*, yet has it self *no form*; it is neither *quantity* or *quality*, it has no *whereness*, or *whenness*, *scite*, or *habit*. If I should say it is the essential shadow of something that is not… To come at a direct and clear understanding of the thing, the best method will be to describe its *operations*, rather than define its *nature*; to show *how it acts* rather than *how it exists*, and *what it does*, rather than *what it is*.[64]

Defoe here pleaded for what could be called today a "pragmatic" approach to public credit. The only possibility to grasp this abstract and shadowy notion was to look at the various techniques, instruments, and practices it gave birth to. Hence the politicization of public debt needs concrete characters and artefacts to be effective. The French revolutionaries created in 1793 the "Great Ledger of the Public Debt" so that all the bondholders of the nation would have their names in a single solemn register. Their purpose was political: this register embodied the Republic's commitment to honor all past and present debts ("by creating this Ledger, you will demonstrate that the Republic, willing to honor the debts contracted by despotism, will recognize them as republican debts"[65]).

The difficulty to make sense of public debt's logic and mechanisms explains why, for such a long time, bankers, financiers, and experts have been criticized for doing their business without consulting the people, or with a view to deceiving the people. The day-to-day management of public debt can hardly be reconciled with the pace of electoral politics, except for debates about the level of public indebtedness or potential repudiation. Financial cycles, economic cycles, and political cycles do not coincide, which may entail deep contradictions. The resort to "financial plebiscites," especially in times of war, was supposed to fill this void, creating a popular consultation that was at the same time political and financial.

However, their results cannot be easily interpreted. In the case of the French Second Empire, newly invented public subscriptions were conceived as a tool for measuring public opinion. Similarly, modern bond auctions have been said to reveal the feeling of investors and produce judgments, about the soundness of a country's finances and reforms—hence the endless reporting about how "markets react" to specific political events and policies.

Current trends of depoliticization of public debt seem to overlap traditional distinctions between political regimes. In a sense, they purport to pursue a democratic commitment to the publicity of public debt, but they simultaneously frame the political debate in the narrow field of acceptable measures. They create a new form of opacity toward populations, while at the same time praising total transparency toward lenders, a fact that has given birth to discussion about a contradiction between citizens and markets as rival constituencies for politicians.[66] Ironically, the discussion of diverging levels of accountability between domestic citizens and markets was at the core of the debt crisis of the 1980s in developing and communist countries. In Poland, the debt crisis that engulfed the country in 1980–1981 elicited criticism of secrecy about the debt in the preceding decades. Politicians and former experts for the Party spoke out condemning the fact that debt figures "became a state secret only for their own population."[67] Debt management was perceived in these years of crisis to reveal the true nature of a state that avoided accountability on key issues.

* * *

Viewing political arguments around public debts as a repertoire helps make sense of how they could circulate, be repeated, and be reconfigured with other arguments in different contexts. Words taken from the past had the power of long-accepted truths, even if specific contexts gave them very different meanings. It also helps historicize arguments and their evolutions even when, at first glance, they sometimes look as if they went unchanged. It thus denaturalizes political arguments, and makes it possible to take them seriously and understand them in their specific contexts at the same time.

The circulation and reconfigurations of discourse meant that public debts are all part of a common historical framework not because they are always the same "thing," but because understanding them as public debts meant that historical actors mobilized concepts and arguments from a common toolbox. Public debts, however, should not be confused with, or reduced to, this political repertoire, which is rather a tool to make sense of discourse while de-essentializing public debts and historicizing its politics. In other words, it resists the recent "economicization" of the debates, against the idea of the "economy" as a separate sphere to be neutrally managed by disinterested experts. It might even give keys to revive and strengthen the politics of public debts in the future.

Acknowledgment Our thanks to Étienne Forestier-Peyrat, who contributed to earlier drafts of this chapter.

Notes

1. On the tropes on the Greek state, see Nicolas Delalande, "The Greek State: Its Past and Future. An Interview with Anastassios Anastassiadis," *Books and Ideas*, 20 March 2012, http://www.booksandideas.net/The-Greek-State-Its-Past-and.html
2. Chapter 7 on Egypt and Chap. 9 on China illustrate this.
3. Friedrich Nietzsche, *Zur Genealogie der Moral. Eine Streitschrift* (Leipzig: C.G. Naumann, 1892), 48–50.
4. Quote in Clare Haru Crowston, *Credit, Fashion, Sex. Economies of Regard in Old Regime France* (Durham: Duke University Press, 2013), 4. See also Laurence Fontaine, *L'économie morale. Pauvreté, crédit et confiance dans l'Europe préindustrielle* (Paris: Gallimard, 2008); Antoine Lilti, "Le pouvoir du crédit au XVIIIe siècle. Histoire intellectuelle et sciences sociales," *Annales. Histoire, Sciences Sociales* 70, no. 4 (2015): 957–78.
5. Michael Tomz, *Reputation and International Cooperation: Sovereign Debt Across Three Centuries* (Princeton: Princeton University Press, 2007). For a critique, see Odette Lienau, *Rethinking Sovereign Debt: Politics, Reputation, and Legitimacy in Modern Finance* (Cambridge, Mass.: Harvard University Press, 2014).
6. Evelyn Baring (Earl of Cromer), *Modern Egypt* (London: Macmillan, 1911), 420, 4.
7. French Diplomatic Archives, 90CCC/103, Constantinople, 12 July 1876.
8. French Diplomatic Documents, *Arrangement financier avec la Grèce. Travaux de la commission internationale chargée de la préparation du projet* (Paris: Imprimerie nationale, 1898). On the ambivalent perceptions of the Balkans, see Maria Todorova's classic study, *Imagining the Balkans* (Oxford: Oxford University Press, 1997).
9. Chapters 6 and 7 in this volume, on the Ottoman Empire and Egypt respectively, are particularly illuminating on this point.

10. See Chap. 5 of this volume.
11. Steven C. Topik, "When Mexico Had the Blues: A Transatlantic Tale of Bonds, Bankers, and Nationalists, 1862–1910," *American Historical Review* 105, no. 3 (2000): 714–38; Pablo Piccato, *The Tyranny of Opinion: Honor in the Construction of the Mexican Public Sphere* (Durham: Duke University Press, 2010), quote 126.
12. The study by Russian legal scholar Alexander Sack, *Les effets des transformations des États sur leurs dettes publiques et autres obligations financières* (Paris, 1927), often presented as the basis for the "odious debt" doctrine in the interwar period, is actually devoid of any moral discourse. Its focus is on the legal, financial, and territorial implications of regime change and state collapse after the First World War.
13. David L. Gregory, "From Pope John Paul II to Bono/U2: International Debt Relief Initiatives 'in the Name of Love,'" *Boston University International Law Review* 19 (2001): 257–71.
14. Picatto, *The Tyranny of Opinion*, 126.
15. Patricia Clavin, *Securing the World Economy: The Reinvention of the League of Nations, 1920–1946* (Oxford: Oxford University Press, 2013).
16. See Chap. 18 of this volume.
17. Adam Smith, *An Inquiry Into the Nature and Causes of the Wealth of Nations* (London: W. Strahan, 1776): bk 5, ch. 3; James Madison, "Political Observations, 20 April 1795," *The Papers of James Madison*, ed. Thomas A. Mason, Robert A. Rutland, and Jeanne K. Sisson (Charlottesville: University Press of Virginia, 1985): 15:511–34.
18. On the French case, see Chaps. 4 and 11 in this volume.
19. See Chaps. 12 and 13 on Germany and the USSR in this volume.
20. Alexander Watson, *Ring of Steel: Germany and Austria-Hungary in World War One. The People's War*, (London: Basic Books, 2014); Kristy Ironside, "Rubles for Victory: The Social Dynamics of State Fundraising on the Soviet Home Front," *Kritika: Explorations in Russian and Eurasian History* 15, no. 4 (2014): 799–828; James T. Sparrow, *Warfare State: World War II Americans and the Age of Big Government* (Oxford: Oxford University Press, 2011); Sheldon Garon, *Beyond Our Means: Why America Spends While the World Saves* (Princeton: Princeton University Press, 2011).
21. *Fenn's Compendium of the English and Foreign Funds* (London, 1874), vi.
22. On the discourse of French economists, see Chap. 4 of this volume. On public demand in the United States and France, see Chap. 10. On the shift from negative to positive views in Germany, see Carl-Ludwig Holtfrerich, "Government Debt in Economic Thought of the Long 19th Century," Freie Universität Berlin, School of Business & Economics Discussion Paper No. 2013/4, 2013, https://ssrn.com/abstract=2255977

23. Some think-tanks have taken up to advise borrowing to invest in infrastructure, to insure future growth. See, inter alia, Elizabeth C. McNichol, "It's Time for States to Invest in Infrastructure," Center on Budget and Policy Priorities report (March 19, 2019), https://www.cbpp.org/research/state-budget-and-tax/its-time-for-states-to-invest-in-infrastructure
24. Herbert E. Sloan, *Principle and Interest: Thomas Jefferson and the Problem of Debt* (Oxford: Oxford University Press, 1995), ch. 2 (including all quotes).
25. Ibid.
26. Quoted in Nicolas Barreyre, *Gold and Freedom: The Political Economy of Reconstruction*, trans. Arthur Goldhammer (Charlottesville: University of Virginia Press, 2015): 59.
27. Edwin Seligman, "Loans vs Taxes in War Finance," *Annals of the American Academy of Political and Social Science* 75 (1918): 69–70. Chapter 11 of this volume deals with this issue for the First World War.
28. Rebecca Spang, *Stuff and Money in the Time of the French Revolution* (Cambridge, Mass.: Harvard University Press, 2015). Also, Chap. 2 of this volume.
29. Sack, *Les effets des transformations des États*; Patrick Dumberry, "Is Turkey the 'Continuing State' of the Ottoman Empire under International Law?" *Netherlands International Law Review* LIX (2002), 258–61; Lyndon Moore and Jakub Kaluzny, "Regime Change and Debt Default: The Case of Russia, Austro-Hungary, and the Ottoman Empire Following World War One," *Explorations in Economic History* 42, no. 2 (2005): 237–58; Kim Oosterlinck, *Hope Springs Eternal: French Bondholders and the Repudiation of Russian Sovereign Debt* (New Haven: Yale University Press, 2016).
30. François Blancpain, *Un siècle de relations financières entre Haïti et la France (1825–1922)* (Paris: L'Harmattan, 2001); Laurent Dubois, *Haiti: The Aftershocks of History* (New York: Henry Hold & Co, 2012). More generally, on the politics of reparations and economic issues, see John Torpey, *Making Whole What Has Been Smashed: On Reparations Politics* (Cambridge, Mass.: Harvard University Press, 2006).
31. Witness the communication blunder of the British Treasury, as it celebrated the debt contracted to abolish slavery being paid off in 2018, while forgetting that it was used to pay slaveowners for "lost property," with former slaves receiving no compensation whatsoever: David Olusoga, "The Treasury's Tweet Shows Slavery Is Still Misunderstood," *The Guardian* (12 February 2018).
32. Philip Harling, *The Waning of "Old Corruption": The Politics of Economical Reform in Britain, 1779–1846* (Oxford: Clarendon Press, 1996).

33. Niall Ferguson, *The World's Banker: The History of the House of Rothschild* (London: Weidenfeld & Nicolson, 1998): 148–73; Nicolas Delalande, *La Lutte et l'entraide. L'âge des solidarités ouvrières* (Paris: Seuil, 2019).
34. See for instance Auguste Chirac, *La Haute Banque et les Révolutions* (Paris: Amyot, 1876).
35. Quote in Barreyre, *Gold and Freedom*, 57. On the Civil War debt, see also Nicolas Barreyre, "Les avatars politiques de la dette américaine: la crise de la sécession et les transformations de l'État fédéral (1861–1913)," in *Les crises de la dette publique, XVIIIe-XXIe siècle*, eds. Gérard Béaur and Laure Quennouëlle-Corre (Paris: IGPDE, 2019), 475–93.
36. Samuel Wilkeson, *How Our National Debt May Be a National Blessing. The Debt Is Public Wealth, Political Union, Protection of Industry, Secure Basis for National Currency, the Orphans' and Widows' Savings Fund* (Philadelphia: M'Laughlin Brothers, printers, 1865): 9; Julia C. Ott, *When Wall Street Met Main Street: The Quest for an Investors' Democracy* (Cambridge, Mass.: Harvard University Press, 2011).
37. On this last example, see Chap. 16 in this volume.
38. Wolfgang Streeck, *Buying Time: The Delayed Crisis of Democratic Capitalism*, trans. Patrick Camiller and David Fernbach, 2nd ed. (London: Verso, 2017). On the importance of redistribution as an economic issue, see Thomas Piketty, *Capital in the Twenty-First Century*, trans. Arthur Goldhammer (Cambridge, Mass.: Harvard University Press, 2014).
39. Keith Dyson, *States, Debts, and Power: "Saints" and "Sinners" in European History and Integration* (Oxford: Oxford University Press, 2014).
40. Richard S. Horowitz, "International Law and State Transformation in China, Siam, and the Ottoman Empire during the Nineteenth Century," *Journal of World History* 15, no. 4 (2004): 472–4. See Chaps. 5, 6, 7, and 8 of this volume.
41. Carlos Marichal, *A Century of Debt Crisis in Latin America: From Independence to the Great Depression, 1820–1930* (Princeton: Princeton University Press, 1989); Emily S. Rosenberg, *Financial Missionaries to the World: The Politics and Culture of Dollar Diplomacy, 1900–1930* (Cambridge, Mass.: Harvard University Press, 1999).
42. Antony Anghie, *Imperialism, Sovereignty and the Making of International Law* (Cambridge: Cambridge University Press, 2007).
43. Juan Flores and Yann Decorzant, "Going multilateral? Financial Markets' Access and the League of Nations Loans, 1923–1928," *Economic History Review* 69, no. 2 (2016): 653–78; Susan Pedersen, *The Guardians: The League of Nations and the Crisis of Empire* (Oxford: Oxford University Press, 2015).

44. António Henrique R. de Oliveira Marques, *A Liga de Paris e a Ditadura Militar, 1927–1928: A questão do empréstimo externo* (Lisbon: Publicações Europa-América, 1976).
45. Murat Birdal, *The Political Economy of Ottoman Public Debt. Insolvency and European Financial Control in the Late Nineteenth Century* (London: I.B. Tauris, 2010), 7; Annette Destrée, *Les fonctionnaires belges au service de la Perse, 1898–1915* (Leyden: E.J. Brill, 1976).
46. Fidel Castro, *Encuentro sobre la deuda externa de América Latina y el Caribe. Discurso, 3 de agosto de 1985*, (Havana: Editora Política, 1985). Several newspapers featured the speeches made at the conference: see *Momento Económico*, no. 17–18 (1985): http://ru.iiec.unam.mx/view/year/1985.html
47. *Thomas Sankara Speaks. The Burkina Faso Revolution, 1983–87* (New York: Pathfinder Press, 2017), 373–81.
48. See Chaps. 15, 16, and 17 in this volume.
49. Voltaire, "Économie," *Questions sur l'Encyclopédie* ([Geneva], 1771–1772), 5:58.
50. On this topic, see Istvan Hont, *Jealousy of Trade: International Competition and the Nation-State in Historical Perspective* (Cambridge, Mass.: Harvard University Press, 2006); Michael Sonenscher, *Before the Deluge: Public Debt, Inequality, and the Intellectual Origins of the French Revolution* (Princeton: Princeton University Press, 2007).
51. Michael Tomz, *Reputation and International Cooperation*.
52. Quote from a speech in the US Senate, but it was a widespread cliché. Barreyre, *Gold and Freedom*, 55.
53. *Agreements on German External Debts*, London (February 23, 1953), 1, https://www.gov.uk/government/uploads/system/uploads/attachment_data/file/269824/German_Ext_Debts_Pt_1.pdf
54. Odette Lienau, *Rethinking Sovereign Debt*.
55. James Steuart, *An Inquiry into the Principles of Political Oeconomy: Being an Essay on the Science of Domestic Policy in Free Nations* (Dublin, 1770), 3:409, 419.
56. James Buchanan, *Public Principles of Public Debt: A Defense and Restatement* (Homewood, Ill.: Irwin, 1958), viii.
57. See Chaps. 15, 16, and 18 of this volume.
58. Alberto Alesina and Silvia Ardagna, "Tales of Fiscal Adjustment," *Economic Policy* 13, no. 27 (1998): 488–545. For the long-term intellectual history of austerity, see Mark Blyth, *Austerity: The History of a Dangerous Idea* (Oxford: Oxford University Press, 2013); Florian Schui, *Austerity: The Great Failure* (New Haven: Yale University Press, 2014); Philipp Ther, *Die Neue Ordnung auf dem alten Kontinent* (Berlin: Suhrkamp Verlag, 2014). On neoliberalism in the United States, Daniel Stedman Jones, *Masters of*

the Universe: Hayek, Friedman, and the Birth of Neoliberal Politics (Princeton: Princeton University Press, 2012); Angus Burgin, *The Great Persuasion: Reinventing Free Markets since the Great Depression* (Cambridge, Mass.: Harvard University Press, 2012). On neoliberalism in France, François Denord, *Néo-libéralisme version française. Histoire d'une idéologie politique* (Paris: Demopolis, 2007); Philippe Bezès, *Réinventer l'État. Les réformes de l'administration française (1962–2008)* (Paris: Presses Universitaires de France, 2015). For a take from the perspective of international organizations, Quinn Slobodian, *Globalists: The End of Empire and the Birth of Neoliberalism* (Cambridge, Mass.: Harvard University Press, 2018).

59. Stephen Gill, *Power and Resistance in the New World Order* (Basingstoke: Palgrave Macmillan, 2002).
60. Lukas Oberndorfer, "Vom neuen, über den autoritären, zum progressiven Konstitutionalismus? Pakt(e) für Wettbewerbsfähigkeit und die europäische Demokratie," *Juridikum. Zeitschrift für Kritik, Recht, Gesellschaft*, no. 1 (2013): 76–86.
61. Rosenberg, *Financial Missionaries to the World*, 187–98.
62. For a recent example, see http://www.telegraph.co.uk/finance/economics/11458161/From-bust-to-boom-How-the-world-became-addicted-to-debt.html. For an in-depth analysis of this language of addiction and dependence, which equates debt with intoxication, see Benjamin Lemoine, *L'ordre de la dette. Enquête sur les infortunes de l'État et la prospérité des marchés* (Paris: La Découverte, 2016).
63. Quoted in Ann Laura Stoler, *Haunted by Empire: Geographies of Intimacy in North American History*, (Durham: Duke University Press, 2006), 409–10.
64. Daniel Defoe, *An Essay upon Publick Credit* (London: 1710), 6.
65. Joseph Cambon and Convention nationale, *Rapport sur la dette publique* (August 15, 1793), reproduced in A. Vührer, *Histoire de la dette publique en France* (Paris: Berger-Levrault, 1886), I:454. In this volume, see Chap. 2.
66. See Wolfgang Streck's distinction between *Staatsvolk* and *Marktvolk*. For a lexical analysis of public discourse, Sandy Brian Hager, "Corporate Ownership of the Public Debt: Mapping the New Aristocracy of Finance," *Socio-Economic Review* 13, no. 3 (2015): 505–23.
67. Stefan Jędrychowski, *Zadłuěenie Polski w krajach kapitalystycznych* (Varsovie: Księčka i Wiedza, 1982), 5. See also Chap. 13 of this volume.

Correction to: A World of Public Debts

Correction to:
N. Barreyre, N. Delalande (eds.), *A World of Public Debts*,
Palgrave Studies in the History of Finance,
https://doi.org/10.1007/978-3-030-48794-2

Chapters 13 and 19 were mistakenly published non-open access. They have now been changed to open access under a CC BY 4.0 license and the copyright holder has been updated to "The Author(s)." The book has also been updated with this change.

The updated version of these chapters can be found at
https://doi.org/10.1007/978-3-030-48794-2_13
https://doi.org/10.1007/978-3-030-48794-2_19

© The Author(s) 2020
N. Barreyre, N. Delalande (eds.), *A World of Public Debts*, Palgrave Studies in the History of Finance,
https://doi.org/10.1057/978-3-030-48794-2_21

Index[1]

A

Accountability, 40, 42, 44, 148, 215, 216, 218, 247, 335, 349, 367, 372, 455, 498, 527, 530, 532, 533
Accounting, 20, 108, 156, 160, 161, 164, 165, 173n50, 176, 215, 226n27, 332, 335, 364, 481–503
Adams, Henry C., 265
Addis, Charles, 273
Aetna Life Insurance Company, 240
Afghanistan, 333
Africa, 103n51, 176, 177, 179–182, 194, 527
Agency for Public Management (*Statskontoret*, Sweden), 63, 64
Agrarian reform, 363
Alawites, 352, 355, 356, 368n21
Albania, 324
Aleppo, 352
Alesina, Alberto, 530, 538n58
Alexandria, 157
Algeria, 80, 88, 278
Amat y Junyent, Manuel, 29
Amato, Giuliano, 412
American Society for the Colonization of Free People of Color (ACS), 184
Amiens, 89, 94
Amortization, 170n11, 215, 297, 409, 496, 501
Amsden, Alice, 377
Amsterdam, 58, 64–66, 68, 70, 500
Andreatta, Beniamino, 406, 414
Andrei, Ștefan, 333
Antwerp, 58, 62, 68, 70, 75n22
Apponyi, Count Rudolph, 80
Aramco oil company, 362
Ardagna, Silvia, 530, 538n58
Argentina, 113, 115–118, 372, 386, 435, 439, 449n16, 455, 461, 473, 509n62, 524

---

[1] Note: Page numbers followed by 'n' refer to notes.

© The Author(s) 2020
N. Barreyre, N. Delalande (eds.), *A World of Public Debts*, Palgrave Studies in the History of Finance,
https://doi.org/10.1007/978-3-030-48794-2

Aristide, Jean-Bertrand, 522
Asante, 182, 184
Ashanti Goldfield Corporation, 187
Asia, 23, 175, 274, 322, 331, 440, 527
Assembly of Notables (France), 42
Asset-backed security (ABS), 468
Assignats, 47–51, 69, 84, 101n23
Atkins, Richard, 155, 170n16
Austerity, 166, 212, 259, 288, 297, 318, 335, 380, 457, 461, 462, 464, 468, 473, 518, 519, 525, 530, 538n58
Austria, 63, 65, 80, 89, 103n52, 140, 145, 262, 263, 271, 272, 431, 526
Authoritarianism, 264, 267, 305, 519
Ayubi, Nazih, 349, 362
al-'Azm, Khālid, 362

B

Baath Party, 365
Babeuf, François-Noël (Gracchus), 43
Baffi, Paolo, 405, 411, 413
Bailout, 118, 372, 431
Baker, Jim, 439
Baker Plan (1985), 438
Bankers, 10, 24, 39, 41, 68, 71, 83, 84, 92, 115, 118, 138–142, 152n16, 158, 160, 167, 171n29, 188, 209, 219, 221, 229n59, 232, 242, 244, 266, 271, 273, 274, 288, 298, 300, 304, 310n34, 330, 331, 380, 388, 390, 391, 407, 413, 429, 436, 437, 440, 453–473, 516, 524, 531
Bank for International Settlements (BIS), 298–300, 303, 313n61, 325, 340n43, 490, 494, 504n9
Bank of British West Africa, 188
Bank of England, 38, 118, 266, 268, 269, 283n27, 299, 413, 463, 464, 470
Bank of France, 90, 104n57, 269, 270, 274, 284n48, 381, 384, 498
Bank of Italy, 406, 408, 410, 411, 413–415, 420, 465
Bank of Japan, 463, 472
Bank of Sweden, 60, 63, 65, 66, 69, 72
Bankruptcy, 24, 25, 41, 43, 51, 79, 84, 86, 147, 157, 169, 206, 290, 293, 428, 429, 432, 441, 444, 451n33, 460, 466, 529
Banks, 240, 262, 266, 292, 295, 297, 301, 330, 331
  commercial banks, 263, 266, 269, 271, 304, 379, 381–383, 389, 408, 412, 435, 436
  nationalized banks, 382, 386, 396
  private banks, 7, 8, 81, 297, 415, 420, 437
  savings banks, 187, 240, 255n20, 262, 266, 292, 295, 297, 301, 330, 331, 524
Banque de Constantinople, 139
Banqueroute des Deux Tiers (1797), 51
Baravelli, M., 161
Barbados, 275
Baring, Evelyn (lord Cromer), 161, 165, 516
Baring Brothers, 83, 121, 122, 221, 360
Baring Crisis (1890), 7, 118
Bark, Nils, 63, 64, 75n26, 76n27
Barker, Alfred, 139, 152n16
Baronnet, E., 245, 246, 256n34
Basel Committee on Banking Supervision, 406
Beijing, 203–205, 207, 210–212
Beirut, 359
Belgium, 89, 103n51, 115, 145, 499
Benchmarking, 488–491, 495, 498–502

Bérégovoy, Pierre, 394
Berlin, 138, 142, 150, 299, 300
Berlusconi, Silvio, 465
Bernadotte, Jean-Baptiste, 2, 59, 71
Bernanke, Ben, 456, 467, 468, 470, 471
Beust, Friedrich Ferdinand von, 80
Biens nationaux, 47–49
Biqdī, Sadr, 354
Blackett, Basil, 270
BlackRock, 458
Blignères, Ernest de, 161, 164, 165
Blinder, Alan, 457
Bloch, Marc, 7
Bloch-Lainé, François, 385, 387
Bloomberg, 456
Board of Revenue (China), 207
Bocconi University, 406
Bolivia, 20, 116, 170n17, 196n21
Bolshevik Repudiation (1918), 260, 280, 528
Bonaparte, Napoleon, 51
Bonar Law, Andrew, 264
Bondholders, 111–121, 123–125, 127, 127n1, 135, 136, 138–141, 144–146, 149, 150, 152n11, 170n18, 180, 190, 265, 266, 270, 278, 280, 288, 29, 300, 329, 331, 430, 445, 459, 523, 526, 528, 532, 57, 70, 71, 96
Bonds, 85, 266, 331, 397, 412, 419
  bond drive, 270, 289, 292, 296
  bond market, 6, 8, 201, 239–241, 248, 386, 394, 396, 397, 410–412, 414, 415, 420, 454–461, 463–469, 471–473
  government bonds, 63, 72, 114, 146, 208, 292, 300, 383, 396, 397, 409–412, 414–416, 419, 459, 468
Bond vigilantes, 372, 453–473, 496
Bono (singer), 517
Bordeaux, 89, 236, 238

Boston, 240, 249, 250, 406
Bourgeois, 38, 317
Bourges, 236, 238
Bouvier, Jean, 155, 169n3, 170n16
Boxer Rebellion (1900), 209, 216, 223
Boxer Indemnities, 209
Brady Plan (1989), 439, 440, 446
Brazil, 6, 31n4, 116, 118, 147, 435, 439
Bretton Woods (1944), 260, 322, 327, 328, 379, 392, 406, 408, 413, 430, 432, 436, 453, 460, 472, 488–491
Breuer, Rolf, 455, 456
Brezhnev, Leonid, 327
Britain, 1, 9, 11, 20, 38, 39, 42, 51n5, 53n20, 53n24, 58, 71, 80, 81, 84–86, 88, 89, 91, 100n14, 108, 113, 114, 116, 117, 120–123, 125, 131n47, 140, 157, 167, 172n40, 173n50, 177, 190, 191, 219, 222, 228n52, 259, 261–280, 291, 300, 303, 322, 349, 350, 352, 358, 369n47, 375, 413, 446, 453, 454, 457, 464, 485, 493, 509n61, 525, 526
Brüning, Heinrich, 288, 297, 313n58
Buchanan, James, 529
Budget
  expenditures, 165, 364, 488
  revenue, 165
Buenos Aires, 115, 130n20
Bulgaria, 141, 151n2, 325, 327, 330, 336, 526
Burbank, Jane, 176, 188
Bureaucracy, 38, 160, 164, 202, 300, 301, 373, 437, 440
Burke, Edmund, 37, 51n1, 520, 521
Burma, 165, 277
Burns, Kathryn, 24, 25, 34n37
Bursa, 142
Byrnes, George, 321

C

Cairo, 158–160, 162, 167
Caisse de la Dette Publique (Caisse, Egypt), 126, 127, 158, 159, 161, 164, 165, 168
Caisse des Dépôts (France), 498
Calonne, Charles Alexandre de, 41, 42, 45, 46
Campion, Henry, 488
Canada, 193, 240, 284n56, 399n3
Canton, 203, 204, 225n19
Cape Colony, 175, 193
Capital
  capital controls, 377, 379, 392, 455
  capital flows, 167, 221, 303–305, 386, 392, 440
  capital market, 6, 13, 61, 66, 81, 121, 126, 131n31, 157, 175, 189, 290, 291, 295, 297, 298, 301, 302, 305, 374, 392–399, 407, 418, 428, 429, 432, 435–440, 453, 455, 459–461, 463, 469, 472, 490, 496
  capital mobility, 420, 454, 455, 460
Capitalism, 375
  gentlemanly capitalism, 156, 224n1, 277
  varieties of capitalism, 375
Cardew, Frederic, 190
Carli, Guido, 411, 413, 414
Carville, James, 455
Casablanca, Comte de, 90
Casa di San Giorgio, 64
Cassel, Gustav, 294
Castro, Fidel, 334, 335, 527
Cave, Stephen, 157, 158
Ceaușescu, Nicolae, 333, 335, 336
Censo (Spanish Empire), 25, 26, 28
Census Bureau (US), 249
Central America, 112, 114, 116, 118, 126
Central and Eastern Europe, 322, 332, 336

Central bankers, 330, 390, 391, 407, 413, 453–473, 524, 531
Central banks, 152n5, 262, 273, 280, 282n25, 297, 298, 301, 302, 327, 371, 389–391, 393, 395, 397, 406–408, 410, 413–416, 423n25, 432, 435, 440, 462–468, 471, 472, 497, 498, 509n61, 531
Ceylon, 275
Chambers of commerce, 229n58
Changlu Salt Mines, 214
Chernyaev, Anatoly, 327
Chevalier, Michel, 87, 88, 91, 92, 94
Chicago, 244, 249
Chicherin, Georgy, 319, 320
Chile, 15, 20, 116, 125, 147, 431
China, 88, 108, 112, 201–224, 232, 274, 318, 322, 329, 331, 447, 468, 469, 496, 509n65, 526
Christian Democratic Party (Italy), 406
Church
  convents, 24, 25
  monasteries, 23–31, 48
Churchill, Winston, 397
Ciampi, Carlo Azeglio, 414
Circuit, 380–382, 384, 385, 396
  circuitist view, 496–498, 500, 501
  Treasury circuit, 380–382, 384, 385, 396
Citizenship
  citizen-investor, 259, 524
  citizens, 3, 45, 58, 62, 93–95, 120, 121, 192, 220, 261, 264, 268, 274, 287, 305, 320–322, 326, 328, 331, 345n101, 347, 353, 381, 395, 459, 492, 502, 519, 524, 529, 533
Civil Code (France, 1804), 427, 443
Civil servants, 60, 160, 294, 300, 351–353, 356, 381, 385
Civil society, 233, 262, 264, 266, 267, 280

Cleveland, 239
Clinton, Bill, 393, 454–456, 467
Club of London, 333, 337
Club of Paris, 333, 336, 490
Cochut, André, 92
Coercion, 93, 95, 112, 123, 177, 224, 263, 266, 267, 271, 289, 301, 304, 318, 320, 321, 328
Cold War, 260, 322, 347–367, 529
Colfax (US), 243
Collateral, 31, 64, 65, 139, 204, 210, 212, 432
Collective Action Clause (CAC), 444, 452n34
Collectivization, 325
Collège de France, 82, 87, 94
Colombia, 85, 147, 431
Colonialism, 126, 155–169, 182, 183, 527
Colvin, Auckland, 161
Comecon, 324, 325, 327, 328
Commission of Inquiry on the Finances of Egypt (CIFE), 161, 163, 164
Commonwealth, 242, 490
Commune (Paris, 1871), 247, 251
Communism, 224, 260, 303, 317–337, 365, 406, 533
Comprador, 221, 438
Comptoir d'Escompte, 91, 94, 137, 171n28
Conditionality, 165, 432, 434–437, 443, 447, 518
Congo Free State, 89, 103n51
Congress (US), 441
Congress of Berlin (1878), 138, 167
Consent, 96, 263, 279
Constantinople, 158, 167, 349, 516
Constitutionalism, 444, 446
  new constitutionalism, 530
Consumption, 5, 19, 25, 38, 206, 217, 263, 264, 268, 303, 323, 331, 354

Continuous borrowing, 268
Contract, 10, 25, 30, 85, 120, 125, 136, 138, 142, 146, 155, 243, 336, 379–381, 385, 386, 388, 393, 427–429, 436, 437, 442–447, 452n35, 496, 531
Conversion, debt, 90, 146
Cooke, Jay, 270
Cooper, Frederick, 176, 188
Coordinated market economy, 378
Corporation of Foreign Bondholders (CFB, London), 115, 124, 132n62, 152n11, 179, 180, 485, 486
Corruption, 12, 166, 219, 336, 431, 516
Council of the Realm (Sweden), 60, 63, 64
Coup, military, 51, 59, 67–70, 322, 354, 355, 358, 361, 365, 394, 522
Cour des Comptes, 64, 90
Credible commitment, 149, 303, 464
Credit, 5–8, 13, 22–27, 29–31, 39, 40, 46, 48, 71–73, 79, 84, 87, 89, 94, 95, , 114, 124, 142, 202–204, 206, 226n29, 244, 249, 259, 262, 265, 269, 272–274, 277, 280, 282n25, 284n48, 288, 291, 295–306, 318, 320, 321, 323–328, 333, 334, 356, 374, 381, 385, 387, 389, 392, 394, 395, 405, 410, 411, 413–415, 450n21, 454, 459, 462, 489, 498, 515–518, 521, 531
  public credit, 57, 72, 73, 79, 80, 82–88, 232, 262, 263, 265, 274, 294, 297, 301, 303, 487, 488, 508n48, 528, 532
Credit Anstalt, 142
Crédit Foncier, 81, 88–90, 157, 171n28
Crédit Générale Ottoman, 139

Crédit Lyonnais, 430, 485, 486, 492, 496, 501
Creditor, 8, 46, 48, 57–59, 64, 65, 69–72, 89, 107, 111, 114, 115, 120, 121, 136, 138–141, 144, 146–150, 157, 159–161, 163, 167, 168, 181, 215, 216, 228n52, 249, 259, 291–294, 296, 299–301, 304, 305, 318, 319, 324, 331, 333, 334, 336, 372, 381, 386, 395, 413, 428, 430, 435, 441, 442, 447, 449n16, 456, 460–462, 473, 482, 502, 517, 518, 520, 523, 525, 526, 528
Creditworthiness, *see* Reputation
Creutz, Carl Johan, 64, 65
Crimean War (1853–1856), 137, 150, 519
Crisis, economic
  crisis of 1873, 138
  crisis of 2008, 336, 420, 453–473
  See also Great Depression
Crown Agents for the Colonies (British Empire), 180, 185
Cuerva, Juan de, 24
Currency, 10, 48, 61, 65, 66, 68, 69, 190, 273, 294, 297, 298, 304, 318, 320, 322, 325, 327, 332, 335, 353, 356, 358, 368n12, 385, 389, 393, 398, 408, 413, 415, 417, 421, 454, 455, 459, 461, 462, 464, 466, 514
Customs, 112, 115, 118, 121, 122, 137, 144, 145, 148, 180, 181, 189–193, 206–210, 213, 216, 224n1, 272, 359, 492, 496
Czechoslovakia, 322, 323, 326

D
Dalberg, Duc de, 86, 87
D'Allarde, baron, 44, 54n33
Damascus, 352, 358, 365
Danish Courant Bank, 61
D'Argenson, René Louis Voyer, 84
Davidson, Nathaniel, 122, 132n52
Davis, Lance E., 176
Dawes Plan (1924), 126, 293, 294, 299
Debt, 10, 19, 41, 80, 82, 84, 86, 88, 96, 103n44, 103n45, 109, 112–114, 116, 121, 126, 137, 150, 151n1, 155, 156, 158, 175, 190, 191, 202, 208, 212, 231, 232, 234–238, 242–244, 248, 249, 251, 252, 259, 267, 271, 287–306, 318, 332, 336, 337n2, 372, 374–376, 393–399, 415, 417, 420, 421, 427–447, 456, 458, 462, 463, 465, 466, 468, 469, 472, 473, 482, 491, 497, 499, 500, 502, 509n68, 511n91, 517, 522, 526–528, 530–532, 535n12
  burden, 324, 352, 356, 457, 492, 501, 502, 511n89
  consolidation, 144, 160
  crisis, 42, 156–159, 331, 333, 334, 371–372, 386, 405–421, 430, 434–439, 441, 445, 446, 450n19, 453, 457, 481, 482, 489, 490, 503n2, 515–517, 527, 533
  external debt, 68–71, 91, 111, 117, 122, 124, 126, 127n1, 139, 141, 149, 153n29, 155, 158, 178, 181, 202, 210, 211, 213, 215, 216, 221, 224n1, 227n34, 228n51, 293, 299, 310n31, 317–320, 322, 324–327, 329, 332–336, 348, 382, 386, 390, 395, 396, 407, 417, 438, 484–486, 494, 496, 497, 501, 507n29, 509n61, 517, 528

floating debt, 158, 245, 246, 262, 263, 269, 289, 292, 297, 390, 395
indebtedness, 41, 80, 82, 84, 86, 88, 96, 103n44, 121, 155, 158, 190, 191, 202, 208, 212, 235, 242–244, 249, 259, 267, 271, 305, 325, 332, 372, 417, 491, 497, 499, 500, 502, 509n68, 522, 528, 530–532
management, 126, 140, 288, 294, 298, 299, 302–305, 371, 373–375, 377, 378, 392, 396, 397, 406, 410, 413–415, 420, 499, 530, 533
marketable debt/non-marketable debt, 375, 487, 488, 495–497, 499, 500
municipal debt, 88, 109, 231, 232, 234, 236–238, 244, 248, 249, 251, 252
odious debt, 260, 296, 318, 336, 337n2, 517, 535n12
restructuring, 72, 127, 427–447, 452n35, 457, 458
sovereign debt, 10, 19, 40, 59, 112–114, 116, 126, 137, 150, 155, 156, 175, 208, 236, 287–306, 372–376, 378, 379, 383, 389, 390, 393–399, 402n41, 415–417, 420, 421, 427–447, 456, 458, 460, 462, 463, 466, 468, 469, 472, 473, 482, 487, 489–491, 494, 502, 504n11, 511n91, 526–528
sustainability, 290, 484, 495, 496, 500, 501
write-off, 68, 324, 334, 336, 435, 438, 439, 442, 513
Debtor state, 293, 502, 529
Debt regime, 88, 89
  dirigiste debt regime, 260, 527
  financialized debt regime, 371, 372
  liberal debt regime, 1, 3, 107, 259
Declaration of the Rights of Man and Citizen (1789), 49
Decolonization, 184, 349
Decree of Muharrem (1881), 140
Default, 2, 6, 7, 30, 46, 51, 58, 70–72, 95, 96, 111–114, 116–123, 125, 126, 127n1, 132n62, 135–141, 144, 146, 150, 151n2, 157, 158, 166, 170n17, 178–181, 188–190, 192, 208, 260, 293, 319, 331, 386, 436, 439–442, 444, 445, 449n17, 461, 465, 466, 489, 500, 502, 511n91, 513, 516, 518, 524, 526
Deficit, 41, 42, 46, 47, 57, 58, 60, 67, 68, 137, 148, 150, 157, 161, 178, 190, 204, 206, 225n8, 324, 330, 352–355, 357, 380, 382, 389, 390, 395, 407, 409–411, 414–421, 453, 457, 458, 464, 468, 519, 529, 530
Deflation, 297, 471
Defoe, Daniel, 532
Delegation Bonds, 245, 246
Delors, Jacques, 394
Democracy
  democratic advantage, xi
  democratic institutions, 372, 406, 439
Denmark, 61, 62, 65, 66, 69, 71, 492
Depoliticization, 429, 530, 533
Deregulation, 371, 372, 394, 395, 412, 420, 429, 437, 440
Desmoulins, Camille, 46
Destutt de Tracy, Antoine, 529
Deutsche Bank, 455
Deutsche Bundesbank, 459
Devaluation, 227n34, 293, 461
Developed economies, 334, 388, 432, 434

Developing economies, 334, 335, 377, 386, 430, 437, 439, 489
Development, 6–8, 12, 13, 23, 27, 30, 31, 58, 59, 72, 80, 81, 87, 88, 97, 101n18, 114, 126, 135, 157, 163, 167, 173n56, 176, 185, 193, 205, 209, 231–233, 235, 239–241, 243, 250, 251, 260, 278, 279, 286n78, 291, 303, 305, 325, 327, 329, 348–350, 352, 354–367, 372, 376–379, 381, 391, 406, 410, 413, 472, 489, 490, 494, 501, 514, 516, 523, 529
  aid, 360, 449n16
Diaz, Porfirio, 192
Dictatorship, 192, 287–306
Diet (Sweden), 60, 62, 63, 65, 67, 72
Dietzel, Karl, 288
Dillon Read, 296
Diplomats, 115, 160, 164, 207, 209, 219, 221, 321, 323, 324, 516
Directorate-General of State Accounts (Egypt), 165
Dirigisme, 298, 302, 304, 305, 373–399, 409, 446
  See also Debt regime
Dollar diplomacy, 526
Doloret, Gabriel, 85, 101n31
Dombrovskis, Valdis, 461
Domestic borrowing, 318, 329, 330, 379
Dornbusch, Rudiger, 462
Draghi, Mario, 406, 465–467, 472
Drago Doctrine, 114
Dreyfus, House of, 124
Drogmans, 162
Druze, 352, 356, 368n21
Dudley-Baxter, Robert, 499, 500
Dulles, John Foster, 365
Dunkerque, 238, 250

E
East Asia, 378
The Economist, 189, 296, 311n41, 351, 485
Economists, 80, 83, 84, 88, 94, 99n8, 255n21, 265, 294, 305, 318, 321, 332, 405, 406, 414, 438, 440, 454, 457, 459, 463, 469, 482, 484–486, 488, 490–493, 495–497, 500–503, 505n15, 519, 522, 529–531, 535n22
Egalitarianism, 97
Egypt, 95, 108, 111, 117, 126, 127, 138, 141, 143, 151n2, 152n10, 155–169, 208, 209, 220, 274, 284n53, 361, 366, 465, 499, 516, 526
Eichengreen, Barry, 440–441, 484
Einaudi, Luigi, 408
Ellensburg, 243
Elliott Associates, 445
Embedded liberalism, 377, 384
Embeddedness, 80, 107, 224
Emerging economy, 178, 193, 439, 440, 455, 468, 470, 473
Émile Erlanger and Co., 180
Empire effect, 108, 147, 176, 181, 188, 189, 194n7
Empires, 22
  British Empire, 156, 188, 275, 276, 284n57, 377
  Spanish Empire, 12, 29, 31, 112
Enfantin, Prosper, 87
Engels, Friedrich, 317
Estates-General (France, 1789), 41, 42, 44, 45
Europe, 1, 2, 12, 23, 29, 37, 58, 80, 84, 85, 107, 117, 123, 124, 141, 157, 167, 201, 244, 274, 289, 296, 322, 392, 408, 413, 435, 458, 464, 466, 472, 486, 499, 500, 519, 523

European Central Bank (ECB), 463–467, 471–473, 490
European Commission, 482
European Monetary System (EMS), 413–415
European Union (EU), 461, 482, 483, 490, 504n7, 504n13, 530
European Community, 414, 416
Eurostat, 482, 489
Eurozone, 372, 420, 457, 460–462, 464–466, 468, 471–473
Exchange rate, 62, 63, 65, 69, 299, 392, 408, 413, 455, 462
Experts, 107, 108, 142, 145, 156, 158–161, 167, 242, 260, 262, 265, 272, 288, 290–292, 294, 295, 298, 301, 303–305, 319, 323, 330, 359, 360, 363, 366, 376, 388, 406, 414, 431, 433, 434, 437, 483, 515, 518, 526, 528, 530–534

F
Farmers, 5, 38, 95, 123, 136, 143, 148–150, 320, 524
Farmers-General, 38
Fascism, 409, 487
Favre, Jules, 93, 105n72
Fawcett, Henry, 218
Faysal I, 351
Federalism, 231–252
Federal Reserve (Fed), 435, 454, 463, 467, 470–472
Fenn's Compendium, 519
Ferdinand VII, 86
Ferguson, Niall, 147, 457
Fernandez, Solomon, 139
Ferrières, marquis de, 46
Ferry, Jules, 236, 238, 239, 247
Financial control, 108, 113, 140, 141, 150, 151n2, 156–165, 167, 168, 173n56, 185, 194, 291, 392

Financialization, 371, 375, 405–421
Financial markets, 6–8, 57, 107, 118, 127n1, 135–138, 149, 150, 151n5, 178, 214, 232, 244, 248, 249, 294, 298, 301, 305, 352, 365, 371–372, 380, 398, 399n3, 407, 411, 412, 415, 420, 453, 455–457, 460, 466, 472, 473, 487, 489, 496–498, 530
Financial orientalism, 516
Financial plebiscite, 264, 265, 292, 295, 299, 532
Financial repression, 260, 415, 460 *See also* Circuit
Financial Revolution (Britain), 38
Financial sector, 24, 128n7, 388, 412, 443, 446, 500
The Financial Times, 189, 352, 458, 470, 471
First globalization, 107, 147, 231, 484, 496, 500
First International, 523
Fiscal-military state, 80, 84
Fisher, Richard, 470
Fitzgerald, Gerald, 165
Flandreau, Marc, 167, 484–486, 506n20, 506n22
Fleury, Joly de, 41
Forlani, Arlando, 414
Foucault, Michel, 290
France, 1, 37, 58, 79–98, 108, 140, 157, 180, 207, 231–252, 261–280, 291, 319, 349, 371, 409, 434, 454, 487, 517
Franco-Prussian War (1870), 138, 236
Frankel, S. Herbert, 193
Fraser, Leon, 300
Free trade, 112, 145, 259, 408, 416
Frémy, Louis, 158
French Africa (West and East), 278
French Revolution (1789), 2, 9, 37–51, 520, 522
Frühling & Goschen, 157, 171n29

Fukien, 204
Fundraising, 273, 276
Funk, Walther, 302
Furet, François, 233
Furetière, Antoine, 515
Future generations, 520–522

G
G7, 437, 439, 446, 449n16, 473
Gaffney, Kathleen, 458
Galata bankers, 139–142, 152n16
Galena, 239
Gallieni, General, 177
G. & C. Marchelli, 64
Gandhi, Indira, 382
Gansu, 212, 227n40
Gaulle, Charles de, 380, 392
Genoa, 58, 61–66, 68, 70
Genoa conference (1922), 319
Gentlemanly capitalism, *see* Capitalism
Germany, 288–290, 296, 297, 303
  German Democratic Republic (GDR), 324, 331, 333, 340n43
  German Federal Republic, 304
  Weimar Republic, 288–290, 296, 297, 303
  See also Nazism
Germiny, Comte de, 92
Ghana, 182
Gibbs, Antony, 123
Gibbs & Sons, 123, 124
Giddens, Anthony, 290
Gierek, Edward, 332, 337
Girard, Louis, 248
Giro banco, 24
Gladstone, William E., 85, 173n50
Globalization, 147, 175, 178, 194, 231, 232, 256n23, 371, 372, 374, 430, 439, 456, 472, 484, 500, 505n15, 514

Glorious Revolution (1688), 38
Gold
  gold clause, 299
  gold reserve, 269, 273
  gold standard, 107, 259, 261, 483
Gold, Joseph, 432
Gold Coast, 177, 180, 186, 187
Goldman Sachs, 466, 482
Goldscheid, Rudolf, 293
Gomułka, Władysław, 324
Goschen, George, 167, 168, 171n29
Goschen-Joubert Mission, 160
Gothenburg, 64
Governance, 7, 9, 10, 12–16, 19, 27, 157, 193, 219, 220, 232, 234, 288, 290, 294, 295, 297, 298, 374, 427–447, 507n33
Graeber, David, 176, 518
Grand Canal (China), 203, 212
Great Compression, xii
Great Depression, 259, 298, 305, 320, 397, 408, 409, 489, 508n46
Greece
  Greek debt crisis (2010s), 457, 516
  International Financial Commission (1898), 118, 126, 516
Greenspan, Alan, 456, 467
Gross, Bill, 458, 469
Gross Domestic Product (GDP), 20, 28, 265, 354, 383, 384, 395, 407, 409, 453, 457, 469, 481, 491, 504n11, 504n12, 505n16, 505n17
Growth, economic, 8, 50, 80, 218, 318, 376, 379, 386, 388, 389, 407–410, 469, 501, 511n89, 519
Guano, 119, 123–125, 127
Guatemala, 170n17, 196n21, 431
Guild, 8, 16, 23–31, 54n33, 166
Gunboat diplomacy, 87, 113, 114, 176

Guomindang, 321
Gustavus III, 59, 67, 68
Gustavus IV Adolphus, 59

H
Haberer, Jean-Yves, 389, 394
Hacienda, 10, 21, 25
Haffar, Lutfi, 353
Hague, The, 64
Haifa, 359, 360
Haiti, 86, 87, 106n85, 170n17
Hall, Peter, 378
Hambros Bank, 118
Hamburg, 63, 66
Hamilton, Alexander, 521
Hamilton, Robert, 83, 139
Hankow, 214, 223
Hanyang Ironworks, 207
Hargreaves, John, 184
Harris, N.W., 242
Hartz, Louis, 233
Hashemite, 361
Haussmann, Georges Eugène, 245, 247, 248
Havana, 21, 28, 29, 527
Hebei, 203
Heinig, Kurt, 287
Helfferich, Karl, 292
Heß, Rudolf, 301
Higginson, Lee, 296
Hilferding, Rudolf, 296, 297
Historiography, 7, 10, 31, 107, 119, 124, 135, 136, 202, 349
Holzman, Franklyn D., 318, 321, 329
Homberg, Octave, 270
Home Front, 263, 264, 285n67
Honecker, Erich, 332, 334, 344n91
Hong Kong, 208, 220, 275
Hongkong and Shanghai Bank (HSBC), 208, 214, 221, 227n33, 229n66
Honor, 43, 45, 49, 58, 62, 92, 203, 207, 259, 324, 515–518, 528, 530, 532
Hoover moratorium (1931), 288
Hope & Co., 64
Horneca, Hogguer & Co, 66
Households, 40, 91, 282n16, 304, 381–383, 385, 407, 410, 415–421, 469, 529
Huang Zunxian, 221
Hume, David, 80, 218, 528, 529
Hungary, 147, 263, 296, 324, 325, 328, 335, 431
Hut Tax War (1898), 184, 186
Huttenback, Robert A., 176

I
Illinois, 242
Imperialism
 imperial war loan, 275, 278
 informal imperialism, 112
Imperial Ottoman Bank (IOB), 137, 139, 142, 151n5, 152n16, 158, 168
Import-substitution, 438
Indebtedness, *see* Debt
Independence, national, 265
India, 161, 165, 172n33, 275–279, 284n56, 285n62, 371, 373–399
Indiana, 242
Indies Company, 44
Indochina, 275, 278
Indonesia, 324
Industrialization, 6, 213, 217, 278, 320, 325, 326
Inequalities, 97, 201–224, 326, 372, 505n15, 520–525

Inflation, 61, 227n42, 259, 263, 266, 268, 289, 292, 293, 301, 302, 328, 331, 354–356, 371, 376, 379, 382, 385–391, 395, 396, 401n26, 408–410, 412, 414, 416–418, 420, 438, 453, 454, 463, 467, 470, 493, 497, 498, 523, 524
  hyperinflation, 280, 320, 438, 439, 522
Information order, 160, 161
Infrastructures, 6, 87, 157, 176, 186, 193, 222, 233, 236, 239, 241, 244, 250, 355, 359, 360, 362, 365, 366, 407, 409, 459, 519, 536n23
Inquisition, 26, 27, 30
Insolvency, 291, 335, 434, 440, 462
Insurance
  insurance companies, 240, 255n20, 301, 302, 382, 396, 411, 412, 439
  insurance funds, 295, 297, 298, 301, 303, 304
  insurance policies, 418
  life insurance, 302, 383
Interest groups, 107, 108, 150, 152n13, 203, 421, 517
Interest rate, 10, 25, 26, 30, 64, 65, 137, 144, 146, 158, 178, 179, 181, 204, 205, 218, 221, 242, 265, 276, 302, 321, 324, 379–381, 385, 389, 392, 394, 397, 408–410, 413–415, 417–419, 423n20, 454, 459, 460, 462, 467, 469–471, 515, 519, 523
Intermediaries, 81, 92, 107, 108, 120, 123, 137, 145, 149, 151n5, 160, 176, 186, 187, 221, 222, 224, 259, 291, 295–298, 300, 302, 303, 330, 383, 495, 497

Intermediary institutions, 259, 291, 295, 297, 302, 303
International Bank for Reconstruction and Development (IBRD), 322, 323, 326–329, 360, 363–366, 369n47, 488
International financial commission, 118, 126, 159–161, 167, 170n18, 516
International financial control (IFC), 105n79, 107, 108, 126, 135, 136, 140, 141, 150, 151n2, 153n31, 155–157, 167–169, 177, 486, 499
International financial institutions (IFI), 323, 333, 334, 483
International financial markets, 6, 127n1, 135–138, 149, 150, 248, 371, 456, 487
International law, *see* Law
International Monetary Fund (IMF), 308n13, 322, 323, 326–328, 333, 334, 344n92, 357, 358, 366, 372, 373, 395, 399n1, 407, 413, 416, 428–437, 440–447, 449n16, 451n27, 453, 455, 457, 461, 463, 472, 484, 485, 488–491, 498, 500, 508n43, 527
International norms, *see* Law
International Trade Union Confederation, 458
Intra-colonial transfers (ICT), 11, 20, 27, 29, 31
Investment, 7, 24–26, 30, 43, 47, 65, 71, 81, 82, 85, 88, 90–97, 100n14, 115–118, 120, 126, 129n10, 131n29, 145, 175, 178, 185, 189, 192, 193, 207, 208, 212, 213, 219, 225n13, 229n58, 238–241, 243–245, 248, 250, 263, 264, 267, 272, 273, 275, 277, 278, 282n17, 284n53, 290–292, 294, 296, 297, 301,

302, 304, 325, 327–331, 352, 364, 380, 382, 387, 391, 407, 409, 410, 418, 419, 429, 439, 440, 445, 469, 488, 497
Investors, 7, 10, 22, 24–27, 41, 43, 48, 62, 64, 65, 72, 81–85, 88–94, 100n14, 112, 113, 115–117, 120, 123, 176–178, 181, 186, 188, 193, 221, 243, 248, 255n21, 264, 269, 272, 274, 276, 278, 288, 290, 291, 293, 295, 301, 335, 374, 380, 396, 407, 412, 416, 419, 420, 428, 430–432, 436, 439–446, 454, 456, 460, 462, 465, 466, 468, 469, 471, 472, 486, 493, 496, 519, 528, 533
Iowa, 242
Iraq, 260, 329, 347–367
Ireland, 457, 461, 462, 464
Ismāʾīl, Khedive, 157, 163, 164, 167, 170n12
Israel, 359, 361, 365, 366
Istanbul, 137, 138, 140–142
Italy, 116, 140, 145, 161, 262, 263, 272, 375, 405–421, 453, 454, 457, 464, 465, 473, 487, 499, 509n61
Ivory Coast, 434, 449n16
Izmir, 137

J

Jackson, Andrew, 72
Jacobsson, Per, 300
Jamaica, 275
Jansenists, 40
Japan, 228n52, 303, 321, 417, 424n49, 446, 463, 465, 472, 473, 486
Jecker, J. B., 121
Jefferson, Thomas, 521
Jiangsu, 203, 211, 213, 215
Johnson, Hilary, 189, 190
Johnston, Harry, 180, 196n29
Joint-stock company, 7, 8, 24
J.P. Morgan, 296
Juárez, Benito, 91
Judicialization
 courts, 442
 judges, 41, 42, 50, 249, 265, 427–452
 jurisdiction, 442
Juros, 10, 22–24

K

Kádár, János, 325
al-Kahhāla, Habīb, 356
Kai Ho, 220, 229n62
Kalecki, Michael, 459
Kansas City, 239
Katushev, Konstantin, 327
Kemmerer, Edwin, 431, 531
Kesner, Richard M., 176
Keynes, John Maynard, 177, 194, 294, 300, 529
Keynesianism, 437, 446
Khrushchev, Nikita, 325, 329
Kindersley, Robert, 268, 273
King, Mervyn, 464
Klein, Herbert S., 22, 33n20
Klotz, Louis-Lucien, 270
Knight, Alan, 114, 129n9
Knights of Labor, 243
Kotkin, Stephen, 319
Kremlin, 332
Kreuger & Toll, 296
Kriegsanleihe, 266, 267
Krosigk, Lutz Graf Schwerin von, 301, 302
Krugman, Paul, 461
Kwass, Michael, 19, 38, 51n6, 52n16
Kytspotter, Jean-Baptiste, 49

L

Laffitte, Jacques, 83–87
Lagos, 186, 187
Landes, David, 155, 169n2
Lang, Robert Hamilton, 139, 142
Latin America, 6, 7, 23, 108, 111–127, 147, 167, 171n18, 232, 274, 435, 438, 455, 527
    Latin American debt crisis (1980s), 372, 489
Latvia, 461
Laufenburger, Henry, 488
Lavrin, Asuncion, 24
Law, 136, 155, 157, 168, 169, 294, 526
    international law, 108, 136, 155, 157, 168, 169, 294, 526
    international norms, xvi, xix
    legal order, 157
Lawyers, 168, 429, 433, 444
Lazarov, Nikola, 330
League of Nations, 126, 170n10, 294, 296, 352, 430, 431, 434, 485, 487–488, 493, 494, 498, 501, 508n46, 526
Leavenworth, 239
Lebanon, 351, 352, 367n8, 368n12
Left (politics), 293
Legal order, *see* Law
Legitimacy
    democratic legitimacy, 517
    political legitimacy, 1–3, 67, 80, 81, 108, 203, 219, 220, 223, 259, 260, 263, 295, 335, 376, 384, 394, 522, 523, 526
    popular legitimacy, 263, 303
Le Moniteur, 245
Lender, 2, 22, 23, 25, 39, 125, 138, 177, 208, 215, 228n52, 241, 246, 318, 319, 323, 326, 332–335, 381, 434, 460, 461, 469, 472, 501, 519, 533
Lend-Lease program (1941), 321
Lenin, Vladimir, 129n10, 156
Le Producteur, 87
Leroy-Beaulieu, Paul, 80, 81, 94, 95, 97, 103n44, 492, 493, 499, 508n48
Le Temps, 92
Leyen, Ursula von der, 461
Liberalism, 1–3, 54n33, 83–85, 94, 107, 108, 163, 165, 166, 173n56, 173n58, 202, 218, 220, 223, 233, 234, 243, 260, 264, 269, 279, 290, 295, 299, 305, 364, 376, 388, 393–398, 409, 427, 444, 446, 519, 523, 529
Liberalization, 93, 111, 372, 378, 383, 386, 396, 398, 402n43, 410, 412, 428, 437–439, 446, 453, 455
Liberia, 112, 175, 177–181, 184, 185, 189–194
Liberian Development Company, 180
Liberty loans (US), 271
Lille, 89, 236, 238
Lima, 12, 24, 27
Lindert, Peter, 484–486
Lipschutz, Neal, 458
Liquidity, 10, 23, 24, 27, 28, 30, 57, 61, 65, 68, 69, 205–207, 213, 214, 297, 301, 360, 374, 379, 380, 382, 384, 387, 391–393, 395, 396, 408, 415, 435, 440, 467
Lloyd George, David, 351
Lloyds, 221
Loan, 6, 39, 60, 79, 113, 136, 157, 175, 204, 239, 261, 288, 318, 348, 382, 408, 431, 483, 519
London, 6, 85, 86, 101n31, 102n37, 109, 118, 119, 121, 124, 127n1, 137, 146, 150, 157, 175, 177, 178, 184, 185, 189, 208, 209,

214, 221, 249, 273–276, 300, 413, 452n34, 466, 500
London Treaty (1953), 529
Lottery bond, 89–94, 96, 97, 103n51, 104n56, 272, 273, 320, 331, 507n32
Louis, Baron, 83
Louis XVI, 39, 43, 46, 68
Löwenhielm, Carl Gustaf, 64
Luther, Hans, 294
Luxemburg, 428
Lyon, 89, 236
Lyon, Ernest, 191
Lyons, Lord, 164

M
Maastricht Treaty (1992), 490
MacDonald, James, 289
MacDonald, Ramsay, 459
Macri, Mauricio, 445
Macroeconomics, 96, 117, 260, 330, 392, 408, 410, 411, 413, 430, 435, 436, 438, 461, 483, 484, 488, 489, 491, 497, 500, 501, 504n9, 510n68
Madagascar, 176
Madison, James, 518, 521
Madras, 165
Madrid, 12, 21, 32n8, 34n44
Manchuria, 223
Mandates, 68, 336, 347–367, 373, 436
Mao Zedong, 329
Markets
  market discipline, 379, 386, 391
  marketization, 82, 390, 407, 412, 421
  market mechanisms, 325, 385
Marseille, 89, 236, 238, 239, 250, 270
Marshall Plan, 323, 360, 408

Massachusetts Institute of Technology (MIT), 406
Massa-Gille, Geneviève, 94, 103n50, 132n52, 256n33
Mass participation, 263, 266, 280, 282n17
Matamoros, 121
Material culture, 271, 277
Maximilian of Habsburg, Emperor, 92, 121, 122
McKenna, Reginald, 275
McManners, John, 47
Meade, James, 493
Mediterranean, 63, 167, 516
Melon, Jean-François, 84, 497
Meltzer, Report, 441
Menichella, Donato, 408
Mercantilism, 80, 220, 497, 500, 529
Metternich, Richard von, 81
Mexican Expedition (1861–1867), 86
Mexico, 13, 25, 27, 28, 31n4, 34n30, 86, 88, 91, 108, 113–116, 119–122, 125, 126, 130n24, 132n52, 147, 192, 440, 449n16, 453, 517, 518, 525
Mexico City, 12, 26
Michelet, Jules, 37, 51n1
Microfinance, 461
Middle class, 89, 264, 268, 394, 395
Middle East, 117, 133n73, 151n2, 155, 201, 232, 348, 354, 357, 361, 366, 367n5
Military intervention, 86, 111–114, 119, 121, 125, 216, 228n52
Mill, John Stuart, 218
Millspaugh, Arthur, 531
Ming dynasty, 205
Mirabeau, comte de, 46
Missale, Alessandro, 482, 504n9
Missouri, 242
Mittag, Günter, 332, 334, 335

556　INDEX

Mitterrand, François, 333, 393, 394, 402n39, 454, 460
Mobilization, 59, 82, 166, 259, 263, 264, 266–273, 275, 276, 279, 281n5, 302, 303, 319–322, 329, 330, 376, 386, 405, 418, 517
Modernity, 81, 244, 376, 519, 527
Modernization, 136–141, 233, 234, 244, 263, 379, 411, 438
Monarchy, 2, 10, 12, 13, 19, 22, 27, 39, 40, 42–46, 50, 59, 84, 86–88, 96, 121, 148, 173n56, 293, 351, 355, 358, 360, 528
Monetarism, 376, 386, 390, 391
Money
　monetary creation, 48
　monetary policy, 48, 117, 295, 384, 395, 406–408, 410, 413–415, 422n11, 463, 470, 471
　monetary regime, 47, 50, 118
　money market, 392, 395, 411, 416
Money doctors, 167, 294, 431
Mongolia, 205, 212, 324, 336
Monnet, Jean, 431, 442
Monopolies, 49, 123, 139, 140, 142, 149, 151n5, 188, 223, 291, 296, 319, 326, 434
Montagu, Edwin, 268
Montélimar, 44
Montesano, 243
Montesquiou, marquis de, 49, 50
Monti, Mario, 406
Moody's, 485
Moral economy, 515–520
Morality, 87, 515–518, 520
Moratorium, 91, 288, 300, 345n101, 368n11, 528
Morocco, 111, 128n2, 499
Mortgage, 25, 88, 255n19, 301, 468
Morton, Peter, 484–486, 505n18, 506n25
Moscow, 324, 332, 334, 468
Multilateralism, 430, 434–437, 442

Municipal debt, *see* Debt
Mur d'argent (France, 1926), 459
Mutual Life Insurance Company, 240

N
Nagy, Imre, 324
Nanjing, 213
Nantes, 44, 236
Naouri, Jean-Charles, 394
Naples, 12
Napoleon III, 88, 122, 333
Natal, 175
National Assembly (France), 45
National City Bank, 271
National Debt Office (Britain), 161
National income, 483, 488, 489, 493
National War Savings Committee (UK), 268–270
Nation-building, 176, 407
Nation-states, 116, 220, 223, 232, 234, 247, 252, 260, 288, 294, 377, 393, 400n6, 526
Natixis, 458
Nazism, 288, 290, 299, 303
Necker, Jacques, 39, 41, 42, 45, 46, 52n7
Neoliberalism
　neoliberal ideology, 387
　neoliberal reform, 393
　neoliberal turn, 529
Netherlands, 11, 20, 70, 140, 399n3
Neutral countries, 262, 273, 274
Nevers, 44
New Deal, 438
New Economic Policy (USSR), 320
New England Mutual Life Insurance Company, 240
New fiscal sociology, viii
New Granada, 16
New Orleans, 28
New York City, 238, 249

INDEX 557

Neymarck, Alfred, 99n12, 272, 492, 493, 499, 506n25
Nietzsche, Friedrich, 515
Nigeria, 177, 180, 182, 184, 187
Norman, Montagu, 299, 300
North, Douglass C., 39, 52n8, 74n6, 232, 252n1, 288
North Korea, 331
Novikov, Nikolai, 321
Nowa Huta, 323
Nützenadel, Alexander, 371, 432

O

Obama, Barack, 456, 457, 462, 467
Odious debt, *see* Debt
Oil
  oil crisis (1970s), 332, 406
  oil revenues, 352, 359, 364, 365
Old Regime, 37–51, 87, 365
Olympia, 242
Opacity, 532–533
Ordoliberalism, 305
Organization for Economic Cooperation and Development (OECD), 393, 407, 409, 432, 437, 453, 455, 458, 489, 491
Orszag, Peter, 456, 457
Ottoman Empire, 89, 108, 112, 117, 126, 135–150, 152n11, 158, 160, 167, 170n12, 177, 180, 226n27, 309n27, 348–350, 357, 363, 516, 522, 526, 527
Ottoman Public Debt Administration (OPDA), 140, 150, 168
Outer Mongolia, 205
Outrey, Maxime, 157

P

Padoa-Schioppa, Tommaso, 405, 406
Paine, Thomas, 521
Palestine, 357, 358, 361

Palmer, Dent, 137
Palmerston, Lord, 120, 125
Panama Canal, 89, 104n56
Panic, financial
  See also Crisis, economic
Paravey, Pierre-François, 85, 86
Pari Passu clause, 444, 445
Paris, 41, 44, 79, 81, 85, 86, 89, 96, 97, 103n44, 103n51, 109, 119, 122, 124, 127n1, 128n1, 137, 150, 236–239, 244–248, 250, 449n16, 450n18, 490, 496, 500
Parker Gilbert, Seymour, 296, 297
Parliamentarism, 11, 38, 39, 58, 59, 61, 74n7, 81, 88, 120, 138, 148, 165, 166, 185, 248, 260, 261, 288, 290, 297, 348, 349, 351, 353, 355–359, 361–367, 384, 455, 456, 458, 464, 517
Pasha, Ismail, 516
Pastré, Jules, 158, 159, 171n20
Peasants, 54n35, 60, 67, 70, 97, 166, 203, 205, 219, 220, 268, 272, 321, 329
Pension, 25, 30, 295, 298, 409, 420, 502, 524
Péreire, Isaac, 92
Persia, 531
Peru, 15, 16, 20, 24, 25, 108, 113, 115–117, 119, 123–125, 127, 180, 431
Picard, Ernest, 93
PIMCO, 458, 469
Planinc, Milka, 334
Planning, 204, 215, 228n49, 327, 332, 336, 375, 380, 397, 405, 409, 411
Plebiscite, financial, 264, 265, 292, 295, 299, 532
Poland, 59, 296, 322–324, 328, 331–334, 336, 343n88, 531, 533
Polanyi, Karl, 397, 459–460
Politburo, 319, 323, 327

Political economy, 7, 11, 23, 43, 47–51, 80, 84, 87, 94, 98, 136, 202, 205, 209, 212, 218–224, 233, 235, 241, 372, 382, 398, 405–421, 437, 453, 459, 461, 469, 472, 473, 484, 495, 516, 528
Politicization, 42, 97, 163, 276, 532
Politics
  political culture, 98, 514
  political discourse, 53n25, 473, 514, 518, 520
  political party, 365, 386, 413, 419, 421
  political regime, 2, 7, 37, 47, 50, 51, 57–73, 79, 88, 108, 109, 113, 117, 121, 122, 126, 154n35, 163, 260, 304, 372, 428, 507n33, 533
Pomerania, 60, 66
Poona, 277
Poor House of Mexico, 25
Popitz, Johannes, 297
Porte, The, *see* Ottoman Empire
Portes, Richard, 441, 484, 505n18
Portugal, 85, 95, 147, 407, 420, 457, 458, 460–462, 464, 499, 509n61
Postcolonial, 303, 318, 348, 527
Priestley, Joseph, 521
Propaganda, 264, 266–268, 270–274, 276, 277, 279, 280, 281n14, 282n25, 285n68, 289, 292, 303, 323, 519
Property
  private property, 12, 21, 164, 319, 429, 528
  property rights, 7, 12, 38, 50, 51n5, 107, 249, 429, 437, 443, 446, 460
Proudhon, Pierre-Joseph, 239
Prussia, 61, 71, 96, 265
Public choice, 529

Public credit, 57, 72, 73, 74n7, 79, 80, 82–88, 101n18, 232, 240, 262, 263, 265, 274, 294, 297, 301, 303, 487, 508n48, 528, 532
Public debt regime, *see* Debt regime
Public finance, 2, 7, 22, 29, 87, 93, 97, 103n44, 120, 156, 160, 161, 163, 164, 166, 177, 203–207, 209, 210, 212, 215–218, 228n48, 260, 261, 263, 273, 280n1, 288, 290, 292, 294, 303, 406, 453, 486, 487, 492, 496, 500, 501, 504n9, 505n14, 508n48, 531
Public opinion, 43, 44, 64, 80, 348, 351, 355, 357, 384, 459, 526, 533
Putin, Vladimir, 336

Q
Qing dynasty, 486
Quantitative Easing (QE), 463, 469–471
Quiroz, Francisco, 125, 132n64

R
Railways, 87, 143–145, 180, 181, 185–187, 213, 214, 217, 219, 223, 230n74, 238, 356, 360, 412, 488, 492, 503, 519
Rákosi, Mátyás, 324
Rathenau, Walter, 320
Rating agency, 226n29, 374, 500, 501
Reagan, Ronald, 333
Real Compania Guipuzcoana, 24
Recession, 462
Reconstruction, 207, 238, 244–248, 250, 321, 322, 374, 376, 377, 385, 406, 408, 484, 487, 507n33

Redistribution, 29, 67, 73, 108, 109, 201, 202, 218, 219, 223, 520, 523–525, 537n38
Régie (Ottoman Empire), 44, 142, 143
Regulation, 97, 128n1, 191, 260, 280, 298, 301, 305, 374, 375, 394, 410, 411, 429, 436, 437, 446
Reichsbank, 266, 292, 294–301
Reichstag, 282n15, 287, 294, 297
Reinhardt, Fritz, 301
Reinhart, Carmen, 457, 484, 485, 500, 506n21, 511n89
Renan, Ernest, 248
Renegotiation, debt, 160, 430–434, 442
Rente, 81, 83, 85, 88–90, 267, 492
Rentiers, 94, 96, 97, 265, 269, 272, 278–280, 349, 364, 523, 524
Rentier state, 349, 364, 366, 367
Reparations, war, 236, 280, 487, 506n29
Repayment, 89, 91, 93, 111, 120, 124, 151n1, 160, 163, 180, 181, 186, 188, 202, 214, 217, 221, 227n37, 277, 289, 320, 331, 335, 362, 376, 482, 489, 490, 494, 495, 517, 518, 522, 528
Representation, 12, 45, 81, 138, 149, 163, 202, 227n48, 260, 290, 302, 348, 366, 376, 444, 505n14, 522
Republic, 6, 98, 190, 283n29, 288, 295, 324, 326, 328, 336, 345n101, 347, 355, 408, 532
Repudiation, 43–47, 122, 124, 224, 260, 280, 318–320, 336, 337n2, 507n32, 517, 522, 528, 532
Reputation, 41, 42, 64, 70, 72, 136, 137, 149, 150, 153n31, 175, 176, 249, 262, 265, 267, 272–274, 280, 288–290, 293, 296, 300, 335, 413, 452n35, 499, 515, 517, 528
Reserve Bank of India (RBI), 383, 389, 391, 396
Revolutionary War, American, 40
Rhodesia, 177
Richelieu, Duc de, 83
Río de la Plata, 15, 16
Risk, 80, 85, 92, 109, 114, 147, 177, 178, 181, 188, 189, 194, 246, 263, 272, 273, 328, 334, 388, 389, 411, 413, 436, 440, 441, 447, 458, 460, 461, 464–466, 493, 495–497, 501, 502
Robespierre, Maximilien de, 45
Rodrigues, Olinde, 87
Rogoff, Kenneth, 457, 484, 485, 500, 505n17, 506n21, 511n89
Romania, 296, 324, 325, 327, 328, 331, 333–336, 344n92, 431
Rothschild, house of, 83, 100n18, 102n37, 101n18, 118, 122, 132n52, 137, 165, 430, 523
Roubaix, 89, 102n35
Rouen, 236
Royal Navy, 351
Roye, Edward James, 189–190
Rubin, Robert, 457
Rueff, Jacques, 388, 392
Russia, 260, 318, 320–324, 326–331, 333–336, 487, 519, 535n19
  Bolsheviks, 318–320, 337n2
  Politburo, 319, 323, 327
  Russian Civil War, 319
  Russian Revolution (1917), 319
  USSR/Soviet Union, 318, 320–324, 326–331, 333–336
Russo-Turkish War, 137–139

S

Sachs, Jeffrey, 441, 505n18
Safe asset, 460, 468–470
Sahlgren, Niclas, 64, 76n30
al-Said, Nuri, 349, 355, 359, 360, 363, 364
Saint-Domingue, *see* Haiti
Saint-Simonians, 87, 88
Sandusky, 239
Sankara, Thomas, 527
Santo Domingo, 118, 181, 196n21
Sarraut, Albert, 278, 279, 286n74, 286n75
Saudi Arabia, 361, 362, 365, 366
Saul, Samir, 155, 169n2, 170n17
Savings, 62, 90, 187, 240, 255n20, 262, 264–266, 268–271, 273–276, 278, 292, 295, 297, 301, 302, 320, 323, 330, 331, 345n101, 380, 382–386, 394, 395, 405, 407, 408, 415–421, 424n49, 459, 468, 497, 507n32, 519, 524
   forced savings, 282n22, 302, 497, 502
   savings banks (*see* Banks)
Saxony, 72
Say, Jean-Baptiste, 83, 84, 100n18
S. Bleichröder, 142
Schacht, Hjalmar, 295, 297, 299, 300
Schäffer, Fritz, 304
Schanz, Georg von, 288
Schlieben, Otto von, 294
Schmidt, Vivien, 378, 402n42
Schroders, 221
Schürer, Gerhard, 332
Seattle, 256n25
Second Empire (France), 80, 87, 88, 91–93, 96, 237, 244, 247, 248, 265, 533
Secrecy, 38, 39, 330, 337, 533
Secular stagnation, 469

Securities, 41, 81, 89–91, 100n14, 141, 146, 164, 179, 207, 208, 240, 249, 255n22, 256n22, 301, 383–385, 410, 412, 414, 417, 456, 460, 468, 469, 490, 495, 497, 508n44, 521
Securitization, 420, 421, 468
Seigniorage, 137
Seligman, Edwin R. A., 522
Serbia, 103n52, 112, 126, 141, 151n2, 492
Serial defaulter, 112, 259
Service des Études Financières, 496
Seven Years' War (1756–1763), 59–67
Sewell, William H., 290, 308n14
Shahīn pasha, 162
Shanghai, 206, 207, 212, 214, 222, 223
Shareholders, 434
al-Shīshaklī, Adīb, 361
Shovlin, John, 40, 52n16
Sichuan, 204, 223
Siegenthaler, Hansjörg, 406
Sierra Leone, 175, 177–180, 184, 186, 187, 190, 191, 198n74
Sieyès, Emmanuel Joseph Abbé, 98
Silent financing, 286n78, 299, 320, 328–331
Silver, 10, 23, 53n24, 61, 62, 67–69, 116, 119, 203, 205, 206, 214, 221, 222, 225n18, 226n20, 227n34, 229n66, 444
Sino-Japanese War (1894–1895), 209, 213, 214, 228n52
Slovenia, 326
Smith, Adam, 221, 497, 510n69, 518, 520, 529, 535n17
Socialism, 94, 218, 318–320, 324, 325, 327, 329, 331, 335, 336, 345n101, 392–395, 454, 523
Social policy, 361, 455
   social insurance, 297, 304
   social spending, 376, 398

INDEX   561

Société de Statistique (Paris), 493
Sokoto Caliphate, 182
Solvency, 247, 436, 496
Sonenscher, Michael, 80, 99n5, 99n6, 252n1, 306n5, 538n50
Soros, George, 466, 470
Soskice, David, 378
South Africa, 175, 509n62
Sovereign debt, *see* Debt
Sovereignty, 8, 74n5, 80, 105n79, 108, 109, 113, 125, 128n3, 138, 144, 150, 151n2, 159, 167, 175–194, 232–234, 251, 252, 289, 291–298, 304, 305, 348–350, 355, 358, 367, 371, 382, 393, 430, 455, 515, 525–530
Soviet Union (USSR), *see* Russia
Spain, 5–31, 63, 69, 85, 91, 95, 121, 147, 152n10, 170n17, 196n21, 274, 399n3, 407, 420, 457, 462, 464, 499, 525, 528
Spanish American Empire, *see* Empires
Special Drawing Rights (SDR), 328
Speculative attack, 462
Spokane, 243, 256n25
Stabilization, 167, 187, 289, 326, 329, 376, 430, 431, 435, 466, 468
Staël, Anne Louise Germaine Madame de, 39
Stakeholders, 12, 13, 29, 33n17, 33n19, 34n44, 525
Stalin, Joseph, 318, 323, 328
Stasavage, David, 52n14, 53n26, 74n6, 252n1, 281n7, 289, 307n7
State, 1, 5, 38, 57, 79, 108, 115, 136–141, 156, 161, 175, 202, 204, 231–252, 260, 261, 287, 291–306, 317, 330, 347, 352, 365, 373, 377, 405–421, 428, 455, 482, 513, 527–530
  state-building, 232, 233, 260, 288, 290, 322, 351, 467, 525

state intervention, 105n79, 115, 213, 348, 372, 497, 500, 502
Statesman's Yearbook, 486, 506n27, 509n65
Statistics, 160, 239, 289, 364, 458, 481–502, 510n68
Statutory liquidity ratio (SLR), 383, 384, 390
Stein, Lorenz von, 103n44, 288
Steiner, Zara, 304, 311n37
Stock markets, 8, 263, 301, 412, 420
Stoler, Ann, 163
Stone-Sweet, Alec, 431
Strasbourg, 236
Strategic game, 372, 461–464, 466, 467, 470–473
Strauss, Franz-Joseph, 333
Streeck, Wolfgang, 402n41, 459–461, 469, 502, 511n90, 525, 537n38
Stresemann, Gustav, 293
Strike, 207, 406, 454, 459
Subscription, 81, 92, 96, 220, 222–224, 230n71, 264, 266, 268, 273, 275–277, 279, 282n17, 284n46, 295, 301, 302, 305, 320–323, 328, 329
  public subscriptions, 88, 221, 223, 302, 304, 519, 523, 533
Suez Canal, 89, 105n72, 157
Sukarno, Achmed, 324
Summers, Larry, 469
Sumner, Charles, 521
Supersanctions, 107, 113–116, 135
  See also Trade sanctions
al-Suwaydī, Tawfīq, 360, 369n33
Sweden, 1, 2, 57–73, 493
Swire and Co., 221
Switzerland, 262
Syria, 137, 260, 329, 347–367
System of national accounts (SNA), 75n26, 490, 501

T

Taiping Rebellions (1850–1860s), 206, 209
Talleyrand, Charles Maurice de, 84, 86, 87, 97, 102n35
Tampico, 121
Tanzimat (Ottoman Empire), 349
Tariffs, *see* Taxation
Taxation, 121, 124, 145, 180, 215, 348, 352, 353, 355, 366
   consumption taxes, 5
   corporate taxes, 300
   income tax, 228n55, 269
   land tax, 5, 161, 162, 203, 205, 206, 212, 214, 217, 353, 354
   likin, 206, 207, 212, 217
   progressive taxation, 358, 371
   tariffs, 348, 366
   tax policy, 38
   tax system, 405
Taxpayers, 13, 19, 136, 149, 176, 241, 249, 435, 492, 502, 523
Technocracy, 335, 363, 371, 378–380, 382, 384, 387–390, 395, 398, 406, 407, 414, 446
TePaske, John J., 22
Thiers, Adolphe, 84, 85, 87, 97, 101n23, 101n24, 101n25
Third Reich, *see* Nazism
Third World countries, 324, 334
   See also Developing economies
Thobie, Jacques, 155
Thrift, 91, 269, 270, 277, 278, 516, 523
Tianjin, 210, 214
Tietmeyer, Hans, 459
The Times, 269
Tito, Josip Broz, 323
Tocqueville, Alexis de, 37
Total war, 261–280, 303, 521
   See also War
Tourcoing, 89

Trade sanctions, xvi
   See also Supersanctions
Transparency, 42, 62, 163, 376, 389, 498, 500, 532
Treasury, 10–12, 19, 21, 22, 24–30, 32n8, 38, 81, 88, 90, 91, 159, 161, 187, 204–208, 210–213, 221, 227n37, 241, 245, 262, 267, 268, 271, 275, 282n25, 352, 371, 373, 379–382, 384–386, 388, 389, 394, 395, 399n1, 401n24, 408, 410, 411, 414, 415, 423n20, 454–456, 458, 462, 463, 468–470, 472, 498
Treasury bills, 262, 297, 301, 384, 410, 411, 415, 416, 419
Treasury circuit (*see* Circuit)
Treasury districts (*caja*), 12–16, 19, 21–31
Treaty of Paris (1815), 79
Treaty of Versailles (1919), 289
Trichet, Jean-Claude, 464–466
Truman, Harry S., 360
Trump, Donald, 467
Trust, 39, 42, 44, 48, 64, 70, 72, 122, 136, 144, 160, 162, 178, 185, 188, 221, 222, 240, 242, 263, 266, 275, 284n48, 287, 289, 298, 320, 407, 457, 459, 462, 509n61, 515, 518, 528
Tunisia, 95, 97, 111, 126, 151n2, 158, 159, 170n17, 171n25, 171n26, 430, 526
Turkey, 95, 120, 147, 168, 296, 351, 430, 499, 501

U

Ukraine, 473
Ulbricht, Walter, 327
Umar Luṭfi pasha, 162

INDEX 563

Unemployment, 454, 467, 471, 489
United Kingdom, see Britain
United Nations (UN), 357, 485, 487, 489, 509n61
United States of America (USA), 262, 270–273, 281n4
Uprising, 138, 184, 186, 350, 351
Urabi revolt, 166, 173n59
Uruguay, 116, 147, 170n17, 196n21
US Civil War, 6, 235, 239, 251, 519, 521, 523, 524
US-Mexican War (1846–1848), 120
Usury, 25, 85

V
Vanderlip, Frank A., 270–271
Varieties of capitalism, See Capitalism
Varoufakis, Yanis, vii
Velde, François, 42
Venezuela, 24, 116, 125, 126, 291, 447, 526
Veracruz, 121
Verdery, Katherine, 319
Vernon, Roland V., 351
Vienna, 63, 99n9, 142, 431
Villèle, Joseph de, 83, 106n85
Villena, Lohmann, 27
Villet, Victor, 159, 171n25
Violence, 44, 46, 48, 291, 363
Vogl, Joseph, 459
Volcker, Paul, 450n21, 463, 464, 467
Vulture funds, 372, 458, 524

W
Wagner, Adolph, 288, 292, 306n4
Wall Street, 289, 428, 431, 454
Walla Walla, 244
Wall Street Journal, 456, 458
Wang Tao, 219

War
  total war, 261–280, 303, 521, 528
  war financing, 271, 321
  war indemnity, 122, 519
  war loans, 261–280, 282n16, 282n17, 282n25, 283n28, 292, 293, 321
  See also Cold War; Crimean War (1853–1856); Franco-Prussian War (1870); Hut Tax War (1898); Reparations, war; Revolutionary War, American; Russia, Russian Civil War; Russo-Turkish War; Seven Years' War (1756–1763); Sino-Japanese War (1894–1895); US Civil War; US-Mexican War (1846–1848); World War I; World War II
Washington, 242, 256n25, 399n1, 435, 449n16, 456, 468
Washington Consensus, 438, 439
Waterloo, 83
Weimar Republic, see Germany
Weingast, Barry R., 39, 232, 288
Weir, David, 42, 53n24
Welfare
  welfare reform, 454
  welfare state, 295, 296, 371, 398, 489, 502, 503
West Africa, 175–194, 232
White, Eugene, 38–39, 42
White, George Henry, 121, 122
Williamson, John, 439
Wilson, Charles Rivers, 161, 162, 164, 165
Wisconsin, 242
Wittfogel, Karl, 349
Wobeser, Gisela von, 24, 25
Woodward, Bob, 454
World Bank, 328, 399n1, 407, 408, 413, 432, 438, 488–490, 501

World Monetary and Economic Conference (1933), 299
World War I, 3, 107–109, 135, 136, 145, 148, 153n27, 184, 191, 235, 261–280, 287, 288, 290–292, 304, 305, 349, 350, 407, 488, 493, 500, 522, 524, 528, 535n12
World War II, 260, 280, 302, 318, 321, 348, 349, 354, 357, 366, 375, 379, 384, 408, 410, 485, 488, 489, 501, 502, 522, 529
Write-off, *see* Debt, write-off
Wuhan, 213
Wyke, Charles L., 121

X

Xinjiang, 205, 207, 208, 212, 226n28

Y

Yangtze Delta, 203, 206
Yardeni, Edward, 454, 456, 469
Yellen, Janet, 471
Yellow River, 203, 212–213, 227n42
Yeltsin, Boris, 336
Yen Fu, 221
Young, E. Hilton, 351
Young Plan (1929), 296–298
Young Turk Revolution (1908), 145, 148
Yugoslavia, 296, 318, 322–324, 326, 331, 332, 334
Yun, Chen, 322

Z

Zamora, 24
Zarifi, George, 139
Zatlin, Jonathan R., 335
Zheng Guanying, 219, 221
Zhili Province, 210
Zhivkov, Todor, 332
Zhou Enlai, 325
Zionism, 358
Žižek, Slavoj, 459
Zumer, Frédéric, 484, 485, 506n20
Zverev, Arseny, 328

Printed by Printforce, the Netherlands